METALWORK IN EARLY AMERICA

COPPER AND ITS ALLOYS FROM THE WINTERTHUR COLLECTION

A WINTERTHUR BOOK

DISTRIBUTED BY ANTIQUE COLLECTORS' CLUB

METALWORK IN EARLY AMERICA

COPPER AND ITS ALLOYS FROM THE WINTERTHUR COLLECTION

BY

DONALD L. FENNIMORE

PHOTOGRAPHY BY

GEORGE J. FISTROVICH

Generous funding for this catalogue was provided by Martha Hopkins Feakes in memory of her husband, L. Russell Feakes.

Claire W. Nagle graciously contributed additional funds for production.

To T.L.

Library of Congress Cataloging-in-Publication Data

Henry Francis du Pont Winterthur Museum.

Metalwork in early America: copper and its alloys from the Winterthur Collection / by Donald L. Fennimore; photography by George J. Fistrovich. Includes bibliographical references and index.
ISBN 0-912724-37-4
1. Copperwork – United States – Catalogs. 2. Brasswork – United States – Catalogs. 3. Copperwork – Delaware – Winterthur – Catalogs. 4. Brasswork – Delaware – Winterthur – Catalogs. 5. Henry Francis du Pont Winterthur Museum – Catalogs.
I. Fennimore, Donald L. II. Fistrovich, George J. III. Title.
NK8112.H46   1996
739.5'1'09730747511–dc20

96-236
CIP

Front cover: Entry 20
Back cover: Entry 76
Frontispiece: Entry 174

Content Editor: Gerald W. R. Ward
Copy Editor: Onie Rollins

Designed and produced by studio blue, Chicago
(Kathy Fredrickson, JoEllen Kames, Cheryl Towler Weese)

Printed by Balding + Mansell, England
Distributed by Antique Collectors' Club

CONTENTS

ACKNOWLEDGMENTS

No WRITING PROJECT of this magnitude is the product of one person alone. That is especially true of this endeavor. Its foundation is built on the work of many who I know only as names on title pages. Yet, their curiosity about copper and its alloys and their willingness to undergo the labor of writing about and publishing their findings have been of immeasurable help to me.

At the same time, my own research required me to reach out to many for help, advice, and direction. To all those who gave so freely, I offer my thanks. This catalogue would not exist had it not been for them.

Many went far beyond merely answering my questions. They remembered me and my work, were supportive and encouraging, and frequently offered unsolicited help. I would, therefore, like them to know that I remember them with gratitude. Thank you James A. Albanese; Mark Allen; Mark J. Anderson; H. Parrott Bacot; Christopher Bangs; the late Harry D. Berry, Jr.; Werner Beyer; Jennifer Blain; Ronald Bourgeault; Richard LeBaron Bowen, Jr.; Norman F. Brazell; Thomas G. Brennan; Lisa L. Broberg; Bradley Brooks; Michael K. Brown; Jean Burks; Shirley Bury; C. D. Chalmers; Richard Champlin; Karel A. Citroen; Mark A. Clark; Heather A. Clewell; Tim Coldren; Teje Colling; Edward S. Cooke, Jr.; Wendy A. Cooper; Gerald Cully; John D. Cushing; John D. Davis, who read the manuscript and offered many helpful suggestions; Ulysses G. Dietz; Richard Doty; Mr. and Mrs. Lee F. Driscoll; Winthrop Edey; Christine Edwards; Gunilla Eriksson; Rosemary Estes; Nancy G. Evans; David J. Eveleigh; Anne Farnam; Deborah Federhen; Jane W. Fisher; Susan Garfinkel; Beatrice B. Garvan; the late Rupert Gentle; Brian Gilmour; Verna A. Gilson; Anne Golovin; A. V. Griffiths; Mr. and Mrs. Otto Haas; J. M. Hamill; Suzanne Hamilton; Roland B. Hammond; Henry Harlow; Don B. Heller; Georg Himmelheber; Stuart Horn; Peter Hornsby; Angela Houstoun; Penelope Hunter-Stiebel; Henry J. Kauffman; Ann Marie Keefer; E. J. Kehoe; A. Van Den Kerkhove; Barry A. Kessler; Carol Kim; Joyce Kim; Daniëlle O. Kisluk-Grosheide; Clare Jameson; Brock Jobe; Marilynn Johnson; Mark Jones; Anizia Karmazyn; the late Scott LaFrance; David Lamb; Jeannette Lasansky; the late Craig Littlewood; Caorl Luan; Ann M. Lucas; Christopher T. Loeblein; Maida H. Loescher; Douglas K. MacDonald; Eugene P. Mahoney; Bruce Manzer; Craig Maue; Jane M. Mellinger; Mr. and Mrs. Karl Miller; Clarence M. Mollett; Virginia Morrow; John Munday; Barbara Nachtigall; D. C. Newton; Eddy Nicholson; Helmut Nickel; Jim Parker; Elizabeth Perkins; Jennifer A. Perry; Christa Pieske; Ronald Pook; Ruth A. Bryant Power; Ian M. G. Quimby; Kathryn Quinn; Bradford L. Rauschenberg; T. D. W. Reid; George J. Reilly; Jack Robrecht; Matthew Roth; Frances G. Safford; Quincy Scarborough; Herbert Schiffer; Peter Schiffer; Karol A. Schmiegel; Theresa A. Singleton; Arnold Skromme; Jeanne V. Sloane; James A. Smith; Duane R. Sneddiker; Ellen M. Snyder; John J. Snyder; P. H. Starling; Helen Stetina; Ned Stinson; Colin Streeter; William G. Strootman; Mary Hammond Sullivan; Susan B. Swan; Scott Swank; Mabel Swanson; Jane C. Sween; Eleanor McD. Thompson; Robert F. Trent; Robert T. Trump; Frank White; Taylor B. Williams; Gillian Wilson; Charles Wilt; Melvyn D. Wolf; John J. Wolfe; Martin Wunsch; and Kathleen H. Young. You all deserve a significant measure of credit.

I particularly thank Janice H. Carlson, who generated all the analytical material in this catalogue and with whom I shared many fruitful discussions that helped greatly with my understanding of metallic alloys. I am also indebted to George J. Fistrovich, who produced all the fine photographs. Furthermore, he very kindly shared his expertise and knowledge, which I believe have helped me greatly in guiding this book to its attractive visual presentation. I am particularly grateful to Gerald W. R. Ward for the impressive knowledge he brought to the manuscript as editor and to the time and effort he put into improving it. I also extend a sincere note of thanks to Onie Rollins, who, as copy editor, effectively transformed my manuscript into a coherent publication. I also offer my thanks to the National Endowment for the Humanities, the American Friends of Attingham, and the Friends of Winterthur for their support.

To Claire W. Nagle, a friend and fellow enthusiast of copper and its alloys, I express a special note of gratitude. Claire and I have often discussed our mutual interest in this attractive metal, and out of those exchanges came the funding for this catalogue. Claire undertook the task of seeking and securing a substantial cash gift that underwrote this work. Without it, the book would still be a fond hope on my part. Her unfailing encouragement and support have been a bulwark to me in seeking as high a level of quality as possible in this publication.

FOREWORD

DWIGHT P. LANMON, DIRECTOR

WHEN HENRY FRANCIS DU PONT began collecting American decorative arts, the idea of assembling more than just a large number of objects guided him. He collected to form a comprehensive record of American artistry and craftsmanship in every material from a period of two centuries–from the time of the first English colonies in North America until 1840. From 1919, when Mr. du Pont acquired the first American-made object, until 1969, when he died, he directed his attention to a wide variety of subjects, amassing a collection that is second to none in quality, quantity, and comprehensiveness. Mr. du Pont procured not just Philadelphia Chippendale high chests and Paul Revere silver but items made of humbler materials such as brass shoehorns and copper kettles, which also shed light on the lives of our ancestors.

Building on that foundation, Winterthur has evolved into an institution where the material culture of early Americans is studied by scholars and students as well as collectors and dealers. The collections have been enhanced by further acquisitions, and the library has grown to provide unmatched written resources that facilitate a greater understanding of the "messages" that objects carry.

The Winterthur trustees and staff have long been committed to documenting the Winterthur collections through a series of specialized catalogues, beginning in 1952 with the publication of Joseph Downs's *American Furniture: Queen Anne and Chippendale Periods, 1725–1788*.

The present catalogue, which focuses on copper and its alloys, continues the tradition, highlighting not just objects but how they were made and used and what people thought about them. Don Fennimore takes us beyond simple antiquarian description to elucidations of the complex and fascinating messages embodied within.

I am personally delighted that this catalogue has come to fruition during my tenure as Winterthur's sixth director, since I was on the staff as a curator when Don joined the Museum Collections Division in 1971 and conceived of producing such a volume. I know that it has been a labor of love and has consumed much of his professional and personal life for some twenty years. That commitment is vividly demonstrated by the quality of the text, which not only showcases the unparalleled Winterthur collections but also reflects both the maturity and depth of his knowledge of the field.

INTRODUCTION

BUILDING A COLLECTION is by definition a personal endeavor. One can couch the acquisitive urge in a variety of objective and dispassionate terms: furnishing a house, saving old things, catering to nostalgia, making an investment, or, as Henry Francis du Pont chose to state, preserving "in some degree the evidences of early life in America."[1] During the process, one can seek the opinion of friends, the recommendation of experts, and advice and direction from professionals. In the end, however, whether for pleasure, hoarding, mercenary, or intellectual purposes, collectors must measure their own likes, dislikes, prejudices, and enthusiasms against each decision to acquire. As such, the collected object becomes an expression of the collector's personality. This is true for an individual object and equally so for the aggregate.

Henry Francis du Pont detailed his acquisitions in four loose-leaf volumes of typed pages, beginning on November 14, 1919, and continuing through the ensuing thirty-five years. Evidenced solely by the entries he recorded, du Pont might appear to have had no special affection for artifacts made of copper and copper alloys. Although his records start in 1919, the first brass object does not appear until December 8, 1923, when he purchased a "Brass Dolphin Knocker." This acquisition was followed on

January 1, 1924, by the second: a "pr. wrought iron & brass American andirons period 1735."[2]

Reading through the purchase book entries that follow, one finds numerous brass and copper objects listed–such as the "Brass Creepers" purchased in 1926; the "Copper Tea Kettle" and "Brass candlestick 17th C.," 1927; the "17th Century cluster column brass candlestick," 1943; the "copper kettle (marked)," 1946; and the "Brass cloak pin with John Wilkes on it," 1950– but identifiable purchases of copper and brass are widely spaced.[3] In addition, with few exceptions, such as the last entry enumerated, most copper and brass acquisitions are so briefly and vaguely described as to suggest only casual interest on du Pont's part.

A more insightful consideration of the purchase books in conjunction with a perusal of the objects represented in those disembodied entries presents quite a different picture, however, when measured against the historical background of collecting during the early twentieth century. Du Pont collected during an era when the acquisition of American decorative arts came into its own as a field of endeavor. Increasing numbers of antiques dealers earned a living selling to those who desired the finest colonial artifacts. Auction houses offered growing numbers of household estates that were described as containing antiques;

some conducted widely advertised sales that consisted entirely of groupings assembled by notable collectors. Publishers began to issue magazines that dealt exclusively with matters of interest to collectors of American decorative arts. Museums began to employ specialists who assembled, studied, and published catalogues of such items. All sought out and lauded the rare and the beautiful. Henry Francis du Pont was no exception. Winterthur is generously endowed with the rare and the beautiful. At the same time he was acquiring his great artifacts, du Pont "came into contact with widely divergent early American materials of all kinds. The problem of giving them appropriate recognition inevitably came to mind." He felt a growing need to make a place not only for those artifacts that most agreed were rare and beautiful but also for those that might generally be overlooked as less significant. The result was that du Pont resolved to preserve "under one roof examples of architecture, furniture, and widely divergent early American materials of all kinds [through which he hoped] interest in this field would be stimulated and . . . the magnificent contribution of our past would be helped to come into its own."[4]

In light of this mission, rereading the purchase books brings into view a host of artifacts that many of du Pont's contemporaries would probably never have considered purchasing–such as the "brass pepper pot, brass tinder box [and] brass snuffer tray" all acquired on October 4, 1946–because they lacked the monumental scale and elaborate decoration of a Philadelphia Chippendale high chest, the name value association of a Duncan Phyfe card table, or the patriotic overtones of a Paul Revere teapot. Perhaps even more enlightening is a whole constellation of entries similar to that dated September 26, 1936, which records the purchase of a "set of Chinese Chippendale brass handles and escutcheons for 3 drawers" or another dated January 9, 1950, that documents the purchase of "16 antique posts for bureau brasses."[5] The question that immediately springs to mind is why bother since reproductions were so readily available and cheaper, and who would know the difference anyway? The only plausible answer is du Pont's commitment to the comprehensive accuracy of the collection. Although many perceived a vast gulf between the relevance and collectibility of furniture and furniture hardware, du Pont did not. Reproduction brass had no more place in a collection that was being assembled to preserve and document early American material culture than did reproduction furniture.

More dramatic evidence of du Pont's concern for accuracy and attention to detail is apparent in the collection itself. Housed in 175 roomlike settings is a virtual panoply of objects–large and small, elaborate and plain, decorative and functional–produced by and for Americans. The period rooms possess a breadth and depth that arise from their creator's conviction that a brass shoehorn or a copper button was just as important in documenting early America as elaborate furniture and spectacular silver. The result is a richness and diversity that is capable of impressing even the most sophisticated, as testified by Luke Vincent Lockwood, a collector, enthusiast, writer, respected student of Americana, and member of the Walpole Society. When Lockwood and that august group visited Winterthur in 1932, he ably recorded their impressions in the *Walpole Society Notebook*: "Imagine a house which records the decorative history of our Country, and that in supreme terms! Are you interested in architecture? Here you will see choicely chosen examples of interior woodwork covering two centuries. Is it silver? The finest examples of distinguished Colonial makers. Pottery? Everything the Country affords. Pewter and brass? A fine collection."[6] Only superlatives properly describe this collection of collections, which in its high level of quality and great quantity tangibly underscore du Pont's commitment to using all the decorative arts in its creation. Its encyclopedic scope poses a daunting challenge to anyone undertaking the cataloguing of one of its many facets.

Like building a collection, writing a catalogue is also a personal endeavor. In the process many choices have to be made, all of which hinge on the author's personality and reaction to objects encountered. That statement is most certainly true with this work. The large number of artifacts available for inclusion required extensive winnowing and were ultimately selected to satisfy several needs. I wanted to use examples that I considered to be the best of their type. I also wanted to select a range of objects that provided a representative overview of the entire collection and, insofar as possible, offered an insight into the variety of forms and uses to which copper and its alloys were put at an early date. I especially wanted to present objects through which I felt I could offer substantive information.

A body of objects containing the number and diversity suggested in the following pages must be organized in some fashion. In contemplating the resolution of this matter, I decided that function might be the most helpful for readers. Accordingly, I have arranged the artifacts into six groups. The first contains objects that are concerned with the preparation, storage, and consumption of food or drink. The second consists of items related to the generation and maintenance of heat, while the third documents those whose purpose is to provide light. The fourth group contains a variety of implements used for measurement. The fifth, admittedly the most diverse, comprises a large number of artifacts that might be perceived as reserved for use by one individual. The sixth, and last, is made up of hardware that is used on both furniture and architecture. Within each section, similar objects are grouped together and arranged chronologically, with European examples generally preceding American.

I believe any individual object, regardless of size or elaboration, can convey many points of information, each of which exists independently but all of which are capable of being integrated into a single story unique to that object. This precept has guided me in writing the catalogue entries. I have attempted to interweave the threads of function, use, technology, economics, trade, and history, adjusting and shifting the balance in each entry to provide the reader with variety and an understanding of each object. At the same time, I have sought to organize all the entries in such a way that they offer, in total, a picture of the multiple uses of copper and its alloys. To infuse a sense of immediacy and vitality, I have quoted the words of the makers, users, and social historians first connected with the objects. I have attempted to build equality and balance into the catalogue entries by making them all approximately the same length. This was done in the belief that all artifacts, regardless of purpose, size, complexity, or elaboration, are capable of informing the curious reader to the same extent.

For the sake of brevity, shortened reference titles are given in footnotes throughout the entries. Full citations may be found in the bibliography.

The composition of every object in the catalogue is included. This information was obtained using the museum's energy dispersive X-ray fluorescence analyzer. Small items such as shoe buckles or buttons required only one analysis. Larger, multipart objects, such as andirons and chandeliers, were subjected to separate analyses on their various parts. In many cases, there is measurable disparity in the quantity of both primary and sec-

ondary components from one part to another in any given object. While this may be attributable to repair or replacement, in many instances it appears to be the result of the relatively loose control of composition at the time the artifact was made. The average content reported is, therefore, only intended to suggest the character of the compositional information available. Those readers wishing to study this aspect in depth may refer to the individual analyses recorded in the museum's analytical laboratory.

The museum's analyzer is capable of accurately detecting elemental constituents as small as 1/100 of 1 percent (0.01). Early metallurgical techniques, however, were not technologically capable of systematically purifying metals to that degree. Even so, I recorded that level of accuracy in documenting composition since it has been demonstrated that very small amounts of secondary elements in silver alloys are capable of providing insights into the date and place of manufacture. The same may prove true for copper alloys. Data on an alloy's composition are given in percentages; because they are a composite, they may not always total 100 percent. Finally, unless otherwise noted in the credit line, all objects were purchased by Henry Francis du Pont or the museum.

This book is not a history of copper and its alloys in early America. It is instead a catalogue of objects selected from those particular collections at Winterthur. As such, the three introductory chapters are intended to supplement the entries. They are designed to provide additional insight into the place these metals had in America from the mid seventeenth through the mid nineteenth centuries. Hopefully, they and the catalogue entries will be useful to the future author of a definitive history on the subject. I would like to think that Henry Francis du Pont, the man who ultimately made this effort possible, would have approved of the catalogue. I sincerely hope that reading it will be as enjoyable and informative for those who have the opportunity and inclination to open its cover as creating it was for me.

1 Joseph Downs, *American Furniture: Queen Anne and Chippendale Periods, 1725–1788* (New York: Macmillan Co., 1952), p. vi.

2 Acquisition records continued to be kept after 1956, but their format changed. The knocker is recorded in the H.F. du Pont purchase books, vol. 1, p. 4, but it is no longer in the museum's holdings. The second item is also in vol. 1, p. 4-A.

3 The objects are listed in the H.F. du Pont purchase books, vol. 1, p. 79-A; vol. 2, pp. 218, 564; vol. 3, pp. 653, 732; vol. 4, p. 853.

4 The history of collecting Americana during the early twentieth century is discussed in Elizabeth Stillinger, *The Antiquers* (New York: Alfred A. Knopf, 1980). Du Pont is quoted in an unpublished foreword to Downs, *American Furniture*, p. 2 (Winterthur Archives), and on p. v of the published volume.

5 The items are recorded in the H.F. du Pont purchase books, vol. 3, p. 726; vol. 2, p. 534; vol. 4, p. 840.

6 Luke Vincent Lockwood, "The Meeting at Winterthur," *Walpole Society Notebook* (Topsfield, Mass.: Wayside Press, 1932), p. 22.

MINING AND
MANUFACTURING

When Elizabeth I granted the incorporation of the Mines Royal Society in 1568, she created an agency to exploit what proved to be significant quantities of copper in England for the economic and political benefit of her kingdom. At the same time, she created the Mineral and Battery Works to oversee and encourage the working of that metal and its alloys, including copper, brass (an alloy of copper and zinc), and bronze (a mixture of copper and tin). Although both were separately incorporated, the agencies operated interdependently, the former involved in mining and refining ore and the latter responsible for fabrication of the metals into usable goods. Through these operations Elizabeth hoped to free England from dependence on its Continental neighbors, who were sometimes unreliable trading partners and sometimes politically hostile. Although early efforts to institute her initiatives were fraught with difficulty and progress was discouragingly slow, these attempts marked a critical point in the history of European base metals, culminating with England's becoming, by the late eighteenth century, the principal center in the Western world for the mining, manufacturing, and marketing of copper and its various alloys. Those sensitive to England's position in this respect were quick to so note, as with the compilers of *The Universal British Directory of Trade, Commerce, and Manufacture*, published in London in 1791. It was with a large measure of pride that they stated editorially, "At present, our wollen manufacture is the noblest in the universe and second to it is our metallic manufacture of iron, steel, tin, copper, lead, and brass, which is supposed to employ upwards of half a million people."[1]

The entrepreneurs who enjoyed Elizabeth's largesse were given a privately owned monopoly and the sole right to mine copper in the English counties of Westmoreland, Cumberland, Lancaster, Cornwall, Devon, Gloucester, Worcester, and York, and the principality of Wales. Where possible, these men, using both native English and imported German labor, mined lodes at or close to the surface, as had been done to a limited extent in Britain since the Roman excavation in Shropshire in the second century.[2] However, with only few exceptions—like the vast copper deposit 7 feet below ground level at Anglesea in Wales—such fields were relatively small and held poor quality ore. Most copper was recovered from shaft mines, some extending to a depth of more than 1,300 feet, which were sunk in considerable numbers, especially throughout Cornwall and Devonshire counties in southwest England (FIG. 1).

SMELTING

Following its extraction from the ground, ore had to be smelted—removing extraneous earthen materials and elemental contaminants—to produce pure copper. This process occurred for the most part in Bristol, Cheadle, Birmingham, and especially South Wales. An early detailed account of the smelting process as practiced in England during the eighteenth century was published by John Henry Vivian and originally printed in the *Annals of Philosophy*. This description provided the basis for a subsequent treatise on the subject by Dionysius Lardner in 1834. Lardner stated:

The processes in a copper work are simple; they consist of alternate calcinations and fusions. By the former, the volatile matter is expelled, and the metals previously combined with the copper oxidised, the general fusibility of the mass being thereby increased. The furnaces in which these operations are performed are reverberatory, and of the usual construction. The substance to be acted upon is placed on the body of the furnace or hearth, which is separated from the fireplace by a bridge about two feet in thickness. The flame passes over this bridge, and reverberating along the roof of the furnace, produces the required temperature, and escapes with any volatile matter that may be disengaged from the ore through

Fig. 1. Cross section and general view of a mine. From Denis Diderot, *Encyclopédie, ou Dictionnaire raisonné des sciences, des arts, et des métiers,* 28 vols. (Paris: Briasson, 1751–76), *Recueil des Planches*, vol. 6, minéralogie, pl. 6.

a flue at the opposite extremity of the furnace, which flue communicates with a perpendicular stack or chimney.

These furnaces are of two descriptions, varying in their dimensions and internal form. The calcining furnaces, or calciners, are furnished with four doors or openings, two on each side of the furnace, for the convenience of stirring the ore, and drawing it out of the furnace when calcined. They vary in their dimensions, but are commonly from 17 to 19 feet in length from the bridge to the flue, and from 14 to 16 in width; the fireplace from 4 1/2 to 5 feet across by 3 feet.

The melting furnaces are much smaller than the calciners, not exceeding 11 or 11 1/2 feet in length by 7 1/2 or 8 feet in the broadest part; the fireplace is larger in proportion to the body of the furnace than in the calciner, being usually from 3 1/2 to 4 feet across, and 3 or 3 1/2 feet wide, as a high temperature [1082°c] is required to bring the substances with as little delay as possible into fusion. These furnaces have only one door, which is in front."[3]

The author then proceeded with a lengthy and well-detailed discussion, which is quoted fully to provide a sense of the many operating steps and level of difficulty involved in obtaining pure copper.

Process I.—Calcination of the ore. The copper ores, when discharged from the vessels in which they are brought from Cornwall, are wheeled into the yards or plots contiguous to the works, and these deposited, one cargo over the other, so that, when cut down perpendicularly, to be carried to the furnaces, a tolerably general mixture is formed. This is always desirable in a smelting work, as the ores being of different qualities and component parts, the one acts as a flux to the other. The ore in the yard is weighed over to the calciner-men in boxes, containing each 1 cwt [100 pounds]. These are carried on men's shoulders to the calciners, and emptied into iron bins or hoppers, formed by four plates of cast iron tapering to the bottom, placed over the roof of the furnace, and supported by wrought iron frames resting on its sides: two of these bins are usually placed over each calciner, and nearly opposite the side doors, so that the charge of ore when let into the furnace may be conveniently spread, which is done by means of long iron tools, called stirring rabbles.

This charge of ore usually consists of three to three and a half tons; it is distributed equally over the bottom of the calciner, which is made of fire bricks or square tiles. The fire is then gradually increased, so that towards the end of the process, which lasts twelve

hours, the charge is drawn out through holes in the bottom of the calciner, of which there is one opposite to each door; and, falling under the arch of the furnace, remains there till it is sufficiently cool to be removed, when water is thrown over it to prevent the escape of the finer metallic particles. It is then put into barrows and wheeled to the proper depots: in this state it is called calcined ore. If the process has been well conducted, the ore is black and powdery.

Process II.—Melting of the calcined ore. The calcined ore is delivered, as in the raw state, to the workmen, in boxes containing 1 cwt each; the charge is deposited in the same manner in a bin placed on the top of the furnace, and from thence passed into the interior as required. When the charge is let down and spread over the bottom, the door of the furnace is put up and well luted [sealed with clay]. Some slags from the fusion of the coarse metal or sulphuret are added, not only on account of the copper they contain, but to assist the fusion of the ore, being chiefly composed of oxide of iron.

After the furnace is charged, the fire is made up, and the main object of the smelter is to bring the substances into fusion; it is, therefore, in this respect, different from the calcining process. When the ore is melted, the door of the furnace is taken down, and the liquid mass well rabbled, or stirred, so as to allow of the complete separation of the metallic particles from the slags or earthy matters, and to get the charge clear of the bottom of the furnace, which is made of sand, and soon becomes impregnated with metal. The furnace being ready, that is, the substances being in perfect fusion, the smelter takes an iron rabble, and skims off, through the front door, the sand or slags, consisting of the earthy matters contained in the ore, and any metallic oxides that may have been formed, which being specifically lighter than the metals in the state of sulphuret, float on the surface. When the metal in the furnace is freed from slags, the smelter lets down a second charge of ore, and proceeds with it in the same manner as with the first; and this he repeats until the metal collected in the bottom of the furnace is as high as the furnace will admit of without flowing out at the door, which is usually after the third charge; he then opens a hole, called the tapping hole, in the side of the furnace through which the metal flows into an adjoining pit filled with water. It thus becomes granulated, and collects in a pan at the bottom of the cistern, which is raised by means of a crane: it is then filled into barrows, and wheeled to the place appointed for its reception.

The slags, received into moulds made in sand in front of the furnace, are removed after each charge, and wheeled out of the work to the slag-bank, where they are broken and carefully examined; any pieces found to contain particles of metal are returned to the smelter to be remelted, and unless the slag is very thick and tenacious, the copper which they may contain is found at the bottom: what is clean or free of metal is rejected. These slags are composed of the earthy matters contained in the ore, and the oxides of iron and other metals that were mixed with the copper. The oxide of iron gives them a black colour; the silex or quartz remains in part unfused, and gives the slags a porphyritic appearance.

In this process, the copper is concentrated, and a mass of stuff with which it was combined in the ore got rid of. The granulated metal usually contains about one third of copper; it is thus four times as rich as the ore, and must consequently have diminished in bulk in the same proportion: its chief component parts are sulphur, copper, and iron. The men work round the twenty-four hours; and commonly melt in this time five charges: under favourable circumstances, as fusible ore, strong coal, furnace in good repair, they even do six charges: they are paid by the ton.

Process III.—Calcination of the coarse metal. This is conducted in precisely a similar manner to the calcination of the ore: the charge is nearly of the same weight; but, as it is desirable to oxidise the iron, which is more readily effected in this process than in the ore calciners, where it is protected from the action of the air by the earthy matters with which it is combined, the charge remains twenty-four hours in the furnace, and during that time is repeatedly stirred and turned. The heat during the first six hours should be moderate, and from that time gradually increased, to the end of the operation.

Process IV.—Melting the coarse metal after calcination. This is performed in furnaces exactly similar to those in which the ore is first melted, and with the calcined metal are melted some slags from the last operations in the works which contain some oxide of copper, as likewise pieces of furnace bottoms impregnated with metal: the chemical effect which takes place is that the oxide of copper in the slags becomes reduced by a portion of the sulphur, which combines with the oxygen, and passes off as sulphurous acid gas, while the metal thus reduced enters into combination with the sulphuret. That there may be a sufficient quantity of sulphur in the furnace to promote these changes, it is sometimes necessary, when the calcined metal is in a forward state, to add a small quantity of raw or uncalcined metal, so that a clean slag may be obtained; the slags from this operation are skimmed off through the front door, as in the ore furnaces. They have a high specific gravity and should be sharp, well melted, and free from metal in the body of the slag. After the slag is skimmed off, the furnace is tapped, and the metal is suffered either to flow into water, as before, or into sand-beds, according to the modes of treatment it is to be subjected to in subsequent operations. In the granulated state, it is called fine metal; in the solid form, blue metal, from the colour of its surface. The former is practiced when the metal is to be brought forward by calcination: its produce in fine copper is about sixty per cent.

Process V.—Calcination of the fine metal. This is performed in the same manner as the calcination of the coarse metal.

Process VI.—Melting of the calcined fine metal. This is performed in the same manner as the melting of the coarse metal; the resulting product is a coarse copper, from eighty to ninety per cent of pure metal.

Process VII.—Roasting. This is chiefly an oxidizing process; it is performed in furnaces of the same description as the melting furnaces, although distinguished by the appellation of roasters. The pigs of coarse copper from the last process are filled into the furnace, and exposed to the action of the air, which draws through the furnace at a great heat: the temperature is gradually increased to the melting point, the expulsion of the volatile substances that remained is thus completed, and the iron or other metals still combined with the copper are oxidized. The charge is from 25 to 30 cwt.; the metal is fused toward the end of the operation, which is continued from twelve to twenty-four hours, according to the state of forwardness when filled into the furnace, and is tapped into sand-beds. The pigs are covered with black blisters, and the copper in this state is known by the name of blistered copper: in the interior of the pigs the metal has a porous honeycombed appearance, occasioned by the gas formed by the ebullition which takes place in the sand-beds on tapping. In this state it is fit for the refinery, the copper being freed from nearly all the sulphur, iron, and other substances, with which it was combined. In some works the metal is forwarded for the refinery, by repeated roastings, from the state of blue metal: this, however, is a more tedious method.

Process VIII.—Refining and toughening. The refining furnace is similar in construction to the melting furnaces, and differs only in the arrangement of the bottom, which is made of sand and laid with an inclination to the front door instead of to one side, as is the case in those furnaces from which the metal flows out; the refined copper being taken out in ladles from a pool formed in the bottom near the front door. The pigs from the roasters are filled into the furnace through a large door in the side. The heat at first is moderate, so as to complete the roasting or oxidizing process, should the copper not be quite fine. After the charge is run down, and there is a good heat on the furnace, the front door is taken down, and the slags skimmed off. An assay is then taken out by the refiner with a small ladle, and broken in the vice; and from the general appearance of the metal in and out of the furnace, the state of the fire, &c. he judges whether the toughening process may be proceeded with, and can form some opinion as to the quantity of poles and charcoal that will be required to render it malleable, or, as it is termed, bring it to the proper pitch. The copper in this state is what is termed dry. It is brittle, is of a deep red colour inclining to purple, an open grain, and a crystalline structure. In the process of toughening, the surface of the metal in the furnace is first well covered with charcoal. A pole, commonly of birch, is then held in the liquid matter, which causes considerable ebullition, owing to the evolution of gaseous matter; and this operation of poling is continued, adding occasionally fresh charcoal, so that the surface of the metal may be kept covered, until, by the assays which the refiner from time to time takes, he perceives the grain, which gradually

becomes finer, is perfectly closed, so as to assume even a silky polished appearance in the assays when half cut through and broken, and it becomes of a light red colour. He then makes further trial of its malleability by taking out a small quantity in a ladle, and pouring it into an iron mould; and when set, beating it out while hot on the anvil with a sledge hammer. If it is soft, and does not crack at the edges, he directs the men to lade it out, which they do in iron ladles coated with clay, pouring it into pots or moulds of the size required by the manufacturer. The usual size of the cakes for common purposes is twelve inches wide by eighteen in length [by about 2½ inches thick]. The operation of refining requires great care; underpoling or over-poling being found injurious to the process.

Sometimes when copper is difficult to refine, a few pounds of pig-lead are added to the charges of copper. The lead acts as a purifier, by assisting, on being oxidized itself, the oxidation of the iron or any metal that may remain combined with the copper, and not, as may be supposed, by uniting with the copper, and thereby increasing its malleability. This is a mistaken notion: indeed the smallest portion of lead combined with copper, renders the metal difficult to pickle or clean from oxide, when manufactured.[4]

ALLOYING

A large portion of refined copper was intended for a multitude of uses, from sheathing for ships to teakettles. An equally substantial amount was converted to brass by alloying it with zinc, and a

Fig. 2. Foundry where copper and calamine are being prepared for making into brass. From Denis Diderot, *Encyclopédie, ou Dictionnaire raisonné des sciences, des arts, et des métiers*, 28 vols. (Paris: Briasson, 1751–76), *Recueil des Planches*, vol. 6, métallurgie, pl. 2.

Fig. 3. Foundry where brass plates are being cast. From Denis Diderot, *Encyclopédie, ou Dictionnaire raisonné des sciences, des arts, et des métiers*, 28 vols. (Paris: Briasson, 1751–76), *Recueil des Planches*, vol. 6, métallurgie, pl. 1.

significant quantity was converted to bronze by mixing it with tin. Zinc combines with a variety of substances in nature to form oxides, carbonates, and sulphurets. These ores exist in two groups known as calamines and blendes. The particular zinc ore that proved most commercially expedient for use in Great Britain was calamine, often called *lapis calaminaris*, a compound of zinc oxide and carbonic acid. Large deposits lay in Devonshire, Derbyshire, and North Wales and were mined extensively by the eighteenth century.

Zinc has a low melting point of 419°c, and it vaporizes at 907°c. Because of this volatility, early English metallurgists had difficulty refining it to its metallic state. Hence, they mixed the ore with copper to make brass until about the second quarter of the eighteenth century, when a process was perfected by which metallic zinc could be obtained. Production began with

the calamine which is received raw from the mines. [It] is first pounded in a stamping mill, and then washed and sifted in order to separate the lead, with which it is largely admixed (FIG. 2). *It is then calcined on a broad shallow brick hearth, over an oven heated to redness, and frequently stirred for some hours. In some places a conical pile is composed of horizontal layers of calamine alternating with layers of charcoal, the whole resting on a layer of wood in large pieces, with sufficient intervals for the draught of air. It is then kindled, and the stack continues to burn till the calamine is thoroughly calcined. The calamine thus prepared is then ground in a mill, and at the same time mixed with about a third or a fourth part of charcoal and is then ready for the brass-furnace. In some places pit-coal is ground with the calamine instead of charcoal, but this is found to injure the malleability of the brass obtained.*[5]

The next step was particularly crucial in the formation of the desired alloy. It was accomplished in a specially designed furnace.

The brass-furnace has the form of the frustrum of a hollow cone, or a cone with the apex cut off horizontally. At the bottom of the furnace is a circular grate or perforated iron plate coated with clay and horse-dung, to defend it from the action of the fire. The crucibles stand upon the circular plate, forming a circular row with one in the middle. The fuel, which in England is coal, is thrown round the crucibles, being let down through the upper opening or smaller end of the cone: over this opening is a perforated cover made of fire

bricks and clay, and kept together with bars of iron so as to fit closely (FIG. 3).

The crucibles are charged with the mixed calamine and charcoal, together with copper clippings and refuse bits of various kinds, and sometimes brass clippings also, most of which are previously melted and run into a small sunk cistern of water through a kind of cullender, which divides the metal into globules, like shot. Powdered charcoal is put over all, and the crucibles are then covered and luted up with a mixture of clay or loam and horse-dung.[6]

It was very important that the crucibles be tightly sealed, for

it is not easy to obtain a perfect union of zinc and copper by mere fusion in open vessels, for at a heat less than is required to melt the copper, the zinc readily takes fire and much of it burns off before it has time to mix with the other metals, so that the proportion of zinc is constantly lessening by volatilization. Even after both metals are fused, the zinc continues to burn off in uncovered vessels, and at last scarcely anything but copper would be left. In order therefore to combine copper most intimately with zinc, and yet to preserve its malleability, the ingenious process of cementation has been resorted to in the manufacture of brass, which is performed by heating in a covered pot alternate layers of copper in small pieces, with zinc ore and charcoal, and continuing the fire till the copper is thoroughly impregnated with the zinc.[7]

"The time required for heating the crucibles and completing the process varies considerably in different works, being determined by custom, by the quantity of materials, the size of the crucibles, and especially the nature of the calamine. In the great way from ten to twenty-four hours are required."[8]

Although very inefficient and time consuming, the process of cementation using calamine continued to be the only way that brass could be made until about the second quarter of the eighteenth century. At that time, the development of sublimation was achieved, by which metallic zinc was obtained from its ores. "Zinc being a volatile metal can only be procured from its ores by sublimation; the process for obtaining it being to strongly heat a mixture of its ore with charcoal in a vessel closed on all sides, except where it admits a tube, the lower end of which dips in water: as soon as the charcoal reduces the oxyde, the metal rises in vapor through the tube and condenses in the water below."[9] Using the pure metal collected through this process, English metalworkers could make brass by combining the zinc with copper through cementation, as had been done earlier using calamine.

"The heat required for brass-making is somewhat less than what would be necessary to melt large masses of copper, brass being the more fusible of the two, and, as it should seem, the vapors of zinc being able to penetrate copper as soon as it is softened by a full red heat. When the brass is judged to be complete, and the saturation of the copper with zinc to be as high as possible, the heat is increased to melt the whole down into one clean mass at the bottom, the crucibles are taken out and the metal poured into moulds."[10]

Red copper and white zinc combine in varying ratios to produce not only differing colors but also different degrees of malleability, ductility, hardness, and fusibility. A 95 percent copper-5 percent zinc mixture produces a red alloy. Increasing amounts of zinc result in a red metal that begins to assume a yellow tinge. As zinc continues to be added, the metal loses its redness until, at about a 75 percent copper to 25 percent zinc ratio, it becomes pale yellow. With still greater amounts of zinc, the yellow deepens and then suddenly turns silver white in color when the ratio stands at about 30 percent copper to 60 percent zinc.

Although technically the metal was brass regardless of the ratio of its constituents, names were created to describe certain alloys. These names not only denoted a specific ratio but also connoted desirable characteristics such as ductility for wire, hardness in solder, or a rich gold color for drawer handles. The more widely used terms during the eighteenth and nineteenth centuries were red brass, similor, tombac, pinchbeck, prince's or Prince Rupert's metal, bath metal, latten, dutch gold, and manheim gold.

Two other related terms that seem to have been largely interchangeable in the eighteenth century were paktong and tutenag. These names and numerous alternate spellings—including pakfong, petong, tin-tina gall, toothenague, tooth and egg, and india metal—describe an alloy of copper, zinc, and nickel that initially was discussed in European writings during the late sixteenth century. The alloy was perfected by the Chinese as early as 200 B.C. and long remained their exclusive provenance; European metallurgists were unable to isolate nickel from its ores until the third quarter of the eighteenth century. Still another seventy-five years were to pass before the copper-zinc-nickel alloy was made in quantity in the West. Not until the 1830s did German metallurgists master commercial production of nickel and its admixture with brass, resulting in large-scale production of the alloy and the addition of another name—german silver—to the many already in use to describe it.

Although base-metal workers were unable to make the three-part alloy until relatively late, Europeans did fabricate paktong objects from imported Chinese metal during the eighteenth century. At the same time, quantities of finished goods in paktong were made in China as well as India and were exported to Western markets.

The ratio of ingredients in paktong varies greatly, just as it does with brass, but copper is always the principal element while zinc and nickel range from 10 to 40 percent each. England did have deposits of nickel ores, principally in Cornwall, but they were for the most part of poor quality. Consequently, English base metal workers depended largely on Norwegian, German, and Dutch imports well into the nineteenth century.

Separating nickel from its ores is a complex multistep process that is more difficult to accomplish than with copper, zinc, or tin, in part because of its 1455°c melting point. The process involves roasting the ore to expel arsenic. The remaining material is then powdered and mixed with nitric acid to remove sulphur. Still remaining in the compound are nickel, iron, cobalt, and copper. The last of these is removed by precipitating it onto a piece of iron, following which the others are precipitated separately using carbonate of potash. Ammonia is then used to dissolve the nickel and cobalt, thereby removing the iron. Lastly, potash is added to the mixture, dissolving the cobalt and leaving nickel oxide, which can be distilled to metallic nickel by heating it in a crucible. At that point the nickel is ready for fusion with brass to make paktong or german silver.[11]

Brass proved to be particularly well suited for a multitude of purposes. Its strength allowed it to serve admirably for making pistol barrels; its color rendered it desirable for personal artifacts like buckles and buttons; its workability made it the preferred metal for clock and watch gears. However, it did not stand up well under extremes of heat or heavy wear. For that, bronze was a much more suitable alloy. Composed of copper and tin in variable amounts, bronze dates to prehistoric use. In Great Britain, tin existed in great quantity in Cornwall and to a somewhat lesser extent in Devonshire. Like copper, zinc, and nickel, tin ores must be cleaned, calcined, and smelted in order to obtain pure, usable metal. Tin's low melting point of 231°c necessitates its being alloyed with copper in such a way that it is not vaporized by the substantially higher temperature needed to melt the latter. This is accomplished by melting copper in a crucible. When the copper is fully liquified, the tin is introduced into the bottom of the crucible and quickly mixed, after which the temperature of the newly made bronze alloy must be immediately reduced, typically accomplished by pouring into molds.[12]

Bronze casts well. It is hard and brittle, so it cannot be easily worked by any other manner. It has proven suitable for casting statuary as well as gears in industrial machinery. Its sonorous nature makes it appropriate for use in bells. It is capable of withstanding extremes of pressure and temperature, allowing it to be used to advantage for cannon and over industrial or domestic fires.

England was fortunate in that it enjoyed ample supplies of copper, zinc in the form of calamine, and tin, which could be used in the making of copper, brass, and bronze implements. These reserves were increasingly exploited throughout the seventeenth, eighteenth, and nineteenth centuries. At the same time, however, the English base-metal industry continued to import Swedish copper, German tin and zinc, and Dutch brass in the form of ore, refined metal, and finished goods, just as had been done prior to Elizabeth's mandate. The British colonies in North America were also viewed as a potential source of these metals. Consequently, exploration commenced soon after settlement. During the seventeenth century, several short-lived attempts to mine copper in the Massachusetts Bay Colony, New Amsterdam, and Virginia were undertaken, but all ended quickly and largely in anonymity.

Among the earliest documented and reasonably successful attempts to extract copper in commercially profitable quantities from American soil were those in the Simsbury area of Connecticut about 1705. While initial efforts were made to smelt the ore at the mine site, English mercantile interests mandated that the ore be shipped across the Atlantic to be worked into pure metal, as was true for all ores mined in America prior to the Revolution. Although the Simsbury mine produced a significant amount of ore, it was only moderately successful, periodically closing and changing ownership until it was eventually shut down in the late eighteenth century.

Belleville, New Jersey, was the site of another early endeavor at copper mining in America that met with marginal success. Ore was discovered there about 1715. The mine contained reason-ably high-grade ore that was sent to Holland and England through the port of New York for smelting. In the middle of the eighteenth century, underground water began to flow into the mine complex more quickly than it could be removed, forcing closure. This situation was temporarily remedied with the importation of an English stationary steam engine to pump out the mine shafts, but when disgruntled workers sabotaged it, the mine closed again for good in the 1770s. Another short-lived copper mining operation was established in Pluckamin, New Jersey, in the early 1770s. Even though its owners ambitiously erected an adjoining smelter and rolling mill to produce wholly American-made sheet copper, the mine closed with the onset of the Revolution.[13]

Prior to the Revolution, Maryland, too, was involved with repeated attempts to mine copper, with some success. The first recorded operation was in the 1740s in Cecil County. A second, about a decade later, occurred in Carroll County, and a third was located in Frederick County. All three produced commercial-quality ore in quantity, which, like efforts in other colonies, ended with the economic turmoil produced by the Revolution.

This short list comprises the best-known successful efforts at copper mining in prerevolutionary America. These attempts were accompanied, however, by a significantly larger number that proved abortive. Records note unsuccessful concerns in virtually every colony along the eastern seaboard. All were failures for a multitude of reasons, including poor-quality ore, lack of capital, inexperienced workers, inaccessible locations, and the high cost of transportation.[14]

Sites known as Mine Hill and Sterling Hill in Sussex County, New Jersey, were discovered to contain zinc ores in the late seventeenth century. Their deposits were quite large, and repeated attempts were made to refine the ores in commercial quantities during the following two hundred years. Another promising deposit of zinc ore was found in the Perkiomen area near Philadelphia during the early nineteenth century. Like the lode in Sussex County, however, it contained a type of ore known as blende—a more complex, tenacious, sulphurous mixture than calamine. It proved difficult to refine, and until the third quarter of the nineteenth century, when improved refining techniques were developed, calamine was preferred for brassmaking. Consequently, these deposits, although initially promising, never proved to be a useful source of zinc until well after 1850.

Tin, like copper and zinc, was sought by base-metal entrepreneurs in America during the colonial era and the early nineteenth century, but, unlike either of the latter, it was never found in quantity.

FABRICATION TECHNIQUES

Copper casts poorly, creating objects with disfiguring surface craters caused by offgasing during cooling. In addition, copper is viscous in its molten state, so it does not flow well into molds. Consequently, copper cakes or pigs, although melted and cast on occasion into finished goods, were for the most part converted into sheet using rolling, flatting, or plating mills. An early description is recorded in Edouard Donovan's *Descriptive Excursions through South Wales and Monmouthshire in the Year 1804 and the Four Preceeding Summers.* Donovan states that

before the copper is converted into plates or bars, the pig of metal is made red hot, when it is closely beaten together under the hammer and cut into pieces of the most convenient length for the purpose wanted, by shears moved by a wheel. Again those pieces are conveyed to the furnace when they become red hot as at first. One of the pieces is carried at a time to the flatting mill, a machine not much unlike the rolling press of a copper plate printer. The two cylinders are of steel, case-hardened and secured within a frame of iron. A man stands on each side, and while the two cylinders revolve, each in a contrary direction, one of them lifts up the piece of red hot copper with a pair of tongs, and thrusts it between the cylinders, the other man on the opposite side securing it with his tongs as it passes through. This he lifts back again over the upper roller to the first man who by the assistance of a strong screw, diminishes the distance between the two cylinders, in order to widen and compress the plate still more; when it is conveyed a second time between them. This screw is turned for the same reason every time before the plate passes between the cylinders, and thus by the most simple process imaginable, the plate is gradually reduced as thin and broad as the workmen may desire. [15]

The metal at this point was ready to be worked by the coppersmith, whose products were "extensive and diversified, as the purposes to which the metal is applied on a large scale are considerable." [16] Little published technical material exists that explains the construction and working techniques of the coppersmith prior to the mid nineteenth century, due in part to word-of-mouth instruction and learning-by-doing practices in crafts shops and manufactories. Those undertaking to earn a livelihood in this profession did so not through books and classroom study but by apprenticing. All instruction took place in the work area by practice at performing the requisite task under supervision.

Upon completion of training and commencement of business, success against competition depended largely upon efficiently practicing the various manufacturing processes and techniques that had been learned and also, when deemed desirable, on developing improvements. Information was not shared. Knowledge of specific practices and improved techniques, if not patented, was purposely limited to the individual, partners (if any), and perhaps a small circle of trusted journeymen and possibly apprentices. Access to work areas and the discussion of processes outside this circle were actively discouraged, as Charles Hatchett discovered on May 25, 1796, when he "stopped at Keynsham 5 miles from Bristol to see the mills for making brass wire and plates also belonging to Messrs. Hanford but were not permitted to see them as we had not a letter from the committee." Hatchett sought admittance to another firm the following day. Of that attempt he recorded in his diary, "At Bristol there is a manufactory for making brass .... We were refused admittance by the proprietors at the brass factory." [17] Numerous others record similar experiences, not having previously provided themselves with letters of introduction or other means of ensuring they were not a threat to the security and privacy of the members of the established copper- and brass-working community.

Some technical accounts concerning coppersmithing do exist, however. That authored by Lardner is particularly useful. Of the metal, he states:

Although copper may be ... cast in sand, like other metals, it is in the state of sheets that the largest consumption takes place. ... Copper, although somewhat difficult to turn at the lathe, or to bore, on account of its clogging the tools, is an exceedingly easy and pleasant metal to fashion by hammering, being at once soft and tenacious. Some articles, being first cast, are afterwards beaten out to the requisite degree of thinness, and to the form intended, advantage being taken of the malleability of the material, by repeatedly heating until red-hot, and then gradually cooling whatever piece of work may be wrought in this manner. Other things, such as kettles, pitchers, and small vessels in general, are soldered.[18]

Large-capacity copper vessels such as stills, which might have to withstand internal pressure, were constructed with overlapping edges that were riveted. The bulk of household objects, however, including but certainly not limited to fry pans, fish kettles, coffeepots, warming pans, boilers, beer mullers, and teakettles, had brazed or soldered seams. Although the design of each is different, their construction is similar and typified by that of the kettle.

A copper tea-kettle presents a familiar but ingenious specimen of the coppersmith's art, both with reference to soldering and hammering: taken, indeed, in all its parts, it exhibits the result of almost every operation of [the coppersmith's] workshop. A piece of metal being cut from the sheet, of a size corresponding with the intended capacity of the kettle, it is brightened by filing over about an inch of the surface at each end. It is then cut with a pair of shears along one end at intervals of [about] an inch, and every alternate portion of the edge bent back a little [often referred to as a dovetail]. It is next bent upon a large mandrel in the manner of a tube, the entire edge being introduced between the cut portions of the other; these when the parts are hammered close, lying alternately inside and out of the vessel. The seam is now to be brazed by the introduction of borax, burnt and titurated with water, and a sprinkling of the solder; the part being held over a coke fire urged with bellows until the solder melts. The vessel, when cooled, is hammered upon a steel head or stake, being lighted occasionally, until the seam is laid smooth, and the body, as to its cylindrical measurement, is correct. Two inches of the tube are next to be turned inward, to form the top of the kettle; this is done by placing it over a little anvil with a sloping face . . . and striking the vessel with the edge of a hammer, until it forms an obtuse angle with the sides. This part being contracted, so as to form a suitable cavity for the lid, the lower end is, by a similar operation, turned inward a little, all round, and then cut with the shears [to form a dovetail joint], the bottom being inserted, and the alternate projecting bits of metal hammered upon it, after which it is soldered in the same manner as the side. The article is now pickled in diluted sulphuric acid and planished to brightness, the marks of the hammer being rendered imperceptible by the intervention of a piece of old moreen, or other woolen stuff, between the copper and the

stake. The lid of the kettle is dished by stamping it in a die; the handle is cast, and the spout, after being soldered up, and rounded a little on a mandrel, is finally shaped upon lead with which it had been filled, and afterwards soldered or riveted into its place. Copper tea urns and saucepans are formed by soldering and hammering in a similar manner, the former being in general finished with a beautiful colour, produced by the application of sulphate of copper or Roman vitriol, previous to the planishing or burnishing.[19]

Since the objects discussed as well as others were sold by weight, standard practice dictated that as thin a gauge as possible be used. If greater strength was needed, as in the bottoms of kettles or saucepans, a heavier-gauge metal would be substituted in these areas. As noted, if still greater strength was needed, as for handles and handle sockets, cast parts could be used.

Thin-walled sheet-metal vessels exemplified by drinking pots, warming pans, and teakettles will, with use, eventually distort and tear at their outer edges. To prevent this from happening, coppersmiths wrapped the outer edge of the object around an iron wire; a small-gauge wire suited smaller lightweight objects, while a larger diameter was needed for vessels of larger size and greater capacity.

Joints in copper vessels are typically dovetailed, but on occasion straight seams were used when particularly complex shapes, such as teakettle spouts, were involved. All were soldered or brazed with a specially formulated copper-zinc alloy called *spelter*. This alloy is purposely high in zinc content, thus giving it a relatively low melting point, which helps prevent melting the copper or brass artifact being brazed.

Appendages such as coffeepot-handle sockets, warming-pan lids, and teakettle handle brackets and spouts were held in place with copper rivets, although on occasion brass and even iron rivets were used. Prior to the late seventeenth century, a typical copper rivet was made of a small piece of sheet metal tightly rolled into a solid cylinder. After insertion into a joint, its ends were hammered flat to form irregular petal-shape heads. By the late seventeenth century, these began to be replaced with solid cylindrical rivets, which also had heads worked onto them with either a hammer or a riveting tool, although the former type continued to be used on occasion. By the late eighteenth century, solid rivets were machine-headed by specialized manufacturers, with either hemispheres or flat disks at the ends.

Brass was worked both as sheet metal and in a molten state. Generally the artisan who fabricated the former was called a brazier. However, "the appellation of brazier, although in strictness applied to an artificer in brass, as contradistinguished from one who works in copper, has long since sunk into a synonym with" the latter.[20] The working techniques and tools he used to fashion his artifacts were virtually the same as those used by the coppersmith (FIG. 4).

The brass or bronze founder, by contrast, made use of very different techniques and tools. Of central importance was the pattern, a wood or metal master of the desired object. If the artifact was a simple shape, like a button or buckle, a single complete pattern would serve. If it was complex in shape, like a candlestick or andiron, the founder would have to use a separate pattern to cast each part individually and then assemble the various parts as a separate step in creating the completed object (FIGS. 5, 6). Castings are made using specially formulated casting sand in flasks.

In working from a pattern in green-sand the object in view is to produce in the finely packed sand a cavity identical in form with that of the pattern; the same being afterwards filled with molten metal and left to cool. To accomplish this the workman is provided with a large assortment of flasks, or molding-boxes of the most various dimensions; they are designed to hold the sand used in making the molds. Small flasks are simply rectangular frames resembling ordinary boxes, but without either top or bottom; each part being 3 to 6 inches high. They are connected together generally in pairs...

by steady-pins, which allow of their separation when full of sand and their restoration to exactly the same relative position afterward.

One flask being laid with its lugs uppermost is filled and rammed up with old-sand, and stricken off level with the joint of the flask: this is called a false-part. [Some] sand in the false-part is cut away roughly, so as to imbed one half of the pattern (FIG. 7). Some dry parting-sand is next scattered over the surface. This adheres to the damp sand, and prevents any union between such a surface and any other sand subsequently rammed upon it. After the parting-sand is blown off the exposed part of the pattern, the other side or drag is put on, its steadying pins entering the holes in the lugs of the false-part easily, but without shake. Newly prepared sand, facing-sand, is next sieved over the pattern in sufficient quantity to cover it completely. The box is filled with old-sand from the floor of the shop and is carefully rammed up and stricken off. After provision is made for the escape of gases from the sand by prodding it all over with a sharp pointed steel wire, known as a vent wire, the two flasks are held together and turned over on a bed prepared for the drag upon the floor, or on a flat board if the boxes are small, and the false-part having done its work, is lifted off and emptied. An exact parting is now made with the trowel along the median line, if the casting be symmetrical, the damp facing-sand being added to or cut away sharply up to the pattern as occasion may require. The parting-line is, as a general rule, that line upon the pattern, as it lies in the sand, above and

Fig. 4. Battery where basins are being formed under trip hammers. From Denis Diderot, *Encyclopédie, ou Dictionnaire raisonné des sciences, des arts, et des métiers*, 28 vols. (Paris: Briasson, 1751–76), *Recueil des Planches*, vol. 6, métallurgie, pl. 4.

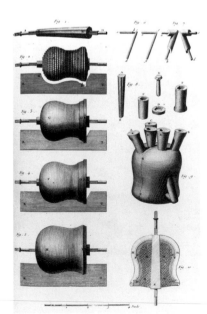

Fig. 5. Cauldron being cast in earth. From Denis Diderot, *Encyclopédie, ou Dictionnaire raisonné des sciences, des arts, et des métiers*, 28 vols. (Paris: Briasson, 1751–76), *Recueil des Planches*, vol. 4, forges, sec. 3, pl. 4.

below which the sides of the pattern run inward from the perpendicular. This is frequently an undulating line, but the parting surface always runs from it in all directions to the horizontal edge of the box. Parting-sand is now strewn over the whole, and the surplus blown off. The upper flask or cope being replaced, a short cylindrical runner-stick is thrust into the sand of the lower part at a convenient distance from the pattern; facing-sand is sieved on, the box filled up with old-sand, rammed up and stricken off as before. The vent-wire is then used as with the drag, the runner-stick withdrawn, and the opening left, through which the metal has ultimately to pass to the mold, is given a bell-mouthed shape.

Having arrived at this stage of the work, the molder, either alone if the box is small, or with the help of other workmen or the crane itself if it be large, lifts the cope steadily upward, leaving the pattern in the sand of the drag. The cope is then usually turned over on wooden blocks for repairs and dressing. The pattern is now to be drawn from the sand. This is done with the help of spikes or screwed rods, temporarily attached to it; with one or more of these it is lifted, being made to vibrate the while by rapid tapping with a piece of wood or iron, for the purpose of causing it to leave the sand readily. The molder has now to repair with suitable tools any broken parts of the sand forming the mold, then cut the runners or channels from the opening left by the gate-stick to the mold, along which the fluid metal finds its way; and lastly to dust finely powdered . . . mill dust or similar farinaceous substance . . . over the facing-sand surface. . . . The excess dust is in every case blown off with the bellows. When the top part is closed, it occupies exactly the position it did before; the space then filled by the pattern being now vacant, and in connection with the gate, the hot metal can therefore make its way so as to fill such space, the form of which it will be found to have taken when cold.[21]

This process was used to create castings of all types of brass or bronze objects except those that had to be hollow, for which additional steps were necessary, usually involving a core. A core is an internal mold which forms the interior of a cylinder, tube, pipe, faucet, or other hollow casting. It is made of various proportions of new sand, loam and horse-dung. It requires to be thoroughly dried, and when containing horse-dung must be burned to a red heat, to consume the straw. This makes it porous and of a brick red color.

The core is made in a core-box and has projecting portions, known as core-prints, which rest in the prints of the mold. The model from which the object is cast is solid and makes an impression, partly in the cope and partly in the drag. When the pattern is removed, the core is laid in its place, the projecting portions resting in the recesses made by the prints of the pattern. Touching the loam of the mold at no other point, it occupies, in the case of a pipe, a central position in the space which is to be run full of metal. When the metal has been poured around it and then cooled, the core is broken out, leaving the casting hollow.[22]

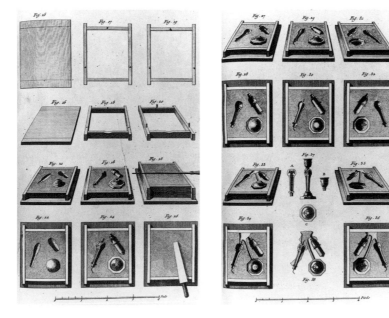

Fig. 6. Candlestick being cast in sand. From Denis Diderot, *Encyclopédie, ou Dictionnaire raisonné des sciences, des arts, et des métiers*, 28 vols. (Paris: Briasson, 1751–76), *Recueil des Planches*, vol. 5, fondeur en sable, pls. 3, 4.

Core casting was the most expeditious for brass- and bronze-wares, but an alternate technique of casting in halves was also used during the eighteenth and early nineteenth centuries, notably for candlesticks and andirons. This process utilized a pattern that was half the object, longitudinally. The pattern was relieved on the reverse side so that two castings made with it, when brazed together, created a hollow object (FIGS. 8, 9).

The need for hollowness was dictated by the fact that copper and its alloys were sold by weight. A competitive coppersmith or brass worker, therefore, fabricated objects with walls as thin as possible. The coppersmith adjusted wall thickness of the various parts of an object according to the demands placed upon them. He might make the side of a teakettle from 1/32-inch gauge sheet. The bottom, which had to withstand considerably greater abrasion and exposure to heat might be of 3/32-inch sheet, while the handle, which had to support the kettle's full weight without distorting or tearing, might be as thick as 1/8 of an inch.

The founder made similar adjustments in his work. A relatively slender object like the bail of a drawer-handle plate or an andiron leg had to be solid for strength. Larger diameter parts, like andiron uprights, if cast solid, consumed far more metal than was needed and became unnecessarily expensive. Making those parts hollow when possible, although complicating the fabrication process, offered the best means of saving metal and reducing cost.

About the middle of the eighteenth century a major advance was made in the production of domestic brasswares that dramatically affected their availability and cost. It is stated to have been "the invention of John Pickering of London, a jeweller, or gilt toy maker, who, on March 7th, 1769, patented a new method of performing that kind of work called chasing for gold, silver, brass, tin, and other metals but more especially to be used in the production of coffin furniture: also ornaments for coaches, chariots, cabinet brass work, and domestic furniture." In his patent specification, Pickering described the new process at length, adding that with it "work is executed in a much more expeditious manner, and far superior in beauty and elegance to anything of the kind (not being actual chasing) ever yet performed by any other method."[23]

The process came to be known as *stamped brassfoundry* and was executed with a downfall or drop press (FIG. 10). Its product

consists of articles of sheet metal figured by stamping. [Through it] at a single stroke, or at most within a single minute of time, an effect is produced on metallic laminae, which, by the tedious methods of chasing or embossing formerly practiced would require thousands of strokes, and many hours, or even days . . . although the expense of the apparatus is very considerable—including dies, often enormously so. . . . The facility of multiplying impressions by this method, and so light, yet stiff the body of metal embossed, that the low price of many brass ornaments of this description would be scarcely conceivable, were it not that cheapness and demand have reacted upon one another until the articles have become universally requisite.[24]

Fig. 7. Paw-foot casting pattern and paw-foot casting, England or northeast United States, 1800–1820. Wood, brass; L. 2 1/8" (5.4 cm), W. 2 1/16" (5.2 cm), H. 1 9/16" (3.9 cm). (Gift of Peter Hill.)

Fig. 8. Andiron upright pattern, probably Boston, 1800–1900. Wood; H. 13 3/8" (34.0 cm), W. 3 1/4" (8.3 cm), D. 1 3/4" (4.4 cm). (Gift of Henry J. Kauffman.)

Speed of replication and light weight were combined in the process of stamping to produce great quantities of stylish yet inexpensive brasswares. Whereas an efficient brass founder may have been able to cast, finish, and chase a few dozen cabinet handles in the course of a day, the brass stamper could easily make five hundred. Similarly, if the founder was careful in fashioning his molds, poured his metal at exactly the right temperature, and took time in grinding and finishing, he might be able to make his cabinet-handle plates between $1/32$ and $1/16$ of an inch in thickness. The stamper routinely worked with sheet rolled to about $1/50$ of an inch, a reduction in thickness of about one half.

The downfall press used in the new production process was a relatively simple device. It consisted of

two upright pillars of wrought iron, about eight feet high, and so placed that their angular edges serve to guide the hammer in its ascent and descent, its ends being grooved for this purpose. This hammer, which is eighteen inches across, and weighs about 100 lbs. is suspended by a rope over the trundle, at the top of the room: it is tufted with worsted in the manner of a bell rope, to form a hand-hold, and at the lower end is attached a stirrup; in this the work-man places his left foot, the right being thrust under [a loop affixed to the floor], during the operation of raising the stamp. [Under the stamp] is a large boss of cast iron, having on its face four stout screws to detain the die: this boss is let into a block of stone, weigh-ing from one to two tons. The stamp hammer is sometimes changed

for one heavier or lighter, according to the description of the work: to accommodate such a hammer, the upright pillars are attached at the top to two beams, and at the bottom to two side screws, by which contrivance they are readily brought nearer together or removed further apart. On the under face of the hammer is fixed a flat piece of iron cut on the surface like a rasp, and called a 'lick-up': its use is, to detain the piece of lead corresponding to the die, and by means of which the material to be impressed is struck into the die; each stroke keeps this lead fast to the lick-up, from which it is, when done with, separated by spiking it downwards. . . . [Tongs are] used when articles are stamped when red hot, which is often the case with copper and plated metal, though never with brass.

The dies of the brass stamper, which vary in size and weight according to the bigness of the article to be operated upon, are made either of steel or cast iron; of the former material when small or when the metal is required to be embossed into designs of very sharp execution; and of the latter when the pieces are large, and, as is generally the case, intended to be afterwards got up with the burnisher on the smooth, and aquafortis on the other parts. What-ever the size, if the metal be thin, and the relief of the design incon-siderable, especially when the parts are roundish, a very few strokes with the stamp are sufficient to produce the impression. But it is far otherwise when the figure is of considerable depth and exhibiting strong angular sections; under these circumstances, the greatest care is required on the part of the workman, not only to select good metal, but likewise to imbed it in the die only by gentle strokes,

and these often repeated, sometimes from a dozen to a score; the metal being frequently lighted, or heated red hot, at intervals during the stamping. If these precautions were not attended to, it would be impossible, even with the most ductile sheet brass, to proceed far without fracturing the article, and thus wasting both time and metal.[25]

FINISHING TECHNIQUES

Following fabrication, copper and sheet-brass objects were polished to present a bright reflective surface. Cast brass and bronze articles were treated similarly but required preliminary cleaning and smoothing. Casting flaws were filled. If irregularly shaped, they were filed to remove flash and surface roughness. The same was accomplished on circular objects or those with circular parts by skimming them on a lathe. When the surface had been worked to a reasonably smooth state, polishing was undertaken with a series of increasingly less-abrasive substances. Among the most commonly used were emery and sand, applied by hand on a piece of soft wood, leather, or cloth. The next in degree of fineness were brick dust and tripoli. These were followed by rottenstone, whiting, or black lead, applied in an oil medium for a very high polish.

If the object so treated were handled on a regular basis, it would remain bright. If not, it tarnished quickly and required periodic polishing. The surface of the metal might be prevented from oxidizing in several ways. The most desirable was to coat the object with gold, a process known as mercury gilding or ormolu. The process begins with heating

some pure quicksilver in a clean crucible, and, when it is nearly boiling, put about a sixth of its weight of fine gold in thin plates heated red-hot, and stir them gently about, till the gold be found melted and incorporated into a mass with the mercury. It is then allowed to cool; and when cold, it is to be put in a piece of soft leather; and by gradual pressure, the fluid part of the amalgam, consisting almost wholly of mercury, may be forced through the pores of the leather, while the gold, combined with about twice its weight of mercury, will remain behind, forming a yellowish silvery mass of the consistence of soft butter. This, after having been bruised in a mortar or shaken in a strong vial with repeated portions of salt and water, till the water ceases to be fouled by it, is fit for use. . . . Copper, and the alloys formed by its combinations with zinc, are gilded [with this mixture]. The piece of copper [or brass] is first cleaned by steeping it in acid and subsequent washing, and it is then burnished in a lathe, or by other means: After this, it is dipped in a neutralized solution of nitrate of mercury, and in a few seconds, on account of the strong affinity of nitric acid for copper, the mercurial salt is decomposed. The copper takes the place of the mercury, and at the same time the mercury is deposited in the metallic state, on the surface of the copper, covering it entirely and strongly adhering to it [when the object is] moderately warm, a little gold amalgam, also warm, is to be evenly spread upon [it], to which it will immedi-

Fig. 9. Dan Berg, unassembled cast candlestick, Williamsburg, Virginia, ca. 1971. Brass; L. 8 7/16" (21.4 cm), W. 3/4" (8.3 cm). (Gift of Dan Berg.)

Fig. 10. Schematic view of a downfall stamp. From Dionysius Lardner, comp., *The Cabinet Cyclopaedia*, 3 vols. (London: Longman, Rees, Orme, Brown, Green, and Longman, and John Taylor, 1834), 3:220, fig. 33.

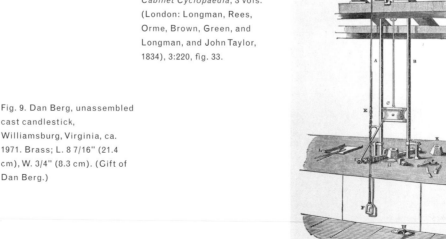

ately adhere. By applying the amalgam, the operator uses a little knife, or a brush made of brass wire, for the purpose; and giving the work a gentle heat before the fire, he dabs or spreads the amalgam with the brush farther and more evenly upon it. Thus far advanced, the metal is set over the fire, upon a grate, or in a sort of cage, under which is a pan of charcoal, yielding a heat just sufficient for evaporating the mercury; by which means the mercury is raised in fumes, and leaves the gold alone adhering to the work.[26]

While this was deemed a most desirable and advantageous process, it was unduly expensive. Consequently, an alternate process producing much the same visual effect, called lacquering, was developed and put widely into practice by the mid eighteenth century. "The Lacquer or varnish is composed of spirits of wine, in which has been dissolved seed-lac. In appearance it presents that of pale French brandy, verging, where coloured, into that of the brown variety of the spirit already named. Tumeric, dragon's blood, or sandal wood, will impart various shades of colour if dissolved in the mixture of spirits of wine and seed-lac already named. The brass articles, having been coated over when cold with the lacquer, are laid on the hot plate, and when sufficiently heated are again coated with lacquer applied with large round camel hair brushes, of sizes varying from five-eight inches to one inch diameter. Delicate and skilful application, and the perfection of lacquering, consist in a uniform coating." If properly executed, the process produces "a rich and lasting gold color unaffected by the action of the atmosphere."[27] Its permanence, affordability, and spectacular appearance were quickly grasped by manufacturers and the buying public alike, with the result that lacquering became a universal means of finishing ornamental brasswares throughout the late eighteenth and nineteenth centuries.

Copper and brass were also silvered. Several means were available by which the transformation could be accomplished. The most basic was known as french plating, and it seems to have been used primarily on brass. "After the goods were polished, and perfectly free from grease, and indeed any other extraneous matter, the part to be plated was heated to a temperature something short of changing the colour of the metal. Silver leaf was now laid upon the part, and, while hot, was rubbed on with a hardened steel-burnisher, perfectly clean and dry. By this means the silver adhered firmly to the brass, which, from the action of the bur-

nisher, assumed a fine polish."[28] As with ormolu, brass objects so treated were relatively expensive and designed to be very stylish.

French-plated wares, including footed salvers, tankards, canns, and candlesticks, experienced their greatest vogue during the late seventeenth through the mid eighteenth centuries, but "this art is scarcely now practiced, from the introduction of the superior plan of plating upon ingots of copper, and forming utensils out of the sheets and wire made from the ingots." That process, termed *fused plate*, was invented in England during the second quarter of the eighteenth century. It proved to be an expeditious and inexpensive method that largely superceded all other types of plating within the span of about fifty years. The process begins with a cast copper ingot

about three inches broad, 1⅛ in thickness, and about eighteen or twenty long. . . . For the ordinary kind of work these ingots are generally cut in two in the middle, being more convenient for plating than long pieces.

The next process is to dress the face of the ingot for the purpose of receiving the silver, on one or both sides, as it may be intended to be single or double plated. This is effected by filing, which is continued till the surface becomes entirely free from the least blemish. . . . If the ingot of copper be 1¼ thick, the silver plate to be laid upon it . . . will be 1/32 of an inch. . . . When the plate of silver is cut to a little less than the size of the copper surface, made flat, and scraped perfectly clean, the copper surface being equally clean, they are laid together, and the silver plate is tied down with wire. A little of a saturated solution of borax is now insulated under the edge of the silver plate on every side: this fuses at a low red heat, and prevents the oxygen of the atmosphere from affecting the surface of the copper, which would prevent the adherence of the silver. In this state the ingot is brought to the plating furnace. . . . When the silver and copper are uniting [in the furnace] the surface of the former begins to be revetted, and this is the sign to remove the ingot from the fire as quick as possible. If it were allowed to stop longer, the silver would become alloyed with the copper, and completely spoiled.

In this process, the silver is, in fact, soldered to the copper, although no solder is expressly employed. . . . The ingot, now being plated, is ready to be rolled. It is flatted to the desired dimension in a mill precisely like that described for use in making sheet copper. This having been accomplished, the sheet is cut to the

appropriate pieces, each of which is then stamped to the neces-
sary shape for assembly.[29]

Most copper and brass objects were intended to be used in their natural color, but large quantities had their surfaces treated in one of the aforementioned ways to make them appear as if they were silver or gold. Additionally, a significant amount was patinated to simulate other colors. "Different tints may be imparted to [copper and] brass, from red to bright yellow, and from dark to light green. Boiling . . . in muriatic acid will give . . . a red colour; and soaking . . . in ammonia renders [them] whiter. [Copper or brass] painted with a thin solution of equal parts of sal-ammonia and oxalate of potash, in a warm room, or in the heat of the sun, gives . . . a fine green colour, particularly if rubbed with it. If a dark blackish bronze colour is required, the foregoing solution is laid on in a room where some liver of sulphur–sulfuret of potassium– is dissolved in water, and set out in flat dishes to generate sulfuretted hydrogren, which will cause a uniform blackish brown colour."[30] These materials and processes provided the brass and copper worker with the means to infuse a strong and diverse range of colors into their products; they were often used.

The foregoing materials outlining mining and manufacturing techniques largely encompass those methods that were developed and used in England and America from the seventeenth through the mid nineteenth centuries. The history of the mining of copper, zinc, tin, and nickel and their manufacture into implements of copper, brass, bronze, and paktong is, however, complex and multifaceted. Summarizing this material briefly is analogous to Lardner's condensing his voluminous material into the statement that "the operations through which brass work, in general, passes in the workshops, are casting, filing, chasing, stamping, soldering, screwing, pickling, turning, burnishing, and lacquering."[31] While the summation is accurate, a comprehensive understanding of the subject requires much additional detail beyond the scope of this catalogue.

1 Maxwell Bruce Donald, *Elizabethan Copper: The History of the Company of Mines Royal, 1568 to 1605* (London: Pergamion Press, 1955), p. 1. Maxwell Bruce Donald, *Elizabethan Monopolies: The History of the Company of Mineral and Battery Works from 1565 to 1604* (Edinburgh, Scot.: Oliver and Boyd, 1961), p. 1. *The Universal British Directory of Trade, Commerce, and Manufacture* (London, 1791), pp. xxiv-xxv.

2 Denys B. Barton, *A History of Copper Mining in Cornwall and Devon* (Truro, Eng.: D. Bradford Barton, 1961), pp. 9, 10.

3 Dionysius Lardner, comp., *The Cabinet Cyclopaedia*, 3 vols. (London: Longman, Rees, Orme, Brown, Green, and Longman, and John Taylor, 1834), 3:141, 142.

4 Lardner, *Cabinet Cyclopaedia*, 3:142-48.

5 Thomas Cooper, comp., *The Emporium of Arts and Sciences* (Philadelphia), n.s., 3, no. 1 (June 1814): 77.

6 Cooper, *Emporium of Arts and Sciences*, pp. 77, 78.

7 Cooper, *Emporium of Arts and Sciences*, p. 76.

8 Cooper, *Emporium of Arts and Sciences*, p. 78.

9 Cooper, *Emporium of Arts and Sciences*, p. 76.

10 Cooper, *Emporium of Arts and Sciences*, p. 79.

11 This process is described in detail in Abraham Rees, *The Cyclopaedia; or, Universal Dictionary of Arts, Sciences, and Literature*, 47 vols. (Philadelphia: Samuel F. Bradford, 1810-24), 26: s.v. "nickel."

12 A detailed description of this process is presented in Cooper, *Emporium of Arts and Sciences*, pp. 100, 101.

13 Johann David Schoepf, *Travels in the Confederation*, 2 vols. (1788; reprint, Philadelphia: William J. Campbell, 1911), 1:26-27.

14 James A. Mulholland, *A History of Metals in Colonial America* (University, Ala.: University of Alabama Press, 1981), pp. 37-54.

15 As quoted in Cooper, *Emporium of Arts and Sciences*, pp. 127-28.

16 Lardner, *Cabinet Cyclopaedia*, 3:154.

17 Arthur Raistrick, *The Hatchett Diary* (Truro, Eng.: D. Bradford Barton, 1967), pp. 49, 50.

18 Lardner, *Cabinet Cyclopaedia*, 3:155.

19 Lardner, *Cabinet Cyclopaedia*, 3:156-58.

20 Lardner, *Cabinet Cyclopaedia*, 3:154.

21 Edward H. Knight, *Knight's American Mechanical Dictionary*, 3 vols. (Boston: Houghton, Osgood, 1880), 2:1460.

22 Knight, *American Mechanical Dictionary*, 1:621.

23 Chasing is discussed in William Costen Aitken, *The Early History of Brass and the Brass Manufacturers of Birmingham* (Birmingham, Eng.: Martin Billing, Son, 1866), p. 68. The Pickering quote appears in Specification of Letters Patent, no. 920, March 7, 1769, British Patent Office, London.

24 Lardner, *Cabinet Cyclopaedia*, 3:218, 219.

25 Lardner, *Cabinet Cyclopaedia*, 3:219, 221.

26 Rees, *Cyclopaedia*, 17:s.v. "gilding on metals by the fire."

27 Lacquering is discussed in Samuel Timmins, ed., *The Resources, Products, and Industrial History of Birmingham and the Midland Hardware District* (London: Robert Hardwicke, 1866), pp. 301-2; J. Leander Bishop, *A History of American Manufactures from 1608-1866*, 3 vols. (Philadelphia: Edward Young, 1866), 3:51.

28 Rees, *Cyclopaedia*, 29:s.v. "plated manufacture in the arts."

29 Rees, *Cyclopaedia*, 29:s.v. "plated manufacture in the arts." An excellent discourse on the complete process of making objects of fused plate is recounted in Frederick Bradbury, *A History of Old Sheffield Plate* (London: Macmillan, 1912), pp. 75-132.

30 Frederick Overman, *The Moulder's and Founder's Pocket Guide* (Philadelphia: Moss and Brother, 1854), p. 242. Additional forumulations are listed in William Norman Brown, *The Principles and Practice of Dipping, Burnishing, Lacquering, and Bronzing Brass Ware* (London: Scott, Greenwood, and Son, 1912).

31 Lardner, *Cabinet Cyclopaedia*, 3:213.

MARKETING

In July 1652, John Mavericke and William Fryer inventoried the salvaged contents of the *Eagle*. The ship had earlier sailed from London for Boston but was wrecked near the Isle of Sable, about six hundred miles from its destination. Among the goods on board were eighty-seven bundles of copper bars weighing 2,506 pounds and eleven brass kettles weighing 187 pounds.[1]

On September 10, 1680, Robert Lord of Salem, Massachusetts, wrote to a correspondent in England "a note of what things we desire to have sent over for our part." His letter listed "a great kettell about 18 or 20 gallons & others les to goe one within another to 3 gallons & 6 skillets the biggest to hold 2 quarts strong such as they call dubble brass [and] 2 doozon occumy spoones."[2]

These and related items of copper, brass, and bronze were a staple in the transatlantic trade between England's industrial-commercial centers and the American colonies. The flow of goods west existed in part because of England's mercantile posture–which used its colonies as markets–but more importantly because immigrants trying to establish a lifestyle in America akin to that which they left behind in England needed them. In short order, their needs gave rise to an extensive network through which both basic and luxury goods in these metals were supplied. So successful was this trading network that in 1783 an interested observer was able to state that "the American market is already glutted with European manufactures. British goods of several kinds were cheaper last year in New York than in London, and the last Letters From Philadelphia mention several articles 25 per cent cheaper."[3]

The quantity of copper, brass, and bronze artifacts available and their affordability meant that they were prevalent in American households. At times they were present in remarkable quantity. When the household of Lord Botetourt–the royal governor of Virginia–was inventoried in 1770, included among its contents were two copper coal scuttles, one copper warming pan, and one brass candlestick in the powder room; a copper boiler, two brass sconces, and two large teakettles in the little middle room; two copper coffeepots in the closet to the little room; one small copper teakettle, eight french-plate candlesticks, three french-plate soup ladles, and one Sheffieldware tea kitchen in the pantry; fourteen copper paste molds, one dutch metal tea oven, two teakettles, one copper boiler, and three dutch metal coffeepots in the second store room; three dozen brass branches, six brass branches for globe lamps, a bunch of large brass curtain rings, two bunches of small brass curtain rings, and a parcel of nails with brass heads in the third store room; one brass brush in the coachman's room; twelve brass saddle buttons and staples in the groom's room; one large boiling copper, four dozen copper molds, a pair of two-pound copper scales and weights, twenty-one copper stewpans and twenty-four covers, one bell-metal mortar and pestle, and three copper chafing dishes in the kitchen; two brass branches in the dining room; and six brass branches in the ballroom. Also listed were numerous other objects such as andirons, shovels, tongs, pokers, and coal grates that, although not specifically described, were probably brass.[4]

Botetourt's close ties to the English court and his use of the governor's palace for entertaining determined the level of his need for copper, brass, and bronze household objects. It was a somewhat atypical American interior, but even on a less grand

scale, these metals could accumulate in significant numbers. Thomas Jefferson's kitchen inventory taken in 1796 listed nineteen copper stewpans and nineteen covers; six small saucepans; three copper baking molds; two small preserving pans; two large preserving pans; two copper fish kettles; two copper brazing pans; two round large brazing pans; one large brass boiling kettle; one copper frying pan; four round, copper baking sheets; four square, copper baking sheets; one copper boiler; one copper teakettle; two copper ladles; four copper spoons; three copper skimmers; twenty-one small, copper baking molds; one brass colander; one old copper fish kettle; one brass mortar and pestle; one old brass kettle; and two brass chafing dishes.[5]

The network that supplied these goods began with manufacturers in Britain's industrial centers, the principal cities involving the copper and brass trades being Bristol and London at the time the American colonies were first settled. "Although the chief dependence of Bristol consists in Foreign trade [it] was the first place where brass was made in England . . . the original workmen [being] brought over from Holland for the purpose, the quantity made here is prodigious . . . from whence it is sent to London, Liverpool and every part of the kingdom." The same was true for London. Although a much larger and more diverse metropolis, "London [was] scarcely acknowledged as a manufacturing city except for objects of furniture or luxury; for metallic works [other centers were better known]. Yet London contains within its streets many [copper and brass working] establishments of much extent, skill and power, scarcely known to the busy throng which pass their doors." These two cities with direct ties to the coast were joined by and began to experience strong competition from the inland town of Birmingham, which came to be "deservedly considered the first manufacturing town in the British empire" by the mid eighteenth century.[6]

Although Birmingham was a landlocked community, it flourished in part because of an extensive canal system. "Birmingham derives considerable advantage from its navigable canals, whereby the expense of land-carriage is much lessened, and the heavy articles are conveyed at a very trifling charge. The first navigation was opened in the year 1769, but has since that time been greatly extended, having now a communication with nearly all the principal canals in the kingdom. . . . The boats [used on them] are long and narrow and carry from 20 to 30 tons; they are drawn by a single horse, and go at the rate of about two miles an hour."[7] Using this extensive canal system, Birmingham and other midland hardware manufacturing towns had easy and inexpensive access to port cities throughout England from where they could ship their goods at will.

Many artisans in these cities and their satellite towns were involved in copper and brass manufacturing. Some presented themselves as generalists, like Sarah Clare of Birmingham, who described herself as a "brass founder," or John and William Turner, also of Birmingham, who called themselves "proprietors of brass works." However, an even greater number of these artisans advertised as specialists. John Hollis of Birmingham was one such man who listed himself in the city directory as a "manufacturer of plated and brass dog collars." Another was John Boulton, who styled himself a "brass candlestick and bell maker." Two others were Joseph Boyce, a brass "bellows pipe maker" and Thomas Bingham, a "brass nutcrack maker."[8]

The many men in the various branches of this craft sought to make and sell their wares directly to the public, but as the geographic size of their market expanded they turned to middlemen, whose job it was to distribute the wares wherever they were wanted, regardless of distance. These men came to be known variously as factors, hardwaremen, hardware merchants, copper merchants, or ironmongers. They opened and maintained lines of communication between producer and consumer through which goods moved according to demand.

The trade these middlemen practiced proved to be very effective, and as a result the merchants flourished. As observed by an early commentator on Birmingham and its trade in 1781: "The practice of the Birmingham manufacturer, for perhaps, a hundred generations, was to keep within the warmth of his own forge. The foreign customer applied to him for the execution of orders, and regularly made his appearance twice a year; and though this mode of business is not totally extinguished, yet a very different one is adopted. The merchant stands at the head of the manufacturer, purchases his produce, and travels the whole island to promote the sale. . . . The commercial spirit of the age, hath also penetrated beyond the confines of Britain, and explored the whole continent of Europe; nor does it stop there; for the West Indies, and the American world, are intimately acquainted with the Birmingham merchant."[9]

In pursuit of the American trade, the Bristol merchant Richard Champion wrote a letter of introduction to the Philadelphia firm of Willing and Morris on July 6, 1774. In it he stated, "Give me leave now to make you an offer of" my services to supply you with English manufactured goods "and to assure you that [for] any business you entrust to my care I hope to give you such satisfaction as will render our correspondence mutually agreeable."[10] Having established a correspondence, Champion or a competitor such as William Eagles, who listed himself as "carolina merchant" in the 1795 Bristol city directory, set about acquiring orders for goods, letting manufacturers know of their availability and shipping those goods as expeditiously as possible. When George Watson, Jr., advertised in the August 2, 1784, issue of *Aris's Birmingham Gazette*, he illustrated the means whereby this process was accomplished handily. "George Watson, junior, merchant in Bristol begs leave to inform the shippers of goods to America that he has the following ships under his direction for the different ports mentioned and solicits the favor of their freights assuring them of the utmost dispatch and punctuality . . . the brig *Sisters* . . . for James River, Virginia . . . the new brig *Petrel* . . . for Baltimore in Maryland, the ship *Tobago Planter* . . . for Philadelphia . . . the ship *Hannah* . . . for New York [and] the new ship *Grace* . . . for New York."

Throughout the seventeenth, eighteenth, and early nineteenth centuries, the movement of ships from England's port cities to those on America's East Coast was constant. Many carried quantities of copper in various forms. On January 23, 1773, the *Restoration*, with James Thomas as its captain, left Bristol bound for Maryland. In its hold, shipped by the merchant T. Pennington, were "14 casks, 4 cases, 3 bales and 24 bundles of . . . brass manufactures [and] unwrought copper." On February 6, 1773, the *America* departed Bristol for New York. It contained 6 casks of brass manufacture shipped by the firm of Peach and Pierce; 3 casks of brass manufacture shipped by Reeve, Son, and Hill; 2 casks of unwrought copper sent by J. Freeman and Company; 4 hogsheads of wrought iron and brass manufacture sent by G. Watson, Jr.; and 7 casks, 1 parcel, 2 baskets, 1 box, and 1 bag of brass manufacture shipped by Cruger and Mallard. On the same day, the *Chalkley* left Bristol bound for Philadelphia. In its hold were 7 tierces, 44 casks, 24 kegs, 14 bundles, 2 boxes, and 8 cases of wrought iron and brass manufacture sent by L. Cowper; 1 tierce, 17 casks, 1 box, and 1 case of wrought iron and brass manufacture consigned by T. Pennington;

2 hogsheads, 1 tierce, and 1 basket of brass manufacture sent by T. Frank; 1 barrel, 3 hogsheads, 4 chests, 3 cases, and 1 tierce of wrought iron and brass manufacture from G. Watson, Jr.; 2 casks of brass manufacture from Cruger and Mallard; 1 tierce of brass manufacture from J. Smith, Jr.; 1 still head, 1 tierce, and 1 basket of copper manufacture from Coghlan, Peach, and Company; 1 cask of solder from S. Munchley; and 1 copper still and brass consigned by Lowbridge, Bright, and Company.[11]

In total, the quantity of English copper and brass consumed in America was extensive, as documented in England's Public Record Office in Kew. The amount of brass shipped to the colonies in the year 1700 totaled about 28 tons and regularly increased during the ensuing decades, rising to 227 tons in 1760. During the Revolution, exports of British-made brass declined, although "trade in general [was stated to be] tolerably good [in spite of] the entire stop [mandated] to the American trade" by the embargo. Following the war, open trade again resumed, and the quantity of English brass arriving in American ports surged to 312 tons by 1795. Copper exports followed the same course, with about 1 ton arriving in the colonies in 1700. In 1760 this figure had risen to about 198 tons, then dwindled to only 6 tons in 1775, but rose quickly to more than 595 tons in 1795.[12]

These figures provide a useful impression of the volume of copper and brass manufactured goods passing from English manufacturers through hardwaremen to Americans prior to the mid nineteenth century, but the general nature of British bills of lading gives no insight into what kinds of objects constituted that trade. Shipping invoices for American importers can be more useful in that respect, as illustrated by an invoice of goods received by the Philadelphia hardware firm of Porter and Fichett dated August 27, 1833, from G. V. Blunt in Birmingham. It itemizes "4 pair of brass candlesticks, 3 dozen brass snuffers, 2 dozen brass snuffer trays, 30 pair of spike head fire irons, 6 pair of brass chamber candlesticks, 1 gross of brass screw nibs, 1 dozen brass trunk locks, 6 sets of brass castors, and 5 dozen pair of brass chimney hooks." On October 23, 1833, the Philadelphia firm received another shipment from the same, the invoice of which itemized 18 pairs of brass candlesticks, 1 gross of brass plate escutcheons, 5 gross of brass fancy escutcheons, 5 gross of brass thread escutcheons, and 30 pairs of brass-head fire irons. Again, on March 1, 1834, an invoice to Porter and Fichett from Blunt listed 15 dozen rim locks with

brass strikers, 15 dozen brass drop padlocks, 6 single bronze trays, 6 double bronze trays, 4 dozen brass curtain pins, 3 dozen brass card table hinges, 3 dozen brass clock hinges, and 5 gross of brass escutcheon pins.[13]

The many urban coastal hardware merchants in America who were receiving these shipments regularly advertised in local newspapers. The bulk of the merchants, like "William Bayley at his stove grate warehouse in Beaker street and at his store in Fly Market," New York, specified that they had

for sale reasonable both wholesale and retail imported in the latest vessels from England . . . India metal, Prince's metal, brass, steel and bath metal stove grates, ditto, shovels, tongs and pokers, India metal, Prince's metal, brass, steel wire and japanned fenders, Prince's metal, brass and steel andirons . . . kitchen and chamber bellows, India metal, Prince's metal, brass, enamelled and japann'd candlesticks, copper and brass warming pans . . . brass & leather dog collars, brass cloak pins and curtain rings, brass savalls and extinguishers, brass scummers, ladles and slices, brass watch stands and wax frames, brass and japann'd flour and pepper boxes, brass arms, double and single, plated and copper sauce pans, copper and iron tea kettles, copper chafing dishes and baisters . . . India metal dish crosses . . . bell metal skillets & mortars, toasting forks . . . box irons and heaters, pocket and candle screens . . . pistol tinder boxes . . . nut crackers, India metal snuffers, with or without pans and stands.[14]

While finished goods for domestic use predominated in the offerings of American hardwaremen, industrial goods and raw materials were also available, as noted by Gerardus Duyckinck, who on August 12, 1773, advertised that he had just "imported from London and Bristol . . . sheet brass & sheet copper in boxes, rolls and bundles." A more graphic instance was spelled out by the metals broker John A. Moore of New York in his advertisement dated May 18, 1820. He offered newly imported "70,000 lbs braziers copper sheets and bottoms, 20,000 lbs first quality spelter, 500 lbs brass wire, No. 16, 10,000 brass cocks . . . 1000 lbs spelter solder, 5000 lbs copper rivets, 10 handsome brass grates, 50 pair andirons, 20 wire fenders, 10 do brass fenders [and] 10,000 copper bolts."[15] The advertisement lists some of the more common forms American craftsmen needed. Copper was almost exclusively shipped unwrought. Sheets and bottoms of standard sizes, tightly packed–like the "8 cases sheet copper, viz. 2 cases 20 by 48 inches, 2 do 26 by 52 do, 2 do 28 by 56 do, 2 do 30 by 60 do [and] 72 raised bottoms, 17 to 40 inches [and] 48 flat do 18 to 24 inches diameter" offered by the Philadelphia merchant John Humes in the November 16, 1812, issue of the *Aurora General Advertiser*–were an efficient, compact, and relatively inexpensive mode of shipping.

Although cast brass was normally transported as finished goods, brass sheet was, like copper, most efficiently shipped in unworked form. "In Birmingham, the brass intended for rolling is run into cast iron molds, the ingot weighing from 20 to 30 pounds; and as this is frequently but little extended in width during the laminating process, the sheet, when thin, is often upwards of 20 yards in length; it is neatly rolled up in the manner of a riband, and tied with wire for the convenience of carriage."[16]

In most instances this vast array of finished goods and raw materials was supplied to the American hardwareman through his English counterpart. On occasion, however, Americans were able to bypass the middlemen and buy directly from the manufacturers. Charles Gilchrist, owner of the Sheffield and Birmingham Button and Buckle Warehouse in Philadelphia, advertised that he had "just imported by the *Manchester* from Liverpool, a large assortment among which is some of the first fashions. He daily expects a further supply from Liverpool and Bristol. His goods coming immediately from the makers enables him to sell them lower then is offered at this market."[17]

Many of the wares fabricated by Britain's coppersmiths and braziers, but particularly by its brass founders and stampers, were intended to appeal to a fashion-conscious market. Many categories of hardware, such as screws, hinges, and the like, were made in varying sizes. As such, a mere printed or verbal description of an object in an inventory did not provide a satisfactorily clear impression for a potential consumer (FIG. 11). Consequently, alternate means were devised to provide American hardwaremen and retail purchasers with a better sense of the specific character of these wares. To this end, pattern cards, although somewhat bulky, were very effective. The cards consisted of wooden or heavy paper boards to which objects were attached (FIG. 12). "Pattern cards and other appendages to the trade [were among the] entire collection of shop tools . . . consisting of 2 stamps . . . with a large assortment of dies, sundry burnishings, turning, turning down and polishing lathes . . . piercing presses and tools, vices, bellows [and] shears" offered at the auction of an anonymous brass buttonmaker on Bath Street in Birmingham on October 9, 1789.[18]

Once the potential of pattern cards as a marketing device was discovered, the cards quickly became an important means for manufacturers to sell their wares widely. Matthew Boulton realized this when he wrote to a prospective client in 1781, stating that "every part of this sett of patterns, that [he] could possibly procure without charge is sent to you free of expense, such as the Buckles,

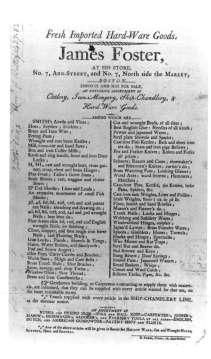

Fig. 11. Broadside issued by James Foster listing some of his imported hardware, Boston, ca. 1800. (Downs collection, Winterthur Library.)

Fig. 12. Scovill Manufacturing Company, pattern card for brass buttons, Waterbury, Connecticut, 1850–1900. Brass, leather, paper, velvet, silk; H. 11 3/8" (28.9 cm), W. (open) 31 1/2" (80.0 cm), D. 1 3/4" (4.4 cm). (Downs collection, Winterthur Library.)

being Single Rings (not in Pairs or Setts) with only Chapes, save one or two in each Card to shew the quality."[19]

These marketing devices were also useful to the hardware merchant, as evidenced by the note the Philadelphia hardwareman Adam Koenigmacher wrote to himself about 1817. In it he stated that he had to "take an assortment of Butt hinges and screw them upon boards to hang in front of the shelves or screw them into the thin shallow boxes" that he had imported from the German manufacturer Walhus "to stand in [the] pattern room." Koenigmacher again underscored their importance for his business when he reminded himself to "have the different patterns & kinds of butts & shutter hinges, plane irons &c &c put upon boards like [his competitors] Askew & Paxson as pattern cards."[20]

As useful as pattern cards were, an even better means of communicating between manufacturer and consumer evolved by the middle of the eighteenth century—trade catalogues. These bound volumes contained printed images of every object offered by a manufacturing establishment. They were issued by lampmakers, silver platers, cutlers, and coppersmiths but seem to have been especially popular for brass founders and stampers. Their wide appeal lay in their small size, easy portability, and modest expense. Trade catalogues were almost exclusively pictorial with only occasional descriptive phrases and indexes. Each image was always accompanied by a number that served as a simple and effective means for proper identification between purchaser and manufacturer (FIGS. 13–18).

Boulton outlined the use of trade catalogues when he wrote to a business correspondent in Russia. He pointed out that "you will find several Books of Copper Plate Prints of Patterns of Brass foundry &c: and small specimens of real work to the greatest part of them . . . the small specimens of work bear a reference to N° of the Book, pattern, and Page, whereto Each belongs and by which each can be ordered."[21]

Trade catalogues were used extensively by American hardware merchants, although few volumes are identifiable as having early American ownership. Winterthur owns two that originally belonged to the eighteenth-century Philadelphia hardware merchant Samuel Rowland Fisher (1745-1834). Peabody Essex Institute owns one that belonged to the Salem, Massachusetts, hardware merchant Samuel Curwen (b. 1719), which passed to Robert Peale, also a hardwareman in the same town, at the former's death, as documented inside the cover by the ink inscriptions "S. Curwen sent to me in January 1774" and "Robert Peele his book 1802."[22]

Both Fisher and Curwen traveled to England visiting manufacturing centers and market towns to find merchandise and make commercial connections. The former's journals recording his trip indicate that he had an agreeable time and encountered no difficulty from those he was attempting to meet. Curwen, by contrast, had a more demanding experience. He noted that "in all the manufacturing towns there is a jealousy and suspicion of strangers; an acquaintance with one manufacturer effectually

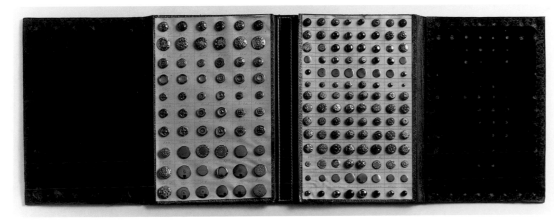

(OPEN)

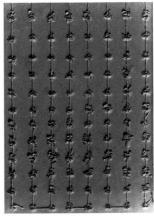

(BACK)

debars one from connection with a second in the same business. It is with difficulty one is admitted to see their works, and in many cases it is impracticable."[23]

Although English manufacturers discouraged visitation in their manufactories, they were eager to sell their goods and made use of trade catalogues to do so. The English entrepreneur's attitude was insightfully stated by Boulton, who was among the first to realize the advantage in selling many inexpensive objects to a wide market instead of a few expensive objects to a small circle of wealthy patrons. It betrayed his low esteem of American's taste when he wrote in 1772 that "it is not necessary to attend to elegance in such articles of my manufacture as are destined for Siberia or America." However, he quickly acknowledged the purchasing power of the masses by noting that it was "of far more consequence to supply the people than the Nobility only; and though [we] speak contemptuously of [them] we must own that we think they will do more toward supporting [my] great Manufactory than all the Lords in the Nation."[24]

Paul Revere, the American silversmith, copper and brass entrepreneur, and importer of English metalwares, documented America's enthusiasm with pattern books when he wrote to Frederick William Geyer, his factor in England, on January 19, 1784. Revere stated that he had just received a parcel of goods from England, and "they enclosed [for] me in the case of plated ware a book with drawings which is a very good direction for one to write by. I should be very glad if you would send me eight pair of plated branches, four of No. 103 and four of No. 178 as marked in said book. If they have drawings different from the book I received [I] should be glad [if] they would send me one more book."[25]

The pattern book proved to be an eminently convenient means of marketing for the metals manufacturer and consumer alike. The demand for books in Birmingham and surrounding towns "extended the occupation of the engraver and copperplate printer to a degree elsewhere unknown."[26] Their product, widely distributed throughout England, Europe, Asia, and America by aggressive metals merchandisers, became a major conduit through which rapidly expanding consumer demand was satisfied.

Trade catalogue images were engraved directly from objects, with every pertinent detail depicted for the sake of accuracy. Even scale was exact, so that mention of measurements was unnecessary unless various sizes of a given object were offered. In most instances this worked admirably, but on occasion the need for a fully informative image resulted in a disjointed composition. Candlesticks, for instance, were sometimes pictured with their base in plan, their shaft in elevation, and the candle cup from a diagonal perspective. Such an image did indeed depict all the information a potential buyer might need except for the unified composition of the candlestick. In spite of the occasional awkward image, however, the trade catalogue system worked well and proved popular.

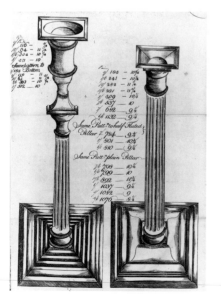

Fig. 13. Candlesticks offered in a 24-page trade catalogue, Birmingham, England, ca. 1777. (Downs collection, Winterthur Library.)

Fig. 14. Trunk handles and upholstery nails offered in a 113-page trade catalogue, Birmingham, England, ca. 1780. (Downs collection, Winterthur Library.)

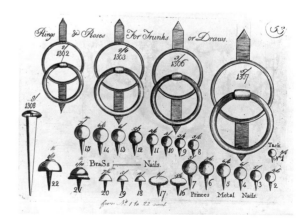

English manufacturers dominated the American market for hardware and related material, but manufacturers in Europe, particularly the Low Countries, France, and Germany, also sent utilitarian and decorative base metals to America. The commercial channels whereby Continental goods arrived were as varied as those from England, though not as extensive. A New York City hardware merchant, Samuel Chace, received £120 worth of Dutch brass including a "Koper Ketel . . . Brass Pan . . . Koper Casserol . . . Koffy Kan [and a] Koper Bengel Lamp" from G. Verhuldsdonck in Rotterdam, Holland, on January 6, 1797. The immigrant cabinetmaker Joseph Brauwers, who worked in New York City during the second decade of the nineteenth century, placed ornamental brass mounts on his furniture and boasted on his trade label that he was an "Ebenist from Paris . . . with the Richest Ornaments just imported from France."[27] German manufacturers also used the popular English practice of marketing with pattern books in America, as documented in the January 26, 1839, issue of the Philadelphia German-language newspaper *Die Alte und Neue Welt*. Advertised there were "patternbooks for Nuremberg and Fürth Manufacturers—one hundred half folio plates with texts and prices. . . . The plates are very neat and correct, painted in colors, and for Fancy ware merchants very useful. They contain, for example, boxes, mirrors, treenware, toys, brassware, writing pens, tin and wooden ware."

American coppersmiths, braziers, and brass and bronze founders also competed for American patronage. Men and women practicing these crafts were to be found in virtually every coastal community as well as inland towns. In the larger cities they advertised their abilities and wares regularly in newspapers, thoroughly detailing the character of their offerings as well as the nature of the competition they faced. On November 16, 1787, Jesse Gooddier, bell founder, placed a lengthy self-congratulatory notice in the *Maryland Gazette; or, the Baltimore General Advertiser*. His composition read: "On Monday last was replaced in the belfry of the Baptist Meeting House in Providence (Rhode Island) a large and noble bell weighing two thousand three hundred eighty-seven pounds lately recast at the furnace Hope in Scituate in this state, about twelve miles from this town with the assistance of Mr. Jesse Gooddier, bell founder of Connecticut. This is the largest bell ever cast in New England and furnishes an additional proof that there is no kind of manufacture but what may be carried to as full perfection in the country as in Europe, not withstanding the predilection which some have in favor of foreign productions to the injury of their native country."

American coppersmiths and brass workers found that they had to compete by making their wares in imitation of those that were being imported. Consequently, those who advertised frequently did so in a comparative context, as suggested by Ichabod Woodruff's notice in the July 30, 1811, issue of the *Kentucky Gazette*. Woodruff stated that he had "lately commenced the Brass Founding business . . . having procured the best workmen from

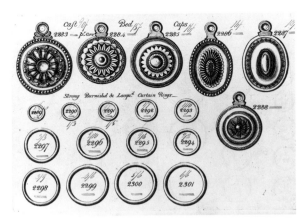

Fig. 15. Bed bolt covers and curtain rings offered in a 152-page trade catalogue, Birmingham, England, ca. 1798. (Downs collection, Winterthur Library.)

Fig. 16. Commode handles offered in a 13-page trade catalogue, Birmingham, England, ca. 1774. (Downs collection, Winterthur Library.)

New York [who make] a general assortment of Brass Andirons, Shovels & Tongs, Door Knockers &c of the newest and most fashionable patterns" equal to any imported. Daniel King, a Philadelphia brass founder, was even more specific when he noted in the July 23, 1772, issue of the *Maryland Gazette* that he made an "assortment of Brass Fire Dogs and Fenders, Fire Shovels and Tongs . . . which he can safely say are neater and more to order than any yet made on the Continent." He then pointed out that he had "served his apprenticeship in London, and worked in some of the best shops in England."

Even though American workers patterned their wares closely on English imports—so closely that it is impossible to distinguish one from the other in the absence of a mark—they still had difficulty competing (FIG. 19). The disadvantage American entrepreneurs experienced was a matter of concern to the federal government. To this end, the political economist Tench Coxe was asked to examine the state of American manufactures during the 1790s. His published findings concluded that "the situation of America before the Revolution was very unfavorable" for the encouragement of native manufactures, "the preference for [British] goods, which habit carried much beyond what their excellence would justify . . . created artificial impediments which appeared almost insuperable." He went on to say that "an extravagant and wasteful use of foreign manufactures has been too just a charge against the people of America since the close of the war. They have been

so cheap, so plenty[ful] and so easily obtained on credit, that the consumption of them has been absolutely wanton."[28]

A later and separate inquiry overseen by Alexander Hamilton drew much the same conclusion and stated that "to multiply and extend manufactures of . . . coppersmiths and brass-founders . . . is worthy of attention and effort. In order to [do] this, it is desirable to facilitate a plentiful supply of materials. And a proper means to this end is, to place" imported raw materials in a duty-free state while putting an ad valorem duty on all finished goods sent from Europe.[29]

In spite of the government's concern and the recommended solutions, little progress seems to have been made to rectify the situation, as indicated by commentary on a federal census of manufactures conducted in 1820. In responding to that census, William Hendricks, a brass founder in New York City, lamented that "during the late war with Great Britain [the War of 1812], I sold nearly 3 times the amount stated [$1,300] & could have sold more if I had the means of manufacturing it, but the enormous influence of foreign goods since has diminished the demand and reduced the price of these articles very much."[30] His observations were reiterated by numerous others.

Throughout the colonial and early federal period in America, England dominated the production and distribution of copper and its alloys through its manufacturing might and aggressive marketing. "Though copper may possibly be bought in the rough

Fig. 17. Drawer handles offered in a 94-page trade catalogue, Birmingham, England, ca. 1813. (Downs collection, Winterthur Library.)

Fig. 18. Door knocker offered in a 112-page trade catalogue, Birmingham, England, 1829. (Downs collection, Winterthur Library.)

cheaper from Sweden than from England, or the copper mines of
America, yet the dearness of labor in the American states will lead
the importer to purchase the article of copper wanted in America
ready made in Europe, and, consequently, the manufacturers
in Great Britain, in that article, must have the preference; and the
American states have so few articles to send to Sweden, or indeed
to any part of the North, that all the articles from the Baltic may
be imported through Great Britain, to greater advantage than
directly from those countries."[31]

In spite of Coxe's aspersions on the quality of English copper
and brass work, the products emanating from that country were
well made and finished, as judged by the objects in the Winterthur
collection. The American preference for English goods seems,
therefore, to have been justified. At the same time, both Continental
and American craftsmen recognized the potential in the American
market for profit and attempted to cultivate it. It was well into the
nineteenth century, however, before they made significant inroads
into the English dominance of the trade.

Fig. 19. Billhead of John
Bailey, New York City,
ca. 1792. (Downs collection,
Winterthur Library.)

1 *Records and Files of the Quarterly Courts of Essex County, Massachusetts*, 8 vols. (Salem, Mass.: Essex Institute, 1911-21), 1:259, 260.

2 *Records and Files of Essex County*, 8:23, 24.

3 John Baker Holroyd, *Observations on the Commerce of the American States with Europe and the West Indies* (Philadelphia: Robert Bell, 1783), p. 4.

4 *An Inventory of the Contents of the Governor's Palace Taken after the Death of Lord Botetourt* (Williamsburg, Va.: Colonial Williamsburg Foundation, 1981), pp. 5-18.

5 Jack McLaughlin, *Jefferson and Monticello* (New York: Henry Holt, 1988), p. 422.

6 On the British trades, see John Reed, *New Bristol Directory for the Year 1792* (Bristol, Eng., 1792); *Art Journal Illustrated Catalogue* (London, 1851), p. 134; *Universal British Directory of Trade, Commerce, and Manufacture* (London: Peter Barfoot and John Wilkes, 1793), p. 201.

7 J. Bisset, *Bisset's Magnificent Directory* (Birmingham, Eng., 1808), p. 4.

8 Charles Pye, *A New Directory for the Town of Birmingham* (1785), pp. 5, 76; J. Sketchley, *Sketchley's and Adam's Tradesman's True Guide* (1770), p. 5; J. Sketchley, *Sketchley's Birmingham, Wolverhampton, and Walsall Directory* (1767), p. 62; M. Swinney, *Swinney's Birmingham Directory* (1775), p. 7.

9 William Hutton, *An History of Birmingham to the End of the Year 1780* (Birmingham, Eng., 1781), pp. 69-70.

10 G. H. Guttridge, ed., *American Correspondence of a Bristol Merchant, 1766-1776: Letters of Richard Champion*, University of California Publications in History, vol. 22, no. 1 (Berkeley, Calif., 1934), p. 23.

11 Documentation on the ships can be found in Bristol presentments, 1660-1840 (Bristol City Library), a microfilm record derived from official sources of the listings on ships inbound and outbound from London, Bristol, Liverpool, and Hull. A hogshead is a cask with the capacity to hold from 1,400 to 1,800 pounds; a cask is a container of about 300 pounds; a bale is a bundle of merchandise more or less round in shape, covered in canvas, and tightly hooped with copper or iron; a tierce is a container equal to about 42 gallons; a parcel is a small package.

12 On brass, see Guttridge, *American Correspondence of a Bristol Merchant*, p. 60. Copper exports are documented in Elizabeth Boody Schumpeter, *English Overseas Trade Statistics, 1697-1808* (Oxford, Eng.: Clarendon Press, 1960), p. 63.

13 Bills of lading, port of Philadelphia, 1784-1850, University of Delaware Library, Newark, Del.

14 *Rivington's New-York Gazetteer*, July 29, 1773.

15 Duyckinck's advertisement is found in *Rivington's New-York Gazetteer*, August 12, 1773. Moore advertised in the *New-York Daily Advertiser*, May 18, 1820.

16 Dionysius Lardner, comp., *The Cabinet Cyclopaedia*, 3 vols. (London: Longman, Rees, Orme, Brown, Green, and Longman, and John Taylor, 1834), 3:185.

17 *Dunlap's American Daily Advertiser* (Philadelphia), May 2, 1792.

18 *Aris's Birmingham Gazette*, October 9, 1789.

19 Matthew Boulton to John Tamesz, May 26, 1781, Boulton and Fothergill letterbook, 1780-81, Birmingham City Library.

20 Notebook of memos and things to be done by A. Koenigmacher, Philadelphia, 1817-19, 56x17.36, pp. 5, 1a, Downs collection, Winterthur Library.

21 Boulton to Tamesz, May 26, 1781.

22 The Winterthur catalogues carry library call nos. NK7899 B61c* and TS1035 W82. The Peabody Essex volume is library call no. 739.4 B82.

23 George Atkinson Ward, *Journal and Letters of Samuel Curwen, an American in England, from 1775-1783* (Boston: Little, Brown, 1864), p. 149.

24 The Boulton quotes are transcribed in Eric Robinson, "Eighteenth-Century Commerce and Fashion: Matthew Boulton's Marketing Techniques," *Economic History Review*, 2d ser., 16, no. 1 (1963): 46, 59.

25 Roll 14, vol. 53, letterbook, 1783-1800, Revere Papers, Massachusetts Historical Society, Boston.

26 William Hawkes Smith, *Birmingham and Its Vicinity as a Manufacturing and Commercial District* (London, 1836), p. 21.

27 The Chace quote can be found in document 74x5, Downs collection, Winterthur Library. The Brauwers label is acc. no. 62.237, Winterthur.

28 Tench Coxe, *A View of the United States of America* (Philadelphia: Printed for William Hall, Wrigley, and Berriman, 1794), pp. 37, 49.

29 *Works of Alexander Hamilton*, 3 vols. (New York: Williams and Whiting, 1810), 1:248.

30 Federal census of manufactures, New York City, 1820, reel 10, National Archives, Washington, D.C.

31 Holroyd, *Observations on the Commerce of the American States*, p. 10.

MARKING AND METALLURGY

Crafts guilds, the origins of which reach back to medieval Europe, were associations of individuals practicing the same livelihood. Guilds existed primarily to promote and protect their members' welfare. A principal means to this end was the establishment and maintenance of standards of quality for the members' work. With such standards, prospective purchasers of goods were assured of full value for money spent and were therefore encouraged to patronize.

Some crafts guilds were organized around an activity, like the ironmongers, barbers, and painter-stainers. Others were established around the manipulation of a particular material, such as goldsmiths, pewterers, and founders. Goldsmiths had the exclusive right to work with the precious metals gold and silver. Pewterers alone had rights over the working of pewter; founders were granted the right to work with copper, brass, and bronze.

In 1363 the Worshipful Company of Goldsmiths of London passed an ordinance stating that every master silversmith must "have a mark by himself, which mark shall be known . . . to survey their work and allay."[1] This mark identified the maker of any given silver object and served as a means of nonverbal communication between maker and consumer, giving the former credit for the artifact's merits and providing the latter with an avenue of redress should the object be found faulty in workmanship or composition.

It is apparent from the wording of the ordinance that the wardens of the company were concerned with both workmanship and composition, but composition seems to have been paramount, since the metal was deemed to have considerable assigned value. Being much too soft in its pure state to survive extended use, however, silver had to be alloyed with the harder metal copper to give it longevity. Since copper was considerably less valuable than silver, a standard had to be devised wherein a specific amount of the base metal was added to provide the necessary strength but still permit the alloy to be accepted as precious. This adherence to the standard was certified through the silversmiths' marks. A potential purchaser, seeing such marks and knowing they were stamped in accordance with the goldsmiths' company ordinance on marking, was assured that the object on which they were placed met the accepted standard of purity.

Base metals were also marked in accordance with statutes instituted by their respective guilds, requiring craftsmen working under their jurisdiction to document their work. The Worshipful Company of Pewterers of London ordained in 1503/4 that "makers of [pewter] wares shall mark the same wares with the several marks of their own to the intent that the [makers] of such wares shall avow the same wares, by them as is abovesaid, to be . . . sufficiently made and wrought."[2]

Although the terminology differs and 140 years separate the writing of the two ordinances, the statutes of the pewterers' company were worded in such a way that it is apparent they also established standards for both composition and workmanship. The need for serviceable wares was obvious, but since pewterers worked with nonprecious metals exclusively, their concern with composition might have been considered gratuitous. The relative value of the metals in the alloy varied, however, and the quantity of lead had to be rigidly controlled because of its toxic effect on the human body.

The Worshipful Company of Founders of the City of London passed an ordinance on January 27, 1614/15, that stated "be yt ordained that every person or persons useing the Art or Mistery of makeing brasse and copper workes, waights or wares within the Citty and three miles compasse thereof shall from tyme to tyme mark the same worke, waights or wares with their owne proper and severall markes which they shall have allowed to them by the Maister, wardens and assistants of this Mistery or the greater part of them, whereby the wares and workmanshipps which they make may be knowne when they shalbe viewed and searched and found defective."[3]

Yet again, specific wording confirms the concerns of those who wrote the ordinance. The need for good workmanship was explained graphically by members of the craft when they observed that "some of the said Mystery do work and make their works of false metal and false solder, so that their said work, to wit Candlesticks, Buckles, Straps, and other such like articles, when exposed to fire or great strain, crack, break and dissolve, to the peril and damage of those who purchase them, and to the great slander of the City and the whole Mystery." Likewise, the need for an unadulterated alloy was spelled out by the company when its members mandated "that no ffounder . . . shall fill or stop with Lead any Brass Works made up by them—whereby the King's liege people may be damnified or any private person cheated in buying the same again for Brasse, when a great part of the same is Lead."[4]

The rationale for good workmanship and standardized metal content was based on the consumer's need for fairly valued reliable goods and the reputable artisan's desire to maintain respectability. Makers' marks proved to be the most readily recognized and acceptable means of documenting goods that satisfied these dual requirements. With the creation of laws mandating and regulating use, it follows that all goods made within that system would be marked. This proves to be so with English silver and pewter. Only infrequently are examples encountered that do not bear marks stamped in accordance with guild regulations.[5] English-made objects of copper and copper alloys fabricated under similar marking constraints, however, rarely reveal their makers' identity.

Perhaps the most significant of the many and complex reasons for this disparity was the relative strengths of the guilds in question. Both the goldsmiths' and pewterers' companies were strong, with substantial incomes and secure political bases. They could, consequently, promulgate regulations governing their members' products and enforce them without hesitation through search, seizure, fines, and the defacement of substandard goods. The founders' company attempted the same control over its members but with considerably greater difficulty; its smaller membership provided only a modest income and a less secure political foundation.

While all London companies that required marking of wares had to bring wayward members to task on occasion, the wardens' accounts of the founders' company contain numbers of assessments of fines, like that against Michael Draper "for not marking of wares" or "Petter Hunsdine for his ware being unmarked" or payment to searchers such as "Mr. Lane, Upper Warden, for expences in taking of distresses for want of marks" by various members.[6] The record of these infractions suggests that English founders did not fear significant recrimination should they overlook identifying their work.

Another difficulty faced by the founders' company was its inability to establish a monopoly over the working of copper, brass, and bronze. Both the pewterers' company and the braziers' company, which joined with the armourers' company, becoming the armourers' and braziers' company about 1708, also worked with the ingredients that went into the making of these alloys. As a result, continual strife existed among them over who had jurisdiction. Costly legal suits depleted guild coffers and produced, for the most part, inconsequential results, adding to the vacuum that allowed workers in copper and copper alloys to ignore marking regulations, with impunity.[7]

It is significant that only two months after the founders' company passed the ordinance mandating marking of members' wares, they felt it necessary to extend its limits. On March 8, 1615, the company stated that "whereas divers persons being free of sundry Companies, and using the Art and Mystery of making Brass and Copper Works and Wares . . . have formerly been warned to have a Mark allowed them, for marking the works and wares which they have made for sale. It was concluded, That the Master and Wardens shall go and take a distress of any person so offending."[8] From this statement it appears that not all founders working in London were doing so as members of the company and that the company was either unwilling or unable to force them into membership. Even so, ordinances like that passed in March 1615 clearly demonstrate the master and wardens' desire to exercise some control over the

workers. However, given the apparent willingness of members to ignore marking provisions, nonmembers surely must have done so to an even greater extent.

Technically, London guilds had jurisdiction over artisans throughout England, but effective control was impossible over great distances because of slow transportation and communication. This fact is acknowledged in the wording of the founders' company ordinance of January 27, 1614/15, which stipulates that its terms apply to founders "within this Citty and three miles compasse thereof."[9] Beyond that three-mile limit founders were technically free of any association and under no guild constraints. There appears to be no similar acknowledgment of geographic limitation in the ordinances of the goldsmiths' and pewterers' companies, but they, too, wielded less control outside London.

Control of the craft in outlying urban areas was, therefore, effected by means of local guilds modeled after those in London. Such guilds were chartered in those cities that had sufficient population and mercantile activity to support them. Prominent cities were Bristol, Coventry, Newcastle upon Tyne, and York, which are estimated to have had upwards of 150 guilds among them by the sixteenth century. Founders companies were assuredly included. They were often of such small membership, however, that they combined with other companies, like the consortium of goldsmiths, smiths, pewterers, plumbers, glaziers, painters, cutlers, musicians, stationers, bookbinders, and basketmakers in Hull who joined forces, because "both for municipal purposes and for mutual protection, union was necessary, and the mere fact of the weakness of their independent position, irrespective of the natural connexion of their trades, seems to have drawn them together into one society."[10] Clearly, circumstances such as these would have encouraged a laxness in enforcement of marking regulations with a commensurate willingness of founders to risk omitting impressment of their mark on finished goods.

Another factor further complicating the task of those whose job it was to enforce the marking of copper and copper alloys appeared in the eighteenth century. As mechanized mass-production techniques began to develop, the guild system, a central factor in medieval and early Renaissance urban life, waned, eventually to the point that by 1795 a social commentator in Bristol could observe that "all kinds of persons are free to exercise their trades and callings here without molestation from the corporation." Even more explicit was the comment made of the preeminent English industrial town of Birmingham. It was stated in 1808 that its population was about 80,000 and that "the town is happily free from chartered institutions (being open for all the sons of industry who wish to display their genius in the Toy-shop of Europe) which has contributed greatly not only to the increase of the buildings, but also to its trade and manufactures."[11] The absence of guilds in this city, judged to be purposeful in light of the above comment, is of particular significance and visible through the numerous trade catalogues issued by Birmingham manufacturers, most of which were published anonymously. The large quantity of copper- and brasswares, identifiable as having originated in Birmingham through the relationship of individual objects to images in the catalogues, are similarly anonymous. It is clear that the apparent need for guilds as enforcers of quality control not only declined in England but, by the late eighteenth century, had been replaced by the perception that they were oppressive. So, too, was the fate of the marking they mandated, resulting in its almost complete abandonment by manufacturers of copper and the copper alloys, with no apparent protest from the buying public.

Against that background there existed an important exception wherein marking was fairly routine. This practice revolved around English laws governing patents and registration of designs, which were of particular significance for the metal trades. Indeed, it was observed in 1866 that "in no department of the great manufacturing system of [England] have patents operated more beneficially than on the manipulation and chemistry of metals, and the present prosperous condition of the local brass manufacture is in no small degree attributable to Patent Law protection."[12] English patent law provided the right of sole use or reward of a licensing fee to anyone who invented a new or improved method or product. That law stipulated that the inventor or licensee place a mark, usually including his name, on each object produced.

Of equal significance was "another form of protection by which the brass trade of Birmingham [and all of England] has been largely benefitted, viz:–The Registration of Ornamental Designs. As the [patent] laws benefit and stimulate invention, so the Ornamental Registration Act has operated very materially in evolving ornamental designs, and in increasing the number and variety of ornamental objects in metal produced, particularly in brass."[13] Here, too, appropriate marking was mandated to ensure that protection was enforceable.

MARKING: AMERICA

During the colonial era, American metalworkers technically practiced their crafts under the auspices of the English guild system and were subject to the same mandates and standards as their counterparts across the Atlantic. The enforcement of those rules, however, was difficult, if not impossible. Consequently,

Fig. 20. The mark of Joseph Wood, an eighteenth-century Birmingham, England, brass founder.

Fig. 21. The mark of William Hunneman, an early nineteenth-century Boston brass founder.

American metalworkers quickly evolved a modified application of the English practice, as evidenced by artifacts they produced.

American silversmiths generally placed a single identifying mark on any object they made. By contrast, four or five marks were required of English silversmiths, documenting maker, date, place of origin, that the object met the sterling standard, and, after 1784, that a tax on it had been paid to the Crown. While English silversmiths, under pain of forfeiture or fine, had to maintain the silver content uniformly at 92.5 percent throughout any artifact they made, American silversmiths rarely met that standard in their work. Silver content typically varied from 80 to 91 percent but could be as high as 95 percent in differing parts of any given American-made object. This same disparity in marking and metal content existed between English and American pewter.[14] Again, the reason appears to have been because English pewterers worked under the close and direct supervision of a strong company while American makers were at a distance sufficient enough to hamper enforcement.

Copper and copper alloys present a different picture. Any distinction between the frequency and method of marking between English and American makers is difficult to perceive (FIGS. 20, 21). Similarly, there is no sharp division between the products of the two countries with respect to metal content. This may be due to the fact that the founders' company and the armourers' and braziers' company were relatively small and comparatively weak.

English founders, braziers, and coppersmiths had less to fear from the threat of search and seizure of faulty goods. They, therefore, exercised greater latitude in their marking technique and metal content, similar to the practices of American silversmiths, pewterers, coppersmiths, and brass workers.

Although American copper and brass workers enjoyed considerable freedom with respect to marking their wares, numbers of them felt obliged to place their names on many of their products, as with the early nineteenth-century New York City brass founder Richard Whittingham (FIG. 22) and the early nineteenth-century Boston brass founder William C. Hunneman. Although the records of these men have not produced the reasoning behind why they routinely marked their work—andirons in particular—some insight is gained into this phenomenon from the Philadelphia coppersmith Benjamin Harbeson (FIG. 23). About 1764 he had engraved and published a broadside advertisement that pictured some of his more popular goods and his name "B. Harbeson" in a scrolled cartouche (FIG. 24). On the broadside he stated that he "Makes and Sells all Sorts of Copper Wares" and went on to say in bold block letters, "My Work is all Stampt as" pictured in the scrolled cartouche.[15] Harbeson clearly wished prospective customers to know that he placed his name on his work, but the brevity of his statement only implies the reasons why. A competitor of his is much more specific. William Bailey, a coppersmith who worked in York, Pennsylvania, and Hagerstown, Maryland, during the late eigh

Fig. 23. The mark of Benjamin Harbeson, an eighteenth-century Philadelphia coppersmith.

Fig. 22. The mark of Richard Whittingham, an early nineteenth-century New York City brass founder.

teenth century, placed an advertisement in the *Maryland Gazette* on May 20, 1773. In it he stated that "he makes for sale all sorts of copperwork such as stills, brewing coppers, wash and fish kettles, tea kettles, sauce pans, coffee and chocolate pots, which he will sell as low as any made or imported in the province of Pennsylvania, Maryland or Virginia . . . and to prevent dispute he stamps his name on all his work, and warrants it to be good . . . it is well known in the province of Pennsylvania, Maryland, Virginia and Carolina, that his work is far superior to any made in these parts."

Harbeson's career spanned more than fifty years, from before 1755 to his death in 1809. Bailey worked for twenty-five years, from 1772 until he died in 1797. Both men advertised their ability to supply a large number and variety of wares throughout their careers. Yet, between the two, only about a dozen examples of copper and brass are currently recorded that bear their names. Many other early American coppersmiths and brass founders also advertised but routinely made no mention of marking their wares. While teakettles, saucepans, andirons, oil lamps, and other forms bearing the names of early American coppersmiths and brass founders do exist, they are extensively outnumbered by unmarked counterparts, suggesting, in spite of Harbeson's and Bailey's advertisements, that marking was only haphazardly practiced.

Even though there was no significant tradition of guild regulation in colonial America that mandated marking, the federal government did consider legislation to that effect prior to the end of the eighteenth century. The report of that wish was communicated to the House of Representatives on December 9, 1791, by Thomas Jefferson, secretary of state. In it he stated that

it would in his opinion contribute to fidelity in the execution of manufacturers, to secure to every manufactory an exclusive right to some [mark] on its wares exclusive to itself; that this should be done by general laws, extending equal right to every case, to which the authority of the Legislature should be competent; that these cases are of decided jurisdiction. Manufactures made and consumed within a state being subject to State legislature, while those which are exported to foreign nations, or to another State, or into the Indian territory, are alone within the legislation of the General Government. That it will, therefore, be reasonable for the General Legislature to provide, in this behalf, by law, for those cases of manufacture, generally, and those only, which relate to the commerce within foreign nations and among the several States and within the Indian tribes. And that this may be done by permitting the owner of every manufactory to enter into the records of the court of the district, wherein his manufactory is, the name with which he chooses to mark or designate his wares, and rendering it penal in others to put the same mark to any other wares.[16]

The wording of this recommendation, while well intentioned, rendered it ineffective, since the authority over marking was to be

Fig. 24. Benjamin Harbeson broadside, Philadelphia, ca. 1764. (Downs collection, Winterthur Library.)

divided between the various states and the federal government. More significant, the recommendation does not say that a given maker must mark all his goods but rather that he may not place his mark on what he does not make. The result was that copper and brass workers continued to be granted considerable latitude in the marking of their wares, a freedom of which they seem to have taken full advantage.

METALLURGY

It has been known since the Bronze Age that metals can be combined to produce alloys that

are more useful than the metals of which they are composed, and possess properties a good deal different from their elements. One of the best known and most serviceable of all the alloys is brass, a compound of zinc and copper: it is harder, more easily melted, more close in the texture, better coloured, and less liable to tarnish than copper; it is less brittle, and in every way more valuable than zinc. Pinchbeck is composed of the same ingredients as brass, but in different proportions, the zinc predominating. Copper and tin are two very soft and flexible metals, which being fused together, form the alloy known as bell-metal, which is harder than iron, very brittle, and very sonorous. The same materials, in different proportions, form speculum metal, and the kind of ordnance improperly called brass cannon.[17]

With this knowledge, metalworkers could mix their ingredients to emphasize particular attributes including strength, hardness, ductility, fusibility, workability, sonority, tarnish resistance, and color. According to James Larkin, a widely read nineteenth-century author on the subject (FIG. 25), 1 pound of copper mixed with $1/8$ to $1/2$ ounce of zinc produced a metal that was good for sound copper castings; if the amount of zinc was increased to 1 or $1\ 1/4$ ounces, the alloy was considered to be a good gilding metal for jewelers. One pound of copper mixed with 2 ounces of zinc produced tombac or red brass, admired for its rich golden-red hue, while 3 to 4 ounces of zinc in combination with 1 pound of copper made what was called red sheet brass, pinchbeck, or bath metal. Five ounces of zinc with 1 pound of copper was termed purback metal, and 6 ounces zinc with 1 pound copper was called bristol brass. If the amount of zinc was raised to 10 or 11 ounces, muntz's metal resulted, which was deemed ideal for ships' fastenings and fittings. Fourteen ounces of zinc with 1 pound of copper made a strong brazing solder for heavy copper work. Equal amounts of zinc and copper made a soft spelter solder.[18] Although there seems to have been general accord concerning the working properties and characteristics of differing alloys, few authors agreed on the precise composition to achieve a given purpose. Consequently, there appears to have been no single universally accepted compositional standard, like that for sterling silver, that was applied to all brass or bronze forms or even to families of a given form such as candlesticks.

Fig. 25. Tables outlining some of the chemical and physical properties of copper and zinc alloys. From James Larkin, *The Practical Brass and Iron Founder's Guide* (Philadelphia: Henry Carey Baird, 1883), pp. 40–41.

In addition to the primary ingredients of copper, zinc, and tin, brass and bronze workers often added secondary metals in small amounts to enhance certain physical properties of their products. Lead was perhaps the most popular since it was inexpensive but, more importantly, made brass alloys much easier to work with a file or on a turning lathe. Silver was another secondary metal that was deemed desirable in small amounts since it was felt to enhance color or sonorous qualities. But, as with the mixing of primary ingredients, there appears to have been no standard or even general agreement regarding the use of these secondary metals, resulting in imprecise alloys when compared to silver or even pewter.

Another complicating factor with respect to determining the acceptance and use of compositional standards in brass and bronze work rests on the ease with which the metal could be recycled. American coppersmiths and brass and bronze workers depended to a large degree upon used and worn objects, which they refashioned into new goods. This practice is readily apparent in advertisements in which workers cite the variety of objects they are capable of making, always followed by the statement that they, like the New York city brazier John Halden, gave "ready money for old Copper, Brass, Pewter or Lead."[19] Another even more detailed instance was stated by the Baltimore coppersmith William Clemm, who advertised in the *Maryland Journal; or, the Baltimore Advertiser* on April 5, 1785, that he "continues to give the highest Price for old Copper, Pewter and Brass, and takes either of said Articles in exchange for new work."

Notices such as these are so common as to be routine and are not unexpected from craftsmen operating small shops where raw materials and cash were in limited supply. But even larger manufacturers depended heavily on used goods. This is graphically illustrated by the base-metals entrepreneur Paul Revere in a letter he wrote to Nathaniel Gorham, supervisor of Massachusetts, on January 26, 1796. Revere had to justify why his losses in making howitzers for the state were larger than those of his competitor, James Byers of Springfield. Revere lamented that "I was obliged to purchase [copper] in small parcels which were utensils that had been burned [making sugar] in the West Indies and their was frequently among it Iron that I could not fond."[20] Not only did he have to refine the iron from the copper, he had to find and purchase additional material to make up the difference. The root of Revere's difficulty was a limited supply of raw materials, necessitating his recycling of old metal of unpredictable quality. It is noteworthy that he encountered his difficulty well after the close of the American Revolution and, therefore, when English mercantile policy with respect to its colonies was no longer in effect. This strongly suggests that the American coppersmiths' and brass workers' traditional and heavy reliance on recycled metal was more affected by limited supply in the face of large demand than by English politics.

Although England was a significant producer of raw copper and brass throughout the eighteenth and nineteenth centuries, English manufacturers, like their American counterparts, also realized the economic expedience of recycling goods. This phenomenon was so extensive that it was noted that a "great deal of the Birmingham sheet brass, being composed of schruff or old metal, with other economical ingredients, is very inferior in colour and ductility to that from Cheadle; it is, however, much cheaper than the latter, and will stand the fire better in soldering."[21] Again, supply and demand were a determining factor that regulated the materials used by coppersmiths and brass workers and had an impact on the composition of their products.

Standards were promulgated by the guilds regulating the composition, workmanship, and marking of copper, brass, and bronze made in England, and by extension the American colonies, but the workers in these metals seem to have exercised considerable latitude in formulating their alloys and fabricating and marking their products, as judged by the written record and examination of objects. In context with the products of English silversmiths and pewterers, the size and wealth of the regulating agency must have been important. Wealth and a strong political base enjoyed by the goldsmiths' and pewterers' companies enabled them to make and enforce membership and regulatory standards. By contrast, the smaller, poorer, and constantly bickering companies that oversaw the making of copper and its alloys experienced greater difficulty with both. Fortunately, this seems not to have compromised the quality or character of the artifacts that have survived to become part of the collection at Winterthur.

1 Statute 37, Edward III, c. 7, as quoted in Charles J. Jackson, *English Goldsmiths and Their Marks* (London: Macmillan, 1921), p. 8. This system evolved into a series of marks, usually four by about 1544, each of which provided a purchaser with specific information about an object's maker, place and year of fabrication, and silver content.

2 Act 19, Henry VIII, c. 6, as quoted in Howard Herschel Cotterell, *Old Pewter: Its Makers and Marks* (London: B. T. Batsford, 1929), p. 24.

3 MS 6360, ordinances of the founders' company, January 27, 1614/15, Guildhall Library, London.

4 Workmanship is addressed in a petition from the founders of the city of London to the mayor, July 29, 1365, as quoted in William Meade Williams, comp., *Annals of the Worshipful Company of Founders of the City of London* (London: Privately printed, 1867), p. 5. The comparison of the alloy is discussed in the ordinances of the founders' company, October 1645, as quoted in Williams, *Annals of the Worshipful Company of Founders*, p. 98.

5 Documentation is provided in numerous twentieth-century publications that depict, organize, and discuss thousands of marks struck on English silver and pewter from the fourteenth century to the present. Two of the most encyclopedic of these are Jackson, *English Goldsmiths* and Cotterell, *Old Pewter*.

6 Guy Parsloe, ed., *Wardens' Accounts of the Worshipful Company of Founders of the City of London, 1497–1681* (London: Athlone Press, 1964), pp. 279, 265, 263. See also William Nembhard Hibbert, comp., *History of the Worshipful Company of Founders of the City of London* (London: Unwin Brothers, 1925), pp. 107-22.

7 Parsloe, *Wardens' Accounts*, pp. ix-xviii.

8 Ordinances of the founders' company, October 1645, as quoted in Williams, *Annals of the Worshipful Company of Founders*, p. 91.

9 MS 6360, January 27, 1614/15.

10 On guilds outside London, see W. Carew Hazlitt, *The Livery Companies of the City of London* (London: Swan Sonnenschein, 1892), pp. 72-73. On the Hull guild, see J. Malet Lambert, *Two Thousand Years of Guild Life* (Hull, Eng.: A. Brown and Sons, 1891), as quoted in Cotterell, *Old Pewter*, pp. 8, 11.

11 For the Bristol quote, see Bristol City Directory, 1795. Comments about Birmingham as found in J. Bisset, *Bisset's Magnificent Directory* (Birmingham, Eng.: J. Bisset, 1808), p. 2.

12 Samuel Timmins, ed., *The Resources, Products, and Industrial History of Birmingham and the Midland Hardware District* (London: Robert Hardwicke, 1866), p. 372.

13 Timmins, *Resources, Products, and Industrial History*, p. 372.

14 Insightful essays into working practices are presented in Victor F. Hanson, "Museum Objects: Analysis of Silver," in H.K. Herglotz and L.S. Birks, eds., *X-Ray Spectrometry*, 17 vols. to date (New York: Marcel Dekker, 1978-), 2:444-54; Victor F. Hanson, "Quantitative Elemental Analysis of Art Objects by Energy-Dispersive X-Ray Fluoresence Spectroscopy," *Applied Spectroscopy* 27, no. 5 (September/October 1973): 301-34. Janice H. Carlson, "Analysis of British and American Pewter by X-Ray Fluoresence Spectroscopy," in Ian M. G. Quimby, ed., *Winterthur Portfolio 12* (Charlottesville: University Press of Virginia for the Henry Francis du Pont Winterthur Museum, 1977), pp. 65-85.

15 Benjamin Harbeson broadside, 65x708, Downs collection, Winterthur Library.

16 *Documents, Legislative and Executive of the Congress of the United States from the first Session of the First to the Third Session of the Thirteenth Congress Inclusive: Commencing March 3, 1789, and Ending March 3, 1815*, vol. 7 of *American State Papers* (Washington, D.C.: Gales and Seaton, 1832), p. 48.

17 James Larkin, *The Practical Brass and Iron Founder's Guide* (Philadelphia: Henry Carey Baird, 1883), p. 32.

18 These formulations are listed in Larkin, *Practical Brass and Iron Founder's Guide*, p. 58.

19 *New-York Weekly Post-Boy*, February 24, 1746.

20 Roll 4, vol. 53, letterbook, 1783-1800, Revere Papers, Downs collection, Winterthur Library.

21 Dionysius Lardner, comp., *The Cabinet Cyclopaedia*, 3 vols. (London: Longman, Rees, Orme, Brown, Green, and Longman, and John Taylor, 1834), 3:185.

COLOR PLATES

A

COLANDER (NO. 20), FLOUR
DREDGERS (NO. 23), NUTCRACKER
(NO. 24), LADLE (NO. 26),
CHAFING DISH (NO. 30)

B

POT (NO. 2), POSNET (NO. 5),
COFFEEPOT (NO. 34),
TOASTING FORKS (NO. 28)

C

WIND-UP JACK (NO. 11), DRINKING
POT (NO. 47), SPOON (NO. 48),
SPOON (NO. 50)

54

D

ANDIRONS (NO. 65), WIRE
FENDER (NO. 81), FRET FENDER
(NO. 76)

E

TRIVET (NO. 40), TRIVET
(NO. 38), COAL SCUTTLE
(NO. 86), WARMING PAN (NO. 98)

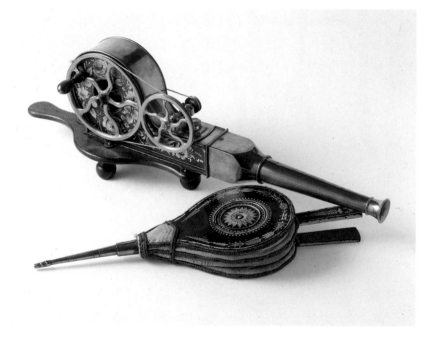

F

BLOWER (NO. 85),
DOUBLE BELLOWS (NO. 83)

G

ANDIRONS, SHOVEL, TONGS
(NO. 52)

H

CANDELABRA (NO. 136),

56

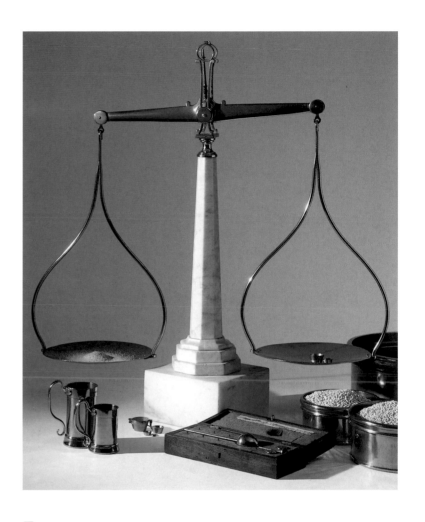

I

ARGAND LAMPS (NO. 168),
CANDLESTICK LAMP (NO. 157),
ARGAND LAMPS (NO. 161), ARGAND
LAMP (NO. 162), READING LAMP
(NO. 163), SOLAR LAMP (NO. 171)

J

COUNTER SCALES (NO. 178),
LIQUID MEASURES (NO. 179),
HYDROMETER (NO. 187),
GRAIN MEASURES (NO. 181)

60

K

MANTEL CLOCK (NO. 199),
WATCH STAND (NO. 195),
SUNDIAL (NO. 190),
EQUINOCTIAL RING (NO. 194)

L

TOBACCO TONGS (NO. 220),
PISTOL TINDERBOX (NO. 227),
FLEAM (NO. 228), BOX
IRON (NO. 254), FLATIRON
TRIVET (NO. 255), FISHING
REEL (NO. 252)

M

STAMP (NO. 237),
MEMORANDUM BOOK (NO. 240),
BOX (NO. 218), DIRK
(NO. 248), INK POTS (NO. 233),
WAX JACK (NO. 234)

N

TOBACCO BOX (NO. 203), TOBACCO
BOX (NO. 201), TOBACCO BOX
(NO. 206), TOBACCO BOXES (NO. 217)

O

COMMEMORATIVE MEDAL (NO. 222),
ADMISSION TOKEN (NO. 224),
MEDAL (NO. 225), SEAL (NO. 235),
SEAL (NO. 236), BUTTON (NO. 242)

P

PIPE CASE (NO. 219), LORGNETTE
(NO. 244), SHOE BUCKLE (NO. 241),
SPECTACLES (NO. 245), SHOEHORN
(NO. 246), WIGMAKER'S COMB
(NO. 247)

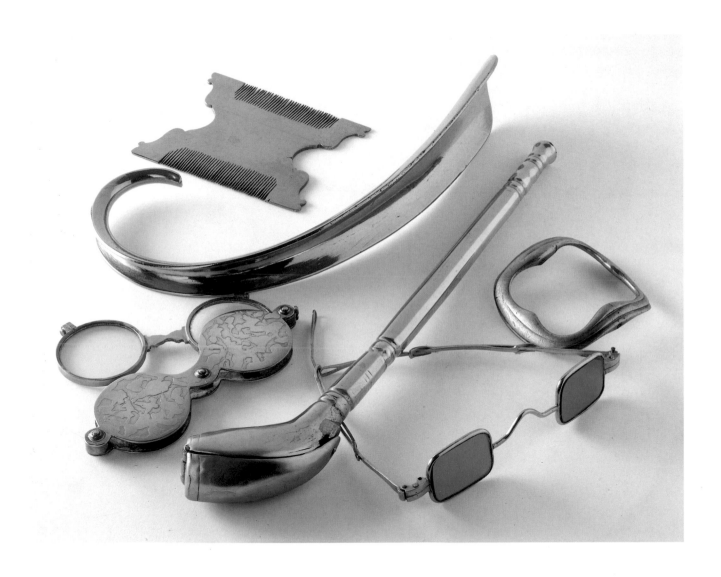

Q

CLOAK PINS (NO. 264), BELL PULL
ORNAMENT (NO. 269), DOOR PORTER
(NO. 270), DOOR LATCH (NO. 274),
DOOR KNOCKER (NO. 277)

CATALOGUE

DETAIL, BRONZE POSNET, 1793–94

ENTRY 4

FOOD AND DRINK

THIS SECTION DETAILS a considerable variety of implements whose primary purpose is the preparation, storage, dispensation, and consumption of food and drink. Those items used for preparation or storage are generally listed first, followed by those used in dispensing and consuming. Represented in the former group are teakettles, coffee mills, stills, cooking pots, posnets, saucepans, stew pans, fish kettles, colanders, funnels, wind-up jacks, pepper casters, flour dredgers, toasting forks, confectioner's and household ladles, skimmers, and nutcrackers. The latter consists of chocolate pots, coffeepots, drinking pots, monteiths, cellarettes, salvers, chafing dishes, plate warmers, trivets, fender footmen, and spoons. In some cases, an object can be interpreted as serving more than one of these functions. A flour dredger, for example, both stores and dispenses. In these instances, I made a subjective decision as to its place in a given group.

POT

1

EUROPE, POSSIBLY GERMANY, 1657
BRONZE (COPPER 75.47, TIN 16.25,
LEAD 4.64, ANTIMONY 2.67, ZINC 0.43,
SILVER 0.28, IRON 0.27), IRON

H. 11 7/8" (30.2 CM), DIAM. 15"
(38.1 CM), W. 16 1/4" (41.3 CM)
61.320
GIFT OF CHARLES F. MONTGOMERY

ONE OF THE MORE POPULAR recipes for preparing a rump of beef in English and American households during the seventeenth and eighteenth centuries was outlined in E. Smith's *The Compleat Housewife*. The recipe involved stuffing "the under part of the beef with forc'd meat made of grated bred, beef-suet, sweet herbs, spice and anchovy, with a little salt, fresh oysters or mushrooms, with two or three eggs beaten fine to mix up with the stuffing; then put it into a pot to stew, with as much water as will near cover it. . . . This requires six or seven hours stewing."[1]

The illustrated pot, with the date 1657 cast near its rim, was the type of vessel used as early as the twelfth century to make such a stew. The form remained popular for more than seven hundred years, finally falling from favor with the advent of the cookstove in the nineteenth century. Iron pots were the cheapest and therefore the most common, but brass and bronze

examples like the "bellmettle pot" inventoried in the kitchen of Samuel Ruggles of Roxbury, Massachusetts, on April 4, 1716, were also used.[2]

The three legs allowed these pots to stand upright directly on or beside a pile of burning logs, peat, or coal. The removable iron handle was used to suspend the pot over the heat source from a pot hook or crane if the contents, like stew, had to be cooked slowly for a long time.

These pots remained an essential piece of equipment as long as householders cooked over an open fire. In America most were imported by men like George Worrall, who had "for sale at his store No. 26 North Second-Street, Philadelphia . . . a large assortment of the best manufactured brass [pots] from 1 to 30 gallons."[3]

POT

2

PROBABLY ENGLAND, 1708
BRONZE (COPPER 80.02, LEAD 7.74,
TIN 5.61, ANTIMONY 4.28,
ZINC 0.75, SILVER 0.39), IRON

H. 14 1/8" (35.8 CM),
W. 18 1/2" (47.0 CM),
DIAM. 17 1/2" (44.4 CM)

61.214

WHEN ROBERT LORD of Salem, Massachusetts, wrote to his factor in England on September 10, 1680, he cited "a note of what things we desire to have sent over for our part. [Prominent among them were] a great kettell about 18 or 20 gallons & others les to goe one within another to 3 gallons & 6 skillets the biggest to hold 2 quarts strong such as they call dubble brass." The vessels he enumerated proved to be of considerable importance for early settlers. Iron, bronze, or brass kettles were used for cooking in most seventeenth-century New England households, and the latter two were often of sufficient value to warrant being itemized in kitchen inventories. The estate of Andrew Dewing of Dedham, Massachusetts, taken on August 8, 1677, typically lists "one brass Kettle, one brass pot & 2 brass posnets" valued at £11.10. William Torrey, who died in Weymouth, Massachusetts, in February 1717, owned "brass Kettles, Pans & Skillets [weighing] 10lb [and] Bell mettle [weighing an additional] 30 [lbs.]" valued at £11.10.[4]

Imported European kettles also became an important trade commodity for early settlers since kettles were highly esteemed by American Indians, who used them primarily for cooking but also broke them up on occasion as a ready supply of metal for weapons, trinkets, and other implements. Numerous Indian communities thought so much of European kettles that they buried them with their dead, often positioned so that the owner's head was inside the pot.[5]

The pot shown here, with two repairs in the base and side and the ends of the three legs burned off and replaced, is of particular interest since it is dated and employs an encircling geometric border. Of equal interest is the survival of the external surface texture. That roughness resulted from the application of a parting material onto the walls of the flask in which the kettle was cast to prevent it from fusing to the mold. Dates, ornament, and surface texture are usually polished away with use.

A.

B.

POSNETS
3 a,b

A. LAWRENCE LANGWORTHY (1692–1739)
NEWPORT, RHODE ISLAND, 1730
BRONZE (COPPER 78.25, LEAD 8.17,
TIN 5.67, ANTIMONY 3.04,
ZINC 1.87, SILVER 0.24)
H. 9 1/8" (23.2 CM), L. 20 7/8" (53.0 CM),
W. 9 7/16" (24.0 CM)
60.918

B. LAWRENCE LANGWORTHY (1692–1739)
NEWPORT, RHODE ISLAND, 1730–39
BRONZE (COPPER 69.55, TIN 14.53,
LEAD 4.39, ZINC 4.30, ANTIMONY 2.71,
SILVER 0.36, ARSENIC 0.21)
H. 10 7/8" (27.6 CM), DIAM.
9 1/2" (24.1 CM), L. 20 1/4" (51.4 CM)
60.921

ENGRAVED ON A headstone in the cemetery of Trinity Church in Newport is the following: "In memory of Lawrence Langworthy of Ashburton in ye County of Devonshire [England] Died Oct ye 19, 1739 in ye 47 year of his age."[6] The year of Langworthy's arrival in Newport is not recorded, but his presence is documented in court records in May 1731. On May 6, 1735, he was admitted a freeman of the town.

Langworthy practiced brass founding, iron founding, and pewtering but is best known for the last of these. Several pieces of his pewter are known, including a quart, a pint, and a gill lidded measure; a 20 3/8-inch dish; and a pint mug. Several iron pots are also recorded that were made in his shop, as are a number of bronze posnets.[7]

A posnet was defined as "a skillet, a kitchen vessel" in the eighteenth century.[8] It always had three splayed legs and a long handle for cooking over an open hearth and can be traced unchanged in design to medieval European antecedents.

Winterthur owns two examples by Langworthy, which are illustrated here. The pans of both are the same size. Each has the remains of a substantial sprue on the center of the underside. The legs are triangular in section with a bead that runs their length along the outermost ridge. The handles, which are brazed to handle stumps, are significantly different. The date 1730 on one handle documents the maker's presence in Newport one year prior to the town's court record.

POSNET

4

SAMUEL AUSTIN AND
ROBERT CROCKER
BOSTON, MASSACHUSETTS, 1790–94
BRONZE (COPPER 78.78, LEAD 11.17,
TIN 9.17, ANTIMONY 0.26, SILVER 0.22)

H. 7 5/8" (19.4 CM), L. 17 5/8"
(44.8 CM), W. 8 1/2" (21.6 CM)
60.47

ON APRIL 17, 1793, Samuel Austin announced: "The copartnership of Samuel Austin and Co. is this day by mutual consent dissolved. All persons having accounts with said company are requested to call and settle them with AUSTIN and CROCKER, Founders, who will in future carry on the business in its various branches at their shop in Market Square." The company apparently had a large foundry and intended to service a sizable segment of Boston's population, for they stated that in their shop "may be had brass and prince-metal Handirons, tongs, shovel, chimney hooks, brass work for ships, viz: pintles and braces, pump chambers, cogs, ships bells, sheathing nails, &c."[9]

About one year later Austin and Crocker placed an advertisement in the same newspaper stating that

"bell metal skillets of the best quality [were] to be had of AUSTIN and CROCKER." But what had promised to be a long and productive business arrangement was ended on October 15, 1794, when the two men concluded that "the copartnership of AUSTIN and CROCKER is dissolved this day by mutual consent."[10]

The posnet shown here, the product of Austin and Crocker's endeavor, is of excellent quality, well cast, and finished with its makers' surnames boldly emblazoned on the handle. Those names are enframed within a border that shows a strong influence from engraved bright-cut borders used on contemporary Boston-made domestic silver.

POSNET
5

MARTIN GAY (1726–1809) AND
WILLIAM C. HUNNEMAN (1769–1856)
BOSTON, MASSACHUSETTS, 1794
BRONZE (COPPER 93.83,
TIN 3.80, LEAD 2.87, ZINC 0.68,
ANTIMONY 0.27, SILVER 0.15)

H. 8 3/4" (22.2 CM), L. 17 5/8"
(44.8 CM), DIAM. 7 7/8" (20.0 CM)
64.31

MARTIN GAY WAS BORN in Hingham, Massachusetts, on December 29, 1726.[11] He was trained in the business of brass founding and was also involved in shipping. During the Revolution he chose the Tory side and remained in Boston when the city was occupied by British troops. When the British departed in 1776, he accompanied them to live in Nova Scotia and then England.

Gay apparently later changed his mind, for in November 1792 he returned to Boston. Within five months he advertised that he "respectfully informs the public in general, and his old customers in particular, that he has re-assumed the coppersmith and brazier's business, which in future will be carried on in all their various branches by GAY and HUNNEMAN at those noted works

No. 19 Union Street, lately improved by Messrs. Cordwell and Wells." Gay and William C. Hunneman remained together, albeit in an increasingly loose working arrangement, until 1799, when they parted, apparently amicably, to pursue coppersmithing and brass founding independently.[12]

The posnet shown here, made during the second year of their partnership, differs little in overall form from those used in Europe since the fourteenth century. Aside from the names, date, and decoration on the handle, the only features that distinguish it from its earlier counterparts are the legs, which are half round in section rather than triangular; the gate or bladed sprue, instead of a sprue on the underside; and a well-detailed architectural molding at the lip.

POSNET

6

JOSEPH SHARE (B. 1780)
AND ARTHUR RIDER
BALTIMORE, MARYLAND, 1812–27
BRONZE (COPPER 79.71,
LEAD 13.60, TIN 4.28, ANTIMONY
1.31, ZINC 0.89, SILVER 0.12)

H. 6 9/16" (16.7 CM), L. 18 1/2"
(47.0 CM), W. 7 5/8" (19.3 CM)
93.13

THIS POSNET IS THE latest in date of ten owned by Winterthur. It is the museum's only southern example and must surely have been made toward the end of this form's use for food preparation. The three short splayed legs and long handle make it suitable for cooking on uneven hearths beside or over open fires. By the second quarter of the nineteenth century, the advent of stoves with enclosed fires and flat-metal cooking surfaces allowed for the development of modern-type saucepans–flat-bottomed, legless, and lidded vessels with handles–that seem to have completely supplanted posnets by about 1850.[13]

This example differs little from its predecessors, except in detail. It is quite thin-walled and has an attenuated handle unlike more massively constructed forms from earlier cen-

turies. The legs have concave backs and pronounced architecturally inspired moldings at the juncture with the pan. The pan wall meets the bottom at a relatively sharp angle. Surprisingly, the pot has the remains of a sprue, rather than a gate, in the center of the bottom.

Joseph Share and Arthur Rider were brass founders in Baltimore, Maryland. Always at separate addresses, the former was listed at various locations in the city directories from 1810 until 1845. The latter was listed intermittently from 1812 until 1827. Both placed advertisements in local and regional newspapers at various times from 1806 to 1820, but always individually.[14] This posnet is currently the only record that documents collaboration between the two.

SAUCEPAN

7

PROBABLY ENGLAND OR
EUROPE, POSSIBLY AMERICA,
1750–1800
COPPER, WOOD, IRON, TIN

H. 19" (48.2 CM),
W. 21" (53.3 CM),
DIAM. 13 1/2" (34.3 CM)
58.1126

THIS 4½-GALLON VESSEL is made of three sheets of copper, two for the body and a third for the bottom, all of which are dove-tailed and brazed. The tubular handle socket is sloppily brazed to the bracket, which is, in turn, held in place with three large die-headed rivets. The rim is wired.

This object is a common eighteenth-century vessel known as a saucepan. "It is probable that among the culinary utensils made by braziers [during the late eighteenth and early nineteenth centuries] there were more saucepans than almost any other article; but later on the French stew pan [a straight-sided flat-bottom vessel] seemed to supersede the sauce pan altogether, excepting in a few instances, such as the smaller sizes, which were made with lips and used for the preparation of little delicacies. . . . Copper sauce pans were made in sizes to hold from 1 pint to four gallons."[15]

Only a few saucepans bearing American makers' names are presently known, and all of those are by men who worked in and around southeast Pennsylvania. Included are a saucepan by the Philadelphia coppersmith Benjamin Harbeson, active between about 1755 and 1809; another by William Bailey, who worked in several Pennsylvania and Maryland towns from about 1762 until his death in 1797; and a third by John Lay, who worked in York, Pennsylvania, between 1791 and 1844. A fourth saucepan bears the mark of two men with the surnames Crabb and Minshall, who are believed to have worked together in Baltimore and possibly southeast Pennsylvania during the late eighteenth century.[16]

STEWPAN

8

PETER BURKHARD (1807/8–71)
NEW YORK CITY, 1836–71
COPPER, IRON

H. 8 1/4" (20.9 CM), W. 16 7/8"
(42.8 CM), DIAM. 8" (20.3 CM)
89.104
GIFT OF WILLIAM J. FLATHER III

IN THE NINETEENTH CENTURY the most commonly used methods of cooking were roasting, frying, baking, broiling, boiling, and stewing. "Stewing differs from boiling in this, that the heat is never to be raised to the boiling point, but only to a very gentle simmering, with a very small quantity of water. . . . Stewing is, therefore, found to be not only a very perfect mode of cooking, but also very economical."[17]

This method of cooking called for a specially designed pan. "The stew-pan . . . is usually made of copper instead of being of tin [tinned sheet iron] like the sauce-pan, and they are less deep. . . . The advice to keep copper stew-pans well tinned on the inside cannot be given too often, since it is well known that fatal accidents have happened through neglect of this precaution [causing food poisoning]. Stew-pans are likewise made of cast iron; these answer for stewing as well as those of copper, and are much cheaper at first, though they do not look so handsome in the kitchen as copper kept bright. A certain thickness of metal appears

to be necessary for stew-pans; for in a common tin sauce-pan, the cooks say it is very difficult to prevent [food from] burning to [it]."[18]

Peter Burkhard fabricated the example shown here from thick, rolled sheet with brazed, dovetailed joints and tinned it heavily on the inside. The point at which he bent the sides to form the lip of the bottom–by hammering over a sharp-edged stake called a forming lag–is called the lag. If not done carefully "many an otherwise good piece of work has been spoiled with the finishing by being cut through, or nearly so, on the sharp edge of" the lag. Burkhard made that mistake on a section of the edge of this pan, which he subsequently repaired. That error suggests that the pan was made early in his career since later examples had the lag formed "on the heel of [a specially designed stake], it being made round and suitable for the purpose. [In even later examples the process] was superceded by a lagging machine, upon which dies or wheels . . . of various sizes" were used to form the bend.[19]

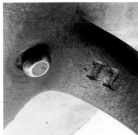

STEWPAN
9

SOLD BY WILLIAM F. DOUGHERTY
PHILADELPHIA, PENNSYLVANIA,
1881–1914
COPPER, IRON

H. 8 1/4" (21.0 CM), L. 21" (53.3 CM),
DIAM. 10 1/4" (26.0 CM)
83.71

"STEWING IS NOTHING ELSE than boiling by means of a small quantity of aqueous fluid and continuing the operation for a long time to make the substance tender, to loosen its texture, to render it more sapid, and to retain and concentrate the most essential parts of animal or vegetable food. If the stewpan be closely shut it is evident that none of the nutritive principles can escape, and must either be found in the meat itself or in the liquid. . . . No scorching or browning of the meat takes place if the process is properly conducted, for the temperature to which it is exposed does not exceed the boiling point of water."[20]

A stewpan "differs from a saucepan in having straight sides, and a flat lid with a handle. This kind of stewpan is much in vogue, it being convenient for many purposes. . . . In French kitchens [the] stewpan is always used. The lid is of bright metal, which forms a nice addition to the kitchen mantlepiece or the pot-board under the dresser. These stew pans are made of copper in all sizes . . . from 1 pint to 22 quarts."[21] The

eleven-quart example shown here, of heavy-gauge rolled sheets assembled with dovetailed joints (but missing the lid), conforms precisely to those used in the most efficient kitchens in France.

William F. Dougherty first appears in the 1880 Philadelphia city directory as a salesman. The following year he was listed at the address stamped on the side of this stewpan and remained there until 1914, after which he was no longer listed. Dougherty recorded himself as a purveyor of stoves, ranges, or heaters for that entire time. This pan suggests that he also sold cooking utensils to householders and restauranteurs, as was done by his competitor, the firm of Cox, Whiteman, and Cox. Their illustrated trade catalogue offers not only a number of differing parlor and kitchen stoves but also a variety of pots, kettles, spiders, and boilers.[22]

FISH KETTLE
10

FORBES CLARK (1779–1835)
HARRISBURG, PENNSYLVANIA,
1807–35
COPPER, IRON, TIN

H. 17" (43.2 CM), W. 13 1/4"
(33.3 CM), L. 28 1/4" (71.7 CM)
90.51
PARTIAL FUNDS FOR
PURCHASE THE GIFT OF EDDY
NICHOLSON

FISH KETTLES WERE a popular kitchen item in the American household during the late eighteenth and early nineteenth centuries. They were almost always made of copper and were offered by men like "William Bailey, Coppersmith of the Borough of York [who] carries on the Coppersmith business in all its various branches [making] all kinds of Copper work, and in particular stills of all sizes, Brewing Coppers, Wash, Fish and Tea Kettles."[23]

Fish kettles "were made shallow . . . oblong, with circular ends and straight sides. . . . The inside was supplied with a perforated fish plate, having two lugs or handles with which to lift it out; the plate was tinned on both sides, planished bright, and then wired around the edge."[24]

Properly used, "the fish-kettle must be large and nicely clean. Lay the fish . . . on the strainer of the kettle. Cover it well with cold water (milk and water in equal portions will be better still), and add a small table-spoon of salt. Do not let it come to a boil too fast, and skim it carefully. When the scum has ceased to rise, diminish the heat under the kettle, and let it simmer for about half an hour or more; not allowing it to boil hard. When the fish is done, take it up carefully with a fish-slice; and having prepared the sauce, pour it over the fish and send it to the table hot."[25]

Forbes Clark was first recorded in the tax lists for Harrisburg in 1807, his property valued at $100. He was subsequently listed in the federal population censuses for 1810, 1820, and 1830. His date of death, February 25, 1835, and age, fifty-six years, were announced one day later in the *Harrisburg Chronicle*.[26]

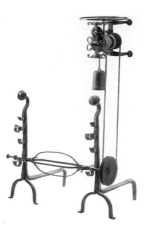

WIND-UP JACK

11

PROBABLY ENGLAND, POSSIBLY
AMERICA, 1750–1810
BRASS (COPPER 72.92, ZINC 21.74,
LEAD 3.17, TIN 0.99, IRON 0.82,
SILVER 0.18, ANTIMONY 0.15),
IRON, ALDER, WILLOW

H. 13 1/2" (34.3 CM), W. 14"
(35.6 CM), D. 18 3/4" (47.6 CM)
60.906

ROASTING JACKS, although not essential, were a desirable part of well-equipped English and American kitchen fireplaces in the eighteenth century. The type pictured here was described as "a compound engine, where the weight is the power applied to overcome the friction of the parts" to rotate beef, mutton, or fowl in front of a fire.[27] The mechanism consists of a series of gears and a worm engaged to a ratcheted spindle in a wall-mounted frame. The spindle is cranked to elevate a weight that, when it descends, causes the large flanged wheel at the back to rotate. This, in turn, rotates the spit hanging on the spithook andirons by means of an endless rope.

England's industrial centers employed numerous specialist jackmakers like "Francis Sadleir, at the Jack and Grate, at Bell Street in Birmingham [who] makes and sells wholesale and retail at the lowest prices all sort of smoak and wind-up jacks, in brass or iron." The demand for his work was sufficient enough for him to note at the end of his advertisement that "a good hand at jack-making or jobbing smith may have constant employment by applying" to him.[28]

Part of the demand for his and other English jackmakers' work was in America, as evidenced in the advertisement of the Philadelphia hardware merchants James and Drinker, who imported and sold "iron and brass roasting jacks." American base-metal workers also supplied them. The New York City craftsmen Lucas and Shepard, who advertised as "whitesmiths and cutlers from Birmingham & Sheffield [noted that they] make . . . winding up and smoak jacks" for New York residents.[29]

COFFEE MILL

12

PROBABLY ENGLAND, 1815–40
BRASS (COPPER 66.87, ZINC
32.74, LEAD 0.33), IRON, WOOD

H. 9 1/4" (23.5 CM), W. 4 7/8"
(12.4 CM), D. 5" (12.7 CM)
65.1442

THE ENGLISH DIARIST John Evelyn recalled in his memoirs for 1637 that "there came in my tyme to the Coll[ege] one Nathaniel Conopios out of Greece. . . . He was the first I ever saw drink coffee, which custome came not into England till 30 years after."[30] From the mid seventeenth century coffee became increasingly popular in England and America.

Coffee beans, imported from the Near East and later the West Indies and Central America, were roasted and ground. The latter was done in a "portable coffee-mill [which] consists of a square box . . . containing in the interior a hollow cone of steel, with sharp grooves on the inside; into this fits a conical piece of hardened iron or steel, having spiral grooves cut upon its surface, and capable of being turned round by a handle. The coffee is put into a hopper, which conducts it into the hollow cone, where it is crushed by the motion of the solid cone as it revolves. The powder ground in this manner falls into a

drawer below. . . . This is a necessary machine in every family, as the goodness of the coffee depends much upon its being fresh ground, which can only be insured by grinding it at home."[31]

Wood was apparently used extensively for the spindles in these and larger commercial coffee mills at an early date, but "the substitution of cast iron for the wooden spindles hitherto used in all coffee mills [was] an improvement which the first Archibald [Kenrick] patented in 1815."[32]

The mill shown here has iron spindles and is housed in a case that has sides held in place by grooved corner posts. Those posts are bolted to the top and bottom plates with urn-shape nuts at each corner so that the entire box can be easily disassembled for adjusting and cleaning when necessary.

TEAKETTLE
13

MARKED "BT"
PROBABLY SWEDEN OR GERMANY,
1720–60
BRASS (COPPER 71.29,
ZINC 27.00, LEAD 1.01, IRON 0.18),
WOOD, IRON, TIN

H. 11 3/8" (28.9 CM),
W. 12 5/8" (32.1 CM),
D. 9 3/8" (23.8 CM)
58.987

THE GLOBULAR BODY of this kettle is fashioned of wrought sheet metal and has a vertical dovetailed joint on the spout side. The bottom is a separate piece, lapped and hard-soldered to a narrow projecting flange. The spout, also made of sheet metal with a straight, brazed seam along its length on the top, is held in place on the body with a large amount of hard solder.

"If such a kettle . . . be put on the fire with a sufficient quantity of water, the solder of the joints would not melt, because [the evaporating water] carries off the greater part of the heat from the metal, and does not become hot enough for the solder to melt. If, however, the kettle should remain on the fire with very little water, it is evident that the solder which fixes the spout [and the bottom] will not be protected [so it becomes] unsoldered wholly or in part, and the kettle leaks, an accident well known to happen too frequently."[33]

The interior of the kettle has been entirely coated with a layer of tin to prevent the brass from imparting a bad taste or poisoning the contents. In doing this, the object "is first scoured bright, and then made hot, and the tin is rubbed on over the fire with a piece of cloth, or some tow [unworked wool or flax]. In this process, nothing ought to be used but pure grain tin; but . . . lead is sometimes mixed with the tin, to adulterate its quality, and make it lie more easily. This is a pernicious practice."[34]

Although the maker and owner of this kettle have yet to be identified, both placed their marks on it. The maker's stamp centered on the bottom of the kettle includes the script initials "BT" flanking a recumbant unicorn and a lobed pot. These motifs, particularly the unicorn, were favored by Swedish and German base-metal workers during the eighteenth century, suggesting that this kettle may have originated there.[35] An owner scratched the conjoined initials "HK" twice on the underside of the lid and again on the bottom of the kettle.

TEAKETTLE ON
STAND WITH TRAY

14

ENGLAND, PROBABLY LONDON,
1730–60; TRAY, CA. 1850
COPPER, TIN, RATTAN

OVERALL: H. 14" (35.5 CM), W. 9 13/16"
(25.0 CM), D. 7 1/4" (18.4 CM);
TRAY: H. 1 1/4" (3.2 CM), W. 9 1/8"
(20.6 CM), D. 8 1/2" (21.5 CM)
59.4.4 PURCHASE FUNDS THE GIFT
OF HENRY FRANCIS DU PONT

ELABORATELY CHASED SILVER KETTLES on stands with spirit burners were made in considerable numbers in London during the second quarter of the eighteenth century. They were disseminated widely, some even to the American colonies, where at least one similar kettle was made by the Philadelphia silversmith Joseph Richardson.[36]

This kettle on stand relates very closely to those in every respect except for the material of which it is fashioned. The body is wrought of sheet metal with a single vertical joint on the spout side. It is tinned on the inside. The chased repoussé ornament on the body and the cast ornament on the stand are technically and stylistically like that on the silver counterparts.[37]

Just as English silver examples were imported by Americans, so too were copper kettles on stands. Robert and Amos Strettell advertised in the July 2, 1752, issue of the *Pennsylvania Gazette* that they had "just imported . . . to be sold at their store in Front Street . . . copper chocolate and coffee pots, tea kettles [and] fine chased ditto."

The inventory of John Penn, Jr., taken in Philadelphia in 1788, included "1 plain brown tea urn." Copper household objects were sometimes patinated in various shades from brown to red to simulate antique bronze and also to prevent tarnish. The process involved dissolving "1 oz. of sulphur and 8 oz. of pearl ash in one gallon of water" and dipping the object to be patinated into it.[38] The longer the item remained immersed, the darker it became.

TEAKETTLE
15

ROBERT REED
LANCASTER, PENNSYLVANIA,
1780–95
COPPER, BRASS, IRON, TIN

H. 13 3/4" (34.9 CM), W. 13 5/8"
(34.7 CM), DIAM. 9 3/8" (23.8 CM)
56.64.1

IN 1790, when the first United States population census was taken, Robert Reed was recorded in Lancaster, Pennsylvania, as the head of a household in which three white males over the age of sixteen, four white females, and one slave lived. Reed was dead by June 24, 1795, when the coppersmith William P. Atlee advertised that he had commenced business in the house of "the late Mr. Reed."[39]

This kettle, made by Reed, conforms in appearance and construction to many made by Pennsylvania coppersmiths and tin-plate workers during the late eighteenth and early nineteenth centuries. Vessels of this type were typically called teakettles and were kept filled by the fire to provide a ready supply of boiling water.

Although there were continuing attempts to find, mine, and refine copper in America for use by men like Reed, none were sufficiently successful to supplant importation from England, like the "152 bottoms, 1 cask [and] 8 cases unwrought copper" sent aboard the *Elizabeth* from Bristol, England, for Maryland on April 21, 1773. These imports were the raw material for American coppersmiths and were bought from men like Alexander Bisland in Philadelphia, who advertised on September 6, 1792, that he had "just received per the ship Adriana . . . from Liverpool for sale . . . sheet copper assorted from 5 to 50 lbs per sheet, Bottoms do from 6 inches diameter to 8 do."[40]

TEAKETTLE
16

JOHN MORRISON (D. 1793)
PHILADELPHIA,
PENNSYLVANIA, 1781–93
COPPER, BRASS, TIN

H. 15 1/4" (38.8 CM), W. 15 3/8"
(39.1 CM), DIAM. 11 1/8" (28.3 CM)
60.585

"TEA KETTLES FOR SUPPLYING boiling water for tea have been employed since the first introduction of this beverage. . . . The largest and strongest for the kitchen are of copper."[41] The illustrated kettle has a ten-quart capacity and is so marked with the numeral 10 on the underside of the handle and outside of the lid flange. The body is made of two sheets of rolled copper that are dovetailed to each other vertically on either side of the spout. The spout is straight seamed and riveted to the body while the bottom, a separate piece, is dovetailed into place. The flanges to which the handle is hinged are riveted to the body. To prevent the thin metal there from bending under the weight

of a full kettle, the maker puddled tin under the shoulder for additional strength.

On September 19, 1781, John Morrison advertised "at his shop in Third Street at the sign of the TEA URN &c nearly opposite Church Alley [that he] has for SALE a variety of COPPER STILLS, TEA URNS of home manufacture, KETTLES, WARMING PANS, and sundry other articles." Although Morrison emphasized the fact that his wares were of home manufacture, it is probable that he used imported parts and materials like the "13 casks, 37 bottoms [and] 137 sheets unwrought copper" consigned aboard the *Concord* bound from Bristol, England, for Philadelphia on March 16, 1773.[42]

TEAKETTLE

17

WILLIAM C. HUNNEMAN
(1769–1856)
BOSTON, MASSACHUSETTS,
1799–1825

COPPER, BRASS
H. 11" (28.0 CM), W. 10 1/2"
(26.7 CM), D. 7 3/4" (19.7 CM)
89.65

ON DECEMBER 15, 1804, William C. Hunneman advertised in *The Democrat* that he had "a Large assortment of Copper Tea Kettles" for sale. His existing accounts document a strong demand for copper teakettles in the greater Boston area. Many were purchased for resale by middlemen, like the "12 [1] gallon tea kettles" he supplied to the Boston hardware dealer John Philips on October 19, 1801. Similarly, on April 20, 1819, Hunneman sold "2 6 qt copper tea kettles, 2 5 qt copper tea kettles [and] 2 4 qt copper tea kettles" to the Salem merchant Edward Farley. On occasion, he even sold outside New England, as with the "6 qt copper tea kettle, 2 5 qt copper tea kettles [and] 3 4 qt copper tea kettles" sent to James Shute and Company of Cincinnati, Ohio, on August 10, 1818.[43]

Alternately, Hunneman supplied teakettles directly to those who wished to use them. He billed "1 copper tea kettle" to the USS *Constitution* on July 7, 1802. On January 10, 1812, he sold one "copper

kettle #22" to Joseph Field of Boston; on July 15, 1815, he "delivered . . . 1 copper kettle [to] John Frost pr order"; on May 28, 1821, he sold "1 copper kettle" to Eliphas Thayer.[44]

Copper teakettles, regardless of size, were designed to heat, boil, and dispense water from kitchen hearths. They were subject to constant and heavy use and eventually wore out. Consequently, Hunneman, like all coppersmiths, enjoyed a brisk demand for his services in repairing them. On June 26, 1819, he charged Joel Whiting for "mending [a] torn tea kettle"; on March 12, 1821, he billed John Limist for "mending [a] tea kettle cover"; and on December 30, 1820, he charged John Doggett for a "new copper bottom to [a tea] kettle."[45]

Whether American coppersmiths made or repaired teakettles, they traditionally depended upon England for their raw material. The English copper industry produced large quantities of rolled sheet copper that was cut into sheets of varying sizes and sent to the United

States. Hunneman was certainly among the many American coppersmiths who used it, as suggested by the "100 sheets of copper [he] bought at auction" in Boston through the auctioneer Thomas Jones in August 1801.[46]

However, Hunneman had an alternate source, due to the initiative of the metal entrepreneur Paul Revere. In 1800 Revere established a copper rolling mill at Canton, Massachusetts, which began to successfully produce and market copper to governmental, commercial, and private customers; Hunneman was among them. His name appears frequently in Revere's accounts, as with the "2 Bottoms, 3 sheets [and] 2 Bottoms" he purchased on February 1, 1821, or the "3 Bottoms [and] 10 Sheets" of copper he bought on February 23, of the same year.[47] The sheet metal from which the handle, lid, body, spout, and bottom of this kettle are made may well have been rolled in Revere's mills.

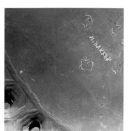

STILL
18

MICHAEL BAKER, JR.
PHILADELPHIA,
PENNSYLVANIA, 1813–24
COPPER, LEAD

H. 33 3/4" (85.7 CM), W. 42"
(106.6 CM NOT INCLUDING
WORM), DIAM. 20 3/4" (67.9 CM)
90.28

"THERE IS PERHAPS no part of the apparatus of the distillery on which more attention should be bestowed by the distiller, than that of the construction of stills. In the United States, the coppersmith becomes the sole agent and artist, he is the distiller's alma mater, in short he regulates the whole destiny of the manufacturer."[48]

American coppersmiths made their stills of sheet metal imported from England. They obtained their raw materials from importing hardwaremen or alternately at auction through commercial merchants like John Humes. Humes noted in the November 16, 1812, issue of Philadelphia's *Aurora General Advertiser* that he would sell to the highest bidder "8 cases sheet copper, viz. 2 cases 20 by 48 inches, 2 do 26 by 52 do, 2 do 28 by 56 do, 2 do 30 by 60 do [and] 72 Raised Bottoms, 17 to 40 inches diameter [and] 48 flat do 18 to 24 inches diameter."

Using these materials, the coppersmith built stills with dovetailed and riveted joints. Creating riveted joints was laborious, but, properly done, it produced a strong and watertight vessel. The process, known

as scrubbing, was accomplished using a specialized tool called a scrubbing hammer. "What is called scrubbing is to . . . first use the pane of the hammer between the rivets; then on each side; then across the four corners made by the previous blows . . . which draws them up . . . and heads them up eight square to the form of a pyramid. If the scubbing is properly done there will be no need of any cement being used to secure the joint against leaking; all that is required is good workmanship."[49]

Stills typically varied in capacity from 5 to more than 200 gallons. Those less than 100 gallons were "for a long time confined to farmers, who only carried on the work during the winter season, and men of small capital" while larger sizes were used by commercial distilleries.[50]

The 42-gallon still shown here, typical of most, "consists of a boiler, which may, for small quantities, be made to fit loosely into any kind of furnace or stove . . . of a head or capital, which consists of a hollow globe fitting upon the boiler, and with its upper part drawn out into a curved pipe [this pipe is straight] of decreasing diameter and

terminates at the upper part of the serpentine or worm into which it fits. The latter, is a long pipe, with a regularly decreasing diameter, which is arranged in a spiral form in the middle of a large tub of cold water, by means of which the [alcoholic] vapor is condensed, and trickles down in a small regular stream from the lower end of the worm where it emerges from the side of the tub."[51] This still was designed to produce alcohol from fermented grains, including corn, rye, and barley; fruit, including apples, peaches, and cherries; or vegetables, including potatoes and beets.

Michael Baker, Jr., first listed himself as a coppersmith at 223 North Second Street in Philadelphia in 1813. He continued to do so annually in the city directories through 1824, making a variety of copper products including, like his competitor Philip Apple, "copper stills, from 35 to 110 gallons."[52] The following year he appears to have given up copper-smithing to join his father in the lumber business.

COLANDER
19

PROBABLY ENGLAND, 1700–1750
BRASS (COPPER 67.80,
ZINC 30.69, LEAD 1.31, IRON 0.15),
IRON, WOOD, COPPER

H. 3 7/8" (9.8 CM), L. 18"
(45.7 CM), W. 11 5/8" (29.5 CM)
60.937

THE LATE SEVENTEENTH-CENTURY English writer Randle Holme described a colander as "usefull for a cooke, or to be in an house, wher there is a considerable familey. [It] is made of Tyn or other mettle, having the bottom full of small round holes: in this Herbs or such like things are washed, whose dirt and filth runs through the holes, leaving them pure and cleane."[53]

There are no seventeenth- or eighteenth-century tinned sheet-iron colanders in the Winterthur collection, but the example shown here is similar to the one pictured in the engraving that accompanies Holme's description. It is of wrought sheet metal, probably beaten into shape with a water-powered tilt hammer of the type in use at the Bristol Brass Company, founded in Bristol, England, in 1702, and pictured in Denis Diderot's *Encyclopédie*.[54]

The edge of the colander is wrapped around a large-diameter iron wire for reinforcement, while the wood handle is pierced with an iron tang whose end is split into two straplike extensions that are held with copper rivets to the side of the colander. Copper rivets also hold the iron loop just under the lip on the side opposite the handle.

Most colanders used in American kitchens during the seventeenth and eighteenth centuries were imported from England. Some American metalworkers did supply them as well, such as "John Haldane, Brasier from London [who] makes and sells all sorts of Copper and Brass . . . cullenders." Similarly, the Alexandria, Virginia, coppersmith William Thompson made and sold "1 cullander" to Thomas Beaty for 5*s*. on April 2, 1796.[55]

COLANDER

20

ENGLAND OR UNITED STATES,
1820–30
BRASS (COPPER 72.00, ZINC 27.20,
LEAD 0.90), COPPER, IRON

H. 5 3/8" (13.7 CM), W. 14 3/8"
(35.9 CM), DIAM. 11 3/8" (28.9 CM)
60.222

IN MAKING BOILED RICE for curry, Isabella Beeton recommended that a cook use "a saucepan of boiling water, drop the rice into it, and keep it boiling quickly, with the lid uncovered, until it is tender but not soft. Take it up, drain it, and put it on a dish before the fire to dry." Similarly, in describing how to prepare sliced carrots, she said to "cut them into slices of equal size, and boil them in salt and water, until half done; drain them."[56]

Although not specifically mentioned in these or any of the other hundreds of recipes in her *Book of Household Management*, the wording clearly implies that Beeton and her readers knew a colander was a necessary part of kitchen equipment for food preparation. The illustrated example is typical of those used in English and American kitchens during the nineteenth century, although tinned sheet iron and pewter colanders, being cheaper, probably outnumbered those of brass. This colander is very similar to one pictured in Thomas Webster's *Encyclopaedia of Domestic Economy*.[57] It is made of thin, rolled sheet metal and was spun to its present shape on a lathe, with the lip wrapped around an iron reinforcing wire. The two handles are made of seamed tubing and riveted to the body. The footrim is a strip of rolled sheet metal, bent to truncated conical form. The ends are brazed with a rabbet joint.

FUNNEL
21

ENGLAND OR UNITED STATES,
1840–70
BRASS (COPPER 64.55, ZINC 34.91,
LEAD 0.40), TINNED SHEET IRON

H. 6 1/2" (16.5 CM),
DIAM. 4 1/2" (11.4 CM)
65.1476

IN 1887 MARIA PARLOA advised all those who aspired to be good housekeepers that they had to have among their kitchen furnishings "one large and one small tunnel for filling bottles, jugs, and cruets." She also stated that they should have a "strainer . . . fine enough to keep back the seeds of small fruits."[58] The brass funnel shown here incorporates a strainer and was probably intended for kitchen rather than industrial or specialized use.

While the funnel itself is made of brass, the strainer is a circular piece of sheet iron pierced with moderate-size holes and soldered into place. It and the interior of the funnel have been coated with tin to prevent the brass from interacting with strongly acidic liquids, like vinegar or citrus juices, and tainting their flavor. For this reason tinning the inside of copper or brass objects that held food or drink was very important. The process involved melting block or ingot tin, "being careful not to allow any part of it to become too hot or get burnt. When the tin is melted . . . warm and dry the vessel to be tinned and pour a sufficient quantity of tin into it. Next take a sal ammoniac wad . . . and with it rub and agitate the liquid tin over the entire inside surface . . . until every part is well covered."[59]

The conical section of the funnel is seamless and has the lip wrapped around an iron wire for strength. The slender tapered tube is straight seamed and has a hollow groove so that air might escape from the narrow-necked vessel it is being used to fill.

PEPPER CASTERS

22

ENGLAND, PROBABLY
BIRMINGHAM, 1730–60

BRASS (COPPER 75.34, ZINC 20.80,
LEAD 3.33, TIN 0.27)

H. 4" (10.2 CM), DIAM. 1 1/2" (3.8 CM)

65.1478 (LEFT)

ENGLAND, PROBABLY
BIRMINGHAM, 1730–60

BRASS (COPPER 72.02, ZINC 21.25,
LEAD 4.92, TIN 0.75, IRON 0.41)

H. 4 1/4" (11.4 CM), DIAM. 2 1/8" (5.4 CM)

65.529

"PEPPER IS A WELL-KNOWN SPICE of an aromatic odour, and an extremely pungent and aromatic taste."[60] It had been a very expensive and highly desirable staple in European and English households since the Middle Ages. By the eighteenth century the cultivation of pepper had spread from its native India to many tropical sites in both hemispheres, making it widely available and affordable.

"This powerful spice [had] become [by then] a necessary article at table, and [was] much esteemed for its flavour, and the quality which it is supposed to possess of promoting the digestion of fish and other kinds of food." The most common variety was black pepper, but by removing the black outer skin, which contained most of the acrid oils, a milder variant was produced known as white pepper. Both were ground to produce a coarse

powder that was dispensed from dredgers or casters like those illustrated or the straight-sided variant pictured in Randle Holme's *Academy of Armory*.[61]

Pepper pots like the ones shown were undoubtedly made in London and many other English urban centers but are currently documentable only to Birmingham, through brass manufacturers trade catalogues. Such catalogues offered pepper casters in two sizes, both priced per dozen. Probably using a trade catalogue, William Bailey, at his stove-grate warehouse in Baker Street and at his store in Fly Market in New York City, ordered and had "for sale reasonable, both wholesale and retail, imported in the latest vessels from England . . . brass, and japanned flour and pepper boxes."[62]

FLOUR DREDGERS
23

ENGLAND, 1750–1800
BRASS (COPPER 68.00, ZINC 28.83, LEAD
2.49, TIN 0.32, SILVER 0.14), COPPER
H. 3" (7.6 CM), W. 2 1/2"
(6.3 CM), DIAM. 1 3/4" (4.4 CM)
65.1447 (LEFT)

ENGLAND, 1750–1800
BRASS (COPPER 73.06, ZINC 24.44,
LEAD 1.48, TIN 0.83), COPPER
H. 4 3/4" (11.1 CM), W. 3 3/4"
(9.5 CM), DIAM. 2 3/4" (7.0 CM)
65.2738

JOHN ASH DEFINED a dredger as "an instrument to scatter flower on meat while roasting."[63] In doing so, he referred to the process of coating a piece of beef, mutton, or pork with a thin layer of flour and then basting it with butter to retain moisture and enhance flavor while the meat was hanging from a hook over a fire or rotating on a spit.

Dredgers like those illustrated here were commonly used in this way and varied little in appearance from the seventeenth through the early nineteenth centuries. Randle Holme, in 1688, pictured a handleless example in his *Academy of Armory* that is otherwise identical to these late eighteenth-century dredgers.[64]

These two are made of heavy sheet metal that is seamed vertically on the handle side. Each has an applied footrim and removable friction-fit lid. The sheet-metal handles are held in place with small copper rivets. The dredgers are pictured in English brass-manufacturers' trade catalogues in two sizes, each sold by the dozen.[65]

By circulating trade catalogues widely, the manufacturers who issued them could sell their wares not only throughout Great Britain but also in America through hardware merchants like Isaac Jones of Philadelphia, who on January 7, 1752, had "just imported (chiefly by the last vessels from London) brass flour and pepper pots."[66]

NUTCRACKER

24

THOMAS BINGHAM (D. 1804)
BIRMINGHAM, ENGLAND, 1770–95
BRASS (COPPER 60.78,
ZINC 38.31, LEAD 0.25)

L. 4 1/4" (10.8 CM),
W. 1 3/8" (3.5 CM)
55.61.5

IN 1737 *The Compleat Housewife: or, Accomplish'd Gentle-woman's Companion* compiled and detailed about six hundred recipes for cakes, meats, jellies, pastries, and confectionaries, many including nuts of various types. One recipe for pickling walnuts recommended taking "walnuts about Midsummer, when a pin will pass through them, and put them in a deep pot." Another recipe for almond pudding suggested taking "a pound of the best Jordan-Almonds, blanched in cold water." Yet another told how to make chestnut pudding by taking "a dozen and a half of chestnuts [and putting] them in a skillet of water."[67]

These and other recipes in the book implied that the cook had ready access to a nutcracker since the nut "consists of a kernel covered by a hard shell" that must be forcefully broken.[68] Although a nut can be opened effectively using a rock, hinged metal nutcrackers had been developed and were in use by the early sixteenth century. Their shape and size and the material of which they are made may vary, but they have remained basically the same since that time.

The nutcracker shown here and two others in the Winterthur collection all bear the same maker's mark. Thomas Bingham listed himself as a "plater and brass nutcrack maker" in the Birmingham city directory for 1770 and 1790, but by 1797 he had apparently given himself over to being the sexton of Saint Phillip's Church in Birmingham. Bingham was one of several brassworkers who made only nutcrackers, the demand for these items apparently being sufficient enough to support such a specialization. Nutcrackers like these appear in Birmingham brassware-manufacturers' trade catalogues in at least four different sizes, each priced by the dozen.[69]

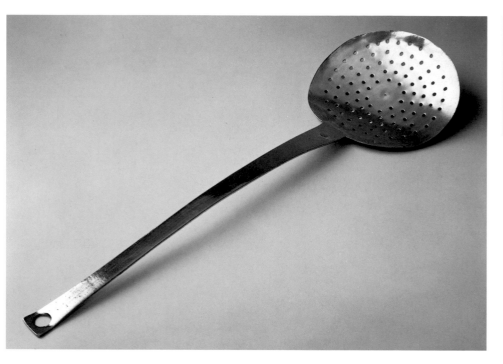

SKIMMER
25

PROBABLY MADE OR
IMPORTED BY WILLIAM KIRBY
PROBABLY NEW YORK CITY,
POSSIBLY ENGLAND, 1760–1804

BRASS (COPPER 70.74, ZINC 27.45,
LEAD 1.09, TIN 0.38)
L. 19 1/2" (49.5 CM), W. 5 13/16" (14.8 CM)
53.21 BEQUEST OF
HENRY FRANCIS DU PONT

ALTHOUGH NOTHING OF William Kirby's early life is known, he was the son of Peter Kirby, a New York City pewterer. William probably apprenticed to his father, for he, too, became a pewterer. He seems to have been quite successful, as attested in a letter written by the merchant John Thurman in his behalf. That letter, dated December 9, 1772, states, "I can recommend him as a safe customer & do not doubt but he may become a considerable one. His business is a Pewterer [and] I don't doubt but he [has] it in his power to Vend more Pewter than any Merch.t in this City."[70]

Thurman's recommendation was apparently well founded for on November 19, 1787, Kirby announced that he "has for sale a large and general assortment of Pewter Ware," listing thirty-seven separate types of objects and "many other articles in the Pewter way too tedious to mention." Another of his advertisements notes that he had for sale "a curious and general assortment of English and Dutch toys . . . amongst

which are a few large humming tops, japan'd waiters, bread baskets, clothes and shoe brushes . . . plated shoe and knee buckles, and a variety of other articles in the toy way, too tedious to mention."[71]

Kirby did not specifically enumerate skimmers, unlike his competitor "William Bailey . . . [who] at his store in Fly Market [did have] for sale reasonable both wholesale and retail . . . brass scummers, ladles and slices." Men like Kirby, although pewterers, dealt in brass and other base metals; they repeatedly noted in their advertisements that they gave "ready Money . . . for old Pewter and Brass."[72]

The simple sheet-metal skimmer shown here would have been easy for Kirby or someone in his shop to make and when completed would have met with a ready sale. Although not often mentioned in household inventories, skimmers were a basic and oft-used kitchen supplement with which "cooks take away all the filth and scume from off a Boiling pott the liquor runing throw the holes, and the dreggs remaineing on the scummer."[73]

A.

B.

LADLES
26 a,b

A. RICHARD LEE, JR. (B. 1775)
PROBABLY SPRINGFIELD, VERMONT, 1795–1830
BRASS (COPPER 91.88, ZINC 5.80,
LEAD 0.93, TIN 0.71, ANTIMONY 0.35), COPPER
L. 16 1/8" (41.0 CM), W. 5 3/4" (14.6 CM)
67.98

B. RICHARD LEE, JR. (B. 1775)
PROBABLY SPRINGFIELD, VERMONT, 1795–1830
BRASS (COPPER 79.35, ZINC 16.59,
LEAD 1.65, TIN 0.92), COPPER
L. 10" (25.4 CM), W. 3 7/8" (9.8 CM)
60.926

DURING THE COURSE OF his lifetime, the elder Richard Lee (1747–1823) tried to earn his living in many ways but was successful at none. He undertook tanning hides, speculating in real estate, manual labor, keeping store, making buttons, preaching, practicing medicine, and making children's books. About 1795 he "attempted pewtering with [his] son," but circumstances soon forced him to give that up and try something else. Following a period of wandering, he noted in his autobiography, "In the year 1805 . . . I went to live with my son and sell pewter and brassware for him again."[74]

Just who taught Richard Lee, Jr., pewtering and brazing while his father wandered about New England in search of success is currently unknown. He had a good master, however, for his work is of fine quality and imaginatively conceived. Of his pewter, many saucers, spoons, ladles, porringers, mugs, plates, and basins survive. The range of forms in brass identifiable as coming from his shop is much more restricted, consisting of ladles and skimmers.[75]

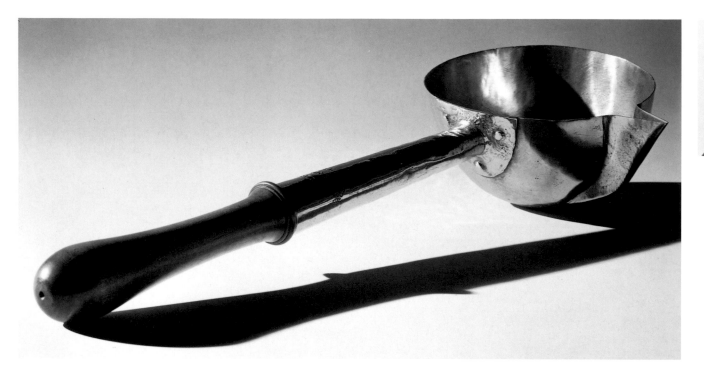

CONFECTIONER'S
LADLE
27

DAVID BENTLEY AND SONS
PHILADELPHIA,
PENNSYLVANIA, 1842–57
COPPER, WOOD

L. 11" (28.0 CM), W. 6 3/8"
(16.2 CM), H. 2 5/8" (6.7 CM)
87.16

NINETEENTH-CENTURY HOUSEHOLDERS were often reminded in print that "copper is . . . fabricated into a variety of household utensils, the use of which, however, for preparing or processing articles of food, is by no means free from danger, on account of the oxidizement to which copper is liable. It has been attempted to obviate this danger by tinning the copper. . . . This method answers the purpose as long as the coating of tin remains entire."[76]

Commercial confectioners used copper pans and kettles extensively for making sweets. The principal ingredient, sugar, liquifies between 215 and 260 degrees Fahrenheit, the temperature at which tin also liquifies. Confectioners therefore used untinned copper vessels "always kept very clean." Their kitchens contained swing pans, batch pans, revolving pans, toy pans, molds, and ladles such as the one illustrated. Such ladles, frequently called mint droppers, had single, double, or triple spouts and were "used for making mint and chocolate drops, and any similar operations."[77]

The makers of the ladle–David Bentley, David Bentley, Jr., and John Bentley–operated an active coppersmithing shop in Philadelphia from about 1813 to 1878, producing a wide array of domestic and industrial material. Among the objects they made were numerous items for the candy trade, including various types of pans: clarifying or sugarplum, candy, confectioner's, toy (mold), rose-almond, bake, sauce, and mint drop.[78]

There were approximately twenty-three confectioners active in Philadelphia during the mid nineteenth century. The sweets they produced were deemed by some to be "the poetry of epicurism [throwing] over the heavy enjoyments of the table the relief of a milder indulgence, and [dispensing] the delights of a lighter and more harmless gratification of the appetite."[79] In pursuit of their art, these confectioners would have turned to the Bentleys and their competitors for the many copper utensils they needed.

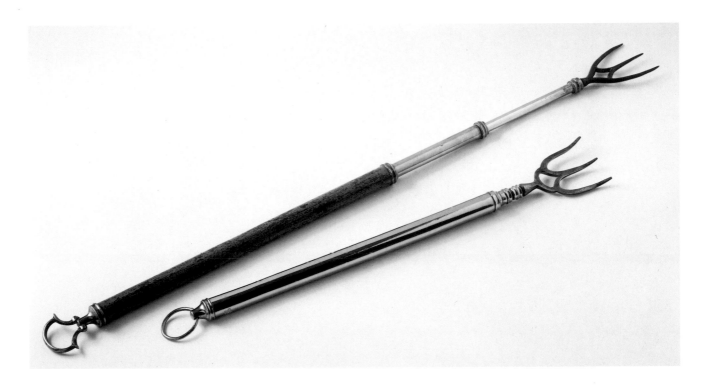

TOASTING FORKS

28

ENGLAND, 1809–38

BRASS (COPPER 73.62, ZINC 25.72,
LEAD 0.36), STEEL, IRON, PAINT

L. 24" (61.0 CM),
W. 1 1/2" (3.8 CM), D. 1/2" (1.2 CM)
64.1019 (TOP)

ENGLAND, 1838–90

BRASS (COPPER 74.19, ZINC 25.20,
LEAD 0.24, IRON 0.16), STEEL

L. 24" (61.0 CM),
W. 1 5/8" (4.1 CM), D. 1/2" (1.2 CM)
61.601

SIR EDWARD THOMASON of Birmingham reminisced in his *Memoirs of Half a Century* that "in 1809 I invented the sliding toasting fork, some with one, two or three slides, within a handsome japanned handle common now in all the shops. . . . [They] were made in silver, gilt, plated and brass and large quantities were sold even by me; but as I did not protect this invention by patent, thousands were made and sold by other manufacturers."[80]

Long-handled forks had been used to brown pieces of bread or other edibles before a flame long before Thomason's invention, but the forks had handles of fixed length. His development was considered a significant improvement in that the length when fully extended allowed the user to stand back from the fire while browning bread, avoiding a scorched hand or face.

The tubes in the fork with the japanned, iron outer section are seamed along their length, while those that are all brass appear to be seamless. "Seamles or solid brass tubes" were developed, after considerable experimentation on the part of many men, by Charles Green of Birmingham in 1838.[81] Tubing, used in many different applications from toasting forks to boiler pipes, could now be manufactured much more quickly and inexpensively. Seamless brass tubing was also stronger than that with a brazed joint along the length.

Americans, like the English, used forks to make toast. One of the New York hardware merchants who helped supply such forks was "William Bailey [who] at his stove grate warehouse in Beaker Street and at his store in Fly Market has for sale reasonably both wholesale and retail imported in the latest vessels from England . . . toasting forks."[82]

CHAFING DISH
29

PROBABLY ENGLAND,
POSSIBLY AMERICA,
1700–1760
COPPER, WOOD, IRON

H. 4 9/16" (11.6 CM), L. 13 1/2"
(34.3 CM), W. 7 7/8" (20.0 CM)
53.151.6

"A CHAFFEING DISH is a kind of round [pan], made hollow like a Bason, set on feet, either 3 or 4 with an handle to move it from place to place; its office is to hold hot coales of fire in, and to set dish-meates thereon, to keep them warme till the time of serving them up to the table, or to heat a cold dish of meate, on the table."[83]

The most desirable chafing dishes were of silver, and several are presently recorded that were made by American silversmiths. These dishes were far outnumbered in American households, however, by those made of base metal, principally copper, iron, or brass, such as the "2 Brass Chaffing Dishes" inventoried in 1760 in the Brookline, Massachusetts, estate of Samuel White.[84]

The illustrated example is made of wrought copper, the lip wrapped around an iron wire. The wood handle is impaled on a copper tang rather than one of iron, which is split into two flanges that are riveted to the pan. The three feet, which also serve as supports for a dish over the coals, are riveted to the pan as well. The pan was originally solid. The holes, crudely punched in a random pattern, were added at a later date, almost certainly by an owner to increase the draft to the coals. This pan is probably similar to the "copper chafing dishes [which the Philadelphia merchant] Isaac Jones just imported (chiefly by the last vessels from London)" in 1752.[85]

CHAFING DISH
30

PROBABLY GERMANY, POSSIBLY THE
NETHERLANDS OR SWEDEN, 1710–60
BRASS (COPPER 78.74,
ZINC 18.00, LEAD 0.97, IRON 0.45,
TIN 0.30), IRON, WOOD

H. 2 3/4" (7.0 CM), W. 11 5/8"
(29.5 CM), DIAM. 8 1/8" (20.6 CM)
64.755

THE WIDE, CIRCULAR CAST PLATE at the top of this chafing dish has a central bolt on its underside that threads into the handled support. Removing the plate exposes a thick circular iron ring that nests snugly inside the cast base. That ring can be lifted out easily and made red hot over a wood or coal fire and then replaced to serve as the source of heat for keeping food warm at the table.

The use of a thick piece of iron to provide heat relates this object to smoothing irons, but it is atypical for chafing dishes. "The old method of keeping the tea-kettle boiling [or heating food] was, to bring it in upon a chafing-dish filled with lighted charcoal. . . . But the fumes of the charcoal were found [to be] very pernicious, and this gave way to the invention of the . . . iron heater [that is] very economical and convenient.[86]

The iron heater was lauded as a significant improvement in safety, but it never entirely superseded burning charcoal or spirit lamps under chafing dishes and hot-water urns. By the early nineteenth century, however, it was acknowledged that "the charcoal chafing-dish ought not to be used except in the open air."[87]

CHAFING DISH
31

PROBABLY FRANCE, POSSIBLY THE
NETHERLANDS OR GERMANY, 1730–80
BRASS (COPPER 66.18, ZINC 31.49,
LEAD 2.15, TIN 0.41), COPPER, IRON

H. 5 1/4" (13.3 CM), W. 9 1/8"
(23.2 CM), DIAM. 8 1/4" (21.0 CM)
59.2878

ON OCTOBER 29, 1773, Richard Sause, a hardware merchant in New York City, advertised in *Rivington's New-York Gazetteer* that he had "just imported . . . brass chafing dishes with and without flaps . . . by the Grace from Bristol [England] and sundry vessels from Europe."

The chafing dish shown here with hinged flaps above the coals "for warming a plate or dish," is one of five of this type owned by Winterthur.[88] It is the only one that retains its removable inner copper liner. The pan appears to be lathe-shaped from sheet brass. The upper lip is wrapped around an iron wire. Below that, the side has been chisel-cut with a scrolled foliate border that serves both to ornament and

provide a draft for burning coals. The feet and flaps are cast and riveted to the body.

The body shape, pierced border, cabriole supports, and hinged flaps are all features that relate to French silver examples date-marked by their makers to the mid eighteenth century.[89] Those features and the use of fleurs-de-lis for the flaps suggest that this chafing dish and others like it, although unmarked, are French as well. The absence of a maker's mark on this object, in combination with eighteenth-century French influence on design in the Netherlands and Germany, render it advisable to also list both the latter as possible places of origin.

CHAFING DISH
32

ENGLAND OR AMERICA,
1740–60
COPPER, IRON, WOOD

H. 7 5/8" (19.4 CM), W. 17 1/2"
(44.4 CM), DIAM. 11 7/8" (30.2 CM)
64.1541

IN HIS TWO-VOLUME BOOK *The Academy of Armory*, Randle Holme describes a chafing dish as being "made of cast brass and of diverse forms." A typical example is illustrated here. "It is used in most houses of any like quality, onely to stand on the Grate neere the fire to keep water always hot for any sudden use."[90] The water it kept hot would have been held in a kettle.

By the middle of the eighteenth century, "houses of any like quality" used hot-water urns with a built-in heat source in the form of a spirit lamp or iron slug for the same purpose. However, "in some Families, a bright tea-kettle on a chafing-dish, to stand on the hearth [was still] used instead of a water-urn" as late as the mid nineteenth century. Eliza Leslie, a prolific American writer on the subject of cookery and house-

hold management, stated that when that was the case, "the chafing-dish [should be] well filled with clear glowing coals, free from ashes; and . . . the water . . . boiling hard at the time the kettle is filled."[91]

The bowl of the capacious chafing dish shown here is of wrought sheet metal, which has had the lip wrapped around an iron wire to prevent it from splitting. The three wrought-iron legs, which also serve as supports for the teakettle, are held to the bowl with copper rivets, as is the flange to which the wooden handle is attached.

CHOCOLATE POT
33

PROBABLY HOLLAND,
POSSIBLY NEW YORK, 1703
COPPER, WOOD, TIN, IRON

H. 6" (15.2 CM), W. 8 5/8"
(21.9 CM), D. 3 3/4" (9.5 CM)
58.989

THIS VESSEL IS similar in shape to contemporary coffeepots but lacks a spout and has a hole in the lid. It was used to brew chocolate, a drink "of a dusky color, soft and oily, usually drank hot, and esteemed not only an excellent food, as being very nourishing, but also as a good medicine; at least a diet, for keeping up the warmth of the stomach, and assisting digestion."[92]

The simplest method of preparing chocolate from cocoa beans involved roasting the beans and grinding them into an oily paste that was shaped and sold in the form of cakes. When making the beverage "a portion of one of the cakes must be scraped fine, added to a sufficient quantity of water, and simmered for a quarter of an hour; but milling is necessary to make it completely smooth. For this purpose [chocolate pots have] a circular wheel of wood or metal within, fixed to a stem that passes through the lid, and which, being whirled about rapidly by the palms of the hand, bruises and mixes the chocolate with the water. The chocolate must be milled off the fire, then put on again to simmer some time, then milled again until it is quite smooth. From the fineness there should be no sediment, and the whole should be drunk; cream is generally used with it. . . . Sugar may be put in with the scraped chocolate, or added afterward."[93]

The wrought pot illustrated here is dovetailed vertically on the handle side, has a folded footrim, and is tinned on the inside. Its owner's initials, "V.R.," which are engraved on the side, probably represent a Dutch surname and suggest that the pot was originally owned in Holland or New York.

COFFEEPOT
34

PROBABLY HOLLAND OR
FRANCE, 1710–50
BRASS (COPPER 72.62, ZINC
25.07, LEAD 1.79, TIN 0.37), TIN

H. 10 3/4" (27.3 CM), D. 8 1/4"
(21.0 CM), W. 7" (17.8 CM)
58.2283

AROUND 1812 ABRAHAM REES wrote that "in the course of three centuries and a half [coffee] which was not before known as an article of food, except to some savage tribes in the confines of Abyssinia, made its way through the whole civilized world." In Europe, where "it has been known little more than a century and a half, it is still regarded rather as a luxury, and is used only by the middle and upper classes. In England . . . tea is most generally preferred; but on the continent, especially in France, coffee is in universal request."[94]

The preparation of coffee evolved into an elaborate ritual during the seventeenth and eighteenth centuries, the proper practice of which was subject to differing opinion. In the Netherlands the type of coffeepot illustrated here seems to have been a favored variety. Examples are recorded in silver, gilt copper, pewter,

japanned sheet iron, and brass. Correctly used, roasted coffee grounds were "put into a linen bag or strainer, suspended at the mouth of a coffee-can . . . boiling water is then poured upon it, till the can is so full as to keep the strainer completely immersed in the hot water. When it has stood a sufficient time, the liquor is conveyed through the spout of the can, clear of the coffee grounds."[95]

The body of this coffeepot is made of wrought sheet metal with a vertically lapped joint on the handle side. It is tinned inside, and the upper edge is folded rather than being wrapped around an iron wire. The removable lid is also of sheet metal, but the finial, handle, legs, and zoomorphic spigot are cast.

COFFEEPOT
35

SKULTUNA MESSINGSBRUK FACTORY
SKULTUNA, SWEDEN, 1825–40
BRASS (COPPER 89.99,
ZINC 7.20, TIN 2.75, LEAD 0.28,
SILVER 0.11), WOOD, TIN

H. 6 1/2" (16.5 CM), W. 7 3/4"
(19.7 CM), D. 5 1/2" (14.0 CM)
60.794

THE SKULTUNA BRASS WORKS, located near the town of Vasteras, northwest of Stockholm, was founded in 1607. It has remained in continuous operation to this day. Its wares have always been intended principally for domestic consumption, with some exports to Finland and Russia. The firm never sought a market for finished goods in England, Western Europe, or America.[96]

Skultuna had no marking system to designate its wares during the seventeenth and eighteenth centuries. This changed during the early nineteenth century, in part as a result of expanding markets fostered by Sweden's political consolidation of the Scandinavian peninsula. Beginning about 1825, the mark stamped on the underside of this coffeepot was used. It was replaced with the full-name mark "SKULTUNA" about 1840, except on small objects, where only the initial mark would fit.

This coffeepot is made of sheet metal with both the body and spout having straight vertical seams. It is substantial in construction, well finished, and tinned inside. Its capacity, marked as $1/4$ K (Kanna) on the underside, is equivalent to about two-thirds of a quart. Skultuna also made larger-capacity coffeepots, teapots, chocolate pots, candlesticks, candelabra, chambersticks, wall sconces, tobacco boxes, and a full range of domestic and personal objects.[97]

COFFEEPOT
36

PROBABLY ENGLAND,
POSSIBLY AMERICA, 1740–1800
COPPER, WOOD

H. 9 5/8" (24.5 CM), W. 11"
(28.0 CM), D. 7 1/2" (9.1 CM)
59.4.14

IN 1657 JAMES FARR, owner of a London coffeehouse, was pros-
ecuted "for makinge and selling of a drink called coffee, whereby
in making the same, he annoyeth his neighbors, by evil smells,
and for keeping of ffier for the most part night and day, whereby
his chimney and chamber, hath been sett on ffier, to the great
danger and affrightment of his neighbors." Within a decade pros-
ecutions for this offense virtually disappeared in London "since
coffee, with most, is become a Morning Refreshment" and has
remained so to this day.[98]

The most common method of brewing coffee in the eighteenth century was to "put fresh-ground coffee into a coffee-pot,
with a sufficient quantity of water, and set this on the fire till it
boils for a minute or two; then remove it from the fire, pour out
a cupful, which is to be returned into the coffee-pot to throw
down the grounds that may be floating: repeat this, and let the

coffee-pot stand near the fire, but not on too hot a place, until
the grounds have subsided to the bottom; in a few minutes
the coffee will be clear without any other preparation and may
be poured into cups."[99]

Coffeepots like the one shown–with dovetailed joinery in
the body, straight-seam construction in the spout, a base rim
wrapped around an iron wire, and tinned inside–were made in
England for use in coffeehouses and private homes. They were
also imported by American hardware merchants like Joseph and
Daniel Waldo, who listed "coffee mills & pots" among the
more than fifty British base-metal objects they offered for sale
to Bostonians in 1748. These items, in turn, served as models
for American coppersmiths who were competing for the same
market, as was the Philadelphian Benjamin Harbeson.[100]

CREAM POT
37

THOMAS WHARTENBY (D. 1861)
PHILADELPHIA,
PENNSYLVANIA, 1825–52
FUSED PLATE OR ELECTROPLATE

H. 4 1/4" (10.8 CM), W. 5 7/16"
(13.8 CM), D. 3 3/8" (8.6 CM)
93.9

THE PHILADELPHIA SILVER MANUFACTURERS Thomas Fletcher and Sidney Gardiner advertised in 1812 that they had just imported "a large assortment of First Quality SHEFFIELD PLATED WARE, consisting of Tea and coffee pots, sugar basons and cream jugs, salt stands, elegant castors, cake baskets, bottle stands, candlesticks" and many other household amenities.[101] Numerous similar advertisements in East Coast metropolitan newspapers indicate there was a considerable demand by Americans for the wares they offered.

Although evidence is meager, a few Americans in whom the entrepreneurial impulse was strong may have attempted to make and sell their own fused plate. In 1811 James Mease published *Picture of Philadelphia*, in which he suggests that some had met with a degree of success.

He recorded that "silver plate fully equal to sterling, as to quality and execution is now made [in Philadelphia], and the plated wares are superior to those commonly imported in the way of trade."[102]

Fused plating, commonly termed *Sheffield plating*, was for a century the most efficient way of depositing silver on base metal. It was superceded in the 1830s by a new process called electroplating. Within a short span of time, a number of Americans were producing electroplate. The most successful was John O. Mead and Sons of Philadelphia, who in 1840 were "producing [electroplate] articles of every kind and variety from the most elaborate Epergne, to the plainest article of Tea or Dinner Service, in the greatest perfection. . . . He instructed others in the process, and was the means of putting into successful operation a number of concerns."[103]

Thomas Whartenby commenced business as a silversmith in Philadelphia in 1811. He was listed in the Philadelphia city directories as such until 1842, when he altered his profession to silverware manufacturer, suggesting he was expanding the quantity and variety of his production and the geographic size of his market. He continued in business until 1852, when he retired. Although he pursued his profession for forty-two years, it seems that success eluded him, as judged by the frequency with which he moved.[104]

The diminutive cream pot illustrated here, the only piece of silver plate currently known bearing Whartenby's name, documents his having worked with metals other than silver. The die-rolled leaf-tip border used as the footrim is identical to borders on numerous pieces of Philadelphia-made silver.[105]

TRIVET
38

ENGLAND OR NORTHERN
EUROPE, 1700–1740
BRASS (COPPER 90.68,
ZINC 3.38, LEAD 3.01, TIN 2.18,
IRON 0.39), IRON

H. 12 3/4" (32.3 CM), L. 12 5/8"
(32.1 CM), W. 12 1/2" (31.7 CM)
52.109
GIFT OF HENRY FRANCIS
DU PONT

TRIVETS ARE FITTED with three legs so they always stand solidly on uneven surfaces. This feature prevents them from wobbling and spilling the contents of any vessel placed on them. Unadorned examples in iron were used directly over a fire to support leg-less cooking pots. If intended for placement beside, rather than over, the fire, brass was usually combined with iron for orna-mental purposes, as with this and two similar examples in the Winterthur collection.[106]

This type of trivet typically held a kettle of hot water, although it could also be used to warm dinner plates or even as a stool for sitting. Its normal location was on a working hearth, as recorded in a lot of four objects consisting of "a gridiron toaster treefeet & fender" inventoried in Jonathan Avery's kitchen in Dedham, Massachusetts, on May 13, 1691. Examples with a number of orna-mental brass appendages like the "brass triffet" recorded in Joseph Loddle's house on January 24, 1754, were usually for the dining room or parlor hearth.[107] When intended for these rooms, their top surface was invariably ornamented. Many were decoratively pierced and had supplemental engraving. Those with solid plates were engraved, as was the case with the three trivets of this type at Winterthur. All had stylized foliate engraving–now almost worn invisible–over the entire upper surface. The upper plate on this example is a single-piece casting with three tabs on the underside, into which the legs are riveted and the handle is threaded. Both the handle and finial surmounting the stretchers were cast hollow in halves and brazed together.

PLATE WARMER
39

PROBABLY ENGLAND, 1740–80
BRASS (COPPER 75.45, ZINC 21.70,
LEAD 1.50, TIN 0.60, NICKEL 0.40)

H. 22 3/4" (57.8 CM), W. 13 1/4"
(33.6 CM), D. 13 1/4" (33.6 CM)
61.606

Stands "with revolving tops are useful to place things on occasionally before the fire to keep hot; by the top being moveable, the several sides of the dish may be presented to the fire very conveniently." The desirability of warmed plates was clearly stated by Catharine Beecher, who maintained that "in winter, the plates and all the dishes used, both for meat and vegetables, should be set to the fire to warm, when the table is being set, as cold plates and dishes cool the vegetables, gravey and meats, which by many is deemed a great injury."[108]

Although there is little evidence to suggest that eighteenth- and nineteenth-century Americans made widespread use of metal frames to warm their plates rather than placing them directly on the hearth, plate warmers were present. "Capucine plate warmers" were among the products offered by James Haldan, "coppersmith from New York [who had] opened shop at the sign of the Still and Golden Tea Kettle" in Philadelphia in 1758. Another copper plate warmer purchased from Haldan's better-known competitor Benjamin Harbeson in 1769 is recorded in Samuel Powel's ledger book.[109]

The capucine plate warmer was made largely of sheet metal in the form of a fixed and partially closed compartment on legs. The name derives from the rounded top, which is related to the hood called *capuche* that is worn by friars of the Catholic Order of Saint Francis.[110] While it performs the same function, the example shown here is markedly different in construction. All the parts are cast. The rotating section has been inserted into a hole at the juncture of the legs and is held in place with a nut at the lower end. The plates to be warmed were put on the rotatable frame and held in place by the four vertical members. The height allowed the stand to hold as many as a dozen plates securely.

TRIVET
40

ENGLAND, POSSIBLY
BIRMINGHAM, 1760–90
BRASS (COPPER 80.18, ZINC 17.25,
LEAD 1.67, TIN 0.51, IRON 0.16),
IRON, WOOD, COPPER

H. 15" (38.1 CM), W. 12" (30.5 CM),
D. 13 1/2" (34.3 CM)
61.1611

THE SEVENTEENTH-CENTURY English author Randle Holme described a trivet as being "made all of iron and . . . set over great fires, for Large potts, or pans, or cauldrons, to be set upon, to boile things in, They are also called Bandretts, Brand Irons, Iron Crowes, with three feet."[111] Three feet rather than four were essential so that the trivet would remain stable on uneven surfaces.

By the mid eighteenth century, trivets had come to be seen as "anything supported by three feet."[112] That change in definition from very specific to general is explained in large part by the evolving nature of cooking pots, pans, and cauldrons, all of which were made in increasing numbers with their own legs. Consequently, the trivet became redundant. Instead, it was put to use as an all-

purpose stand to support other things near the fire, such as kettles for hot water or plates for warming.

The trivet shown here is made almost entirely of wrought iron with a cast brass riveted facing. Trivet facings were cast in sand flasks in exactly the same manner as fret fenders made for the parlor, often incorporating the same motifs into their designs. As stated by Holme, trivets intended for use directly in the fire had to be completely of iron. Only when used on the hearth away from the intense heat could they have brass facings and wooden handles.

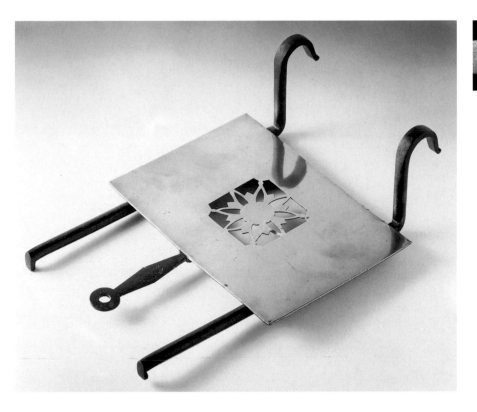

FENDER FOOTMAN

41

PROBABLY WILLIAM C. HUNNEMAN
(1769–1856),
POSSIBLY WILLIAM C. HUNNEMAN,
JR., OR SAMUEL H. HUNNEMAN
BOSTON, MASSACHUSETTS, 1799–1856

BRASS (COPPER 68.99, ZINC 27.62,
LEAD 2.03), IRON
H. 4 3/4" (12.1 CM), W. 10 1/16"
(25.5 CM), D. 14 1/8" (35.9 CM)
66.603

THE DEVICE ILLUSTRATED HERE, usually associated with teakettles, is, in reality, multipurpose. "Smoothing irons may be heated, a saucepan boiled, water warmed, bread toasted, apples roasted, and a tea or coffee-pot, or a small kettle kept hot on a footman."[113]

This fender footman is made principally of iron, as are most examples of its counterpart, the freestanding trivet. The wrought-iron frame supports a sliding rectangular platform that appears to be entirely of brass. However, the brass is thin sheet metal unable to support any weight on its own, so it serves only as a decorative covering for a piece of sheet iron.

Examples made entirely of brass are illustrated in Birmingham trade catalogues that are dated to the early nineteenth century.[114] Unlike this footman, which is only usable when hung from a fender or grate, brass examples usually have a hinged support that can be folded out of the way of three short legs so that they can double as decorative table trivets for hot dishes.

William C. Hunneman, who had worked with Martin Gay, commenced his career independently about 1799. He listed himself in the Boston city directories as a coppersmith and brass founder until 1825. At that time he added the term *engine builder*, thus marking a significant shift in his career. With the purchase of a patent for a hand-pumped extinguisher from Jacob Perkins, he devoted most of his attention to the building of municipal fire engines, transferring the business of coppersmithing and brass founding to his sons Samuel H. and William C. Hunneman, Jr.[115]

MONTEITH
42

HOLLAND OR ENGLAND, 1680–1720
BRASS (COPPER 71.03,
ZINC 24.22, LEAD 3.23, TIN 0.70,
IRON 0.53, SILVER 0.19)

H. 9 1/2" (24.1 CM), L. 18 1/2"
(46.5 CM), W. 15 7/8" (40.3 CM)
59.2564

IN 1683 THE ENGLISHMAN Anthony Wood wrote in his diary that "this year in the summer time came up a vessel or bason notched at the brim to let drinking glasses hang there by the foot so that the body or drinking place might hang in the water to coole them. Such a bason was called a 'Monteigh' from a Fantastical Scot called 'Monsieur Monteigh,' who at that time or a little before wore the bottome of his cloake or coate so notched U U U U."[116]

Wood was probably referring to English monteiths made of silver and copied from Dutch and German examples of silver, brass, pewter, glass, and porcelain.[117] The body of the illustrated example consists of three pieces of wrought brass sheet. The two pieces that make up the sides are dovetailed to each other vertically behind the lion-mask handles while the bottom is brazed in place with a straight seam. The ornamental parts are all cast—the dolphins in halves—and applied.

These decorative features derive directly from late sixteenth- and seventeenth-century European architecture. The Dutch in particular were fond of scrolled gable ends, which architects and builders incorporated into their private, civic, and ecclesiastical buildings. One of Holland's most creative architects and sculptors who worked in this late Renaissance style, Hendrick de Keyser (1565-1621), executed a design for an entrance to the Admiralty Office in Amsterdam that relates intriguingly to this monteith. Both combine lion masks, dolphins, and arched scrolls with flat volutes in their composition. These Dutch designs were readily incorporated into London architecture through avenues of influence such as de Keyser's visits to London or his taking of an English apprentice, thus providing influential material on both sides of the English Channel for the anonymous maker of this monteith.[118]

MONTEITH
43

ENGLAND OR HOLLAND,
1720–90
COPPER, IRON

H. 7 3/4" (19.7 CM), L. 16 1/4"
(41.3 CM), W. 12 7/16" (31.6 CM)
58.2144

THIS TYPE OF VESSEL was first noted in an English language dictionary in 1721. It was called a monteith and described as "a scallopt bason to cool glasses in" by suspending them from the rim, bowl down, in water. By 1785 Samuel Johnson, who compiled another dictionary of the English language, described the object as "a vessel in which glasses are washed."[119] In doing so, Johnson apparently confused the form with French *verrières*, a similar shallow, scalloped-rim container in which wine glasses were indeed washed.

While monteiths experienced their greatest vogue in late seventeenth- and early eighteenth-century England, Holland, and Germany, the form was also brought to America. The Virginian William Fitzhugh stipulated in his will, dated 1701, that "I Give to my son Henry Fitzhugh my Silver Moonteeth Bason which I have brought out of England." The 1742 inventory of the estate of Henry

Hacker of Williamsburg, Virginia, listed "I Monteth 10 [shillings] in the kitchen."[120] Its modest value and location in a service area indicate it was probably made of pewter, brass, or copper.

The body of this monteith is made from one sheet of wrought copper. It is supported on a wrought footrim, which has a vertical dovetailed joint at one end. The bottom edge has been wrapped around an iron wire for strength. A cast decorative molding serves the same purpose at the lip, which is a separate piece brazed to the body just above the cove. The absence of highly charged decorative motifs, unusual construction features, and a maker's mark make it difficult to positively identify this monteith as either English or Dutch, since the two countries were closely aligned in taste and trade at the time it was made.

CELLARET LINER
44

UNITED STATES, POSSIBLY
CHARLESTON, SOUTH CAROLINA,
1790–1820
COPPER, BRASS, LEAD

H. 11 1/2" (29.2 CM), W. 24 1/2"
(62.2 CM), D. 19 7/8" (50.5 CM)
57.698

A CELLARET IS A "convenience for wine, or a wine cistern" constructed to hold a number of bottles, unlike a wine cooler, which holds only one and sometimes two bottles. The cellaret "should be lined with lead [or tinned sheet iron or copper], if meant to contain water." The metal liner served as a watertight receptacle and was fitted into the piece by "the tinman," whose business it was to provide this amenity, regardless of the metal from which it was made.[121]

Its use derived from "the principal object to be attended to in the management of wine vaults, [which was] to keep [the wine] of a temperate heat. . . . In the winter, it is necessary to have a chafingdish, to keep up a proper degree of warmth. . . . In the summer time it will be best to keep them as cool as you can."[122] Prior to the modern era of refrigeration, a wine bottle was best kept at a constant temperature by being immersed in cool water after removal from the vault.

The liner in this cellaret is made of sheet copper with its joined edges leaded so they will remain waterproof. It has been constructed around a wooden medial brace so that the bottom consists of two shallow compartments, each of which is capable of holding about five bottles. The liner is not removable from the frame, necessitating a brass petcock, leaded into the bottom of each well, so that water can be drained without having to tip the cellaret.

Although unmarked, this type of object was made by artisans like John Crawford, who, on August 5, 1774, advertised in the *South Carolina and American General Gazette* that as a "coppersmith & plumber, from London [he] makes and sells all sorts of copper and plumber's work such as brewing coppers, stills, pots for kitchens of all kinds and sizes, coffee pots, chocolate pots, tea kettles, sauce pans, stew pans, French stew pans, coal scuttles, plate warmers, Turbot pans, camp kettles, Decanters, Copper pumps, Lead pumps, copper chambers for ship pumps, and . . . other articles too tedious to mention."[123]

SALVER
45

PROBABLY ENGLAND, POSSIBLY
THE NETHERLANDS, 1700–1725
BRASS (COPPER 71.81,
ZINC 24.57, LEAD 1.48, SILVER 0.80,
TIN 0.78, IRON 0.24), SILVER

H. 3 1/2" (8.9 CM), W. 13"
(33.0 CM), D. 11" (28.0 CM)
59.1867

IN 1717 ELISHA COLES, schoolmaster and teacher of English to foreigners, published *An English Dictionary* in London. In it he defined the term *salver* as "a broad Plate (with a Foot) used in giving Beer, &c to save the Carpet or Cloaths."[124]

The finest salvers were made of silver, but silvered-brass examples were available for those who were unable or unwilling to underwrite the cost of the former. The illustrated salver has a cast tray to which a molded rim is brazed. The underside has a threaded projection that screws into the separately cast foot. Only traces of the french plating that originally covered the entire object are in evidence on the underside of the base. Both the base and tray were chased with narrow borders of flower clusters against a matted

ground, and like the silvering, their most-apparent remains are on the lower portion.

This salver may have been part of a set, as evidenced by the six deep parallel grooves filed into the threads on both parts. Sets of salvers, although not common, do occur in household inventories, as with the "4 [silver] salvers [and] 6 small hand do . . . in the Pantry, [the] 19 japanned Waiters [in the] Little middle Room [and the] 13 japann'd hand waiters [in the] Physic closet" listed in the estate appraisal of Norborne Berkley, first Baron Botetourt and royal governor of Virginia, on October 24, 1770.[125]

TRAY
46

JAMES DIXON AND SONS (1804–PRESENT)
SHEFFIELD, ENGLAND, 1835–51
GERMAN SILVER, FUSED PLATE

L. 36" (91.5 CM), W. 23 1/4"
(59.1 CM), H. 2 1/4" (5.7 CM)
93.6 GIFT OF C. WILLIAM MARSHALL
IN MEMORY OF JENNIE
DICKINSON CAUSEY MARSHALL

JAMES DIXON (1776–1852) was one of the most success-ful entrepreneurs in the city of Sheffield. He founded his firm in 1804 for the production of pewter, silver plate, and silver. It eventually grew into a manufacturing com-plex that comprised "about four acres of land [employing] more than 700 workpeople" by 1879.[126]

Dixon distributed wares throughout Great Britain, Europe, and the United States, where "up to the middle of the 19th century [the] firm's trade with America was so considerable that it was worth while for one of the senior partners [James Wallis Dixon] to live there, and besides that they also had four agents in America."[127]

When Dixon first opened his firm, he used fused plate (silver fused to copper) of the type made in England since the early eighteenth century. The fused plate process produced relatively inexpensive artifacts that appeared to be silver, until the thin silver coating wore through, exposing the copper underneath. In 1879 the author of a history of the city of Sheffield noted that "Messrs. Dixon, who for the last twenty years have abandoned copper as a basis for plating, [use] instead the modern metal, nickel silver. This is a composition of nickel, copper and zinc. Nickel possesses the property of whitening the copper when mixed with it in proper proportions. The compound called nickel silver [paktong, india metal, or german silver] proves to be very valu-able in use. It is employed not only as a substitute for copper in the old plating process, but also as a basis for electroplating."[128]

The firm's wares were marketed widely through printed trade catalogues. Trays of the type illustrated here were described as "oblong chased coffee tray[s] with handles." They were available with tinned or more expensive plated backs and "with silver mountings and shields for engraving." This example is among the largest made by the firm. The inset silver reserve in the center is engraved "RAVH," for R. A. Virginia Handy (1823–97), who married Henry Dickinson (1812–45), in Wilmington, Delaware, on December 8, 1840. Marks imitative of those used on English silver are also on the front of the tray. The "I," "D," and "S," each in a shaped cartouche, stand for James Dixon and Sons. The "PNS" in a shield stands for plated nickel silver. The pattern num-ber 356 and workman's symbol, a crown, are on the back of the tray, as is an embossed applied label with the British royal coat of arms and the Dixon firm's name and location.[129]

DRINKING POT
47

JOHN W. SCHLOSSER
(1785–1860)
YORK, PENNSYLVANIA, 1810–60
COPPER, TIN

H. 5 1/2" (14.0 CM), W. 6"
(15.2 CM), DIAM. 4 3/8" (11.1 CM)
85.93
GIFT OF HENRY J. KAUFFMAN

JOHN WILLIAM SCHLOSSER was born on November 16, 1785, the eighth child of Ernst and Anna Maria Schlosser, in York, Pennsylvania. When of sufficient age, he was apprenticed to a coppersmith. Although his master is unknown, it may have been William Bailey, who operated shops in York and Chambersburg, Pennsylvania, and Hagerstown and Fredericktown, Maryland. In the 1790s Bailey advertised that "he has complete workmen in each shop, regularly bred to the business, as many of them have been taught by himself."[130]

Upon completion of his apprenticeship, Schlosser established himself in York making many of the objects then in demand, which included "stills of all sizes; brewing kettles; fish-and washing ditto; sauce pans; coffee and chocolate pots; and all other sort of copper and tin ware too tedious to mention," among which was the drinking pot shown here.[131] He remained in York as a coppersmith and tinplate worker until his death on April 6, 1860. He left a wife, daughter, and five sons, through whom evidence of Schlosser's interest in the War of 1812 remained. He named his sons Hazard Zebulon, Lafayett Bainbridge, Perry Decatur, Thomas Coates, and Columbus Oliver.

In his will Schlosser stipulated: "I give to my son Perry Decatur the use of my shop and sale room free for the term of one year after my death . . . also the uninterrupted right to pass from my shop to my sale room and back as often as necessary in prosecuting his business. I give and bequeath unto my said son Perry Decatur my copper and tin smith tools, patterns and conveniences thereunto. . . . He shall also have the privilege of taking any part of or all of my work made up, and my material on hand at the time of my death. . . . The tools and patterns are a free gift to my son Perry Decatur over and above his share of my estate, provided that if [he] declines following the business . . . I give [them] to my son Thomas Coates."[132]

The drinking pot here is of good quality and typical of the small number of Schlosser-marked objects known. The body is of sheet metal dovetailed vertically on the handle side. The lip and handle edges are wrapped around iron wire for strength, and the bottom edge is folded to form a low lip into which the body is set and brazed. The interior is tinned.

SPOON

48

PROBABLY THE NETHERLANDS,
POSSIBLY ENGLAND, 1600–1680
BRASS (COPPER 76.12, ZINC 22.09,
LEAD 1.40, TIN 0.16, SILVER 0.11)

L. 6 3/4" (17.2 CM),
W. 2 1/8" (5.4 CM)
58.28.10
GIFT OF CHARLES F. MONTGOMERY

FROM THE LATE fifteenth century to the end of the seventeenth century, spoons with figures of apostles on the handle were made in England and Europe. Of these, silver examples are the most common, with some still existing in sets of twelve and, on occasion, thirteen. Pewter and brass apostle spoons are considerably rarer and when encountered are almost invariably not part of a set. Each of the thirteen possible figures on this type of spoon is identifiable through an accoutrement. Saint Paul is always depicted with keys or fish while Saint Mark is accompanied by a lion. The saw held in the hand of the figure shown here identifies him as Saint Simon the Zealot.

Spoons were often made by hammering to shape from a thick billet of metal, but when incorporating a figure they were cast into their final form in sand flasks. Cast examples had a porous surface as well as flash—which adhered to the edges created by the gates and joints in the mold—and had to be properly dressed before the spoon was marketable. Flash was removed by filing, and porous surfaces were hammered to smoothness. Some makers attempted to bypass some or all of the finishing steps to save time. This was frowned upon by more fastidious competitors, as evidenced by a complaint brought before London's Worshipful Company of Pewterers by the spoonmaker Daniel Barton. On December 20, 1683, he charged that "John Clark, Thomas Waight & Joseph Higdon [were] makeing spoones w[th]out beating, being only cast, grated [filed] & burnished."[133]

A.

B.

C.

SPOONS

49 a–c

A. ATTRIBUTED TO RICHARD
SHELLDRAKE
LONDON, ENGLAND, 1620–80
BRASS (COPPER 74.17, ZINC 22.54,
LEAD 2.10, TIN 0.85)
L. 6 1/2" (16.5 CM), W. 1 7/8" (4.8 CM)
58.28.11
GIFT OF CHARLES F. MONTGOMERY

B. ATTRIBUTED TO RICHARD
SHELLDRAKE
LONDON, ENGLAND, 1650–80
BRASS (COPPER 76.71, ZINC 20.31,
LEAD 1.52, TIN 1.06, SILVER 0.10)
L. 6 1/2" (16.5 CM), W. 1 13/16" (4.6 CM)
58.28.12
GIFT OF CHARLES F. MONTGOMERY

C. ATTRIBUTED TO RICHARD
SHELLDRAKE
LONDON, ENGLAND, 1650–80
BRASS (COPPER 76.72, ZINC 18.04,
TIN 3.13, LEAD 1.63, ANTIMONY 0.13)
L. 7 1/4" (18.4 CM), W. 1 7/8" (4.8 CM)
58.28.13
GIFT OF CHARLES F. MONTGOMERY

IN 1567 LONDON'S large and influential Worshipful Company of Pewterers noted that the use of brass for making spoons was "lately invented by [the spoonmaker] John God." The company did not look favorably on his development, however, because it threatened to curtail the extensive and lucrative production of pewter spoons by many of its members. Consequently, "it was agreed by the whole Company that there should be no spones made of Brass or laten or any yellow metall" in England.[134] Anyone caught violating that edict would be fined, but demand was sufficient to warrant the risk, and yellow metal spoons eventually came to be widely made in England throughout the seventeenth century.

Richard Shelldrake was a maker of such spoons. He earned the right to cast them under the auspices of the Worshipful Company of Founders of the City of London in 1619, at which time he commemorated his master's status by presenting the company with "one gilt spoone . . . marked with R & S."[135]

Each of the three cast spoons in this entry are marked with Shelldrake's initials. Two also include the phrase DOUBLE WHITED, referring to their having been tinned. Latten spoons were routinely tinned to prevent the poisonous effect they would otherwise have upon food. "Sometimes also they gave the [spoons] a double layer, as they would have them very thickly covered. This they do by dipping them into the tin, when very hot, the first time, and when less hot the second. The tin which is to give the second [coat], must be fresh covered with suet" so that it will properly adhere.[136]

A.

B.

SPOONS
50 a,b

A. ATTRIBUTED TO JOHN BALLARD
LONDON, ENGLAND, 1663–1700
BRASS (COPPER 79.69, ZINC 16.83,
LEAD 2.87, TIN 0.30, SILVER 0.13)
L. 7 1/4" (18.4 CM), W. 1 7/8" (4.8 CM)
58.28.14
GIFT OF CHARLES F. MONTGOMERY

B. DANIEL BARTON
LONDON, ENGLAND, 1670–1700
BRASS (COPPER 73.80, ZINC 24.17,
LEAD 1.90, TIN 0.31)
L. 8" (20.3 CM), W. 1 3/4" (4.4 CM)
58.28.15
GIFT OF CHARLES F. MONTGOMERY

SAMUEL JOHNSON DEFINED the word *alchymy* as "a kind of mixed metal used for spoons." The metal was an alloy of copper and zinc with small amounts of lead, tin, and iron and was commonly known as brass or latten.[137]

Brass, latten, or alchemy spoons were made extensively in England from the mid sixteenth to the end of the seventeenth centuries. Many were stamped with marks by their makers, almost two hundred of whom have been recorded. These spoons were used throughout England, and many were brought to the British colonies in America. "Eight brass spoones" were recorded in the estate of Lt. Philip Curtice of Roxbury, Massachusetts, on November 9, 1675, and "one doz: Alcamy Spoons" were item-

ized among the household effects of Peter Hobart of Hingham, Massachusetts, on January 20, 1678.[138]

Spoons of this type have been unearthed from American Indian burial mounds and the sites of early white settlements in this country. Some are marked and have been identified as the work of the London spoonmaker Daniel Barton, whose initials are stamped into the handle of one of these spoons. Barton was a member of the Worshipful Company of Pewterers, receiving his freedom from them to practice metalworking in 1670. He continued to do so until at least 1699, when he was elected by that company to the office of upper warden.[139]

1 Smith, *Compleat Housewife*, p. 7.

2 As recorded in Cummings, *Rural Household Inventories*, p. 92.

3 *Pennsylvania Gazette* (Philadelphia), July 4, 1810.

4 On Lord, see *Records and Files of the Quarterly Courts of Essex County, Massachusetts*, 8 vols. (Salem, Mass.: Essex Institute, 1911-21), 8:23, 24. The Dewing estate is documented in Cummings, *Rural Household Inventories*, p. 19. For the Torrey inventory, see Cummings, *Rural Household Inventories*, p. 95.

5 Timothy L. Dilliplane, "European Trade Kettles," in Susan G. Gibson, ed., *Burr's Hill: Seventeenth-Century Wampanong Burial Ground in Warren, Rhode Island* (Providence, R.I.: Brown University, 1980), pp. 79-83; "Indian Graves Unearthed at Charlestown," *Rhode Island Historical Society Collections* (January 1922): 18, 19.

6 As recorded in Laughlin, *Pewter in America*, 1:87.

7 Laughlin, *Pewter in America*, 1: 88; 3:49, pls. 88, 89.

8 N. Bailey, *An Universal Etymological English Dictionary* (London: Printed for J. and A. Duncan, J. and M. Robertson, and J. and W. Shaw, 1794). The stump of a sprue is visible on the illustrated detail, acc. no. 60.767.

9 *Columbian Centinel* (Boston), April 17, 1793.

10 *Columbian Centinel* (Boston), March 19, 1794; October 15, 1794.

11 Frederick Lewis Gay, "John Gay, of Dedham, Massachusetts, and Some of His Descendants," *New-England Historical and Genealogical Register* 33 (1879): 48, 52.

12 The advertisement appeared in the *Columbian Centinel* (Boston), March 2, 1793. The exact date they separated is unknown, but the Boston city directory for 1800 was the first to cease carrying the joint Gay and Hunneman listing. Hunneman's accounts, which are owned by the Boston National Historical Park, Charlestown Navy Yard, Boston, contain several entries that suggest they had a formal parting in 1799 but continued to cooperate in the exchange of goods, jobbing, and advertising.

13 Five posnets, all American, are illustrated in this catalogue. Winterthur owns a sixth American example, acc. no. 70.287, and four English posnets, acc. nos. 60.50, 60.51, 64.73, and 66.531. A Roman posnet owned by the British Museum in London is described in Wills, *Collecting Copper and Brass*, p. 136. The demise of posnets seems to have been quick and complete. They merit not a single mention in the extensive treatise on cooking in Webster, *Encyclopaedia of Domestic Economy*.

14 The advertisements in the Baltimore and Easton, Md., and Norfolk, Va., newspapers are in the research files of the Museum of Early Southern Decorative Arts, Winston-Salem, N.C.

15 Fuller, *Art of Coppersmithing*, p. 87.

16 The Harbeson example is privately owned; the Bailey is owned by the National Museum of American History, Washington, D.C.; the Lay saucepan is in the collection of the Rockford-Kauffman Museum in Lancaster, Pa.; and the Crabb and Minshall saucepan is in the collection of the Historical Society of Dauphin County, Harrisburg, Pa.

17 Webster, *Encyclopaedia of Domestic Economy*, p. 805.

18 Webster, *Encyclopaedia of Domestic Economy*, p. 825.

19 Fuller, *Art of Coppersmithing*, pp. 93, 97.

20 *Book of the Household*, 2:464.

21 Beeton, *Book of Household Management*, pp. 24, 25.

22 A copy of the Cox, Whiteman, and Cox catalogue published in Philadelphia in 1880 is in the Downs collection, Winterthur Library, TS425 C88* TC. Appropriate city directories and newspapers were surveyed for advertisements by Dougherty that might have indicated the range of his wares, but none were found.

23 *Pennsylvania Herald, and York General Advertiser*, July 25, 1792.

24 Fuller, *Art of Coppersmithing*, p. 102.

25 Miss Leslie, *New Receipts for Cooking* (Philadelphia, 1854), p. 21.

26 Biographical information on Clark was provided by Peter Seibert, former director, Dauphin County Historical Society, August 1990.

27 M. Hinde, W. Squire, J. Marshall, and Rev. Thomas Cooke, *A New Royal and Universal Dictionary of Arts and Sciences*, 2 vols. (London: Printed for J. Cooke, 1771), 2:s.v. "jack."

28 *Aris's Birmingham Gazette*, April 20, 1762. A smoke jack operates by means of a horizontal fan installed in the chimney. Rising heat causes the jack to rotate and drive the spit in a manner similar to the weight-driven jack.

29 On James and Drinker, see *Pennsylvania Gazette* (Philadelphia), October 1, 1761. Lucas and Shepard advertised in the *New-York Gazette, and Weekly Mercury*, May 20, 1771.

30 John Evelyn, *Diary, 1603-1714*, ed. E. S. de Beer, 3 vols. (Oxford, Eng.: Clarendon Press, 1955), 2:18.

31 Webster, *Encyclopaedia of Domestic Economy*, pp. 709, 710.

32 R. A. Church, *Kenricks in Hardware: A Family Business, 1791-1966* (London: David and Charles, 1969), p. 38.

33 Webster, *Encyclopaedia of Domestic Economy*, p. 705.

34 Webster, *Encyclopaedia of Domestic Economy*, p. 705.

35 For marks incorporating these motifs, see Birger Bruzelli, *Tenngjutare I Sverige* (Stockholm: Alb. Bonniers Boktryckeri, 1967); Ludwig Mory, *Schönes Zinn* (Munich: Verlag F. Bruckmann, 1972).

36 A fine and complete silver example dated 1747/48 is pictured in Davis, *English Silver at Williamsburg*, pp. 93-94. The Richardson example is pictured and discussed in Kathryn C. Buhler and Graham Hood, *American Silver: Garvan and Other Collections in the Yale University Art Gallery*, 2 vols. (New Haven: Yale University Press, 1970), 2:189-91.

37 The tray is a later addition, probably dating from the mid nineteenth century.

38 "Inventory of the Household Effects of John Penn, Jr., 1788," *Pennsylvania Magazine of History and Biography* 15 (1891): 374. Brown, *Principles and Practice of Dipping*, p. 36.

39 *Heads of Families at the First Census of the United States Taken in the Year 1790-Pennsylvania* (Washington, D.C.: Government Printing Office, 1908), p. 136. The Atlee advertisement appeared in the *Lancaster Journal*, June 24, 1795.

40 On the *Elizabeth*, see Bristol presentments, gleanings from ship manifests 1770-80, 1790-1820, exports, Bristol City Library, Bristol, Eng. Bisland advertised in the *Pennsylvania Packet, and Daily Advertiser* (Philadelphia), September 6, 1792.

41 Webster, *Encyclopaedia of Domestic Economy*, p. 705.

42 The Morrison advertisement appeared in the *Freeman's Journal*, September 19, 1781. On the *Concord*, see Bristol presentments, gleanings from ship manifests 1770-80, 1790-1820, exports, Bristol City Library, Bristol, Eng.

43 On Hunneman's sales, see William C. Hunneman account book, October 19, 1801; April 20, 1819; August 10, 1818, Boston National Historical Park, Charlestown Navy Yard, Boston.

44 Hunneman account book, July 7, 1802; January 10, 1812; July 15, 1815; May 28, 1821.

45 Hunneman account book, June 26, 1819; March 12, 1821; December 30, 1820.

46 Hunneman account book, August 1801.

47 Roll 6, vol. 7, waste book, Boston 1818-25, Revere Family Papers, 1746-1964, Massachusetts Historical Society, Boston.

48 Michael Krafft, *The American Distiller* (Philadelphia: Printed for Thomas Dobson, 1804), p. 30.

49 Fuller, *Art of Coppersmithing*, pp. 30, 31.

50 Harrison Hall, *Hall's Distiller* (Philadelphia, 1813), p. 10.

51 Rees, *Cyclopaedia*, 12:s.v. "distillation."

52 John A. Paxton, *The Philadelphia Directory and Register for 1813* (Philadelphia: B. and T. Kite, 1813). On Apple, see *Poulson's American Daily Advertiser*, July 14, 1812.

53 Holme, *Academy of Armory*, 2:11.

54 Hamilton, *English Brass and Copper Industries*, p. 148. Diderot, *Encyclopédie*, 4:564.

55 On Haldane, see *New-York Weekly Post-Boy*, February 24, 1746. William Thompson daybook, manuscript collection, New York Public Library.

56 Beeton, *Book of Household Management* (1861), pp. 677, 563.

57 Webster, *Encyclopaedia of Domestic Economy*, p. 840.

58 Maria Parloa, *Miss Parloa's Kitchen Companion* (Boston: Estes and Lauriant, 1887), pp. 41, 45. *Tunnel* is an archaic synonym for *funnel*.

59 Fuller, *Art of Coppersmithing*, p. 20.

60 Webster, *Encyclopaedia of Domestic Economy*, p. 520.

61 Webster, *Encyclopaedia of Domestic Economy*, p. 520; Holme, *Academy of Armory*, 2:opp. p. 18.

62 The illustrated casters are in trade catalogue TS573 T76 F, Downs collection, Winterthur Library. An almost identical silver example made in London in 1737/38 is illustrated in Davis, *English Silver at Williamsburg*, p. 150. On Bailey, see *Rivington's New-York Gazetteer*, July 29, 1773.

63 Ash, *New and Complete Dictionary*, 1:s.v. "dredger."

64 The example is illustrated in Gentle and Feild, *English Domestic Brass*, p. 27.

65 They can be seen in trade catalogue TS573 T76 F, Downs collection, Winterthur Library.

66 *Pennsylvania Gazette* (Philadelphia), January 7, 1752.

67 Smith, *Compleat Housewife*, pp. 79, 101, 112.

68 Johnson, *Dictionary of the English Language*, 2:s.v. "nut."

69 The other nutcrackers by Bingham are acc. nos. 60.74 and 60.1109. Trade catalogue NK7899 B6IC* TC, Downs collection, Winterthur Library, depicts and prices nutcrackers almost identical to this example.

70 A discussion of William's output is in Laughlin, *Pewter in America*, 2:17-18; 3:105. The letter is quoted in Laughlin, *Pewter in America*, 2:17.

71 *New-York Daily Advertiser*, November 19, 1787; *New-York Gazette, and Weekly Mercury*, September 26, 1774.

72 On Bailey, see *Rivington's New-York Gazetteer*, July 29, 1773. The advertisement is that of New York pewterer Cornelius Bradford, *New-York Mercury*, November 13, 1752. The mark on this skimmer is not identical to those found on Kirby's pewter to date, but it is sufficiently close to allow a comfortable attribution. Kirby's pewter marks are to be seen in Laughlin, *Pewter in America*, 2:pl. 62, figs. 499, 502, 503.

73 Holme, *Academy of Armory*, 2:6.

74 Richard Lee, *A Short Narrative of the Life of Mr. Richard Lee; Containing a Brief Account of His Nativity, Conviction, and Conversion*, 1821, as quoted in Harold G. Rugg and Homer Eaton Keys, "Richard Lee, Pewterer," *Antiques* 13, no. 6 (June 1928): 494.

75 On his pewter, see Laughlin, *Pewter in America*, 1:121-24. The larger of these two ladles is stamped with a full-name touchmark, identical to that on a pewter porringer, acc. no. 58.676, and plate, acc. no. 65.1526. The mark on the smaller ladle was also used on a pewter ladle, acc. no. 66.1189, and spoon, acc. no. 60.101.

76 Jacob Bigelow, *Elements of Technology* (Boston: Billiard, Gray, Little, and Wilkins, 1831), p. 407.

77 *The Candy Maker* (New York: Excelsior Publishing House, 1901), p. 489.

78 *Candy Maker*, p. 495. The Bentley shop is the subject of Brian M. Sipe, *Coppersmithing in Nineteenth-Century Philadelphia: The Bentley Shop* (Master's thesis, University of Delaware, 1987).

79 On confectioners, see Archibald McElroy, comp., *McElroy's Philadelphia City Directory* (Philadelphia: Printed by Sherman, 1865), p. 761. As quoted in Robert B. and J. W. Parkinson, *The Complete Confectioner, Pastry-Cook, and Baker* (Philadelphia: Leary and Getz, 1849), p. 3.

80 Sir Edward Thomason, *Memoirs of Half a Century*, 2 vols. (London, 1845).

81 Aitken, *Early History of Brass*, p. 103.

82 *Rivington's New-York Gazetteer*, July 29, 1773.

83 Holme, *Academy of Armory*, 2:11.

84 Winterthur owns one American silver chafing dish, made in Boston by John Potwine (1698-1792), acc. no. 65.1347. On White, see Cummings, *Rural Household Inventories*, p. 170.

85 *Pennsylvania Gazette* (Philadelphia), January 7, 1752.

86 Webster, *Encyclopaedia of Domestic Economy*, pp. 705-6.

87 Webster, *Encyclopaedia of Domestic Economy*, p. 705.

88 Ash, *New and Complete Dictionary*, 1:s.v. "chafing dish." Winterthur's other chafing dishes of this type are acc. nos. 58.988, 58.1566.1, 65.2455, and 66.749.

89 A French silver example made by Antoine Bailly in Paris in 1750 was offered in London at Sotheby's (February 11, 1985), lot 155. Four others are illustrated in Dennis, *Three Centuries of French Domestic Silver*, 1:238, 291, 306, 360.

90 Holme, *Academy of Armory*, 2:282.

91 Leslie, *House Book*, p. 276.

92 Rees, *Cyclopaedia*, 8:s.v. "chocolate."

93 Webster, *Encyclopaedia of Domestic Economy*, p. 717.

94 Rees, *Cyclopaedia*, 9:s.v. "coffee."

95 An example of this type of coffeepot in silver is pictured in Th. M. Duyvené de Wit-Klinkhamer and Milt. Gans, *Geschiedenis Van Het Nederlandse Zilver* (Amsterdam: J.H. De Bussy, 1958), fig. 56; an example in gilt copper is in Hanns-Ulrich Haedeke, *Metalwork* (London: Weidenfeld and Nicolson, 1970), opp. p. 80. Rees, *Cyclopaedia*, 9:s.v. "coffee."

96 On the brass works, see Teje Colling to Ned Cooke, November 1, 1978, object folder 60.794, Registration Office, Winterthur; Eva Lillienberg Olssen to Donald L. Fennimore, April 4, 1986, object folder 60.794, Registration Office, Winterthur.

97 These and other Swedish brass-works products are presented in Sigurd Erixon, *Gammal mässing* (Västeras, Swe.: ICA-Förlaget, 1964).

98 As quoted in Edward Forbes Robinson, *The Early History of Coffee Houses in England* (London: Kegan Paul, Trench, Trübner, 1893), pp. 92, 82.

99 Webster, *Encyclopaedia of Domestic Economy*, p. 710.

100 The Waldo advertisement is on a broadside owned by the American Antiquarian Society, Worcester, Mass. Harbeson's trade card, engraved by Henry Dawkins and dated about 1776, depicts a coffeepot of this type. A copy of that trade card is in the Downs collection, Winterthur Library. A similar coffeepot, marked by Harbeson, is owned by the Phildelphia Museum of Art.

101 *Aurora General Advertiser* (Philadelphia), July 7, 1812.

102 Diana Cramer, "Philadelphia Silverplaters," *Silver*, pt. 1 (May–June 1990): 35-40; pt. 2 (July–August 1990): 17-22. James Mease, *Picture of Philadelphia* (Philadelphia: B. and T. Kite, 1811), p. 74. Mease's use of the term *silver plate* almost certainly refers to what is known today as sterling silver. His use of the term *plated wares* is less definite, referring either to close plate or fused plate.

103 Edwin T. Freedley, *Philadelphia and Its Manfactures* (Philadelphia: Edward Young, 1858), p. 350.

104 He is recorded at eleven separate addresses between 1811 and 1853.

105 See, for example, the presentation ewer and stand dated 1841 made by the Philadelphia silversmiths Conrad Bard and Robert Lamont and illustrated in David B. Warren, Katherine S. Howe, and Michael K. Brown, *Marks of Achievement: Four Centuries of American Presentation Silver* (New York: Harry N. Abrams, 1987), p. 113.

106 The other examples are acc. nos. 59.44 and 61.1323.

107 The Avery inventory is recorded in Cummings, *Rural Household Inventories*, p. 59. On Loddle, see MS 53.190, Downs collection, Winterthur Library.

108 Webster, *Encyclopaedia of Domestic Economy*, p. 841. Catherine E. Beecher, *Miss Beecher's Housekeeper and Healthkeeper* (New York: Harper and Brothers, 1873), p. 110.

109 On Haldan's advertisement, see *Pennsylvania Gazette* (Philadelphia), January 19, 1758. On Harbeson, see *Philadelphia: Three Centuries of American Art* (Philadelphia: Philadelpha Museum of Art, 1976), p. 79.

110 A plate warmer of this type is pictured in Gentle and Feild, *English Domestic Brass*, p. 158.

111 Holme, *Academy of Armory*, 2:7.

112 Johnson, *Dictionary of the English Language*, 2:s.v. "trevet."

113 Leslie, *House Book*, p. 132.

114 Several examples are illustrated in the anonymous trade catalogue TS573 M58i*, watermarked 1811, Downs collection, Winterthur Library.

115 Tufts, *Hundreds of Hunnemans*, p. 16.

116 Anthony Wood, *The Life and Times of Anthony Wood, Antiquary, of Oxford, 1632–1695, Described by Himself, Collected from His Diaries and Other Papers* (Oxford, Eng.: Clarendon Press, 1894), as quoted in Davis, *English Silver at Williamsburg*, pp. 43-44.

117 A variety of these can be seen in Jesse McNab, "The Legacy of a Fantastical Scot," *Bulletin* 19, no. 6 (New York: Metropolitan Museum of Art, 1961): 172–80; see also Georgina E. Lee, *British Silver Monteith Bowls, Including American and European Examples* (Byfleet, Eng.: Manor House Press, 1978).

118 The Admiralty Office design can be seen in Wouter Kuyper, *Dutch Classicist Architecture* (Delft: Delft University Press, 1980), p. 571. A discussion of Dutch architectural influence in England is in Henry-Russell Hitchcock, *Netherlandish Scrolled Gables of the Sixteenth and Early Seventeenth Centuries* (New York: New York University Press, 1978), pp. 95-98.

119 Nathaniel Bailey, *Household Dictionary* (London, 1721), as cited in Georgina E. Lee, *British Silver Montieth Bowls, Including American and European Examples* (Byfleet, Eng.: Manor House Press, 1978), p. 11. Johnson, *Dictionary of the English Language*, 2:s.v. "monteith."

120 The Fitzhugh quote and Hacker inventory are cited in Davis, *English Silver at Williamsburg*, p. 44.

121 The cellaret is defined and discussed in Sheraton, *Cabinet Dictionary*, 1:142. George Smith, *A Collection of Designs for Household Furniture* (London: J. Taylor, 1808), p. 17.

122 William Beastall, *A Useful Guide, for Grocers, Distillers, Hotel and Tavernkeepers, and Wine and Spirit Dealers* (New York: By the author, 1829), p. 124.

123 The attribution to South Carolina is based on the design of the decoration inlaid into the wooden case containing this liner, as recorded in Montgomery, *American Furniture*, pp. 431, 432.

124 Elisha Coles, *An English Dictionary* (London, 1717), s.v. "salver."

125 *Inventories of Four Eighteenth-Century Houses in the Historic Area of Williamsburg* (Williamsburg, Va.: Colonial Williamsburg Foundation, n.d.), pp. 6, 7. Those that are recorded as being japanned could be painted sheet iron or brass chased with oriental motifs, as suggested in Davis, *English Silver at Williamsburg*, p. 125.

126 The firm's history, emphasizing its pewter production, is ably discussed in Jack L. Scott, *Pewter Wares from Sheffield* (Baltimore: Antiquarian Press, 1980), pp. 39-54; John Taylor, ed., *The Illustrated Guide to Sheffield and the Surrounding District* (Sheffield, Eng.: Pawson and Brailsford, 1879), p. 286.

127 Frederick Bradbury, *History of Old Sheffield Plate* (London: Macmillan, 1912), p. 58.

128 Taylor, *Illustrated Guide to Sheffield*, pp. 287-88.

129 Trade catalogue NK7252 D62* TC, Downs collection, Winterthur Library. This tray is en suite with a covered vegetable dish, acc. no. 93.7; the ownership history was provided by the donor, a descendant of the original owner. Copper, zinc, nickel, gold, and lead are present in the tray, but their absolute amounts cannot be determined because of the silver plating.

130 On Schlosser, see register of the First Moravian Congregation, York, Pa., 1751-1899, trans. Henry James Young, 1938, MS JJ2, Historical Society of York County. On Bailey, see *Pennsylvania Herald, and York General Advertiser*, July 25, 1792.

131 *Pennsylvania Herald, and York General Advertiser*, June 1, 1793.

132 John William Schlosser, will book 5, pp. 240-48, York County Court House. Schlosser's tools and marking dies still exist in the collection of the Historical society of York County. They are photographed and recorded in DAPC.

133 Charles Welch, *History of The Worshipful Company of Pewterers*, 2 vols. (London: Blades, East, and Blades, 1902), 2:156.

134 Court records of the Worshipful Company of Pewterers, London, September 23, 1567, as quoted in F. G. Hilton Price, *Old Base Metal Spoons* (London: B. T. Batsford, 1908), p. 12.

135 Parsloe, *Wardens' Accounts*, p. 270.

136 On tinning, see Webster, *Encyclopaedia of Domestic Economy*, p. 231; Rees, *Cyclopaedia*, 21:s.v. "lattin."

137 Johnson, *Dictionary of the English Language*, 1:s.v. "alchymy." Ronald F. Homer, *Five Centuries of Base Metal Spoons* (London: By the author, 1975), p. 7.

138 On makers, see F. G. Hilton Price, *Old Base Metal Spoons* (London: B. T. Batsford, 1908). On Curtice and Hobart, see Cummings, *Rural Household Inventories*, pp. 9, 25.

139 Percy E. Raymond, "Latten Spoons of the Pilgrims," *Antiques* 61, no. 3 (March 1952): 242-44. On Barton, see Howard H. Cotterell, *Old Pewter: Its Makers and Marks* (London: B. T. Batsford, 1929), p. 156.

DETAIL, COAL GRATE, 1760–80
ENTRY 74

HEAT

This section contains artifacts for the generation and maintenance of heat. In most instances the rationale is obvious, as with andirons or coal grates. In other cases, fenders or curfews, for example, it may not be as apparent. Such items have been included in this section because they have no reason for being outside the context of heating. Represented here are andirons, shovels, tongs and pokers, fret and wire fenders, bellows, curfews, coal grates, coal scuttles, blowers, and warming pans.

ANDIRONS
51

ENGLAND, 1725–75
BRASS (COPPER 75.45, ZINC 17.53,
LEAD 2.73, TIN 2.34, IRON 0.86,
ANTIMONY 0.26, SILVER 0.14), IRON

H. 21 3/8" (54.3 CM), D. 19 1/2"
(49.5 CM), W. 12 3/8" (31.4 CM)
58.25.9, .10

AMERICA HAD ALWAYS BEEN an important market for English manufacturers of base-metal goods. Although American craftsmen met an increasingly large portion of the demand for household metalwork through the eighteenth and nineteenth centuries, English manufacturers retained a competitive edge until the mid 1800s. Consequently, as late as 1833 it was observed that "as an article of manufacture, andirons are little known in England [but are] made at Birmingham for exportation; in the United States they constitute a considerable item in traffic with the various parts of America, where wood is the only fuel of the inhabitants." The author went on to quote the English writer and engraver Joseph Strutt (ca. 1742-1802), who observed in 1775 that English andirons "stand on the hearth, where they burn wood. . . . Their fronts are usually carved, with a round knob at the top: some of them are kept polished and bright."[1]

These knobs are related to the round knobs at the top of each of the illustrated andirons, which are cast hollow in halves, vertically seamed, and threaded to the cast baluster uprights, which are constructed in the same manner. The single-piece trestle that supports each is bolted to a horizontal tabular projection at the base of the upright, while the circular boss used to disguise the end of the billet bar just above that juncture is held in place with two small rivets. This type of andiron is often found in American base-metal collections, providing some insight into the quantity that was imported from England during the mid eighteenth century. Hardware merchants such as William Bailey "at his stove grate warehouse in Baker Street and at his store in Fly Market" offered "for sale reasonable both wholesale and retail imported from the latest vessels from England . . . Prince's metal, brass, and steel andirons" of this type.[2]

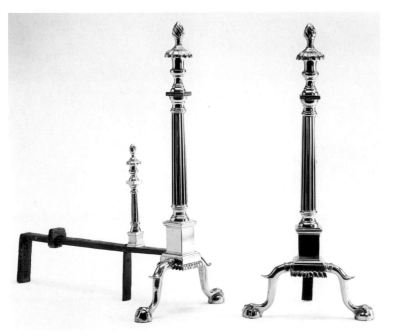

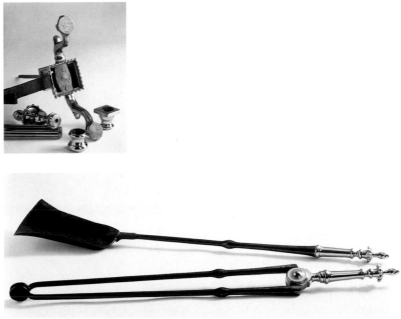

ANDIRONS, SHOVEL, TONGS

52

PROBABLY ENGLAND, POSSIBLY
PHILADELPHIA, PENNSYLVANIA, 1760–80
BRASS (COPPER 83.31,
ZINC 8.56, LEAD 4.23, TIN 2.43, IRON 1.08,
ANTIMONY 0.21, SILVER 0.11), IRON

ANDIRONS: H. 28 3/8" (72.1 CM), W. 12 1/2"
(31.7 CM), D. 25" (63.5 CM);
SHOVEL: L. 36 7/8" (93.7 CM), W. 8 7/8" (22.5 CM);
TONGS: L. 36 1/8" (92.1 CM), W. 3 1/2" (8.9 CM)
54.92.1–.4

ON APRIL 7, 1784, the Philadelphia bookseller and druggist John Sparhawk advertised "a few pair of handsome brass dogs, fender, shovel and tongs to match." He may have come to own those fireplace implements by accepting them as barter goods with the thought that he could sell them advantageously. They might have been made in Philadelphia; local brass founders offered such items individually and in sets, but hardware merchants in every major American coastal city also imported English examples. William Zane noted in 1792 that he "has just imported, in the late arrivals from Europe . . . brass head andirons, shovels and tongs." Similarly, the New York merchants Garrit Abeel and John Byvanck imported "from London and Bristol . . . andirons, neat brass and iron head shovels and tongs."[3]

It is difficult to distinguish between English and American andirons and fire tools since they are so infrequently marked and because American founders made their "articles from the newest patterns now in vogue in London."[4] The illustrated andirons look like many of those

attributed to Philadelphia, but their construction is different in several respects. While Philadelphia andirons have their internal iron rod peened at the top to hold the multipart brass uprights in place, the five-part uprights on these are held in place by the urn, which is threaded at its base to the internal iron rod. Philadelphia andirons have individually cast legs brazed to a solid plinth block, on which the plinth rests separately. These legs are a single piece casting, and the plinth block, integral with the plinth, is hollow and cut out on the side to fit over the legs. A separate gadrooned border is soldered to the bottom edge.

All parts of the uprights are cast hollow in halves and seamed vertically, as are the handles of the shovel and tongs. The fluted portion of the columns, however, is cast in three vertical sections, and the gadrooned canopy on the andirons and tools is a single casting that has been brazed in place.

ANDIRONS
53

ATTRIBUTED TO EDWARD TAYLOR AND
THOMAS BAILEY
LONDON, ENGLAND, 1784–97
PAKTONG (ZINC 56.00, COPPER 34.00,
NICKEL 6.82, IRON 0.99), IRON

H. 28 7/8" (73.3 CM),
W. 14 1/8" (35.9 CM), D. 20 3/4"
(52.7 CM)
61.1413.1, .2

THE UPRIGHTS OF THESE ANDIRONS relate to illustrations published by the English designers William Ince and John Mayhew in *The Universal System of Household Furniture*. Robert Sayer also included similar patterns in *Genteel Household Furniture*. The andirons have an extensive amount of engraving that closely parallels the designs created by the Scottish architect Robert Adam for architecture, furniture, and other household furnishings during the second half of the eighteenth century.[5]

The andirons have equally interesting construction features. The most visible of these are the hollow blocks attached with iron screws to the underside of the feet. Equally unusual are the blocks between the urns and trapezoidal capitals of the piers. Each is cast solid with four projecting blunt points on the underside used to align the corners with those of the elements below. English fire-dog founders rarely used washers like these between adjoining parts and infrequently cast their work as thickly.

The most unusual feature is the manner in which the iron rods inside the uprights are attached to the legs. Typical eighteenth- and early nineteenth-century English andirons had a wrought, tapered, internal iron rod, square in section and shouldered near the lower end. During assembly the billet bar and legs were slid over the lower end, abutting the shoulder. The lower end was then peened, forming a permanent joint.

The andirons shown here employ a drawn iron rod, circular in section, which is threaded at the upper end. The lower end is also threaded into a square nut through the billet bar and finally into the legs. The first known Western reference to this mode of construction is a United States patent for "a new and useful improvement in the Mode of Manufacturing andirons in a Detachable Manner" issued to Joseph D. Sargeant of New Britain, Connecticut, on August 17, 1858.[6]

Sargeant acknowledged in his patent specifications that he was "aware that andirons have been made having a bolt with a screw on the upper end for the purpose of securing the ornamental pillar and also having a shoulder on the lower end passing through the legs and fire iron, and riveted on the underside, which [is not] detachable." He went on to say that his improved andiron was held together with an internal iron bolt threaded at both ends so that it could be "more cheaply made and easily detached, to be packed closely in crates or boxes, thereby preventing the great amount of breakage in the transporting."[7]

Sargeant was referring to the suitability of his andirons for shipment throughout the United States. In doing so, he was clearly unaware of andirons like these, which had long been a staple in the transatlantic trade between England and America. These particular andirons are of a type that has been documented with frequency in and around Charleston, South Carolina. They are specifically described as "very neat large new make d[ou]ble Fire dogs with neat Eng[rave]d Princes metal obelisk pillars Claw Feet vase heads" in the cargo of the *Castle Douglas* bound from London to Charleston in 1785. They were consigned by the London braziers and ironmongers Edward Farmer Taylor and Thomas Bailey.[8]

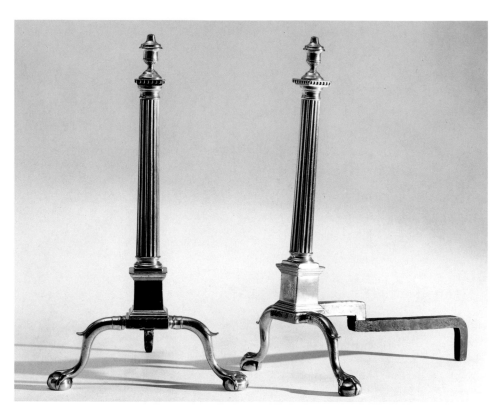

ANDIRONS

54

DANIEL KING (1731–1806) OR
DANIEL KING, JR. (1757–1836)
PHILADELPHIA, PENNSYLVANIA,
1760–1800

BRASS (COPPER 78.91, ZINC 18.51,
LEAD 1.44, TIN 0.90), IRON
H. 23 1/4" (59.0 CM), W. 13 5/16"
(33.8 CM), D. 15 13/16" (40.5 CM)
58.1997.1, .2

"WHEN WOOD [WAS] THE ONLY kind of fuel in use, . . . [it] was burned upon irons called dogs laid upon the hearth." The demand for andirons or fire dogs in America during the eighteenth century was so great that most urban American brass founders and importers of English hardware routinely offered them in their newspaper advertisements. Daniel King or Daniel King, Jr., both brass founders in Philadelphia, advertised in the December 19, 1793, issue of Philadelphia's *Dunlap and Claypoole's American Daily Advertiser* "an elegant assortment of brass andirons of American manufacture, superior in quality and taste to whatever has been offered of the kind at this or any other market." The appearance of this elegant assortment is partially specified in the elder's bill, dated 1770, to the prominent Philadelphia merchant John Cadwalader. The bill lists "a pare of the best rote fier dogs with Corinthen coloms, A pare of the best fluted do with counter flutes, one pare do plane fluted [and] one pare of the best plane chamber dogs."[9]

The andirons pictured here, according to King's bill, are a pair of plain, fluted fire dogs. Although they have undergone major restoration, they are significant because they are the only pair presently recorded that are signed by King. "Daniel King Fecit" is engraved in script on a square plate riveted to the top of the dentiled section of each capital. A heraldic crest of a rampant, collared, and chained demi-lion is also engraved on the front of each plinth. This crest was associated with the Meredith family. Its presence on these andirons might indicate that they were the property of Joseph Meredith of Philadelphia, who specifically listed a pair of "brass andirons, shovel and tongs" among his best household goods, which he willed to his wife, Elizabeth, in 1803.[10]

The five brass elements constituting the upright are vertically seamed and held in place with an internal wrought-iron rod peened at the top. The solid cast legs, one of which is a modern replacement, are brazed to the plinth block, relating them in construction to numerous other andirons attributed to Philadelphia.[11]

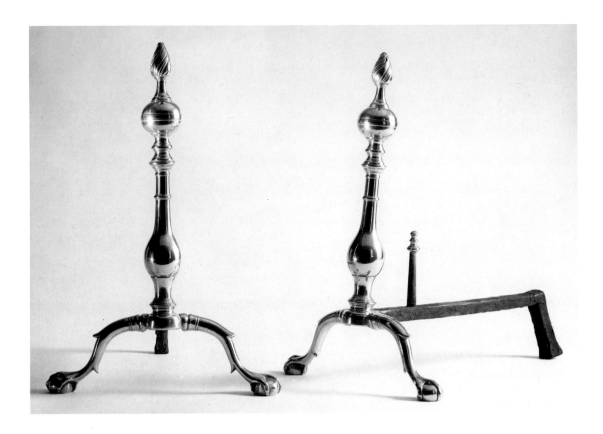

ANDIRONS
55

PROBABLY PHILADELPHIA,
PENNSYLVANIA, 1770–1800
BRASS (COPPER 71.36, ZINC 26.00,
LEAD 2.34), IRON

H. 20 1/3" (51.4 CM), W. 14 1/8"
(35.9 CM), D. 18 1/2" (47.0 CM)
58.2811.1, .2

THESE ANDIRONS and a second pair at Winterthur are part of a small, undocumented group that was probably made in Philadelphia during the last few decades of the eighteenth century. They employ broadly stanced cabriole legs with ball-and-claw feet that relate closely in design to a pair of andirons signed by the Philadelphia brass founder Daniel King or his son of the same name.[12] A thick, circular disc at the juncture of the legs is pierced by a wrought-iron rod that extends through the upright and, being peened at both ends, holds the legs, billet bar, and upright together.

The upright consists of two parts, the baluster and the sphere with stylized flame. Both were cast hollow in halves and seamed vertically, and each relates closely in design to turned elements in Philadelphia candlestands, pole screens, tea tables, and Windsor chairs. As such, they strongly evidence the influence of the turner.

Urban brass founders often looked to turners to provide them with patterns, which they used in casting. Philadelphia had many turners during the late eighteenth century, a few of whom were Joseph Anthony, Bernard Schomo, and George Stow. While a large portion of their time was devoted to making furniture, they also made "billiard balls, backgammon men [and] everything that can demand the application of their art."[13]

Many of their products were for use by other craftsmen, as stated by John C. Kinnan, a machinist and turner in iron, brass, ivory, and hardwood in Philadelphia. Kinnan advertised that he did "cutler's turning . . . Silversmith's and Jeweller's turning [and] Printing Press Maker's turning . . . at the shortest notice, and on the lowest terms." He also "made . . . Founder's iron or wooden patterns" of the type used in casting the brass parts of these andirons.[14]

ANDIRONS
56

PROBABLY PHILADELPHIA,
PENNSYLVANIA, 1770–1800
BRASS (COPPER 78.17, ZINC 16.53,
LEAD 2.53, TIN 1.44, IRON 0.45,
ANTIMONY 0.17, SILVER 0.11), IRON

H. 19 1/2" (49.5 CM), W. 13 1/4"
(34.9 CM), D. 26 3/8" (67.0 CM)
51.69.1, .2

"DANIEL KING INFORMS THE PUBLIC . . . [that] he has on hand a general assortment of fashionable Andirons, among which are the approved French Fire dogs."[15] The low height and curved billet bars of the illustrated andirons may be the features that King and his fellow Philadelphians perceived as being French. If so, this Philadelphia interpretation has a strong English accent, using opposed cabriole legs flanking a block and plinth surmounted by an upright element.

The contour of the legs and detailing of the hairy paw feet are practically identical to those on a set of four Philadelphia mahogany fire screens that have been identified in the accounts of the Philadelphia cabinetmaker Thomas Affleck.[16] While Affleck was surely responsible for supplying the wood and form of the screens, he appears to have subcontracted

their decoration to the Philadelphia carvers Nicholas Bernard and Martin Jugiez.

Bernard and Jugiez worked together from about 1760 until approximately 1783, executing "all sort of carving in wood and stone . . . in the neatest manner." Following their separation, Jugiez continued to carve alone until his death in 1815. The architectural and furniture carving of the pair is well documented, but they also supplied metalworkers with models to be used in casting, the best-known instance of which is "the pattern for the back of a chimney" made for Isaac Zane, who owned Marlboro Furnace in Virginia. They and their competitors also supplied brass founders with carved patterns, as suggested with the entry "by a carved foot for the andirons" in a bill Daniel King submitted to John Cadwalader for brass fireplace equipment in February 1771.[17]

ANDIRONS
57

WILLIAM TUSTON (D. 1812)
PHILADELPHIA, PENNSYLVANIA, 1802–12
BRASS (COPPER 84.78,
ZINC 9.18, LEAD 2.20, TIN 2.20, IRON 1.37,
SILVER 0.15), IRON

H. 22 1/2" (57.2 CM), W. 11 1/2"
(29.2 CM), D. 22" (55.9 CM)
93.29.1, .2

ON DECEMBER 19, 1793, the Philadelphia brass founder Daniel King, or his son Daniel King, Jr., advertised "an elegant assortment of Brass Andirons of American manufacture, superior in quality and taste to whatever has been offered of the kind in this or any other market."[18] The predominant taste in andirons in the United States at that time was urn-shape uprights, usually on a short pedestal, supported by two opposed cabriole legs.

The pair of andirons shown here conforms to that description generally but with some significant variation. Being signed, they document one maker's interpretation of the style then in vogue. They stand on legs that differ from the traditional cabriole: they have pointed knees, created by casting the legs in the form of two C scrolls instead of an S-shape profile, and the legs join the pedestal from below instead of from the side. Both features seem to be present only on andirons signed by William Tuston. In other respects his andirons conform to the norm in the principal centers for andiron production: Philadelphia, New York, and Boston. The billet bar is held to the legs with an iron rod concealed in the two-part brass upright, which is peened at the lower end and threaded at the upper end. The two parts of the brass upright are cast hollow in halves vertically and brazed together. The stamped "2" next to the maker's mark may refer to a size or pattern number.

Little is currently known of Tuston, who first appears in 1802 in the Philadelphia city directories as a brass founder. He continues to be listed annually through 1811. On April 4, 1812, Tuston signed his will in a very debilitated hand; it was probated on May 9. He seems to have met with marginal success in his profession, for the inventory of his estate totaled only $205, 10 percent of which was "Sundry Brassfoundering tools & c. in the Shop."[19]

A.

B.

ANDIRONS

58a,b

A. PROBABLY NEW YORK CITY, 1760–80

BRASS (COPPER 78.40, ZINC 18.23,

LEAD 2.23, TIN 0.54, ANTIMONY 0.11), IRON

H. 24 3/4" (62.9 CM),

W. 13 1/8" (33.3 CM), D. 19 3/4" (50.2 CM)

59.2872.1,.2

B. PROBABLY NEW YORK CITY, 1760–80

BRASS (COPPER 77.79, ZINC 18.03, LEAD 2.87,

TIN 0.64, IRON 0.27, ANTIMONY 0.13), IRON

H. 25 9/16" (64.9 CM),

W. 13 1/4" (33.7 CM), D. 19" (48.2 CM)

61.178.1, .2

ON MAY 18, 1775, the New York City brass founder Richard Skellorn advertised that he "makes . . . brass andirons . . . from the newest patterns now in vogue in London." About a decade before, "James Byers, Brass Founder next-door to Mr. Heyman Levy's in Bayard Street" noted that he did the same, as did "Jacob Wilkins at the sign of the gold andiron and candlestick."[20]

Charleston, South Carolina, although about eight hundred miles south of New York City, was closely connected to it through the coastal trade. By using that connection, the Charleston hardwareman James Duthie advertised in the pages of that city's principal newspaper on March 1, 1768, that he had "just imported . . . a few pair of Chamber Dogs, the handsomest that were ever brought into this province, with large brass twisted, plain and fluted pillars . . . made in New York."[21]

The andirons that constitute this entry represent two of the three types enumerated in Duthie's notice. While the spiral reeded columns of one are clearly different from the fluted piers of the other, the tetradecagons with flame finials and ball-and-claw–footed cabriole legs are almost identical not only in design but also in dimension and detail, strongly suggesting that all were made in the same foundry.[22]

The uprights of the twisted column pair are composed of six parts: plinth, square washer, column base, column, column capital, and polyhedron with finial. All parts except the washer are cast hollow in halves and seamed vertically. The same applies to the five-part upright of the other pair. On both, all parts are held in place on the plate between the legs with a slender, internal, wrought-iron rod peened at both ends.

ANDIRONS

59

PROBABLY NEW YORK CITY, 1760–80
BRASS (COPPER 77.10,
ZINC 20.20, LEAD 1.24, IRON 0.82,
TIN 0.35), IRON

H. 24 3/4" (62.9 CM), W. 13 5/8"
(34.6 CM), D. 19 1/2" (49.5 CM)
61.580.1, .2

IN 1753 the English artist, satirist, social commentator, and connoisseur William Hogarth published an essay on taste entitled *The Analysis of Beauty*. Among the many illustrations, he pictured three horns. The first was perfectly straight along its length. The second he shaped into an S and noted that "the beauty of this horn is increas'd . . . where it is . . . bent two different ways." To the third he added a spiral twist and observed "the vast increase of beauty, even to grace and elegance . . . where it is . . . twisted round, at the same time, that it was bent two different ways." He concluded his presentation of these horns by stating that objects that incorporate the lines inherent in the last of these "are extremely beautiful and pleasing to the eye."[23]

Using this design concept, English metalworkers, during the third quarter of the eighteenth century, fashioned silver coffeepots and brass candlesticks into baluster shapes with spiral twists. That same approach was taken by the founder of these and two similar pairs of andirons in the Winterthur collection.[24] Their swirled balusters are a striking instance of Hogarth's design philosophy adapted for domestic artifacts by an artisan-mechanic.

The polyhedron with flame finial and cabriole legs with ball-and-claw feet relate these andirons very closely to others (see entry 58) by founders such as Richard Skellorn, who "makes . . . brass andirons . . . from the newest patterns now in vogue in London." The square plinth, swirled baluster, and polygonal-flame finial that constitute the upright are all cast hollow in halves and seamed vertically. They are held in place on the front of the billet bar and the legs with a slender internal iron rod peened at both ends.[25]

ANDIRONS

60

POSSIBLY PETER ALLISON
(1769–1836),
PROBABLY SAMUEL ALLISON (B. 1790)
NEW YORK CITY, 1804–40

BRASS (COPPER 79.48, ZINC 17.43,
LEAD 1.36, TIN 1.23), IRON
H. 25 5/8" (65.1 CM), W. 11 1/2"
(29.2 CM), D. 24 3/4" (62.9 CM)
59.513.1, .2

PETER ALLISON WAS BORN in Haverstraw, New York, on November 19, 1769.[26] The events of his early life are unrecorded, but at the age of thirty-five he appears in the 1804 New York City directory as a brass founder. The rigors of the craft apparently did not agree with him. Within five years he gave it up for the less arduous professions of grocer and eventually dry goods merchant.

His cousin Samuel Allison, also born in Haverstraw, on January 29, 1790, followed brass founding but seemingly with greater success. At age twenty-three he listed himself in the 1813 New York City directory and continued to do so through 1840. In addition to brass founding on his own, he is said to have been a foreman in a bell foundry in New York during all or part of that time.[27]

The illustrated andirons are presently the only pair recorded that bear the Allison surname. Although either of the aforementioned men might have made them, the latter is more likely, due to the greater number of years he was in business. The heads and matching log stops, described as "andiron spears" in the estate inventory of the New York brass founder David Phillips, occur on numerous New York andirons, many of which bear the name Richard Whittingham.[28]

While these andirons are typical in style and construction to those made by Whittingham, they are coarsely fabricated with repaired casting flaws. The surfaces are finished in a cursory manner. Moldings and other details are simplistic and not well integrated into the overall design. It also appears as if the maker's name may have been cast incuse rather than stamped into the andirons, an unusual practice.

ANDIRONS
61

PROBABLY RICHARD
WHITTINGHAM, JR. (B. 1776),
POSSIBLY RICHARD
WHITTINGHAM (1747–1821)
NEW YORK CITY, 1807–55

BRASS (COPPER 84.01, ZINC 12.42,
LEAD 1.50, TIN 0.57), IRON
H. 26 1/8" (66.3 CM), W. 11 5/8"
(29.5 CM), D. 20 1/2" (52.0 CM)
60.225.1, .2

THE BRASS PARTS OF these andirons were cast in sand flasks. The legs were cast solid, but the urn-shape finials, columns, and plinths were each cast as hollow vertical halves and then brazed together. This was the standard manner in which hollow castings were made in America during the eighteenth and early nineteenth centuries. All the parts of these andirons are held together with an internal iron rod to which the urn-shape finial is threaded.

While the same wooden, lead, or brass pattern was used to create all like parts, the resultant castings were not necessarily identical. Small differences caused by finishing meant they might not be interchangeable. Consequently, many parts were individually fitted and had to be coded so that they did not become mixed during assembly. Those codes were typically a series of punched dots, filed grooves, or engraved lines. This pair of andirons uses a combination of the above.

One has a single straight line punched into each part while the elements of the other are marked with a cluster of four small dots, which, when paired with the dots stamped on the underside of the plinth on which it rests, serves as an assembly guide.

In addition to these markings, andirons were often coded to indicate their size, which determined their price. The larger the size, the greater the weight of brass, resulting in a higher price. Arabic numerals were sometimes used to designate size, but marks such as those described earlier were more common. These andirons have a line of five large circular depressions stamped into the underside of the plinths, recording them as size five.

ANDIRONS

62

PROBABLY RICHARD WHITTINGHAM,
JR. (B. 1776), POSSIBLY RICHARD
WHITTINGHAM (1747–1821)
NEW YORK CITY, 1807–55

BRASS (COPPER 76.15, ZINC 20.26,
LEAD 2.17, TIN 0.74), IRON
H. 24 7/8" (63.2 CM), W. 11 1/2"
(29.2 CM), D. 21 5/8" (54.9 CM)
59.614, .615

RICHARD WHITTINGHAM WAS BORN in 1747 in Birmingham, England, where he learned the craft of brass founding. Presumably hoping to better his situation, he left England for the United States at the age of forty-four, arriving in Philadelphia on September 22, 1791. Shortly thereafter he moved to Passaic Falls, New Jersey, as a member of the Society for Establishing Useful Manufactures, a short-lived industrial community. The records of that organization note that he was a poor but "very usefull and deserving mechanic."[29]

Upon leaving that ill-fated venture, Whittingham settled in New York City and is recorded as a brass founder in the city directories beginning in 1795. He continues to be listed thereafter at 95 Henry Street until 1818. He died in 1821, leaving a modest estate of just over $3,500. Although his inventory, taken on October 16, 1821, included no tools or shop equipment, there were "2 pr shovel & tongs [and] 3 pr Brass andirons."[30]

His son Richard Whittingham, Jr., was also born in England, in 1776, and came to the United States with his father. He, too, established himself as a brass founder in New York City, in 1807, probably having learned the trade from the elder Whittingham, as did his brothers Isaac, Joseph, and Charles. Father and son are listed at different addresses until 1818, when the younger Whittingham is believed to have taken over his father's business. After that the son continued to list himself as a brass founder working on Henry Street through 1855, at which time he retired.

It has not yet been determined positively whether the father, the son, or both used the misspelled "R. WITTINGHAM" mark stamped into these and numerous other andirons made in various styles. Richard, Jr., successfully spent forty-eight years in the profession, while his father devoted less than half that time, suggesting that the son is more likely to have been the principal user of the stamp. This type of andiron, described as having a "spear" in the 1818 estate inventory of the New York brass founder David Phillips, commonly bears Whittingham's stamped mark.[31] The brass parts are all cast, the two-part uprights in hollow halves vertically and brazed.

ANDIRONS
63

PROBABLY RICHARD WHITTINGHAM,
JR. (B. 1776), POSSIBLY
RICHARD WHITTINGHAM (1747–1821)
NEW YORK CITY, 1807–55

BRASS (COPPER 83.32, ZINC 13.89,
LEAD 1.06, TIN 0.53), IRON
H. 24" (61.0 CM), W. 11 1/4" (28.6 CM),
D. 23 1/2" (59.7 CM)
61.604.1, .2

ANDIRONS WITH CURVED BILLET BARS, or dogs, as they were usually called, are described as "circular" in early nineteenth-century brass founders' inventories.[32] Although no contemporary discussion of their purpose has been found, they may have served to increase radiated heat by moving the uprights to either side of the burning logs. This feature seems to have experienced its greatest popularity during the first half of the nineteenth century and was incorporated into andirons made in all the major coastal centers of the northeast United States.

Most andirons of this type use an undecorated cast brass cover over the curved portion of the billet bar only. The pair shown here is one of a few that have that area further embellished with a fret, pierced probably to match an accompanying fender. Frets were described as "an elegant ornament, of ancient invention, appropriate [when] applied in narrow pannels [and of] endless variety, which, under skillful hands, may be conducive of producing a better proportion in Design." Examples are illustrated in furniture design books from as early as Thomas Chippendale's *Gentleman and Cabinet-Maker's Director* and, as Thomas Sheraton stated, could be adapted to be "cast in brass."[33] Most consisted of interlocking geometric patterns like the upper third of these frets, but animal forms amid foliate scrolls were also used. While this fret has no exact published counterpart, it does have a related precedent on plate 108 of Robert Sayer's *Household Furniture in Genteel Taste for the Year 1762*, published in London.

The row of four dots stamped to the left of the maker's mark were used in the proper assembly of various parts. The parts of its mate are stamped with two dots.

ANDIRONS
64

PROBABLY RICHARD
WHITTINGHAM, JR. (B. 1776),
POSSIBLY RICHARD WHITTINGHAM
(1747–1821)
NEW YORK CITY, 1807–55

BRASS (COPPER 78.83, ZINC 17.84,
LEAD 2.13, TIN 0.64), IRON
H. 19 3/4" (50.1 CM), L. 20 7/8"
(55.5 CM), W. 10 1/4" (26.0 CM)
74.122.1, .2

THE LANDSCAPE SCENES engraved on the plinths of these andirons
are not commonly found on fireplace equipment. Although simple
and stylized, they and the flowers that flank them are expertly executed
and bespeak an accomplished artisan. Richard Whittingham, Jr., the
probable maker of the andirons, became closely associated with such an
artisan when he married on January 4, 1805. His wife's father, William
Rollinson (1762–1842), arrived in New York from Birmingham, England,
in 1789 and almost immediately established a reputation for himself
as a competent engraver, being asked to decorate "the Arms of the United
States upon a set of gilt buttons which was worn by General Washington
on the . . . day of his inauguration as President." Rollinson subsequently
followed a successful career engraving "all kinds of devices, ornaments, arms, names, cyphers, &c &c . . . on gold and silver, seals or
copper [and] brass." Among his documented work are bank notes, coats
of arms, membership certificates, and portraits on copper as well as

commemorative presentation inscriptions and cyphers on silver.
Although Rollinson did not place his name on these andirons, circum-
stantial evidence supports the contention that the landscape scenes
were executed in his shop.[34]

The multipart uprights of these andirons are cast hollow in halves
vertically. The halves are brazed together with almost invisible seams.
Square castings, such as the engraved plinths, are purposely joined at
the corners to make the seams even more difficult to see. All parts
of the brass uprights are held together by an internal iron rod, peened
to the juncture of the legs at the lower end and threaded to the base
of the ball at the upper end.

The two short lines above and to the left of the maker's mark were
used in the correct assembly of the andirons. The parts of its mate
are stamped with one line.

A.

ANDIRONS
65 a,b

A. POSSIBLY ISAAC CONKLIN
PROBABLY NEW YORK CITY, 1807–17
BRASS (COPPER 81.40, ZINC 16.25,
LEAD 1.72, TIN 0.39), IRON
H. 16 1/2" (41.9 CM), W. 8 3/4" (22.2 CM),
D. 12 1/4" (31.1 CM)
64.944.1, .2

B. POSSIBLY ISAAC CONKLIN
PROBABLY NEW YORK CITY, 1807–17
BRASS (COPPER 77.11, ZINC 19.45,
LEAD 2.78, TIN 0.36, ANTIMONY 0.11), IRON
H. 22 1/2" (57.1 CM), W. 8 1/16" (20.5 CM),
D. 16 1/8" (41.0 CM)
66.1213.1, .2

THE IDENTITY OF THE MAN who stamped his initals into the plinths of these andirons is presently unknown. He may have been Isaac Conklin (Concklin), a smith who worked between 1807 and 1817 on Manhattan Island at various addresses, all of which were in close proximity to the brass founders Richard Whittingham and his sons Richard, Jr., and Isaac.

The urns, which are cast hollow in halves, seamed vertically, and peened on top of the uprights of the shorter pair, were probably made in the same foundry as those by Richard Whittingham, Jr. (see entry 61). They are similar except in size, being 2 3/4 inches shorter than the urns atop the Whittingham andirons. The urns on the taller of the two pairs illustrated here have a counterpart on other marked Whittingham andirons, even in size.[35]

While the nature of Whittingham's involvement in the fabrication of these andirons is not yet known, he probably cast the urns and other brass parts and sold them wholesale or used them as barter. The exchange of specialty items among craftsmen whose work was closely interrelated, such as brass clockworks makers and cabinetmakers or those who made brass and iron andirons, was a common practice.

Heads for andirons were among the most marketable items for the makers of fireplace equipment. They were often specifically cited in base-metal advertisements, like that of Herbert Van Wagenen, who was located at the sign of the golden broad-ax in Beekmans-Slip in New York City. He noted in the *New-York Mercury* that he had "for sale . . . brass and iron heads [for andirons] at various prices."[36]

ANDIRONS
66

EDWARD SMYLIE	H. 23 3/8" (59.4 CM), W. 11 1/2"
NEW YORK CITY, 1827–49	(29.2 CM),
BRASS (COPPER 74.98, ZINC 23.10,	D. 24 1/8" (61.3 CM)
TIN 0.70, IRON 0.20), IRON	78.5.1, .2

EDWARD SMYLIE FIRST LISTED HIMSELF in the New York City directories in 1817 as a brass founder at the corner of Pike and Henry streets. He continued to be listed at various addresses until 1849, when he apparently turned the business over to his son Charles. During his thirty-two-year career Smylie developed several improvements in andirons, which he then patented. On February 1, 1827, he was granted a "patent for pedastal feet for andirons." Less than a month later he received another "patent for preparing and finishing andirons." On July 12, 1843, he acquired a third patent for a safety bar that was to be placed "on the top of the horse [to prevent] the possibility of the andiron upsetting and causing damage by embers being thrown on the hearth or burning children . . . by the falling of the hot irons."[37]

The specifications for the first two patents were destroyed when the United States Patent Office burned in 1839. Smylie

seems not to have resubmitted them; consequently, their details are unknown. The specifications and drawing for his third patent have survived, but they do not relate to this pair of andirons, which were, therefore, presumably made and stamped under the protection of one of his first two patents.

The multiknopped and faceted uprights, log stops, and feet are cast hollow in halves and seamed vertically. The billet bar covers are also cast, in keeping with traditional practice. Both covers were incorrectly stamped with the number 7 and subsequently overstruck with the number 9. Single-digit numbers like these appear often in the shop inventory of the early nineteenth-century New York brass founder David Phillips, serving as a shorthand method for designating the size of any given object in relation to others of the same pattern. The numbers were undoubtedly used in the same capacity on this pair.[38]

ANDIRONS
67

BOSTON, MASSACHUSETTS,
1780–1810
BRASS (COPPER 93.43, ZINC 2.58, TIN
2.09, LEAD 1.50, SILVER 0.12), IRON

H. 28" (71.1 CM),
W. 12 5/8" (32.0 CM),
D. 20 1/16" (51.0 CM)
59.1142.1, .2

THE ABSENCE OF a maker's mark on these andirons would seem to prevent specific identification of their date and place of origin.

Within a broad context, the use of two graduated urns, one atop the other, was a popular design formula for American silversmiths during the last two decades of the eighteenth and first part of the nineteenth centuries. Many of those smiths–including Charles L. Boehme (1774–1868) of Baltimore, Samuel Williamson (ca. 1772–1843) of Philadelphia, William Garret Forbes (1751–1840) in New York, and William Moulton (1772–1861) and Joseph Loring (1748–1815), both of Boston–fashioned graduated urns into teapots, coffeepots, sugar bowls, and presentation vases. Similarly, the delicate swagged ornament encircling the urns on these andirons was created with the same type of rouletting tool used by many of those silversmiths to decorate their wares.

More specifically, the urns atop these andirons are similar in appearance to those on a set of attributed Boston fire tools in the Winterthur collection (see entry 90). Both are made of relatively uncommon red brass, which was used more frequently to make hearth equipment by documented Boston founders than by those elsewhere in the United States. Furthermore, the legs of these andirons are one-piece castings that have been relieved on the back sides to save metal, making the backs distinctively hollow and unfinished in appearance. This feature is common to virtually all cabriole leg andirons–whether ball-and-claw or pad footed–presently documented to Boston brass founders, including John Clark, James Davis, William C. Hunneman, Nathaniel Johnson, John Molineux, John Stickney, and Barnabas Webb.[39]

ANDIRONS
68

PROBABLY WILLIAM C. HUNNEMAN (1769–1856),
POSSIBLY WILLIAM C. HUNNEMAN, JR., OR
SAMUEL H. HUNNEMAN
BOSTON, MASSACHUSETTS, 1799–1825

BRASS (COPPER 74.85, ZINC 22.53,
LEAD 1.10, TIN 0.23), IRON
H. 16 1/4" (41.3 CM), W. 12 1/4"
(31.1 CM), D. 23" (58.4 CM)
54.560.1, .2

WILLIAM C. HUNNEMAN'S surviving business accounts date from 1793 to 1821 and contain numerous entries documenting the production of andirons. He sold large quantities to householders like Joseph Bancroft, who bought "1 sett brass handirons" for $20 in May 1812. Greater numbers were sold through middlemen, however, one of whom was Edward Farley in Salem. Hunneman consigned "sundry articles" to Farley on April 20, 1819, among which were three sets of brass andirons.[40] They were followed by nine more pairs on April 23.

While most of his mercantile connections were within a small radius of Boston, Hunneman did on occasion send his goods considerable distances. On August 10, 1818, he sold fourteen "setts of brass andirons" to James Shute and Company of Cincinnati, Ohio, consigned through George and John Rich in Baltimore.[41]

In addition to finished andirons, Hunneman also sold a lesser amount of unfinished castings to others in the foundry trade. James

Davis, who commenced the coppersmithing and brass-founding business in 1801, purchased "40 lb. handiron mettle" from Hunneman on May 23 of that year. They were undoubtedly coarse castings that Davis finished and assembled to market, possibly with his name stamped into them.[42]

A number of Hunneman's andirons bear stamped numbers in conjunction with his name. Their meaning is conjectural. All those presently recorded are three digit and range from 324 to 842. They appear on several differing sizes and styles of andirons, a few of which duplicate each other. Yet, none of the numbers duplicate, so it is likely each represents the total number Hunneman made at any given time. If this is so, Winterthur's was apparently the 474th pair of andirons he made during his working career.

ANDIRONS
69

JOHN MOLINEUX (D. 1829)
BOSTON, MASSACHUSETTS, 1806–29
BRASS (COPPER 80.60, ZINC 14.01,
LEAD 1.97, TIN 1.12), IRON

H. 19 1/4" (48.9 CM), W. 12 1/4"
(31.1 CM), D. 22 1/2" (57.2 CM)
60.226.1, .2

JOHN MOLINEUX FIRST APPEARED in the Boston city directories in 1805 with Samuel Cook in the hardware business. One year later he was listed by himself, again in hardware. Not until 1810 did he describe himself as a founder, which he then continued to do until his death in 1829. Molineux was listed continuously except for a four-year hiatus from 1811 to 1815. He appears to have left Boston during that time for Camden, Maine, as documented by one pair of andirons marked "MOLINEUX/CAMDEN." Camden, a small community about forty miles southeast of Augusta on Penobscot Bay, was described as having a "good harbor [with] considerable navigation employed in the coasting trade."[43] In spite of that town's apparent economic promise, Molineux returned to Boston.

Numerous andirons that bear his name are extant. The inventory of his estate also lists a preponderance of andirons, shovels, tongs, pokers, and jamb hooks, indicating he specialized in fireplace equipment. Itemized are "circular andirons, double bar andirons, [andirons

in the] French pattern, andirons with feet [and andirons of a] new pattern."[44] Others were differentiated numerically, including sizes 8, 9, 16, 22, and 26.

All were noted as being "in the possession of the Furniture Commission Company [a cooperative retail outlet] and . . . subject to the rules and regulations of said Company of which the deceased was a stockholder." That organization offered one-stop shopping for Bostonians seeking "a variety of . . . goods, necessary for the furnishing of households" and provided Boston's artisans with a useful additional outlet for their wares.[45]

The andirons shown here were a popular type made in Boston throughout the nineteenth century. The cabriole legs are cast hollow and unfinished on the back, typical of Boston andirons. The multipart uprights are cast hollow in halves vertically and brazed. They are held together with an internal iron rod to which the lobate finial is threaded.

ANDIRONS
70

JOHN MOLINEUX (D. 1829)
BOSTON, MASSACHUSETTS, 1806–29
BRASS (COPPER 77.25, ZINC 18.46,
LEAD 2.82, TIN 1.04, IRON 0.25), IRON

H. 14 1/8" (35.9 CM), W. 8 3/4"
(22.3 CM), L. 26 1/4" (66.7 CM)
90.50.1, .2

THE INVENTORY OF JOHN MOLINEUX'S SHOP, taken at the time of his death on October 12, 1829, lists numerous andirons and fire tools but little else. It is apparent that he specialized in fireplace equipment, a fairly narrow branch of brass founding. Many different types of andirons are itemized, including circular andirons, double-bar andirons, small andirons, andirons with feet, and several identified by numbers only. In addition, there are a few described as being either a french pattern with square feet or french pattern with round feet.[46]

The last of these probably describes the subject of this entry. These andirons are unusual in that their upright element is not supported on opposed cabriole legs or a trestle. Both were long-established means of providing stability under a load of burning logs and, like any tripod, insured a wobble-free stance on uneven surfaces. The substitution of this type of pedestal for opposed legs or trestle base on andirons seems to have been unique to Boston and its environs. It occurs on andirons marked by William Hunneman, James Davis, and John and Henry Noyes, but most extant examples are marked by Molineux. The allusion to French counterparts might indicate that their pedestal support is a simplified version of the feet on French andirons of the type sent to Boston by Col. James Swan during the 1790s.[47] In any event, their popularity was short lived, lasting only through the first quarter of the nineteenth century, probably because they were less stable and were more easily knocked over and damaged than those with opposed legs.

ANDIRONS
71

BARNABAS EDMANDS (1778–1872)
CHARLESTOWN,
MASSACHUSETTS, CA. 1799–1811

BRASS (COPPER 77.34, ZINC 19.27,
LEAD 1.35, TIN 1.22,
SILVER 0.18, IRON 0.12), IRON
H. 14 1/4" (36.2 CM), W. 10" (20.4 CM),
D. 16 3/4" (42.5 CM)
59.132.1, .2

BARNABAS EDMANDS was a sixth-generation American descended from Walter Edmands, a London-born distiller who arrived in Concord, Massachusetts, in 1639.[48] His father was a housewright, so Barnabas must have learned brass founding under the instruction of another craftsman, most likely in Boston.

The precise date he commenced business for himself is unknown, but it was probably around 1799. Shortly thereafter he took Thomas Whittemore as an apprentice. The foundry business seems to have lost its appeal, however, for Edmands gave it up by 1811, when he purchased a stoneware manufactory with his brother-in-law, William Burroughs.[49]

Only andirons are presently documentable to his short career as a brass worker. The illustrated pair is typical of his work and is quite similar to those of his competitors William C. Hunneman, James Davis, and John Molineux. Their diminutive size indicates they were most likely intended for use in a chamber rather than a parlor. The two parts of the upright are vertically seamed. The two cabriole legs are cast as a unit, being hollow and unfinished on the back, also typical of Edmands's and other Boston brass founders' work.

ANDIRONS

72

MURDOCK PARLOR GRATE COMPANY
BOSTON, MASSACHUSETTS, 1875–CA. 1903
BRASS (COPPER 78.91, ZINC 17.81,
LEAD 1.27, TIN 1.07), IRON

H. 16 1/2" (41.9 CM), W. 10 1/2"
(26.0 CM), D. 20 1/2" (52.1 CM)
67.959.1, .2

WARREN MURDOCK COMMENCED BUSINESS as an ironmonger and merchant in Boston in 1834. In 1842 he took Lewis Bullard into partnership. The two are listed together in the city directories until 1848, when the former may have retired or withdrawn from active participation. Bullard continued to operate the firm until 1875, when it was incorporated as the Murdock Parlor Grate Company, under which name it remained until about 1903, when it was renamed the Murdock Corporation.[50]

One of the firm's trade catalogues issued about 1890 indicates that they were specializing in the production of household heating apparatus, with the manufactory located in Middleborough, Plymouth County, Massachusetts, and the wareroom at 18 Beacon Street in Boston.[51] The catalogue pictures numerous brass and iron andirons, grates, and stoves. Other hearth accessories including fenders, cordwood boxes,

coal hods, fire screens, bellows, hearth brushes, and jamb hooks are also offered.

The andirons shown here are on page thirty of the catalogue and were offered in two sizes—seventeen inches high at $8 and twenty inches high at $9. They were also available with curved billet bars at a cost of $12, as pictured on page thirty-seven.

This pair of andirons consists of a cast one-piece leg element held to the billet bar with two pan-head bolts. They are surmounted by a single-piece hollow seamless baluster shaft, which is held in place with an internal drawn iron rod threaded at both ends. A brass finial screws to the upper end, while the lower end is held in place with a hexagonal nut. The brass billet bar covers are of thin rolled sheet.

COAL GRATE
73

ENGLAND, PROBABLY LONDON, 1720–50
BRASS (COPPER 76.29, ZINC 18.50,
LEAD 2.89, TIN 0.85, IRON 0.78,
ANTIMONY 0.13), IRON

H. 20" (50.8 CM), W. 18 1/8" (46.0 CM),
D. 16 1/8" (41.0 CM)
63.643

THE CABRIOLE-SHAPE UPRIGHTS of this grate closely follow the form of legs on side chairs, arm chairs, and easy chairs made in England between 1710 and 1740. Their "waving line, or line of beauty, being composed of two curves contrasted [was considered to be most] ornamental and pleasing." By adding cabriole ornaments to the front of this grate, the anonymous maker created a stylish artifact. As observed by the prolific social commentator William Hogarth, in mid eighteenth-century England "there is scarce a room in any house, whatever, where one does not see the waving-line employ'd in some way or other."[52]

Scallop shells with pendant honeysuckle were often carved on the knees of English cabriole chair legs during the first half of the eighteenth century. They, too, have been transferred with the uprights to the front of this grate, inasmuch as shells were believed to be suitable for "entertaining the eye with the pleasure of variety."[53]

Basket grates of this type were used to burn peat, wood, or sea coal, so called because it was shipped by sea from the coal fields of Northumberland and South Wales to England's major port cities. English coal was also shipped to America, as with the "46 tons of best house coals" that arrived in Philadelphia aboard the *Levant* from Liverpool.[54] As in England, coal was burned in containers like the "Fashionable Chamber or Parlor Grate" offered for sale in the *Boston Gazette* on December 6, 1736.

COAL GRATE
74

ENGLAND, POSSIBLY LONDON, 1760–80
BRASS (COPPER 74.51, ZINC 17.93,
LEAD 4.82, TIN 1.82, IRON 0.65,
ANTIMONY 0.14, SILVER 0.11), IRON

H. 26" (66.0 CM), W. 31 1/8" (79.1 CM),
D. 14 3/4" (37.5 CM)
60.384
GIFT OF JOHN JUDKYN

PLATES 90 AND 91 in Thomas Chippendale's *Gentleman and Cabinet-Maker's Director* picture eight coal grates. In discussing them, the author states that "I would recommend the ornamental Parts to be of wrought Brass, and as they may be made to take off, will be easily cleaned." Chippendale was not the only author to offer designs for stylish fireplace grates. Similar examples are pictured by Robert Sayer under the guise of a society of craftsmen and tradesmen in *Household Furniture in Genteel Taste for the Year 1762*. William Ince and John Mayhew also included grates in *The Universal System of Household Furniture*.[55]

Stove or coal grates properly fitted into an English fireplace were always accompanied by a fender designed en suite. While most have frets pierced with abstract geometric or stylized foliate motifs, the example shown here incorporates uncommon winged dragons that appear to be modeled after a similar design in Sayer's book.[56]

Another unusual feature in the design of this grate is the pointed ogee arch in the front feet. Such arches are pictured on many of the stove grates in *The Stove-Grate Makers Assistant* published in London in 1771. It may, therefore, be a design element attributable to that publication's author, the stove-grate maker William Glossop. He and his competitors found an active market not only in England but also in America through hardware merchants like Walter and Thomas Buchannan of New York City, who, in 1767, "just imported . . . from Glasgow . . . brass mounted grates, with shovels and tongs."[57]

COAL GRATE

75

PETER JACKSON (D. 1829)
NEW YORK CITY, 1820–29
BRASS (COPPER 70.75, ZINC 25.29, LEAD 3.05,
TIN 0.65, SILVER 0.10, IRON 0.10), IRON

H. 25 3/4" (65.4 CM), W. 33"
(83.8 CM), D. 10 3/4" (27.3 CM)
83.175

IN 1790 Alexander Hamilton observed that "fossil coal . . . as an article of household fuel . . . is an interesting production; the utility of which must increase in proportion to the decrease of wood." By 1845 it was noted that "the grate has become an essential part of our chimney fireplaces, since coal has been the general fuel." Although andirons continued to be used extensively in less populous areas, coal grates appeared in increasing numbers in town houses during the early nineteenth century, burning imported "Liverpool, Orrel & New Castle Coal of a superior quality selected expressly for family use."[58]

Peter Jackson was one of many smiths who foresaw the growing demand for these heating fixtures, advertising himself as a gratemaker and fendermaker, rather than general blacksmith or founder, when he first appeared in the New York City directories

in 1820. Within a decade he was joined by James L., Jesse, George R., Nathan H., William, and William H. Jackson. All seem to have worked within a loose confederation in which each had his own address. By 1854, however, most had consolidated under the name of William Jackson and Son, "manufacturers and dealers in every variety of Plain, Enameled and German Silver Parlor Grates and Fenders." By 1884 it was noted that "the sole surviving proprietor [of that firm was] Peter Jackson, who is held in the highest estimation in social and mercantile life."[59]

The illustrated grate, designed to be built into the masonry of a fireplace and probably missing its ash pan and fender, is one of Jackson's earliest productions. It has decorative sheet-metal uprights with cast finials seamed in halves vertically.[60]

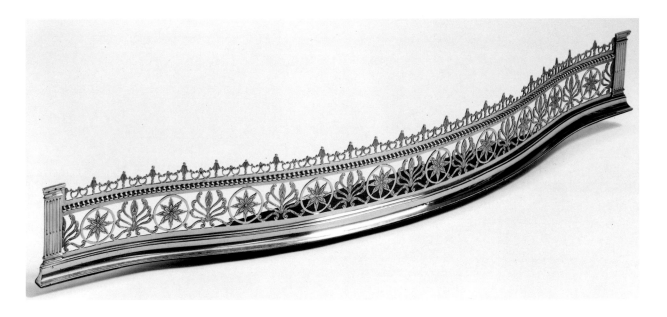

FRET FENDER

76

ENGLAND, PROBABLY LONDON OR
BIRMINGHAM, 1770–90
BRASS (COPPER 59.64, ZINC 35.24,
IRON 2.62, SILVER 1.95, TIN 0.49), IRON

L. 50" (127.0 CM), H. 7 1/2"
(19.0 CM), D. 13 1/4" (33.6 CM)
61.849

ROBERT AND JAMES ADAM "adopted a beautiful variety of light mouldings, gracefully formed, delicately enriched and arranged with propriety and skill" for the decoration of their clients' houses. In 1778 they published the first volume of their work, which they felt would be useful not only in formulating "designs in architecture, but also in every kind of ornamental furniture."[61]

A stylized honeysuckle blossom and patera—a circular or oval flowerlike ornament—figured prominently in many of their designs, as with the "chimney piece . . . for one of the rooms in St. James Palace." The opening is surrounded with a prominently displayed and well-detailed border of anthemia. The fender shown here is

of the type that the brothers would have designed to place in front of it. The profile is purposely curved in accordance with the Adams' belief that curvilinear outlines "blend and mingle themselves more harmoniously . . . and attain more delicacy and elegance." Each end is defined with a counter-fluted pier, "one of the noblest and most graceful pieces of decoration," which is riveted to the single piece cast fret.[62] The sheet-iron pan was later enlarged with another fitted section, probably at the same time the five Marlboro feet were added.

FRET FENDER
77

UNITED STATES OR ENGLAND, 1780–1800
BRASS (COPPER 77.00, ZINC 20.90,
LEAD 1.00, TIN 0.56), IRON

H. 9 1/8" (23.2 CM), L. 50"
(127.0 CM), D. 9 1/4" (23.5 CM)
58.2477

IN 1803 Thomas Sheraton observed that "frets are used to fill up and enrich flat empty spaces. [They are often] cast in brass, which is doubtless much to the advantage of the work, as they are both durable and pleasing to the eye."[63]

Fretwork was commonly incorporated into fireplace fenders—for both decorative and practical reasons—by myriad craftsmen who specialized as fendermakers in Birmingham, Sheffield, Wolverhampton, Walsall, Stockport, and other lesser English cities.[64] Some of them left England, such as "Richard Skellhorn brass founder late from London," who advertised in *Rivington's New-York Gazetteer* on May 18, 1775, that he "makes and sells . . . brass andirons [and] fret fenders . . . from the newest patterns now in vogue in London."

The fender shown here is cast in five units, which are held together with rivets and iron braces. The central section is ornamented with a pierced and chased oval design of Neptune with his trident in a horse-drawn chariot. Classical subjects of this type were popular during the late eighteenth century, and the maker may have been inspired by Josiah Wedgwood, who was among their most active proponents. Beginning in 1759, Wedgwood produced a large body of widely marketed, influential porcelain plaques and medallions featuring mythological and antique subjects. Some of these were intended to be set into mantels. Listed among the offerings in his first catalogue, published in 1773, was "Neptune upon his chariot drawn by four sea horses," which may have served as the inspiration for the primary ornament on this fender.[65]

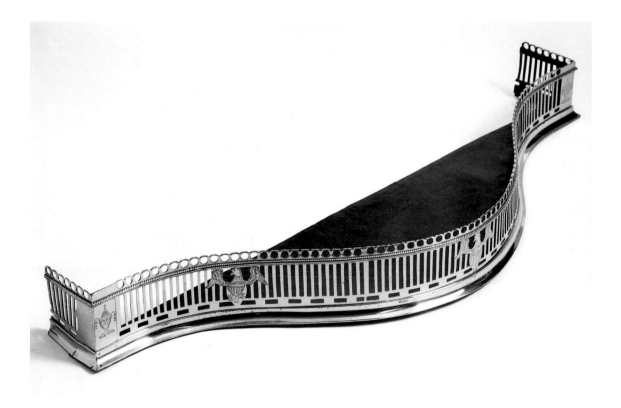

FRET FENDER

78

PROBABLY UNITED STATES, 1785–1810
BRASS (COPPER 77.77, ZINC 14.07,
LEAD 3.37, TIN 3.05, IRON 0.53, SILVER
0.33, ANTIMONY, 0.14), IRON

H. 6 1/8" (15.6 CM), L. 56 1/2" (143.5 CM),
D. 15 3/4" (40.0 CM)
61.605

ON JULY 4, 1776, the Continental Congress established a committee "to bring in a device for a seal of the United States of
America." During the following six years, the motif of a displayed
or spread eagle with shield-shape body, holding an olive branch
in one talon and arrows in the other, evolved. The final design,
created largely by Charles Thomson and William Barton, was
approved by Congress on June 20, 1782. That design, slightly
modified, forms the principal iconography of the fender
illustrated here.[66]

    The fender itself consists of three cast sections–each centered
with an eagle–brazed end to end. A cove molding has been riveted along the bottom length, and a gadroon molding is similarly
attached near the top. The fender measures only six inches
in height and is pierced with numerous rectangular and circular
holes because "fenders should not be higher than safety requires
as they thus stop much of the radiant heat of the fire, and that where
it is most wanted, namely, in the lower part of the room, and
keep it from the feet: to prevent this, they are always made with
some open work."[67]

    While brass fret fenders were imported from England during
the eighteenth century, they were made by Americans as well. One
of these men, "John Barrett begs leave to inform the Publick . . .
that he makes all sorts of Brass Founders work in the neatest and
best manner, such as . . . fenders and fronts for graits."[68]

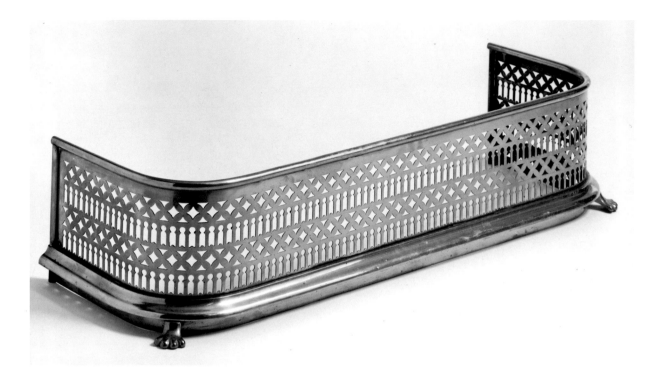

FRET FENDER
79

PROBABLY BIRMINGHAM, ENGLAND,
POSSIBLY UNITED STATES, 1820–60
BRASS (COPPER 89.93, ZINC 23.80,
LEAD 0.72, TIN 0.30)

H. 8" (20.3 CM), L. 36 1/8"
(91.7 CM), D. 12" (30.5 CM)
77.232
GIFT OF
CHARLES VAN RAVENSWAAY

"THE FIRST FENDERS were mere bent pieces of sheet iron, placed in front of the fire, to prevent . . . cinders from rolling . . . upon the wooden floors. Fashion and ingenuity, however . . . combined [by the 1820s] in the production of that elegant and standard ornament of the hearth, the polished cut [brass] fender."[69]

"The rich and varied open work exhibited in . . . these . . . is produced by . . . the fly-press [using] loose dies and [two] perforated plates" in a technique known as book piercing. The perforations in the plates vary according to the desired pattern for the piercing in the fender, in this instance, alternating rows of x's and arches. The loose dies are shaped to fit precisely in these holes. After placing the brass sheet between the two plates, the entire assembly is put in the press. Using the momentum of heavy weights, the dies are forced through the holes in the plates. In doing so, they punch corresponding holes in the brass sheet. Following that, "the [sheet is] rearranged, and another stroke is made [and] repeated until the perforation of the [sheet] is completed throughout its length."[70]

With that finished, the fender front is "buffed on a leather covered wheel with sand . . . then bent into the shape desired, and . . . finished by the riveting of a tube of brass drawn upon an iron rod, along the top and in like manner by affixing . . . a molding . . . upon the bottom. The whole is usually supported upon . . . lackered claw or ball feet."[71]

WIRE FENDER

80

ENGLAND OR UNITED STATES, 1790–1840
BRASS (COPPER 79.19, ZINC 18.05, TIN
1.27, LEAD 1.17, IRON 0.26), IRON

H. 15 1/4" (38.7 CM),
L. 54 1/4" (137.8 CM),
D. 16" (40.6 CM)
58.1712

EARLY "FENDERS WERE . . . very low, to correspond with the wood fires on the dogs. . . . The cheapest [were made] of wire painted and with iron or brass tops and bottoms."[72] This accurately describes wire fireplace fenders, which were made in great quantity in both England and the United States from the late eighteenth through the nineteenth centuries.

Numerous examples pictured in a trade catalogue owned by Winterthur are described as "green wire fenders" and priced "per foot" in length.[73] The least expensive were entirely of iron with the wires perfectly straight, upright, and parallel. If the wires were interlaced into a more elaborate pattern, the price increased. Thin-sheet brass coverings on the top and bottom rails also added to the cost, as did cast brass finials and feet.

Fenders are rarely marked by their maker, and there seems to be little apparent difference between those made in England and the United States. Consequently, assigning a country of origin to any given example is problematic. The uprights of the fender pictured here are rectangular in cross section, a feature normally assigned to English-made examples. The fender also uses brass wire to hold the iron wire fabric to the frame, an uncommon feature. Most fenders use iron wire throughout. Although undocumentable, this use of brass wire might indicate an English origin, in light of the availability of "brass wire fenders" in English trade catalogues.[74]

WIRE FENDER
81

UNITED STATES OR ENGLAND,
1790–1840

BRASS (COPPER 75.29, ZINC 21.24,
LEAD 1.55, TIN 0.96, IRON 0.30), IRON

H. 14 1/4" (36.2 CM), L. 40 1/2"
(102.9 CM), D. 14 1/2" (36.9 CM)

59.520

IN 1794 THE PHILADELPHIA brass founder Daniel King, or his son of the same name, advertised that he had "for sale, a neat assortment of fashionable green fenders, with brass mouldings." That same year in Boston, Joseph De Blois offered "fire fenders with brass tops, from 4 1/2 to 5 feet long, some very high to prevent children from falling into the fire."[75]

King and De Blois were just two of many men in the United States and England who met the demand for wire fireplace fenders. Some made numerous other wire household objects as well. John Cluley, who owned a wire-fender manufactory at 17 South Fourth Street in Philadelphia from 1805 to 1823, sold "WIRE MEAT SAFES, to keep out flies, BRASS WIRE WORK, for Libraries, Book Cases &c, Neat and Durable WIRE FENCE, for Gardens and

Pleasure Grounds, Neat WIRE BIRD-CAGES, of all sorts, WIRE-WORK for Aviaries, Cellar Windows, &c, SCREENS for Gravel, Lime, &c, Land-Chains, RAT and MOUSE TRAPS &c."[76]

Wire workers rarely marked their fireplace fenders, making attribution difficult. Even so, the cylindrical cross section of the uprights in this fender has been traditionally assigned American authorship. That feature, coupled with the acorn-shape finials, which relate closely to finials on American andirons, handles on fire tools, and fonts on oil lamps, might support an American attribution for this fender.[77]

CURFEW
82

NORTHERN EUROPE OR ENGLAND,
1742
COPPER, IRON

H. 16 1/2" (41.9 CM), W. 23"
(58.4 CM), D. 11 7/8" (28.0 CM)
61.1318

IN 1785 THOMAS JOHNSON described the curfew as "an evening-peal [of bells] by which [William] the Conqueror willed that every man should rake up his fire, and put out his light; so that in many places, at this day, where a bell is customarily rung toward bedtime, it is said to ring curfew." He listed the word's second definition as "a cover for a fire."[78] Even so, the use of those covers had apparently become so rare that many observers of English customs at that time refused to believe the form had ever existed.

William Hone, who wrote a two-volume book on English habits during the early nineteenth century, was intrigued with the question and pursued its answer until he found a published interview of a man who owned a curfew that he claimed had belonged to his ancestors for generations. The owner stated that it was "called a curfew, or couvre-feu, from its use, which is that of suddenly putting out a fire: the method of applying it was thus;—the wood and embers were raked as close as possible to the back of the hearth, and then the curfew was put over them, the open part placed close to the back of the chimney; by this contrivance, the air being almost totally excluded, the fire was of course extinguished." His curfew, like the example shown here, "is of copper, rivetted together, as solder would have been liable to melt with the heat." He also observed that "it is 10 inches high, 16 inches wide and 9 inches deep [and that] some others of this kind are still remaining in Kent and Sussex" counties.[79]

The repoussé ornament surrounding the date on this example follows French prototype and is closely related to a design by Paul Van Somer published in London in the 1740s as part of Thomas Bowles's *Compleat Book of Ornaments*.[80]

DOUBLE BELLOWS
83

ENGLAND, 1800–1830
BRASS (COPPER 66.69,
ZINC 31.34, LEAD 1.70), WOOD,
LEATHER, FABRIC, PAINT

L. 20 3/8" (51.8 CM), W. 6 5/8"
(16.8 CM),
D. 2 3/4" (7.0 CM)
58.2481

"THE DOUBLE BELLOWS is mostly used for the forge; but it is occasionally employed in a portable form in the same way as the single . . . there is another board in the space between the upper and lower ones; and there is a valve opening upward [in it]. By this means a continuous blast is produced; but this construction is generally too heavy for domestic use."[81]

The handsomely painted double bellows with silk-covered leather illustrated here is light in weight and was made for no other than parlor use. It is constructed as described above, but the third board is outside the two with handles. Another unusual feature is the pipe, which is made of seamed sheet metal. Bellows pipes were usually cast hollow in halves and then brazed together.

Although pipes could be readily made by the general founder, they were often the product of a specialist, such as George Field, "bellows pipe maker," and his competitor Joseph Boyce. These men sold their wares to the bellowsmaker, who made and decorated the boards, attached the leather, and fitted the pipe. They, in turn, would offer their products for sale retail or through a fancy hardware merchant such as Benjamin Taylor of Philadelphia, who had "a large assortment of elegant Patent Japanned Convex and Flat-top, Satin-wood, Bird-eye, Cherry, Walnut, and Gum, Turned-top, Common, Kitchen, and Smith's bellows, of any required size . . . in his store at 90½ North Front Street."[82]

BELLOWS

84

JOHN ECKSTEIN AND ROSS B. RICHARDSON
PHILADELPHIA, PENNSYLVANIA, 1818–23
BRASS (COPPER 71.43, ZINC 26.61, LEAD 1.09,
TIN 0.70), WOOD, LEATHER, PAINT

L. 18 5/8" (47.3 CM), W. 6 1/2"
(16.5 CM),
D. 3 3/8" (8.5 CM)
59.685

"To MAKE A WOOD FIRE, lay a large . . . stick across the andirons, and upon it, place the live coals and chunks for kindling. Then pile on two or three other sticks, take the bellows and blow the fire into a flame till the wood is well ignited."[83]

As seen in this recommendation, the bellows were helpful to efficiently start a fire and were an essential part of the well-equipped fireplace. Consequently, numerous men supplied "brass and iron pipe bellows" to householders. One of these was Ross B. Richardson, a brushmaker in Philadelphia who, on August 22, 1817, was granted a United States patent for "japanned bellows." One year later he and John Eckstein, another brushmaker, opened a bellows manufactory at 36 North Third Street, where they offered

"a large stock of common bellows of various sizes; Bird-eye, Curled Maple, Mahogany, Cherry, Satinwood and Gum Chamber Bellows; [and] Elegant Convex Japanned Parlor Bellows (for which they have Letters Patent)."[84]

Richardson's specifications for this patent were lost when the Patent Office burned in 1839, but his stressing the convex shape of the upper board and japanned finish suggests the improvement had something to do with these two features. These bellows otherwise appear similar in design and construction to those of their competitors.[85]

BLOWER
85

ENGLAND, 1820–50
BRASS (COPPER 65.00, ZINC 34.50,
LEAD 0.30), IRON, WOOD, PAINT

L. 27 3/4" (70.5 CM), W. 9 5/8"
(24.4 CM), H. 9 1/4" (23.5 CM)
57.789

"EVERY GRATE SHOULD BE FURNISHED with a poker, shovel, tongs, blower, coal-scuttle and holder for the blower. The latter may be made of woolen covered with old silk, and hung near the fire." The author of this passage was referring to "a great improvement on the double bellows, producing a continuous blast [by means of] a circular fan . . . driven round by a wheel. Air enters at the holes on the sides and . . . is expelled in a continuous stream through the tube."[86]

This device seems to be principally associated with the coal grate, although it might on occasion have been used to start wood fires as well. The strength of its constant stream of air, however, "if used injudiciously, sometimes puts the fire out." Although its merits are acknowledged, its use was recommended only with reservation. As stated by Robert Roberts in his directions for making a fire of Lehigh or anthracite coal, "If you are in a hurry [to kindle a fire] put up the

blower; if not do not use it, for the hard coal kindles much better without forcing. The blower makes a quicker fire but a worse one."[87]

The United States Patent Office records that a coal-grate blower was patented by Robert Fuller and Thomas Thomas, gratemakers in New York City, on May 27, 1827. Its specifications did not survive the Patent Office fire of 1839. Fortunately, details of a similar British effort do survive. British patent 6365 for "certain improvements in blowing machines" was issued to Alexander Clark of North Wales on July 11, 1833. Although his drawings detail a fan driven by friction, he did "not intend to confine [his patent] to that mode, as a toothed wheel and pinion may be employed . . . or the fan may be driven by a band and pulley." The example shown here operates using the latter mechanism, while another in the Winterthur collection uses a variant of the former.[88]

COAL SCUTTLE
86

PROBABLY WILLIAM C. HUNNEMAN (1769–1856),
POSSIBLY WILLIAM C. HUNNEMAN, JR.,
OR SAMUEL H. HUNNEMAN
BOSTON, MASSACHUSETTS, 1799–1825
COPPER, IRON, BRASS (COPPER 82.69, ZINC 7.72,
LEAD 5.80, TIN 3.04, IRON 0.55, SILVER 0.13)

H. 15 1/2" (38.1 CM),
W. 13" (33.0 CM),
L. 18 1/2" (47.0 CM)
91.1

IN 1845 THOMAS WEBSTER observed that "the grate has become an essential part of our chimney fireplaces, since coal has been the general fuel."[89] A proper coal fire needed a number of implements different from those used with a wood fire, including the grate, poker, blower, and hod. The last of these, also known as a scuttle or scoop, and typically in the form of a lipped bucket, was used to carry, store, and dispense coal.

"Bright copper coal scoops have been considered an adornment for the parlor, as well as a necessary accompanying adjunct for the fireside, as long as any article which has been wrought out from" the metal. They were in use in America as early as 1770. The estate of Norborne Berkeley, Baron de Botetourt and royal governor of Virginia, inventoried in that year,

included "2 Copp.r coal scuttles."[90] Scuttles were made in a variety of shapes, the simplest being a vertical cylinder with handle.

The body and foot of this hod are made of sheets of rolled copper assembled with a combination of cramped and brazed dovetailed joints. The edges are wired. The bail is a seamed tube held in place with thick sheet-metal brackets, while the tilting handle is cast brass.

Coal hods like this require "as much art and painstaking care as . . . any other thing upon which the brazier has been called to exercise his skill. There is however little profit in coal scoops; that is, in those ordinarily in use, for they were among the goods which were paid the least for, considering the labor

necessary to produce them in such a manner as the purchaser desired. On this account men sought the assistance of a good careful boy when the opportunity offered, and in this labor a pathway was opened for the boy which was closed in other instances where better wages were given for the work."[91]

Two surviving William Hunneman account books record his production for a portion of his career. They include entries dating from 1793 to 1821. Among the hundreds of objects listed are a "copper coal hod" sold to John Bazine (Bazin, Bazen), a Boston hardware merchant, on October 5, 1809, and "1 new copper coal scoop" sold to the Boston attorney Charles Davis on December 9, 1816.[92] The example illustrated here might be one of those.

COAL SCUTTLE
87

RETAILED BY
DANIEL E. DELAVAN (1808–70)
AND BROTHERS
NEW YORK CITY, 1827–49
COPPER, BRASS, IRON

H. 14 1/2" (36.8 CM), W. 11 1/8"
(28.2 CM), D. 17 1/8" (43.8 CM)
93.2

THE DELAVANS–Robert I., Henry C., Charles H., Christian S., and Daniel E.–were in business in New York City at various addresses from 1827 to the 1870s. They were located at 489 Broadway between 1827 and 1849 only and always listed themselves during that twenty-two-year period as hardwaremen. The use of that term without exception strongly suggests they were middle-men, not coppersmiths. The variety of their offerings would have been substantial, including "Silver Plated ware, Table Cutlery, Planished Tin-ware, Bathing Apparatus, Japanned Iron and Tin-Ware, Brass & Copper Utensils, Brushes, Brooms, Wooden-ware, Willow-Ware, Refrigerators . . . & c."[93]

Coal scuttles of copper, brass, or japanned sheet iron were in demand as house-furnishing hardware at the time the Delavans were active. Their great popularity fostered the production of various designs. The type shown here, with pear-shape body and arched spout on molded footrim, was known as the helmet. It "was considered at one time by old braziers as the summit of excel-lence in this line [which demanded] proficiency and a long, careful training with much patience to acquire the skill necessary for the execution of the various steps through which [it must] pass to completion."[94] Hammering the compound curves of the body and footrim from one piece of metal required great skill.

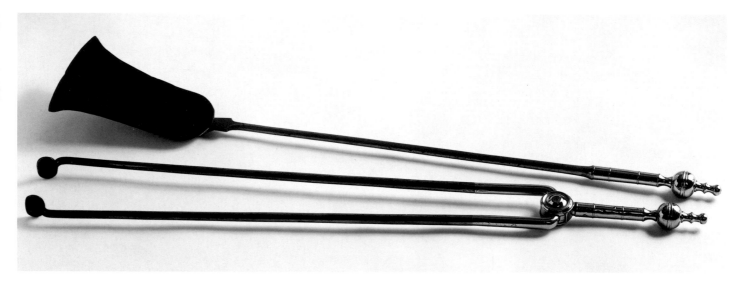

SHOVEL AND TONGS

88

PROBABLY RICHARD WHITTINGHAM,
JR. (B. 1776),
POSSIBLY RICHARD WHITTINGHAM (1747–1821)
NEW YORK CITY, 1807–55
BRASS (COPPER 78.80, ZINC 18.70,
LEAD 1.68, TIN 0.40), IRON

SHOVEL: L. 37 7/8" (96.2 CM), W. 7 5/8"
(19.4 CM), D. 2 5/8" (6.7 CM);
TONGS: L. 37 1/4" (94.6 CM), W. 3"
(7.6 CM), D. 1 3/4" (4.5 CM)
61.851.1, .2

RICHARD WHITTINGHAM, JR., followed his father's profession, commencing business as a brass founder in New York in 1807. He was apparently a good craftsman and businessman, for his career spanned forty-eight years, and numerous well-designed and well-made andirons bear his name.

On June 8, 1821, he was issued a patent for "tongs, fire irons, &c" by the United States Patent Office. Eighteen years later the specifications for that patent were destroyed when the Patent Office burned. Inventors were immediately invited to resubmit, but Whittingham did not, so the details of his invention are cur-

rently unknown. Some of his fire tools are identifiable, however, since he was one of a few founders to mark his work. He used the same name stamps on the tips of his log tongs and andirons.[95]

Whittingham also designed the handles of his fire tools to match the uprights of the andirons. The illustrated shovel and tongs and another pair of marked tongs in the Winterthur collection match two pairs of marked andirons also owned by the museum.[96] The brass handles, cast hollow in halves and seamed, are miniature versions of the andiron uprights in style and construction.

SHOVEL AND
TONGS
89

DAVID PHILLIPS (D. 1818)
NEW YORK CITY, 1806–18
BRASS (COPPER 76.70, ZINC 21.30,
LEAD 1.24, TIN 0.49), IRON

SHOVEL: L. 29 1/4" (74.3 CM),
W. 6 1/4" (15.8 CM);
TONGS: L. 29 1/2" (74.9 CM),
W. 2 1/4" (5.7 CM)
67.37.1, .2

DAVID PHILLIPS FIRST LISTED HIMSELF in the New York City directory in 1802, recording his profession as blockmaker or pulleymaker. He continued to list himself annually thereafter but changed his profession to brass founding in 1806. He remained a brass founder at 65 Division Street and later at 112 Henry Street until his death in 1818.

His estate was inventoried on August 19, 1818, by Richard Whittingham and Benjamin Thomas, brass founder and shopkeeper, respectively.[97] They listed on seven pages a total of 763 shovels, 488 pairs of tongs, and 29 pokers in various stages of completion. Each is grouped into units described as "size 1," "size 2," "size 3," and "old pattern." Listed separately are 94 shovel pans and 199 tong pins. Shovels, tongs, and pokers with lower numbers were priced more cheaply than those assigned a higher number, the price differential being related to weight.

The 131 pairs of andirons in his inventory are similarly grouped into "size 1," "size 2," "size 3," "size 4," "size 5," and "Philadelphia pattern." Aside from the obvious exceptions of the "old" and "Philadelphia" patterns, there is no evidence in the inventory listings that Phillips was making a large variety of andiron and fire-tool styles. Most examples marked by him conform in appearance to the tools that are illustrated here and another pair of marked tongs in the Winterthur collection. Aside from one entry in his inventory that reads "10 pr brass knockers," the stock in his shop consisted entirely of andirons and fire tools, strongly suggesting that he specialized in fireplace equipment.[98]

The brass handles of these tools were designed en suite with Phillips's andirons, of which a number are recorded that have uprights with the same graduated elements decorated with beaded borders. Additionally, these brass handles are cast hollow in halves vertically, brazed together, and peened to an internal iron rod, as was done with matching andiron uprights, which were threaded to an internal iron rod.

SHOVEL AND TONGS
90

PROBABLY BOSTON, MASSACHUSETTS, 1785–1810 BRASS (COPPER 87.74, ZINC 6.40, LEAD 3.34, TIN 1.82, ANTIMONY 0.16, SILVER 0.11), IRON

TONGS: L. 32 1/2" (82.5 CM), W. 2 5/8" (6.7 CM); SHOVEL: L. 31 1/8" (79.0 CM), W. 7 3/4" (19.7 CM) 58.2478,.2479

THE HANDLES OF THIS SHOVEL and tongs and another similar set at Winterthur are cast hollow in halves and seamed vertically. They are held in place with an internal iron rod that is peened on the end. This construction is typical of eighteenth- and early nineteenth-century English and American fire-iron handles. In the industrial centers of England they were made by specialists who called themselves fire-iron makers, but in America brass founders like William Coffin made and sold such items including "Knockers for Doors, Brasses for Chaises and Sadlers, Brass Doggs of all Sorts, Candlesticks, Shovels and Tongs, Small Bells, and all sorts of Founders ware."[99]

The tools shown here are unmarked, but they bear a stylistic relationship to attributed Boston andirons, which suggests they were made in that city. A Boston attribution is further supported by the presence

of the initials of retailer John Coffin Jones (1750–1829) stamped inside the pads of the log tongs and on the back of the shovel pan support.[100]

Jones was a prominent Boston merchant active in the Maine coastal trade. He "settled into a Boston store from which he sent supplies to a branch managed in Machias," Maine, by a cousin. Because of his extensive privateering, international and local business connections, and political activity, he was among those who voted to ratify the federal constitution on February 7, 1788. "It was [also] Jones who led the section of 'Merchants & Traders' in the welcoming procession . . . when President Washington visited Boston" in 1789.[101]

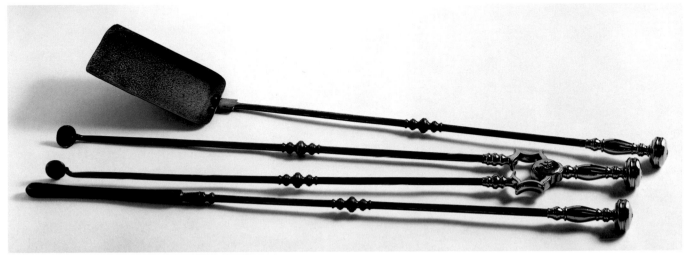

SHOVEL, TONGS,
POKER

91

POSSIBLY PEARSON-PAGE COMPANY
(1897–1933)
ENGLAND, PROBABLY BIRMINGHAM,
1897 1900
BRASS (COPPER 73.78, ZINC 20.45, LEAD 4.26,
TIN 1.04, IRON 0.25, SILVER 0.12), STEEL

TONGS: L. 36 1/4" (92.1 CM), W. 4 1/8" (10.5 CM);
SHOVEL: L. 36 1/2" (92.7 CM),
W. 5 5/8" (14.3 CM);
POKER: L. 36 3/8" (92.4 CM),
DIAM. 1 7/8" (4.8 CM)
61.602.1–.3

THESE FIRE TOOLS and another related pair at Winterthur are hand-somely designed, well finished, eminently functional, and embellished with a variant of the great seal of the United States.[102] All these features gave them particular appeal for late nineteenth-century Americans who were acutely aware of their country's centennial and the country's grow-ing industrial character.

The latter, while lauded, generated a wave of nostalgia for life in a seemingly simpler time with its attendant trappings, like the "beloved old-time fire-place, with its hospitable warmth and eye-and-heart-delighting glow." Although household heating had progressed significantly dur-ing the nineteenth century from open fireplaces to central heating, it was noted by the 1870s that "much has been done of late to re-instate the open fire in public favor."[103]

Many thought American fireplaces were best furnished with English hardware and agreed with the tastemaker Clarence Cook, who urged

householders to buy English fire grates. "The English grates I am praising come provided with the prettiest appendages in the shape of andirons, brass shovels, tongs, and pokers."[104]

The Pearson-Page Company of Birmingham and London was one of England's largest brass-working firms from the mid nineteenth through the early twentieth centuries. The company had an extensive domestic market but also produced household wares exclusively for the United States. The firm retailed these through affiliates such as the Skinner-Hill Company in New York City.

Following long-established Birmingham brass-manfacturing tradi-tion, the company published trade catalogues that pictured their wares. Number 10658 pictures a shovel, tongs, and poker closely related to this entry. They were offered "polished bright or [with a] special old finish. A specialty of [theirs] in great demand as it harmonizes very well with Reproduction and Antique Furniture in vogue today."[105]

WARMING PAN
92

PROBABLY HOLLAND, POSSIBLY
ENGLAND, 1670–1720
BRASS (COPPER 70.79, ZINC 27.69,
LEAD 1.07, IRON 0.18), IRON

L. 42 1/2" (107.9 CM), DIAM. 13 1/4"
(33.6 CM), H. 4 5/8" (11.7 CM)
58.1116

MANY WARMING PANS for beds were made by braziers throughout northern Europe, England, and America during the seventeenth, eighteenth, and early nineteenth centuries. They were not necessarily a familiar bedroom implement, however, as recorded in the journal of the Scot John Harrower when he traveled to London in 1774. On January 12 he took a room at a tavern near Portsmouth. He wrote in his journal that following supper, he "paid 3d for my bed, and it was warmed with a warming pan, this being the first time I ever seed it done."[106]

While warming pans were specifically designed to drive the cold and moisture out of bedsheets with hot coals, travelers who were familiar with them might also be surpised at their various uses, as was the case with Alexander Hamilton, a Scot who traveled in America in the 1740s. In the midst of eating supper at a tavern outside New York City, his "landlady called for the bed-

pan. [He recalled that] I could not guess what she intended to do with it unless it was to warm her bed to go to sleep after dinner, but I found that it was by way of a chaffing dish to warm our dish of clams" that she wished to use it.[107]

The bedwarmer pictured here is unmarked but is closely related to myriad Dutch examples in that its lid is ornamented with piercing, chasing, and repoussé work. English and American warming-pan lids are embellished with less decoration, which usually consists of piercing and chasing only.

The pan is made, like most, of relatively thin sheet metal. It is hung from and riveted to a thick, flat iron collar attached to the end of the handle. Also attached to the handle is the widely overhanging sheet-metal lid, which is reinforced at the edge by being wrapped around an iron wire.

WARMING PAN
93

MARKED "I:ST"
ENGLAND, PROBABLY LONDON, 1730–60
BRASS (COPPER 66.70, ZINC 31.00,
LEAD 1.70), IRON

L. 49" (124.5 CM), DIAM. 11 1/2"
(29.2 CM), H. 5 1/4" (13.3 CM)
60.1140

"THE WARMING PAN should be as large at the bottom as at the top. It must shut down perfectly close, and must on no account possess those absurd, irrational holes [in the lid]. Not an exit must be allowed whereby a stray coal may expend its smoke; and this preeminent pan, being half full of clear, brisk, bright red cinders . . . must be passed hastily and sharply all over the bed, the left hand being employed in lifting and wafting the bed clothes repeatedly to allow the damp . . . to escape."[108] The warming pan shown here, which probably dates from the middle of the eighteenth century, would not have met with the above author's approval. Typical of those made during the seventeenth and early eighteenth centuries, the lid is pierced with numerous holes, closes at an oblique angle, and widely overhangs the pan. By the mid eighteenth century, lids had few or no holes and fit snugly into the rim of the pan.

This pan and three others in the Winterthur collection have iron handles, each with a large flat ring at one end into which the brass pan is fitted. The hinged lids are chased in a hexafoil pattern of clustered circles alternating with pointed petals. While all four relate closely in design and construction, only this one is marked.[109]

The maker is unknown. He may have been Dutch, suggested largely by the character of the mark, which is unusual in that it employs three letters with a colon. This type occurs on Dutch silver, exemplified by the "I:BS" mark of Johannes Bartels and the "B:DP" mark of Bernardus du Pré, both late eighteenth-century Amsterdam silversmiths. The maker, however, was more likely English, an attribution strongly supported by the existence of closely related warming pans bearing the three-initial mark of the early eighteenth-century London brazier Charles Appelby. There were also numerous other London braziers active about the same time who used three-initial marks. Among them was John Stiller, whose "IST" mark is recorded in a book of London braziers' marks believed to date from the early eighteenth century.[110]

WARMING PAN
94

ATTRIBUTED TO JOHN WELLS (D. 1832)
BOSTON, MASSACHUSETTS,
1796–1832
COPPER, WOOD

L. 41 5/16" (105.0 CM),
D. 11 1/8" (28.2 CM),
H. 4" (10.1 CM)
85.141

JOHN WELLS first listed himself as a coppersmith in the Boston city directories in 1796. He is recorded continuously after that, sometimes in partnership with Benjamin T. Wells, until 1831. He was a founding member of the Massachusetts Charitable Mechanic Association, which was organized in 1795 for the purpose of "promoting mutual good offices and fellowship . . . assisting the necessitous; encouraging the ingenious; and rewarding the faithful." The published annals of that organization, which was limited to mechanics and manufacturers, state that Wells was a native Bostonian and "carried on an extensive business" until his death on October 14, 1832.[111]

In spite of his reputed extensive business, Wells is credited with just this warming pan and another similarly marked example in the National Museum of American History. Both are fabricated in the traditional manner, being "raised up and formed from a disc. [They were made] in five sizes, namely 10, 10 1/2, 11, 11 1/2, and 12 inch" diameters.[112] As with the signed Hunneman example (see entry 95), the low-domed lid has the edge wrapped around an iron reinforcing wire. A cast handle socket serves as the element to which the pan and lid are riveted independent of each other, apparently typical of Boston warming pans. The turned wood handles of both pans seem to be original and, although not identical, are similar enough to indicate that Hunneman and Wells were supplied with warming-pan handles from a single turner.

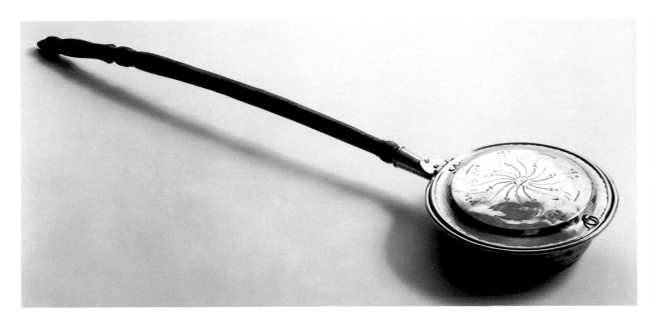

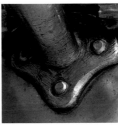

WARMING PAN

95

PROBABLY WILLIAM C. HUNNEMAN
(1769–1856),
POSSIBLY WILLIAM C. HUNNEMAN, JR.,
OR SAMUEL H. HUNNEMAN
BOSTON, MASSACHUSETTS, 1799–1825

BRASS (COPPER 71.66, ZINC 26.72,
LEAD 1.35), WOOD, COPPER, IRON
L. 41 1/2" (105.0 CM), D. 10 1/2"
(26.7 CM), H. 3 5/8" (9.2 CM)
57.581

WILLIAM C. HUNNEMAN became a junior partner to Martin Gay in the "coppersmith's and brazier's business" in Boston in 1793 at the age of twenty-four.[113] By 1797 he began working concurrently on his own as a coppersmith at Scott's Court and became fully independent by 1799.

He recorded in his business ledgers that he made a considerable quantity and variety of wares, including liquid and dry measures for the state of New Hampshire, copper tubes for the necessary on the USS *Constitution*, and a weather vane for the Randolph Meeting House. The bulk of his work, however, consisted of household objects. Among them was a warming pan purchased by Daniel Lewis, a Boston blacksmith. Another billed to John Doggett and Co., a looking-glass warehouse, hints at Hunneman's involvement in the wholesale trade.[114]

Warming pans were a staple in Hunneman's inventory, since they "were once quite largely in demand, and kept men busy at work for a considerable time during the year, as almost every household, rich or poor, possessed a warming pan."[115] In addition to their utility, warming pans were often ornamental, with pierced, repoussé, engraved, or chased decoration on the lids. The illustrated example employs a simple radiating pattern created with four different steel dies, some of which Hunneman used to decorate the lid of a similar, but unsigned, copper warming pan (see entry 96). Both the pan and lid have the edges wrapped around iron wire for reinforcement since they are made of relatively thin sheet metal. Each is separately riveted to the cast handle socket. The number 6 stamped into the lid above the maker's name, near the edge, probably indicates that it was the 6th (or 9th) warming pan that Hunneman made.

WARMING PAN
96

ATTRIBUTED TO WILLIAM C. HUNNEMAN
(1769–1856), WILLIAM C. HUNNEMAN, JR.,
OR SAMUEL H. HUNNEMAN
BOSTON, MASSACHUSETTS, 1799–1825

COPPER, WOOD, IRON
L. 41 1/2" (105.0 CM), D. 10 1/2"
(26.7 CM), H. 3 5/8" (9.2 CM)
60.186

THIS WARMING PAN bears no maker's name, but instructive parallels can be drawn between it and a signed Hunneman example (see entry 95). The pans and lids of both have the same dimensions and profile. The hinge mechanisms, except for five knuckles on this example and three on the other, are constructed identically. The rivets are shaped in the same way with extra-broad flat heads inside the thin-walled pans to help prevent them from tearing free of the handle sockets. Their cast handle sockets and flanges are identical in size, shape, and coarsely filed finish.[116]

The lid bears the stamped number 4, while the other lid has the numeral 6 in conjunction with Hunneman's name. Such numbering is uncommon, and its meaning in this instance is conjectural. It might relate to the way Hunneman marketed some of his wares. In 1821 George Baker opened a furniture commission company warehouse in Boston. Soon thereafter, Hunneman consigned some of his andirons, fenders, teakettles, and warming pans, which Baker offered for sale, "with a variety of other goods, necessary for the furnishing of houses."[117]

Yet another means for Hunneman and his sons to market their wares was through the New England Society for the Promotion of Manufactures, also in Boston. The group was incorporated in 1826 to hold semiannual "public sales and exhibitions of the products of the arts." A provision governing objects in these sales stated that they "must be distinguished by a private mark, any known or public mark being concealed."[118] If this warming pan had been sold through that society, the rules may account for the fact that its lid bears only the number 4 and not Hunneman's name.

WARMING PAN
97

PROBABLY ENGLAND, POSSIBLY
AMERICA, 1770–1810
BRASS (COPPER 68.70, ZINC 30.60,
LEAD 0.50), WOOD

L. 35 3/4" (90.8 CM), DIAM. 9 3/4"
(24.8 CM), H. 3 3/4" (9.5 CM)
62.191

HOT COALS were traditionally used to warm bedsheets dur-ing cold weather. While effective, they could quickly scorch the sheets or even set the bed afire if not watched closely.

In 1762 John Wood, a smith in York, England, claimed to have invented a warming pan that obviated this danger. He was granted patent number 778 for his ingenuity. In out-lining the details of his development, Wood stated that "the body of the warming pan or engine . . . consists of two thin circular plates . . . made hollow and . . . fastened close together, with their concave sides inward, in size and shape nearly similar to the pans now in use for warming beds with coals . . . [through a] neck or pipe a proper amount of boyling water [is] introduced by a funnel, and the neck or pipe being closed . . . the engine is to be used as other com-mon warming pans."[119]

Wood's patent specifications state that the opening was "in the border or rim" of the pan and that it was "closed with a common cork and made with a screw [to attach] a common warming pan handle." The pan shown here appears to be an improved model with its opening on top to help prevent the contents from leaking or spilling.[120]

While seemingly a significant improvement in safety over those using coals, few warming pans of this type are recorded. At least one signed American example exists. It was made by the New Bedford, Massachusetts, brass founder and cop-persmith Anthony D. Richmond and dates from the second quarter of the nineteenth century.[121]

WARMING PAN
98

PROBABLY GERMANY, POSSIBLY
SWITZERLAND, 1820–70
COPPER, BRASS
(COPPER 66.27, ZINC 32.44,
LEAD 0.79, IRON 0.34)

H. 3 7/8" (9.9 CM), L. 11 1/2"
(29.2 CM), W. 8" (20.3 CM)
65.1438

ABOUT 1870 THE EDITORS of *The Book of the Household* stated that "the best [warming pan] is made watertight and filled with boiling water as the source of heat." The bed warmer illustrated here operates on that principle, being made of two pieces of rolled sheet copper crimped with a watertight joint and a screw cap with watertight washer.[122]

Although unmarked, this warming pan is identical to others that are stamped incuse on the threaded cap "GARANTIET MASSIV-REINKUPFER" [guaranteed solid pure copper]. The pan was probably made somewhere in the large mining and manufacturing district of Germany that extended from Nuremburg 150 miles west northwest to Aachen. "The mines of Germany are very productive, particularly those of Erzgebirge, the Hartz [and] the Sudetes in Bohemia and Silesia. The rich materials which Germany offers for national industry have not been neglected, and that country may . . . be placed next to Great Britain in respect to national industry [but only because Britain's]

superior machinery [allows them] to furnish . . . goods much cheaper than the German manufacturer."[123]

Germany is "intersected by a number of navigable rivers [making] external as well as internal commerce . . . of great importance. The internal commerce is partly carried on at great fairs and partly by purchasers in the manufacturing districts." Numerous German Americans were among those who purchased goods for exportation to the United States, such as the firm of "Lewis and Conger, Importers and Dealers in House-Furnishing Hardware, etc" in New York City. They "are completely stocked with a splendid assortment of house furnishing hardware, cutlery, fire-irons, tin . . . and a vast array of articles too numerous to particularize. The firm imports directly from European manufacturers" and probably included warming pans like this among its wares.[124]

1 *The Cabinet of Useful Arts* (London: Longman, Rees, Orme, Brown, Green, and Longman, and John Taylor, 1833), 2:163, 161. Strutt's original publication was *A Compleat View of the Manners, Customs, Arms, Habits, etc. of the Inhabitants of England from the Arrival of the Saxons till the Reign of Henry the Eighth (-to the Present)* (London, 1796).

2 *Rivington's New-York Gazetteer*, July 29, 1773. This type of andiron is found in all three metals enumerated, prince's metal being a designation for red brass. Andirons of this type have long been assigned a Rhode Island origin by American writers, presumably because they were associated with that area in the early twentieth century. I have attempted to identify a basis for the attribution that would allow me to substantiate this contention, but I have been unable to do so.

3 *Pennsylvania Gazette* (Philadelphia), April 7, 1784; on Zane, see *Pennsylvania Gazette*, October 10, 1792; on Abeel and Byvanck, see *New-York Mercury*, November 14, 1768.

4 *Rivington's New-York Gazetteer*, May 18, 1775.

5 William Ince and John Mayhew, *The Universal System of Household Furniture* (London, 1760), pl. 92. Robert Sayer, *Genteel Household Furniture* (London, 1765), pl. 105. The wall decoration that Adam created for Luton Park House in Bedfordshire between 1767 and 1775 is strikingly close in composition. That design is illustrated in Oresko, *Works in Architecture*, p. 143.

6 Specification of Letters Patent, no. 21,218, August 17, 1858, U.S. Patent Office, Alexandria, Va. Bennett Woodcroft, *Alphabetical Index of Patentees of Inventions* (London: Evelyn, Adams, and Mackay, 1854) lists no comparable English patent between 1617 and 1852.

7 Specification of Letters Patent, no. 21,218, August 17, 1858, U.S. Patent Office, Alexandria, Va. The relationship of these andirons to the specifications in Sargeant's patent might suggest a late nineteenth-century American origin. Construction, wear, and stylistic features, however, all strongly point to an eighteenth-century date.

8 Bradford L. Rauschenberg, "A School of Charleston, South Carolina, Brass Andirons: 1780-1815," *Journal of Early Southern Decorative Arts* 5, no. 1 (May 1979): 26-74. On the *Castle Douglas*, see James Douglas account book, July 10, 1785, William L. Clements Library, University of Michigan, Ann Arbor; see also Bradford L. Rauschenberg, "Reconsidering Charleston Brass Andirons, Types II and III," *Journal of Early Southern Decorative Arts* 17, no. 2 (November 1992): 37-52. Taylor and Bailey listed themselves at various addresses in London city directories from 1784 to 1797.

9 Webster, *Encyclopaedia of Domestic Economy*, p. 93. John Cadwalader section: bills and receipts, 1770, Cadwalader Papers, Historical Society of Pennsylvania, Philadelphia.

10 On the Meredith crest, see Arthur Charles Fox-Davis, *Fairbairn's Book of Crests* (Edinburgh, Scot.: T.C. and E. C. Jack, Grange Publishing Works, 1892), 1:pt. 1, 306; 1:pt. 2, 99; 2:pl. 10, fig. 12. Joseph Meredith will, 1803, bk. 1, p. 114, Philadelphia City Hall.

11 An almost identical pair of unsigned andirons is in the Bayou Bend collection of the Museum of Fine Arts, Houston, Texas.

12 The second pair of andirons, acc. no. 59.2457.1,.2, have pad feet. The King andirons are entry 54.

13 *Desilver's Philadelphia Directory and Stranger's Guide* (Philadelphia: Robert Desilver, 1828), adv. supp.

14 The Kinnan advertisement is in *Desilver's Philadelphia Directory*, 1828.

15 *Dunlap and Claypoole's American Daily Advertiser* (Philadelphia), March 6, 1794.

16 Morrison H. Heckscher, *American Furniture in the Metropolitan Museum of Art*, 3 vols. (New York: Random House, 1985), 2:204-5. A pair of andirons with identical legs and feet is owned by the American Philosophical Society in Philadelphia and is pictured in the exhibition catalogue *Philadelphia: Three Centuries of American Art* (Philadelphia: Philadelphia Museum of Art, 1976), p. 103. The illustrated detail, acc. no. 60.1065, is from one of the 4 screens.

17 Luke Beckerdite, "Philadelphia Carving Shops, Part II: Bernard and Jugiez," *Antiques* 128, no. 3 (September 1985):

499. On Zane, see John Bivens, Jr., "Decorative Cast Iron on the Virginia Frontier," *Antiques* 101, no. 3 (March 1972): 539. John Cadwalader section: bills and receipts, 1771, Cadwalader Papers, Historical Society of Pennsylvania, Philadelphia.

18 *Dunlap and Claypoole's American Daily Advertiser* (Philadelphia), December 19, 1793.

19 His name was spelled variously as Tustin, Tustan, and Tustian. He may have changed professions, for a William Tustman, gunsmith, appeared in the city directories in 1799 and 1800. William Tuston will, 1812, bk. 4, p. 126, Philadelphia City Hall. The peened joint on one of the andirons failed. It was restored with a threaded extension and nut, as pictured in the detail.

20 The Skellorn advertisement appeared in *Rivington's New-York Gazetteer*, May 18, 1775. On Byers, see *New-York Mercury*, February 22, 1762; on Levy, see *New-York Journal, or General Advertiser*, August 11, 1774.

21 *South-Carolina Gazette, and Country Journal*, March 1, 1768, as quoted in Bradford L. Rauschenberg, "A School of Charleston, South Carolina, Brass Andirons: 1780-1815," *Journal of Early Southern Decorative Arts* 5, no. 1 (May 1979): 68.

22 The slight differences that do exist are due to hand filing and skimming.

23 Hogarth, *Analysis of Beauty*, pp. 67, 68, 70.

24 The other Winterthur andirons are acc. nos. 59.2668,.2669 and 58.5215.1,.2.

25 On Skellorn, see *Rivington's New-York Gazetteer*, May 18, 1775. A pair of andirons closely related to these bears the stamp "REVERE & SON" on the plinth of one and "BOSTON" on the other. They are pictured in Kauffman, *American Copper and Brass*, p. 149. It is generally conceded that they were not made by Paul Revere.

26 Leonard Allison Morrison, *The History of the Alison or Allison Family* (Boston: Damrell and Upham, 1893), p. 260. Peter was brother to the well-known New York City cabinetmaker Michael Allison.

27 Morrison, *History of the Alison or Allison Family*, p. 267.

28 That inventory, MS 54.67.171, is in the Downs collection, Winterthur Library. Stylistically similar examples also occur on occasion in Boston. A pair marked by James Davis is pictured in Schiffer, Schiffer, and Schiffer, *Brass Book*, p. 52.

29 As cited in George H. Kernodle and Thomas M. Pitkin, "The Whittinghams: Brass Founders of New York," *Antiques* 71, no. 4 (April 1957): 351.

30 Inventory of Richard Whittingham, New York City, October 16, 1821, MS 54.67.227, Downs collection, Winterthur Library.

31 Inventory of David Phillips, New York City, August 19, 1818, MS 54.67.171, Downs collection, Winterthur Library.

32 Circular andirons are itemized in the inventory and appraisement of the goods and estate of the Boston, Mass., brass founder John Molineux, October 12, 1829, county probate, Suffolk, Mass., M-165, Downs collection, Winterthur Library. They are also listed in the estate of the New York brass founder David Phillips, dated 1818, MS 54.67.171, Downs collection.

33 On frets, see George Smith, *A Collection of Designs for Household Furniture* (London: J. Taylor, 1808), p. 33. Sheraton, *Cabinet Dictionary*, 2:214.

34 Another pair of andirons by Whittingham with almost the same landscape scene is illustrated in George H. Kernodle and Thomas M. Pitkin, "The Whittinghams: Brass Founders of New York," *Antiques* 71, no. 4 (April 1957): 350. On the Whittingham family, see Kernodle and Pitkin, "The Whittinghams," p. 352. On the gilt buttons, see William Dunlap, *A History of the Rise and Progress of the Arts of Design in the United States*, 3 vols. (New York: G. P. Scott, 1834), 1:158. Rollinson advertised in the *Royal Gazette* (Charleston, S.C.), October 24, 1781. On Rollinson, see Robert W. Reid and Charles Rollinson, *William Rollinson, Engraver* (New York: Privately printed, 1931), pp. 25-61. A superlative silver bowl made by the New York silversmith Hugh Wishart and extensively engraved by William Rollinson is pictured and discussed in the catalogue for Sotheby's sale no. 4268 (June 21, 1979), lot 102. On August 13, 1802, Rollinson advertised for an engraver in the *New-York Evening*

Post. He employed at least one man, William Satchwell Leney (1769–1831), who was as celebrated as Rollinson himself. Either man could have done the engraving on these andirons.

35 Kauffman and Bowers, *Early American Andirons*, p. 51, pictures these urns on a pair of Whittingham andirons contrasted with a pair marked "I C."

36 *New-York Mercury*, January 11, 1768. Marked andirons of this type have been attributed to the late eighteenth-century New York City blacksmith John Constantine. See Kauffman and Bowers, *Early American Andirons*, pp. 50, 52; see also Frederick D. Hill, "Living with Antiques," *Antiques* 121, no. 2 (February 1982): 467, for an iron thumb latch, stamped with the same initials, on an interior door of the Philo Beardsley house near Kent, Conn.

37 On the first two patents, see M.D. Leggett, comp., *Subject-Matter Index of Patents for Inventions Issued by the United States Patent Office from 1790 to 1873, Inclusive*, 3 vols. (Washington, D.C.: Government Printing Office, 1874), 1:15. On the safety bar, see Specification of Letters Patent, no. 3,170, July 12, 1843, U.S. Patent Office, Alexandria, Va.

38 Inventory of David Phillips, New York City, August 19, 1818, MS 54.67.171, Downs collection, Winterthur Library.

39 The Boston fire tools are acc. no. 58.2478,.2479. Winterthur also owns a second set of fire tools like these, acc. no. 64.150.1,.2, which are decorated with swags on the urns. Other Boston brass founders possibly responsible for these andirons, but whose work has not yet been identified, are Thomas Cater, John Cutler, Samuel Drew, Richard Farrell, Robert Holmes, Thomas Leach, and Thomas Lillie.

40 Hunneman's account books dating intermittently from March 1, 1793, to December 26, 1821, are owned by the Boston National Historical Park, Charlestown Navy Yard, Boston.

41 Hunneman account book, August 10, 1818.

42 On Davis, see Hunneman account book, May 23, 1801. Davis's andirons use cabriole legs with spurs and pad feet that appear to be similar, if not identical, to those on these andirons.

43 The Camden andirons are recorded in DAPC. On Penobscot Bay, see Daniel Haskel and J. Calvin Smith, *A Complete Descriptive and Statistical Gazetteer of the United States of America* (New York: Sherman and Smith, 1844), p. 98.

44 Inventory and appraisement of the goods and estate of John Molineux, October 12, 1829, Suffolk County probate, M-165, vol. 127, no. 2:346–48, Downs collection, Winterthur Library.

45 Molineux inventory. *The Boston Directory* (Boston: H. A. Frost and Charles Stimson, Jr., 1821), adv. supp., p. 25.

46 Inventory and appraisement of the goods and estate of John Molineux, October 12, 1829, Suffolk County probate, M-165, vol. 127, no. 2:340–48, Downs collection, Winterthur Library.

47 Howard C. Rice, "James Swan: Agent of the French Republic, 1794–1796," *New England Quarterly* 10 (September 1937): 464–86; *Paul Revere's Boston: 1735–1818* (Boston: Museum of Fine Arts, 1975), p. 161.

48 Thomas Bellows Wyman, *The Genealogies and Estates of Charlestown*, 2 vols. (Boston: David Clapp and Son, 1879), 1:324–29.

49 Timothy T. Sawyer, *Old Charlestown* (Boston: James H. West Co., 1902), pp. 417, 416.

50 This information was gleaned from Boston city directories.

51 Trade catalogue TH7427 M97 TC, Downs collection, Winterthur Library.

52 Hogarth, *Analysis of Beauty*, pp. 55, 65.

53 Hogarth, *Analysis of Beauty*, p. 34.

54 Inbound ship manifests, port of Philadelphia, September 20, 1789, National Archives, Washington, D.C.

55 Robert Sayer, *Household Furniture in Genteel Taste for the Year 1762* (London, 1762), pp. 103, 104, 105. William Ince and John Mayhew, *The Universal System of Household Furniture* (London, 1762), pls. 85, 87, 89, 90, 91, 94, 95.

56 A steel fender matching this grate is pictured in *Antiques* 131, no. 3 (March 1987): 579; a brass fender of the same design is pictured in Schiffer, Schiffer, and Schiffer, *Brass Book*, p. 241. Sayer, *Household Furniture*, p. 108.

57 The ogee arch is reproduced in Christopher Gilbert and Anthony Wells-Cole, *The Fashionable Fireplace, 1660–1840* (Leeds, Eng.: Leeds City Art Galleries, 1985), pp. 54–58. *New-York Journal; or, The General Advertiser*, August 13, 1767.

58 *Works of Alexander Hamilton*, 1:249. Webster, *Encyclopaedia of Domestic Economy*, p. 95. The advertisement appeared in the *New-York Commercial Advertiser*, January 2, 1830.

59 *The New-York City Directory* (New York: Charles R. Rode, 1854), adv. supp., p. 33. Richard Edwards, ed., *New York's Great Industries* (New York: Historical Publishing Company, 1884), p. 164. This Peter is almost certainly a son or nephew of the Peter who is the subject of this entry.

60 A complete example is pictured in *Antiques* 93, no. 1 (January 1968): 31. Another, standing in the fireplace, is recorded in Kauffman and Bowers, *Early American Andirons*, p. 84.

61 Oresko, *Works in Architecture*, 1:45–46.

62 Oresko, *Works in Architecture*, 1: no. 5, pl. 4 (a somewhat more elaborate version of this border is depicted in vol. 52 of the Adam papers owned by the Sir John Soane Museum, London); 1:no. 2, pp. 50, 51, 52.

63 Sheraton, *Cabinet Dictionary*, 1:214.

64 Among the many men recorded as fendermakers in England during the eighteenth and nineteenth centuries are Edward Day and John Allday of Birmingham; William Batty of Sheffield; and Charles Lavendar, John Baker, and Thomas Bradney of Wolverhampton.

65 Alison Kelly, *Decorative Wedgwood* (London: Country Life Limited, 1965), pp. 56–70. As quoted in Eliza Meteyard, *The Wedgwood Handbook* (1875; reprint, Peekskill, N.Y.: Timothy Trace, 1963), p. 80.

66 Richard S. Patterson and Richardson Dougall, *The Eagle and the Shield* (Washington, D.C.: Department of State, 1976), p. 6. Frank H. Sommer, "Emblem and Device: The Origin of the Great Seal of the United States," *Art Quarterly* 24, no. 1 (Spring 1961): 73.

67 Webster, *Encyclopaedia of Domestic Economy*, p. 98.

68 *Pennsylvania Journal; and the Weekly Advertiser*, July 17, 1760.

69 Lardner, *Cabinet Cyclopaedia*, 2:195.

70 Lardner, *Cabinet Cyclopaedia*, 2:195, 197.

71 Lardner, *Cabinet Cyclopaedia*, 2:197–98.

72 Webster, *Encyclopaedia of Domestic Economy*, p. 98.

73 Trade catalogue TS285 B61s, 1827, Downs collection, Winterthur Library.

74 The only documented English wire fender I have seen is privately owned. It is marked by William Oldfield, a whitesmith who worked in Stockport, England, during the early years of the nineteenth century. The uprights of that fender's frame are rectangular in cross section. Trade catalogue TS285 B61s, 1827, Downs collection, Winterthur Library.

75 King advertised in the *Pennsylvania Packet, and Daily Advertiser* (Philadelphia), December 6, 1794. De Blois advertised in the *Columbian Centinel* (Boston), March 8, 1794.

76 *Paxton's Philadelphia Annual Advertiser*, supp. to *The Philadelphia Directory and Register, for 1819* (Philadelphia: John Adems Paxton, 1819).

77 I have seen only a few documented American fireplace fenders. All were marked by John W. Howard and David R. Morse, who were in partnership as wire workers in New York City from 1864 to 1905. The uprights are all circular in cross section.

78 Johnson, *Dictionary of the English Language*, 1:s.v. "curfew."

79 William Hone, *Every-Day Book*, 2 vols. (London: Hunt and Clarke, 1820), 1:243–44.

80 This design is on an unnumbered plate in the copy of Bowles's book NK1530 B78*, Downs collection, Winterthur Library.

81 Webster, *Encyclopaedia of Domestic Economy*, p. 840.

82 On Field and Boyce, see James Sketchley, comp., *Sketchley's Birmingham, Wolverhampton, and Walsall Directory* (Birmingham, 1767), pp. 7, 62. On Taylor, see *Paxton's Philadelphia Annual Advertiser*, supp. to John Adems Paxton, *The Philadelphia Directory and Register, for 1818* (Philadelphia: E. and R. Parker, 1818).

83 Leslie, *House Book*, p. 122.

84 Retailer Joseph Surmon advertised in the *Pennsylvania Chronicle* (Philadelphia), December 19, 1793. On Richardson, see *A List of Patents Granted by the United States, for the Encouragement of Arts and Sciences, Alphabetically Arranged from 1790 to 1828* (Washington, D.C., 1828), p. 9. On Eckstein, see *Paxton's Philadelphia*

Annual Advertiser, supp. to John Adems Paxton, *The Philadelphia Directory and Register, for 1818* (Philadelphia: E. and R. Parker, 1818). Eckstein's and Richardson's partnership was not long lived. They remained together only through 1823.

85 Three examples are in the Winterthur collection. One is labeled by John Smith, acc. no. 66.1013; a second is by Myers Bush, acc. no. 61.1240; another is by George W. Metz, acc. no. 69.1969. All were working in Philadelphia during the 1820s.

86 Beecher, *Treatise on Domestic Economy*, p. 281; Webster, *Encylopaedia of Domestic Economy*, p. 840.

87 Webster, *Encyclopaedia of Domestic Economy*, p. 840; Roberts, *House Servant's Directory*, p. 162.

88 M. D. Legett, comp., *Subject-Matter Index of Patents for Inventions Issued by the United States Patent Office* (Washington, D.C.: Government Printing Office, 1874), p. 99. Specification of Letters Patent, no. 6,365, July 11, 1833, British Patent Office, London. The other Winterthur example is acc. no. 59.519.

89 Webster, *Encyclopaedia of Domestic Economy*, p. 95.

90 Fuller, *Art of Coppersmithing*, p. 122. *An Inventory of the Contents of the Governor's Palace Taken after the Death of Lord Botetourt* (Williamsburg, Va.: Colonial Williamsburg Foundation, 1981), p. 6.

91 Fuller, *Art of Coppersmithing*, p. 122.

92 William C. Hunneman account book, October 5, 1819; December 9, 1816, Boston National Historical Park, Charlestown Navy Yard, Boston.

93 On the brothers, see Judy M. Giuriceo, research paper, object folder 93.2, Registration Office, Winterthur; *The New-York City Directory* (New York: Charles R. Rode, 1854), adv., p. 45.

94 The importance of scuttles to nineteenth-century American coal-burning householders is amply evidenced by John Fuller, who devotes twenty-five pages to them in his *Art of Coppersmithing*, more than twice the space he gives to any of the twenty-two other objects he discusses, including the ever-popular teakettle. Quoted in Fuller, *Art of Coppersmithing*, p. 147.

95 *A Digest of Patents Issued by the United States from 1790 to January 1, 1839* (Washington, D.C., 1840), p. 81. The size and character of this mark are so close to that used by David Phillips, whom Whittingham knew, as to indicate both were cut by the same die sinker.

96 The tongs are acc. no. 58.1921; the andirons are acc. nos. 61.604.1,.2 and 74.112.1,.2.

97 That inventory, MS 54.67.171, is in the Downs collection, Winterthur Library.

98 The inventory also includes numerous andiron parts, including feet, heads, spears, and billet bars. The marked tongs are acc. no. 68.661. A pair of andirons that match these fire tools and bear the identical stamp is pictured in Schiffer, Schiffer, and Schiffer, *Brass Book*, p. 79.

99 The similar set carries acc. no. 64.150.1,.2. Coffin advertised in the *Boston News-Letter*, February 12, 1736.

100 The similar Boston andirons are acc. no. 59.1142.1,.2. A pair of andirons, shovel, and tongs of the type made by the Boston brass founder John Molineux also carry the stamped initials of Jones. They are pictured in *Antiques* 100, no. 1 (July 1971): 39.

101 On Jones, see Clifford K. Shipton, *Biographical Sketches of Those Who Attended Harvard College*, 17 vols. (Boston: Massachusetts Historical Society, 1975), 17:49, 50. "Ratification of the Federal Constitution by Massachusetts," *New-England Historical and Genealogical Register*, 148 vols. (Boston: Samuel G. Drake, 1847), 1:232.

102 The related pair has acc. no. 58.3056, .3057. The eagle differs significantly from that on the great seal in that it faces the talon that grasps arrows, a warlike depiction. The eagle on the great seal always faces the talon that grasps the olive bough, a peaceful gesture. All English depictions of the great seal in brass thus far identified by the author exhibit this anomaly.

103 Clarence Cook, *The House Beautiful* (New York: Scribner, Armstrong, 1878), pp. 112, 113.

104 Cook, *House Beautiful*, p. 117.

105 Section 41, p. 4, MS TS575 P36* TC. Downs collection, Winterthur Library.

The Pearson-Page Company dates from 1897. It continued in operation under that name until 1933, when it was acquired by John Jewsbury and Company and was renamed Pearson-Page Jewsbury Company Limited. In 1978 the company was again renamed to Peerage of Birmingham Limited; it currently operates under that name.

106 Edward Miles Riley, ed., *The Journal of John Harrower* (Williamsburg, Va.: Colonial Williamsburg Foundation, 1963), p. 12. I am grateful to Gerald W. R. Ward for apprising me of this information.

107 Carl Brindenbaugh, ed., *Gentleman's Progress: The Itinerary of Dr. Alexander Hamilton, 1744* (Williamsburg, Va.: Institute of Early American History and Culture, 1948), p. 40.

108 *Book of the Household*, 2:551.

109 The three pans have acc. nos. 58.1560, 58.1975, 58.2344. Winterthur owns a fifth warming pan, acc. no. 93.41, that relates to these. It and two recorded photographically in DAPC bear the "I:ST" mark, but they differ significantly from those listed in this entry. The lids fit into the lip, and each has a turned wooden handle that fits into a cast brass socket. These features postdate those of Winterthur's iron-handled pans and suggest the maker worked at a time when warming pans were evolving to a more efficient design. See E. E. Hopwell, "Summary of a Discussion on Warming Pans at the 1991 Spring Meeting, Including Information That Has Since Come to Hand," *Base Thoughts* (Journal of the Antique Metalware Society), no. 4 (Spring 1992): 11–28.

110 K. A. Citroen, *Amsterdam Silversmiths and Their Marks* (Amsterdam: North-Holland Publishing Co., 1975), pp. 16, 82. Hopwell, "Summary of a Discussion," pp. 21–23. Hornsby, *Collecting Antique Copper and Brass*, pp. 265–75.

111 Joseph T. Buckingham, *Annals of the Massachusetts Charitable Mechanic Association* (Boston: Crocker and Brewster, 1853), pp. 6, 10, 46.

112 Kauffman, on p. 88 of *American Copper and Brass*, tentatively attributes the "I:W" mark to Joshua Wetherle, who was listed as a coppersmith in the 1789 and 1803 Boston city directories. Wetherle, however, called himself a pewterer on land deeds and lists himself variously as "wire manufacturer," "brass founder," and "candle mould maker" in the city directories. Wells, by contrast, was always listed as a coppersmith. Fuller, *Art of Coppersmithing*, p. 112.

113 Columbian Centinel (Boston), March 2, 1793.

114 William C. Hunneman account book, intermittant entries, Boston National Historical Park, Charlestown Navy Yard, Boston.

115 Fuller, *Art of Coppersmithing*, p. 112.

116 The attribution of an unmarked object to a given maker based on castings that are identical to those in a marked counterpart has proven important in the study of American pewter; see Charles V. Swain, "Interchangeable Parts in Early American Pewter," *Antiques* 83, no. 2 (February 1963): 212-13.

117 The consignment of these articles is recorded in William C. Hunneman's account books, Boston National Historical Park, Charlestown Navy Yard, Boston. The advertisement quoted is in *The Boston Directory* (Boston: H.A. Frost and Charles Stimson, Jr., 1821), adv. supp., p. 25.

118 *Acts of Incorporation and Bylaws of the New England Society for the Promotion of Manufactures of Mechanic Arts* (Boston: Beals and Homer, 1826), pp. 4, 13.

119 Specification of Letters Patent, no. 778, October 30, 1762, British Patent Office, London.

120 Patent no. 778.

121 The pan is owned by the Henry Ford Museum and Greenfield Village. It is pictured in Kauffman, *American Copper and Brass*, p. 92.

122 *Book of the Household*, 2:551. The joint subsequently leaked and was repaired with lead solder.

123 Charles Partington, ed., *The British Cyclopaedia*, 10 vols. (London: William S. Orr, 1838), 5:147.

124 On German topography, see Partington, *British Cyclopaedia*, 5:147. On Lewis and Conger, see Richard Edwards, ed., *New York's Great Industries* (New York: Historical Publishing Company, 1884), p. 271.

DETAIL, CANDELABRUM, 1785–1800

ENTRY 135

LIGHT

CANDLESTICKS, OIL LAMPS, GAS LIGHTING, and their variants are represented in this section. Information on candle lighting precedes that on oil lighting and is supplemented with entries on a few of the implements necessary for candle maintenance and use. Included here are candlesticks, chambersticks, candelabra, wall sconces, hall lanterns, chandeliers, save-alls, snuffers, and candle screens. In addition, fat lamps, oil lamps, candlestick lamps, burning-fluid lamps, argand lamps, annular lamps, sinumbra lamps, and solar lamps are listed.

CANDLESTICK
99

UNIDENTIFIED MAKER'S MARK
NUREMBERG, GERMANY, 1650–90

BRASS (COPPER 79.51, LEAD 8.24,
ZINC 6.58, TIN 3.90, ANTIMONY 0.41,
IRON 0.36, SILVER 0.15)
H. 8" (20.3 CM), DIAM. 6 1/4" (15.9 CM)
64.693

THIS CANDLESTICK is surprisingly light in weight for its size. The shaft has been cast hollow except for the narrow portion that threads into the base. The base is also cast. When removed from their molds, "the excrescences which may happen to have been formed in the partings or core-joints are broken off. . . . The gates [remains of the channels through which molten metal flows into the mold] are, at the same time broken off by the moulder."[1]

After the castings are sufficiently cool, they are finished in a brazier's lathe. "Braziers that turn Andirons, Pots, Kettles [and candlesticks fit] their Work on a small Iron Axis. . . . They begin to work first with the sharp point of a Graver . . . directing the point to the Work, and lay Circles upon it close to one another, till they

have wrought it pretty true: Then with one of the broad Edges of the Graver they smoothen down what the point left, and afterwards with Sculpters, Round or Flat, or great or small, they work their intended Moldings."[2] The result is a candlestick like this one, which has a smooth reflective surface and sharply defined profile.

The maker stamped his mark–which appears to be a spread eagle in a conforming outline–on the outside base rim, as was commonplace among Nuremberg candlestick makers at that time. The mark registered incompletely, however, so the maker's identity is unknown.[3]

CANDLESTICK
100

ATTRIBUTED TO HANS GEORG BECK
NUREMBERG, GERMANY, 1670–1700
BRASS (COPPER 81.66, ZINC 7.75,
LEAD 4.52, TIN 3.75, ANTIMONY 0.68,
IRON 0.61, SILVER 0.17)

H. 7 7/8" (20.0 CM),
DIAM. 5 1/2" (14.0 CM)
ONE OF A PAIR
64.708.1

THIS CANDLESTICK TYPIFIES those made in Germany, particularly Nuremberg, during the second half of the seventeenth century. The shaft was cast as a single piece, and the large-diameter knop and candle cup were made hollow to save metal and reduce the cost of the object, since metal objects were sold by weight.

Single-piece hollow castings were possible using cores that were "commonly composed of rock-sand and sea-sand. The former, having a proportion of clay in its composition to which it owes its powerful cohesiveness when dried, serves very well for short cores," like that in this candlestick.[4]

Cores must be centered in the mold to obtain a flawless casting with uniformly thick walls. They are "sustained [in place] by [iron wires called] staples stuck into the sand at several places in their length and projecting above it just as much as the thickness of metal. . . . The staples are, of course, buried in the casting, and the projecting points outside cut off in the course of dressing it."[5] The ends of those staples are visible on the knop of this candlestick as two small, vertically aligned dots.

The shaft is threaded to the base, which is also cast. The floral ornament on the base and knop is engraved and has a chased matted ground. It modestly follows the bold, balanced foliate scrollwork patterns that were being devised by the French painter and designer Charles Le Brun (1619–90) for Louis XIV at Versailles.

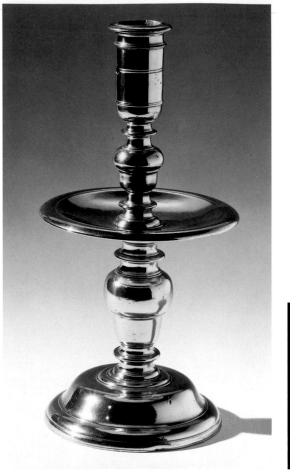

CANDLESTICK
101

GERMANY OR THE NETHERLANDS,
1650–1700
BRASS (COPPER 74.09, ZINC 11.68,
LEAD 7.59, TIN 3.12, ANTIMONY
2.40, IRON 0.25, SILVER 0.16)

H. 10 9/16" (26.8 CM),
DIAM. 4 3/4" (12.1 CM)
61.1470

WINTERTHUR OWNS twenty-three candlesticks of the type shown here. This particular example is characteristic, being very heavy for its size. It was cast in four separate parts: the upper shaft and candle cup, the drip pan, the lower shaft, and the base. An extension of the topmost casting passes through the drip pan, lower shaft, and base, where the bottom end is peened.[6]

Candlesticks such as this were popular from the mid seventeenth through the mid eighteenth centuries and perhaps longer. Judging from the number of extant examples, they were apparently made in many European base-metalworking centers. They cannot, however, be documented securely to known makers since they appear to have been rarely, if ever, marked. A candlestick of this type was prominently pictured in the interior of a candlemaker's shop that appeared in a Nuremberg, Germany, 1698 publication and again in Amsterdam, Holland, in 1718, thus providing a geographic and temporal framework.[7]

Another indication of the widespread and long popularity of this type of candlestick has been documented. In 1596 a Dutch merchant fleet under the command of Jacob van Heemskirk and William Barentz attempted to navigate a route to China over the Eurasian continent. Their expedition got as far as Novaya Zembala, two Arctic islands off the coast of Russia, and became stranded. About three hundred years later their encampment was discovered and the remains returned to Holland. Candlesticks of this type were among the artifacts.[8]

Again, about 1750, a European merchant ship on its way from Canton to Batavia (now Djakarta), Java, carrying Chinese porcelain for the Dutch market, sank in the South China Sea. The ship was discovered and salvaged in 1985. Among the contents was a candlestick almost identical to the one shown here.[9]

CANDLESTICK
102

NORTHERN EUROPE OR ENGLAND,
1650–70
BRASS (COPPER 64.76, ZINC 33.97,
LEAD 0.66, IRON 0.22)

H. 6 3/16" (15.7 CM),
DIAM. 5 1/2" (14.0 CM)
64.736

THE SHAFT OF THIS CANDLESTICK is designed as a cluster of six columns bound along the length by three molded fillets. The form derives from monumental cluster columns like those that line the nave of London's Westminster Abbey, built between 1245 and 1270, and old Saint Paul's Cathedral, begun about 1250. When the latter burned in the great London fire of 1666, Christopher Wren designed and oversaw its rebuilding but in a radically different Renaissance style supported on classically inspired columns. That event marked the terminus for cluster-column architecture in England and, concurrently, candlesticks derived from it.

This example is made almost entirely of sheet metal, the column being hammered to shape over an iron or wood swage and seamed vertically. It is attached to a large upright bolt with a hand-filed thread that has been peened to the center of the base.

Cluster-column candlesticks made of silver, pewter, and brass were used in many northern European countries and England during the sixteenth and seventeenth centuries. They were present on the banqueting table at The Hague for the great feast that the estates of Holland made to the king (Charles II of England) and to the royal family in May 1660, just before Charles crossed the channel to assume the throne in England.[10]

CANDLESTICK
103

GERMANY, THE NETHERLANDS,
OR ENGLAND, 1660–90
BRASS (COPPER 66.75, ZINC 26.71,
LEAD 1.39, TIN 0.24), STEEL

H. 7 1/8" (18.1 CM), W. 3 7/8"
(9.8 CM), D. 3 7/8" (9.8 CM)
64.706

SQUARE CANDLESTICKS with fluted shafts were made in France, Germany, and the Netherlands during the late seventeenth century. They were also fashioned in England by silversmiths such as Jacob Bodendick, "a native of Limburg in Germany" granted citizenship by Charles II in October 1661.[11] Those silver candlesticks that bear legible datemarks were from the 1660s through the 1680s, thus establishing a context for unmarked brass examples of the same type.

The shaft of this candlestick is sheet metal that has been shaped over a swage. The seam was placed vertically on one corner to minimize its visibility. The fillets encircling it at the lip, midpoint, and lower end were drawn to create surface contour while the base and drip pan were cast. The three parts were originally held together with a threaded brass bolt peened to the base, now replaced with one of steel.

This candlestick is similar in appearance to a more elaborately decorated pair in silver gilt–made by an unidentified Parisian silversmith between 1669 and 1670–that bears the engraved cypher of William of Orange and Mary, princess of England. Those candlesticks are part of a large and elaborate twenty-two-piece toilet service that was probably acquired by William and Mary at the time of their marriage in 1677.[12]

CANDLESTICK
104

NORTHERN EUROPE, 1670–1700
BRASS (COPPER 74.03, ZINC 10.10,
LEAD 9.69, TIN 4.72, ANTIMONY 1.09,
IRON 0.91, SILVER 0.12)

H. 8 3/4" (22.2 CM),
DIAM. 4 13/16" (12.2 CM)
ONE OF A PAIR
61.1314.1

WILLIAM SALMON, JR., recorded in *Palladio Londinensis* that the term "spira is properly Latin for the folds of a serpent laid at rest or the coil of a cable, rope, &c. In Architecture 'tis sometimes used for the base of a column."[13] The gigantic baldacchino designed by Cian Lorenzo Bernini, cast in bronze and erected under the dome of Saint Peter's Basilica in Rome, is a spectacular use of this motif. The construction began in 1625 and continued to completion in 1633, making it one of the earliest examples of the spiral column in Europe. Numerous others were built into ecclesiastical and secular architecture throughout Europe from the mid seventeenth century to the first decades of the eighteenth century.

Since "all the arts . . . are either improved or ornamented by architecture," it naturally followed that contemporary furniture came to incorporate similar columns for structural or ornamental purposes.[14] The same spiral column was also used on a more modest scale for date-marked German, Dutch, and Swedish silver candlesticks from the 1660s through the 1680s as well as for their unmarked counterparts in brass.

The spiral shaft of the candlestick shown here was cast hollow and uses iron staples, the stumps of which are visible, to hold a core in place. The shaft was subsequently peened to the base. The base, possibly not the first to support this candlestick, is engraved with a coat of arms, tinctured as a silver shield with a blue chevron.[15] This shield was assigned to a number of Continental and English surnames, making a positive assignment of original ownership difficult.

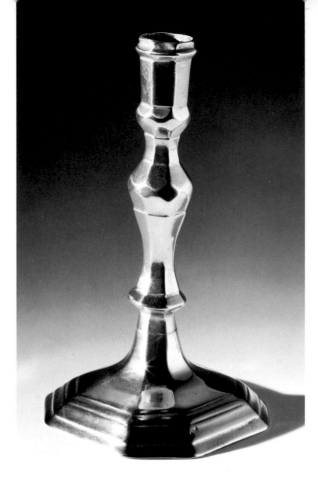

CANDLESTICK
105

PROBABLY PROVINCIAL
FRANCE, 1700–1730
BRASS (COPPER 77.20,
ZINC 15.78, LEAD 4.95,
TIN 1.71, ANTIMONY 0.22)

H. 7 1/8" (18.1 CM), W. 3 7/8"
(9.9 CM), D. 3 7/8" (9.9 CM)
66.1339

THIS CANDLESTICK and another at Winterthur are almost identical to one owned by the Victoria and Albert Museum that bears its maker's mark–"I*B" within a rectangle–stamped on the outside edge of the base. Although that candlestick has been tentatively ascribed an English origin, it could also be French. The upright portion appears to be seamless. English candlestick shafts of this era are invariably cast in vertical halves and seamed. The casting is quite thin walled, also unlike English technique. The deep octagonal candle cup and inverted baluster shaft relate closely to French silver candlesticks of provincial origin.[16]

Eighteenth-century brass candlesticks invariably had separately cast shafts and bases that were brazed, peened, or screwed together. The joint between the two parts was typically hidden insofar as possible–usually with a decorative fillet–by specialized makers in urban areas. The undisguised joint between the stem and base of this candlestick and its counterparts support a probable provincial origin, as does the unsophisticated proportion and greater-than-expected amount of hand finishing under the base.

CANDLESTICK
106

STAMPED WITH A CROWNED "C"
FRANCE, PROBABLY PARIS, 1700–1749
BRASS (COPPER 77.40, ZINC 18.70,
LEAD 2.30, TIN 1.10)

H. 6 1/4" (15.9 CM), W. 3 1/2"
(8.9 CM), D. 3 1/2" (8.9 CM)
59.2455

IN FEBRUARY 1745 Louis XV issued an edict stating that casters, braziers, sword cutlers, mercers, metal dealers, manufacturers of weighing machines, and others involved in the fabrication and sale of copper, brass, and bronze were obligated to pay a royal tax. That duty was payable "on all works, old or new, of pure copper, cast bronze, brass and so forth, mixed copper, cast, ground, beaten, forged, engraved, gilded, silvered over and [lacquered], with no exception whatever."[17] The amount of the tax was figured on the basis of weight and applied to all objects that passed through the artisan's or merchant's hands.

As proof of payment, tax collectors were to stamp each object brought to them with a crowned "c," the letter presumably

standing for *cuivre*, the French word for copper. Makers were also expected to strike their own identifying stamp on each object they made. The law remained in effect only four years; in February 1749 it was revoked because of the country's improving financial condition.[18]

The candlestick illustrated here has most of its outer surface chased with reserves of diaperwork and stylized foliate motifs that relate to Parisian silver candlesticks date marked from 1690 to 1724.[19] It retains minimal traces of original silvering on the underside of the base, to which the seamed shaft is threaded.

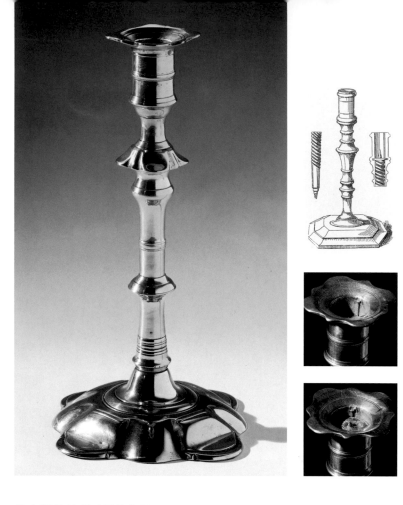

CANDLESTICK
107

ENGLAND, PROBABLY BIRMINGHAM,
1740–70
BRASS (COPPER 73.00, ZINC 27.02,
LEAD 2.10, IRON 1.12, TIN 0.49,
ANTIMONY 0.10)

H. 8 1/2" (21.6 CM), W. 4 1/8"
(10.4 CM), D. 4 1/8" (10.4 CM)
ONE OF A PAIR
65.1647.1

UNTIL THE DEVELOPMENT of the tubular wick by Aimé Argand in 1784, the oil lamp never equaled the candle in popularity. Candles were generally cleaner, easier to use, and somewhat less expensive.[20] A common complaint, however, was that the flame moved as the candle was consumed, unlike the flame in a lamp, which remained fixed. Also, the portion of the candle within the socket had to be recycled to be usable.

One of the earliest attempts to remedy these drawbacks is recorded in the minutes of the Academy of Sciences in Paris. In 1730 a Mlle Duchâteau presented before that body a candlestick, the shaft of which was "double walled and contains a screw fitted with a nut, onto which is attached a movable plate that is raised and lowered the length of the bobeche, by rotating the double walled shaft. . . . In this manner [one can] push up the candle at will, easily remove it or burn it completely."[21]

English manufacturers quickly incorporated this device into their work, as exemplified by the candlestick shown here. Even so, the first

English patent seems not to have been issued until 1779. In that year the Sheffield goldsmith Edmund Greaves was awarded a patent for a candlestick that had a nut "fastened into the bottom of the sockett . . . thro' which the screw rises by turning the nossil, and is kept in its proper place . . . by means of a square . . . which falls into a square box or tube . . . and upon the end of the screw is fixed a round piece of metal with a point in the center for the candle to rest upon . . . to raise and lower the candle when burning . . . until the whole is consumed" thus providing "a considerable saving in candle as well as cleanliness and utility."[22]

Such candlesticks were offered in the American colonies at an early date, as evidenced by the Philadelphia merchant Edward Penington, who advertised "brass screw candlesticks . . . at his store on Edward Warner's warf" in 1752. In the same year Isaac Jones, also of Philadelphia, "just imported, chiefly by the last vessels from London . . . brass screw up . . . candlesticks."[23]

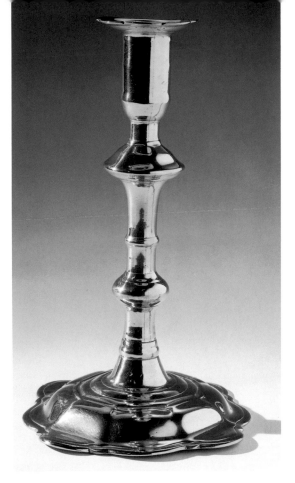

CANDLESTICK
108

GEORGE GROVE (D. 1768)
BIRMINGHAM, ENGLAND, 1748–68
BRASS (COPPER 70.12, ZINC 26.88,
LEAD 2.06, IRON 0.44, TIN 0.26), IRON

H. 7 1/2" (19.0 CM), W. 4 1/4"
(10.8 CM), D. 4 1/4" (10.8 CM)
ONE OF A PAIR
61.830.1

ON DECEMBER 5, 1768, *Aris's Birmingham Gazette* announced that "Mr. George Grove, of Birmingham, brass candlestick maker" had died. Among the many candlestick makers in that city was his son Daniel, to whom he left "all the shop tools and patterns belonging to my trade and which shall be in use at the time of my decease." The estate was administered by "Mr. Henry Kempson, Plater, in Birmingham."[24]

A sizable number of candlesticks exist that have Grove's name impressed under the base either as "GEORGE GROVE" or "GEO. GROVE." The example illustrated here (and another pair also at Winterthur) typifies not only the work of Grove but also most brass candlesticks made by his competitors in Birmingham during the mid eighteenth century.[25]

The shaft is cast hollow in halves vertically and brazed together. It is peened to the base, which is also cast. Within the shaft is a spiral mechanism, which when activated by turning the base against the shaft, raises or lowers the floor of the candle cup.

CANDLESTICKS
109

PROBABLY LONDON, ENGLAND,
POSSIBLY CANTON, CHINA, 1750–65
PAKTONG (COPPER 66.45,
ZINC 21.64, NICKEL 11.41)

H. 11" (27.9 CM), W. 5 3/8"
(13.6 CM), D. 5 3/8" (13.6 CM)
94.99.1–.4

THESE CANDLESTICKS ARE CAST in the expected manner for mid eighteenth-century English examples—the shafts in vertical halves that are brazed to separately cast bases. The bobeches are removable. Their anonymous maker departed remarkably, however, from the standard design formula for brass-alloy candlesticks. He created a strongly textured, writhing composition of scrolls, volutes, leaves, and flowers from base to bobeche. Furthermore, each design element is depicted against a void and is given striking clarity through chasing to sharpen outline and enhance detail.

Their character ultimately derives from a design aesthetic that is best known in a French context, now called rococo. In essence, it consists of gravity-defying, logic-confuting, illogical juxtapositions of disparate imaginings that could not possibly exist. Even so, a number of individuals did translate impossible designs into successful artifactual contexts. Among the most creative was the French designer, artist,

sculptor, and architect Juste Aurèle Meissonnier (1695-1750), as seen in a catalogue of his works entitled *Oeuvre de Juste Aurèle Meissonnier*, first published about 1750 in Paris by Gabriel Huquier. Among the images depicted therein are candlesticks (pls. 6-8, 31-35) that although somewhat more architectural in character, contain the salient design elements that indisputably lead to these rather more effusive examples.[26]

These candlesticks and an identical pair in brass are given geographic and temporal context by comparison to London silverwork of the 1750s, as exemplified by a set of six sweetmeat dishes made by Fuller White in 1757.[27] Although London appears to be the most probable place of origin, it must be conceded that they could have been made in Canton for the English market, since China was the primary source for the exotic and difficult-to-make alloy called paktong.

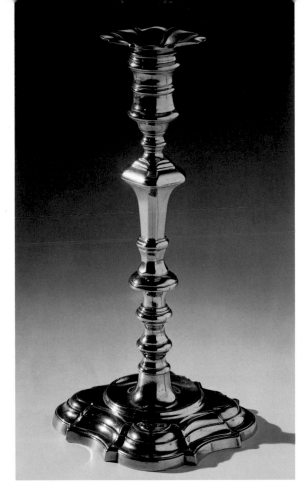

CANDLESTICK
110

STAMPED WITH PSEUDO ENGLISH
SILVER HALLMARKS
PROBABLY CANTON, CHINA, 1750–84
PAKTONG (COPPER 44.00, ZINC 41.00,
NICKEL 11.00, LEAD 1.00, SILVER 0.10)

H. 9 1/4" (23.5 CM), W. 4 1/2"
(11.4 CM), D. 4 1/2" (11.4 CM)
ONE OF A PAIR
61.240.1

THIS CANDLESTICK RELATES very closely to mid eighteenth-century English silver examples. The shape of the base is common for the 1740s while the profile of the shaft is more typical of the 1750s.[28] The nozzle is removable. The shaft is cast in vertical halves, and the underside of the base bears evidence of having been skimmed and scraped in finishing.

This candlestick and its mate have been stamped with four small marks on the top of the base. Although these relate in size and number to the hallmarks routinely stamped on English silver prior to 1784, they are completely nonsensical within an English context, like similar marks on Chinese export silver.[29] Some of the marks seem to relate to Chinese characters.

In 1775 the *Annual Register*, published in England, recounted that the late John Blake, a resident supercargo for the East India Company in Canton, sent a sample of Chinese paktong together with "the processes by which this beautiful metal is made in China into utensils of various sorts for the table, sideboard, etc." to England for experimentation. This candlestick was probably among those made in China for the Western market, as was the case with quantities of Chinese porcelain, furniture, silks, paintings, and other artifacts.[30]

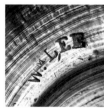

CANDLESTICK
111

WILLIAM LEE (D. 1800)
BIRMINGHAM, ENGLAND, 1759–80
BRASS (COPPER 67.32, ZINC 28.75,
LEAD 2.40, IRON 0.65, TIN 0.22)

H. 8 7/8" (22.4 CM), W. 4 1/2"
(11.4 CM), D. 4 1/2" (11.4 CM)
ONE OF A PAIR
64.1.1

WINTERTHUR OWNS TWO PAIRS of candlesticks marked by William Lee, who worked as a brass candlestick maker and founder from 1759 until he gave up his business in 1780.[31] Shortly thereafter, he sold his entire stock in trade, tools, and material and spent the remaining twenty years of his life in retirement until he died on January 8, 1800.

His candlesticks, like those of his contemporaries, are of good quality, well designed, and well finished.[32] In the example shown here, the two halves of the shaft are fitted and brazed together so that the vertical seam is practically invisible. The shaft is peened to the base, which has been fully skimmed on the underside to remove excess metal.

This candlestick and its mate have removable bobeches, which were necessary prior to the development of the woven self-con-

suming wick, especially if tallow candles were used. Prior to that time wicks were made of twisted cotton or flax and could contain many knotlike irregularities. "The portion . . . within the flame became charred by the heat, but not consumed [necessitating constant snuffing] in the course of time, however, if the candle be left unsnuffed, the wick will project beyond the flame, and coming in contact with the air, be partly consumed; but the soot, collecting as a spongy mass at the top, will darken the flame, and at length, falling into the cup [of the candle], will break down its edges, and cause the tallow to overflow," a process known as guttering.[33] Bobeches did not prevent guttering but did serve to catch the runoff.

CANDLESTICK
112

ENGLAND, PROBABLY BIRMINGHAM,
1760–80
BRASS (COPPER 78.00, ZINC 19.10,
LEAD 1.83, TIN 0.75)

H. 10" (25.4 CM), DIAM. 4 13/16"
(12.3 CM)
ONE OF A PAIR
52.189.1

WINTERTHUR OWNS A TOTAL of six and a half pairs of candlesticks like the one shown, all with slightly differing details. Brass candlesticks with spiral decorated bases, knops, and bobeches have been documented to George Grove (d. 1768), William Lee (d. 1800), and Edward Durnall (d. 1812), all of whom worked in Birmingham. There were others making them as well, as suggested by an anonymous Birmingham brass-manufacturer's catalogue that pictures a candlestick like the one shown here and notes that it is available in four heights–8 1/4, 8 3/4, 9 1/4, and 10 inches.[34]

Although this design might initally appear to be peculiar to brass, the London silversmiths John and William Cafe made silver candlesticks that relate conceptually in that their principal decorative motifs are radiating spiral elements on the base, primary knop, and bobeche. Silver candlesticks of the type were also made in Birmingham in Matthew Boulton and John Fothergill's Soho manufactory, providing a convenient and probable immediate source of inspiration for this design in brass.[35]

CANDLESTICK

113

PROBABLY ENGLAND, POSSIBLY
AMERICA, 1760–90
BRASS (COPPER 72.95, ZINC 24.54,
LEAD 1.75, TIN 0.50)

H. 8 1/2" (21.6 CM), W. 4 1/4"
(11.4 CM), D. 4 1/4" (11.4 CM)
ONE OF A PAIR
59.2869

THIS CANDLESTICK CONFORMS in many ways to those with a documentable Birmingham origin. The shaft was cast in vertical halves, brazed together, and peened to the base. The underside of the base has been skimmed on a lathe to remove excess metal. The shaft was originally fitted with an internal screw mechanism, now defunct, to eject unusable candle stumps. Stylistically, the candlestick resembles those from Birmingham.

There are, however, differences between this and Birmingham candlesticks. All other published brass candlesticks that employ a spiral ornament–some of which are signed by George Grove, William Lee, and Edward Durnall–have the swirl oriented in a clockwise direction.[36] This example uses diagonal elements that swirl counterclockwise. In addition, the base of this candlestick is almost square in plan, whereas all other related examples are circular. The principal knop has angular instead of sloping shoulders. The swirls in the base are somewhat less well defined than those to which they are related.

The reason for these differences is speculative. The candlestick may represent the work of a founder who was attempting to create fashionable examples following the mode of those being made in and exported from Birmingham. He may have worked in Sheffield, England, or Philadelphia, Pennsylvania. Herinemus Warner, brass founder on Eighth Street, Philadelphia, who made "andirons and candlesticks of various patterns" was such a man who, with many competitors in all East Coast cities, made brass objects using English imports as models.[37]

CANDLESTICK
114

ROBERT BUSH, SR. (D. 1807)
BRISTOL, ENGLAND, 1760–90
BRASS (COPPER 76.18, ZINC 17.00,
LEAD 3.70, TIN 1.39, IRON 0.84,
ANTIMONY 0.21, SILVER 0.10)

H. 7 1/2" (19.0 CM), W. 4" (10.2 CM),
D. 4" (10.2 CM)
95.14

THE SHAFT OF THIS CANDLESTICK was cast in halves vertically and subsequently peened to the separately cast base. It was originally fitted with an internal screw mechanism that ejected unburned candle stumps from the socket when the shaft was rotated in one hand and the base was held immovable in the other. The bobeche is integral with the socket, and all cylindrical portions, including the center of the underside of the base, were skimmed on a lathe.

In all these respects, as well as in its style, this candlestick is virtually identical to many brass candlesticks documented to mid to late eighteenth-century Birmingham candlestick makers.[38] It does, however, differ in several respects from the prototypical Birmingham brass candlestick of the type made by George Grove or Joseph Wood. The most apparent is its proportion. While the stick conforms to similar Birmingham examples in overall height, the candle socket is deeper, and the shaft is shorter. This unusual proportion might be presumed to

be the work of an unidentified Birmingham candlestick maker were it not for the second feature, the maker's mark. Stamped incuse on the underside of the base is "R. Bush." Robert Bush, Sr., who worked in Bristol, England, from 1755 until his death in 1807, is well known as a prolific and successful manufacturer of pewter, a significant proportion of which he sent to America. He did, however, work in other metals, as recorded in the July 27, 1765, issue of the Bristol newspaper *Felix Farley's Journal*. Bush noted that he was a "pewterer, brazier, and brass founder, in High Street." Additionally, he listed himself as "Robert Bush and Company, pewterers, brass and coppersmiths," in the Bristol city directory for 1775. Judging from the relative paucity of brass and copper documented to Bush, as compared to the large amount of pewter, it might be presumed that the bulk of his production was devoted to the latter.[39]

CANDLESTICK
115

PROBABLY CANTON, CHINA, 1760–80
PAKTONG (ZINC 42.57,
COPPER 42.25, NICKEL 11.39,
IRON 1.46, LEAD 0.82)

H. 12 1/4" (31.1 CM), W. 5 5/8"
(14.3 CM), D. 5 5/8" (14.3 CM)
ONE OF A PAIR
56.22.2

PAKTONG IS A MIXTURE of copper, zinc, and nickel. "The addition of nickel decolorizes brass or bronze, and when 10 percent or more is added, a white alloy is produced, at the same time the resistance to corrosion is increased." The alloy was first made in China at an undetermined but apparently very early date. Although knowledge of its existence is first recorded in Europe in 1597, Europeans were not able to isolate nickel in commercial quantities and, therefore, make paktong until 1824.[40] Prior to that date they imported the metal as finished objects or, less commonly, as coin or in unfinished form.

The European demand for paktong grew considerably during the eighteenth century. The Swedish scientist and metallurgist Gustavus von Engström observed in 1776 that "a lot of workmen are occupied [in Canton making] different household things such as spoons, dishes, boxes, candlesticks, etc." These and more were displayed in shops clustered on New and Old China streets in Canton, "where foreigners might ramble and purchase."[41]

The candlestick illustrated here is of substantial weight, well finished, and constructed like those from England. The square base, removable bobeche, multiple knops, and gadrooned borders are typical of English silver and brass examples dating as early as the 1750s. With the absence of a maker's mark, this candlestick might easily be assumed to have been made in England. However, it has been observed that Chinese export silver is "almost indistinguishable from Western examples of the same period, so that identification as export can only be made through their marks."[42] This is also true of most paktong.

CANDLESTICK
116

EDWARD DURNALL (D. 1812)
BIRMINGHAM, ENGLAND,
1766–1812
BRASS (COPPER 73.62,
ZINC 22.05, LEAD 1.73, TIN 0.19)

H. 6 11/16" (17.0 CM), DIAM. 3 7/8"
(9.8 CM)
ONE OF A PAIR
67.1382.1

ON NOVEMBER 3, 1766, Edward Durnall informed "the Public that he . . . opened a shop at the Bell and Two Candlesticks opposite the Bear-in-Bull Street, Birmingham, where he sells all sorts of brass, copper, pewter and cast iron goods, he has also made an entire new set of brass candlesticks of the most elegant patterns."[43]

Durnall (or Durnell) was identified in city directories as a candlestick maker, brazier, tinplate worker, and ironmonger. His advertisements in the local newspaper indicate that he divided his time among these activities and selling imported "Nankeen richly gilt . . . fine pearl spoons, fish and counters, India fans . . . flint glasses, cut and plain . . . Dutch Tea Urns [and a] great variety of Children's and other toys."[44]

Four styles of brass candlesticks are presently documented with Durnall's name. He noted that "Merchants [and] Factors [who supplied overseas markets] may be served with any quantity [of them] at the shortest notice and on the most reasonable terms." Most use an internal screw ejector to ease stump removal after a candle had burned to the rim of the bobeche, reflecting Durnall's desire to provide useful and up-to-date lighting. This is underscored in an advertisement of "Mr. Pinchbeck of Charing Cross, London, [who] obtained His Majesty's Royal Letters Patent for . . . a new invented candlestick nossel which [holds] the spilling the wax or tallow on the floor in walking about and of holding candles of various sizes firm . . . without being papered. [He] transferred the whole power of making them in iron or brass, japann'd or not japann'd, and polished steel to messrs, John Gibbons and Henry Clay, of Birmingham . . . in Enamel of Mr. Isaac Waterhouse of Birmingham . . . and in brass and Prince's metal of Mr. Edward Durnall."[45]

CANDLESTICK
117

ENGLAND, 1770–1800
BRASS (COPPER 88.39,
ZINC 10.73, LEAD 0.86)

H. 11 1/4" (28.6 CM),
DIAM. 4 3/4" (12.1 CM)
ONE OF A PAIR
59.1359

A CANDLESTICK VERY SIMILAR to this one is illustrated in an anonymous Birmingham brass-manufacturer's trade catalogue that dates from the 1770s.[46] Just as with all the candlesticks shown in that catalogue, it is offered in several different sizes, 9 1/4, 10 1/2, and 11 inches, priced at 6s., 8s., and 9s. the pair, respectively. Wishing to accurately present all details of the candlestick in the catalogue fully, the engraver chose to depict the base in plan, the shaft in elevation, and the bobeche in a three-quarter view. The result is a disjointed image, but it provides the viewer with a full and complete rendition of the object and all its details.

This candlestick has four narrow borders of pearlwork on the base and shaft. All the remaining ornament is in the form of gadrooning, a motif that seems to have made its first appearance on European and English silver at the end of the seventeenth century, possibly deriving as an adaptation of the echinus or egg-and-dart border used extensively in the pediments of Greek and Roman buildings. The gadrooned border became very popular as a decorative motif on silver and silver plate, particularly candlesticks, during the second half of the eighteenth century. Its extensive use here relates the candlestick to silver examples made in London by John and William Cafe–candlestick specialists–and in Birmingham by Matthew Boulton.

CANDLESTICK
118

ENGLAND, PROBABLY
SHEFFIELD, 1780–1800
FUSED PLATE

H. 13 1/4" (33.6 CM), W. 6"
(15.2 CM), D. 4 1/4" (10.7 CM)
ONE OF A PAIR
59.1598

ALTHOUGH COPPER AND BRASS wire had been used to make a variety of utilitarian wares as early as the sixteenth century, they were not common components of ornamental objects. That situation changed significantly in 1768 when George Whately, a Birmingham silver-plater, invented and patented a "method of Plating silver upon mettal wire, and drawing the same into wire of very fine sizes, both round, flat, and square" and other more complex profiles as well. Prior to his invention, plated wire was created by wrapping a thin sheet of hammered silver foil around a copper wire and then burnishing it under heat to adhere the two metals. Whately suggested making a copper wire "about two or three inches in circumference, and about four or five inches in length . . . then take the finest virgin silver, run it into a flat ingott, and roll it to the thinness of a sixpence or shilling [about 1/16 of an inch]. When the silver is so rolled, cut thereout so much as will nearly cover . . . the mettal wire . . . then put . . . the rolled silver . . . round the mettal wire and draw it through . . . the draw-plate . . . till the silver is

entirely closed round the mettal wire." The resultant plated wire could then be drawn to great length, producing a large quantity of quickly made low-cost material suitable for use in stylish objects such as cake baskets, glass-lined cream pots, sugar bowl and mustard pot frames, wine bottle coasters, wax jacks, epergnes, and candlesticks.[47]

The frame of the lyre shown here consists of silver-plated copper wire that is oval in section, while the five lyre strings are circular in cross section. The bobeche is removable and fits into a candle socket that was stamped to shape as two vertical halves and then soldered together. The base was also stamped to shape and pitch filled.

A close variant of this candlestick is pictured in plate 30 of a Sheffield trade catalogue datable to about 1800. That candlestick is 8 inches high and is described as being item number "578 oval [priced] at 20/ pr pair [but] if 10 inches high 30/," the price differential being based on the weight of metals in each.[48]

CANDLESTICK
119

THOMSON WARNER
LONDON, ENGLAND, 1782–98
BRONZE (COPPER 90.00,
TIN 4.30,
ZINC 3.50, LEAD 1.10), IRON

H. 9 3/4" (24.8 CM), W. 4" (10.2 CM),
D. 4" (10.2 CM)
ONE OF A PAIR
83.171.1

THOMSON WARNER, "son of Jacob Warner, citizen and tin plate worker of London, but by trade a founder," attained freedom to practice bronze and brass founding on May 4, 1761. His foundry, located in the Cripplegate section of London, was apparently large, as he took in at least thirteen apprentices between October 9, 1786, and September 13, 1787. He also appears to have been successful, for his work was known in the United States. Paul Revere imported one of Warner's bells as a model for the first example he cast in his Boston foundry in 1792.[49]

While most of Warner's activity was presumably devoted to heavy castings such as cannons, bells, and cauldrons, several pairs of candlesticks bearing his name are known.[50] All celebrate the British victory in the last siege of Gibraltar.

That garrison was taken from Spain in 1704 by England; during the eighteenth century, Spain attempted to win it back several times. Their final siege began in July 1779 and lasted forty months. It ended after the arrival of "the combined fleet of France and Spain . . . on the 12th" of September 1782 to displace the British, as recounted by Adm. Richard Lord Howe in the London publication *Gentleman's Magazine*. That fleet contained "ten battering ships . . . of different sizes from 1400 to 1600 tons. . . . Their guns . . . were brass twenty-six pounders and entirely new."[51] In spite of this formidable armada, the British sank most of the vessels within twenty-four hours.

The successful reversal of the lengthy siege "had a great impact on the British public." It generated numerous written and pictorial accounts, some of which were even available in America.[52] Spanish cannons, as a prize of war, were brought to London and recast, mostly into ordnance and possibly bells. A small amount of the metal was used to make souvenir candlesticks like this example, which has a seamed shaft, an internal push-up rod, and an unfinished underside.

CANDLESTICKS
120

MATTHEW BOULTON'S SOHO
MANUFACTORY
BIRMINGHAM, ENGLAND, 1784–1830
FUSED PLATE, IRON, GLASS, PITCH

H. 21 1/16" (53.5 CM),
DIAM. 6 7/16" (16.3 CM)
64.528.1, .2

ON JANUARY 18, 1772, Matthew Boulton wrote to his patron, Lady Mary Montague, that "it is not necessary to attend to elegance in such articles of my manufacture as are destined for Siberia or America." Even though he did not concern himself with criticism from Americans over the products of his factory, Boulton was sensitive to their purchasing power. He thought "it of far more consequence to supply the people than the Nobility only; and though [we] speak contemptuously of [them] we must own that we think they will do more toward supporting [my] great Manufactory than all the Lords in the Nation."[53]

The examples illustrated here may be like "Boulton and Fothergill's best plated candlesticks of the newest patterns . . .

just imported in the ship Betsy . . . and to be sold by Timothy Chandler in Arch Street between Second and Third streets" in Philadelphia in 1772. They employ an internal screw in the shaft "to heighten it as the candle burns down, so as to preserve the flame at the same actual height. This construction is only used in plated or silver candlesticks, as it is expensive." The candle socket is fitted with an inverted bell-shape glass shade "to protect the flame from the wind."[54] Whenever a globe of this type encircles a candle or oil lamp, the socket that holds it in place must be pierced to ensure a constant flow of air for the flame.

CANDLESTICK

121

ENGLAND, PROBABLY BIRMINGHAM,
1796–1810
BRASS (COPPER 73.36, ZINC 22.57,
LEAD 2.80, NICKEL 0.30, TIN 0.20)

H. 5 3/4" (14.6 CM), DIAM. 3 1/2"
(8.9 CM)
ONE OF A PAIR
57.57.3.1

FEW BRASS CANDLESTICKS can be said to have identical silver counterparts. The one illustrated here resembles a pair in silver that bears marks indicating they were made in the Soho manufactory of Matthew Boulton in 1796. Their design has been attributed to the architect James Wyatt, who is known to have supplied Boulton with patterns for silverware as early as the 1770s. Wyatt, however, was only one of several designers, including Robert Mylne, James Stuart, and William Chambers, who provided Boulton with source material. Additionally, Boulton employed at least one draftsman in his manufactory, a man named Hooker, whose task was presumably to execute designs.[55]

Regardless of the source, once designs were put into production and were successful, they were quickly imitated by competitors, especially if they derived from someone of Boulton's stature. Several brass candlesticks of this type, some of fixed height and others telescoping, are marked by Birmingham manufacturers, including William Fiddian and Company, John Turner and Company, and James Harrison and Son. The last of these advertised in the May 2, 1791, issue of *Aris's Birmingham Gazette* that "two or three steady industrious men may have constant work by applying to James Harrison & Son, candlestick makers and cock founders." This candlestick that shows no seam in the shaft, which is peened to the base, could have been made by any one of these men or their numerous competitors.

CANDLESTICKS
122

BIRMINGHAM, ENGLAND, 1798–1820
BRASS (COPPER 86.51, ZINC 5.09,
TIN 4.87, LEAD 2.52,
IRON 0.49, ANTIMONY 0.12)

H. 12" (30.5 CM), W. 4 5/8"
(11.8 CM), D. 4 5/8" (11.8 CM)
94.80.1, .2
GIFT OF BENJAMIN EDWARDS III

IN 1785 JAMES TATE, brazier and ironmonger in the County of Middlesex, was granted a patent that acknowledged his inventing "candlesticks and Nozells for Sconces, Chandeliers, Girandoles, and other things used for holding Candles, upon entire new Construction, which will receive, keep upright, and hold fast, Candles of every Size, without the trouble of Pareing, or the addition of Paper, and without Damaging the Candles either in putting in or taking out."[56]

In 1798 Samuel Roberts, silversmith and plater in the parish of Sheffield, County of York, was granted a patent acknowledging his inventing an alternate version of an adjustable nozzle that fit into, but was detachable from, a candlestick. It had a bottom that could be raised or lowered by a spiral thread, and it could "be made to contain and hold firm candles of different dimensions by means of movable or sliding pieces of metal within the nozzle without obstructing the working of the screw to raise the candle."[57]

Such a device is pictured in an English candlestick pattern book watermarked to the year 1803. The book is one of a group in the Peabody Essex Institute that was originally owned by the Salem, Massachusetts, hardware merchants Samuel Curwen and Robert Peele.[58] The device is described as a "patent nozzel," and it could be ordered for a candlestick of "any pattern at two shillings six pence pr pair extra," while candlesticks with the standard nozzle varied in price from 3s. 9d. each for a 3¼-inch-high example, to 10s. 9d. for one that was 10 inches in height. The candlesticks shown here, which have unfinished undersides and appear to have unseamed shafts that are attached to the bases with a tubular rivet, incorporate a nozzle that conforms in part to the specifications of Roberts's patent. There are three flanges in the bobeche that are attached to a mechanism that constricts them to grip candles of different diameters when the edge of the nozzle is rotated. The nozzle has no adjustable bottom.

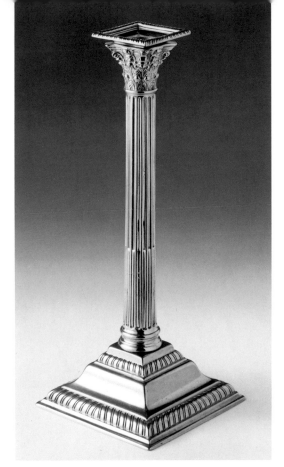

CANDLESTICK
123

ENGLAND, PROBABLY BIRMINGHAM
OR LONDON, 1810–30
PAKTONG (ZINC 43.75,
COPPER 42.28, NICKEL 8.48, IRON 4.74,
LEAD 0.31, TIN 0.14)

H. 12" (30.5 CM), W. 4 3/4"
(12.1 CM),
D. 4 3/4" (12.1 CM)
ONE OF A PAIR
64.960.1

IN 1781 BISHOP WATSON wrote that "he who imports tutenag from the East Indies or white copper from China or Japan, is sure of meeting with a ready market for his merchandize." The white silverlike nature of this alloy and its resistance to tarnish were widely admired, and European metallurgists put considerable effort into reproducing the alloy by determining its ingredients. Production was not accomplished on a commercial scale until the early nineteenth century, but Watson did observe that "imitations have . . . been made . . . and we have European tutenag, and European white copper, differing in some qualities from those which are brought from Asia, but resembling them in so many other that they have acquired their name."[59]

Although no documentable imitations have been identified, Watson may have been referring to attempts by the famed Soho manufactory of Matthew Boulton and James Fothergill begun in 1762 outside Birmingham. The range of their wares was extensive and, as noted in a 1772 advertisement, included "teutenaque buckles" and "teutenaque candlesticks." The pages of the firm's pattern books depict numerous candlestick designs, one of which, like the example illustrated here, utilizes a Corinthian capital atop a counterfluted column on a gadrooned base.[60] This style first became popular in the 1760s but continued to be made well after 1800, as shown by this example, which has a seamed shaft but also a tubular rivet to hold the shaft to the base, a typical nineteenth-century feature.

Most paktong was purchased and used in England and Europe, but it was also available in America during the eighteenth century. In 1773 the New York hardware merchant William Bailey advertised that he had "just imported in the latest vessels from England . . . India metal candlesticks." His competitor Richard Sause offered "tutenaque candlesticks . . . just imported by the *Grace* from Bristol."[61]

CANDLESTICK

124

ATTRIBUTED TO JAMES BARLOW
BIRMINGHAM, ENGLAND, 1842–56
BRASS (COPPER 71.66, ZINC 22.83,
LEAD 2.47, TIN 1.26)

H. 7 3/8" (18.7 CM),
DIAM. 4 1/8" (10.5 CM)
85.142

JAMES BARLOW listed himself as a "tea & house bell founder, tea urn and brass candlestick manufacturer" in the 1831 Birmingham, England, city directory. He was one of countless men engaged in the brass trade and would probably have no place in any history of the subject were he not issued a patent in 1839 for "certain improvements in the construction of candlesticks."[62]

His patent specification describes two innovations. The first was a ring of spring-steel fingers attached to a sliding disc in a candlestick socket. The steel fingers flexed to accommodate any diameter candle and constricted to hold the candle securely in an upright position. The sliding disc served as an elevator, raising the candle as it burned so that it would consume itself entirely with no waste. The patent specification describes and pictures a slender iron rod within the candlestick shaft, called a "pusher-up," which when pushed from beneath, raises the elevator. The candlestick shown here incorporates an improved version

that functions with an internal spiral mechanism attached to an oval-headed thumbscrew that passes through the apparently seamless shaft.[63]

Barlow's second improvement offered a new method of "connecting the parts of a candlestick together without solder." During the early nineteenth century, soldering (brazing) was the preferred means of joining a candlestick shaft to its base. Somewhat less frequently the two parts were riveted together, and even more rarely the shaft was screwed to the base. Barlow proposed that the lower end of the shaft have a hollow cylindrical extension that, when fit into the neck of the base, was flanged to hold the two together securely. He called the invention a "tubular rivet or hollow bolt."[64]

While little seems to have come from the first feature in his patent, the second appears to have eventually supplanted all other methods of joining candlestick shafts to their bases, being a simple, inexpensive, and easily assembled yet effective joint.

CANDLESTICK

125

RETAILED BY GREENHILL AND COMPANY
LONDON, ENGLAND, 1831–39
BRASS (COPPER 74.33, ZINC 20.13,
LEAD 2.86, TIN 2.19, IRON 0.23,
SILVER 0.14), STEEL, PAINT

H. 17 1/8" (43.5 CM), W. 9 1/2"
(24.1 CM), DIAM. 4 7/8" (12.4 CM)
57.902

GEORGE GREENHILL, probably the son of Joseph Greenhill, a wax and tallow chandler, listed himself in partnership with Eusebius Say as a tallow chandler and melter at 7 Bury Street, St. James, from 1824 through 1831. In 1831 he listed himself singly at the same address and continued to do so until 1839, when the directory entry recorded him as "Greenhill & Co., wax chandlers" and at the same time "Greenhill, Barrett & Co." The latter of these continued as the annual entry until 1844, when the firm obtained a royal license to list itself as "wax bleachers, manufacturers and oil merchants to the Queen and Queen Dowager."[65]

Chandlers made candles. Tallow chandlers made them of animal fat by dipping and molding. Their work was "a nauseous greasy Business, but the Profits attone for that Inconvenience; it is a healthy business enough, few of them die of Consumptions; yet . . . People, not used to it, find much difficulty to breathe near the Scent of a Tallow-Chandler's Work-House." Wax chandlers made candles of vegetable oils by rolling and drawing. They also made "sealing Wax and Wafers, and Flambeaus,

Links [and other related objects]. The business is still more profitable than that of the Tallow-Chandler, and reconed a more genteel Trade."[66]

Prior to the early nineteenth century, it was generally believed that "candles are preferable to lamps, as their light is less injurious both to the eyes and lungs. [Even so, they were not without their drawbacks], for as all candles burn downwards, the eye becomes necessarily more Fatigued and strained during the latter hours of candle-light [and] if the air be agitated ever so little, or if the candles are made of bad materials, they injure the eye by their flaring light."[67]

The candle arm on the fixture illustrated here, which can be adjusted along the height of the upright, answers the first of these problems. The adjustable painted shade above it resolves the second. The fixture itself, consisting mostly of cast parts with a sheet-brass shade, was probably made by a London founder for Greenhill, who had his name and address engraved under the base.

CANDLESTICK
126

PROBABLY ENGLAND, POSSIBLY
UNITED STATES, 1840–70
BRASS (COPPER 64.00, ZINC 33.50,
LEAD 1.30, TIN 0.50)

H. 10 1/8" (25.7 CM), W. 4 1/4"
(10.8 CM), D. 3 3/4" (9.5 CM)
ONE OF A PAIR
61.1564.1

THIS CANDLESTICK, with no apparent seam in the shaft, is almost identical to one drawn in the Birmingham brass founder James Barlow's English patent specification, dated April 25, 1839. Barlow describes it as "an ordinary cast-metal table candlestick . . . in the manufacture of which I propose no novelty," implying it is a typical and commonly made type.[68]

In outlining the details of his patent, Barlow states that his proposed improvements were "partly the communication from a foreigner abroad." That foreigner must certainly have been William Church, "citizen of the United States, now residing in Birmingham," who on October 17, 1839, applied for a United States patent virtually identical to Barlow's.[69]

Both patents protected two features. The first was "a new mode of holding the candle securely in the socket" by means of a spring metal insert. That portion of this candlestick is now missing. The second feature detailed "peculiar methods of connecting the parts of a candlestick together without solder." This was accomplished by means of a "tubular rivet or hollow bolt," a cylindrical extension of the lower end of the shaft that, when inserted through the base, was flanged to permanently attach the two. A further advantage noted by both Barlow and Church was that "a cork being firmly driven into the hollow bolt, prevents the tallow from leaking out when melted and also provides a convenient passage for the stem of the 'pusher up.'"[70] Although both items have been stripped from this example, the hollow rivet is clearly visible, as is the typically mid to late nineteenth-century incompletely skimmed and unfinished underside.

CANDLESTICK
127

MARKED "E6K"
PROBABLY ENGLAND, POSSIBLY
EUROPE, 1830–90
BRASS (COPPER 78.08, ZINC 19.53,
LEAD 1.32, TIN 0.41, IRON 0.20)

H. 9" (22.8 CM), DIAM. 4 1/2"
(11.4 CM)
ONE OF A PAIR
58.2758

IN 1894 IT WAS OBSERVED by J. M. O'Fallon that "brass is to be found everywhere; and chiefly of Birmingham manufacture. Forty thousand people are engaged producing it in Birmingham and its immediate vicinity. Though the supply of ordinary goods [like machine parts, boiler fittings, and other industrial brasswork] undoubtedly forms a great part of its trade, the best brass work in the world has been and is made there."[71]

Household objects, including furniture hardware, kitchen and cooking utensils, ornamented dining room and parlor objects, fireplace fittings, and lighting devices made up a large portion of this industry, with many and varied examples recorded pictorially in late nineteenth- and early twentieth-century brass-manufacturer's trade catalogues, such as those of W. Tonks and Sons, Evered and Company, R. Mansell and Son, Pearson-Page Company, and B. and S. H. Thompson.[72]

Many of the objects pictured therein are recognizably late nineteenth century in appearance. However, a large number were also designed after earlier styles in response to demand for "renewal of old fashions."

As a result of widening demand, there was a "large quantity of brass manufactured in [England] and sold as [antique]. And so well is some of this done that the fraud is only detected with difficulty."[73]

The candlestick illustrated here relates stylistically to those that were made during the third quarter of the eighteenth century. However, a number of features argue persuasively in favor of its having been manufactured about one hundred years later. The shaft is cast hollow and is apparently seamless. Eighteenth-century candlesticks of this type were seamed vertically. The proportion is poorly conceived, and details are awkwardly executed when compared to eighteenth-century examples. The underside of the base is skimmed in a cursory manner, and it lacks the attention to detail in finishing expected on earlier candlesticks. When made in the late nineteenth century, this candlestick may or may not have been intended to deceive. Now with several decades of wear, it could easily be misread by the casual observer as dating from the eighteenth century.[74]

CANDLESTICK
128

JAMES CLEWS AND SONS
BIRMINGHAM, ENGLAND, 1893–1914
BRASS (COPPER 64.40, ZINC 32.40,
LEAD 3.30, TIN 0.60, IRON 0.60), IRON

H. 10 7/8" (27.6 CM), W. 4 1/4"
(10.8 CM), D. 4 1/4" (10.8 CM)
ONE OF A PAIR
71.807.1

HORIZONTALLY REEDED KNOPS are a distinctive and apparently exclusive feature of nineteenth-century brass candlesticks and initially appear in Birmingham trade catalogues that bear watermarks dating them to the first quarter of that century. The feature is described as a "scrol vause" (scroll vase) and is always depicted in catalogues with the large end up, although actual candlesticks have this vase form both right side up and inverted.[75]

Most nineteenth-century brass candlesticks are unmarked, but this thinly cast example with seamless shaft, internal push-up, and unfinished underside is stamped on the outside of the base "ENGLAND/R^D 223580." The first part of this mark was placed on the candlesticks in accordance with the McKinley Tariff Act of 1890 and indicates they were intended for the American market. Section 6 of that act stipulates that

"all articles of foreign manufacture [imported into the United States] shall be plainly marked, stamped, branded or labeled in legible English words, so as to indicate the country of origin."[76]

The latter part of the mark is in accordance with parlimentary law that provided exclusive right of reproduction for designs submitted to the Patent Office as early as 1787. In 1883 that law was updated by the Patents, Designs, and Trade Marks Act, which allowed five years protection for designs of ornamental and useful articles. The design for this candlestick was registered and assigned the number stamped thereon on December 7, 1893, to James Clews and Sons, brass founders, and chandelier and gas-fitting manufacturers, in Birmingham.[77]

CANDLESTICK
129

MARKED "FS"
VIENNA, AUSTRIA, 1825–40
PAKTONG (COPPER 60.30, ZINC 20.80,
NICKEL 9.20, IRON 4.40,
COBALT 1.70), PLASTER

H 10 5/8" (26.7 CM),
DIAM. 4 5/8" (12.0 CM)
86.81
GIFT OF J. WILLIAM AND
JONATHAN D. INSLEE

"PACKFONG IS A CHINESE ALLOY." The term *packfong*, a variant of paktong–derived from the Chinese *pai-t'ung* (white brass)–was first coined by the Swedish chemist Gustavus von Engström in 1776. His spelling of the word was subsequently adopted by many Continental and English writers. He observed that "Pack-fong has a beautiful aspect, especially in ornaments, and is of great use for such household things that never come in contact with anything acid or salt, for it does not easily get tarnished."[78]

Prior to the nineteenth century, the alloy, consisting of copper, zinc, and nickel, was rarely made in the West because metallurgists had difficulty separating the last of these metals from its ores. Commercial production was accomplished in Berlin and Saxony in the 1820s.[79] At that time the term *german silver* became a popular synonym for the alloy, and a number of European, English, and American centers began its production.

During the ensuing decades various formulations were developed for different applications. When german silver is "intended as a substitute for silver, it should be composed of 25 parts of nickel, 25 of zinc, and 50 of copper. Castings, such as candlesticks, bells &c., may be made of an alloy, consisting of 20 of nickel, 20 of zinc, and 60 of copper; to which 3 of lead are added. An alloy better adapted for rolling consists of 25 of nickel, 20 of zinc, and 60 of copper."[80]

The candlestick shown here is fabricated of thinly rolled sheet metal. The shaft is seamed vertically while the candle cup and base are spun to shape and their edges folded. The entire candlestick is plaster filled, and an iron rod was probably imbedded for strength. The maker stamped his initials on the underside, but he is currently unidentified.[81]

CANDLESTICK
130

CORNELIUS AND BAKER
PHILADELPHIA, PENNSYLVANIA, 1851–70
BRASS (SHAFT: COPPER 70.10, ZINC
28.90, LEAD 0.70; BASE: COPPER 76.50,
ZINC 22.90), IRON

H. 9 3/8" (23.8 CM),
DIAM. 5 1/16"
(12.8 CM)
61.115

ROBERT CORNELIUS and Isaac F. Baker were not formally listed together in the Philadelphia city directories until 1851, but both were working at 176 Chestnut Street as early as 1842. Their firm was credited with "introducing a new era in the line of their manufactures in America. The beauty and variety of their patterns, and the substantial elegance of their work, entitle them to distinction."[82]

Although the candlestick shown here might not be described as beautiful or elegant, its type is notable as the earliest documentable American brass candlestick. It is made of sheet metal, and the tubular shaft contains an iron spring that automatically maintains a flame at a constant height by holding a candle against the removable cap as it burns. This concept is traceable to Benjamin Dearborn of Boston, who was granted a patent on October 9, 1804, for a spring-loaded candle-

stick.[83] Although innovative, the idea apparently never proved practical because melted wax or tallow quickly clogged between the candle and tube, overriding the upward push of the spring.

In 1860 Henry Rogers of South Manchester, Connecticut, patented an "elastic spring thimble," which he maintained would "prevent the grease running down between it and the body of the candle." Furthermore he stated that it would "prevent the drop of grease while being carried, or inclined, as would necessarily occur in the old way."[84] But the invention was offered when kerosene was becoming widespread as an illuminant. That fact, coupled with the ease of using paraffin candles atop the traditional type of candlestick, doomed his innovation and the spring-loaded candlestick to obscurity.

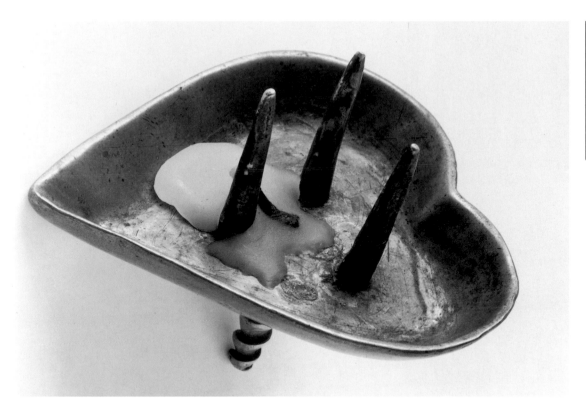

SAVE-ALL
131

PROBABLY ENGLAND, 1700–1770
BRASS (COPPER 74.67, ZINC 23.39,
LEAD 1.25, IRON 0.34, TIN 0.12,
SILVER 0.12)

H. 2 1/16" (5.2 CM), W. 2 1/4"
(5.7 CM), D. 2 5/8" (6.7 CM)
59.2735

CANDLES WERE THE PRINCIPAL source of artificial light in Europe, England, and the American colonies prior to the increased use of oil lamps at the end of the eighteenth century. Although burned in virtually every public and private building, candles did have drawbacks. Their light was feeble; they could easily be extinguished, even by a slight breeze; and they were messy. They also left stumps after the candle had burned down to the top of the candlestick socket. Discarding stumps was wasteful and even expensive, so many were recycled by the cost-conscious householder. This process saved wax or tallow, but what was left of the wick was still unusable.

An anonymous individual presented a simple solution to the problem at an early date. The device was called a save-all. In the late seventeenth century, Randle Holme described save-alls as "things made after the forme of a candle sockett, and are set in the stick as the sockett is, and the candle that is almost burnt is set upon the point

of iron, set in the middle of it, where it will burne, to the last sight of the wick, and drop of Tallow, and much better and Longer, then if it remained in the stick."[85]

Save-alls were still in use more than one hundred years later, although apparently on the decline as noted by Thomas Webster, who stated that "economical housewives use, for burning their ends of candles, a little apparatus called a save-all, which deserves much more patronage than it meets with. It is usually made with a socket to fit into the candlestick, on which is a circular cup, with three projecting wires to fix the piece of candle between. These wires bend and are soon out of order, which may be one reason why this is not a favorite" household amenity.[86] The cast, heart-shape example shown here has a hand-cut thread onto which a piece of wood, cork, or other material may be screwed. That, in turn, fits into a candle socket.

CHAMBERSTICK
132

ILLEGIBLE MARK ON HOOK
PROBABLY BAVARIA, POSSIBLY
SWITZERLAND, 1770–1830
COPPER, IRON

H. 8" (20.3 CM), W. 9 1/8" (23.2 CM),
D. 5 1/2" (14.0 CM)
60.583

A CHAMBER OR BEDCHAMBER candlestick was designed to be the most portable of all lighting devices. It was the preferred type of candlestick to bring light into a darkened room; from it other candles or a fire would be lit if needed. It always has a deeply dished base to catch the drippings that invariably resulted from its being carried from place to place. The large diameter and low height help prevent it from overturning and accidently starting a fire. Although absent from the example shown here, chamber candlesticks were often fitted with a conical extinguisher and sometimes a scissorslike snuffer. More expensive models had a glass shade to keep the flame steady and bright while it was being carried.

In most chamber candlesticks, "the bottoms of the sockets are made to rise up to burn the last portion of the candle."[87] In this example, the bottom can be adjusted to five different positions by sliding the handle along the vertical slot as the candle is consumed.

This chamber candlestick is made of relatively thin sheet metal. Consequently, the perimeter of the drip pan has been wrapped around an iron wire to prevent it from splitting. The maker stamped a mark on the hook that extends from the bobeche, but it is not fully legible. The character of this mark and the design of the candlestick relate closely to silver examples made in lower Germany and Switzerland in the late eighteenth and early nineteenth centuries.[88]

CHAMBERSTICK
133

MARKED "IC"
ENGLAND, PROBABLY BIRMINGHAM, 1800–1820
BRASS (COPPER 82.85, ZINC 14.20,
LEAD 1.37, TIN 0.44, SILVER 0.09,
ANTIMONY 0.04)

H. 4 1/2" (11.4 CM), W. 6 3/4"
(17.2 CM), DIAM. 5 5/8" (14.3 CM)
ONE OF A PAIR
69.275.1
GIFT OF MRS. ALFRED C. HARRISON

SHORT CANDLESTICKS with wide-dished bases, often fitted with a handle, were used to carry a lit candle from one place to another. They were usually called chamber candlesticks but could also be identified as hand candlesticks or "sheet hand" candlesticks, when made of rolled or stamped sheet metal.[89]

Most candlesticks of this type have no identifying marks. The example illustrated here has the initials of the maker, "IC," stamped on the top of the ejector tab, similar to iron candlesticks made by William and Thomas Bill; Mary, Thomas, and William Dowler; John and Durant Hidson; and Charles and James Shaw, all of whom were working in the Birmingham area during the early nineteenth century.

An anonymous English trade catalogue datable to about 1803, now in the collection of the Peabody Essex Institute and having a long history of American ownership, pictures chambersticks that are like this example in every respect. The notation accompanying the illus-

tration states that they were made in three sizes, with or without beading. The conical douter was included in the purchase price, but scissors-like "snuffers to suit," which could be fitted into the void below the candle cup, were optional.[90]

Although the douter is made of seamed sheet metal, this chamber candlestick is cast, with no apparent seams in the candle socket, typical of those made during the first few decades of the nineteenth century. By the 1830s this type was almost completely replaced by less expensive stamped or spun "sheet hand" candlesticks, which like earlier cast examples, were shipped in large numbers from Birmingham to the United States. The sixty pairs of "brass chamber candlesticks" listed in the February 4, 1847, invoice from Joshua Scholefield and Sons of Birmingham to the Philadelphia hardware merchants Samuel and Jacob A. Scheble serve to suggest the extent of this trade.[91]

CHAMBERSTICK
134

SKULTUNA MESSINGSBRUK FACTORY
SKULTUNA, SWEDEN, 1825–40
BRASS (COPPER 68.05,
ZINC 31.05, LEAD 0.31)

H. 2" (5.1 CM),
DIAM. 4 1/4" (10.3 CM)
ONE OF A PAIR
59.678

IN 1827 ROBERT ROBERTS published a small book entitled *The House Servant's Directory* in which he proffered information to help the various members of a household staff take care of their employers' needs. With respect to lighting, Roberts stated that "you should always make it a regular rule to set up your candles in the morning, and particularly your chamber candlesticks, as they are often called for in the course of the day to send letters, &c."[92]

Chamber candlesticks were always designed with a short shaft and a large diameter base because they were more frequently moved than any other type of candlestick. The example shown here is made of thin sheet metal. The base appears to be spun. The rim is simply folded, not wrapped, around an iron reinforcing wire, and the sheet metal candle cup is held in place with three simple tubular extensions that are bent at 90 degrees and riveted to the pan. As such, they were a very inexpensive utilitarian product.

The Skultuna brass factory was founded in 1607, at the direction of Karl IX, King of Sweden. The firm's principal production consisted of wire and sheet brass, a considerable percentage of which was sent to Great Britain, France, and Russia. Additionally, the firm made a wide range of domestic wares, including kettles, pots, bowls, candlesticks, chandeliers, and mortars.

CANDELABRUM

135

ENGLAND, PROBABLY
SHEFFIELD, 1785–1800
FUSED PLATE

H. 13 5/16" (34.6 CM), W. 15"
(38.1 CM), D. 4 3/8" (11.1 CM)
ONE OF A PAIR
65.1376.1

ON JANUARY 21, 1797, the New York City silversmith and merchant Daniel Van Voorhis stated in the *New York Daily Advertiser* that he had in stock the "best London plated lyre candlesticks, do brackets [and] do branches with 3 lights." In doing so, he accurately described this candelabrum for three lights.[93]

The bases, candle cups, and bobeches of the candelabrum and its mate are fabricated of fused, plated sheet metal, which had been used extensively by the manufactories in Sheffield, Birmingham, and London since its invention by Thomas Boulsover about 1743.[94]

The uprights and arms are composed of plated wires that are either circular or oval in section. The use of plated wires in domestic objects was as old as the technique of making fused plate but had always been an expensive process and was therefore used sparingly. That changed in the late 1760s when new manufacturing techniques were introduced, involving bending a "strip of fine silver $1/32$ of an inch thick [around] a copper bar about five inches long by 1 inch thick which had previously been drawn into a round form by the end of a whortle. The two metals were then wired together and united by fusion. After being plated the bar was repeatedly drawn through a whortle until it assumed the form of wire. This also gave it rigidity and smoothness, whilst at the same time it brought the two edges of silver together, these being purposely left slightly apart to facilitate the process of fusion."[95] With that development it became possible for the first time to inexpensively make wire cake baskets, cruet frames, toast racks, bottle coasters, epergnes, and this type of candelabrum.

CANDELABRA

136

SHOP OF PIERRE-PHILIPPE THOMIRE
(1751–1843)
PARIS, FRANCE, 1810–15
BRASS (COPPER 70.00, ZINC 25.87,
TIN 1.62, SILVER 1.45),
MERCURY GILDING

H. 22 1/4" (56.5 CM), DIAM. 7"
(17.8 CM)
EACH ONE OF A PAIR
61.1224.1 (LEFT)
61.1223.1

THE ORIGINAL DESIGN for these candelabra was executed by the Parisian artist Pierre-Paul Prud'hon in 1810 for Empress Marie-Louise. His design was translated into silver and lapis lazuli by silversmith Jean-Baptiste Claude Odiot and brass worker Pierre-Philippe Thomire. These two are among the many gilt brass examples closely copied after that royal commission in silver.[96]

The female figures probably represent the sister goddesses Aglaia, Thalia, and Euphrosyne–commonly called the three Graces–who, in Greek mythology, were bestowers of beauty and charm. Each holds a torch that serves as a candle socket when the fruit clusters are removed. These fixtures, in conjunction with

a plateau that formed a group known as a "surtout de table," were designed to illuminate a dining table.[97] The reverse of several pieces shown here illustrate assembly marks of grooves, dots, and numerals, and a workman's initial that is incised.

Lighting of this type is usually associated with the severe and monumental French interiors developed under Napoleon's reign from 1804 to 1815, but such items were also exported. A "pair of candelabra dorée" was among the many stylish French goods ordered by the Philadelphia merchant Thomas Fletcher from the factors Poirier and Rouge when on a buying trip in Paris in 1825.[98]

GIRANDOLES
137

CORNELIUS AND COMPANY (1839–51)
PHILADELPHIA, PENNSYLVANIA,
1848–51
BRASS (COPPER 82.09, ZINC 16.20,
LEAD 1.49), MARBLE, GLASS

CANDELABRA: H. 21 1/4" (54.0 CM),
W. 15 7/8" (40.3 CM), D. 6" (15.1 CM);
CANDLESTICKS: H. 16 7/8" (42.9 CM),
W. 5 3/4" (14.6 CM), D. 3 3/8" (8.1 CM)
91.43.1–.3

CHRISTIAN CORNELIUS listed himself as a silversmith in the Philadelphia city directory in 1810. In 1813 he had changed his listing to silver plater, which he retained until 1825, when he changed again to silver plater and patent lamp manufacturer. He was joined by his son Robert about 1831. By 1837 they listed themselves as lamp and chandelier manufacturers. From that point the firm grew and by 1866 was "an immense factory, requiring as its motive power several hundred workmen, and two large steam engines" devoted to the manufacture of all forms of lighting.[99]

The firm produced a large variety of oil, gas, and candle lighting from simple, tubular, spring-loaded sheet-brass candlesticks to the massive chandelier in the Hall of Representatives in Nashville, Tennessee. The chandelier "is a mammoth of its kind—it is fifteen feet in diameter; on it, and used as decorations, are buffalos, Indians,

corn, cotton, and tobacco plants, thus representing the products of the State in the last three mentioned articles."[100]

The ornamental motifs incorporated into that chandelier typify much of the firm's work, which was lauded as being artistically highly developed. Their lighting was stated to have "enriched and adorned thousands of private and public buildings with masterpieces of beauty, whose influence has been felt throughout society, and aided in awakening a taste for objects of art."[101]

By the 1840s, candles had fallen from favor for lighting interiors as oil and gas rose in popularity. This did not prevent candlesticks from serving as a vehicle for artistic and, in some instances, historic and literary expression. This set of girandoles, being a case in point, depicts five figures drawn directly from James Fenimore Cooper's *The Last of the Mohicans*, first published in 1826.

Dominating the central fixture is Chingachgook, chief of the Mohican tribe. He is introduced early in Cooper's novel, "seated on the end of a mossy log. His closely shaved head . . . was without ornament of any kind, with the exception of a solitary eagle's plume, that crossed his crown, and depended over the left shoulder, a tomahawk and scalping knife . . . were in his girdle." Beside him sits Natty Bumppo, also known as Hawkeye, who "wore a hunting-shirt of forest green, fringed with faded yellow, and a summer cap of skins which had been shorn of fur. He also wore a knife in a girdle of wampum, like that which confined the scant garments of the Indian, but no tomahawk. His moccasins were ornamented after the gay fashion of the natives, while the only part of his under-dress which appeared below the hunting frock, was a pair of buckskin leggings, that laced at the sides."[102] Behind them stands Chingachgook's son, Uncas, the last of the Mohican tribe.

The flanking fixtures depict Cora Munro and Maj. Duncan Heyward, the former abducted in Cooper's novel by hostile Indians and rescued by Natty Bumppo, Chingachgook, and Uncas, with the aid of Major Heyward.

The Last of the Mohicans proved to be a very popular and widely read novel. Its influence extended beyond the realm of literature to have an impact on the design of household amenities. This particular interpretation was created in 1848 and 1849 by Isaac F. Baker, a partner in the Cornelius firm. Baker drew and described what he called designs for furniture ornaments in two separate applications to the United States Patent Office. The design patent for his three-figure grouping was approved on December 5, 1848, while those for the flanking figures were approved on April 10, 1849.[103] With approval of the design patents, Cornelius and Company began production of these girandoles in quantity for use on mantels and pier tables in stylish households.

CANDELABRUM
138

BAKER, ARNOLD AND COMPANY
PHILADELPHIA, PENNSYLVANIA, 1871–78
BRASS (COPPER 79.21, ZINC 19.53,
LEAD 1.04), SHEET IRON, PAINT

H. 26" (66.0 CM),
DIAM. 16 3/4" (42.5 CM)
59.506

"WILLIAM C. BAKER was successor to his father [Isaac] in the old firm of Cornelius & Baker; while Crawford Arnold occupied for a number of years a position . . . with the same." These two men entered into a partnership and built a large fireproof brick factory on Twelth Street between Brown and Olive when the firm of Cornelius and Baker dissolved in 1870. Before Baker, Arnold and Company closed in 1878, their factory employed as many as five hundred workmen making chandeliers, gas fixtures, other lighting devices, ornaments, and statuettes, which were shipped to "every part of the United States, Cuba, South America, Mexico, China and India."[104]

The firm supplied lighting to many Pennsylvania buildings, including "the opera houses at Easton, Reading, and Erie," but their most celebrated commission was for the Masonic Temple in Philadelphia.

"Viewing the gas fixtures of this magnificent structure with its gas jets not counted by hundreds but thousands, its gorgeous chandeliers, candelabras, brackets and pendants, with their chaste original designs, [proved] that Messrs. Baker, Arnold & Co. [were] able to undertake the largest contracts."[105]

This candelabrum is modeled on early nineteenth-century French examples, which were imported into the United States. The candle holders "rise or fall, in order to keep the light always at the same height." The conical shade "japanned, white within, to reflect the light strongly" down, conceals the flame from the eyes. The foliate candle arms and cups are cast; the base with internal iron weight is spun; the upright shaft is a section of seamed gas tubing supported on a cylinder with die-rolled strips of ornament.[106]

SCONCE

139

PROBABLY FRANCE, POSSIBLY
THE NETHERLANDS, 1650–90
BRASS (COPPER 84.90, ZINC 12.08,
TIN 1.40, SILVER 0.50,
ANTIMONY 0.29, IRON 0.22)

H. 6 3/8" (16.2 CM), D. 6 5/8"
(16.8 CM), W. 2 5/8" (6.7 CM)
ONE OF A PAIR
64.530.1

THE FRENCH ANTIQUARY and student of lighting Henri-René d'Allemagne commented in his book that "in addition to candlesticks intended for use on tables, there were, during the seventeenth century [in France], small sconces with one arm [called *appliqués*] which were normally intended to be placed on a chimney breast to either side of a Venetian mirror [and] was considered to be a very valuable object."[107] The illustration accompanying that observation depicts five *appliqués*, one of which is almost identical to the example pictured here.

Although surrounded by bold and distracting motifs, the center of the backplate is significant in that it depicts implements of war–a bow, a quiver of arrows, and a flaming torch. Such arrangements of artifacts, called trophies, came to be an important part of French architectural design. As stated by the architect François Blondel (1618–86), "trophys of arms or of war [and] trophys of peaceful activities, such as the sciences, the arts and

other amusements, arranged for instance as a group of musical instruments [heighten a building's interest], their beauty consisting principally in the choice and disposition, and in the appropriateness which these ornaments must have to the general design of the building."[108]

As the trend grew in popularity, practitioners began to define the rationale. For instance: "It would be inappropriate to represent in trophy form the trappings of a church, the candlesticks, the chalice, the cruets and other similar things, unless they had traditionally been assigned the meaning embodied by their use in those trophys."[109] Furniture and furnishings were increasingly being seen as an integral part of an interior design scheme. It logically followed that the decorative allusions had to be en suite with the purpose and tone of the architecture, as philosophically embodied in the decorative features of this cast sconce.

SCONCE
140

PROBABLY FRANCE, POSSIBLY THE
NETHERLANDS, 1680–1710
BRASS (COPPER 74.55, ZINC 22.42,
TIN 1.17, LEAD 0.98, IRON 0.46)

H. 9" (22.8 CM), W. 2 7/8"
(7.3 CM), D. 8 7/16" (21.4 CM)
ONE OF A PAIR
54.66.1

Marcus Vitruvius Pollio was a Roman architect and engineer who is thought to have lived during Caesar Augustus's reign between 27 B.C. and A.D. 14. Little else is known about him except his authorship of *De Architectura Libri Decum*, a book that became the undisputed authority on all architectural matters in Renaissance Europe. His observations, which dealt with every aspect of the subject from the proper education of an architect and the fundamental principles of architecture to the specifics of building materials and construction techniques, were accepted as the final word from the fifteenth through the eighteenth centuries.

In discussing the importance of an architect's education, Vitruvius stated that "wide knowledge of history is requisite because, among the ornamental parts of an architect's design . . . there are many [features for which] the underlying idea of [their use] he should be able to explain . . . for instance, suppose [he erects] marble statues of women . . . called Caryatides, to take the place of columns. . . . [He would have done so knowing that] Caryae, a state in Peloponnesus, sided with . . .

Persian enemies against Greece, later the Greeks, having . . . won . . . the war . . . declared war against . . . Caryae. They took the town, killed the men . . . and carried off their wives into slavery. The architects of the time designed . . . statues of these women [for public buildings] placed so as to carry a load, in order that the sin and punishment of the people of Caryae might be known and handed down . . . to posterity."[110]

Renaissance and post-Renaissance European architects from Michaelangelo to Robert Adam used female figures in this manner for ornamental and historical purposes. At the same time, other craftsmen and artisans, including brass workers, labored under the premise that their work was "either improved or ornamented by Architecture," mandating that the latter be used to not only regulate proportion but also provide a source of decorative motifs.[111] The cast sconce shown here exemplifies correct architectural proportion and the adaptation of architectural motifs, including a caryatid supporting the candle arm.

SCONCE
141

FRANCE, 1725–49
BRASS (COPPER 76.96, ZINC 17.06,
LEAD 2.83, TIN 2.13, IRON 0.66,
SILVER 0.18, ANTIMONY 0.16)

H. 6 5/8" (16.8 CM), W. 3"
(7.6 CM), D. 8" (20.3 CM)
ONE OF FOUR
59.1869.1

ALTHOUGH THIS SCONCE has no evidence of silvering on it, another pair in the Winterthur collection, which is identical, retains a substantial amount. This example was probably originally silvered and covered with a coat of lacquer to retard tarnish, in a method known as french plating. The process "consisted of burnishing a beaten leaf [or sheet] of silver at a low heat on the metal before oxidation [of the object's surface] took place."[112]

Each sconce in the set is a composite assembly. The back plate, corbel, arm, and bobeche were individually cast. The candle cup was cast in two vertical halves that were then brazed together. That cup is connected to the end of the cantilevered arm with a threaded brass bolt, while the arm, although it appears to be supported by the corbel, passes through and is bolted to the octagonal plate.

Although Paris was the center of the brass industry in eighteenth-century France, it is unlikely that this sconce and others like it in collections elsewhere were made there. The simplicity of the form, poor definition and integration of the design elements, and coarse workmanship suggest fabrication in a less demanding center.

Only three of the four sconces in this set are stamped with a crowned "c" within a conforming cartouche, in accordance with French law. That law, in effect throughout France between 1745 and 1749, levied a tax on all newly made objects of copper or copper alloys. It also stipulated that older objects, fabricated before the law was promulgated, were taxable if taken in trade.

SCONCE

142

ENGLAND, PROBABLY LONDON OR
BIRMINGHAM, 1760–80
BRASS (COPPER 74.90, ZINC 22.12,
LEAD 1.29, TIN 0.99, IRON 0.57)

H. 12 7/8" (32.7 CM), W. 11"
(28.0 CM), D. 9 3/8" (23.8 CM)
ONE OF A PAIR
57.126.26

ARABESQUE WAS DEFINED by Ephriam Chambers in 1751 as a term "applied to such paintings, ornaments of freezes, &c . . . which consist . . . of imaginary foliages, plants, stalks, &c."[113] In conjunction with the cartouche and the trophy, it constituted the essence of the style known as rococo.

The style was brought to its peak in France by Gilles-Marie Oppenord (1672–1742), Nicholas Pineau (1684–1754), and Juste-Aurèle Meissonier (1695–1750) as well as a host of lesser artists, designers, sculptors, and metalworkers. Two who are identified as having created designs for wall sconces that relate closely to the one illustrated here are René-Michel Slodtz (1705–64) and Francois de Cuvilliers (1695–1768).[114]

The designs of Slodtz, Cuvilliers, and their competitors, created for the French court and aristocracy, were published in France, Germany, the Netherlands, and London. Those designs and the ideas brought by craftsmen emigrating from the Continent provided source material for Englishmen like Matthias Lock (ca. 1710–65) and Thomas Johnson

(1714–ca. 1778) who, in turn, created and published designs for Britons who coveted objects in the French taste.

This sconce, or girandole, is an excellent interpretion of the French *genre pittoresque* made for the English market. Cast in separate parts, the decorated surfaces have been chased and the plain areas burnished. The sconce was then coated with tinted lacquer to simulate gilding. There is no maker's mark, but the form is closely related to an illustration in an anonymous English brass-founder's pattern book, through which sconces of this type were marketed widely.[115]

The "double and single branches . . . imported in the latest vessels from London and Bristol" by Peter Goelet in New York in 1768 were probably much simpler. However, the "pair of elegant sconces . . . just imported in the New-York from London and the last vessels from Bristol by William Neilson" may have begun to approximate the arabesque fantasy embodied in this example.[116]

SCONCE
143

PROBABLY ENGLAND, 1770–1800
BRASS (COPPER 68.30, ZINC 29.00,
LEAD 1.13, IRON 0.22), IRON

H. 14 1/2" (36.8 CM), W. 16 3/8"
(41.6 CM), D. 13" (33.0 CM)
ONE OF FOUR
65.2875.1

ROBERT ROBERTS OFFERED two suggestions about wall sconces in *The House Servant's Directory*. In the first he stated, "If you have branches around your drawing room, and they are to be lit up when there is a party, you must trim your wax candles sublimely, with some white paper cut in the form of a rose, to go round the socket of the branch." He averred that "this looks very well at night."[117]

Apart from that recommendation, and in a much more practical view, he suggested that the servant "should likewise have a piece of taper tied on the end of a piece of rattan, on purpose for lighting [candles in wall sconces], as it is very awkward to bring steps into the room."[118] In recommending tapers, Roberts probably had in mind breaking off a piece of the slender coiled candle kept in a brass or silver-plated wax jack for use in melting sealing wax. Rattan had probably been conveniently

at hand when this idea came to him, but a splint of wood would have served just as well.

The three-armed sconce shown here and its mates were cast in parts. The stylized leafy decoration was then textured, and the detailing of the design elements was sharpened with chasing tools. The undecorated areas were burnished. After assembly, the entire sconce was coated with tinted lacquer to retard tarnish and provide a semblance of gilding. None of that lacquer remains.

As Roberts noted, sconces of this type were suitable for use in drawing rooms. It may be that the "pair of branches" inventoried in the parlor of the Philadelphian Peter Glenworth in 1793 was similar to these.[119]

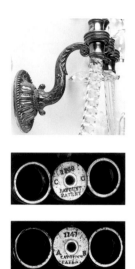

SCONCE
144

MOSES LAFOUNT
PENTONVILLE, ENGLAND,
1796–1810
BRASS (COPPER 80.03, ZINC 16.78,
LEAD 2.50, IRON 0.30, TIN 0.24,
SILVER 0.12), GLASS

H. 22" (44.9 CM),
W. 14 5/8" (37.2 CM),
D. 9 7/8" (25.1 CM)
ONE OF A PAIR
61.901.1

ON DECEMBER 23, 1796, Moses LaFount, lustremaker in Pentonville, Middlesex, was granted a patent for assembling glass parts of lighting devices. The invention consisted of a "plate, and Hoop or Band, of a Circular or other Form, either Attached to or Detached from each other, to be made use of in the Mounting of Glass Chandeliers, Gerandoles or other Lustres." With this device, he maintained that glass lighting fixtures "had a much more elegant form than any which had been theretofore used, [since] the Upper and Lower Branches had the appearance of being one Branch only."[120]

The wall sconce illustrated here, its mate, and a closely related pair of mantel or table lustres employ a variant of that invention in their construction.[121] Although the description and drawings for LaFount's patent specify a flat circular plate with piercings surrounded by a ring to hold the upper and lower glass arms in place, these fixtures affect the same result with opposed brass sockets.

This sconce and its mate are numbered sequentially 1147 and 1148, while the similar pair of mantel lustres are numbered 499 and 500, probably representing production figures.

HALL LANTERN
145

ENGLAND, 1810–30
BRASS (COPPER 75.26,
ZINC 23.42, LEAD 0.50),
GLASS, PAINT

H. (EXCLUDING HANGER) 26"
(66.0 CM),
DIAM. 13 1/2" (34.3 CM)
64.783

LANTERNS "are generally made of Brass, cast from Wooden Moulds" and designed to hang "under Landings of stairs and between Columns or from the centers of Arches in Halls, Passages, &c."[122]

While they vary considerably in size, shape, and detail, usually they "are either of the vase kind or consist of panes of glass in frames. . . . The lights [they contain] may be, in the first case, [candles or] simple lamps with one or more wicks, or Argand lamps, when a stronger light is required. Of course, it is essential that a supply of air shall be given to the light by proper openings in the [base of the] containing vessel. A glass [dome] is suspended over the lamps, when they are not Argand's to collect the smoke, which otherwise would blacken the ceiling."[123]

Access to the candle or lamp contained within lanterns was essential for proper operation and was accomplished with a counterbalanced elevator mechanism of chains that pass over pulleys, the lantern attached at one end and a lead weight at the other. With this device a lantern could be lowered to light or extinguish the fixture, trim the wick, or replace a spent candle or lamp fuel and then returned to the proper height. Lanterns of the vase kind were fitted with a removable base to facilitate these chores. Those with panes of glass in brass frames had hinged doors for the same purpose.[124]

The frosted and polychrome-painted lantern shown here employs a combination of cast and die-rolled brass parts. The suspension ring consists of three cast strips brazed end to end forming a circle of palmettes that is brazed to three cast satyr's heads, which serve as suspension hooks. The foliate strip encircling the lantern's base is a single thin-walled, die-rolled strip with removable cast element consisting of a candle cup, pierced breather, and pendant bud-shape handle.

CHANDELIER
146

PROBABLY NORTHERN EUROPE,
POSSIBLY ENGLAND, 1650–1800
BRASS (COPPER 85.35, ZINC 5.02,
TIN 4.79, LEAD 4.70, IRON 0.83,
ANTIMONY 0.60, SILVER 0.23)

H. 16 3/4" (42.5 CM),
DIAM. 17 3/4" (45.1 CM)
69.774

IN 1434 THE FLEMISH ARTIST Jan Van Eyck painted a double portrait of the newly married Giovanni Arnolfini and his wife.[125] Hanging above the subjects is an elaborate brass chandelier with each upwardly curved branch held to the central shaft by a sliding dovetail. The candle cups and bobeches are screwed into an offset tab at the end of each branch.

At that time chandeliers were largely the prerogative of the church and the wealthiest of individuals. As their use gradually became more widespread during the following two centuries, their design evolved. By the mid seventeenth century sliding dovetail joints were replaced by angular hooks, square in section, fit into individual spherical sockets that projected from the shaft or, alternately, a single flat circular disc incorporated into the shaft. Branches curved downward in a pronounced S shape with candle cups and bobeches that threaded centrally on their ends.[126]

These changes probably first took place in base-metal workers' shops in major production centers like Antwerp, Paris, Dinant, and London. From there, new techniques and styles spread to influence makers in smaller, less affluent cities.

The shaft of the chandelier shown here is a single-piece hollow casting from the trefoil hanging loop to just below the branches. The removable pendant, bulbous, reeded knop is held in place by two small opposed tabs that fit through recesses in a circular lip. All these features are atypical of up-to-date chandelier construction in the seventeenth and eighteenth centuries. In conjunction with the retarditaire sliding dovetails and tabular ends to the branches, they suggest fabrication in a tradition-oriented small European town or in the west of England.

CHANDELIER

147

ENGLAND, 1770–1800
BRASS (COPPER 75.63, ZINC 16.81,
LEAD 5.37, TIN 1.00, IRON 0.84,
SILVER 0.16, ANTIMONY 0.12), IRON

H. 29" (73.7 CM),
DIAM. 35" (88.9 CM)
59.109.1

THE RECTOR AT BALDOCK, HERTFORDSHIRE, complained that "it was inconvenient for him to finish the Afternoon Service in the Winter Months without a greater number of Candles [and suggested] that if a pair of Chandeleers were placed in the body of the Church they would not only answer the intended purpose, but also very much ornament the Church."[127] In doing so, the rector identified a type of lighting device that had become popular for places of public gathering, especially churches, in England by the mid seventeenth century.

Chandeliers were considered so appropriate for churches that it has been estimated that by 1830 upwards of one thousand places of worship in England had them. Most were brass with from three to forty-two branches arranged radially in one, two, and sometimes three tiers.[128]

The example illustrated here is typical of those produced during the mid to late eighteenth century in many English centers north to Chester and Wigan, south to Bridgewater and Totnes, and west to

Bristol, but principally London. The shaft consists of eleven cast parts held together by an internal iron rod threaded at both ends. The six cast branches bolt through a band encircling the knop.

Unmarked, it could have been from any of the aforementioned cities. Birmingham is another possible source, as evidenced in a brass-founder's trade catalogue in the Winterthur Library. One of the engraved plates depicts a very similar chandelier that is described as a "Church Chandelier" and is available with 6, 8, 10, 12, or 18 lights.[129]

American founders occasionally advertised their ability to make chandeliers, such as Daniel King of Philadelphia, who stated that he "makes . . . all kinds and sizes of chandeliers or branches, for Places of Worship or shop use." Similarly, John Robertson, brass founder in King Street, Charleston, South Carolina, noted that he "continues to make in the neatest manner, all sorts of brass candlesticks, and church lustres or branches."[130]

CHANDELIER
148

ENGLAND, 1760–1800
BRASS (COPPER 74.18, ZINC 21.59,
LEAD 2.66, TIN 0.81, IRON 0.51,
SILVER 0.12), IRON

H. 51" (127.5 CM),
DIAM. 50" (125.0 CM)
57.47

THIS CHANDELIER, the largest at Winterthur and the only one with two tiers of branches, has a central shaft composed of twenty separate but interlocking castings held together with an internal wrought iron rod threaded at both ends. It weighs 176 pounds and has twenty-four branches.[131]

The branches bolt through collars incorporated within the maximum circumference of the shaft's two main knops, a construction feature first recorded in English chandeliers in 1739. Fully developed gadrooning, present below the flaming finial and also below the primary knop, is a stylistic feature first recorded in English brass chandeliers in 1747. Foliate bobeches and borders bolted to the secondary knop and central fillet on the shaft seem to first appear in conjunction with the other two features about 1760.[132]

In England and Europe large chandeliers were used in public gathering places such as churches, meeting halls, banqueting rooms,

and state reception areas. Smaller examples were used similarly, it being "customary with barbers to have their shops lighted by candles in brass chandeliers of three, four and six branches."[133] Smaller varieties were also used in a domestic context, best recorded in seventeenth- and eighteenth-century Dutch genre paintings.

Affluent American congregations often imported English and, to a lesser degree, Dutch brass chandeliers. Fine documented examples remain in Christ Church, Boston, installed in 1725; Christ Church, Philadelphia, installed in 1740; Touro Synagogue, Newport, Rhode Island, installed in 1769; and other churches in American coastal cities.[134]

American brass founders competed for patronage, as did Frederick Weckerlin, brazier in Philadelphia, who announced in 1771 that he "practices all sorts of fine and coarse brass work, namely . . . chandeliers for churches of 12 to 36 lights made of the finest and newest styles and varnished."[135]

A.

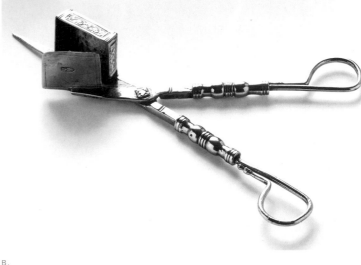

B.

SNUFFERS
149 a,b

A. GERMANY OR
THE NETHERLANDS, 1650–1700
BRASS (COPPER 74.07, ZINC 23.69,
LEAD 1.15, IRON 0.53, TIN 0.30)
L. 6 3/8" (16.2 CM), W. 3" (7.6 CM),
H. 1 1/4" (3.2 CM)
56.512

B. THE NETHERLANDS
OR ENGLAND, 1650–1700
BRASS (COPPER 82.44, ZINC 14.83,
LEAD 0.86, IRON 0.42, TIN 0.35)
L. 8 5/16" (21.2 CM), W. 1 15/16" (5.0 CM),
H. 1 1/4" (3.2 CM)
64.729

IN HIS *Directions to Servants*, first published in London in 1745, the social satirist Jonathan Swift offered some tongue-in-cheek recommendations to the butler on the extinguishing of candles because he maintained that "there is nothing where in the skill of a butler more appears." Swift stated that the butler should "snuff the candles at supper as they stand on the table, which is much the securest way; because, if the burning snuff happens to get out of the snuffers, you have a chance that it may fall into a dish of soup, sack-possett, rice-milk, or the like, where it will be immediately extinguished with very little stink." He further elaborated by writing that "when you have snuffed the can-

dle, always leave the snuffers open, for then the snuff will of itself burn away to ashes, and cannot fall out and dirty the table, when you snuff the candles again."[136]

Although the author was being perverse, his writing is useful, for if the recommendations are reversed, an accurate picture of the intent and proper use of snuffers appears. The examples that make up this entry function like scissors, with a box to house the snuffed portion of the wick until it cooled enough to be discarded. The pointed end of each was used to pick up an unburnt wick that might have fallen over prior to snuffing.

A.

B.

SNUFFERS AND
SNUFFER STAND

150a,b

A. EUROPE, POSSIBLY ENGLAND, 1720–50
BRASS (COPPER 67.04, ZINC 28.53,
LEAD 1.97, TIN 1.26, IRON 0.48), SILVER
L. 6 7/8" (17.1 CM), W. 2 1/4"
(5.7 CM), H. 1 1/4" (3.2 CM)
58.2786

B. PROBABLY ENGLAND, 1710–40
BRASS (COPPER 76.50, ZINC 18.71,
LEAD 2.97, TIN 0.89, IRON 0.51,
ANTIMONY 0.22, SILVER 0.19)
H. 4 7/8" (12.4 CM), W. 4"
(10.1 CM), D. 4" (10.1 CM)
64.127

THOMAS WEBSTER DEVOTED a generous amount of space in his *Encyclopaedia of Domestic Economy* to the humble candle snuffer. He observed that "snuffers, so essential a domestic implement for cleanliness and safety, in all classes of society [were made] of great variety of forms and prices."[137]

The most basic was a hinged iron implement with pads on the ends of the arms that extinguished a flame when closed against each other. The illustrated example is the next most complicated, being "in reality, a kind of scissors, constructed to cut off the excrescence which accumulates on the wick of the candle during combustion, retaining the snuff in a box or cavity." Webster would have considered the snuffers shown here to be cheap since they contained "no con-

trivance to prevent them from opening and letting the snuff fall out." However, he was writing from a nineteenth-century viewpoint, by which time "all the best sorts [of snuffers had] a coiled spring fixed in a cell in the shanks where the rivet is placed, to keep the box closed by the cutter when it is not in use."[138]

Other specialized and more expensive base-metal snuffers had complex multiarm extendable scissors or a long offset shaft to snuff candles in a chandelier, wall sconce, or within a deep glass shade. Many were fitted to holders, such as the "brass snuffers with neat stands" that Herbert Van Wagenen offered for sale in New York.[139]

SNUFFER AND TRAY
151

PROBABLY FRANCE, POSSIBLY THE
NETHERLANDS OR ENGLAND, 1720–60
BRASS (COPPER 71.72, ZINC 24.67,
LEAD 2.61, TIN 0.69, IRON 0.58,
ANTIMONY 0.25), SILVER

TRAY: H. 2 3/8" (6.0 CM),
L. 8" (20.3 CM), W. 4" (10.1 CM);
SNUFFERS: H. 1 1/8" (2.8 CM),
L. 6 5/8" (10.0 CM), W. 2 1/4" (5.7 CM)
66.1085, .1086

UNTIL THE END of the eighteenth century, candles, whether made of tallow or wax, dipped, molded, or rolled and drawn, all had "wicks . . . made of cotton spun for that use." Care had to be exercised in the making of candle wicks, since wick diameter affected the efficiency with which a candle burned; "the thinner the wick the less fluid it will draw up," causing melted wax or tallow to accumulate and eventually overflow the top of the candle. Conversely, too thick a "wick occasions a good deal of smoke, from the escape of unburned carbon vapor in the interior of the flame [if left unattended] a deposition of this unburned carbon takes place upon it as it lengthens, and . . . projects into the hollow of the flame; and at last it becomes covered with great quantity of soot, in a sort of fungus or mushroom form, that still farther increases the evil; a candle in this state does not give above one tenth of the light [of

a newly lit one]. It is necessary, therefore, to take off this accumulation, together with the upper part of the wick, now lengthened by the diminution of the tallow [or wax], which process constitutes the snuffing of the candle."[140]

Snuffers in the form of scissors were developed as the preferred means of trimming and extinguishing a candle during the eighteenth century. The snuffers with tray illustrated here typify those used at that time. The blades, one having a box and the other fitted with an opposing door to the box, were designed to efficiently cut the unwanted portion of wick and catch it for disposal. This cast pair with fitted cast snuffer tray, both of which were originally french plated, although unmarked, is closely related in appearance and construction to a silver example made in Paris by Achille Bellanger in 1718.[141]

CANDLE SCREEN
152

PROBABLY ENGLAND, 1797–1838
BRASS (COPPER 72.81,
ZINC 26.07, LEAD 0.94), SILK

H. 20 1/4" (51.5 CM),
DIAM. (SCREEN) 9 1/4"
(23.5 CM)
57.904

IN 1849 CATHERINE E. BEECHER, a celebrated home economist and prolific author, observed that every "parlor should be furnished with candle and fire screens, for those who have weak eyes." The candle screen shown here is typical of many made in Birmingham and elsewhere during the first half of the nineteenth century, in some cases by specialists such as John Matthews, maker of telescopic toasting forks and fire and candle screens at Steelhouse Lane.[142]

The vertically seamed outer tube is cloth lined and contains a second seamed tube, which can be extended as needed. When the folding silk screen is not in use, it can be closed and placed within the inner tube, as shown here, thus converting the object to a mantel ornament. The principle on which it works was patented in England by Anthony George Eckhardt and Richard Morton on February 23, 1797, as "a new invented method of making candlesticks, lamps and girandoles by means of sliding pillars." Although numerous types were made, the best known are the elaborately decorated examples that follow Benjamin Ager Day's patent dated June 3, 1817, and termed "certain improvements in chimney ornaments which . . . are so constructed that they may be used for fire screens, flower or sweet jars, time piece cases, candlesticks, toast stands, and various other purposes."[143]

Although the type and quantity of ornament varied from maker to maker, all such stands were constructed of seamed sheet metal until 1838, when Charles Green of Birmingham developed "the production of seamless or solid brass tubes" from short, thick cylinders.[144]

FAT LAMP

153

J. EBY
PROBABLY LEBANON OR
LANCASTER COUNTY,
PENNSYLVANIA, 1820–60

BRASS (COPPER 75.00, ZINC 22.00,
LEAD 1.00), IRON, COPPER
H. 8" (20.3 CM), D. 5 1/4" (13.4 CM)
60.339

THE MAKER OF THIS table lamp probably considered himself an iron-worker although he used mostly copper and brass in the fabrication. Similar table lamps as well as hanging lamps originating in southeast Pennsylvania were marked by men such as Peter Derr, who was taxed as a blacksmith; Benjamin Sebastian, also a blacksmith; and John Long, who was assessed as a locksmith. There were at least three Ebys recorded as blacksmiths in Lancaster County alone, and any one of them could have made this lamp: John, first recorded in Hampfield Township in 1820; Jacob, present in Warwick Township in 1821; and another John, listed in Conestoga Township beginning in 1829. There were, however, nine J. Ebys present in the Lebanon, Lancaster, and Franklin county areas of Pennsylvania in 1820. By 1840 that number had risen to nineteen, including Cumberland, Dauphin, and Centre counties as well. Consequently, the identity of the particular J. Eby who made this lamp cannot be stated with certainty.[145]

This lamp and a similar but unmarked example at Winterthur were designed to burn mutton tallow and beef tallow, laboriously rendered from animal fats by the Pennsylvania German householder, who saved all "the scummings of her bacon pot." It is among the most primitive of man-made lighting devices, unchanged in fuel and function from center-wick pottery lamps used more than 2,500 years earlier in Egypt and China. In spite of this unbroken tradition of use, the grease lamp was not without its drawbacks, principally "the smoky light that's fed with stinking tallow." These handicaps were endemic although house-holders could reduce any noxious smell by the quick and thorough melting of animal fats to remove putrescent material. They could also avail themselves of the following advice: "To prevent lamp wicks from smoking, soak them in vinegar and dry thoroughly."[146]

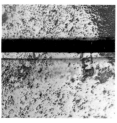

FAT LAMP
154

H. AND R. BOKER
REMSCHEID, GERMANY,
1839–70
IRON, COPPER

H. 7 3/4" (19.7 CM), W. 2 7/8"
(7.3 CM), L. 4 1/4" (11.4 CM)
83.237 GIFT OF MR. AND MRS.
IRVIN SCHORSCH, JR.

THE CULTURAL ANTHROPOLOGIST Henry Chapman Mercer stated that the hanging fat lamp was "easily traceable backward by way of the Crusie of Scotland, the brass lard lamps of Holland, and the people's lamps of sheet iron and tin of Germany, Dalmatia, Italy, and Majorca to Roman times." In doing so, Mercer outlined not only its ubiquitous character but also its ancient lineage. Yet this form has come to be associated with Germany and those people of central European extraction as is epitomized by the German settlements in Pennsylvania, where numerous such lamps, signed by their makers, were "in general use."[147]

The lamp illustrated here bears the names "H & R BOKER" stamped incuse on the cover with a single die. Hermann Boker was first recorded in New York City in 1839 as an "importer of German hardware, cutlery, guns, pistols and percussion caps." Although England had traditionally been the principal overseas source of industrial and household articles for America, Germany became a major supplier by 1860, when it was observed that "not many years back nearly all goods appertaining to the hardware business were imported from England and Germany, and it is but twenty years since that Germany became a competitor with England for the American trade, and with great success, too, for at this time large importations are made from Germany."[148]

This mercantile activity depended in part on the influx of Germans into the United States–647,273 of whom settled in New York alone between 1851 and 1855. Many retained their language, social customs, and way of life, providing an active market for several dozen importers, of which Hermann Boker and Company, agent for H. and R. Boker, was "the heaviest house in [the] city directly engaged in the importation of German hardware."[149]

The copper plating on this lamp was probably electrolytically deposited, but iron objects were copper coated prior to the invention of electroplating in 1840 to retard rust and provide a bright finish. The usual technique involved "dipping [the object] in a thin solution of sulphate of copper, or muriate of copper, and when sufficiently covered with copper, it is washed and painted with oil varnish."[150]

FAT LAMP
155

PETER DERR (1793–1868)
BERKS COUNTY, PENNSYLVANIA, 1838
BRASS (COPPER 72.00, ZINC 27.00,
LEAD 1.20), COPPER, IRON

H. 8 7/8" (22.5 CM), W. 2 7/8"
(7.3 CM), L. 3 3/4" (9.5 CM)
83.241 GIFT OF MR. AND MRS.
IRVIN SCHORSCH, JR.

PETER DERR WAS BORN on June 21, 1793–the fourth of thirteen children–into a farming and metalworking family of Germanic extraction in Tulpehocken Township, Pennsylvania. During his youth he was apprenticed to his father, Johann, to learn pewtering, ironworking, and coppersmithing and went on to assume control of the family forge when his father died in 1831.[151] As early as 1818 he had begun making a large variety of objects for local use, including sheet-iron cookie cutters and grain bag stencils, pewter spoons and flasks, brass dough scrapers and crimpers, and copper kettles.

Derr is best known for his many standing and hanging fat lamps fabricated with iron that he bought from the neighboring Charming Forge and copper and brass that he purchased from the Reading hardware dealer Joseph L. Stichter. The hanging lamps closely follow long-standing Germanic prototypes, having a small shallow reservoir. A loosely twisted cotton wick held in place with an iron support burns tallow obtained from the seasonal rendering of butchered farm animals.[152]

While Derr was making these lamps, all of which are date stamped from 1832 to 1860, the quality and quantity of light sources available to American households were increasing through experimentation with more volatile fuels and the development of more efficient burners. At the same time, lighting fixtures were being made in an extraordinary array of elaborate and stylish shapes. Even though Derr was aware of this progress through his knowledge of Philadelphia lampmakers and his access to United States Patent Office journals, he chose to make, and his customers chose to buy, only these traditional lamps.

Unlike contemporary factory-made sheet-iron examples imported into the Berks County area, Derr made his lamp bodies of copper and brass. These were quite bright when new but tarnished quickly, so purchasers were advised to polish them with "whiting well saturated with ammonia [or] 6 oz. finely pulverized limestone with 1 oz. of sweet oil and 1 oz oxalic acid" applied with a flannel cloth.[153]

WALL LANTERN
156

ENGLAND, 1770–90
BRASS (COPPER 75.61, ZINC 18.30,
LEAD 4.94, TIN 0.60,
IRON 0.32, SILVER 0.15), SHEET IRON,
MAHOGANY, GLASS

H. 23" (58.3 CM),
W. 9 1/4" (23.5 CM),
D. 6" (15.2 CM)
59.779

DURING THE EIGHTEENTH CENTURY, hall and stairway lanterns were typically hung from the ceiling. They were "either of the vase kind [an inverted glass bell] or . . . of panes of glass in frames." Their frames were "generally made of Brass, cast from wooden Moulds."[154]

Less commonly, as with the example illustrated here, they were mounted to walls. This wall lantern has a lacquered brass frame with half a glass cylinder plastered into it to prevent drafts from extinguishing the flame. The frame, in turn, is nailed to the edges of a mahogany panel. A removable painted sheet-iron canopy adorns the top but serves more importantly to "collect the smoke, which otherwise would blacken the ceiling" and wall.[155]

The lamp, a simple fluted vase with a small reservoir, would have provided only a moderate amount of light from the two wicks by burning various types of oil: sperm whale, herring, cod, lard, rape, and colza. The base is in the form of a pendant leafy patera, the petals of which are cast with voids because it was "essential that a supply of air shall be given to the light by proper openings in the containing vessel" so that the oil burned as efficiently as possible.[156] The lamp and its base are held by tabs within a circular opening in the bottom of the lantern and can be easily removed by rotating one-quarter turn for cleaning and refilling.

CANDLESTICK
LAMP
157

UNITED STATES, POSSIBLY BOSTON,
MASSACHUSETTS, 1810–40
BRASS (COPPER 70.60, ZINC 26.78,
LEAD 1.50, TIN 0.52, IRON 0.38),
COPPER

H. 3 7/8" (9.8 CM), DIAM. 2 1/4"
(5.7 CM)
ONE OF A PAIR
65.1440.1

"CANDLESTICK LAMPS ... are often made and sold separate, so as to fit into any candlestick, either japanned or of brass. They form cheap lights for kitchens and other places where economy is much an object."[157] Such lamps proved very popular during the first half of the nineteenth century and were made in great quantity, often of brass but also of tinned sheet iron, glass, and occasionally silver plate. Their extensive use was directly tied to the prodigious rise in availability of animal and vegetable oils as illuminants, including seal oil, lard, colza oil, and occasionally olive oil. A mixture of turpentine and alcohol was also common from the 1820s to the 1850s.

Whale oil was by far the most popular illuminant for lamps of this type because of its cleanliness, efficiency, affordability, and availability. Although whaling had been practiced for some time, it reached its zenith during the nineteenth century. New England ports, particularly New Bedford and Nantucket, were among the most active with as many as 257 ships hunting in 1834, netting 128,000 barrels of whale oil in that year alone.[158]

With this plenteous and inexpensive supply, old-fashioned candlesticks could continue to be used by simply fitting a candlestick lamp into the candle socket. The font of the illustrated lamp was cast integrally with the cylinder in halves and brazed vertically, a typical construction for American brass hollowware dating from the early nineteenth century. This lamp is somewhat unusual in the quality of its finish, with a fillet encircling the font, beading on the screw cap, and copper wick tubes. Most such lamps were much cruder and simpler and were fitted with tinned sheet-iron wick tubes.

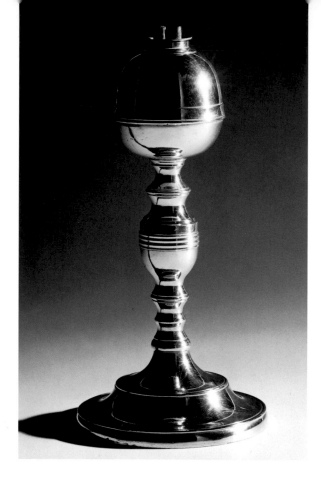

OIL LAMP

158

WILLIAM HOMES WEBB
(1773–1868)
WARREN, MAINE, 1800–1868
BRASS (COPPER 73.03, ZINC
23.33, LEAD 2.66, TIN 0.44)

H. 8 1/8" (20.6 CM),
D. 3 7/8" (9.8 CM)
64.781

WILLIAM HOMES WEBB was born in Boston, Massachusetts, in 1773, the son of Barnabas Webb, silversmith. When fourteen, he was apprenticed to Thomas Leach, brass founder, with whom he remained four years. Following that, he worked with Samuel Austin, also a founder, until twenty years of age, when he entered into business for himself.

After about five years of self-employment he failed through "imprudent conduct" so he "left Boston about four hundred dollars [in debt] and arrived in Warren, State of Maine, in October 1799."[159] Webb undoubtedly chose Warren because his father had moved to Thomaston, Maine, just a few miles from there, about 1786.

In Warren, Webb established himself "in business . . . in a very small way, under very embarrassed and discouraging circumstances . . . but through industry and perseverance . . . struggled through and began to get a little ahead." He apparently felt the need to explore the British brass industry, for he traveled to England in 1803 and worked

in Birmingham for several months, during which time he gathered information about manufacturing processes and marketing techniques. Upon his return to the United States in 1805, he applied his knowledge to the operation of his foundry. By the 1820s the success with which his business was operating proved his reasoning. He was making "between $1,000 and $2,000 worth of brass lamps, fire sets, and etc for the Boston Market" as well as supplying a more modest local demand.[160]

The scope of his production was broad, including andirons, fire tools, harness and carriage fittings, ship hardware, clockwork parts, branding irons, candlesticks, oil lamps, and anything else a customer might wish. His shop also repaired all of the above. The lamp illustrated here is typical of his work, being substantially made and well finished. The shaft and font were cast hollow in halves and brazed together, after which they were peened to the circular base. The rivet head has been drilled to accommodate an electrical wire.

LAMP TOP
159

PATENTED BY LUTHER C. WHITE
MERIDEN, CONNECTICUT, 1852–65
BRASS (COPPER 69.91, ZINC 29.62,
NICKEL 0.15, LEAD 0.10)

H. 1 3/4" (45.0 CM), DIAM. 1 1/4"
(3.2 CM)
69.3402

IN 1820 ROBERT HARE reported his work with a new lamp illuminant to the *American Journal of Science and Arts*. His creation contained one part spirits of turpentine mixed with seventeen parts of alcohol and burned "with a highly luminous flame . . . without smoke like a gas light." It was not until October 16, 1830, however, that the first United States patent for burning fluid was issued to Isaiah Jennings of New York City. His fuel, a mixture of one part turpentine with eight parts alcohol, burned with a flame that was "clear, dense and brilliant. The light may be made greatly to exceed that from oil, without the escape of any smoke and there is not the slightest odour of the turpentine."[161] Furthermore, it was cheap.

The fluid's efficiency and economy made it popular and ideal as a household illuminant, with one important exception. It was highly explosive. The rise in use of burning fluid from the 1830s through the 1860s occasioned an equal increase in accidents like that involving "Miss Mary Weston [who] was burned to death in Philadelphia last week while attempting to fill a fluid lamp when it was burning," as reported in the June 19, 1847, *Scientific American*.[162]

Among the more effective innovations to reduce the risk of explosion was a change in design for the wick tubes. Oil lamp wick tubes, which were short, parallel to each other, of large diameter, and extended deeply into the font, needed to be modified. They were lengthened, flared away from each other, tapered along their length, and terminated flush with the underside of the cap. These alterations, by keeping heat farther from the fuel reservoir and reducing vapori-

zation, helped to make burning-fluid lamps somewhat safer to use.

The lamp cap shown here incorporates all these design features, but none are the subject of Luther White's patent. His contribution was stated to be "a new and Improved Method of Making Lamp-Tops . . . from a disk or plate of metal by bending it and forming it, so that the rim is formed of two thicknesses of metal and the center and flange of one thickness." White maintained his development made much better, less expensive, and cleaner lamp tops than those fabricated in the usual manner of casting and pressing. While laudable, his and all burning-fluid lamp tops quickly became useless with the advent of clean, efficient, cheap, and safe kerosene in the 1860s.[163]

ARGAND LAMP
160

ATTRIBUTED TO MATTHEW
BOULTON'S SOHO MANUFACTORY
BIRMINGHAM, ENGLAND, CA. 1786
FUSED PLATE, TINNED SHEET
IRON, PITCH

H. 7 1/8" (17.9 CM),
DIAM. 3 3/4" (9.5 CM)
58.2950

THIS DIMINUTIVE fused-plated argand lamp has a number of historical associations that render it noteworthy. It was recorded in this country at a very early date. The celebrated historian John Fanning Watson (1779–1860) states in the *Annals of Philadelphia, and Pennsylvania in the Olden Time*, first published in 1830, that this lamp is "the first [of its type] which ever came to this country [and] is in my possession–originally a present from Thomas Jefferson [1743-1826] to Charles Thomson [1729-1824]," first secretary to the Continental Congress.[164]

The lamp was apparently purchased by Jefferson when he was living in Europe. His correspondence offers substantive information to that effect, as in his letter to Matthew Boulton, dated January 7, 1787, requesting information and prices of household articles "plated in the best manner." Even more provocative is an entry in

his memorandum book dated March 27, 1786, recording that he paid 31*s*. 6*d*. for a "plated reading lamp."[165] Shortly thereafter, on April 30, 1786, Jefferson purchased two additional lamps, one of them being this example, which he sent to Thomson.

The lamp was apparently secured by Watson directly from Thomson because of its historical association. It subsequently passed through several generations of Watson's descendants, as suggested in an article written by Harrold E. Gillingham in *Antiques* magazine in 1928. Gillingham proudly records that "a few years ago, my wife, on entering a smelter's shop, recognized a direct descendant of John F. Watson leaving the place. Within, she found the lamp here illustrated, for the Watson descendant had just sold it to the smelter. Needless to say, to a collector's heart this was a veritable find; and it has been one of our cherished pos-

sessions ever since." He went on to add that "attached to the lamp was a small paper tag, bearing, in Watson's own handwriting, the inscription, 'The First Argand lamp, a present from Thos. Jefferson to Chas. Thomson.'"[166]

Gillingham's estate was dispersed at his death in 1945. The York, Pennsylvania, antiques dealer Joe Kindig, Jr., acquired the lamp for Henry Francis du Pont.[167] It is in reasonably good condition with its plating largely intact and a portion of its original burner mechanism extant, undoubtedly due to its having passed through the hands of a number of persons who were sensitive to its historical associations. The lamp provides useful insight into a facet of lighting in early America as well as the beginnings of collecting in this country and some of the personalities associated with it.

ARGAND LAMPS
161

ENGLAND, PROBABLY SHEFFIELD
OR BIRMINGHAM, 1785–95
FUSED PLATE, BRASS, TINNED
SHEET IRON, GLASS

H. 5 7/8" (14.9 CM), DIAM. 5"
(12.7 CM)
61.1692.1, .2

THESE COPPER LAMPS have their outer surface, which is silver plated, chased in imitation of engraving. The interiors are tinned. Both lamps retain their internal mechanism, which is an improved variant of the type of oil burner patented by François-Pierre Aimé Argand in 1784. Argand's lamp used gravity to feed the illuminant to the burner, which dictated that the font always be located above the wick. Initial attempts to alter this arrangement by placing the font below the burner, thereby reducing the shadow it cast, proved unsatisfactory. The viscosity of fuels that were not highly refined prevented them from readily rising up the wick of their own accord, resulting in a flame no better than that of a candle.[168]

Two methods were developed to overcome this design limitation. The simpler works on a hydrostatic principle to elevate the fuel up a column, while the second uses a clockwork pump to attain the same end. The former was first applied successfully in English lighting by Peter Keir about 1800. His innovation used two tubes of differing heights; one supplied a constant and even amount of oil to the wick through pressure exerted by a saline solution of greater specific gravity than the oil, hence the name fountain lamp. Prior to Keir's invention, efficient argand lamps like these depended on highly refined fuels–typically olive, ox-foot, colza, or spermaceti oil–to burn efficiently. These lamps are fitted with a removable arrangement of tubes that provide a vertical current of air, hold the wick in place, and anchor the rack-and-pinion elevator mechanism. Their comparatively bright light and relatively low need for maintenance freed them from "the evil arising from the smoke and smell of lamps [which] was formerly so great, as to prevent their introduction into domestic use, notwithstanding the strong inducement of convenience and economy." Such lamps, both convenient and stylish, were among the "variety of Keir and Argand's patent lamps" offered in Philadelphia in 1790 by the hardware merchants Isaac Paxson and John Bringhurst.[169]

ARGAND LAMP

162

MATTHEW BOULTON'S SOHO
MANUFACTORY
BIRMINGHAM, ENGLAND, 1784–1809
FUSED PLATE, IRON, PITCH, GLASS

H. 24 1/2" (62.2 CM), W. 11 1/4"
(28.6 CM), D. 6 1/2" (16.5 CM)

61.1725

FRANÇOIS-PIERRE AIMÉ ARGAND (1750–1803) was introduced
to Matthew Boulton in February 1784. One month later, Argand's
revolutionary lamp "producing neither smoke nor smell, and giving more light than any before known" was patented in London.
Boulton, the consummate entrepreneur, realized its marketing
potential and agreed to produce it in his Soho works, "situated
in the Parish of Handsworthy, in the County of Stafford, two Miles
distant from Birmingham. . . . It consisted of . . . Shops . . . for a
Thousand Workmen, who, in a great variety of Branches, excel in
their several Departments; not only in the fabrication of Buttons,
Buckles, Boxes, Trinkets, &c . . . but in many other arts, long
predominant in France."[170]

Many lamps were undoubtedly made by the firm, but the
illustrated example is one of the few that can be documented to
Boulton's factory.[171] It is composed of many fused-plate parts,
each stamped up separately using steel dies in downfall presses.
The various parts were hard soldered together, and the entire
lamp base was filled with pitch surrounding an internal iron rod
that stabilized the bottom.

The central globular font was designed to hold spermaceti
oil that was gravity-fed out the horizontal arms to the burner tubes,
each of which held a cylindrical wick that could be elevated as
necessary with a rack and pinion, now missing. The lamp "has an
appearance of solid silver, more especially when compared with
that of any other Manufactory, [showing] that Taste and Elegance
of Design prevail [in his factory] in a superior degree, and are,
with Mechanism and Chymistry, happily united."[172]

READING LAMP
163

THOMAS MESSENGER AND SONS
BIRMINGHAM, ENGLAND, 1835–40
RETAILED IN BOSTON, MASSACHUSETTS,
BY JONES, LOW AND BALL

BRASS (COPPER 79.37, ZINC 17.48,
LEAD 1.83, TIN 0.77, IRON 0.35,
SILVER 0.14), IRON, GLASS
H. 19 3/4" (50.2 CM), W. 10 7/8"
(27.6 CM), D. 6" (15.3 CM)
85.95

IN HIS *Encyclopedia of Domestic Economy*, Thomas Webster calls this type of lamp a "university lamp," noting that it "is much used as a reading lamp; it is on the Argand principle, with a small wick; but as the reservoir is not above the light, it does not burn many hours without replentishing." The lamp was made at the celebrated and long-lived firm of Thomas Messenger, founded in Birmingham, England, about 1797 and continuing in business until the 1920s. Messenger advertised as a brass founder in 1797. By 1808 he presented himself as a manufacturer of church candlesticks and patent lamps, but by 1825 that list had been lengthened to include "chandeliers, candelabra, tripods, lamps of every description, and other ornamental work in bronze and ormolu."[173]

Messenger's business acumen and the high regard for his work encouraged virtually every major American fancy hardware merchant to import and offer his products. The retailer of this lamp was the Boston, Massachusetts, firm of Jones, Low and Ball, which noted in 1835 that it imported "from the best makers bronzed lamps of all kinds." This partnership of John B. and George B. Jones, John J. Low, and Samuel S. and True M. Ball lasted from 1835 to 1840, although the firm traces its beginning to 1796 with the Boston merchant John M. McFarlane and continues to this day as Shreve, Crump and Low.[174]

The largely intact finish on this lamp is noteworthy, since it was widely used on brass as an inexpensive substitute for gilding. English trade catalogues dating from the 1770s refer to objects coated in this way as "burnished & gold lacquered" or "of a fine burnished gold colour." Nineteenth-century American publications discuss the process in detail, stating that the objects were dipped in nitric acid whereby "a rich pale gold color is imparted to the brass."[175] Following that, selected areas were burnished with steel or bloodstone to create contrasting reflective highlights. Finally, they were coated with lacquer and often tinted with turmeric, dragon's blood, or saffron to color and protect the surface from tarnishing.

ARGAND LAMP
164

GEORGE ALEXANDER MILLER
AND WILLIAM ADAMS
LONDON, ENGLAND, 1834–50
BRASS (COPPER 76.00,
ZINC 21.00, LEAD 2.00, TIN 0.50),
STONEWARE, IRON, GLASS

H. 17" (43.2 CM), W. 9" (22.9 CM),
D. 4 1/2" (11.4 CM)
ONE OF A PAIR
68.1167

CHARLES TAVERNER MILLER was first recorded in the London city directories in 1825 as a wax chandler and oil merchant. In 1831 he moved to 179 Piccadilly under the name Charles Miller and Sons. One of the firm's members was George Alexander Miller, who called himself a wax chandler, spermaceti refiner, and dealer in lamps. He was granted a patent in 1834 for "an alteration in the construction of Argand burners having the spiral movement, so as to adapt the same to the convenient use of several detached wicks in each burner, in lieu of the one entire cylindrical wick now ordinary in such burners."[176]

His modification was complex and required removal of the wick and its supporter. In their place he suggested multiple miniature wicks. Eight are depicted in the patent drawing and each is a miniature version of

the larger original, which was discarded. Miller further stated that "as the wick supporter used in my improvement requires more room between the inner tube and the loose tube than the cotton holder used in the Argand burner, I obtain part of the additional space by using an inner tube of smaller diameter than that now used in the Argand burner, and the rest of the required space I obtain by using an outer tube and loose tube of larger diameter than those used in the Argand burners." Miller maintained his improvement provided "a purer and more brilliant light from such lamps than is produced by the Argand burner with one entire cylindrical wick from the same quantity of oil."[177] Even so, its complicated and expensive nature discouraged widespread adoption.

Miller's burner has been removed from this lamp, which is unusual because of the variety of materials. Cut glass was used for the font in an attempt to reduce the undesirable shadow cast by the more common metal counterparts. The blue and white jasper drum in the base has the name "ADAMS" stamped on one end, believed to be William Adams. The presence of Miller's and Adam's names on the lamp hallmarks a manufacturing and mercantile relationship like that documented to the potter Josiah Wedgwood and the metals entrepreneur Matthew Boulton. The Millers apparently shared Boulton's ambition and talent, for they became "lamp manufacturer to her Majesty" in 1856, and continued in operation until after World War I.[178]

ANNULAR LAMP

ENGLAND, PROBABLY SHEFFIELD,
1790–1815
FUSED PLATE, IRON, PITCH, GLASS

H. 36 1/2" (92.7 CM), W. 20 3/4"
(52.8 CM), D. 20 3/4" (52.8 CM)
69.590

165

THE ANNULAR FRENCH LAMP "has been for many years generally used in England as a table lamp. . . . The ring of metal . . . contains the oil, which descends below the burner . . . by the tubes
. . . a construction which is extemely simple, and, consequently, not
liable to be out of order. . . . The construction of the burner is on
Argand's principle. This lamp was placed upon an elegant stand . . .
and the flame concealed by a [shade] of ground glass."[179]

"Although the object of the French lamp was to do away the
shadow cast by the reservoir of the Argand lamp, this was not
completely effected, for still a slight shadow was projected by the
thickness of the annular reservoir, which, coming just about
the level of the eyes of those at table, had an unpleasant effect. This
fault was corrected by an improvement made by [Samuel] Parker,
for which he took out [an English] patent in 1820. In his lamp,
called the Sinumbra, or shadowless lamp . . . the reservoir is sloped
away from the light by reducing the breadth of the ring in front."[180]

The lamp illustrated here represents an earlier attempt to
reduce the font's shadow by using candles. Each removable arm
is stamped with a numeral, 1 through 4, to aid in assembly. The
lamp is made of fused plate, and all the corners have been covered
with slender separate silver wires to hide the edges of the red
copper. The radiant ovals on each side of the plinth are die stamped.

SINUMBRA LAMP
166

THOMAS MESSENGER AND SONS
BIRMINGHAM, ENGLAND, 1829–46
RETAILED IN NEW YORK CITY BY
BALDWIN GARDINER
BRASS (COPPER 76.30, ZINC 22.30,
LEAD 0.90), IRON, GLASS

H. 27 3/4" (70.5 CM),
D. 11 1/2" (24.2 CM)
75.223
FUNDS FOR PURCHASE THE GIFT
OF THE CLANEIL FOUNDATION

THE TERM *sinumbra lamp* is derived from the Latin phrase *sine umbra*, meaning "without shadow." The shadowless oil lamp was first attempted in France during the late eighteenth century by encircling the burner with a ring-shape font. Samuel Parker, an Englishman, improved the device by patenting a thinner streamlined font in 1820, making a considerable advance in domestic lighting by combining the argand burner, which gave a brighter light than previously possible through improved combustion of animal and vegetable oils, with a shadowless oil reservoir. Even so, by 1845 it was "no longer made, being superseded by" improved models.[181]

The burner tube of the lamp shown here has the name plate of its New York City retailer, Baldwin Gardiner, prominently affixed to it, while the maker's name is hidden from view, cast into the underside of the base.

Also covered by the internal iron weight of the base is the statement "PUBLISHED AS THE ACT DIRECTS," in conformity with the provisions of "An Act for encouraging the Art of making new Models and Casts of Busts" made law in England on June 21, 1798. This law and its amendment, dated May 18, 1814, encouraged artists and artisans to "make any new and original sculpture . . . of the Human Figure . . . Animal . . . or any Animal combined with the Human Figure" by granting exclusive right to its use for fourteen years, provided the maker placed his name and the date on each copy.[182]

That law protected the design of the cast ornament applied to the circular plinth of this lamp. Amid a foliate cluster are griffins and mythological beasts—part eagle and part lion—picked out in burnished and lacquered brass on a bronze patinated background.

ARGAND LAMP
167

JOHN PHIPSON AND ABRAHAM LAMBLEY (W. 1828–39)
BIRMINGHAM, ENGLAND, 1828–39
WHOLESALED IN BIRMINGHAM, ENGLAND, BY
THOMAS COX (W. 1816–53)
RETAILED IN NEW YORK CITY BY JOHN AND
JOSEPH COX (W. 1816–51)

BRASS (COPPER 76.10, ZINC 23.10,
LEAD 0.48), GLASS, IRON
H. 20 1/2" (52.0 CM), W. 10 3/4"
(27.3 CM), D. 6 1/2" (16.5 CM)
ONE OF A PAIR
73.40.1

ONLY THE NAMES of the retailers John and Joseph Cox are easily seen on this lamp although those of several others who were involved in its fabrication and shipment to the United States are also present. The iron weight fitted into the base has the names "PHIPSON AND LAMBLEY" cast into it, recording fabrication during the twelve-year partnership of John Phipson and Abraham Lambley, the Birmingham lamp and chandelier manufacturers. This mark is overstruck with the name "T. COX BIRMH. " Thomas Cox, also working in Birmingham, established himself as a brass founder and lamp manufacturer in 1816 and was probably related to John and Joseph Cox, who opened their lamp store the same year in New York City, where they offered "a handsome and general assortment of brass, bronzed and japanned Liverpool and Argand Lamps."[183]

The argand burner, around which this lamp was built, was almost certainly the single most important advance in lighting prior to the application of electricity. Deceptively simple in principle, it ended thousands of years of life by candlelight and presaged a century of intense and rapid development culminating in the creation of the incandescent bulb.[184]

In 1784, the inventor François-Pierre Aimé Argand, a Swiss, conceived the idea of making a cylindrical wick that increased the amount of air fed to a flame. When used with a glass chimney to force a constant draft, light output was strikingly increased.[185] His model quickly became the standard burner on practically all lamps made during the first half of the nineteenth century. The argand, sinumbra, solar, carcel, fountain, vesta, and table lamp as well as chandeliers and wall brackets all use a variant of the argand burner.

ARGAND LAMP
168

THOMAS MESSENGER AND SONS
BIRMINGHAM, ENGLAND, 1827–40
RETAILED IN NEW YORK CITY BY BALDWIN GARDINER
BRASS (COPPER 78.80, ZINC 20.00,
LEAD 0.59), IRON, GLASS

H. 20 3/4" (52.7 CM), W. 18 3/8" (46.7 CM),
D. 10 1/4" (26.0 CM)
ONE OF A PAIR
76.195.1
GIFT OF CHARLES VAN RAVENSWAAY

BALDWIN GARDINER began his career apprenticing to the mercantile trade about 1809 under his brother Sidney Gardiner and his partner Thomas Fletcher. In 1827 he decided to establish himself in New York City. There he opened a furnishing warehouse, advertising that "young Householders, and others, will find . . . a complete and choice assortment of lamps, chandeliers, and girandoles" in addition to silver, plated wares, china, glass, table cutlery, and other amenities for well-appointed households.[186]

He assembled his shop inventory seasonally from English and American manufacturers, his role being that of a retailer providing a convenient grouping of stylish and useful objects for customers' ease. He made none of his wares, but his name is often found on them, as exemplified by the label embossed "B. GARDINER/N • YORK" on the burner tubes of this lamp. The labels were added at the request of the retailer by the manufacturer, in this instance Thomas Messenger, whose name is cast into the lamp's internal iron weights. On occasion, the retailer

declined to have his name so placed, as with Gardiner's mentor, Fletcher, who, upon ordering lamps from Thomas Cox in Birmingham, stipulated "I wish the lamps now ordered to have *no name* on them."[187]

Argand lamps were made of brass, usually patinated. A dark greenish bronze was achieved when the object was "painted with a thin solution of equal parts of salammonia and oxalate of potash . . . where some liver of sulpher is dissolved in water." Contrasting highlights in imitation of gilding were created by dipping the parts in nitric acid followed by colorless or tinted lacquers.[188]

Often these lamps were ornamented with foliate borders and anthropomorphic or zoomorphic appendages, including paw feet and animal or human heads. The seasonally updated stylish nature of these imported lamps provided American artisans, particularly lampmakers and silversmiths, with a useful array of decorative motifs to incorporate into their work.

ARGAND LAMP
169

CORNELIUS AND SON (1831–39)
PHILADELPHIA, PENNSYLVANIA,
1835–39
BRASS (COPPER 77.40, ZINC 18.50,
LEAD 1.80, TIN 0.48), IRON, GLASS

H. 21" (53.3 CM), W. 13 1/4"
(33.6 CM), D. 7 1/2" (19.0 CM)
ONE OF A PAIR
78.2

CHRISTIAN CORNELIUS is said to have emigrated from Amsterdam to Philadelphia in 1783, but his name does not appear in the city directory until 1810, when he is recorded as a silversmith. By 1813 he listed himself as a silver plater, with no apparent involvement in lighting until 1822, when he was issued a patent for an "improvement in lighting."[189] In 1825 he made public note of this by calling himself a "silverplater and patent lamp manufacturer" in the Philadelphia city directory. From that point his interest and activities became increasingly devoted to lighting.

About 1831 he was joined by his son Robert who, through business acumen and an inventive nature, was instrumental in making Cornelius and Son, later Cornelius and Company, "confessedly without a superior in Europe or America" by the 1850s. The firm is best known for its lard-burning solar lamps first patented by Robert on April 6, 1843, and its gas chandeliers, which were described as "the most attractive,

artistic and brilliant feature . . . of nearly every Exhibition of American manufactures, which has been held in the last quarter of a century."[190]

Prior to the development of the solar lamp in the 1840s, the argand lamp was the most popular form for stylish domestic oil-burning illumination, and as noted by a contemporary observer, the whole trade in lighting in the United States was in the hands of foreign importers until 1830. This contention is supported by the close relationship between the uncommon American-made example shown here and the numerous argand lamps bearing English manufacturers' names in conjunction with American retailer labels. More graphic are the foliate ornaments on the arm and atop the urn, which are cast copies of originals from English lamps.

ARGAND LAMP
AND BOUQUET

170

HENRY N. HOOPER AND COMPANY (1832–68)
BOSTON, MASSACHUSETTS, 1839–49
RETAILED IN BOSTON, MASSACHUSETTS, BY
WILLIAM HARRIS AND HENRY B. STANWOOD

BRASS (COPPER 78.00, ZINC 20.18,
LEAD 1.22, NICKEL 0.42), IRON, GLASS
H. 19 3/4" (38.1 CM), W. 18" (45.7 CM),
D. 9" (22.9 CM)
ONE OF A PAIR
85.1.1, 93.54.1

UNTIL "THE YEAR 1830, the whole trade in [lighting in the United States] was in the hands of foreign importers."[191] English lamps were retailed in virtually every major American coastal city by fancy hardware merchants, among the more active of whom were Robert and Andrew Campbell of Baltimore; Lewis Veron of Philadelphia; John and Joseph Cox and Baldwin Gardiner, all of New York City; and Alfred and George Welles of Boston. While American brass workers advertised that they would make candlesticks, lamps, and other lighting, few could compete with the inexpensive, mass-produced, and stylish brass lighting from Birmingham.

In the 1830s, however, American entrepreneurs were attempting to supplant English manufacturers. Henry N. Hooper exemplifies them. He began his career as a maker of mathematical instruments in the early 1820s, but in 1826 he became an agent for the Boston Copper Company. By 1832 he had established himself as Henry N. Hooper and

Company, copper dealers, in partnership with William Blake and Thomas Richardson, and was "prepared to supply . . . sheathing copper . . . bells for factories, ships or railroads [and] castings of every kind in copper, composition, brass [and] German silver."[192]

In addition to industrial products, the firm made an extensive array of domestic lighting devices, the styles and finishes of which could be tailored to individual taste. Many are depicted in the Hooper sixty-two-page catalogue dated 1858.[193] No argand lamps are included, however, the form having passed from favor about a decade earlier.

By 1854 the firm had achieved sufficient stature to warrant comment by an English author, who observed that Hooper's products were "generally in good taste [with] more artistic breadth of effect in the ornamental portion of the articles manufactured . . . than in those produced at Philadelphia; the latter being florid and showy, whilst the former are more massive and simple."[194]

SOLAR LAMP
171

CORNELIUS AND COMPANY (1839–51)
PHILADELPHIA, PENNSYLVANIA, 1849–51
BRASS (COPPER 79.45, ZINC 19.18, LEAD
1.12), MARBLE, GLASS, IRON

H. 23 1/4" (59.1 CM),
DIAM. 8" (20.3 CM)
92.111

ON APRIL 6, 1843, Robert Cornelius of Philadelphia was granted a United States patent for a lard lamp with argand burner. He described his invention in detail, observing that "in the lamps hitherto constructed for the burning of lard and other fatty substances, the general aim has been to conduct a large portion of the heat, produced by the flame, immediately onto the body of the lamp so as to produce a complete fusion of the lard. . . . When this has been affected, there has necessarily resulted such a diminution of heat at the point of ignition as has interfered materially with the intensity of combustion upon which the brilliancy of the light is dependent." Cornelius found a way to correct this by conducting "no more heat down from the flame than is necessary to fuse the lard in the vicinity of the wick . . . to obtain a light from lard equally intense with that usually obtained from the best sperm oil."[195] He designed a mechanism for raising and lowering

the wick that had minimal contact with the lamp body. The reduction of unwanted heat transfer produced a lamp that burned inexpensive fuel brightly and efficiently.

On July 24, 1849, Cornelius and an employee, Charles Wilhelm, were awarded another patent for this lamp involving a method of making wick elevator tubes inexpensively. Elevators of this type previously had been made by cutting a spiral groove along the outside diameter of a thick-walled tube, a process requiring considerable talent on the part of a lathe operator and generating wasteful brass shavings. Cornelius and Wilhelm proposed fabricating elevators much more speedily and inexpensively by making "use of thin sheets or laminae of metal . . . which we cut into strips or ribbons of such breadth that they can readily be wound around a cylindrical core or mandrel the edges forming a spiral. . . . The manner in which we unite the [spiral] with the tube, is

by inserting the latter within the former. . . . The two tubes may then be permanently united, either by dipping them into melted solder or by passing the soldering tool along the whole length of the groove." This advance did nothing to increase the solar lamp's efficiency, but it did help reduce its cost.[196]

The commercial success and artistic fame enjoyed by Cornelius and Company encouraged the firm to exhibit at the Great Exhibition of the Works of Industry of All Nations, commonly known as the Crystal Palace Exhibition, in London in 1851. Among the thirty-three objects they displayed were "24 damask solar lamps [which were] exhibited for their graceful shape, tasteful ornament and rich color."[197]

Rich color was important to the firm. Considerable effort was spent on this feature, and the results were a matter of great pride. The lamp shown here retains a well-preserved gold and blue damask pat-

tern of reserves, flowers, leaves, scrolls, and dripping water, which served to prevent tarnish and to decorate. Both were largely accomplished with "lacquers [which] are used upon polished metals . . . to impart the appearance of gold."[198] Colorants typically included turmeric, gamboge, gum-sandarach, and dragon's blood.

The blue color was created by dissolving sulphide of antimony and calcined soda in water and adding "the kermes mineral, then filter separately, dissolve . . . tartar and soda hyposulphate in [a like] quantity of water and then mix the two solutions. For use, warm the mixture and immerse the polished brass in it until it assumes a steel-blue color."[199]

SOLAR LAMP

172

ATTRIBUTED TO HENRY N. HOOPER
AND COMPANY (1832–68)
BOSTON, MASSACHUSETTS, 1850–60
BRASS (COPPER 77.27, ZINC 12.80,
LEAD 0.82), GLASS

H. 24 3/4" (62.9 CM),
DIAM. 11" (27.9 CM)
92.99

IN HIS LENGTHY ENTRY on lamps, Abraham Rees stated that "in the original lamp of [Aimé] Argand [invented in 1784], a perpendicular column of air was perpetually ascending through the glass chimney of the lamp. . . . With this perpendicular current alone, it is well known that the Argand lamp would not burn whale oil . . . but an improvement was made in the lamp itself which effectually answered the desired purpose. For this discovery we are indebted to an ingenious and scientific manufacturer of Derby. It is curious to observe, however, that no advantage was taken of this invention for twenty years, during which time it had been used in the cotton mills of this discoverer, and now the same end is accomplished by a simpler contrivance. The above improvement consisted in placing over the mouth of the [wick] tube a plate of metal about the diameter of the tube, and at such a height as to be a little short of the apex of the flame. By this means the ascending column of air was turned out of its perpendicular course, and thrown immediately into

that part of the flame where the smoke was formed, and which, by this means was consumed, producing at the same time a more than ordinary brilliant light."[200]

Numerous individuals had tried to capitalize on the use of a deflector to increase the efficiency of oil lamps during the first quarter of the nineteenth century. Those attempts culminated with Jeremiah Bynner, who patented an efficient variant in 1837 that came to be known as the solar lamp. Although the general configuration of the solar burner proved quite satisfactory, it underwent numerous adjustments in its design in quest of increased efficiency. "The most usual form in which this improvement of Argand's lamp has been executed is what is termed the vase solar lamp." It was typically configured like the lamp illustrated here, with an inverted pear-shape font atop a base, fitted with a removable cap that deflected air into the flame and held a glass chimney and shade. While early variants used cylindrical glass chimneys with and without shoulders, a conical shoulderless chimney that improved air flow and reduced heat breakage was developed by another English inventor, Thomas Quarrile of London.[201]

Solar lamps were fabricated in an array of designs and materials, with brass seemingly the most popular. The solar lamp shown here represents the acme of its type insofar as ornamental elaboration is concerned. Although unmarked, it appears to be identical to a design for a lamp base published by Henry N. Hooper and Company of Boston in 1850 and again in 1858. The cast parts are assembled in a convoluted assymetric composition of flowers, scrolls, falling water, acanthus leaves, and shells. Their character and integration demonstrate a clear understanding and mastery of the style as it was developed and executed by its most accomplished eighteenth-century practitioners.[202]

CHANDELIER
173

PERRY AND COMPANY
LONDON, ENGLAND, 1817–35
BRASS (COPPER 75.93, ZINC 20.52,
LEAD 2.79, TIN 0.73, IRON 0.26),
IRON, GLASS

H. 46" (116.8 CM), W. 21 1/2"
⌐.6 CM), D. 21 1/2" (54.6 CM)
86.137

IN 1844 ANDREW JACKSON DOWNING contended that "there is no style which presents greater attractions being at once rich in picturesque beauty and harmonious in connection with surrounding forms of vegetation [than] the Rural Gothic."[203] The three-light argand chandelier shown here well illustrates that belief translated into brass and glass. The font, a Gothic lantern with spires, crockets, and blind-pointed arch panels, is complemented by the interlaced pointed arches engraved into the glass shades and drip pan and the trefoil piercings of the shade holders.

The maker, William Perry, first listed himself as "glass manufacturer to the Prince Regent" in London in 1817. When the prince became George IV in 1820, Perry changed his advertisement to read "glass manufacturer to his Majesty." In 1824 William was joined by his brother George, and the two continued in the business of lamp- and lustremak-

ing at 72 New Bond Street until the 1850s. Their firm was entitled to advertise that they enjoyed royal patronage as a result of the £11,523.15.1 worth of extravagant fixtures they made for the Marine Pavilion in Brighton between 1817 and 1823, the most famous of which is the thirty-foot-tall dragon chandelier in the banqueting room.[204]

The brass of this more modest chandelier has contrasting textured and burnished areas, all of which are patinated with tinted lacquer simulating gilding. It is characterized as "a suspended lamp of [an] elegant kind, with a cut glass basin, to prevent accident from the oil dropping: it has . . . ground glass shades, over the lights [which] are not only agreeable in concealing the flame, and preventing the disagreeable dazzling effect of a strong light, but they appear to increase the light by dispersing it and softening the shadows."[205]

CHANDELIER
174

ATTRIBUTED TO HENRY N. HOOPER
AND COMPANY (1832–68)
BOSTON, MASSACHUSETTS,
1850–60

BRASS (COPPER 85.66, ZINC 14.01,
LEAD 0.22), IRON, GLASS
H. 50" (127.0 CM), DIAM. 34" (86.4 CM)
91.41

HENRY NORTHEY HOOPER (1799–1865) began his professional career as a mathematical instrument maker and agent for the Boston Copper Company. In 1832 he started his own firm, which, in partnership with William Blake and Thomas Richardson, he named Henry N. Hooper and Company. He and his partners called themselves copper dealers, founders, and manufacturers, and advertised that they could supply fittings and sheathing for ships, bells for churches and factories, and lanterns for locomotives.

They also noted that they made "Chandeliers, girandoles, candelabra, and lamps, in great variety of patterns, and of the most approved styles, for GAS, Oil, and CANDLES, finished in Plain, Olive, and Antique Bronze, Ormolu, or Gold and Silver Plate, as may be wanted. Great care has been taken to bring this Branch of business to a high state of perfection, and no pains spared to insure a thorough finish in every particular."[206]

Their trade catalogue, of which copies dated 1850 and 1858 survive, pictures an eight-arm variant of the fifteen-light gas chandelier shown here.[207] The many ornamental parts of this example are individually cast in the form of flowers, tendrils, and leaves and are bolted or threaded together. The gas pipes appear to be seamless tubes. All parts have been given a matte or burnished finish and coated with tinted lacquer to prevent tarnish and simulate gilding. The entire assemblage is a spirited and striking interpretation of the rococo style reminiscent of the work of the Parisian brass founders François-Thomas Germain (1726–91) and Philippe Caffieri (1714–74).

The use of gas for illumination in America commenced with demonstrations of its merit in 1816 by Rembrandt Peale in Baltimore and Charles Willson Peale in Philadelphia. Between

then and 1860, a total of 420 gas companies were chartered. Of them, 1 produced wood gas, 3 made water gas, 30 supplied rosin gas, and the balance of 386 generated coal gas.[208]

These figures demonstrate the overwhelming preference for coal gas as an illuminant, largely explained by its plentiful supply, easy access, and cheapness. The hydrogen it generates when it is burned and united with carbon produces a clear, steady, bright, dense flame. Coal gas was piped from its source through a system of underground pipes to houses using gas-burning fixtures. In this instance, the chandelier is fitted with simulated candles made of white glass. Their tips are "furnished with burners having small apertures, out of which the gas issues with a velocity corresponding to its degree of pressure. Near the termination of each tube there is a stop-cock, upon turning which, when light is required, the gas instantly flows in an equable stream, and instantly inflames, on the approach of a lighted taper, into a brilliant, soft and beautiful flame, requiring no trimming or snuffing, to keep up equal brightness; and the quantity of gas that issues, and of course, the height of the flame, is regulated simply by turning the stop-cock: it may be made to give a considerable flame, or one so low and dim as scarcely to be perceived."[209]

The merits of gas were manifold. Indeed, "the superiority of gas over every other invention for the production of artificial light . . . is obvious to all; the advantage of a handsome room being well lighted in every corner from one concentrated point can need no argument. A five-light chandelier, suspended from the center of a room, will give as much light as 65 ordinary sperm candles."[210]

1 Overman, *Moulder's and Founder's Pocket Guide*, p. 219.

2 Joseph Moxon, *Mechanick Exercises* (London: Printed for Daniel Midwinter and Thomas Leigh, 1703), pp. 215-17.

3 Stengel, *Die Merkzeichen der Nürnberger Rotschmiede*, p. 11, pictures this mark with and without maker's initials, but the identity is not positively established.

4 Larkin, *Practical Brass*, p. 209.

5 Larkin, *Practical Brass*, p. 211.

6 The ends of slender iron wire staples, used to hold the core in place while casting, are visible on the side of the candle cup near the candle stump removal holes.

7 The first of these is in Jarmuth, *Lichter Leuchten im Abendland*, p. 239; the second is in Geoffrey Wills, *Candlesticks* (New York: Clarkson N. Potter, 1974), p. 13.

8 These candlesticks are pictured in Michaelis, *Old Domestic Base-Metal Candlesticks*, pp. 71-72.

9 This candlestick was sold at Christie's in Amsterdam, "The Nanking Cargo" (April 28-May 2, 1986), lot 2920.

10 This banquet scene was recorded by the Dutch engraver Pieter Philippe, apparently after a painting by the Dutch artist Jakob Toorenvliet. A depiction of that engraving can be seen in Richard Barber, *Samuel Pepys, Esquire* (London: National Portrait Gallery, 1970), p. 16.

11 A pair of square candlesticks made by the silversmith Charles or Christopher Vassadel in Clermont-Ferrand, France, was offered in New York at Christie's sale 5982 (October 15-16, 1985), lot 58. A pair of silver candlesticks bearing Jacob Bodendick's mark and dated 1667-68 is in the collection of the Victoria and Albert Museum. The information concerning Bodendick's background and work in London was obtained from the records of the metalwork department at the Victoria and Albert Museum.

12 Those candlesticks are pictured in Dennis, *Three Centuries of French Domestic Silver*, 1:190, 231.

13 William Salmon, Jr., *Palladio Londinensis* (1734; reprint, Westmeade, Eng.: Gregg International Publishers Limited, 1969). Salmon's definition is recorded in an alphabetical addendum entitled "The Builder's Dictionary."

14 Chippendale, *Gentleman and Cabinet-Maker's Director*, preface.

15 The basis for hypothesizing that the shaft and base might not be original to each other rests on compositional and color differences among upper and lower parts and the atypical pronounced overhang at their juncture.

16 The other Winterthur example is acc. no. 69.1338. On the marked candlestick, see Turner, *Introduction to Brass*, pp. 40, 41. An unmarked example is pictured in Kauffman, *American Copper and Brass*, p. 236; a related French provincial candlestick in silver is pictured in Dennis, *Three Centuries of French Domestic Silver*, 1:297, fig. 467.

17 Verlet, "A Note on the 'Poinçon' of the Crowned C," p. 22.

18 Geoffrey de Bellaigue, *The James A. De Rothschild Collection at Waddesdon Manor; Furniture, Clocks, and Gilt Bronzes*, 5 vols. (London: National Trust, 1974), 5:33.

19 Dennis, *Three Centuries of French Domestic Silver*, 1:94, 100.

20 A classic study of the comparative cost of lighting was conducted by the English naturalist Gilbert White, *Natural History of Selborne* (1789).

21 Henri-René d'Allemagne, *Histoire du Luminaire* (Paris: Alphonse Picard, 1891), pp. 350-51.

22 Specification of Letters Patent, no. 1,241, December 17, 1779, British Patent Office, London.

23 On Penington, see *Pennsylvania Gazette* (Philadelphia), December 14, 1752. On Jones, see *Pennsylvania Gazette*, January 7, 1752.

24 *Aris's Birmingham Gazette*, December 5, 1768. Information on Daniel's legacy was noted in the Joint Record Office, Diocese of Litchfield, Staffordshire, transcribed in Burks, *Birmingham Brass Candlesticks*, p. 57.

25 The other Winterthur pair, with a square base and incurved corners, is acc. no. 67.1381.1, .2. Grove's marks are fully pho-

tographed and discussed in Burks, *Birmingham Brass Candlesticks*, pp. 56–76.

26 *Oeuvre de Juste Aurèle Meissonnier* (1750; reprint, New York: Benjamin Blom, 1969).

27 See Christie's sale "Fine Silver, Objects of Virtu, and Portrait Miniatures" (May 11, 1994), lot 206. The brass candlesticks were offered in London at Phillips (June 16, 1992), lot 151. I am grateful to Christopher Bangs for bringing these candlesticks to my attention. A very important set of eight gilt brass candlesticks that also aid in placing the catalogued set in context were made by the London founder Jon White in 1757 as a gift to the Worshipful Company of Armourers and Braziers in London. Although not pierced through overall, they are cast as lavish sculpted compositions of natural motifs that relate conceptually to those illustrated here. Six remain in the company's guildhall, and two are in a private collection in the United States.

28 John P. Fallon, "The Goulds and the Cafes–Candlestick Makers," *Antiques Dealer and Collector's Guide* 27, no. 4 (November 1974): 100-105.

29 As recorded in Charles J. Jackson, *English Goldsmiths and Their Marks* (London: Macmillan, 1921), pp. 72, 88-90, five hallmarks were required on all silver made in England from 1784 to 1890.

30 As quoted in Bonnin, *Tutenag and Paktong*, p. 21. H. A. Crosby Forbes, *Shopping in China: The Artisan Community at Canton, 1825–1830* (Washington, D.C.: International Exhibitions Foundation, 1979), ent. 29.

31 The other pair is acc. no. 59.790.1, .2. On Lee, see *Aris's Birmingham Gazette*, November 27, 1780.

32 See Burks, *Birmingham Brass Candlesticks*, pp. 76–83, for a discussion of his work.

33 Charles Tomlinson, ed., *Cyclopaedia of Useful Arts*, 2 vols. (London: George Virtue, 1854), 1:296.

34 In addition to this pair, the others are acc. nos. 55.100; 59.2862, .2863;

59.2866, .2867; 59.2886.1, .2; 59.2918, .2919, and 59.2920, .2921. The candlesticks of Grove, Lee, and Durnall are pictured and discussed in Burks, *Birmingham Brass Candlesticks*, pp. 50-94. Birmingham catalogue TS573 T76 F TC, Downs collection, Winterthur Library.

35 On the Cafe designs, see John P. Fallon, "The Goulds and the Cafes–Candlestick Makers," *Antiques Dealer and Collector's Guide* 27, no. 4 (November 1974): 103. Eric Delieb and Michael Roberts, *Matthew Boulton: Master Silversmith* (New York: Clarkson N. Potter, 1971), between pp. 88 and 89.

36 Many of these are pictured and discussed in Burks, *Birmingham Brass Candlesticks*.

37 *Federal Gazette* (Philadelphia), April 20, 1791.

38 Burks, *Birmingham Brass Candlesticks*, is an excellent pictorial reference for candlesticks of the type made in Birmingham relating stylistically to this example.

39 A pair of brass candlesticks marked by Bush is pictured in Gentle and Feild, *Domestic Metalwork*, p. 150, fig. 95.

40 *Uses of Nickel in the Brass Foundry*, p. 1. Bonnin, *Tutenag and Paktong*, pp. 19, 73.

41 Von Engström is quoted in Bonnin, *Tutenag and Paktong*, p. 22. Gertrude Z. Thomas, *Richer than Spices* (New York: Alfred A. Knopf, 1965), p. 153.

42 H. A. Crosby Forbes, John D. Kernan, and Ruth S. Wilkins, *Chinese Export Silver, 1785 to 1885* (Milton, Mass.: Museum of the American China Trade, 1975), p. 57.

43 *Aris's Birmingham Gazette*, November 3, 1766.

44 *Aris's Birmingham Gazette*, December 13, 1784.

45 Durnall is quoted in *Aris's Birmingham Gazette*, November 13, 1760. These candlesticks are pictured and discussed in Burks, *Birmingham Brass Candlesticks*, pp. 83-94. The advertisement appears in *Aris's Birmingham Gazette*, November 28, 1768.

46 Trade catalogue TS573 T70 F, pl. 21, Downs collection, Winterthur Library.

An even closer match is pictured in Gentle and Feild, *English Domestic Brass*, p. 120.

47 On Whately's invention, see Specification of Letters Patent, no. 905, November 8, 1768, British Patent Office, London. Whately was granted a related patent, no. 908, on December 6, 1768, which he described as a "New-Invented Method of Plating Gold upon Silver-plated Metal Wire." Winterthur also owns a pair of three-socket lyre-form candelabra, acc. no. 65.1376.1, .2 (entry 135).

48 Trade catalogue NK7240 T76, Downs collection, Winterthur Library.

49 Vol. 2, MS 6336, Register of Freemen, Founders Company, London, 1730-1801, Manuscript collection, Guildhall Museum, London; vol. 6, MS 6330, audit books of the Worshipful Company of Founders, 1497-1916, Manuscript collection, Guildhall Museum, London. *Paul Revere's Boston, 1735–1818* (Boston: Museum of Fine Arts, 1975), p. 200.

50 A pair with engraved ornament and inscription is owned by the Chrysler Museum in Norfolk and another is illustrated in Gentle and Feild, *English Domestic Brass*, p. 123.

51 "Lord Howe's Account of the Relief at Gibraltar," *Gentleman's Magazine* (November 1782): 511-14.

52 Jules D. Prown, *John Singleton Copley*, 2 vols. (Cambridge: Harvard University Press, 1966), 2:323. Robert Campbell, "The History of the Siege of Gibraltar," *Pennsylvania Packet, and Daily Advertiser* (Philadelphia), July 18, 1789.

53 Both quotes are transcribed in Eric Robinson, "Eighteenth-Century Commerce and Fashion: Matthew Boulton's Marketing Techniques," *Economic History Review*, 2d ser., 16, no. 1 (August 1963): 46, 59.

54 The Chandler advertisement is in the *Pennsylvania Packet, and Daily Advertiser*, May 4, 1772. While this type of candlestick could date as early as 1772, the mark struck on the base was not registered with the Sheffield Assay Office until 1784. On the screw mechanism and

glass shade, see Webster, *Encyclopaedia of Domestic Economy*, pp. 174, 178.

55 On the related pair in silver, see Delieb, *Great Silver Manufactory*, p. 97. On Wyatt, and the other designers, see Goodison, *Ormolu: The Work of Matthew Boulton*, p. 53. On Hooker, see Delieb, *Great Silver Manufactory*, p. 131.

56 Specification of Letters Patent, no. 1,467, February 26, 1785, British Patent Office, London.

57 Specification of Letters Patent, no. 2,263, October 30, 1798, British Patent Office, London. The candlestick is dated based on the latest features, which are the apparently seamless shafts and hollow rivets joining shafts to bases. The numbers stamped incuse into the base next to the word "PATENT" may be a production code.

58 Sample book 739.3 S19, vol. 2, watermarked by Evans and Sons, Peabody Essex Institute, Salem, Mass.

59 As cited in Bonnin, *Tutenag and Paktong*, p. xii.

60 The advertisement is cited in Goodison, *Ormolu: The Work of Matthew Boulton*, p. 11. Burks, in *Birmingham Brass Candlesticks*, has documented other English makers of paktong. She records that Thomas Dowler and Richard Sharp offered "white India metal candlesticks called Tooth and Egg" (tutenag) in *Aris's Birmingham Gazette*, February 5, 1770. Delieb, *Great Silver Manufactory*, p. 134. This candlestick is pictured in a Birmingham brass-manufacturer's trade catalogue dated about 1777, TS573 T76F, Downs collection, Winterthur Library.

61 On Bailey, see *Rivington's New-York Gazetteer*, July 29, 1773. On Sause, see *Rivington's New-York Gazetteer*, October 28, 1773.

62 *Wrightson's Annual Directory of Birmingham* (Birmingham, Eng.: R. Wrightson, 1831), p. 307. Specification of Letters Patent, no. 8,049, April 25, 1839, British Patent Office, London.

63 This improvement was invented by Thomas Clive, iron founder, in Birmingham in 1842. He called it a rack and pinion and fully described and pictured it in Specification of Letters

Patent, no. 9,316, October 7, 1842, British Patent Office, London.

64 Patent no. 8,049. Parenthetically, patents were intended to recognize an individual's new idea and assure the patentee appropriate remuneration. If a proposed idea could be proven to have been in general use previously, it was not patentable, but there seem to have been exceptions. Tubular rivet construction was present in English candlesticks prior to the date of Barlow's patent. Apparently this was not known by the patent office, or its use was not so widespread as to prevent Barlow's being issued his patent.

65 London city directories, Guildhall Library, London.

66 On chandlers, see Campbell, *London Tradesmen*, p. 271.

67 A. M. F. Willich, *The Domestic Encyclopaedia*, 3 vols. (Philadelphia: Abraham Small, 1821), 1:373.

68 Specification of Letters Patent, no. 8,049, April 25, 1839, British Patent Office, London.

69 On the foreigner, see patent no. 8,049. For Church's patent, see Specification of Letters Patent, no. 1,528, March 28, 1840, United States Patent Office, Alexandria, Va.

70 Patent no. 1,528.

71 J. M. O'Fallon, *The Art Journal* (London: J. S. Virtue, 1894), p. 313.

72 Catalogues of these firms are in the Winterthur rare book collection.

73 On the renewal of old styles, see *The Housekeeper's Quest* (New York: Sypher, 1885), p. 3. A. Beresford Riley, "Old Flemish and Dutch Brass," *Connoisseur* 8 (April 1904): 212.

74 The identity of the manufacturer or partnership whose initials are cast in conjunction with the number 6 on the base has not been determined. Another pattern marked with these initials flanking the number 5 is pictured in Michaelis, *Old Domestic Base-Metal Candlesticks*, p. 114. Other examples are marked in a similar manner with the numbers 1, 2, and 3. Although England has been noted as the country of origin for this group,

Germany has been suggested by others knowledgeable on the subject.

75 Birmingham brass trade catalogues 739.3 S19 v.4 and 739.3 S19 v.9, Peabody Essex Institute, Salem, Mass., depict numerous such knops, including 739.3 S19 v.9, pl. 27.

76 As quoted in Louise A. Boger, *The Dictionary of World Pottery and Porcelain* (New York: Charles Scribner's Sons, 1971), p. 209. In 1914 the law was modified requiring imported objects to be marked with the country of origin following the phrase *Made in*. A pair of brass candlesticks, closely following this English design, is owned by the Peale Museum, Baltimore. They are marked "China" on the underside and not only demonstrate the widespread dissemination of this design but also the global scope of the American market for foreign goods at this time.

77 On the 1883 law, see "Designs and Trademarks: Registers and Representations," Public Record Office, London. Design registration record BT 50/202, no. 223580, Public Record Office, London. Another registration, 263297, appears infrequently on similar candlesticks and was awarded to James Clews and Sons on October 9, 1895.

78 Knight, *Knight's American Mechanical Dictionary*, 2:1590. Von Engström is cited in Bonnin, *Tutenag and Paktong*, p. 23.

79 Bonnin, *Tutenag and Paktong*, p. 73.

80 Robert Hunt, ed., *Ure's Dictionary of Arts, Manufactures, and Mines*, 3 vols. (London: Longman, Green, Longman, and Roberts, 1860), 2:331.

81 Correspondence with the Austrian Museum of Applied Art, the Historical Museum of the City of Vienna, and the Museum of the History of Art, all in Vienna, produced no identification of the maker.

82 William C. Richards, *A Day in the New York Crystal Palace* (New York: G. P. Putnam, 1853), p. 37.

83 This type of candlestick also bears the label of Ellis H. Archer and Redwood F. Warner, competitors of the firm in Philadelphia from 1849 to 1857, and several are known with the label of Michael

B. Dyott, lampmaker in Philadelphia from 1842 to after 1881. On the Dearborn patent, see *A List of Patents Granted by the United States for the Encouragement of Arts and Sciences, Alphabetically Arranged from 1790 to 1828* (Washington, D.C., 1828), p. 16.

84 Specification of Letters Patent, no. 29,341, July 24, 1860, United States Patent Office, Alexandria, Va.

85 Holme, *Academy of Armory*, 2:5.

86 Webster, *Encyclopaedia of Domestic Economy*, pp. 176–77.

87 Webster, *Encyclopaedia of Domestic Economy*, p. 173.

88 Marcel Grandjean, *L'Argenterie du Vieux-Lausanne* (Lausanne, Switz.: Editions du Grand-Pont, 1984), p. 32.

89 Specification of Letters Patent, no. 1,528, March 28, 1840, United States Patent Office, Alexandria, Va., notes the common use of the term *sheet hand candlestick*, as do numerous other similar patents dating from the mid nineteenth century.

90 Trade catalogue 739.3 519 v.2, Peabody Essex Institute, is part of a sizable group of such books believed to have been owned by the early Salem hardware merchant Robert Peele.

91 United States Customs House Papers, Philadelphia, 1790–1869 (microfilm of original material owned by the University of Delaware).

92 Roberts, *House Servant's Directory*, p. 27.

93 The description also fits a pair of lyre candlesticks owned by Winterthur, acc. no. 63.694.1, .2.

94 A full explanation of the process of making fused plate is in Bradbury, *History of Old Sheffield Plate*, pp. 11–12.

95 Bradbury, *History of Old Sheffield Plate*, pp. 79–81.

96 On Odiot, see David Harris Cohen to Donald L. Fennimore, January 7, 1985; Juliette Niclausse, *Thomire* (Paris: Librairie Gründ, 1947), p. 57.

97 A grouping that incorporates these candelabra is pictured in "Thomire le Talleyrand du bronze doré," *Connaissance des Arts*, no. 50 (April 15, 1956): 79.

98 Thomas Fletcher letterbook, 75x10.1-2, Downs collection, Winterthur Library.

99 On Christian and Robert, see Horace Greeley, *The Great Industries of the United States* (Hartford, Conn.: J.B. Burr and Hyde, 1872), p. 315. Bishop, *History of American Manufactures*, 3:50. The firm went through a number of name changes. They were Cornelius and Son from 1831 to 1839; Cornelius and Company from 1839 to 1851; Cornelius and Baker from 1851 to 1870; Cornelius and Sons from 1870 to 1886; Cornelius and Hetherington from 1886 to 1888; and Cornelius and Rowland from 1888 to 1900, when the company ceased doing business.

100 *Description of the Establishment of Cornelius and Baker* (Philadelphia: J.B. Chandler, n.d.), p. 24.

101 Bishop, *History of American Manufactures*, 3:49.

102 James Fenimore Cooper, *The Last of the Mohicans* (1826; reprint, New York: Bantam Books, 1981), pp. 21, 22.

103 Specification of Letters Patent, no. 206, December 5, 1848; Specification of Letters Patent, no. 216, April 10, 1849, United States Patent Office, Alexandria, Va.

104 *The Manufactories and Manufactures of Pennsylvania of the Nineteenth Century* (Philadelphia: Galaxy Publishing Co., 1875), pp. 242, 243.

105 On the Pennsylvania buildings, see *Manufactories and Manufactures of Pennsylvania*, p. 243. *A Description of the New Masonic Temple, Broad Street, Philadelphia* (Philadelphia: M'Calla and Stavely, 1873), p. 21.

106 As quoted in Webster, *Encyclopaedia of Domestic Economy*, p. 176. Scott La France, "A Philadelphia Brass Candlestand: American Antique or 'Age of Decline,'" research paper, object folder 59.506, Registration Office, Winterthur.

107 Henri-René d'Allemagne, *Musée du Luminaire* (Paris: J. Schemit, 1900), p. 31.

108 François Blondel, *Cours d'Architecture* (Paris, 1683), as quoted in Fiske Kimball, *The Creation of the Rococo*

(Philadelphia: Philadelphia Museum of Art, 1943), p. 27.

109 Transactions of a June 3, 1697, meeting of the Academy of Architecture in Paris, as quoted in Kimball, *Creation of the Rococo*, p. 78.

110 Marcus Vitruvius Pollio, *De Architectura Libri Decum*, trans. Morris Hicky Morgan (Reprint, New York: Dover Publications, 1960), pp. 6, 7.

111 Chippendale, *Gentleman and Cabinet-Maker's Director*, preface.

112 The other pair is acc. no. 65.945.1, .2. On french plating, see Bradbury, *History of Old Sheffield Plate*, p. 4.

113 Ephraim Chambers, *Cyclopaedia; or, An Universal Dictionary of Arts and Sciences*, 2 vols. (London, 1751), 1:s.v. "arabesque."

114 On the French artisans, see Fiske Kimball, *The Creation of the Rococo* (Philadelphia: Philadelphia Museum of Art, 1943), pp. 114, 132, 134, 154. The sconce designs are in Kimball, *Creation of the Rococo*, fig. 256, and Gabriel Henriot, *Encyclopédie du Luminaire*, 2 vols. (Paris: R. Panzani, 1934), 2: pl. 182, fig. 2.

115 Illustration 1788 in unbound trade catalogue NK8360 C35c PF TC, Downs collection, Winterthur Library.

116 On Goelet, see *New-York Journal, or General Advertiser*, May 5, 1768. On Neilson, see *New-York Journal, or General Advertiser*, April 30, 1767. Winterthur also owns a closely related pair of sconces, acc. no. 61.542.1, .2, which are said to have belonged to Gen. Epaphroditus Champion (1756–1834) of East Haddam, Conn.

117 Roberts, *House Servant's Directory*, p. 28.

118 Roberts, *House Servant's Directory*, p. 28.

119 Peter Glenworth inventory, will 404, 1793, City Hall Annex, Philadelphia.

120 Specification of Letters Patent, no. 2,153, December 23, 1796, British Patent Office, London.

121 The related pair is acc. no. 61.902.1, .2.

122 Chippendale, *Gentleman and Cabinet-Maker's Director*, p. 17. Oresko, *Works in Architecture*, 1:pl. 8.

123 Webster, *Encyclopaedia of Domestic Economy*, p. 193. Designs for lanterns

with glass panes in brass or gilded wood frames are pictured in Chippendale, *Gentleman and Cabinet-Maker's Director*, pls. 42, 43. Designs for vase-shape lanterns can be seen in George Hepplewhite, *The Cabinet-Maker and Upholsterer's Guide* (London: I. and J. Taylor, 1794), pl. 112.

124 The adjustable elevator, acc. no. 63.861, from which this lantern is suspended uses a gilded lead dove as its counterweight. The braided silk cords, which pass through holes in the dove's body to attach to the lantern, have probably been shortened.

125 The portrait is owned by the National Gallery in London.

126 Sherlock, "Chandeliers, Fine and Handsome," p. 45.

127 Sherlock, "Churches and Candlelight," p. 44.

128 Sherlock, "Chandeliers and the Scrap-Yard," p. 91.

129 Trade catalogue TS573 B61F* no. 2, Downs collection, Winterthur Library.

130 On King, see *Pennsylvania Chronicle*, April 20, 1767. On Robertson, see *South-Carolina Gazette*, December 16, 1760.

131 Larger chandeliers were made having three tiers with 30 arms; one is recorded at Saint Michael's Church, Charleston, S.C., with three tiers and 42 arms. It was imported from London and installed in 1804. Each of the twenty elements in the shaft of Winterthur's example has a roman numeral filed into the inside surface. These numbers are organized sequentially from top to bottom. In addition, the rings to which the arms are bolted are stamped with numbers 1 through 12 beside each bolt hole. Each arm has a corresponding stamped number. These numbers were used to facilitate assembly.

132 On the collar construction, see Sherlock, "Churches and Candlelight," p. 44; on gadrooning, see Sherlock, "In Search of Chandeliers," p. 80; on foliate bobeches and borders, see Sherlock, "Chandeliers and Posterity," p. 30.

133 William Hone, *The Every-Day Book*, 2 vols. (London: Hunt and Clarke, 1826), 1:1271–72.

134 Oman, "English Brass Chandeliers in American Churches," pp. 110–13; Rabbi Theodore Lewis, "Touro Synagogue, Newport, R.I.," *Newport History* 48, no. 159 (Summer 1975): 284, 295.

135 *Wochentliche Philadelphische Staatsbote* (Philadelphia), February 5, 1771.

136 Jonathan Swift, *Directions to Servants* (1745; reprint, New York: Pantheon, 1964), pp. 35, 42, 44.

137 Webster, *Encyclopaedia of Domestic Economy*, p. 171.

138 Webster, *Encyclopaedia of Domestic Economy*, p. 171.

139 *New-York Mercury*, January 11, 1768.

140 On wicks, see Campbell, *London Tradesmen*, p. 270. Webster, *Encyclopaedia of Domestic Economy*, p. 170.

141 That silver example is pictured in Dennis, *Three Centuries of French Domestic Silver*, p. 59.

142 Beecher, *Treatise on Domestic Economy*, p. 353. On Matthews, see Birmingham City Directory, 1809–11, Birmingham City Library.

143 On the Eckhardt and Morton patent, see Bennett Woodcroft, *Titles of Patents of Invention*, 2 vols. (London: Queen's Printing Office, 1854), 1:398. On Day's invention, see Woodcroft, *Titles of Patents of Invention*, 1:721; a pair of these, owned by the Victoria and Albert Museum, is pictured in Turner, *Introduction to Brass*, p. 43.

144 Aitken, *Early History of Brass*, p. 103.

145 On the makers, see Jeannette Lasansky, *To Draw, Upset, and Weld* (Lewisburg, Pa.: Union County Historical Society, 1980), pp. 47, 49. On the Ebys, see Elmer Z. Longenecker, *The Early Blacksmiths of Lancaster County* (Lancaster, Pa.: Lancaster Theological Seminary, 1971), pp. 32, 35, 44. Ronald V. Jackson, Gary R. Teeples, and David Schaefermeyer, eds., *Pennsylvania 1820 Census Index* (Bountiful, Utah: Accelerated Indexing Systems, 1977), p. 96. Ronald V. Jackson, Gary R. Teeples, eds., *Pennsylvania 1840 Census Index* (Bountiful, Utah: Accelerated Indexing, Systems, Inc., 1978), p. 179.

146 The other example is acc. no. 60.340. William T. O'Dea, *The Social History*

of Lighting (London: Routledge and Kegan Paul, 1958), p. 213. The advice is quoted in Lester Breininger, Jr., "The Works of Peter Derr," *Spinning Wheel* (July-August 1972): 49.

147 Henry Chapman Mercer, *Light and Fire Making* (Philadelphia: Press of MacCalla Co., 1898), pp. 7, 3.

148 Hermann Boker is noted in Thomas Longworth, *Longworth's American Almanac, New York Register, and City Directory* (New York: By the author, 1839), p. 107. Hermann is presumably related to Heinrich Boker, whose initial is stamped into the lamp. On Germany as a supplier, see John C. Gobright and James Pratt, *The Union Sketchbook: Reliable Guide, Exhibiting the History and Resources of the Leading Mercantile and Manufacturing Firms of New York* (New York: Pudney and Russell, 1860), p. 15.

149 Robert Ernst, *Immigrant Life in New York City: 1825–63* (New York: King's Crown Press, 1949), p. 187. James Twitt, *Twitt's Directory of Prominent Business Men in New York* (New York: By the author, 1858), p. 39.

150 Overman, *Moulder's and Founder's Pocket Guide*, p. 243.

151 James F. Spears, *A Picture Story of the House of Derr* (Myerstown, Pa.: Church Center Press, 1949), pp. 12, 49, 69.

152 Spears, *Picture Story*, pp. 74, 94. The Reverend F. J. F. Schantz, "The Domestic Life and Characteristics of the Pennsylvania German Pioneer," in *The Pennsylvania-German Society Proceedings and Addresses* (Lancaster, Pa.: By the society, 1900), p. 72.

153 On new light sources, see Lester Breininger, Jr., "The Works of Peter Derr," *Spinning Wheel* (July-August 1972): 49. Spears, *Picture Story*, pp. 37, 162.

154 Webster, *Encyclopaedia of Domestic Economy*, p. 193. Chippendale, *Gentleman and Cabinet-Maker's Director*, p. 17.

155 Webster, *Encyclopaedia of Domestic Economy*, p. 193.

156 Webster, *Encyclopaedia of Domestic Economy*, p. 193.

157 Webster, *Encyclopaedia of Domestic Economy*, p. 178.

158 William Chambers, *Chambers's Information for the People*, 2 vols. (Philadelphia: J. and J.L. Gihon, 1853), 1:127.

159 William H. Webb notebook, 1828, privately owned, as quoted in Ackerman, "William Homes Webb," *Maine Antique Digest* 11, no. 4 (April 1983): 1-c.

160 Webb, as quoted in Ackerman, "William Homes Webb," p. 1-c. On his business, see Cyrus Eaton, *Annals of Warren* (Hallowell, Maine: Masters and Livermore, 1877), pp. 307, 370, as quoted in Ackerman, "William Homes Webb," p. 2-c.

161 Hare is quoted in Russell, *Heritage of Light*, pp. 94, 95. On the Jennings patent, see C. Malcom Watkins, "Artificial Lighting in America," in *The Smithsonian Report* (Washington, D.C.: United States Government Printing Office, 1952), pp. 398, 399.

162 As quoted in Watkins, "Artificial Lighting in America," pp. 399, 400.

163 Specification of Letters Patent, no. 9,250, September 7, 1852, United States Patent Office, Alexandria, Va. Russell, *Heritage of Light*, p. 153.

164 John Fanning Watson, *Annals of Philadelphia, and Pennsylvania in the Olden Time* (1830; reprint, Philadelphia: Leary, Stuart Co., 1927), 1:204.

165 The Jefferson quote is cited in Marie Kimball, "The Furnishing of Monticello," *Antiques* 12, no. 5 (November 1927): 342. Letter and memorandum book transcription sent by Ann M. Lucas to Donald L. Fennimore, August 15, 1991. A similar lamp bearing Boulton's label is pictured in Bradbury, *History of Old Sheffield Plate*, p. 395.

166 An account of Watson's historical research and collecting is in Frank Sommer, "John F. Watson: First Historian of American Decorative Arts," *Antiques* 83, no. 3 (March 1963): 300–303. Harrold E. Gillingham, "An Historic Lamp," *Antiques* 13, no. 4 (April 1928): 293. The location of the paper is unknown.

167 Gillingham's lamp is pictured and described in the auction catalogue of Samuel T. Freeman and Company, Philadelphia (April 16-20, 1945), lot 442. H. F. du Pont purchase books, vol. 3.

168 On Argand, see Russell, *Heritage of Light*, p. 76. Michael Schroder, *The Argand Burner* (Odense, Den.: Odense University Press, 1969), pp. 126-31.

169 On Keir, see Rees, *Cyclopaedia*, 21:s.v. "lamp." The fountain lamp is discussed in Webster, *Encyclopaedia of Domestic Economy*, pp. 187-88. On the argand lamp, see Rees, *Cyclopaedia*, 21:s.v. "lamp." The advertisement is found in the *Federal Gazette* (Philadelphia), November 16, 1790.

170 On Boulton, see Delieb, *Great Silver Manufactory*, p. 107. Specification of Letters Patent, no. 1,425, March 15, 1784, British Patent Office, London. *Swinney's Birmingham Directory* (Birmingham, Eng.: Printed by Myles Swinney, 1775), preface.

171 A pair bearing the Soho manufactory label, acc. no. 59.671.1, .2, is also owned by Winterthur. A fourth example is pictured in Bradbury, *History of Old Sheffield Plate*, p. 395. A fifth is at Colonial Willamsburg.

172 *Swinney's Birmingham Directory* (Birmingham, Eng.: Printed by Myles Swinney, 1775), preface. This lamp appears as pl. 1331 in Boulton's 1790 pattern book, housed in the Birmingham City Library. I am grateful to John J. Wolfe for this information.

173 Webster, *Encyclopaedia of Domestic Economy*, pp. 191-92. Robert Wrightson, *Wrightson's Triennial Directory* (Birmingham, Eng.: By the author, 1825), p. 100.

174 On the firm, see *Stimpson's Boston Directory, The Boston Annual Advertiser* (Boston: Charles Stimpson, Jr., 1835). Dorothy T. Rainwater, *Encyclopedia of American Silver Manufacturers* (New York: Crown Publishers, 1975), p. 155.

175 Trade catalogues TS573 M58h* TC and NK7899 B61a TC, Downs collection,

Winterthur Library. Bishop, *History of American Manufactures*, 3:51.

176 Specification of Letters Patent, no. 6,551, February 6, 1834, British Patent Office, London.

177 Patent no. 6,551.

178 A lamp closely related to the Miller lamp is depicted in the portrait of the Philadelphian James Peale painted by his older brother Charles Willson Peale, now in the Detroit Institute of Arts. On Adams, see Geoffrey Godden, *An Illustrated Encyclopedia of British Pottery and Porcelain* (New York: Crown Publishers, 1964), p. 21. On Boulton, see Goodison, *Ormolu*, pp. 74, 77. London city directory, 1856, Guildhall Museum, London.

179 Webster, *Encyclopaedia of Domestic Economy*, p. 181.

180 Webster, *Encyclopaedia of Domestic Economy*, p. 182. Specification of Letters Patent, no. 4,475, June 15, 1820, British Patent Office, London.

181 On Parker, see Russell, *Heritage of Light*, p. 83. Webster, *Encyclopaedia of Domestic Economy*, p. 182.

182 O. Ruffhead, *The Statutes at Large*, 14 vols. (London: George Eyre and Andrew Strahan, 1798), 13:833. John Raithby, comp., *The Statutes of the United Kingdom of Great Britain and Ireland*, 6 vols. (London: George Eyre and Andrew Strahan, 1814), 5:577.

183 *New-York Daily Advertiser*, April 25, 1820.

184 Howard G. Hubbard, "A Complete Check List of Household Lights" (South Hadley, Mass., 1935), an unpublished monograph, enumerates the patents granted for household lamps, lanterns, candlesticks, and burning fluids from 1792 through 1862, as recorded in document 688, United States Patent Office, Alexandria, Va.

185 The argand burner is fully described and illustrated in David Brewster, comp., *Second American Edition of the Edinburgh Encyclopaedia*, 36 vols. (New York: Samuel Whiting and John Tiffany, 1819), 11:658-59, 12:pl. 342.

186 Letters from Thomas Fletcher to Timothy Fletcher, November 21, 1809,

August 30, 1812, Thomas Fletcher Papers, Athenaeum of Philadelphia. Thomas Longworth, *Longworth's Almanac, New-York Register and City Directory* (New York: T. Longworth and Son, 1842), adv. supp.

187 Letter from Fletcher to Cox, October 28, 1833, Thomas Fletcher Papers, Athenaeum of Philadelphia.

188 Overman, *Moulder's and Founder's Pocket Guide*, p. 242. The pseudo-gilding process was quite complex and required strict temperature and time limits. A fuller discussion of the steps involved is in Timmins, *Resources, Products, and Industrial History*, pp. 299-300.

189 On Cornelius, see Denys Peter Myers, *Gaslighting in America* (Washington, D.C.: United States Department of the Interior, 1978), p. 39. *A List of Patents Granted by the United States, for the Encouragement of Arts and Sciences, Alphabetically Arranged from 1790 to 1828* (Washington, D.C., 1828), p. 52.

190 On the company, see Bishop, *History of American Manufactures*, 3:49. On gas chandeliers, see Edwin T. Freedley, *Philadelphia and Its Manufactures* (Philadelphia: Edward Young, 1858), p. 352.

191 *Great Exhibition of the Works of Industry of All Nations, 1851. Official Descriptive and Illustrated Catalogue*, 3 vols. (London: Spicer Brothers and W. Clowes and Sons, 1851), 3:1435.

192 Henry N. Hooper and Company trade catalogue (Boston: Henry W. Dutton and Son, 1858), cover, copy in Peabody Essex Institute, Salem, Mass.

193 Hooper trade catalogue, Peabody Essex Institue. This catalogue is one of three presently recorded. There are a few other early American lighting catalogues known: one issued by Dietz and Company of New York about 1860; another published by Mitchell, Vance, and Company, also in New York City, about 1876; one published by Archer and Pancoast of New York City about the same time; and one published by Cornelius and Sons, also about 1876.

194 Whitworth and Wallis, comps., *The Industry of the United States* (London: George Routledge, 1854), p. 130.

195 Specification of Letters Patent, no. 3,028, April 6, 1843, United States Patent Office, Alexandria, Va.

196 Specification of Letters Patent, no. 6,603, July 24, 1849, United States Patent Office, Alexandria, Va. Even though solar lamps simplified the matter of obtaining light from solid fuels, they, like their predecessors, required specific directions and constant attention to operate efficiently. The directions for operating Cornelius and Company's solar lamps were detailed and extensive. A printed copy, which almost certainly accompanied every lamp the company sold, is in the Downs collection, Winterthur Library, 74x209.

197 *Great Exhibition of the Works of Industry of All Nations, 1851. Official Descriptive and Illustrated Catalogue*, 3 vols. (London: Spicer Brothers and W. Clowes and Sons, 1851), 3:1435.

198 The many steps and processes involved in coloring brass lamps are outlined in Bishop, *History of American Manufacturers*, 3:51-53. Larkin, *Practical Brass and Iron Founder's Guide*, p. 114.

199 Brown, *Principles and Practices of Dipping*, p. 31.

200 Rees, *Cyclopaedia*, 21:s.v. "lamp." The unnamed inventor to whom Rees was referring may have been Jedediah Strutt (1726-97), an innovative cotton hosiery manufacturer in Derby.

201 On the Bynner development, see Specification of Letters Patent, no. 7,503, December 9, 1837, British Patent Office, London. The interesting and convoluted story of the development of the solar lamp is well detailed in a series of articles by Robert E. Calvin in *The Rushlight* (Breeksville, Ohio): "Evolution of the Solar Lamp: Part I," 47, no. 4 (December 1982): 12-17; " Part II," 49, no. 1 (March 1983): 2-8; "Part III," 49, no. 2 (June 1983): 8-14; "Part IV," 49, no. 3 (September 1983): 2-9; "Levavasseur and Neuburgers

Solar Lamps," 49, no. 4 (December 1983): 6-11; "More on British Solar Lamps," 50, no. 1 (March 1984): 7-11; and "The Bynner Solar Lamp Trial," 50, no. 4 (December 1984): 13-14. For more on the solar lamp, see Webster, *Encyclopaedia of Domestic Economy*, pp. 186-87.

202 The lamp base appears in Henry N. Hooper and Company trade catalogue, fig. 611, Peabody Essex Institute, Salem, Mass. This lamp was originally electroplated with gold.

203 Andrew Jackson Downing, *A Treatise on the Theory and Practice of Landscape Gardening Adapted to North America; With a View to the Improvement of Country Residences* (New York and London: Wiley and Putnam, 1844), p. 374.

204 William Holden, *London City Directory* (London: Thomas Underhill, 1817). On the Brighton fixtures, see Henry D. Roberts, *A History of the Royal Pavilion* (London: Country Life Limited, 1939), pp. 128-29.

205 Webster, *Encyclopaedia of Domestic Economy*, p. 181.

206 Cover of Henry N. Hooper and Company trade catalogue, Peabody Essex Institute, Salem, Mass.

207 An 1858 copy is owned by the Peabody Essex Institute, and one copy each of the 1850 and 1858 catalogues are currently in a private collection.

208 *American Gas-Light Journal* (January 1862): 198-99.

209 Webster, *Encyclopaedia of Domestic Economy*, p. 200.

210 Alfred H. Wood, *A Guide to Gas-Lighting* (Hastings, Eng.: George P. Bacon, 1860), p. 4.

DETAIL, EQUINOCTIAL RING, 1810–15

ENTRY 194

MEASUREMENT

This section presents a variety of objects, all of which were used for measuring. Measurement, in this instance, is defined in its broadest sense and includes implements designed to deal with time, temperature, purity, direction, elevation, distance, weight, and volume. Included are hydrometers, thermometers, barometers, scales and weights, liquid and dry measures, hourglasses, clocks and timepieces, equinoctial rings, watch stands, rulers, gunners' quadrants, and compasses.

WEIGHT
175

ATTRIBUTED TO PETER STRETCH (1670–1746)
PHILADELPHIA, PENNSYLVANIA, 1709–46
BRASS (COPPER 76.23,
ZINC 17.41, LEAD 3.05, TIN 1.80, IRON 1.10,
ANTIMONY 0.29, SILVER 0.12)

H. 5/8" (1.6 CM), W. 1 1/16"
(2.7 CM),
D. 1 1/16" (2.7 CM)
58.1592

PETER STRETCH WAS BORN in Leek, Staffordshire County, England, in 1670. When of age he was apprenticed to his uncle Samuel Stretch to learn the craft of clock- and watchmaking. Having done so, he moved to Philadelphia in 1702 and established himself in business.[1]

Stretch impressed those in the political community with his civic-mindedness, and in 1708 he was appointed to the city's Common Council, serving until his death in 1746. As a council member, he helped "make all such laws and ordinances as were necessary and convenient for the government of the city."[2]

In 1709 the General Assembly of the Commonwealth of Pennsylvania passed "an act for ascertaining the rates of money for payment of debts [by] reducing foreign coins to the same current rate. [It was ordained that] foreign silver coins except Peru's [could not exchange] at any other rate than at nine shillings and one penny by the ounce Troy-weight, either by the single ounce or in greater quantities, and for any sum under a piece of eight at five pence halfpenny each pennyweight."[3]

The many denominations of clipped and unclipped English, Dutch, German, Austrian, French, Spanish, Swedish, and Italian coins circulating in the colony made such a standard cumbersome. Consequently, it was further enacted, to render "payments according to the rates enjoined more easy and expeditious, [that] there shall be sets of weights of all sorts necessary, exactly proportioned, according to the said rates, from one halfpenny worth of silver to any sum that shall be thought fit, which weights shall be prepared and sold by Peter Stretch and George Plumly of Philadelphia, who shall stamp their respective marks thereon and be accountable for their exactness."[4]

Under the provisions of this act, both Plumly and Stretch made up sets of weights for sale to any who needed them. Among the latter's customers was William Penn, who bought "a box of Scales & Weights for gold & silver" on November 10, 1733. Each of the fourteen graduated weights was marked and signed, one of which would have been identical to the example illustrated here.[5]

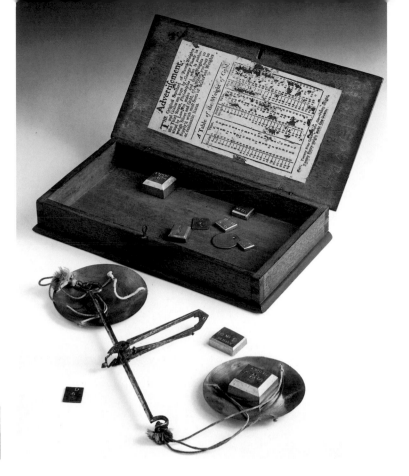

SCALES AND WEIGHTS
176

GEORGE PLUMLY (D. 1754)
PHILADELPHIA, PENNSYLVANIA, 1717–54
BRASS (COPPER 70.00, ZINC 25.47,
LEAD 2.31, TIN 0.18), WOOD, IRON,
COTTON, WALNUT, PAPER

BOX: L. 9" (22.8 CM), W. 4 3/4"
(12.1 CM), H. 1 1/2" (3.8 CM)
58.2279

GEORGE PLUMLY WAS GRANTED freedom to work in Philadelphia on May 6, 1717. From that time until his death in 1754, he practiced the craft of a cutler, making edged tools and weapons. His estate inventory listed "44 doz & 6 sickles, 6 ½ doz sickles finished [and] a sickle cutting bench with its irons and dish" with little else in the way of standard cutlers' wares, clear evidence that he was a specialist.[6]

There is scant material that hints at his working with brass, but interspersed in the list of the contents of his shop are "an anvil, a pr bellows, 23 lb brass & copper, 4³/4 [lb.] brass weights [and] a box with scales & wts."[7] The last of these was surely similar to the group pictured here. Within the walnut box are a pair of hand-held balance pans and nine graduated weights. All are stamped with either Plumly's initials or full surname. Additionally, each weight is designated. The largest, marked "58 8" weighs 2 ounces, 18 pennyweight, 8 grains, while the smallest is marked with five circles and weighs 1 pennyweight, 5 grains.

These designations are in the troy scale, reserved for weighing precious metals and stones. According to the printed table on the box lid, gold was valued at £5.10.0 per ounce. Undoubtedly, those who bought these scales used them for weighing gold–usually in the form of coin–but more often would have weighed silver coin, valued at the same time at 18*d*. per ounce.[8]

SCALES AND
WEIGHTS
177

ENGLAND, PROBABLY LONDON, 1774
RETAILED IN PHILADELPHIA,
PENNSYLVANIA, BY
JOSEPH RICHARDSON, SR. (1711–84)

BRASS (COPPER 80.61, ZINC 15.52,
LEAD 1.60, TIN 0.92), STEEL,
COTTON, WHITE OAK, PAPER
BOX: L. 7 1/16" (18.0 CM), W. 3 1/4"
(8.3 CM), H. 1 3/8" (3.5 CM)
59.899

ON APRIL 11, 1769, the Philadelphia silversmith Joseph Richardson, Sr., wrote to John Masterman, a merchant in London, ordering "6 Doz Pair Gold Scales & Weights from 9 dwt to 1/2 dwt. & a Set of Grains in Shagreen Cases." He specifically requested that the weights be made "about 1 gr. over weight that I may regulate them myself." Sixteen days later he again wrote to Masterman requesting only "2 Doz of the Scales & Weights [in] Shagreen Cases, the other 4 Doz to be in Wooden Boxes."[9]

Richardson imported many sets of scales and weights during his career. In spite of his request that the weights be slightly heavy, he often found that his needs were not met. On October 16, 1771, he wrote to Thomas Wagstaff in London that a "Parcel of Scales & Weights . . . came in good order & to Satisfaction except the Weights which are most

of them too light. I have sent [you] some weights & Desire for the future they may be made exactly the same weight. If they are 1/20 of a Grain Lighter they will not suit."[10]

Richardson advertised these as "a Parcel of money Scales & Weights" for sale in the September 13, 1770, issue of the *Pennsylvania Gazette*. In addition to correctly calibrating each weight, he placed a printed label with his advertisement inside each box lid, outlining the current weight/value for the most common English, French, and Spanish coins circulating in Philadelphia at that time. The stamped lion within a reserve indicates that the weight has been calibrated and certified correct.

COUNTER SCALES
178

HENRY TROEMNER (1809–73)
PHILADELPHIA,
PENNSYLVANIA, 1838–73
BRASS (COPPER 77.57, ZINC 17.09,
TIN 3.26, LEAD 1.75), MARBLE

H. 30" (76.2 CM),
W. 29" (73.7 CM),
D. 9" (22.9 CM)
60.587

HENRY TROEMNER, born and trained in the electorate of Hesse-Cassel, Germany, immigrated to the United States in 1836. Following two years working as a journeyman, he established himself as a scalemaker at 240 Market Street in Philadelphia. His business began modestly, but by 1875 it had grown to "the largest manufactory [of scales, weights, and measures] in the United States," with annual sales of $165,000.[11]

Troemner's success was in large part attributed to his having "paid special attention to the careful manufacture of counter-scales for druggists . . . who insist on perfect accuracy in their weights and balances."[12] The balance-pan scale illustrated here is the type used to measure medicinal and pharmaceutical prepa-rations, including patent medicines, elixirs, powders, extracts, syrups, and magnesias.

While druggists' scales may have been Troemner's principal line, he also supplied bankers, jewelers, grocers, and confectioners with scales capable of measuring "twelve tons [to] the thousandth part of a grain." In addition, his firm "constructed all the Balances, Weights, etc., required for the U.S. Mint, Custom Houses and Repositories and several scales for the Mexican Mint."[13] After his death, his sons John L., Frederick W., and Edward carried on the business under the name Henry Troemner's Sons; the firm is still in operation today.

LIQUID MEASURES

179

JOHN W. CLUETT
ALBANY, NEW YORK, 1830–57
BRASS (COPPER 77.22, ZINC 19.33,
LEAD 1.62, TIN 0.62), COPPER

LEFT: H. 3 3/4" (9.5 CM), W. 3 1/4"
(8.3 CM), DIAM. 2 1/4" (5.7 CM);
RIGHT: H. 4 3/4" (12.1 CM), W. 3 7/8"
(9.8 CM), DIAM. 2 5/8" (6.7 CM)
58.1594, .1596

JOHN W. CLUETT AND CHAUNCY WHITNEY, tin and sheet-iron workers, were together as early as 1830. They remained in partnership until 1855, when the former advertised that as the "successor to Whitney and Cluett, coppersmith, plumber and metallic roofer, [he] makes all kinds of copper work."[14] Cluett continued to list himself alone as a tinmaker, coppersmith, and plumber through 1857, after which time he was no longer recorded in the Albany city directory.

The liquid measures shown here, of 1/2 and 1/4 pint capacity, were made by Cluett as standards for Dutchess County, New York. They were probably part of a larger set that would have included a minimum of "the gallon . . . the half gallon, quart, pint, half pint and gill all to be made of brass," as mandated by federal law.[15] Although standards of weight, capacity, and length were established in Washington, each

state had the responsibility for making and distributing those standards used by their counties.

New York took an active role in regulating and standardizing weights and measures. Its statutes stipulated that "the unit or standard measure of capacity . . . for liquids . . . shall be the gallon, which shall be a vessel of such capacity, as to contain, at the mean pressure of the atmosphere at the level of the sea, ten pounds of distilled water . . . such standard shall be made of brass. . . . All other measures . . . shall be derived from the gallon, by continual multiplication or division by the number two, being in the descending scale, half gallons, quarts, pints, half pints and gills." The illustrated measures were made under the provisions of that statute and were used to dispense "milk, beer, ale, cider, . . . vinegar," and other consumables.[16] The stamped spread eagle certifies that the measures are of accurate volume.

HALF-PINT MEASURE
180

JAMES A. AND JOHN H. KISSAM
BROOKLYN, NEW YORK, 1852–82
BRASS
(COPPER 77.60, ZINC 21.80,
LEAD 0.33), STEEL, LEAD

H. 3 5/8" (9.2 CM), W. 4 1/2"
(11.4 CM), DIAM. 3 9/16" (9.5 CM)
84.28

ON APRIL 11, 1851, the New York state legislature passed an act adopting the United States standard weights and measures for the state of New York. Entitled "An Act in Relation to Weights and Measures," the first section stated that "the standard weights and measures now in charge of the secretary of state, being the same that were furnished to this state by the government of the United States, in accordance with a joint resolution of Congress, approved June 14, 1836, and consisting of . . . one set of standard liquid capacity measures, consisting of one wine gallon of two hundred and thirty-one cubic inches, one half gallon, one quart, one pint and one half pint measure . . . shall be the standards of weights and measures throughout this state."[17]

Measures were to be made cylindrical with plain and even bottoms. They were to be in the custody of a superintendent of weights and measures chosen by the governor, lieutenant governor, and secretary of state. The superintendent was to have copies made of the originals to use in checking the county standards. The state superintendent was to pro-

vide standards for all cities and counties in the state and, as often as once every ten years, compare them with those in his possession. County sealers were, in turn, to provide all towns with copies of standard measures and compare them with county standards as often as once every five years. Town sealers were to see that all measures used for commercial purposes in their town agreed with the standards in their possession.

The half-pint measure illustrated here, almost certainly meant for commercial use within a town, was made in accordance with the 1851 act. It is fashioned of thinly rolled sheet brass; has a straight, folded, and lead-soldered joint along the height of the body; and has wired handle edges. It was undoubtedly part of a graduated five-part set made by James A. and John H. Kissam, who operated a manufactory and store at 81 Fulton Street in Brooklyn and advertised that they were able to provide "grocer's scales and tinware" at the shortest notice.[18]

GRAIN MEASURES
181

POSSIBLY JOHN W. CLUETT
ALBANY, NEW YORK, 1830–57
COPPER

LARGEST: H. 5 1/2" (14.0 CM),
DIAM. 12 1/8" (30.8 CM);
SMALLEST: H. 2 7/8" (7.3 CM),
DIAM. 6 1/4" (15.9 CM)
58.1597, .1598; 65.3002.1, .2

THESE FOUR DRY MEASURES of wrought copper with dovetailed joints hold 1 (1/4 peck), 2, 3 1/2, and 6 1/2 dry quarts. While they bear no maker's mark, they are struck with a spread eagle, which certifies that each measure is volumetrically correct, and the initials "N. Y.," because "no weights or measures . . . shall be used for buying or selling, unless they are duly stamped or marked." The statutes of the state of New York stipulated that "the state sealer shall cause to be impressed on each [standard measure and copy thereof for county and town use] the letters N. Y. and such other additional device, as he shall direct."[19]

Inspectors and sealers of weights and measures were appointed by the governor of each state. They often served in their capacities while pursuing a full-time profession. They provided their ser-

vices competitively, as evidenced by "William Welling, Sealer of Weights and Measures . . . [who] would specially like to thank the numerous manufacturers of weights and measures for the preference they have given him in his official capacity."[20]

The measures brought to Welling and sealers throughout the country consisted of "the half bushel . . . the peck, the half peck and quarter peck, to be of a cylindrical form, made of stout sheet brass." After certification that they were of correct volume, they were used principally for "salt and grain," although other solids were measured in them as well.[21]

HALF-BUSHEL AND HALF-PECK MEASURE

182

WILLIAM ORVILLE HICKOK (B. 1815)
HARRISBURG, PENNSYLVANIA,
1848–83
COPPER, BRASS (COPPER 71.19,
ZINC 28.10, LEAD 1.21, TIN 0.11)

HALF BUSHEL: H. 9 3/4" (24.7 CM),
W. 15 1/2" (39.4 CM),
DIAM. 12 3/4" (32.4 CM);
HALF PECK: H. 7" (17.8 CM), W. 11 3/8"
(28.9 CM), DIAM. 8 3/8" (21.3 CM)
89.51, .52

WILLIAM ORVILLE HICKOK was born October 6, 1815, in Genesee County, New York. In 1823 he moved with his family to Union County, Pennsylvania. He worked for his father in the bookbinding business and also manufactured blank books. In 1839 he moved to Harrisburg to pursue that business on his own, but by 1848 he had redirected his efforts toward the "manufacture of ruling-machines and minor articles." In 1854 he built his Eagle Works, which, following an expansion in 1869, consisted of a brick manufactory four stories in height and about two acres in size on the corner of Canal and North streets. His firm employed about ninety workers who specialized "in making machine castings, cider mills, mechanics' tools, ruling machinery, etc." valued at about $1,500,000 annually.[22]

The measures illustrated here were made to conform to the dry-measure standards made by the United States government for distribution to each state. The government mandated that those standards "consist of the half bushel to contain 1075.21 cubic inches; the peck, the half peck and quarter peck, to be of a cylindrical form, made of stout sheet brass, one tenth of an inch in thickness, and thickened at the top by a band, to be one fifth of an inch. The bottom also to be of stout sheet brass, one fifth of an inch thick, and slightly concave, to prevent the spring in the bottom, which might occur if the bottom were a plane. The interior diameter of each measure, should be equal to the height from the centre of the bottom to the plane of the rim. The half bushel should have handles for the convenience of handling. . . .

The form proposed, it is believed, will be found to be preferable to that of shallower vessels, or even to any other. It is similar to the French dry measures. It is more convenient for striking and handling than a shallower measure. It is to be hoped that the introduction of this form will be a step toward the final abolition of the practice of heaping measures."[23]

The measures shown here are variably marked with an "MS," probably indicating the sealer who certified the capacity; "PA 1818," referring to a Pennsylvania act establishing a standard weight for grain and foreign salt; "47," indicating that a bushel of barley was forty-seven pounds avoirdupois; and "4," for four pecks in one bushel.

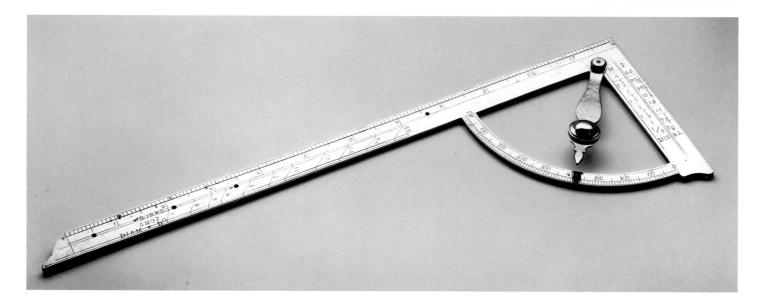

MADE + BY × ISAAC + GREENWOOD + N + YORK.

GUNNER'S QUADRANT
183

ISAAC GREENWOOD (1758–1829)
NEW YORK CITY, 1810–27
BRASS (COPPER 83.58, ZINC 12.78,
LEAD 1.84)

L. 12 5/8" (32.1 CM), H. 4 1/8"
(10.5 CM), D. 1/2" (1.2 CM)
60.1009

ISAAC GREENWOOD WAS BORN in Boston and, when old enough, apprenticed to his father, an "ivory turner, mathematical and musical instrument maker [and] dentist." In 1783 he established himself as a dentist in New York, but having no success moved to Charleston, South Carolina, in 1785. He experienced similar difficulty there, so returned to Boston and then went on to Providence, Rhode Island, by 1787. He remained in Providence, curing "all complaints incident to the Teeth and Gums," until his brother Clarke died in 1810. He then moved to New York City to take over the mathematical-instrument making business that Clarke had established twenty-two years earlier; he remained there until his death.[24]

Greenwood's trade card states that he "imports and makes all kinds of mathematical instruments." It pictures a sextant, gyro-scope, hourglass, telescope, nautical spy glass, and etui and lists thermometers and gauging rods. Although gunners' quadrants are not specifically mentioned, Greenwood made them when called upon to do so. His quadrant, like most, was "introduced into the mouth of [a cannon] to know its elevation" but was deemed to "be of little advantage" in combat because computing from it was too time consuming. In battle, seasoned gunners determined elevation and distance much more quickly "by eye."[25]

The quadrant illustrated here has a twelve-inch rule, each inch divided into twelfths, and a 90 degree protractor. It also has a scale that is believed to relate the elevation of a cannon barrel in degrees to the distance a projectile is shot in meters and another scale that apparently relates shot diameter to barrel bore.[26]

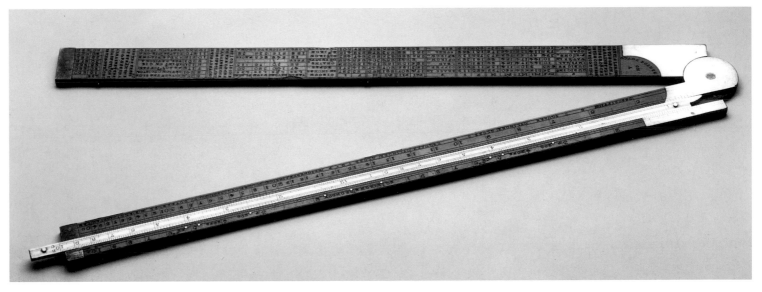

RULER
184

SAMPSON ASTON
BIRMINGHAM, ENGLAND, 1833–47
BRASS (COPPER 72.13, ZINC 25.91,
LEAD 1.24, TIN 0.60), WOOD, STEEL

L. 24" (61.0 CM), W. 1 3/8"
(3.4 CM), D. 1/8" (0.3 CM)
60.379

ALL FOUR SIDES of this folding rule are covered with different graduated scales. The rule is also extensively marked with notations on the load-bearing limits of structural materials; tables of lineal, square, and cubic measure; specific gravities; and the physical properties of various building materials. When opened, it measures twenty-four inches but can be extended to thirty-six inches with a sliding-brass segment set into one arm. It was used by a civil engineer when building roads, bridges, buildings, towers, and other structures.[27]

According to the inscription on one end of the closed rule, the information and format were formulated by Robert Hawthorn, a civil engineer living in Newcastle upon Tyne.

The rule itself was made by Sampson Aston in Birmingham. Aston advertised himself as a "box and ivory rule maker and [operated a] bacon warehouse" on Jennens Row in 1833. By 1843 he appears to have expanded his business, describing himself as a "Manufacturer of Box and ivory rules of every description . . . and [a] wholesale home cured ham and bacon dealer." However, within seven years he seems to have decided that foodstuffs were more profitable than rulemaking; in 1850 he had become a "cheese monger."[28]

YARD STANDARD
185

PROBABLY NEW YORK STATE,
CA. 1822
BRASS (COPPER 71.09, ZINC 26.84,
LEAD 1.47, TIN 0.21, IRON 0.13)

L. 36" (91.4 CM), W. 3/4" (1.9 CM),
D. 9/16" (1.4 CM)
64.1026

THE FEDERAL GOVERNMENT REALIZED the importance of a universal system of measurement as early as 1781, when it gave itself the authority of "fixing the standard of weights and measures throughout the United States."[29] Even so, it was slow in implementing any laws to that effect until the 1830s. Several states, including New York, sought to fill the need during the interim.

On March 22, 1822, New York state authorized the making of a standard "yard . . . divided into three equal parts, called feet, and each foot into twelve equal parts called inches; and for measure of cloth . . . it may be divided into halves, quarters, eighths and sixteenths. . . . The original standard . . . shall be deposited in the office of the state sealer [in Albany] . . . copies . . . shall be deposited in the offices of the clerks of the supreme court at New-York, Albany

and Utica [and] copies . . . for general use . . . shall be deposited in the offices of the assistant state sealers of the city and county of New-York, and the several county sealers."[30]

The rule shown here, one of those for general use, was made for Tioga County, located between Elmira and Binghamton. It bears the seal of the state of New York stamped into one end and the great seal of the United States in the other. The rule is cast and finely finished, with one side divided into inches and the other into eighths of a yard. The nail, a British unit equal to 1/16 of a yard was, like most American weights and measures, adopted in this country "for measuring cloth." When a yard is so used, "it is divided into four quarters, and each quarter subdivided into 4 nails."[31]

PLAIN COMPASS
186

ATTRIBUTED TO BENJAMIN
RITTENHOUSE (1740–AFTER 1820) AND
WILLIAM L. POTTS (1771–1854)
PHILADELPHIA, PENNSYLVANIA,
CA. 1796–98

BRASS (COPPER 77.25, ZINC 21.03,
LEAD 1.15, TIN 0.18), GLASS, STEEL
L. 14" (35.6 CM), H. 7 7/8" (20.0 CM),
DIAM. 6 1/4" (15.9 CM)
57.646

"SURVEYING IS THAT ART which enables us to give a Plan . . . of any Piece . . . of Land." It is accomplished with a circumferentor (compass), which "is composed of a Brass circular box . . . within which is a Brass Ring, divided . . . into 360 Degrees . . . in the center of the Box is . . . a Steel Pin . . . which . . . always points to the North . . . [it is] fixed on a Ball and Socket . . . on the head of a three-legged Staff."[32]

The compass was the principal instrument that land surveyors used in determining property boundaries. A surveyor placed the compass and an object to be sighted through it at the necessary points, turned the north cardinal point to his "eye, and looking through the small aperture" in the upright, turned "the index . . . 'till [he cut] the . . . object . . . with the Horse hair or Thread of the opposite [upright]. . . . The South End of the Needle [would then tell] the Number of Degrees the . . . Line [between those two points] is from the North."[33]

Computing from that, a surveyor could establish accurate permanent boundaries for any size and shape piece of land.

The plain compass illustrated here is typical of many made by American instrument makers during the late eighteenth and early nineteenth centuries. Its probable makers, Benjamin Rittenhouse, a mathematical-instrument maker, and William Lukens Potts, began working together about 1796. Their joint venture apparently lasted for only two years; they then separated and worked independently. Both remained in the Philadelphia area. Potts eventually became an iron merchant between 1818 and 1822.[34]

Lightly engraved on one arm is a partially legible inscription that reads "C. B. Jacob . . . Chester Co. Pa." This may be Benjamin Jacobs, who was a surveyor, related through marriage to the Rittenhouse family.[35]

HYDROMETER

187

CHRISTOPHER COLLES (1739–1816)
NEW YORK CITY, 1774–1816
BRASS (COPPER 76.13, ZINC 21.26,
LEAD 2.04, TIN 0.39), COPPER,
WOOD, FELT, PAPER

L. 8 5/8" (22.0 CM),
DIAM. 1 3/8" (3.6 CM)
59.3353

CHRISTOPHER COLLES arrived in Philadelphia from Ireland in 1771. He described himself as an engineer and architect and offered to build mills of various kinds, design and construct hydrostatic engines, survey land, take levels for the conveyance of water, ornament buildings, and "instruct young Gentlemen . . . in the different Branches of . . . Mathematics and Natural Philosophy." By 1774 he was in New York, where he proposed to build a system for the city that would "bring water to every street and lane . . . where water might be drawn any time of Day or Night, and in case of fire."[36]

While in New York City, Colles made the hydrometer shown here. It was used to "measure the densities of liquors, especially spiritous liquors. . . . If [it] be immersed in any fluid, and the

point to which it sinks in the surface be marked; it shews the density of it, and its goodness. For it sinks deepest in the lightest liquor and the lightest is best."[37]

The scale on the wider shaft reads from -10 to 0 in units of one. Interchangeable discs of differing thickness, which screw onto the end of the narrow shaft, have numbers and temperature notations stamped into them. The thinnest disc reads "75" and "VERY HOT" while the thickest reads "40" and "COLD." The box was originally fitted with ten discs, seven of which are now missing.

Colles supplied hydrometers of his own making in competition with New York merchants like Garret Noel who "imported from London . . . hydrometers in copper for proving spirits."[38]

THERMOMETER

188

PROBABLY ENGLAND OR FRANCE,
POSSIBLY NEW YORK CITY, CA. 1817
RETAILED IN NEW YORK CITY BY
SPENCER, CRANE AND CO.

BRASS (COPPER 81.97, ZINC 16.64,
LEAD 0.68, TIN 0.26, IRON 0.19),
WOOD, GLASS, MERCURY
L. 15 1/8" (38.4 CM), W. 2 3/8"
(6.0 CM), D. 1 1/8" (2.8 CM)
63.68

THE SHEET-BRASS PLATE of this thermometer is engraved with the Fahrenheit scale to the left and the Reaumur scale to the right. The former was invented by the German Daniel Gabriel Fahrenheit (1686–1736) and became the preferred scale for temperature measurement in Great Britain and America. The latter was developed by René Antoine Ferchault de Réaumur (1683–1757) of France. While it never became popular in America, it was "still the only one used in France" as late as 1819.[39]

Along the scales of each are joint reference points based on natural phenomena and human body temperatures. These include freezing, 32°F or 0°R, which is self explanatory; temperate, 55°F or 10.3°R, a temperature considered to be neither too hot nor too cold; and sun heat, 76°F or 19.5°R, normal daytime temperature during summer. Spirit boil, 178°F or 65°R, is the boiling point of alcohol, while water boil, 212°F or 80°R, is the equivalent for water. Blood heat, 98°F or 29.3°R, is the maximum heat a thermometer can attain from contact with a healthy human body, and fever heat, 112°F or 35.5°R, is the high temperature of the body in fever.[40]

The use of both English and French scales on this thermometer perhaps represents an attempt by the New York retailers Spencer and Ambrose Crane at a universal instrument that would satisfy both English and French consumers. The thermometer was certainly among those they offered, which "graduated from 80 degrees below zero to 700 above for the use of chymists [with] a general assortment for halls, greenhouses, baths, brewers and in morocco cases for travellers [which they had] just received from London and Paris" in 1817.[41]

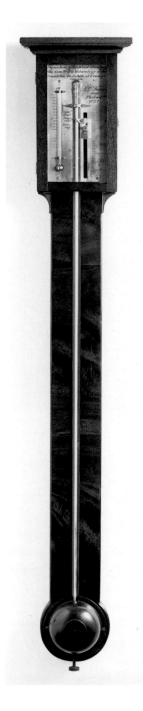

BAROMETER
189

LAWRENCE C. FRANCIS
PHILADELPHIA, PENNSYLVANIA, 1839–45
BRASS (COPPER 68.58, ZINC 30.07,
LEAD 1.12, SILVER 0.19), WOOD, GLASS,
LEATHER, COTTON, MERCURY

L. 38 1/4" (97.1 CM), W. 6 5/8"
(16.8 CM), D. 3 3/8" (8.6 CM)
59.112

IN 1834 THE FRANKLIN INSTITUTE and the American Philosophical Society jointly initiated a project to study and record weather on a national scale. Their intent was to determine the "progression of weather patterns, primarily for the benefit of agriculture and the furtherance of scientific knowledge." In support of this endeavor the state of Pennsylvania appropriated $4,000 to furnish "each county of [the] commonwealth with the necessary instruments for the observation of such atmospheric changes and phenomena as may be useful for the promotion of knowledge in the science of meteorology."[42]

The barometer illustrated here, originally having a silver-plated face with thermometer attached, is one of those commissioned by the Franklin Institute (the American Philosophical Society withdrew from the project in 1838). It was made to be used by a volunteer observer in Bedford County and was accompanied by a thermometer and rain gauge.[43] It was the thirty-seventh barometer made by Lawrence C. Francis during a forty-two-year career that extended from 1839 to 1881.

To aid volunteer observers who used these barometers, the Committee on Meteorology at the Franklin Institute, which included Francis, published directions stating that "when taking an observation, the barometer should be . . . tapped, to obviate the effects of friction. The movable index . . . should then be set to the top of the mercury, and its height be read off to the nearest 1/100 of an inch. . . . The thermometer . . . should always be noted at the time of observation."[44]

The collection of weather information became increasingly widespread and was eventually nationalized with the founding of the United States Signal Weather Corps in the 1870s.

PORTABLE COMPASS
AND SUNDIAL
190

PROBABLY CHRISTIAN TEETS
WASHINGTON COUNTY,
PENNSYLVANIA, 1796–1810
BRASS (COPPER 66.38, ZINC 31.29,
LEAD 1.38), MAHOGANY, GLASS, IRON

H. 1 1/16" (2.6 CM), W. 2 5/16"
(5.9 CM), L. 3 7/8" (9.8 CM)
61.1689

EGYPTIANS WERE USING SUNDIALS as early as 1450 B.C. The instruments proved to be one of the best means of telling time by daylight until clockworks were developed about A.D. 1000. When Christiaan Huygens improved their accuracy using an oscillating pendulum in 1657, he initiated an era of intense development for clockworks. Sundials then fell into decline, in spite of William Emerson's maintaining that "clockworks and watches . . . are often out of order . . . and . . . require frequently to be regulated by some unerring instrument as a [sun] dial; which being rightly constructed will always . . . tell us truth and therefore whether we have any clocks or not, we should never be without a dial."[45]

Small portable sundials continued to be useful for travelers until the mid nineteenth century, when accurate inexpensive watches finally became a reality. A typical example is shown here, owned by Samuel Ralston (1758–1851), minister to the Mingo Creek Presbyterian Congregation in Monongahelia, Washington County, Pennsylvania,

from 1796 until his death. It was made for him by Christian Teets (Deets, Tietz), also a resident of Washington County.[46]

Sundials must be calibrated to read correctly at differing latitudes by adjusting the angle of the gnomon and the graduations of the dial. If the parts are fixed, as on this example, the dial will read accurately only within about thirty miles north or south of the latitude for which it is set. The inclination of this gnomon and the graduations on the face are set to a latitude of about 40 degrees 30 minutes, which passes through Washington County.[47] The dial's gnomon must point north to cast a readable shadow, which is accomplished with the compass.

Although the engraved initials "L," "T," "G," and "s" are enigmatic, they may refer to the ancient names of four of the earth's principal winds: levanter (east), tramontana (north), graecus (northeast), and sierocco (southeast).[48] The reverse of the sundial case shows patriotic and allegorical symbols.

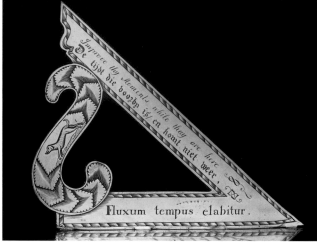

SUNDIAL

191

PROBABLY JOSEPH LEDDELL, SR.
(CA. 1690–1754),
POSSIBLY JOSEPH LEDDELL, JR. (1718–54)
NEW YORK CITY, 1751

COPPER
H. 4 5/8" (11.6 CM), W. 9 1/4"
(23.5 CM), D. 9 1/4" (23.5 CM)
95.41

For Europeans, sundials have been fertile ground for allegory since the Middle Ages because of their time-telling capacity
and the implications of time for mortality. They provide a continual reminder of morality as a determinant for one's place in the
hereafter, where time no longer matters. Numerous examples
are recorded that exhort and entertain viewers with complex
rhyming verses and allegorical figures about the sun's movement
as a measure of mankind's mortality and the need to be ever
mindful of life after death.[49]

For Americans, sundials were the most readily available means
of telling time prior to the advent of inexpensive clocks and timepieces during the mid nineteenth century. They could be fixed on
either vertical or horizontal surfaces, and some were portable.
The example pictured here was intended for placement on a dial

post, probably outside the front door of its owner's house.[50] The
gnomon, set at a forty-one degree angle, indicates that it was
designed to cast an accurate shadow near the forty-first parallel,
which passes just above New York City.

On and around the gnomon, the maker engraved a plethora
of verbal and pictorial imagery.[51] Paramount is the chapter ring,
enclosing all, that depicts daylight hours from five in the morning
to seven in the evening, divided into one-minute intervals. The
twelve lines of verse to the left of the gnomon, written in the third
person, encourage the user to regulate his or her activity and
temperament to the predictable, virtuous pace of the dial. Those
to the right, written in the first person, laud the dial's helpful
nature, in a punning way.

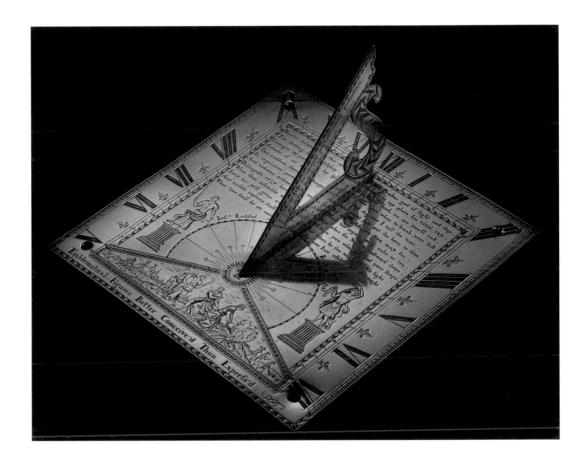

Additional phrases translate as follows: Latin, "Time flows back and slips away"; German, "The time which is gone it comes not back"; French, "If we give it serious thought"; Greek, "Temporary futile time."

Emblematically, a radiant sun, shining on the path of the just to a more perfect day, is flanked by the pillars of strength and beauty, which serve as the gateway to the millennium. They support the figures of justice and wisdom, necessary attributes of the virtuous person destined for heaven. Below, within a classical pediment, figures symbolic of industry and amity, with the coat of arms of New York City, enjoy the proverbial thousand years of peace.

Reader behold how this machine,
The fleeting hours display.
Unurg'd by passion, or by spleen,
Admits of no delay.
This emblem should our tempers give,
Its regulative power.
And virtuous action while we live,
Distinguish ev'ry hour.
When thus inflexible we'r found,
Envy her yell gives o'er,
And endles raptures shall us crown,
When time shall be no more.

When Phaebus god of Light and day,
Moves o'er my plain his vivid ray.
If a slight look on me you'll cast.
I'll shew you when to break your fast
By just degrees I tell the time.
And point you out the hour to dine.
By my assistance you may see,
When too regale with cake or tea.
And when the Sun to westward drops.
I'll shew you when to shut your shops.
But when he dos withdraw his light,
Like you I am useless all the night.

SUNDIAL
192

SPENCER AND COMPANY (1783–1838)
LONDON, 1793–1804
RETAILED IN PHILADELPHIA,
PENNSYLVANIA,
BY WILLIAM RICHARDSON

BRASS (COPPER 78.36, ZINC 17.19,
LEAD 2.85, IRON 0.84, TIN 0.51, SILVER 0.17)
H. 5 1/16" (12.8 CM),
DIAM. 8 13/16" (22.4 CM)
92.122

JOHN FANNING WATSON (1779–1860), one of America's first historians and an early collector of material culture, recorded in his book *Annals of Philadelphia and Pennsylvania in the Olden Time* that "it was once a convenience to have sun-dials affixed to the walls of houses. To appreciate this thing, we must remember there was a time when only men in easy circumstances carried a watch, and there were no clocks, as now, set over the watchmaker's door to regulate the time of street passengers."[52] Judging from his comment, Watson lived during an era when clocks and watches grew in general use. However, they were often unreliable, causing many to prefer sundials. The fact that sundials could only be used during daylight hours was no handicap, since most people rose with the sun and retired when it set.

Sundials were reliable time-telling devices as long as they were designed for the proper latitude and the sun shone. They were widely

made, used in many variations–including vertically mounted, horizontally mounted, and portable types–and were constructed of stone, slate, wood, copper, silver, and stoneware, but were most frequently of brass.

Numerous craftsmen in America made sundials. They were also a significant component of the transatlantic trade in consumer goods, as evidenced by the Philadelphia merchant Thomas Biggs, who advertised in 1793 that "he has just received by the Pigou, in addition to his usual assortment; a very elegant supply of Mathematical, Philosophical and Optical Instruments [including] a few large and highly finish'd brass horizontal dials for garden posts." They were almost certainly like the example illustrated here, made by Spencer and Company–mathematical-instrument makers in London–and imported into Philadelphia by the optical-instrument maker William Richardson.[53]

HOURGLASS
193

PROBABLY GERMANY OR
HOLLAND, 1781
BRASS (COPPER 69.97, ZINC 28.00,
LEAD 1.92), GLASS, SAND,
COTTON

H. 8 1/2" (21.6 CM),
W. 3 13/16" (9.7 CM)
58.2324

IN 1738 EPHRAIM CHAMBERS described an hourglass as "a popular kind of chronometer or clepsydra (water-operated timekeeper) serving to measure the flux of time by the descent or running of sand out of one vessel into another." More than one hundred years later William and Robert Chambers added that "for the measurement of the time of [a] sermon, hour-glasses were frequently attached to pulpits."[54]

The hourglass shown here empties its sand from the upper half to the lower in fifty-five minutes. The glass container is held within a brass frame that consists of six drawn rods to which sections of thinly rolled sheet metal with pierced collars are soldered. The end sections are framed with segments of drawn molding to strengthen and ornament their edges.

Within the frame on one end is expertly engraved a flaming heart bound with a crown of thorns, the Christian symbol for Christ's passion and suffering. Surrounding that and the foliate composition is a Latin inscription: "QUI EST ANNOS ATENAM CAETERA SUMES DET TIBI," which translates as "Let He who is God give you years, for you will get the rest from yourself." The opposite end is similarly engraved with a second Latin inscription "TEMPORA LONGA TUAE 1781 SINT MODO VIRTUTI," translated as "Let the time be long only for your virtue."[55]

Hourglasses like this, although gradually displaced by imported and locally made brass clockworks during the eighteenth century, continued to have limited use, as outlined above and illustrated by the "1 Hhd [hundred] time glasses" aboard the *Ellen* bound from Bristol, England, to New York on April 22, 1773.[56]

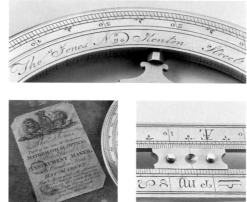

EQUINOCTIAL RING
194

THOMAS JONES
LONDON, ENGLAND, 1810–15
BRASS (COPPER 77.27, ZINC 16.60,
LEAD 4.80, IRON 0.58, SILVER 0.11)

H. 8 3/8" (21.3 CM),
W. 6 1/8" (15.5 CM),
DIAM. 5 1/4" (13.3 CM)
70.725 A, B

THE EQUINOCTIAL RING, universal dial ring, or sectograph was invented in the early seventeenth century to tell time using the sun. This typical dial ring consists of an outer ring that has two 90-degree scales engraved on one side, representing the meridians or degrees of latitude of the northern and southern hemispheres. A hanging loop is affixed to the outer edge and can be slid around the circumference. A second and smaller ring is hinged to the inner edge of the first so that the two can be rotated 90 degrees to each other. One of the sides is divided into two twelve-hour units. Suspended within it is a bridge that has a scale with the signs of the zodiac on one side and a scale for the days of every month on the other. Within the bridge is a sliding cursor, the center of which is pierced by a tiny hole.

To determine the time, "place the line (on the middle of the sliding-piece) over the degree of latitude of the place [where one is located] put the line which crosses the hole of the cursor to the degree of the sign, or day of the month. Open the instrument so as that the two rings be at

right angles to each other, and suspend it by the ring, that the axis of the dial, represented by the middle of the bridge, may be parallel to the axis of the world. Then turn the flat side of the bridge toward the sun, so that his rays, striking through the little hole in the middle of the cursor, may fall exactly on a line drawn round the middle of the concave surface of the inner ring; in which case the bright spot shews the hour of the day in the said concave surface of the ring."[57]

The maker of this ring, Thomas Jones, apprenticed to the optician and mathematical-instrument maker Jesse Ramsden, as noted on the trade card inside the lid of the box for the ring. Upon completion of his training, Jones and his brother William entered business at 30 Mary le Bon Street, about 1803. They remained together until 1805, after which time Thomas seems to have moved frequently. He was located at 21 Oxendon Street, the address on his label, only during the year 1815. He was apparently at 20 Kenton Street, the address engraved on the instrument, for such a short time that solicitors for city directories never had an opportunity to record his being there.[58]

WATCH STAND
195

ENGLAND, PROBABLY
BIRMINGHAM, 1750–80
BRASS (COPPER 72.90,
ZINC 26.50, LEAD 0.18)

H. 14 1/2" (38.8 CM), W. 5 3/8"
(13.7 CM), D. 3 3/4" (9.5 CM)
84.29

IN HIS PREFACE TO THE SERIES of designs published by Thomas Johnson beginning in 1758, the author stated that they "were meant as assistants to young artists . . . and when honoured by the hand of the skillful workman . . . will give entire satisfaction."[59] Among the 150 engravings are 3 watchcases and 5 bracket and tall-case clocks. Like all the objects depicted, these cases are elaborate and fanciful agglomerations of humans, animals, architectural elements, water, rocks, and plants. As such, they represent the mature expression of the rococo style in England.

It seems that watchcases in this style had fairly broad appeal; additional designs were published in London in 1764 or 1765 by Robert Sayer. Several examples have been recorded in wood and porcelain. Brass also served well in this capacity, as is seen in a number of Birmingham trade catalogues. Although ideal-ized rococo motifs are the dominant visual feature in all these watch stands, allegory is important as well. Typically featured are allusions to the passage of time personified as a benign but remorseless grim reaper; a cock, symbolic of morning; and an owl, representing night.[60]

The actual and symbolic focus of their highly charged ornament renders these stands purposeless without a watch face and indicates they were not temporary but permanent receptacles for watches intended as a mantel, shelf, or wall timepiece. While the makers of these elaborate cast holders may have found England to be their principal market, stands were part of the transatlantic trade, as evidenced by the New York merchant William Bailey, who offered "brass watch stands . . . for sale reasonable both whole-sale and retail imported in the latest vessels from England."[61]

CLOCKWORKS
196

MACOK WARD (1702–83)
WALLINGFORD, CONNECTICUT, 1724–40
BRASS (COPPER 72.85, ZINC 18.80,
LEAD 2.81, TIN 2.18, ANTIMONY 1.86,
SILVER 0.63, IRON 0.55;

BELL: COPPER 66.34, TIN 33.03, SILVER 0.23,
ZINC 0.15, LEAD 0.12, ANTIMONY 0.12), STEEL, WOOD
H. 47" (19.4 CM), W. 8 1/8" (20.6 CM)
D. 6 1/4" (15.9 CM)
69.228 PARTIAL FUNDS FOR PURCHASE
THE GIFT OF CHARLES K. DAVIS

MACOK WARD lived his entire life in Wallingford, Connecticut. Although he is best known as a clockmaker, he was also a lawyer and a politician. He manufactured reeds for handlooms, farmed, made cabinetwork, and served as a soldier.[62]

A clock wheel engine, used to cut gear teeth, and other clockmaking tools are included in the inventory of his estate. The presence of "shears for cutting brass . . . crucibles [and] one pair old bellows" indicates that he was capable of casting his own clock parts rather than buying blanks from founders for machining, as many of his contemporaries did.[63]

Ward decoratively engraved his name on the clockworks face illustrated here and also cast it into the bronze bell, an uncommon feature, which testifies to his self-sufficiency as a founder. Although primitive in appearance–using wooden drums (instead of brass) that are wound by pulling the weight cords instead of a key–the works follow the standard format for Anglo-American clocks made during the eighteenth century. Between the plates is an anchor recoil escapement, and behind the face, which was originally fitted with a day-of-the-month wheel, is a rack-and-snail striking mechanism.

The bell's high tin and low zinc content, with significant trace amounts of silver, provide a useful insight into the purposeful control of alloy in an eighteenth-century American brass-worker's shop. Instead of altering the standard brass alloy he used for his clockworks, Ward formulated a specific bronze alloy for the bell's tone.

CLOCKWORKS
197

JAMES WADY (D. 1759)
NEWPORT, RHODE ISLAND, 1736–59
BRASS (COPPER 76.66, ZINC 18.06,
LEAD 3.26, TIN 0.57, IRON 0.61,
SILVER 0.13, ANTIMONY 0.13);

BELL: (COPPER 77.14, TIN 19.72,
LEAD 1.51, ZINC 0.83, IRON 0.54,
ANTIMONY 0.14, SILVER 0.13), PAINT, IRON
H. 51 1/2" (130.8 CM), W. 12" (30.5 CM),
D. 6 1/4" (15.8 CM)
51.28

ON MAY 27, 1736, JAMES WADY married the daughter of William Claggett, a Newport, Rhode Island, clockmaker, which may indicate that Wady had apprenticed to the man who was to become his father-in-law, a common occurrence. A master-apprentice relationship is further supported by a construction feature common to both men's clocks that is rare elsewhere: "the striking train is stopped by a projection on the rack pawl instead of by the tailpiece of the much more fragile gathering pallett."[64]

Although little manuscript material exists that aids in understanding Wady's life and work, he can be connected to the brassmaking community at large through another feature of the clock shown here. Each of the four ornamental spandrels surrounding the silvered chapter ring is identical to an engraved image in a Birmingham, England, brass-founder's trade catalogue. The illustration, *Clock Corner Pieces*, notes that the spandrels were sold in sets of four and is assigned catalogue number 224 for easy ordering.[65]

A copy of that catalogue was almost certainly owned by a Newport merchant and used to order these spandrels from an English manufacturer or factor, only a small part of the extensive trade that active shipping communities on the Atlantic seaboard, like Newport, conducted with England prior to the American Revolution.[66]

The nautical activity of the Newport community, where this clock originated, is evidenced by its unusual feature of a dial in the upper-left quadrant of the face that records the movement of the tides. It registers tidal reverses every six hours and twelve minutes, the hand making a complete revolution once every fifteen days.

CLOCKWORKS
198

DANIEL BURNAP (1759–1838)
EAST WINDSOR, CONNECTICUT, 1786–1805
BRASS (COPPER 75.57, ZINC 19.58,
LEAD 2.55, SILVER 1.50, TIN 0.45,
IRON 0.30), STEEL, IRON

H. 51" (129.6 CM),
W. 12" (30.5 CM),
D. 6 1/2" (16.5 CM)
64.585

DANIEL BURNAP WAS BORN in Coventry, Connecticut, on November 1, 1759. Upon coming of age, he is thought to have apprenticed with Thomas Harland, an English-trained clockmaker who immigrated to Norwich, Connecticut, in 1773.[67] After completing his apprenticeship and a few years as a journeyman, Burnap established himself in business as a clock- and watchmaker in East Windsor, Connecticut.

Within a short time he could claim that "clocks of various kinds may be had at his shop . . . on short notice on the most reasonable terms (warranted)." The daybooks, ledgers, and correspondence generated during his nineteen-year career record that he built "chime clocks," "moon age clocks," "small clocks," "small timepieces," "eight day clocks," "eight day timepieces," and at least one "tower clock."[68]

The subject of this entry is an eight-day clock. Typical of his clockworks and those made throughout the United States at that time, it is weight driven with separate but interworking time and strike trains. It uses an anchor recoil escapement with the seconds hand on the escape

wheel arbor. A rack-and-snail regulates the strike. The mechanism is housed within two cast brass plates behind a sheet-brass face, which has been handsomely engraved and silvered. Burnap's recipe for silvering is recorded in his memorandum book as taking "an equal quantity of alum, saltpetre & sal ammoniac crude. Pound them together fine. Then take silver lace or silver filings & put a laying of the powder before mentioned & a laying of the silver until you have mixed the quantity of silver to be dissolved with the powder. Then put it to a moderate fire & heat it 'till it ceases to smoke. Then pour it off & pound it fine & apply it to the brass. To be washed with clean water."[69]

Elihu Colton (1753–1825) was a fourth generation resident of Longmeadow, Massachusetts, and among those who ratified the Constitution in Boston on January 9, 1788.[70] When he purchased this clock from Burnap, he must have considered it a significant acquisition, for he had his name engraved on the brass cover of the pendulum bob.

MANTEL CLOCK
199

JEAN-BAPTISTE DUBUC
PARIS, FRANCE, 1804–17
BRASS (COPPER 73.70, ZINC 22.40,
LEAD 1.04, TIN 0.70), STEEL, GLASS

H. 20 1/4" (51.5 CM), W. 18 3/8"
(46.7 CM), D. 5 7/8" (15.0 CM)
57.744

THIS MERCURY-GILDED BRASS CASE houses an eight-day spring-powered clockworks with silk-thread pendulum suspension. It strikes the hour and half hour. The silvered face is engraved with the surname of the maker. Jean-Baptiste Dubuc, Parisian clockmaker, made many clocks for the American market, as evidenced by numerous examples bearing his name and sometimes street address—Rue Michel-le-Compte No. 33—which incorporate features intended to appeal singularly to American sensibilities.[71]

The principal iconography of this mantel clockcase lauds the achievements of George Washington. He is dressed in the uniform he wore while commander in chief of the American military and is depicted holding his resignation, which he offered to the United States Congress on December 23, 1783. The stance and dress are derived from John Trumbull's portrait of Washington at the Battle of Trenton, painted in 1792.[72]

Under the clockface is the popular phrase coined by Maj. Gen. Henry Lee when he gave Washington's funeral oration before Congress on December 26, 1799: "WASHINGTON:/First in WAR, First in PEACE/First in the HEARTS of his COUNTRYMEN."[73] To the left, the spy glass, protractor, and globe refer to his surveying activities before being called to war.

The plaque in the center of the base shows Washington receiving a sword from the head of state, symbolic of the authority given him as commander in chief of the Revolutionary forces. In doing so, he was likened to the great Roman citizen-soldier Cincinnatus, around whom the Society of the Cincinnati—an American military order composed of American and French officers who served during the Revolution—was founded.[74]

The Franco-American silversmith-jeweler Simon Chaudron offered "for sale . . . seventy marble and gilt brass time pieces" of this type in Philadelphia as early as 1802. His competitor, the American-born merchant Thomas Fletcher, also supplied Americans with these clocks. When on a buying trip to Paris in 1815, Fletcher stipulated that "the gilding on the clocks . . . must be of the best quality." Clocks of this type were held in high esteem by Americans who owned them, as evidenced by the Philadelphia cabinetmaker Joseph B. Barry (1759–1838), who specifically gave his "daughter Ann Barry, the Washington Clock" when he wrote his will.[75]

TIMEPIECE
200

SIMON WILLARD (1753–1848)
ROXBURY, MASSACHUSETTS, 1809–18
BRASS (COPPER 77.32, ZINC 17.78,
LEAD 2.95, TIN 1.53, IRON 0.27, SILVER 0.24,
ANTIMONY 0.12), IRON,
LEAD, WOOD, GLASS, PAINT

H. 41 1/2" (105.4 CM), W. 10 3/8"
(26.4 CM), D. 3 3/4" (9.5 CM)
57.952

ON NOVEMBER 25, 1801, Simon Willard was granted a United States patent for "a new and useful improvement in a Time Piece. . . . [Its] power of motion is a weight instead of a spring. . . . The weight falls only fifteen inches in eight days . . . without winding . . . the pendulum is brought forward . . . of the weights, by which means it may be made longer and will consequently vibrate more accurately. . . . The pendulum is suspended on pivots by which it is prevented from [wobbling]."[76]

Such a timepiece quickly became popular and was widely manufactured by New England clockmakers in spite of patent protection. The Willards–Simon, Benjamin, Aaron, and Aaron, Jr.–carried on an extensive trade as manufacturers of these and "every kind of clock work; such as Clocks for Steeples . . . eight day clocks . . . Time pieces which run 30 hours . . . Spring Clocks of all Kinds . . . Clocks that will run one year . . . Time pieces for Astronomical purposes [and] Chime clocks."[77]

It is assumed that they made all their clockworks. Simon, however, did have the Boston brass founder William Hunneman supply him with castings. Hunneman and Willard had a long-standing agreement wherein the former manufactured large amounts of brass castings that he sold to the latter, who then finished and assembled them. Illustrative of this is an entry in Hunneman's account book on July 2, 1818, which notes the sale of "34 lb. clockwork [and] 16 1/4 lb. timepiece do" to Simon Willard.[78]

Hunneman also supplied Willard with clock-case decoration, as with the "10 lb. circles & side ornaments" noted in his account book on January 10, 1819.[79] These are recorded in numerous entries and were used by Willard to hold the glass window over the face of his patent timepieces and to ornament each side of the neck under the face. Hunneman also sold the identical clockwork castings and clock-case ornaments to Willard's competitor William Cummings.

1 Carolyn Wood Stretch, "Early Colonial Clockmakers in Philadelphia," *Pennsylvania Magazine of History and Biography* 56 (1932): 229–30. *Philadelphia: Three Centuries of American Art* (Philadelphia: Philadelphia Museum of Art, 1976), p. 15.

2 Edward P. Allinson and Boies Penrose, *Philadelphia, 1681–1887* (Philadelphia: Allen, Lane and Scott, 1887), pp. 17–18.

3 J. T. Mitchell and S. Flanders, eds., *The Statutes at Large of Pennsylvania, 1700–1790* (Harrisburg, Pa.: State printer, 1896–1908), p. 296. I am indebted to Eugene Mahoney for bringing this material to my attention.

4 Mitchell and Flanders, *Statutes at Large of Pennsylvania*, p. 297.

5 On Penn, see "Notes and Queries," *Pennsylvania Magazine of History and Biography* 19 (1905): 111. This weight has previously been attributed to the Philadelphia and Annapolis brass founder Philip Syng (1737–92) because of the initials and material. Although he is not the maker and very little is known about him, he did advertise in the March 15, 1759, issue of the *Maryland Gazette* that he made domestic wares. Syng was the son of the silversmith John Syng (1705–38), first cousin of the silversmith Philip Syng (1733–60), nephew of the silversmith Philip Syng (1703–89), and grandson of the silversmith Philip Syng (1676–1739). The stamped numbers indicate the object's weight: 5 grains, 20 pennyweight.

6 *Minutes of the Common Council of the City of Philadelphia, 1704–1776* (Philadelphia, 1847), p. 123, photocopy, Downs collection, Winterthur Library. George Plumly will, 1754, book K, p. 140, City of Philadelphia Archives.

7 Plumly will.

8 1 troy ounce (oz) = 20 pennyweight (dwt) = 480 grains (gr). Martha Gandy Fales, *Joseph Richardson and Family: Philadelphia Silversmiths* (Middletown, Conn.: Wesleyan University Press, 1974), p. 60.

9 Joseph Richardson letterbook, Historical Society of Pennsylvania, Philadelphia, as quoted in Martha Gandy Fales, *Joseph Richardson and Family:*

Philadelphia Silversmiths (Middletown, Conn.: Wesleyan University Press, 1974), pp. 253, 254.

10 As quoted in Fales, *Joseph Richardson*, p. 208.

11 *The Manufactories and Manufactures of Pennsylvania of the Nineteenth Century* (Philadelphia: Galaxy Publishing Co., 1875), pp. 205, 264.

12 *Manufactories and Manufactures of Pennsylvania*, p. 265.

13 On Troemner's business, see Edwin T. Freedley, *Philadelphia and Its Manufactures* (Philadelphia: Edward Young, 1858), p. 335.

14 *Munsell's Albany Directory* (Albany, N.Y.: J. Munsell, 1855), p. 69.

15 *Report of the Secretary of the Treasury Communicating in Compliance with a Resolution of the Senate of the 14th of August 1856, a Report of the Progress on the Construction and Distribution of Standards of Weights and Measures* (Washington, D.C.: Government Printing Office, 1857), p. 6.

16 *Revised Statutes of the State of New-York* (Albany, N.Y., 1822), pt. 1, chap. 9, p. 608. "Extracts of Albany City Ordinances," *Hoffman's Albany Directory, and City Register* (Albany, N.Y.: Printed by L.G. Hoffman, 1839), p. 39. Another set of four graduated liquid measures marked by Cluett is owned by the Albany Institute of History and Art; see Mary Ellen W. Hearn, "Copper Measures 58.1594 and 58.1596 by John W. Cluett, Albany," research paper, object folder 58.1594, Registration Office, Winterthur.

17 U.S. Congress, *Report of the Secretary of Treasury*, 34th Cong., 3rd sess., S. Ex. Doc. 27, 1857, p. 52.

18 W. H. Smith, comp., *Smith's Brooklyn Directory* (Brooklyn, N.Y.: Charles Jenkins, 1857), adv. supp., p. 14.

19 "Extracts of Albany City Ordinances," *Hoffman's Albany Directory, and City Register* (Albany, N.Y.: Printed by L.G. Hoffman, 1839), p. 39. *Revised Statutes of the State of New-York* (Albany, N.Y., 1822), pt. 1, chap. 9, p. 609. Each county and town had an individual mark. Since the signed Dutchess County liquid mea-

sures, entry 179, bear the identical sealers' marks as these dry measures, the latter were also probably used in Dutchess County.

20 Donald L. Fennimore and Charles V. Swain, "Sealers' Marks on Boardman Measures," *Pewter Collectors Club of America* 8, no. 6 (September 1982): 226, 227.

21 *New-York Annual Advertiser*, supp. to *Longworth's American Almanac, New-York Register and City Directory* (New York: David Longworth, 1817). *Report of the Secretary of the Treasury Communicating in Compliance with a Resolution of the Senate of the 14th of August 1856, a Report of the Progress on the Construction and Distribution of Standards of Weights and Measures* (Washington, D.C.: Government Printing Office, 1857), p. 6. *Hoffman's Albany Directory, and City Register* (Albany, N.Y.: Printed by L. G. Hoffman, 1842).

22 On Hickok's Harrisburg business, see Charles Robson, *Biographical Encyclopaedia of Pennsylvania of the Nineteenth Century* (Philadelphia: Galaxy Publishing Co., 1874), p. 284. William Henry Egle, *History of the Counties of Dauphin and Lebanon in the Commonwealth of Pennsylvania* (Philadelphia: Everts and Peck, 1883), p. 358.

23 U.S. Congress, *Report of the Secretary of the Treasury*, 34th Cong., 3rd sess., S. Ex. Doc. 27, 1857, pp. 6, 7.

24 The father's advertisement is in the *United States Chronicle* (Providence, R.I.), June 1, 1786, December 14, 1786. Greenwood's advertisement is in the *Providence Gazette; and Country Journal*, June 21, 1788. A complete history of the Greenwood family is the subject of Isaac John Greenwood, *The Greenwood Family of Norwich, England, in America* (Concord, N.H.: Privately printed, 1934).

25 The trade card is pictured in Greenwood, *Greenwood Family of Norwich*, facing p. 96. On quadrants, see John Muller, *A Treatise of Artillery*

(1780; reprint, Ottowa, Can.: Museum Restoration Services, 1985), p. 150.

26 Wade Lawrence, research paper, object folder 60.1009, Registration Office, Winterthur; see also Silvio A. Bedini, "Isaac Greenwood III, Dentist and Mathematical Instrument Maker," *Rittenhouse Journal of the American Scientific Instrument Enterprise* 3, no. 3 (1989): 73–85. I am grateful to Charles Hummel for bringing this article to my attention.

27 This type of rule is pictured and discussed in William Pain, *The Builder's Companion* (London: William Pain and Robert Sayer, 1762), p. 29.

28 Aston is noted in *The Directory of Birmingham* (Birmingham, Eng.: Wrightson and Webb, 1843), pp. 4, 11. The reference to cheesemonger can be found in *Slater's (Late Pigot and Co.) Royal National and Commercial Directory . . .* (Manchester, Eng.: Isaac Slater, 1850), p. 14.

29 As quoted in Lewis V. Judson, *Weights and Measures Standards of the United States* (Washington, D.C.: Government Printing Office, 1963), p. 2.

30 *Revised Statutes of the State of New-York* (Albany, N.Y., 1822), pt. 1, pp. 607, 609.

31 On the British nail, see George Gregory, *A New and Complete Dictionary of Arts and Sciences*, 3 vols. (New York: William T. Robinson, 1822), 2:s.v. "nail." Gregory, *New and Complete Dictionary*, as quoted in Charles Venable, research paper, object folder 64.1026, Registration Office, Winterthur.

32 Robert Gibson, *A Treatise of Practical Surveying* (Philadelphia: Joseph Crukshank, 1785), pp. 1, 148, 149.

33 Gibson, *Treatise of Practical Surveying*, p. 149.

34 The vernier compass, unlike the plain compass, is equipped with a mechanism to compensate for the difference between true and magnetic north (declination). That factor must be calculated separately with a plain compass. Both men also made compasses on their own. While Rittenhouse, like his older brother, David, spent his entire productive career in Philadelphia, Potts was

located in Bucks County, Pa., prior to settling in Philadelphia; see Bruce R. Foreman, "The Worcester Workshop of Benjamin Rittenhouse," *Rittenhouse* 2 (1988): 82.

35 On the inscription, see Bradley C. Brooks, research paper, object folder 57.646, Registration Office, Winterthur. J. Smith Futhey and Gilbert Cope, *History of Chester County* (Philadelphia: Louis H. Everts, 1881), p. 612.

36 Colles advertised in the *Pennsylvania Chronicle*, August 26, 1771. Martha Gandy Fales and Robert L. Raley, "Christopher Colles, Engineer and Architect," *Winterthur Newsletter* 5, no. 7 (September 25, 1959): 1.

37 William Emerson, *The Principles of Mechanics* (London: Printed for J. Richardson, 1758), p. 227.

38 *New-York Gazette, or Weekly Post-Boy*, June 13, 1768.

39 Rees, *Cyclopaedia*, 30:s.v. "thermometer."

40 These are outlined by Aline Zeno, research paper, object folder 63.68, Registration Office, Winterthur.

41 *New-York Evening Post*, April 14, 1817.

42 On the joint effort, see Gretchen Townsend, research paper, object folder 59.112, Registration Office, Winterthur. *Laws of the General Assembly of the Commonwealth of Pennsylvania*, sess. 1836-37, sec. 4, p. 73.

43 Bruce Sinclair, *Philadelphia's Philosopher Mechanics* (Baltimore: Johns Hopkins University Press, 1974), p. 146.

44 *Directions for Making Meteorological Observations by the Committee on Meteorology* (Philadelphia: Franklin Institute, 1854).

45 René R. J. Rohr, *Sundials* (Toronto: University of Toronto Press, 1965), p. 5. On the development of clocks, see Tom Robinson, *The Longcase Clock* (Woodbridge, Eng.: Antique Collectors' Club, 1981), p. 24. William Emerson, *Dialing* (London: Printed for J. Richardson, 1779), p. iii, as cited in Kathleen Higgins, "The Classification of Sundials," *Annals of Science* 9, no. 4 (December 1953): 342-43.

46 Stacia Gregory, "'Mark How Time Passeth': The Sundial of Samuel S. Ralston," research paper, object folder 61.1689, Registration Office, Winterthur. Ronald Vern Jackson, Gary Ronald Teeples, and David Schaefermeyer, eds., *Pennsylvania 1800 Census Index* (Bountiful, Utah: Accelerated Indexing Systems, 1972), p. 72.

47 Gregory, "'Mark How Time Passeth,'" p. 4.

48 Gregory, "'Mark How Time Passeth,'" p. 6.

49 T. Geoffrey Henslow, *Ye Sundial Booke* (London: W. and G. Foyle, 1935); Horatia K. F. Gatty, *The Book of Sun-Dials* (London: George Bell and Sons, 1890).

50 The original owner of this sundial is unknown. Scratched into the back, however, is "Jos D. Koecker, Phila 1860," an architect who was the apparent owner as of that year.

51 Biographical and historical information about Joseph Leddell, also spelled Liddel, Leddel, and Ledell, is to be found in Laughlin, *Pewter in America*, 1:45; 3:96-98. See also Janine E. Skerry and Jeanne Sloane, "Images of Politics and Religion on Silver Engraved by Joseph Leddel," *Antiques* 141, no. 3 (March 1992): 490-99; Christie's sale "Nicholson-8082" (January 27, 28, 1995), lots 622, 623.

52 John Fanning Watson, *Annals of Philadelphia and Pennsylvania in the Olden Time*, 3 vols. (Philadelphia: Leary, Stuart Co., 1927), 1:218.

53 Biggs advertised in the *Federal Gazette and Philadelphia Daily Advertiser*, May 15, 1793. Richardson advertised his abilities and goods in the *Pennsylvania Packet, and Daily Advertiser*, December 11, 1788, and in *Dunlap's American Daily Advertiser*, May 28, 1791, but did not mention sundials. He listed himself in the Philadelphia city directories from 1793 to 1804.

54 Ephraim Chambers, *Cyclopaedia: or, An Universal Dictionary of Arts and Sciences* (London, 1738), 1:s.v. "hour glass." William and Robert Chambers, *Chambers English Dictionary* (London, 1872).

55 I am grateful to Dr. Gerald E. Culley for providing me with the translations.

56 Outward bound manifests, Bristol to America, Bristol City Library.

57 Rees, *Cyclopaedia*, 12:s.v. "dial."

58 Fragmentary remains of a ring similar to this are at Shadwell, Peter Jefferson's (1708-57) home in Virginia. That ring was excavated on the property and is believed to have been owned by Jefferson, a surveyor.

59 As cited in Helena Hayward, *Thomas Johnson and English Rococo* (London: Alec Tiranti, 1964).

60 Robert Sayer, *One Hundred and Ten Capital New Designs, Being All the Most Approved Patterns of Household Furniture in Genteel Taste* (London, 1764), fig. 99. Wooden watch stands in the rococo taste can be seen in Edward H. Pinto, "Watch-holders for Bedside and Mantel," *Country Life* 128, no. 3326 (December 1960): 1353. A porcelain watch stand in the same style is pictured in David S. Howard and John Ayres, *China for the West*, 2 vols. (London: Sotheby Parke Bernet, 1978), 1:136. The Victoria and Albert Museum owns a number of Birmingham trade catalogues (M61b, M61f, and M60b) that depict brass watch stands. They are also pictured in catalogues NK7899 H26 and TS573 M58a F, Downs collection, Winterthur Library. The arrangement of decorative and allegorical elements exemplified by this stand seems to be the norm in both trade-catalogue illustrations and extant examples. A variant is pictured in Michael Snodin, ed., *Rococo: Art and Design in Hogarth's England* (London: Victoria and Albert Museum, 1984), p. 152.

61 *Rivington's New-York Gazetteer*, July 29, 1773.

62 Details of Macok Ward's life and work are outlined in Penrose R. Hoopes, *Connecticut Clockmakers of the Eighteenth Century* (Hartford, Conn.: Edward Valentine Mitchell, 1930), pp. 119-21.

63 Hoopes, *Connecticut Clockmakers*, p. 121.

64 Richard L. Champlin, "James Wady," *Newport History* 48, no. 160 (Fall 1975): 354.

65 Trade catalogue NK7899, B61c*TC, Downs collection, Winterthur Library.

66 The nature and extent of this trade is well detailed in Ford, "Commerce of Rhode Island."

67 Hoopes, *Shop Records of Daniel Burnap*, p. viii.

68 The advertisement appeared in the *Connecticut Courant*, March 14, 1791. Hoopes, *Shop Records of Daniel Burnap*, pp. 38, 39, 44-52.

69 Hoopes, *Shop Records of Daniel Burnap*, p. 126.

70 Carol Laun, Salmon Brook Historical Society, to Donald L. Fennimore, March 25, 1985; *New-England Historical and Genealogical Register*, 148 vols. (Boston: Samuel G. Drake, 1847-), 1:233; 34:32.

71 I am grateful to Dana J. Blackwell for supplying me with Dubuc's given names and other particulars of his life and work. Winterthur owns two other clocks by Dubuc, acc. nos. 57.795 and 57.1035.

72 Helen A. Cooper, *John Trumbull: The Hand and Spirit of a Painter* (New Haven, Conn.: Yale University Art Gallery, 1982), p. 121. See also p. 88 for Trumbull's 1824 painting of Washington offering his resignation in which the subject is depicted almost unchanged.

73 "Funeral Oration on Washington," in *Old South Leaflets* (Boston: Old South Leaflet Association, 1896), p. 7.

74 This scene was inspired from the logo of Cincinnatus being presented with a sword by Roman senators, described in the articles of the institution of the Order of the Cincinnati and depicted on its medal; see William S. Thomas, *The Society of the Cincinnati, 1783-1935* (New York: G.P. Putnam's Sons, 1935), p. 47.

75 Chaudron's advertisement appeared in the *Philadelphia Gazette, and Weekly Advertiser*, December 29, 1802. The Annapolis cabinetmaker John Shaw is said to have received a small number of choice French gilt clocks made by Dubuc in 1805, but no documentation to substantiate this has been found; see Mrs. N. Hudson Moore, *The Old Clock Book*

(New York: Frederick A. Stokes Co., 1911), p. 86. Thomas Fletcher to Charles Fletcher, August 31, 1815, Fletcher Papers, Athenaeum of Philadelphia. Thomas Fletcher to Poirier and Bouge, December 30, 1829, Thomas Fletcher letterbook, 75x10.1-.2, Downs collection, Winterthur Library. Joseph B. Barry will book (transcription), 1838, Office of the Register of Wills, City Hall, Philadelphia.

76 Specification of Letters Patent, United States Patent Office, illustrated in John Ware Willard, *A History of Simon Willard, Inventor and Clockmaker* (Boston: Privately printed, 1911), pls. 5, 6. This clock is assigned its date based on an inscription "Willard & Nolen" in red paint on the reverse of the pendulum door, which probably refers to Simon's brother Aaron or his nephew Aaron, Jr., and Spencer Nolen, who worked together on Washington Street in Boston ca. 1809-18.

77 As quoted on a Simon Willard broadside advertisement printed in Worcester, Mass., by Isaiah Thomas, Jr. Illustrated in Richard W. Husher and Walter W. Welch, *A Study of Simon Willard's Clocks* (Nahant, Mass.: By the authors, 1980), p. 239.

78 William C. Hunneman account book, July 2, 1818, Boston National Historical Park, Charlestown Navy Yard, Boston.

79 Hunneman account book, January 10, 1819.

DETAIL, SHOEHORN, 1700–1800

ENTRY 246

PERSONAL

A VERY BROAD and loosely constructed cross section is represented in this group. Form and function vary widely, from ceremonial medals to recreational fishing reels to medicinal bleeding bowls. Yet there is a philosophical connection linking them all. They are all implements reserved for use, for the most part, by a single individual, many in a daily context. While it is true that everything in this catalogue was owned by an individual, the concept "for personal use" is strongly implied in both the form and function of these artifacts in particular. Represented are boxes of varying types, tobacco tongs, plaques, medals, slave tags, admission tokens, strikers, pistol tinderboxes, fleams, bleeding bowls, barbers' basins, standishes, ink pots, wax jacks, seals, stamps, pastille burners, harness bells, and memorandum books. Also included are shoe buckles, buttons, spectacles and lorgnettes, shoehorns, combs, dirks, speaking horns, dog collars, fishing reels, flatirons and trivets, goffering irons, shot molds, eprouvettes, and spoon molds.

TOBACCO BOX
201

ENGLAND, 1679
COPPER, BRASS (COPPER 77.90,
ZINC 19.20, LEAD 1.22), TIN

L. 3 7/8" (9.8 CM), W. 3" (7.6 CM),
H. 3/4" (1.9 CM)
64.717

UPON THOMAS HARIOT'S return to England from America in 1588, he published a tract entitled *A Briefe and True Report of the New Found Land of Virginia*. In it he discussed "an herbe [called] Tobacco. The leaves thereof being dried and brought into powder: [the natives] use to take the fume or smoke thereof by sucking it through pipes made of claie into their stomack and heade; from whence it purgeth superfluous fleame & other gross humors . . . whereby their bodies are notably preserved in health, & know not many greevous diseases wherewithall wee in England are oftentime afflicted. . . . We our selves during the time we were there used to suck it after their manner, as also since our returne, & have found manie rare and wonderful experiments of the vertues thereof."[1]

Following that introduction of tobacco into England, smoking grew so quickly in popularity that it was observed in 1660 that "he's no good-fellow that's without burnt Pipes, Tobacco, and His [tobacco] Box."[2] The wrought-copper tobacco box illustrated here is lined with

a coating of tin to prevent the copper from interacting with the contents, thus providing an insight into the esteem with which its owner held his tobacco. Lightly engraved around the perimeter twice, alternating with calligraphic flourishes, is the phrase "Com fill your pyp & merie be & thank my masters Courtisie." Jovial social sentiments of this type were frequently placed on smoking and drinking paraphernalia during the seventeenth century, worded as if the object itself, rather than the owner or maker, were communicating with the user. Such sentiments reflect the general use of tobacco at that time as a social rather than solitary pastime.

The owner's initials and the probable date of acquisition are engraved on the removable lid. The box seems to have retained its value for a subsequent owner—whose initials "WM" are engraved on the bottom—as evidenced by the three riveted repair strips, which rendered it of continued use after the bottom had split away from the side.

TOBACCO BOX
202

PROBABLY ENGLAND, POSSIBLY
NEW YORK CITY, CA. 1724
BRASS (COPPER 67.82, ZINC 30.28,
LEAD 1.56)

L. 5 1/16" (12.8 CM), W. 2 15/16"
(7.5 CM), H. 1 9/16" (4.0 CM)
57.98

JOHN MOORE, JR. (1686–1749) was a wealthy man who bene-
fited from mercantile activities and a lucrative appointment as
collector for the port of New York. When he died, he left his
heirs eleven separate lots in the city of New York, more than
2,800 acres near West Point, worth £6,495; property and a house
in Philadelphia; and a lengthy list of personal possessions, including the tobacco box shown here.[3]

The engraving on the lid was probably executed by a specialist,
such as the New York pewterer Joseph Leddel, Jr. (1718–54), who
advertised that he "engraves on Steel, Iron, Gold, Silver, Copper,
Brass, Pewter, Ivory or Turtle-shell, in a neat manner and reasonably." In addition to heralding Moore's ownership of the box

in script, the engraving does so pictorially with his coat of arms—
a shield containing a chevron between three griffins' heads, the
upper half tinctured gold and the lower blue. The winged death's-
head below, commonly found on gravestones, was also frequently
associated with smoking and alludes to human mortality. The
thistles on calligraphic knots above, expressly noted by pointing
fingers on dismembered hands, are somewhat more enigmatic, as
is the meaning of the date at the lower right. Although both clearly
represent important parts of Moore's life, which he wanted
recorded, their meaning is currently unknown.[4]

TOBACCO BOX

203

ENGLAND, PROBABLY LONDON, 1772
BRASS (COPPER 66.90,
ZINC 31.74, LEAD 1.16)

L. 4 1/8" (10.5 CM), W. 2 11/16"
(6.9 CM),
H. 1" (2.5 CM)
61.1755

THIS BOX and its engraved decoration clearly demonstrate that "tobacco has been employed, in ordinary use, by snuffing, smoking and chewing; and these practices have been common for more than 200 years to all Europe." Tobacco was first introduced to Europeans during the sixteenth century by the Spanish, who discovered it in America. Even though some thought "there cannot be a more base, and yet hurt-full, corruption . . . than . . . the vile use . . . of taking tobacco," its popularity as a pastime and medicine grew rapidly.[5]

Although many European countries laid claim to parts of the Americas, one that proved well suited to the cultivation of tobacco belonged to England. Consequently, British tobacco lords became the principal beneficiaries of an extensive trade starting in the tobacco fields of Maryland, Virginia, and the Carolinas through British ports

to all of Europe. Annual tobacco exports from the James River basin alone "rose from about five million pounds in the mid-1730s to above thirty million pounds in the early 1770s." Of that trade, Scottish, par-ticularly Glaswegian, tobacco merchants garnered the greatest share, which amounted to well over 50 percent. In 1775 alone, Scotland directed 45,863,154 pounds of tobacco from America to English and European snuffers, smokers, and chewers, which is pictorially under-scored on the reverse of this box by the tartan-clad tobacco merchant.[6]

The owner of the box had his initials engraved in German script on the lid and again in round hand with his name in Roman print on the back. Although he has not been positively identified, he was prob-ably Cornelius Willson, who lived in the St. Mary Aldermary section of London during the late eighteenth century.[7]

TOBACCO BOX

204

PROBABLY BRISTOL, ENGLAND,
CA. 1790
BRASS (COPPER 66.37, ZINC 32.76,
LEAD 0.46)

L. 5 1/8" (13.0 CM), W. 1 13/16"
(4.6 CM), H. 13/16" (2.1 CM)
56.558

THE ANCIENT AND ACCEPTED Scottish Rite of Freemasons is "an oath-bound fraternal and benevolent association of men whose purpose is to nurture sound moral and social virtues among its members and all of mankind." The organization traces its operative or craft history to at least the fourteenth century in Great Britain. Its speculative or symbolic side, although filled with lore, dates more accurately from the seventeenth century, by which time elaborate ceremony, symbolism, and organizational secrets hallmarked its every aspect.[8]

While numerous different devices were used with symbolic intent, stonemason's implements figured prominently in Masonic iconography. Often included were the square and compass, symbolic of Reason and Faith and emblematic of the office of the senior deacon in a lodge when used in conjunction with the sun, whose light guided "men to, at and from their labor." The senior

deacon in a lodge served to "bear the Master's messages and commands to the Senior Warden."[9]

J. (John) Gillot (Gaillot), whose name is engraved on the box illustrated here, is present in the Bristol city directories in 1793, 1797, and 1798. He is recorded as a mariner, which may account for his being listed as an inhabitant during those three years only. Bristol was home to no fewer than eight Masonic lodges in 1790. Although Gillot is not mentioned in the records of the United Grand Lodge of England in London, he may have belonged to the Sea Captain's Lodge, which was originally warranted in Bristol in 1752 but lapsed through the oversight of its members. It was reinstituted in 1782 and incorporated into the Lodge of Hospitality, also in Bristol, in 1788.[10]

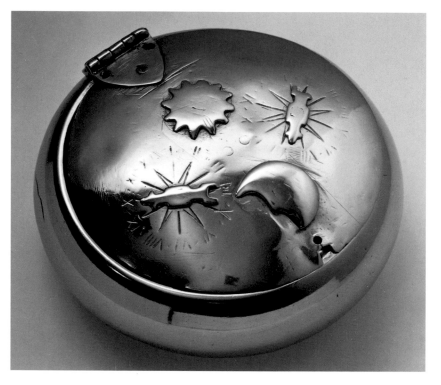

TOBACCO BOX
205

ENGLAND, PROBABLY
LANCASHIRE, 1800–1850
BRASS (COPPER 63.96, ZINC
34.68, LEAD 1.28)

H. 1 5/8" (4.1 CM),
DIAM. 3 1/2" (8.9 CM)
59.2910

THE LID OF THIS wrought pocket tobacco box has been fitted with an ingenious locking mechanism that requires no key. Both arrows and the sun above them rotate freely and are part of what Edward H. Knight describes in *Knight's American Mechanical Dictionary* as a dial lock. Such a lock was "provided with one or more dials, having a series of letters or figures on them. Each dial has a hand or pointer connected to a spindle with a wheel inside the lock; on the wheel is a notch which has to be brought into a certain position before the bolt can be moved."[11]

The box is opened by pointing the left arrow to the roman numeral X and the right arrow midway between VII and VIII. At the same time, the ray of the sun with III engraved on it has to point to II in the chapter ring encircling the left arrow. When the three are properly positioned, the crescent moon can be slid toward the sun, releasing a double-pronged catch from under the lip of the box that opens the lid.[12]

TOBACCO BOX

206

PROBABLY HOLLAND OR
GERMANY, 1672–1702
BRASS (COPPER 82.52, ZINC 11.01, TIN 2.93,
LEAD 1.37, SILVER 0.42, ANTIMONY 0.12)

L. 2 3/8" (6.0 CM), W. 1 11/16"
(4.3 CM), H. 7/8" (2.2 CM)
51.60

WILLIAM III (1650–1702), whose profile adorns the lid of this diminu-tive box, was born eight days after his father died. Because his father had attempted a coup d'etat of the Dutch Republic, his position as stadtholder had been abolished, and William III, although the heir, was raised as a state figurehead. In 1672, however, when William was twenty-two years old, Louis XIV invaded the Dutch Republic. To lead the counterattack, the Dutch named William their stadtholder, captain-general, and admiral for life.

Through marriage to Mary, eldest daughter of James II of England, William assumed the English throne with her in 1689. In England his statesmanship was principally concerned with his adopted country's domestic and international activities. In those he met with only limited success and popularity. His military triumphs were few, and, although he fared better diplomatically, he was continually at odds with the English Parliament, against whom he scored few victories.[13]

William's autocratic demeanor and frequent presence on the battle-field surely account for his depiction here in armor. Although the print or painting from which this hand-raised and chased repoussé image was copied has not been identified, it was probably not done in England, since his British subjects never became sufficiently fond of him to create a market for bibelots of this type. The Dutch felt more strongly about William "as the great founder of their freedom and indepen-dence" from the French. As such, they would have more eagerly bought and used a tobacco box ornamented with his profile.[14] At the same time, Germany was an active producer of brass artifacts like this for both local consumption and export. It is possible that this box was made in Germany and tailored for the Dutch market.

TOBACCO BOX
207

PROBABLY HOLLAND, POSSIBLY
NEW YORK CITY, 1730–50
BRASS (COPPER 68.32, ZINC 30.28,
LEAD 1.01, IRON 0.22)

L. 4 3/4" (12.1 CM), W. 2 1/4"
(5.7 CM), H. 1 9/16" (4.0 CM)
61.1608

ABOUT 1739 CHARLES FOREMAN wrote to the Right Honorable Sir Robert Walpole, prime minister of England, complaining that because of "efficient smuggling carried on by the Dutch in the various parts of the British Empire . . . a Dutchman has now the Prerogative of smoaking English Tobacco Cent. per Cent, cheaper in Amsterdam . . . than an Englishman can in London."[15]

Tobacco's increasing affordability during the eighteenth century helped spawn widespread use with a commensurate growth in attendant paraphernalia. The tobacco box was essential not only to carry tobacco in its various forms but also to keep it fresh. It also reflected its owner's taste and economic status. Consequently, tobacco-box owners came to expect as great a variety "in the shapes of their boxes as in the man-

ner of taking what they contain. Some will have them circular, others oval, some in the form of a Parallelogram or oblong [or] square."[16]

The example illustrated here, which might be described as an astragal-ended rectangle, is virtually identical in shape to one of silver that was made and marked by Leendert Beekhuysen, an Amsterdam silversmith who became a master in 1731 and specialized in tobacco boxes. The Beekhuysen box was originally owned by Jeremias Van Rensselaer (1705-45), sixth patroon of the manor of Rensselaerwick near Albany. Imported boxes like it or this brass example provided a ready design source for local craftsmen such as the New York silversmith Daniel Fueter, who "informs the Public that Mr. John Anthony Beau, Chaser, from Geneva, works with him; where Chaising [on] Snuff Boxes . . . is done in the best and cheapest manner."[17]

TOBACCO BOX

208

HOLLAND, 1740–1800
BRASS (COPPER 67.51, ZINC 31.21,
LEAD 0.80)

L. 7" (17.8 CM), W. 2" (5.1 CM),
H. 1 3/8" (3.5 CM)
59.2558

THIS TOBACCO BOX is made of engraved sheet metal. The scene depicted on the lid is identified in Dutch as "the Greenland fishery." A complementary scene on the bottom is described, also in Dutch, as "Greenland boats setting out among the ice."[18]

The Norwegians first began whaling in the Greenland fishery–an area extending from the North Sea to the island of Svalbard and west to Greenland–in the ninth century. The English followed suit by the sixteenth century. They found that "the whales, never having been disturbed, resorted to the bays near the shore, so that their blubber was easily landed at Spitzbergen. . . . The Holanders coming later, were obliged to find bays farther to the north." Because of extensive harvesting between then and the eighteenth century, "the whales are

less frequently in the bays, and are commonly among the openings of the ice farther from the land."[19]

Even with heavy English whaling, "the Dutch carried it on with much greater success . . . and it became one of the principal branches of their flourishing trade. The chief [Dutch] merchants of the several provinces associated themselves into a body for carrying it on, and sent every year a great fleet of vessels to the North seas for that purpose. [They fixed their] fishery about the western coast of Spitzbergen. . . . In the year 1725, there were two hundred and twenty-six [European] vessels [involved in whaling]; one hundred and forty-four were Dutch. . . . Their captures were 349 fish."[20]

TOBACCO BOX
209

HOLLAND, 1800–1830
BRASS (COPPER 69.14, ZINC 29.26,
LEAD 1.26), TIN

L. 6 1/8" (15.5 CM), W. 2 11/16"
(6.8 CM), H. 1 1/8" (2.8 CM)
61.1606

THIS COMMODIOUS TOBACCO BOX is made of thin, rolled sheet metal and has been tinned on the inside. The full-length hinge along the back side has knuckles that are alternating bent-over extensions of the body and lid. A sham hinge has been affixed to the front edge, but the box opens in a straightforward manner, so that feature is simply ornamental.

All the outer surfaces of the box have been fancifully engraved. The owner's initials, "AL" in script, are centered within a circular surround of foliate motifs on the underside. On the lid, a moralistic vignette of Adam and Eve in the Garden of Eden is enframed with winged angels similar to those on seventeenth- and eighteenth-century Dutch altarpieces, where they focus the worshiper's attention on the Virgin, the Crucifixion, or the Ascension. Below is a lengthy Dutch inscription that translates as "Let the first person eating with satisfaction in the lust court [Garden of Eden] think of God's image with content/now life is like a lamb, everything equally tame, the cruelty ocurred when the first sin was done."[21]

Instructive ornament derived from the Old or New Testament was often placed on tobacco boxes of this type, reflecting a timeless concern with man's place in the unknown. These views, whether expressed religiously from a pulpit or secularly using a tobacco box, were often simplistic, with original sin figuring prominently. God "made a man, named Adam, and a woman whose name was Eve; and he put them in a garden. . . . The beasts were playful and tame. . . . There was but one tree of which God said they should not eat; yet they partook of the fruit of that very tree . . . and disobeyed God [and] became very wretched. . . . Disobeying God always makes people wretched."[22]

TOBACCO BOX

210

HOLLAND, 1800–1830
BRASS (COPPER 72.92, ZINC 22.88,
LEAD 2.39, IRON 0.25), TIN, LEAD

L. 6 5/8" (6.8 CM), W. 3 5/8"
(9.2 CM), H. 1 1/8" (2.9 CM)
61.895

CHAPTERS 13 THROUGH 16 in the Book of Judges of the Old Testament tell the story of Samson. Before he was born, his father, Manoah, and his mother had been without children. An angel visited them and announced that they would have a son. In celebration Manoah made a burnt offering. As that took place, "it came to pass, when the flames went up toward heaven from off the altar, that the angel of the Lord ascended in the flame of the altar, and Manoah and his wife looked on it, and fell on their faces to the ground."[23]

That event is depicted in the central reserve on the lid of this tobacco box. The secondary reserves describe the scene in Dutch as "parents of Samson offering a sacrifice as the angel appears in the flame Judges Chapter 13 Verse 20." The faces and foliage that surround these reserves appear to derive from the work of the Dutch artist and

engraver Lucas Jacobsz, known as Lucas van Leyden (1494–1533). Although he died at a young age, he was accomplished and prolific, and his work remained influential long after his death.

The hinged lid opens to reveal a tin-lined interior. On the underside is a holder for a pipe stem cleaner and a dollop of lead into which is impressed the initials of the owner, "AV," between a stylized crown and a fish. Just above them a suggestive couplet has been lightly scratched in Dutch, probably by the owner. It translates as "a certain young woman when first touched by love did not know what happened to her or what she might miss." Although quite different from the religious sentiments offered on the other side of the lid, bawdy writing like this or "obscene and lascivious" pictures often decorated Dutch tobacco boxes.[24]

TOBACCO BOX
211

JOHN HEINRICH GIESE
ISERLOHN, GERMANY, CA. 1757
BRASS (COPPER 69.27, ZINC 29.92,
LEAD 0.68), COPPER

L. 6 1/4" (15.9 CM), W. 2" (5.1 CM),
H. 1 1/4" (3.2 CM)
59.3571
GIFT OF H. RODNEY SHARP

FREDERICK III (1712–80) was born in Berlin to Frederick William, King of Prussia, and Sophia Dorothea, daughter of the elector of Hanover. When his father died in 1740, Frederick ascended the throne of Prussia, a vast confederation of states in central Europe extending along the entire southern coast of the Baltic Sea as far south as the city of Cracow, in what is now Poland.

Almost immediately, Frederick became embroiled in war with Silesia and emerged victorious. In 1744 he again marched at the head of his armies, this time into Bohemia; the battle concluded in his favor with the signing of the Treaty of Dresden in 1745. At that time he came to be called Frederick the Great.

After about a decade of progressive peace, the year 1756 saw the commencement of "the Seven Years' war between the Prussian monarch and the great and power-ful princes [of Europe]. It was one of the most sanguine contests that ever desolated the globe [and because of it] the military fame acquired by Frederic was very great." The tobacco box shown here, celebrating Frederick's military might, is one of many made by John Heinrich Giese in the ancient Prussian metalworking town of Iserlohn in the district of Westphalia. It was probably created shortly after Frederick conquered Prague in 1757.[25]

The lid's die-stamped ornament depicts Frederick's profile flanked by Justice on the left and Atlas on the right. The lettering under Justice translates as "The tight rein of the eagle the fight for the Austrians is shown in this print with the image of Frederick the father to his population the advisor to his counsels famous in the war due to his inimitable deeds." The lettering under Atlas translates as "An Atlas who carries his kingdom on his own shoulders a miracle of this century a true model of the souvereign a German Hercules who could rule as formerly Caesar did I came I saw I won."

The reverse of the box depicts and describes three critical battles that Frederick won in 1757 at the beginning of the Seven Years' War: "victory of Reichenberg April 21st 1757," "complete victory of Prague fought by the Prussians May 6th 1757," and "bombardment of Prague May 30th 1757." Their importance is underscored in the text's first line, which serves as a chronogram of roman numerals for the year 1757. The legend "Fredericus Borussorum Rex" translates as "Frederick the Great, King of the People of the Borysthenes." This box was most certainly intended for the Dutch market since the text is entirely in that language rather than in German.[26]

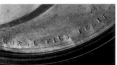

SNUFF BOX
212

EUGÈNE MOREL, JR.
PARIS, FRANCE, 1799–1825
GILT COPPER, GLASS,
COMPOSITION, TORTOISE SHELL

H. 1 1/4" (3.2 CM),
DIAM. 3 1/4" (8.3 CM)
60.507

WE KNOW LITTLE about Eugène Morel, a French sculptor and medalist. The signature on the gilt copper insert in the lid of this snuffbox and that on another identical example in the Winterthur collection indicate that he passed his profession on to his son of the same name.[27]

Their work consists principally of medals and plaquettes like the one set into the lid of this box. The subjects depicted are primarily European notables, including Napoleon Bonaparte; Marie Louise, his wife; William Frederick George Lewis, crown prince of Holland; George, prince regent of Great Britain; and Joseph Francis Oscar, crown prince of Sweden. Each box was intended for sale in its respective country, as was the case with this snuff box, which lauds the just-deceased George Washington.[28]

The thin gilt copper image set under the low glass dome in this lid was stamped using a pair of steel dies cut by a specialist engraver known as a die sinker. His principal work involved cutting dies for specie, but commemorative medals and plaquettes were also his domain. In making these images, "the first thing done, is that of designing the figures; the next is the moulding them in wax, of the size and depth they are to lie, and from this wax the punch is engraven. When the punch is finished, they give it a very high temper, that it may better bear the blows of the hammer with which it is struck to give the impression to the matrice."[29]

SPONGE BOX

213

PROBABLY FRANCE, 1740–60
BRASS (COPPER 75.95, ZINC 18.40,
LEAD 2.66, TIN 1.67, IRON 0.87),
SILVER

H. 3 3/4" (9.5 CM),
DIAM. 3 3/8" (8.6 CM)
61.246

IN 1738 EPHRIAM CHAMBERS defined the toilet as "the dress-ing-box, wherein are kept the paints, pomatums, essences, patches, &c. the pin-cushion, powder-box [and] brushes" used in personal grooming and hygiene.[30] It also often included a looking glass, candlesticks, a ewer and basin, and a soap and sponge box. The most expensive were of silver or silver gilt. Less expensive examples were of silver-plated brass. Most are French in origin.

The cast and french-plated sponge box shown here was origi-nally part of a set and undoubtedly had a matching soap box, which would have been identical except for an unpierced lid. The latter contained "ball soap . . . made with lees from ashes and tallow [which when] dissolved with spirit of wine [was used] in the cure of cold humors [skin maladies] besides being used in suppositories, and in the composition of a kind of plaster com-monly called *emplat de sapone*," a type of facial cream.[31]

The lid of the soap box was always unpierced. That of the sponge box, however, had to be pierced so that the sponge within could dry properly after use, which in addition to cleans-ing often consisted of its being "saturated with a composition of egg yellows beaten together to give the color of gingerbread" when rubbed on the face.[32]

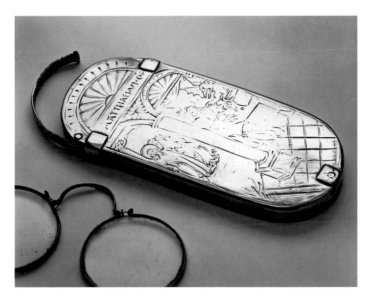

BOX AND
SPECTACLES
214

PROBABLY HOLLAND, POSSIBLY
GERMANY, 1700–1750
BRASS (COPPER 71.31, ZINC 24.67,
TIN 2.31, LEAD 1.35, IRON 0.28), COPPER,
GLASS

L. 4 3/16" (10.6 CM), W. 1 7/8" (4.7 CM),
D. 5/16" (0.8 CM)
59.4.7 A,B

THE FRAGILE NATURE of spectacles and the ease with which the lenses can be scratched mandated that they be kept in a protective box when not worn. Spectacle boxes were made of silver, gold, wood, leather, papier-mâché, sheet iron, silvered copper, and brass. While most were quite plain, some, like the example illustrated here, were elaborately decorated.

The two sides are engraved with biblical scenes from the New Testament. The Book of Matthew, chapter 6, verse 19–identified as "MATTHAEI VI CAP"–advises readers to "lay not up for yourselves treasures upon earth, where moth and rust doth corrupt, and where thieves break through and steal." That thought is depicted on this box by a man who has turned his back on Christ and his followers to steal from a money bag, while he is in the clutches of a demon.

The opposite side is identified as coming from the Book of Luke, chapter 16, verses 19, 20, and 21–"LUCAE XVI CAP"–which moralize that "there was a certain rich man which was clothed in purple and fine linen, and fared sumptuously every day and there was a certain beggar named Lazarus which was laid at his gate full of sores and desiring to be fed with the crumbs which fell from the rich man's table: Moreover the · dogs came and licked his sores."

The box is made of sheet-metal parts riveted together; the spectacles are pince-nez. The lenses are loosely held into narrow strips of sheet copper that are formed into open loops and bound with wire. Although it cannot be stated with certainty that the spectacles are original to the box, based on stylistic and construction features, both date to early eighteenth-century northern Europe.

A.

B.

BOXES
215 a,b

A. BIRMINGHAM, ENGLAND, 1790–1810
FUSED PLATE
H. 1" (2.5 CM), DIAM. 2 1/8" (5.4 CM)
67.503

B. BIRMINGHAM, ENGLAND, 1790–1810
BRASS (COPPER 78.10,
ZINC 19.99, LEAD 1.00)
H. 1" (2.5 CM), DIAM. 2 1/8" (5.4 CM)
61.1017

JOSEPH WRIGHT WAS BORN in Bordentown, New Jersey, on July 16, 1756. When he was sixteen, his widowed mother moved the family to London, where Joseph became immersed in the artistic community. He remained in London until 1782, when, with a letter of recommendation from his mother–Patience Wright, a well-known artist–he went to Paris to paint Benjamin Franklin's portrait. Within a year, he was back in the United States, where he "painted both . . . General [George Washington] and Mrs. Washington. He afterwards drew a profile of Washington and etched it."[33]

That etching, which depicts Washington in uniform and wearing his hair in a queue, was executed in 1790. "It had the flattery of frequent imitations [among which was one by] Thomas Holloway in London for the *Literary Magazine*, August 1792." Holloway's engrav-

ing may have served as the model for a profile medallion of Washington by Josiah Wedgwood and also for the image stamped into the lids of these two boxes. Although the maker of the boxes is anonymous, he was without doubt "an ingenious young man capable of designing and sinking button and other dyes in the most perfect manner."[34]

His work is illustrated in an early nineteenth-century Birmingham brass-manufacturer's trade catalogue in the form of a box identical to these two but with the profile of Adm. Lord Horatio Nelson (1758-1805) and a "Black Papier Maché frame with convex glass and gilt pendant ring and rim" picturing the British statesman and orator Charles James Fox (1749-1806). As seen here, accompanying the engravings is the notation that "the Frames & Box may be had with the Head of Nelson, Pitt, Fox, Washington, Jefferson, or Bonaparte."[35]

BOX
216

ENGLAND, PROBABLY
SHEFFIELD, 1797
BRASS (COPPER 67.12, ZINC 30.83,
LEAD 1.59, NICKEL 0.32), TIN

L. 3 3/8" (8.6 CM), W. 1 1/2"
(3.8 CM), H. 3/4" (1.9 CM)
60.1207

SOLOMON GORGAS WAS BORN January 22, 1764, the second son of Jacob Gorgas, in Ephrata, Pennsylvania.[36] Jacob was a clockmaker in Cocalico Township, Berks County, as were three of his sons: Jacob, Jr., Solomon, and Joseph.

Solomon made thirty-hour and eight-day clockworks in Ephrata from 1787 through 1804; they were typical of those being made by numerous competitors throughout southeastern Pennsylvania. He also supported himself as a "retailer of goods" but apparently felt that greater opportunity lay west of the Susquehanna River and so moved to Lower Allen Township, Cumberland County, where he operated the area's first tavern and store. He was also active politically, serving in the state legislature at Harrisburg in 1821 and 1822.[37]

The engraving on the pocket-size brass box shown here is in the same flowing script as the name "Solomon Gorgas" painted on the clock dials he made. Although he probably engraved it himself, the box is almost certainly English in origin. The box bears no stamped maker's mark but is depicted in the catalogue of Broadhead, Gurney, Sporle and Company. The members of this firm, although working individually in Sheffield for several decades, were only in partnership from 1792 to 1800.[38] Their principal products were fashionable Britannia-metal household objects.

In the catalogue, this object is described as a "yellow metal secret box," referring to the fact that it can be opened only by someone who knows the secret of the hinge mechanism, which when opened reveals a tinned interior containing a second lidded compartment.[39]

A.

B.

BOXES
217 a,b

A. ENGLAND, PROBABLY
BIRMINGHAM, 1816–25
BRASS (COPPER 80.99, ZINC 18.43)
DIAM. 2 1/16" (5.2 CM), H. 15/16" (2.4 CM)
58.2931

B. ENGLAND, PROBABLY
BIRMINGHAM, 1816–25
BRASS (COPPER 80.52, ZINC 18.92)
DIAM. 2 1/16" (5.2 CM), H. 15/16" (2.4 CM)
64.1101

WITH THE SIGNING of the Treaty of Paris on September 3, 1783, the United States formalized its independence from Great Britain. Even so, during the following decades Americans felt they they were being treated "in a slavish subjection" through trade restrictions, political intrigue, and impressment of their sailors.[40] Dissatisfaction grew until Congress finally declared war on England on June 18, 1812. Almost immediately the two countries commenced armed conflict on the Atlantic and the Great Lakes. Numerous confrontations ensued between the British and American navies, the details of which were patriotically discussed in American periodicals.

Commodores Oliver Hazard Perry and Stephen Decatur were among the country's most celebrated naval heroes during the conflict. The former, famed for his declaration "we have met the enemy and they are ours," defeated the British fleet on Lake Erie on September 10, 1813, with a remarkable "display of skill and gallantry." On October 25, 1814,

Commodore Decatur, in command of the frigate *United States* "fell in with and captured . . . the British Frigate Macedonian" in the Caribbean. He "received from all quarters the congratulations of his countrymen" for this brilliant victory.[41]

Interest in these and other events of the war was so great that "the publick mind was . . . continually excited by some series of naval exploits." This enthusiasm provided enterprising businessmen with a ready market for timely commemorative artifacts. One such merchant in Philadelphia was Thomas Fletcher, who wrote to his brother in 1815 while on a European buying trip, "If you can send me . . . things that I can turn to advantage–such as the portraits of our naval officers . . . it will be well."[42] The diminutive sheet-metal boxes with die-stamped decoration shown here, probably intended for snuff, are among the many objects Fletcher and his competitors imported that not only celebrated American heros but also served routine daily needs.

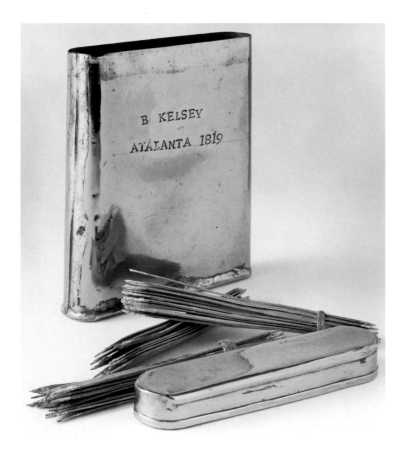

BOX
218

ATTRIBUTED TO
BENJAMIN KELSEY (1796–1876)
EAST HADDAM, CONNECTICUT, 1819
COPPER

H. 6 1/8" (15.6 CM), W. 5 1/2"
(14.0 CM), D. 1 1/4" (3.2 CM)
61.248 A,B

IN GREEK MYTHOLOGY the goddess Atalanta was renowned as a swift-footed huntress who always bested those against whom she ran, whether male or female. Her name was synonomous with speed. It followed that Atalanta was a favored name for schooners, which were among the fastest of sailing ships in the nineteenth century. Between 1784 and 1864 no fewer than twenty-four schooners, ships, sloops, brigs, brigantines, and even towboats in the United States were named Atalanta.[43]

These vessels were built in many East Coast ports from Freetown, Maine, to Perquimons, North Carolina. One, an eighty-one-ton, square-sterned sloop that was sixty-two feet in length was built in East Haddam, Connecticut, in 1815. Coincidentally, East Haddam is the only coastal city that records a B. Kelsey whose life dates and profession coincide. Benjamin Kelsey was born in 1796. When he came of age, he worked as a carpenter and shipwright in the shipyards of Higganum, Haddam, and East Haddam. As a shipwright, he worked largely with wood, but on occasion he would have to fashion metal fittings, such as

iron door hinges or copper sheathing nails. Apparently Kelsey eventually decided that metalworking agreed with him, for family tradition records that he gave up shipbuilding in 1846 to become a blacksmith, a profession he pursued until his death in 1876.[44]

The box illustrated here is assembled in a simple manner from pieces of rolled sheet metal with the edges folded or lap-jointed and sloppily lead soldered, all of which suggest that it was made by some-one like Kelsey, who was not a professional coppersmith. This assumption is underscored by the letters and numbers, each of which is struck with a separate die. Professional coppersmiths used full-name dies. Kelsey may have fashioned the box about 1819 from scraps of sheet copper used in resheathing the *Atalanta*'s hull, rebuilding its bilge pumps, or replacing its neccessary. The purpose of the box is unknown, although at the time of its acquisition it contained bundles of large sulphur-tipped splints of the type used as matches during the early nineteenth century.[45]

PIPE CASE

219

PROBABLY HOLLAND OR
ENGLAND, 1680–1720
BRASS (COPPER 69.27, ZINC 29.65,
LEAD 0.55, TIN 0.33)

L. 10 3/4" (27.3 CM), W. 1"
(2.5 CM), D. 1 3/4" (4.4 CM)
52.8

In 1688 William Harrison recalled in his *Chronologie* that as early as 1573, "the taking in of the smoke of the Indian herb called Tobacco by an instrument formed like a little ladell [was] greatly taken up and used in England."[46] The ladle to which he referred was the tobacco pipe. Many were made of metal and wood, but clay seems to have been the preferred material from the onset of smoking in European culture in the sixteenth century, remaining so until the eventual eclipse of the pipe by the cigar and cigarette during the late nineteenth century. Clay was used for good reason. It was readily obtained, easily worked, inexpensive, undamaged by heat, and light in weight. It fell short of perfection, however, for clay pipes broke. Consequently, if owners valued a clay pipe, they had a pipe case as well.

The Dutch and English were "generally the greatest consumers of the weed."[47] Their clay tobacco pipes passed through a discernible evolution from the mid sixteenth to the mid nineteenth centuries, characterized by changes in bowl diameter, stem length, and the angle between bowl and stem. The pipe case shown here was designed to accommodate a clay pipe of the type that was in use between 1680 and 1720. The shaft is wrought of sheet metal brazed with a straight seam. The portion that houses the pipe bowl was fabricated separately, and the two were joined by brazing.

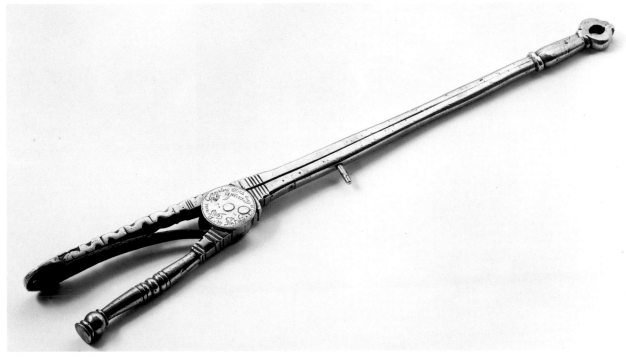

TOBACCO TONGS
220

ENGLAND OR AMERICA, 1755–63
BRASS (COPPER 77.11,
ZINC 19.47, LEAD 2.10, TIN 0.81,
IRON 0.32), IRON

L. 15 3/4" (40.0 CM), W. 2 1/8"
(5.4 CM), D. 1" (2.5 CM)
90.34

TOBACCO TONGS WERE USED to retrieve a hot ember from a fireplace for lighting a pipe or for other purposes. They were designed to be easily manipulated with one hand and were often spring loaded to clamp securely around the ember. They were frequently made of iron but also of brass. English-made examples were common in the American colonies during the eighteenth century, as documented in the broadside of the Boston hardware merchants Joseph and Daniel Waldo, who advertised in 1748 that they had just "imported from London [and would sell] by wholesale and Retail at the cheapest Rates . . . brass . . . tobacco tongs." At the same time, the American brass worker Mary Jackson of Boston noted that she "makes and sells all sorts of Brass and Founders ware, as Hearths, Fenders, Shovels and Tongs."[48] Although she was almost certainly referring to log tongs, she would have been capable of making tobacco tongs as well.

Tobacco tongs seem to have been popular in New England households, as judged by their frequent appearance in eighteenth-century inventories. Robert Oliver of Dorchester, Massachusetts, had "1 tobacco tongs in [his] setting parlour," as noted in his inventory dated January 11, 1763. Consider Leeds of Dorchester owned a pair of "tobacco tongs in [the] kitchen," recorded in his July 3, 1772, inventory.[49]

The tobacco tongs pictured here–cast in four separate parts, brazed together near the base of the arms, and double riveted at the hinge–were almost certainly part of the household effects of Daniel Greenleaf at the time of his death in Boston on August 27, 1763. They are engraved "The Revd Mr. Daniel Greenleaf obed Augst 27./1763 aged 85 years." They were presumably a cherished personal amenity, making them a suitable vehicle for one of his ten surviving children to use as a memento mori.

Greenleaf graduated from Harvard College in 1699. He then taught school for about two years in Portsmouth, New Hampshire. By 1705 he was ministering to a congregation at Star Island in the Isles of Shoals off the coast of Maine. In 1707 he was invited to Yarmouth to preach. At the same time he was a practicing physician and apothecary. He remained in Yarmouth until 1728, when he moved to Boston and became a "very noted apothecary."[50]

Greenleaf was apparently close to his family. In 1847 his great-grandchild, Elizabeth L. Sewell, wrote to a relative that Greenleaf "was in the habit of going around once a week to see all his married children who were settled in Boston. I often heard my mother say how many pleasant hours she passed in her grandfather's sick chamber; he was always so cheerful and so instructive."[51]

PLAQUE
221

BIRMINGHAM, ENGLAND,
1766–1810
BRASS, GLASS, MARBLE

DIAM. 3 15/16" (10.0 CM),
D. 3/4" (1.9 CM)
61.1207

IN FEBRUARY 1759 eleven professors and the rector of the University of Saint Andrews in Scotland "conferred the degree of Doctor of Laws on Mr. Benjamin Franklin famous for his writings on Electricity and appoint his diploma to be given him gratis, the Clerk and Arch Beadle's dues to be paid by the Library Questar."[52]

Franklin had been living in London for two years prior to receiving that honor and would remain in residence there until 1762. During that time and from 1764 to 1775, when he was again living in London, he was a celebrated and controversial figure not only for his work with electricity but also for his other numerous scientific, humanitarian, and political activities.

Fame caused his likeness to be widely circulated in engravings on paper, Staffordshire pottery, and other media. As noted in the

July 4, 1775, issue of the *London Chronicle*, a full-size likeness in wax "of that excellent and public spirited philosopher Dr. Benjamin Franklin, of Philadelphia" had been executed by Patience Wright and was on exhibit in her popular London studio.[53]

Another artist, Isaac Gosset (1713-99), was among the most celebrated English miniaturists who "excelled in modelling cameo portraits . . . of many distinguished persons from the reign of George II to 1780." Franklin sat for him in 1766. The resulting wax profile is virtually identical to the one on the stamped brass plaque shown here and probably served as its inspiration, as it did for similar ceramic likenesses by Josiah Wedgwood and James Tassie.[54]

COMMEMORATIVE
MEDAL
222

UNITED STATES MINT
PHILADELPHIA, PENNSYLVANIA,
1814–34
COPPER

DIAM. 2 19/32" (6.6 CM),
D. 1/4" (0.6 CM)
79.30

ON FEBRUARY 24, 1813, while sailing north in the Atlantic from Bahia, Brazil, the American sloop *Hornet*, commanded by Lt. James Lawrence, encountered and sank the British brig *Peacock* near Surinam.[55] For this feat Lawrence was promoted to captain and given command of the frigate *Chesapeake*, on which he was killed in a battle with the British ship *Shannon* outside Boston on June 1, 1813.

On January 11, 1814, the United States Senate and House of Representatives resolved "that the President of the United States be requested to present to the nearest male relative of Captain James Lawrence, a gold medal, and silver medal to each of the commissioned officers who served under him in the sloop

of war Hornet, in her conflict with the British vessel of war the Peacock in testimony of the high sense entertained by congress of the gallantry and good conduct of the officers and crew in the capture of that vessel."[56]

These medals were struck at the United States Mint in Philadelphia using dies that were cut by Moritz Fürst (b. 1782), the profile of Lawrence possibly taken from a portrait by Thomas Sully. They were part of a series commissioned by the United States that Fürst executed to honor eleven army heros and twelve naval heros of the War of 1812. At the time these medals were made, copper examples were struck from the same dies and offered for sale at the Mint.[57]

SLAVE BADGE
223

JOHN JOSEPH LAFAR (1781–1849)
CHARLESTON, SOUTH CAROLINA, 1819
COPPER

H. 2 1/8" (5.4 CM),
W. 2 1/4" (5.7 CM)
77.152
GIFT OF MRS. SAMUEL SCHWARTZ

THE SLAVE TAX BADGE, commonly known as the slave badge, was worn by slaves in the southern United States when their owners allowed them to be hired out or self-employed. Working arrangements of this type were practiced throughout the South, but a system of badges seems to have evolved only in an urban context. Savannah, New Orleans, Mobile, and Norfolk all had slave badge laws, but Charleston is the only city for which badges exist.[58]

The use of such tags arose as a means of controlling slave labor, which when unchecked, proved detrimental (it was thought) to self-employed white artisans such as carpenters and mechanics. Consequently, a "certificate, note or memorandum" detailing the specifics of employment was mandated by law in Charleston as early as 1722. Continued difficulty generated a municipal ordinance in 1751, 1764, and again in 1783, that blacks "wear [a public badge] suspended by a string or ribband and exposed to view at his breast," to be renewed annually upon payment of a fee by their owners.[59] After periodic repeal, this ordinance was finally reinstated in 1800 and remained in effect until the Civil War.

In 1806 the law was revised to stipulate that each badge had to have a "number as well as the specific trade or employment to be performed by any slave working out for hire." In 1818 the City Council of Charleston decreed that "no negro or other slave shall be permitted, to own any boat or vessel except fishermen or fisherwomen [and only by obtaining] a license for fishing and selling fish."[60]

The badge illustrated here, issued in 1819 and marked in accordance with those specifications, was made by the Charleston silversmith and city marshall John Joseph Lafar. It is one of fifty such badges presently recorded, dating between 1812 and 1863, worn by fishermen, carpenters, fruit vendors, porters, mechanics, and servants.[61]

ADMISSION TOKEN

224

UNITED STATES MINT
PHILADELPHIA, PENNSYLVANIA,
1829–45
COPPER

DIAM. 1 1/4" (3.2 CM),
D. 3/32" (0.2 CM)
66.78

IN 1794 CHARLES WILLSON PEALE's museum in Philadelphia, an outgrowth of his painting studio, attracted among its visitors an Englishman named Henry Wansey, who observed that he "was entertained for two or three hours, in viewing his collection of artificial and natural curiosities." Among those items that Wansey found most interesting were birds' nests used to make soups, a pair of Chinese women's shoes only four-inches long, scalps, and "portraits . . . of all the leading men concerned in the late revolution."[62]

By 1818 the museum's founder advertised that "thirty-three years of unremitted exertion has rendered [it] one of the most valuable in the world [and noted that it] contains at present upwards of 100,000 articles." He went on to state that "the whole Museum is brilliantly illuminated with Gas Lights . . . and during the winter season a number of chemical and philosophical experiments are exhibited . . . price twenty-five cents."[63]

Peale, with his sons Rubens and Rembrandt, oversaw the operation of the museum until 1821, when the formation of a board of trustees was authorized. After the elder Peale's death in 1827, that board appointed a committee to inquire about having a medal made at the United States Mint in Philadelphia. By 1833 silver impressions were engraved and presented to each trustee of the museum and also to Samuel Moore, director of the Mint; William Kneass, the Mint's engraver who probably cut the dies for the medal itself; and Adam Eckfeldt, the Mint's chief coiner.[64]

Copper impressions were also struck that, although identical on the obverse, contain the impression "ADMIT THE BEARER" on the reverse instead of the engraved name of the recipient. These were probably "awarded to the subscribers and stockholders [of the Philadelphia museum] to provide them with a reusable pass . . . which would distinguish them from the occasional visitor." Prior to that time, paper admission tickets had been used.[65]

MEDAL
225

DESIGNED BY SALATHIEL ELLIS (B. 1760)
AND PETER PAUL DUGGAN (D. 1861),
ENGRAVED BY CHARLES
CUSHING WRIGHT (1796–1854)
NEW YORK CITY, 1848

COPPER
DIAM. 2 9/16" (6.6 CM),
D. 3/8" (0.9 CM)
79.137
GIFT OF DR. RICHARD H. ZESCHKE

"The American Art-Union, in the city of New York, was incorporated [in 1847] by the Legislature of the State of New-York, for the PROMOTION OF THE FINE ARTS in the United States," The union proposed to fulfill its lofty goal by maintaining a "free Picture Gallery" for members to visit and by producing a "large and costly Original Engraving from an American Painting," copies of which would be sold to members for a nominal sum. In addition, members could purchase "paintings and Sculpture, Statuettes in bronze and Medals, by native or resident artists." These were "publicly distributed by lot among the members, each member having one share for every five dollars paid by him."[66]

The first medal, commemorating the artist Washington Allston, was made in 1847. It was "a costly bas-relief [of which] fifty [copies] in silver and two hundred fifty in bronze [were] distributed amongst" the organization's 9,666 members. The following year the Art-Union's

Committee of Management "caused a second medal to be struck for the purpose of distribution, in honor of GILBERT STUART, and his early conceded prominence in the History of American Art."[67]

The dies for both medals and a third, honoring John Trumbull, struck in 1849, were made by Charles Cushing Wright. The subject's profile in high relief was placed on the obverse, while the seal of the American Art-Union, Genius crowning an artist and a sculptor, appears on the reverse in low relief. Stuart's profile is modeled after a portrait executed by the cameo portraitist, sculptor, and designer Salathiel Ellis, and the composition of the reverse was created by the portrait artist and designer Peter Paul Duggan.

The medal shown here and its two mates were the only ones issued, for in 1852 the New York Supreme Court declared its lottery offerings illegal, and the American Art-Union was disbanded.[68]

STEEL
226

PROBABLY FRANCE, POSSIBLY
THE NETHERLANDS OR GERMANY, 1660–1700
BRASS (COPPER 77.42, ZINC 21.17,
LEAD 0.65, TIN 0.21, IRON 0.48), STEEL

L. 2 1/2" (6.3 CM), W. 1 1/4"
(3.2 CM), D. 1/4" (0.6 CM)
53.80.3C

FLINT IS A SILICEOUS STONE that is known for "the quality it posseses in an eminent degree of giving . . . copious . . . sparks" when struck against a piece of steel.[69] For this reason, a flint and steel (or striker) were an essential part of any household before the development of the chemical match during the early nineteenth century.

For convenience, the two items were usually kept in a small metal box with tinder and brimstone, all of which were needed to light a fire. Properly used, the steel was held over cotton wadding, scraps of linen, wood shavings, or some other tinder. The flint was struck downward against the steel to produce a shower of sparks, some of which would eventually ignite the tinder and provide a glowing ember. At that point a brimstone match (a sliver of wood that had been dipped in molten

sulphur) would be touched against the ember. With judicious blowing, it could be ignited. That match would, in turn, be used to fire larger sticks, culminating in a usable fire.

Most steels used for this purpose were simple hand-held, U-shape objects with no embellishment. The example illustrated here, however, is unusual in that it has a cast brass handle. The design of the brass portion appears to derive from the work of the Parisian painter-designer Nicolas Loir (1624–79) and his brother, the goldsmith-engraver Alexis (1640–1713). Although none of the designs currently known to have been created by them are exactly like that of this steel, most are a balanced sculpted composition of winged putti and fantastic animals amid bounteous foliage.

PISTOL TINDERBOX

227

THOMAS MORTIMER AND SON
LONDON, ENGLAND, 1809–17
BRASS (COPPER 68.80, ZINC 29.24,
LEAD 1.75), WOOD, STEEL, FLINT

L. 6 3/4" (17.2 CM), H. 5"
(12.7 CM), W. 3" (7.6 CM)
59.2864

HENRY WILLIAM and Thomas Mortimer both enjoyed royal patronage, entitling them to advertise as "gunmakers to his Majesty" George III. London city directories record them working together in 1805 at 89 Fleet Street, but by 1809 Mortimer had moved to 4 Ludgate Hill and entered partnership with his son Thomas, Jr. They were together until about 1817, when the latter began working independently.

Flint was a crucial part of European, English, and American firearm design during the eighteenth and early nineteenth centuries because it gave off sparks when struck against steel. It was put "into a vice made at the top of the cock, of a musquet or pistol lock; so that when impelled against a piece of steel called the hammer [frizzen], it may strike fire, and ignite the gun-powder contained in a pan concealed by the hammer, until the latter is forced backwards on a pivot, by the great force with which the cock strikes against it; when it not only produces fire, but, by its peculiar form directs the sparks towards the priming in the pan."[70]

That mechanism was adapted almost exactly by Mortimer for the fire starter illustrated here. The trigger, hammer, and frizzen work just as on a flintlock firearm but strike into a shallow pan filled with cotton wadding or fine wood shavings instead of gunpowder. From that the candle kept in the candle cup is lit and used like a modern match. Extra wadding or shavings were stored in the box under the pan until needed.

Many gunmakers made these as an aside, although they were also fashioned by specialists, like "William Bullock, pistol tinder box maker" on Barn Street in Wolverhampton, England.[71] These devices were also an item of international trade as recorded in *Rivington's New-York Gazetteer*. The hardware merchant William Bailey noted in the July 29, 1773, issue that he had "for sale reasonable both whole-sale and retail imported in the latest vessels from England . . . pistol tinder boxes."

FLEAM
228

EUROPE OR ENGLAND, 1680–1730
BRASS (COPPER 66.89, ZINC 29.34,
LEAD 3.26, IRON 0.27, TIN 0.11), STEEL;
HOUSED IN A FITTED MAPLE BOX

L. 2 1/8" (5.3 CM), W. 15/16"
(2.4 CM), D. 1/2" (1.3 CM)
52.266

BLEEDING WAS A WIDELY used medical practice during the seventeenth and eighteenth centuries. It was "a species of evacuation, frequently resorted to, as a principal remedy in inflammatory affections, such as pleurisy, peripneumonia, phrenitis, quinsey, entaritis [and] acute rheumatism. . . . In all these cases, the earlier this is employed the better . . . Nor is the timing of this remedy the only circumstance that requires attention. [Others] of equal moment are . . . the quantity of evacuation, and the suddenness with which it is effected. . . . Leeches are often applied to a part of the body requiring the local evacuation of blood." Medical authorities frequently advised withdrawing greater amounts of blood than leeches could extract. In such a case, "the instrument used . . . for bleeding the human subject [was] a Lancet" or fleam.[72]

The illustrated example is typical. The engraved case houses a simple spring-loaded mechanism that can be exposed by a sliding cover on one side. Affixed to the opposite side is a trigger used to plunge the curved steel blade into a vein. "In general [it was used] at the bend of the elbow, or upon the foot."[73]

Most of the fleams used in America were made in England, like the "brass fleams [and] lancets . . . imported from London" by Isaac Greenleaf, but a few American-made examples are recorded. They were by John Vogler (1783–1881), a silversmith and gunsmith who worked in Salem, North Carolina; Peter Derr (1793–1868), a Berks County, Pennsylvania, metalworker; and George Tiemann, cutler and surgical-instrument maker, whose company was active in New York City from 1827 to 1899.[74]

BLEEDING BOWL
229

EUROPE OR ENGLAND, 1750–1800
BRASS (COPPER 67.98, ZINC 31.12,
LEAD 0.42), IRON

H. 1 7/8" (4.8 CM), DIAM.
6 1/2" (16.5 CM)
58.1118

"THE OPENING OF A VEIN is termed Phlebotomy . . . also venesection or bleeding. Venesection is commonly applied to blood-letting at the bend of the arm," although sites at every part of the body were used from the temple to the ankle. The quantity of blood let at any given time could vary depending on the physician's judgment about the nature of the illness, its severity, or the location of the infection. Generally it was performed in conjunction with "active purging, tobacco enemata, warm bath, low diet, perfect rest and the apartment kept darkened. Blood is to be abstracted from the system [and] should be allowed to flow until fainting ensues . . . whenever the constitution has rallied from the effects of the first bleeding, which generally happens in four or six hours, . . . a second bleeding should be repeated . . . but the quantity required then to produce fainting, will generally be very small."[75]

The wrought bleeding bowl shown here was used to catch small amounts of blood from the arm of a patient in a second or subsequent bloodletting. The outer rim is reenforced by being wrapped around an iron wire, while the cutout has had a half-round fillet brazed to the lower edge for the same purpose.

Some larger bleeding bowls have graduations like those on measuring cups. The lack of graduations in this example suggests its use by a skilled physician who knew when to stop the flow of blood simply by monitoring the patient's state.

BARBER'S BASIN
230

PROBABLY EUROPE OR ENGLAND,
POSSIBLY AMERICA, 1700–1800
BRASS (COPPER 64.03, ZINC 28.51,
LEAD 3.06, IRON 0.16, TIN 0.11)

L. 13 11/16" (34.7 CM),
W. 10 1/2" (26.7 CM),
H. 2 1/4" (5.8 CM)
66.1455

SAMUEL JOHNSON defined a barber as "man who shaves the beard" and a barber chirurgeon as "man who joins the practice of surgery to the barber's trade; such as were all surgeons formerly, but now it is used only for a low practiser of surgery."[76]

Among the essential tools of a barber were "a basin for the Beard of tin or china." He also needed a razor, "a strip of calves leather . . . impregnated with . . . emery, crushed slate, brick-dust [or] razor stone [used for sharpening], to make the razor cut more sweetly [and] a piece of white soap [which] is better for the beard than compounded soap, rendering it softer so that the razor cuts more sweetly."[77]

The wrought basin illustrated here is identical in appearance to that pictured by François-Alexandre-Pierre Garsault and described by Randle Holme in his *Academy of Armory* as a "barbers Washing Bason or Trimming Bason [which] generally have rounds cut in the rim or edge thereof, to compass about a mans Throat or Neck."[78]

Although brass seems not to have been the preferred material for barbers' basins–probably because it was more expensive than tinned sheet iron or earthenware–it was used on occasion, and must certainly have been among "all sorts of brass . . . Barbers Trimmings [which] William Scandrett, Brass-Founder, living about the center of the Fly-Market [in New York City] makes and sells."[79]

STANDISH
231

ENGLAND, 1720–50
BRASS (COPPER 71.09, ZINC 26.91,
LEAD 1.07, TIN 0.39, IRON 0.32)

H. 5 3/4" (14.6 CM), W. 9"
(22.8 CM), D. 8 1/8" (20.6 CM)
64.584

THE STANDISH (inkstand) was an essential part of a literate individual's personal possessions during the eighteenth and nineteenth centuries. As illustrated here, most had an inkwell, a container for sealing wax, and a sand or pounce pot. They were almost always arranged on a rectangular tray.

The example here, being trefoil shape, is quite unusual. The conjoined semicircles that form the edge of the tray were also used in the design of a number of three-, six-, eight-, ten-, and twelve-lobe silver salvers made in London during the 1720s.[80]

It was precisely at that time that Richard Boyle, third earl of Burlington (1694–1753), built Chiswick House near London. In the design he used conjoined semicircles.[81] In doing so, Lord Burlington followed prototypical designs published by the architect Andrea Palladio (1518–80), which he encountered at the end of his grand tour in Italy in 1715.

Lord Burlington was the most active proponent of Palladian architecture in England during the first half of the eighteenth century, but many less-well-known and anonymous artisans incorporated Palladian design precepts into their work as well. Those features, as they relate to this standish, were specified among the marginal notes of the English architect Inigo Jones's (1573–1651) personal copy of Palladio's *I Quattro Libri dell' Architettura*. He wrote under the engraving of the Roman temple of Galluce that it was "formed all out of circles [being of] a . . . perfectly . . . round form . . . divided into ten faces [semicircular niches] which, next to the Pantheon, is the greatest round [building] in Rome."[82]

An English language edition of the volume was published in 1715 and was championed by Lord Burlington and others for decades. Palladian influence is visible in this standish. The lobed tray is cast with an integral border and applied feet; the inkpot, wafer box, and removable sander are made of seamed sheet metal. The inkpot and box have removable cast lids.

STANDISH

232

PROBABLY CHINA, POSSIBLY
ENGLAND, 1750–70
PAKTONG (COPPER 37.53, ZINC 60.32,
NICKEL 10.37, LEAD 0.90, IRON 0.23)

H. 8 1/4" (21.0 CM), W. 15 3/4"
(40.0 CM), D. 6 1/4" (15.9 CM)
60.509

"BEFORE DEMONSTRATING the principles of handwriting, it is necessary to explain the manner in which one places oneself and how one must hold the quill. These two things are important; one consists of holding the body in a correct posture and the other with the ease of execution."[83] These observations preceded a sixteen-page explanation about how to write correctly, in Denis Diderot's monumental mid eighteenth-century encyclopedia.

The length and detail of the explanation underscore the fact that literacy and the ability to write were available to only a few prior to the advent of widespread public education in the nineteenth century. For those who did know how to write, it was as much an art as a form of communication. Properly done, it required a number of accoutrements including "a choice pen-knife . . . a store of quills . . . pure white smooth grain'd, well gum'd paper . . . the best Ink . . . Gumsandrick

beaten into Powder . . . and tyed up in a fine Linen-cloth [to] pounce your Paper . . . a flat Ruler [and] Indian Black dust, or fine sand, to throw on Letters."[84]

The standish housed many and sometimes all of these necessary objects in an organized fashion. Most standishes were small and had containers for ink and blotting sand only. The example illustrated here, composed almost entirely of cast parts riveted together and originally silvered, is larger and more elaborate. Its portable nature is indicated by the centrally located bail. The frame also houses a vessel for sealing wax and one for a small hand bell. The cantilevered candle arms rotate in their sockets and hold candles that provide light for writing and heat for melting sealing wax. The frame may have originally been fitted with a candle screen.[85]

A.

B.

INK POTS

233 a,b

A. PROBABLY ENGLAND, CA. 1766
BRASS (COPPER 66.11, ZINC 32.27,
LEAD 1.40), LEAD
H. 1 1/2" (3.8 CM), W. 2 1/8"
(5.4 CM), D. 2 1/8" (5.4 CM)
64.88

B. PROBABLY ENGLAND, CA. 1771
BRASS (COPPER 76.92, ZINC 18.03,
TIN 2.77, LEAD 1.72, IRON 0.47), LEAD
H. 1 1/2" (3.8 CM), W. 2 3/16"
(5.6 CM), D. 2 3/16" (5.6 CM)
61.941

THESE SMALL, lead ink pots with engraved sheet-brass tops, one with interior compartments and one without, were among the least expensive and most popular metal containers of their type. Made in England, they were imported in quantity by American hardware merchants, as evidenced in the October 5, 1752, edition of the *Pennsylvania Gazette*, which carried advertisements by three men–John Ogdon, Randle Mitchell, and John Smith–each of whom proclaimed that he had "just imported . . . brass ink-pots . . . from London." Similarly, the accounts of their New York City counterparts, Jonathan and John Holmes, record the sale of "1 doz. [English] brass ink pots" to Hendrick Wessels on July 18, 1749, and "1/2 doz. brass japanned ink pots" to Mrs. Garty Willson the day after.[86]

William Bradford (1722–91), the famous author, journalist, founder, and editor of the *Weekly Advertiser, or Pennsylvania Journal*, America's most widely circulated eighteenth-century newspaper, was closely connected with these diminutive vessels. He sold "brass and leather Ink-Pots [as well as an extensive variety of other writing materials and books] at the sign of the Bible in Second Street," Philadelphia.[87] The example pictured here bearing the initials "WB" is believed to have been owned by him personally and may have been used when he coined and first wrote the phrase "join or die" as well as influential editorials strongly in favor of the colonial cause prior to and during the American Revolution. The identity of the owner of the other example pictured here is unknown.

WAX JACK
234

ENGLAND, PROBABLY BIRMINGHAM, 1750–1800
BRASS (COPPER 72.07,
ZINC 23.80, LEAD 3.32, TIN 0.35,
IRON 0.24, SILVER 0.14), IRON

H. 5 7/8" (14.9 CM), W. 4 1/4"
(10.8 CM), DIAM. 3 1/4" (8.3 CM)
61.1629

PRIOR TO THE INVENTION of the envelope with gummed flap in 1840, letters were folded on themselves and closed with a lump or disc of sealing wax.[88] That wax was a hard, brittle, tenacious, and adhesive mixture of venice turpentine, beeswax, shellac, and a colorant, usually vermilion. In order to render it soft and sticky, it had to be heated. An ordinary table candlestick would have sufficed, but in the eighteenth century small taper sticks and wax jacks were used. The former were nothing more than normal candlesticks reduced in size by about two-thirds. The latter were of a completely different design and held a candle that was also radically different from those used for light.

The jacks were made in silver and silverplate, but cheaper brass examples were more widespread. English wax jacks made in Birmingham were marketed widely using trade catalogues.[89] The simplest examples were like the one shown here. More expensive models had the taper mounted horizontally on a revolving drum. Both types consisted of a cast base that was bolted or peened to an upright that supported the framework for the taper. They were made in at least three different sizes and were also offered with or without the wax. For a few pence more, a small conical extinguisher with chain, like that on this example, could be included.

The underside of this example has an engraved "H," probably the initial of an owner.

SEAL
235

UNITED STATES, POSSIBLY
PHILADELPHIA, PENNSYLVANIA, 1796–1800
BRASS (COPPER 76.51, ZINC 20.90,
LEAD 1.60, TIN 0.29, IRON 0.11), BOXWOOD

H. 2 1/8" (2.8 CM),
DIAM. 1 3/8" (3.5 CM)
66.79

A SEAL IS A "PUNCHEON, or piece of metal . . . usually either round or oval, on which are engraven the arms, device, &c. of some prince, state, community, magistrate, or private person, often with a legend or inscription; the impression of which in wax serves to make acts, instruments, &c. authentic."[90]

Their production was considered to be an area of specialty within the craft of silversmithing, even though they were often made of brass or semiprecious stone. Joseph Cook, goldsmith and jeweler at the Federal Manufactory and European Repository Wholesale and Retail Warehouse in Philadelphia, was a member of that fraternity. He advertised in the March 2, 1793, issue of the *Aurora General Advertiser* that "counting house and watch seals [were] to be had ready made of the best pinchbeck, not inferior in colour to gold, with the initials of any person's name elegantly engraved from the famous Lockington London cypher-book for the moderate price of one dollar." He also stated that "Company, Church, State and County-seals and all manner

of engraving [were] executed [by him] in a masterly style and proportionately low" in price.

The diminutive seal illustrated here came from a workshop like his and may have been made for the prickly political journalist William Cobbett (1763–1835). An Englishman by birth, Cobbett became so outspoken against social injustice that he felt obliged to leave England in 1792 for his safety. After a brief sojourn in France, he settled in Philadelphia, where he adopted the pseudonym Peter Porcupine and published his *Political Censer* and *Porcupine's Gazette*. His acerbic writing style gained him strong support but even stronger criticism, sometimes from members of his own party, as with Benjamin Russell, editor of the *Boston Centinel*, who commented that "Cobbett was never supported by the Federalists as a judicious writer in their cause; but was merely [kept as a] Fretful Porcupine . . . to hunt Jacobinic skunks, foxes, and serpents." American political cartoonists also depicted Cobbett as a porcupine dispensing verbal quills against opponents. His bombastic style forced him to return to England in 1800.[91]

SEAL

236

UNITED STATES, PROBABLY
NEW HAMPSHIRE, 1803–38
BRASS (COPPER 74.20, ZINC 21.51,
LEAD 2.50, TIN 0.74, IRON 0.38)

DIAM. 1 3/8" (3.5 CM),
H. 13/16" (2.1 CM)
61.6

THE CHARLESTOWN TURNPIKE CORPORATION was founded in
New Hampshire in 1803. It oversaw a 15-mile road that extended from
Charlestown, on the Connecticut River, east to Lempster. The turnpike
was part of a general effort in road building that began in the 1790s
and lasted through the first decade of the nineteenth century. In New
England alone during that era, 240 incorporated turnpike companies
were responsible for more than 3,700 miles of road.[92]

   The builders of the Charlestown turnpike had probably hoped to
link it to a then-developing hub of roads radiating out of the Boston area
to the nether reaches of northern and western New England, but alternate routes through Manchester, New Hampshire, and Brattleboro,
Vermont, siphoned traffic and revenues away. That and increasing public
dissatisfaction with private turnpikes caused New Hampshire to enact
a law in 1838 that permitted town selectmen to condemn turnpikes and

take them over as public roads, dooming the Charlestown Turnpike
Corporation and many others to closure.[93]

   The seal illustrated here, a cast slug that has been engraved with the
turnpike corporation's emblem intaglio and in reverse, was used by its
officers to impress that image into a disc of sealing wax on official documents, thereby certifying their legitimacy. Seals of this type, whether
personal, corporate, state, or federal, were not engraved by brass founders
but by silversmiths such as James Smithers, who "performs all Manner
of Engraving in Gold, Silver, Copper, Steel, and all other Metals–Coats
of Arms, and Seals, done in the neatest Manner." John Ward Gilman
(1741–1823), working in Exeter, New Hampshire, also made seals,
although he is not known to have advertised that he did so. One example
engraved by him for a notary public is presently recorded.[94]

STAMP
237

PROBABLY ENGLAND, POSSIBLY
AMERICA, 1750–1800
BRASS (COPPER 79.71, ZINC 14.93,
TIN 1.79, LEAD 2.93, IRON 0.33,
ANTIMONY 0.18, SILVER 0.13), WOOD

L. 3 1/4" (8.2 CM), H. 1 7/8"
(4.7 CM), W. 1 1/4" (3.1 CM)
59.146

ON APRIL 25, 1768, James Smithers, like many of his competitors, proclaimed his ability to execute any kind of engraving. In addition, he "cuts Stamps, Brands and metal cuts for Prints."[95]

Smithers cut his seals intaglio so that when pressed into sealing wax, a three-dimensional image was created. By contrast, he cut his stamps cameo-fashion so that when their surfaces were inked, they printed a flat, two-dimensional image. Edward H. Knight, who defined a hand stamp as "an engraved block by which a mark may be delivered by pressure," noted that "they are made for several different purposes, among which are canceling, dating, addressing and official."[96]

The example here was probably a personal stamp, with its owner's initials "GM" flanking the dog, the central and most important visual and symbolic element in its design. Below, the motto in Latin, "FIDELITAS IPSA," always the favored language for stamps and seals, translates as "faithfulness itself." This is a clear and direct allusion through a pictorial device and the scholar's language to the most desirable attribute of the dog. Having "a natural share of courage, an angry and ferocious disposition, . . . the dog in his savage state [is] a formidable enemy to all other animals; but these readily give way to very different qualities in the domestic dog . . . he is more faithful even than the most boasted among men." The owner of this seal saw himself in the same light and, through its impression, sought to convince others of the same.[97]

PASTILLE BURNER
238

PROBABLY NORTHERN EUROPE,
POSSIBLY ENGLAND, 1670–1740
BRASS (COPPER 72.58,
ZINC 25.45, LEAD 1.63, TIN 0.17),
WOOD, IRON, COPPER

H. 5 3/4" (14.6 CM),
L. 12 1/2" (31.7 CM),
W. 5 3/4" (14.6 CM)
59.2904

PASTILLE IS "A DRY COMPOSITION, composed of odorous resins, mixed with aromatic woods or drugs pulverized, and incorporated with mucilages of gum tragacanth, yielding a fragrant smell when burnt in a perfuming pan, to clear and scent the air of a chamber."[98] Pastille was typically formed into a small lump or cone, which, when lighted, would smolder for a period of time diffusing its pleasing scent.

Pastille burners, also called cassolettes, were made of silver, porcelain, earthenware, brass, or iron and are distinct from the perfume burner, which vaporizes a liquid perfume from a container set above and heated by a small spirit lamp. While the latter seem to have been favored in Germany and to a lesser extent in France,

the former had more widespread popularity. Pastille burners were recorded in European and British household inventories. The example shown here may not be much different from the "p[er]fuming panne of brass" itemized in the winter parlor of the Englishman Sir Thomas Kyston's house, Hengrave Hall, in 1603.[99] Kyston and his contemporaries would have considered such amenities very desirable in households that had open cooking fires but lacked central plumbing. The example shown here, with a wrought body and lid and cast legs and finial, differs little in usage from modern incense burners. The lid hinged opposite the handle opens to expose a removable iron liner, which contained the smoldering perfumed charcoal.

HARNESS BELL

239

WILLIAM BARTON, JR. (1762–1849)
EAST HAMPTON, CONNECTICUT, 1808–46
BRONZE (COPPER 80.89, TIN 16.40,
LEAD 1.77, SILVER 0.45)

DIAM. 2 1/8" (5.4 CM),
H. 2 5/8" (6.7 CM)
53.155.46

WILLIAM BARTON, JR., was born near Windsor, Connecticut, on November 26, 1762. When of age, he apparently worked with his father, an armorer in Springfield, Massachusetts, during the Revolution. At the war's end "he returned to [his birthplace] and manufactured pistols and other warlike implements until 1790 when he went to New York."[100] In New York he listed himself in the city directories as a blacksmith until 1801. The following year he was recorded simply as a smith, and finally in 1806 he was termed a brass founder.

From New York City "he came to . . . East Hampton in the spring of 1808, and commenced the manufacture of hand and sleigh-bells." He is reputed to have been the first artisan in this country to devise single-piece castings for bells of this type, as "prior to this time they had been cast in two parts and soldered together."[101]

Spherical harness bells are not peculiar to America. They have a long tradition of use in England, documented to the fifteenth century and possibly earlier. Called rumblers, because of the constant noise made by a loose internal clapper when in motion, they were made by numerous English founders including Edward Sellers of York; Robert Wells of Aldbourne, Wiltshire; and John Latham of Wigan. Even though Sellers was working from 1678 to the late 1750s, Wells from 1760 to 1780, and Latham from 1759 to 1783, their rumblers are virtually indistinguishable in appearance from the harness bells made in Connecticut.[102]

MEMORANDUM BOOK
240

JEFFREY LANG (1707–58)
SALEM, MASSACHUSETTS, 1746
BRASS (COPPER 71.03, ZINC 27.54,
LEAD 0.82), IVORY

L. 3 3/4" (9.5 CM), W. 2 1/8"
(5.4 CM), D. 1/4" (0.6 CM)
52.127

ON SEPTEMBER 29, 1768, Peter Goelet advertised in the *New-York Journal, or General Advertiser* that he had "just imported in the last vessels from London and Bristol . . . ivory leaved memorandum books." Similarly, Joseph and Daniel Waldo of Boston let it be known in 1748 that they had "imported from London [to be] sold by Wholesale or Retail at the cheapest rates . . . Memorandum Books [and] Pencils."[103]

When the silversmith Jeffrey Lang, who worked in Salem, Massachusetts, from about 1727 until his death, was asked to supply a memorandum book, he undoubtedly had in mind imported English examples when he fabricated the diminutive one shown here. The two covers are made of sheet metal and rotate on a small rivet that pierces them near the bottom edge. The chased, hinged clasp riveted near the top edge holds the two covers in alignment to protect five ivory pages, and the left edge of the top cover is shaped into a slender tube for a pencil.

The owner, Daniel Gott, was born a fourth-generation American on September 2, 1724, to Samuel and Hannah Gott. He spent his entire life in Wenham, a town founded six miles north of Salem in 1643 but that still in the 1840s, with "no compact village," had a population of only 698 persons who discouraged new settlement. Its citizens elected Gott "constable for the east end of the town" in 1748, "deer reef" in 1749, and "surveyor of highways for the west district in 1755."[104] In each of these tasks he would have had occasion to use his memorandum book. Gott had his name and town engraved on the cover to distinguish him from his cousins of the same name who lived in neighboring towns.

SHOE BUCKLE
241

ATTRIBUTED TO JAMES SMITH
PHILADELPHIA, PENNSYLVANIA, 1750–77
BRASS (COPPER 71.95, ZINC 24.99,
LEAD 1.71, IRON 0.60, TIN 0.20)

L. 2 9/16" (6.5 CM),
W. 2 3/8" (6.0 CM),
D. 3/4" (1.9 CM)
83.60

WHEN SAMUEL PEPYS penned "this day I began to put buckles on my shoes" in his diary on January 22, 1659, he marked the beginning of a change in fashion. Gold, silver, silver plate, brass, steel, paste, and even earthenware buckles ornamented the shoes of the fashion conscious from that time until the 1790s. In 1791 Birmingham's bucklemakers, who had "supplied the whole demand [in much of England and] for America, Holland, France, Germany, Italy and Spain," petitioned the Prince of Wales for protection for their declining fortunes, but to no avail.[105] The humble shoelace prevailed.

When buckles were the preferred mode of fastening shoes, numerous American hardware merchants stocked them, such as Joseph and Daniel Waldo of Boston, who "imported from London . . . a great variety of Shoe and Knee and other Buckles [to be] sold by Wholesale or Retail at the cheapest Rates."[106]

For those who chose to buy from an American craftsman, James Smith provided an alternative. On December 14, 1752, he advertised

that he had relocated his shop "to within three doors of the corner of Market Street in Second Street, at the sign of the Founders Arms, where he continues to make all sorts of brass work [including] sleeve buttons [and] shoe buckles."[107] Smith advertised fairly regularly in the Philadelphia newspapers, sometimes in conjunction with John Winter, and always included shoe buckles among his offerings.

His customers' perceptions aside, Smith was only partly responsible for the complete buckles he sold. His efforts would have involved casting the brass frame and fitting the iron chape and tongue, which is missing on the example shown here. The iron fitting was almost certainly made in Birmingham, Sheffield, or one of their smaller satellite towns, where "a great number of men, women and children are employed . . . as chape makers, filers and forgers. . . . large quantities [of their work] are vended both at home and abroad."[108]

A.

B.

BUTTONS

242 a,b

A. UNITED STATES, POSSIBLY
PHILADELPHIA, PENNSYLVANIA, 1811–32
BRASS (COPPER 94.00, ZINC 4.80,
LEAD 0.80, ARSENIC 0.10)
DIAM. 1 5/16" (2.9 CM), D. 3/8" (0.9 CM)
GG.505

B. UNITED STATES, POSSIBLY
PHILADELPHIA, PENNSYLVANIA, 1811–32
BRASS (COPPER 74.08, ZINC 22.10,
LEAD 0.52, ARSENIC 0.17)
DIAM. 1 5/16" (2.9 CM), D. 3/8" (0.9 CM)
GG.506

GEORGE WASHINGTON "on the day of his inauguration appeared dressed in a complete suit of HOMESPUN CLOATHS." The New York City engraver William Rollinson was employed "to chase the arms of the United States upon a set of gilt buttons for the coat which was worn by" him.[109]

Upon completion of his first term, Washington was popularly reelected, and with his death on December 14, 1799, "veneration for the most illustrious hero that ever graced the annals of time" began. In 1811 the Washington Association, composed entirely of young men, was formed to "perpetuate the political and moral virtues of the founding fathers." The Washington Benevolent Society, organized one year later, "celebrated Washington's birth by a numerous procession, the ringing of bells,

a display of appropriate banners and ensigns."[110] The association, a uniformed military corps, joined about two thousand of the Benevolent Society, the Washington Artillery, and five companies of Washington's Guards to march the streets of Philadelphia on February 22, 1815, in annual celebration of their hero's birth.

Their uniforms were probably similar to the "blue cloth coat with two rows of yellow buttons" of the Light Artillery Corps of Washington Grays. The buttons illustrated here, two of twenty-three related patterns presently recorded, were most likely those worn by members of these various organizations. The designs and mottos stamped on the buttons capsulize the esteem their owners had for the country's first president and the ideals that his memory embodied.[111]

The design incorporating the initials of the thirteen original states within interlocking circles is adapted from that of the fugio cent, the first coin minted under the authority of the United States government, struck at New Haven, Connecticut, and possibly elsewhere. On July 6, 1787, Congress stipulated that one side of those coins be struck with thirteen circles linked together with a small circle in the middle.

The design of the circular reserve enclosing "LONG LIVE THE PRESIDENT" is conceptually very close to the design of marks used by the Philadelphia silversmiths Samuel Williamson (w. 1794–1813) and Thomas Fletcher and Sidney Gardiner (w. 1808–27) and the Philadelphia coppersmiths and pewterers Benjamin and Joseph Harbeson, Jr. (w. 1783–1824).

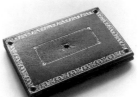

BUTTON PATTERN
CARD

243

SCOVILL MANUFACTURING COMPANY
WATERBURY, CONNECTICUT, 1850–1900
BRASS (COPPER 80.61, ZINC 17.99, LEAD 0.89,
TIN 0.17, IRON 0.16, SILVER 0.15), LEATHER,
PAPER, VELVET, SILK

H. 11 3/8" (28.9 CM), W. CLOSED: 7 5/8"
(19.3 CM), OPEN: 31 1/2" (80.0 CM),
D. 1 3/4" (4.4 CM)
DOCUMENT 77

BRASS ROLLING was first undertaken in Waterbury, Connecticut, in 1802 by the firm of Abel Porter and Company, makers of gilt brass buttons. In 1806 Porter's company was purchased by Frederick Leavenworth, David Hayden, and James Mitchell Lamson Scovill. That partnership lasted until 1827, when the first two partners sold their interest to the latter's brother, William H. Scovill. In 1850 the brothers created a joint stock corporation with several others to form Scovill Manufacturing Company, which continued brass production until 1974.

"Their business continued to grow steadily from its beginning, and many new branches of manufacture have been added. Besides sheet brass and German silver in all its varieties, they also made gilt and covered buttons, brass hinges, coal-oil burners and lamps, brass thimbles, and a variety of other small articles of brass. . . . Their works at Waterbury are very large, the buildings extending in one line nearly a thousand feet, being for the most part three stories in height, and all

built of brick. They have fine water power with a fall of thirty-six feet, operating one large overshot wheel and two turbines. In addition to these they have an engine of one hundred horsepower. Besides their work in Waterbury, they have a large factory in New Haven, where they make brass clocks and photograph cases and trimmings and one in New York for photographic apparatus."[112]

Buttons made up an extensive portion of the firm's business. Many of the company's work areas were devoted solely to this production, which numbered into millions per year. A visitor to the Scovill button shop in 1836 described it, having "witnessed [there] most of the numerous processes in making buttons. The melted red-hot liquid is turned into molds, making narrow plates say 15 or 18 inches long, 4 to 5 inches wide and half or 3/4 of an inch in thickness. These plates are then rolled down to the proper thickness for buttons between cylinders which are nearly a foot in diameter. Then the buttons are cut out. Then the buttons are stamped in a mold. The mold gives the figures, let-

ters, or whatever is desired for the outside of the buttons, and gives them the flat, convex or concave shape. . . . The eyes cut from wire are then applied to their place and fastened there; the solder is then placed around the eye, and being laid on a plate, the buttons are heated, so as to appear red-hot. They then undergo various processes–fixing round the eye–fixing the edge, making the sides smooth, encasing on the outside of figured buttons, etc. They are then gilded by dipping them in an amalgum of gold and mercury or quicksilver and then made smooth and bright. Everything is done by machinery. Every process upon the buttons is done in an instant, as it were."[113]

The pattern card illustrated here, with 172 separately numbered buttons, served as a portable eye-appealing means of marketing the company's vast production. The plain, die-stamped, chased, engraved, flat, convex, gilt, silvered, and lacquered buttons were a convenient and precise reference for potential customers–probably fancy hardware merchants and haberdashers–to use in ordering stock.[114]

LORGNETTE
244

PROBABLY FRANCE, 1810–50
BRASS (COPPER 68.21,
ZINC 30.85, LEAD 0.66),
GLASS, STEEL

CLOSED: L. 4 1/2" (11.4 CM),
W. 1 3/4" (4.5 CM),
D. 1/2" (1.3 CM)
59.154

WE DO NOT KNOW who invented eyeglasses or when, but an Italian monk, "Friar Jourdan de Rivalto, in a Sermon written in the Year 1305, says that it is not twenty years since the Art of making Spectacles was found out, and that it is indeed one of the happiest and most useful Inventions in the World."[115] Prior to that, literate persons suffering from defective or degenerating sight read through water-filled globes or, more often, had sighted people read to them.

"Spectacles are made in great varieties of forms, and ornamented according to fashion, or to the fancy of the wearer. The frames are made of all kinds of materials, such as gold, silver, steel, pearl, tortoise-shell, ivory, bone . . . wood [and brass]. The lenses are usually made of glass, but the better sorts are made of natural crystal, and are known by the name of pebble-spectacles."[116]

Twin lenses hinged into a hand-held case were known as a lorgnette. They were popular throughout the nineteenth century, particularly in France, and were not always for corrective purposes. In 1870 Robert Tomes observed that "the functions of . . . eyeglasses are much abused. . . . Nine tenths of the people, male and female, who are constantly eyeing the universe and each other through glass, require no other medium than the one provided by Nature. Nothing can be more ill bred . . . than . . . surveying an opposite neighbor at the theatre with a lorgnette."[117]

The example shown here has the magnifying lenses held into the frames with small tabs bolted together on the circumference. The case is ornamented with a vermicelli-like pattern that was probably stamped. The two halves are held together by short rivets with steel washers.

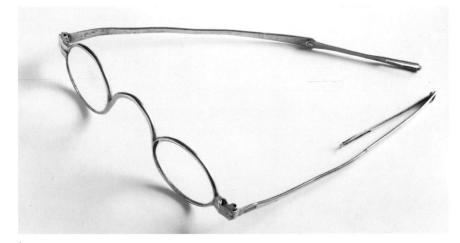

A.

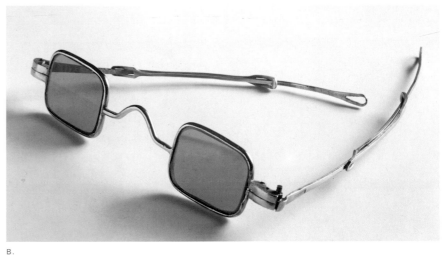

B.

SPECTACLES
245 a,b

A. ATTRIBUTED TO PETER HALL
PHILADELPHIA, PENNSYLVANIA, 1818–24
BRASS (COPPER 72.19, ZINC 25.09,
TIN 1.83, LEAD 0.61), GLASS
H. 1 1/8" (2.8 CM), L. 6 1/2" (16.5 CM),
W. 6 3/8" (16.2 CM)
67.1384

B. ATTRIBUTED TO EDWARD H. SCHILD
BALTIMORE, MARYLAND, 1870–90
BRASS (COPPER 73.12, ZINC 24.96,
TIN 0.96, LEAD 0.81), GLASS
H. 1 1/4" (3.2 CM), L. 6 1/8" (15.6 CM),
W. 4 3/4" (12.1 CM)
61.1170

"SPECTACLES ARE AN OPTIC MACHINE, consisting of two lenses set in a frame, and applied on the nose, to assist in defects of the organ of sight." They vary considerably in size, shape, material, and the manner in which they are held in place. However, during the eighteenth century nothing was "more common than to meet with spectacles, the glasses of which are of a dark muddy Colour (which are imperfectly ground) and generally mounted in Copper-Frames silvered, of which very large quantities are every Year imported, and dispensed all over England [and America], and which are very detrimental to the Eyes."[118]

By the nineteenth century, England and the United States had numbers of men practicing optometry. Even more sold spectacles, which were usually chosen by a customer after trying on many pairs to deter-

mine which was liked best. One such vendor was Charles Pool of New York City, who offered thermometers, barometers, clocks, hydrometers, and "spectacles for long and short sighted eyes, mounted in gold, silver and steel, with the finest white or colored glasses, or Brazil pebbles. Tortoise shell spectacles, peculiar for their lightness and uninterruption of dressed hair [and] Spectacles with shades to screen weak and inflamed eyes from too intense light."[119] Many of those he offered were similar to these two pairs, both of which have lenses set into slender yet strong and adjustable frames.

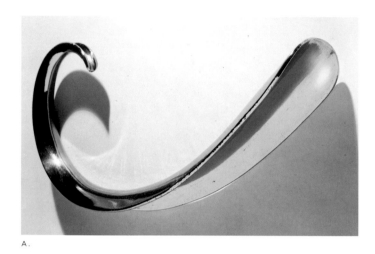

A.

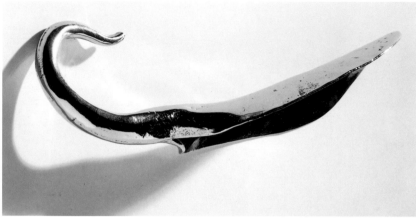

B.

SHOEHORNS

246 a,b

A. PROBABLY ENGLAND, 1700–1800

BRASS (COPPER 65.90,

ZINC 31.88, LEAD 2.06)

L. 8 3/8" (21.2 CM), W. 1 3/4" (4.5 CM),

D. 4 1/2" (11.4 CM)

58.2373

B. ENGLAND OR AMERICA, 1740–1800

BRASS (COPPER 68.21, ZINC 25.37,

LEAD 3.60, TIN 2.03)

L. 6 1/2" (16.5 CM), W. 2"

(5.1 CM), D. 2 1/4" (5.7 CM)

58.1117

WHEN CHARLES II ENDED ten years of exile in Europe and reclaimed the English throne for the Stuarts in 1660, he brought with him a Spanish wife and many up-to-date Continental styles. Among them was a heightened interest in the shoe as fashionable footwear for men. Prior to that time, boots, often extending to the knee, were worn as often as shoes.

Neither was more difficult than the other to put on, but the backs of close-fitting shoes usually broke down, became frayed, and lost their shape quickly when put on feet unaided. This situation was easily corrected–thus extending the life of a pair of shoes–with a shoehorn, which was defined by Samuel Johnson in *A Dictionary of the English Language* as "a horn used to facilitate the admission of the foot into a narrow shoe."[120]

As indicated by its name, many were made of animal horn, but silver, wood, and brass were also used. The examples illustrated here, although simple in appearance, were difficult to fabricate. Their anonymous makers, who hammered them to shape, had to simultaneously stretch and bend the metal longitudinally and latitudinally, a technique requiring considerable experience and dexterity.[121]

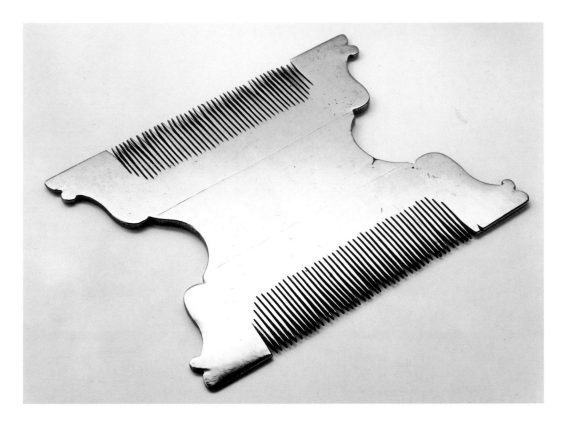

WIGMAKER'S COMB
247

EUROPE OR ENGLAND, 1680–1720
BRASS (COPPER 62.16, ZINC 36.28,
LEAD 1.44)

L. 3 3/4" (9.5 CM), W. 3"
(7.6 CM), W. 3/32" (0.3 CM)
59.29

WHEN LOUIS XIV, king of France from 1643 to 1715, and Charles II, England's king from 1660 to 1685, began wearing long, flowing, fully curled wigs, many of their subjects hastened to do the same. As a result of that vogue, wigmakers in Europe, England, and even America enjoyed an unprecedented period of activity for the following one hundred years.

Using human hair and horsehair, wigmakers created and dressed a great variety of wigs from simple to complex, curled or straight, powdered or in natural colors. To do so they required, as part of a fully equipped salon, "a wigmaker's wooden head of elm or ash, sissors, large and small . . . iron screws . . . a loom for braiding, a wigmaker's vice, a wooden ruler . . . wooden curlers . . . a cylindrical oven, pressing irons [and] combs, coarse and fine."[122]

The illustrated example is one of five different types of wigmakers' combs, which were categorized by the eighteenth-century French encyclopedist Denis Diderot as "dressing combs, dressing the tail combs, banded [curved] chignon combs, unravelling combs [and] two sided unravelling combs."[123]

The two sided unraveling comb is pictured and discussed a second time in Diderot's *Encyclopédie* in an explanation of the combmaker's craft. While such combs were often of animal horn or wood, this example is made from a thick plate of rolled sheet metal. After the ends were cut to shape, the straight edges were chamfered, and the teeth were sawn individually. The teeth on both sides are spaced in a fine pattern, but most were fine on one side and coarse on the other.[124]

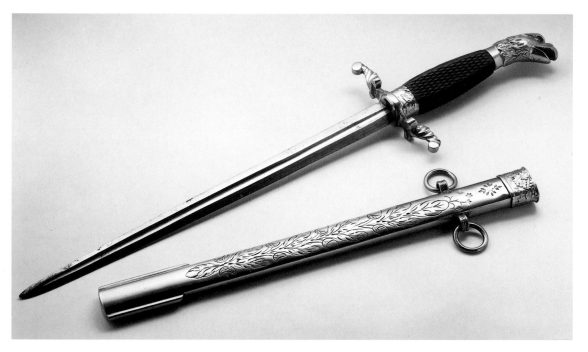

DIRK AND SCABBARD

248

UNITED STATES, PROBABLY
NEW YORK, 1797–1803
BRASS (COPPER 74.67, ZINC 20.91,
LEAD 3.02, TIN 0.94,
IRON 0.32), STEEL, HORN

L. 15" (38.1 CM), W. 3 1/4"
(8.2 CM), D. 5/8" (1.6 CM)

55.96.4.2

DIRKS WERE WORN by United States naval personnel soon after that branch of the service was instituted in 1775. Even so, they were mentioned in regulations only sporadically between 1802 and 1876 and were never a prescribed part of the uniform. As an option, worn at the officer or midshipman's discretion, they could and did vary considerably in design, shape, length, and embellishment. Not until 1869 do regulations provide any record of their appearance, which was very similar to the example shown here, having a straight, double-edge blade and an eagle-head pommel.

This dirk is much earlier in date, as judged by its ownership, construction, and ornament. When acquired by the museum, it had a history of ownership in the Pickman family of Salem, Massachusetts. The original owner may have been William Pickman (1747–1815), who "with the

establishment of the Federal government . . . was appointed Naval Officer for the Port of Salem and Beverly," a post he held until 1803.[125]

Eagle-head pommels were quite popular on American edged weapons throughout the nineteenth century and were made by silversmiths and swordmakers in Washington, D.C.; Baltimore; Philadelphia; New York; Middletown, Connecticut; and Chicopee, Massachusetts. The pommel shown here relates closely to those on swords documented to John Targee, who worked in New York City between 1797 and 1828.[126] The pommel on this example is cast in halves, which is typical of brass hollowware during the eighteenth and early nineteenth centuries. The die-rolled grapevine borders encircling the throat of the scabbard and hilt of the dirk were often used on early nineteenth-century domestic silver and also by Targee on his swords.

A.

B.

STAFF HEADS

249 a,b

A. UNITED STATES, POSSIBLY
MASSACHUSETTS, 1790–1830

BRASS (COPPER 64.80, ZINC 33.11,
LEAD 1.23, IRON 0.27, TIN 0.20), WOOD

H. 6 3/4" (17.2 CM), DIAM. 2 3/0" (6.1 CM)
60.93.1–.4

B. UNITED STATES, PROBABLY
BOSTON, MASSACHUSETTS, 1760–90

BRASS (COPPER 79.05, ZINC 18.30,
LEAD 1.68, TIN 0.77), WOOD

H. 8 1/4" (21.0 CM), DIAM. 2 1/8" (5.3 CM)
51.65.4

ON FEBRUARY 26, 1656, "the Burgomasters of the City of [New York] observed that . . . there is little attention paid to the subject of fire and to the necessity of keeping the chimneys clean." They therefore "appointed . . . Fire Wardens . . . who [were] authorized to visit all the houses and chimnies within the city jurisdiction" and inspect them.[127] If the chimneys were found to be a fire hazard, the wardens had the power to levy a fine on the owners.

Boston also used fire wardens and by 1711 had created a board of ten to direct operations at fires, order citizens into the bucket brigade, and arrest looters or other troublesome persons. These wardens held considerable emergency power, even extending to "blowing up or pulling downe of houses," if they deemed it would help put out a fire.[128]

Symbolic of that authority, Boston's fire wardens were assigned staffs, which they were required to have at the scene of a conflagration so that no one would question their right to direct all activities. These staffs were of wood, between five and six feet long, and each had a carved gilt wood or brass flame at the top.[129]

The metal tips were made by brass founders such as William Hunneman (1769-1856) of Charlestown, Massachusetts, who on April 12, 1820, sold "2 brass heads for fire wardens staffs" to the neighboring town of Roxbury. Again, on August 29, he sold a head for "1 fire warden's staff" to Dorchester, another nearby town.[130] Although no fire-warden staff tips by Hunneman have been identified, when they are, they will probably be similar to the illustrated examples, which relate in design to finials on Massachusetts case furniture. All five are cast hollow in halves vertically and brazed together.

SPEAKING HORN

250

UNITED STATES, PROBABLY
PHILADELPHIA, PENNSYLVANIA, 1851–64
BRASS (COPPER 67.26, ZINC 31.99,
LEAD 0.42), GERMAN SILVER

L. 14 3/4" (37.4 CM),
DIAM. 5 13/16" (14.8 CM)
67.943

THE NATIVE AMERICAN HOSE COMPANY was instituted on July 4, 1844, in Philadelphia "for the purpose of benefiting our Citizens by preserving their property from the ravages of fire." Its members changed the name shortly thereafter and incorporated it as the Vigilant Hose Company on April 12, 1851. It remained active, with one suction hand engine, two hose carriages, and a total of 1,400 feet of hose, until 1864, when it was disbanded.[131]

Like the Good Will Fire Engine Company, also in Philadelphia, the company consisted of "active members [each of whom] shall be subject to a monthly contribution of twelve and a half cents [and] shall equip himself, at his own expense, with a hat, cape and coat." The organization was run by an elected president, vice president, secretary, treasurer, board of trustees, and directors. The constitution and bylaws stipulated that "each Director shall be provided with a speaking trumpet, at the expense of the Company, to be kept in condition for immediate service, and to be delivered to the Company at the expiration or their removal from office."[132]

The plug director was in charge of selecting the hydrant or plug the company was to use for their water supply when fighting a fire. He used a megaphone like the illustrated example to call his commands to members under his direction. Unlike elaborate silver or silver-plated speaking trumpets, which were used ceremonially during parades or for presentation, this horn is unadorned and functional. The mouth-piece and cone are dovetailed of heavy-gauge metal. They and the flaring horn are brazed together. The interior of the cone has the remains of red japanning.

DOG COLLAR
251

ENGLAND OR UNITED STATES,
1790–1830
BRASS (COPPER 69.60,
ZINC 29.34, LEAD 0.65)

CIRC. 12 5/8" (32.0 CM), W. 9/16" (1.4 CM)
68.67
GIFT OF MRS. SAMUEL SCHWARTZ

ON MARCH 22, 1762, *Aris's Birmingham Gazette* advertised that "journeymen collar makers wanting employ, by immediately applying to Mr. John Cook, collar-maker at Bow near London, shall meet with great encouragement, with a hot Dinner and strong beer every day, great advance to their wages and for no small time." Specialists in collarmaking worked in all of England's major metropolitan centers. John Hollis of Birmingham was listed as a "manufacturer of iron tinned spoons, ladles and skewers [and] fancy, plated and brass dog collars."[133]

Although America seems not to have spawned similar specialists, its brass and copper workers did number dog collars among their work. Daniel Burnap, the East Windsor, Connecticut, clockmaker, recorded making "one brass strap & bell for a dog." Similarly, the daybook of William Thompson, an Alexandria, Virginia, coppersmith, records "1 dog collar" sold to Andrew McDonald.[134]

These men supplied dog collars in direct competition with the likes of William Bailey of New York, who had "for sale reasonable both wholesale and retail imported in the latest vessels from England . . . brass and leather dog collars." Purchasers of imported or locally made work could have their items personalized by men such as "John Hutt from London, engraver in general [who] engraves all sorts of arms, crests, seals & cyphers, shop bills, door plates, spoons, all sorts of plate, dog collars [and] stamps."[135]

Dog owners did not always collar their pets by choice. As early as 1765 Connecticut stipulated that "each dog permitted to go at large in this state shall wear a collar with the name of the owner." The common council of Philadelphia also enacted a law that "no dog shall be permitted to run at large in the city . . . without having a collar composed in the whole, or in part of hard metal, on which shall be distinctly engraven the name of the owner. . . . Every dog found at large, contrary to the provisions of this ordinance . . . shall be liable to be seized and killed."[136]

The collar shown here is engraved "Pray kind people let me jog, For I am Josiah Smith's good Dog" in script.[137] The name Josiah Smith was commonplace throughout England and the United States when this collar was made, making specific identification of the owner and location impossible.

FISHING REEL
252

JABEZ B. CROOK (D. 1882)
NEW YORK CITY, 1837–60
BRASS (COPPER 78.70, ZINC 17.07,
LEAD 2.73, TIN 0.12), COPPER,
STEEL, IVORY

W. 3" (7.6 CM), L. 2 7/8" (7.3 CM),
H. 2 1/4" (5.7 CM)

60.245

JABEZ B. CROOK first listed himself in New York City directories in 1837 as a machinist, but by 1843 he had added "fishingtackle" to his entry. Following that, his name continues to be listed at various addresses until 1915 as J. B. Crook and Co., importers and manufacturers of fishing tackle, with "Green Hart, Split Bamboo, Log Wood, Fly and Salmon Rods a Specialty."[138]

When Crook sold the reel shown here, he probably placed it on a rod between eight and eleven feet in length. It was designed for freshwater bait casting with a capacity of about one hundred yards of line. Within its thicker barrel plate are a series of gears that cause the spool, around which the line is wound, to revolve twice for every turn of the winding arm. This type of reel is known as a multiplier; it was used

extensively for bass, "inch for inch and pound for pound the gamest fish that swims."[139] It incorporates a ratchet, known as a click, which allows the reel to unwind and prevents the winding arm from rotating backward, inadvertently letting out line.

The reel was originally purchased from Crook's establishment by Thomas Hazard Roe (1806–1907). He was the son of William and Marie (Hazard) Roe, who settled in Newburgh, New York, in 1827 after a successful career in the wholesale grocery and import business. Thomas, a lifelong bachelor, worked for his father and apparently enjoyed sufficient leisure to pursue the "gentle art" of angling.[140]

FISHING REEL
253

GEORGE KARR
RETAILED BY JOHN J. BROWN AND CO.
NEW YORK CITY, 1846–57
BRASS (COPPER 81.35, ZINC 15.05,
LEAD 1.60, TIN 0.57), STEEL

W. 4 3/4" (12.1 CM), L. 4 1/4"
(10.9 CM), H. 2 3/4" (7.0 CM)
60.246

DURING THE NINETEENTH CENTURY, makers of fishing hardware like this freshwater, bait-casting multiplier preferred using brass because it did not rust. Consequently, it is apparent that the winding arm on this example is a replacement. The arm is equipped with a knopped counter-balance, thereby making the reel easier to use in casting. Balanced winding arms, like adjustable clicks, drags, and level winds (which are absent on this model), were nineteenth-century innovations that came about as a result of increased interest in fishing as a recreational pastime.

George Karr, the maker of this reel, entered business as a turner in 1834. By 1843 he began specializing in fishing tackle and continued to do so through 1862, after which he is no longer present in New York City directories. John J. Brown, whose name was stamped into this reel by Karr, retailed it through his "Angler's Depot and General Emporium for Hardware, Fishing Tackle & Fancy Goods [where he also sold] Superior Trout & Bass Rods, Flies, Floats, Sinkers, Flax & Green Silk Lines, Fishing Stools [and] Silver Plating Fluid for plating or replating any article of Brass, Copper or German Silver with pure Silver."[141]

Brown operated his fishing tackle business from 1846 to 1857 and might not have been included in any historical consideration of the subject were it not for the fact that he wrote America's first useful fishing manual in 1845. Entitled *The Angler's Guide*, the manual contains "a description of the more important American fish and the methods of their capture, observations on the practice of angling with extracts from English angling books, a chapter on tackle and baits with a few contributions by American fishermen, and some account of the author's own limited experience with a rod."[142] His book proved to be popular; a second edition was issued within a year, and, in all, it was reprinted seven times.

BOX IRON
254

EUROPE, POSSIBLY
SWITZERLAND, 1700–1750
BRASS (COPPER 71.98, ZINC 22.80,
LEAD 2.87, TIN 2.15), IRON, WOOD

H. 5 5/8" (14.3 CM), L. 7"
(17.7 CM), W. 3 7/8" (9.8 CM)
65.1479

BOX IRONS—variously known as flatirons, smoothing irons, and sad irons—were made throughout Europe and England and used extensively in most households. They were probably made on occasion in America during the seventeenth and eighteenth centuries but are rarely mentioned in American brass-workers' or iron-workers' advertisements and inventories. In contrast, hardware merchants such as Peter Goelet of New York did offer "smoothing irons . . . just imported in the last vessels from London and Bristol." John Smith, a hardware merchant in Philadelphia, also sold "floodgate box irons . . . just imported." These irons typically had a hinged or sliding door at the back and contained "an iron heater, which is made nearly red hot, occasionally as the iron cools."[143]

Their straightforward utilitarian purpose discouraged extensive handworked embellishment. The example shown here is, there-fore, somewhat unusual, having a thin brass plate fitted into a shallow well on the top. The plate is extensively pierced and competently engraved as a symmetrical foliate framework with birds and a seminude recumbent woman. The design follows the fashion associated with the French designers Jean Berain (ca. 1638-1711) and Daniel Marot (ca. 1663-1752) but seems to have a particular affinity to the work of Alexis Loir (1640-1713), as seen in his *Divers Pannaux d'Ornements et Rinceaux de Feuillages*.[144]

The plate is held in place by two cast handle supports that screw into the top plate of the box. They were originally supplemented by five small rivets around the edge. The scrolled supports that terminate with human heads also parallel the designs of Loir as seen in his *Desseins de Brasiers dont les Ornements peuvent servir aux Cuvettes, Tables, et autres Ouvrages d'Orfevrerie*.[145]

FLATIRON TRIVET
255

PROBABLY HIRAM BARTON
(1798–1878), POSSIBLY HUBBARD
BARTON (1797–1860)
EAST HAMPTON, CONNECTICUT,
1826–70

BRONZE (COPPER 81.32, TIN 10.57,
LEAD 5.90, ZINC 0.70, ANTIMONY 0.30,
MERCURY 0.29, SILVER 0.24)
H. 1 1/4" (3.2 CM), L. 8 1/4" (21.0 CM),
W. 4 1/8" (10.5 CM)
84.136

"IRON RINGS OR IRON-STANDS, on which to set the irons, and small pieces of board to put under them, to prevent scorching" were among the various necessities enumerated by Catherine E. Beecher for the properly equipped laundry. "The best iron-stands are those with feet and handles. If a mere ring, they are likely to scorch the blanket, and to burn the fingers when removing them."[146]

The flatiron trivet illustrated here, although a simple one-piece casting now missing the wood handle, readily illustrates its purpose. The stamped mark "H. BARTON" is similar in character to the "W. BARTON" mark used by William Barton, Jr. (1762–1849), who is credited with having been the first brass founder in East Hampton, Connecticut, in 1808. Two of his three sons, Hubbard and Hiram, are stated to have assumed responsibility for their father's workshop when he moved in

1826 to work in Cairo, New York. However, only Hiram is listed as living in Middlesex County by the 1830 Connecticut population census. Hubbard, who is believed to have given up brass founding for farming, does not appear as the head of a household until the 1840 census.[147]

Hiram "carried on the business of [brass founding] in a shop near his late residence on Barton Hill, and afterward in the factory on the road leading west from . . . East Hampton, where his son William E. Barton, carried on the same business until the factory was destroyed by fire in 1874."[148] Hiram Barton is, therefore, the more likely maker of this trivet.

FLATIRON TRIVET
256

UNITED STATES, POSSIBLY
CONNECTICUT, 1840–80
BRASS (COPPER 73.37, ZINC 25.24,
LEAD 0.85, TIN 0.34)

H. 7/8" (2.2 CM), L. 9 1/2"
(24.1 CM), W. 5 1/4" (13.4 CM)
65.1483

ANYONE WHO IRONS "must be provided with an iron-stand on which to rest the iron . . . iron stands are of different kinds, the simplest being those made of strong wire supported on four legs. Others are made of a plain ring of iron, and some of more elaborate design; but in any case they should stand high enough above the table to prevent the heat of the iron from scorching the ironing sheet."[149]

The flatiron stand shown here is a one-piece casting. Its triangular shape with handle on three short legs is typical of many that were mass-produced in Germany, Sweden, England, and the United States during the mid to late nineteenth century. Most such stands were made of iron and modestly decorated with simple abstract geometric or floral motifs.

The heart-shape outline of this trivet accords very well with the inscription it encloses, almost certainly the words of Ann Lee (1736–84), founder of the religious sect known as Shakers. Born in England, Lee immigrated to the United States when she was thirty-eight and estab-

lished at Niskeyuna (now Watervliet), New York, the beginnings of what was to grow into many Shaker communities throughout New England, the South, and the Midwest. Although illiterate, she possessed a fertile mind and strong religious conviction, enabling her to propound simple but spellbinding religious rules around which her followers built their communities and by which they lived. She offered one of the most important of these when she admonished her followers to "put your hands to work and give your hearts to God."[150]

Although the motto on this flatiron stand probably sprang from Shaker dogma, the trivet was in all likelihood not intended for use in a Shaker community. It was instead a commercial product, possibly made in one of Connecticut's many brassworking communities, for popular consumption.

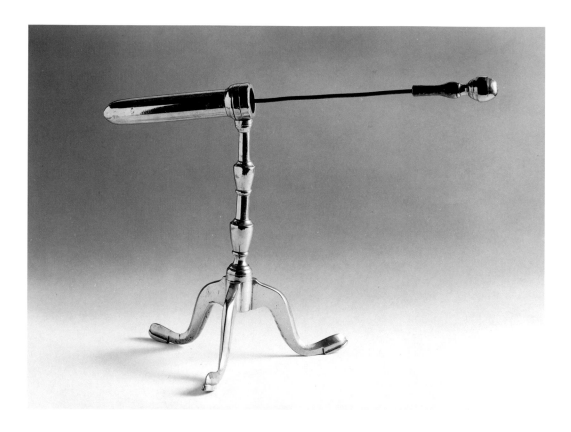

ITALIAN IRON
257

PROBABLY ENGLAND, 1760–1820
BRASS (COPPER 72.56, ZINC 24.62,
LEAD 2.65, TIN 0.18), IRON

H. 9 7/8" (25.1 CM), W. 6 3/4"
(17.1 CM), D. 14 1/4" (36.2 CM)
59.2464

ITALIAN OR GOFFERING IRONS "are fixed to a stand, and have smooth tubes diminishing toward one end which is closed, and open at the other to admit the heater. There are always two heaters, they have long handles and somewhat resemble a poker. While . . . using one, the other is heated by putting the thick end into the fire till it becomes nearly red-hot. It is then slipped into the hollow tube."[151]

When the tube has heated sufficiently, "the ruffles of gingham, chintz, or painted muslin dresses and pelerines" are stretched over it a little at a time. Properly done, the fabric is held "tightly with both hands between the thumb and fingers, and as you go along pinching it down at the sides close against the iron, taking care to keep it quite straight. The gathered part of the frill must go upon the point of the iron." Care must be taken "to have one

of the heaters always in the fire, so that it may be hot by the time the other has become too cool for use."[152]

Italian irons were used in this fashion from the sixteenth to the nineteenth centuries. Examples described as Italian irons and patent Italian irons made of iron, brass, or a combination of the two are pictured in nineteenth-century English and German base-metal trade catalogues.[153] The iron illustrated here is cast entirely of brass except for the heater, which is cast iron. It has been designed with three radiating legs for stability. The design of the cabriole legs with pad feet and urn-shape shaft closely relates to candlestands and tea tables made during the late eighteenth and early nineteenth centuries on both sides of the Atlantic.

SHOT MOLD
258

NATHANIEL DOMINY IV (1737–1812)
EAST HAMPTON, LONG ISLAND, 1779
BRASS (COPPER 75.57, ZINC 21.90,
LEAD 1.65, TIN 0.16), WOOD, STEEL

CLOSED: L. 10 1/8" (25.7 CM),
W. 1 1/2" (3.8 CM), D. 7/8" (2.2 CM)
57.84.1

SHOT—SMALL LEAD BALLS—was used principally for bird hunting with long-barreled, large diameter, smooth-bore shotguns called fowling pieces. From as early as the sixteenth century, shot was found to be more reliable at bringing down a small, fast-moving target than a bullet from a rifle.

Shot, "otherwise called hail, by reason of its figure and size," was made in two ways. One involved pouring molten lead mixed with orpiment (arsenic trisulfide) onto "a copper plate, hollow in the middle, and three inches in diameter, bored through with thirty or forty small holes . . . over a tub of water . . . the lead . . . will make its way through the holes [and fall] into the water in round drops."[154]

The second and slower method involved casting the round drops in shot molds, which consisted of two or more hinged plates. The inside faces had opposed hemispheres that were "first punched, being blood-red hot, with a round ended-punch, of the shape and size of the intended" shot. Then to make the inside of these depressions uniform, "a steel shank having a globe at one end," called a shot-bore, was used.[155]

The mold shown here, when closed, has a V-shape trough on each side that connects via narrow-neck gates to the cavities. It is designed to cast six $9/32$-inch balls and nine $7/32$-inch balls on one side and nineteen $7/16$-inch balls on the other, all of which must be cut from their gates before they can be used.[156]

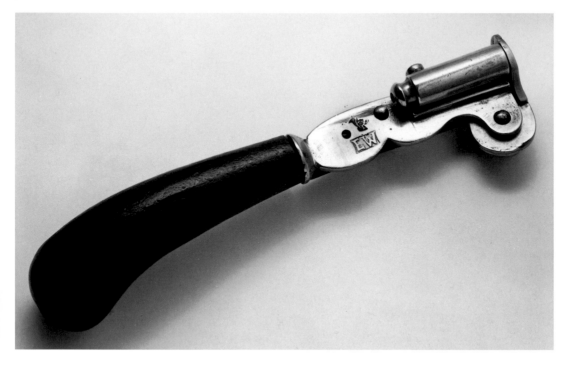

EPROUVETTE
259

MAKER'S MARK "EW"
PROBABLY UNITED STATES, POSSIBLY
ENGLAND, 1820–50
BRASS (COPPER 77.82, ZINC 20.48, LEAD 0.85,
IRON 0.10), STEEL, WOOD, LEATHER

H. 1 1/2" (3.8 CM), L. 6 1/4"
(15.4 CM), W. 1 1/16" (2.7 CM)
65.1965

GUNPOWDER is "a composition of nitre, sulphur, and charcoal, mixed together and usually granulated. . . . it is to this powder we owe all the action and effect of guns, ordnance, &c. so that . . . military art, fortifications, &c. depend almost wholly upon it."[157]

The three ingredients were mixed together in differing ratios depending upon the use. A strong force was needed to eject a sixty-four-pound iron ball from a mortar, while a weaker compound served to shoot a three-ounce lead ball from a pistol. It was important to know the explosive force in any given sample of gunpowder for precision shooting and the prevention of the inadvertent bursting of a gun barrel.

An eprouvette was used to measure this force. It resembled "a pistol, of which the barrel is very substantial, and the bore not more than the eighth of an inch in diameter. Over the barrel is a circular plate, acted upon strongly by a spring, which offers considerable resistance to

the revolution caused therein, by the action of the powder on a projection which shuts down close upon the muzzle. The bore being filled with powder, and the wheel, or plate, turned so that its projection closes the muzzle, the explosion will, in proportion to its force, throw up the projection, and cause the wheel to revolve; the power of the powder is . . . ascertained by means of figures on the circumference, which indicate how much the wheel has been thrown round."[158]

The maker of the example shown here, which appears to have been designed to use percussion caps, stamped his initials and the fanciful figure of a bird on the side. The maker also graduated the wheel by engraving the numbers 1 through 5 around the perimeter, with each interval divided into fourths.

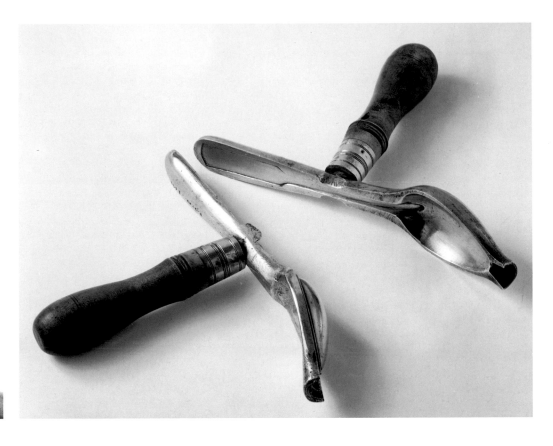

SPOON MOLD
260

USED BY PETER DERR (1793–1868)
PROBABLY PHILADELPHIA, POSSIBLY
BERKS COUNTY, PENNSYLVANIA, CA. 1841
BRASS (COPPER 75.57, ZINC 21.90,
LEAD 1.65, TIN 0.16), WOOD, STEEL

L. 9" (22.9 CM), W. 11 3/8"
(28.9 CM), D. 1 15/16" (4.9 CM)
55.621

PEWTER SPOONS were produced in large quantity throughout the seventeenth, eighteenth, and nineteenth centuries. Most were made by pewterers who cast and sold them wholesale and retail. At the time of his death in 1742, Simon Edgell, a Philadelphia pewterer, had 1,183 pounds of brass molds, some of which he had used to make the 1,968 tablespoons, 1,296 teaspoons, and 4 soup spoons remaining in his shop. Thomas Byles, another Phildelphia pewterer, died in 1771 leaving 4,300 tablespoons and 552 teaspoons in his workplace. By the mid nineteenth century American pewter manufacturers, still using brass molds, had significantly raised their production, as represented by the East Haddam, Connecticut, firm of Luther Boardman and Company, which by 1860 was making 2,592,000 spoons a year.[159]

Not all pewter spoons were made by specialists. Because the process of casting was quite simple and the necessary tools few, persons with only a limited knowledge of metalworking techniques could make them. Those people were the object of the brass founder John Stow's advertisement in the March 17, 1752, issue of the *Pennsylvania Gazette*, when he stated that he had "spoon molds of all fashions" for sale. His competitors, James Smith and Thomas Gregory, also sought the same market with advertisements.[160]

Peter Derr, who stamped his name and date on the top half of the spoon mold shown here, made copper, brass, and iron fat lamps; dough scrapers; apple peelers; pie wheels; butchering tools; pipe tongs; mousetraps; and other objects. Almost all are of sheet or wrought metal. The substantially cast mold shown here might be his handiwork as well, but he more likely bought it from a Philadelphia brass founder to cast pewter spoons for those in Berks County who used him as a supplier of necessary household goods.[161]

1 Thomas Hariot, *A Briefe and True Report of the New Found Land of Virginia* (London, 1588), p. 25. A reprint edition is entitled *Narrative of the First English Plantation of Virginia* (London: Privately printed, 1893).

2 As quoted in Berthold Laufer, *Introduction of Tobacco into Europe* (Chicago: Field Museum of Natural History, 1924), p. 35.

3 Abstract of John Moore's will, Surrogate's Office, New York, as published in William S. Pelletreau, ed., *Collections of the New-York Historical Society* (New York: By the society, 1895), pp. 248–51.

4 Leddel advertised in the *Weekly Post-Boy*, June 1, 1752. See William Macintire, research paper, object folder 57.98, Registration Office, Winterthur, which notes that the thistle is the emblem of Scotland. It also indicates retaliation and in this instance might be suggestive of Moore's political activities in New York and his attitude toward England.

5 As quoted in Rees, 37:s.v. "tobacco." James I, *A Counterblaste to Tobacco* (London, 1604), as quoted in Count Corti, *A History of Smoking* (London: George G. Harrap, 1931), p. 77.

6 On the James River exports, see Allan Kulikoff, *Tobacco and Slaves* (Williamsburg, Va.: Institute of Early American History and Culture, 1986), p. 52. T. M. Divine, *The Tobacco Lords* (Edinburgh, Scot.: John Donald, 1975), p. 108.

7 The surname Willson occurs with some frequency in England and America during the eighteenth century but rarely in combination with the given name Cornelius. The only Cornelius Willson whose dates seem to encompass the date on this box is recorded in the International Genealogical Index as having married Elizabeth Pryor on June 10, 1760, at St. Aldermary in London. The lid of the box depicts a Frenchman, German, and an Englishman. The Frenchman asks, "Voule vous de Rippe" (Will you have some snuff?); the German responds, "No dis been better," while the Englishman asks, "Will you have a quid?" Below is the couplet "Thes

three unite in the same Cause/This snuffs that Smoaks the other Chaws."

8 On the Masons, see Barbara Franco, *Masonic Symbols in American Decorative Arts* (Lexington, Mass.: Scottish Rite Masonic Museum of Our National Heritage, 1976), p. 9. Albert Gallatin Mackey, *The History of Freemasonry*, 7 vols. (New York and London: Masonic History Company, 1906), 1:15. Bernard E. Jones, *Freemason's Guide and Compendium* (London: George E. Harrap, 1965), pp. 93, 427.

9 As quoted in Jones, *Freemason's Guide*, pp. 360, 379.

10 Arthur Cecil Powell and Joseph L. Littleton, *A History of Freemasonry in Bristol* (Bristol, Eng.: Privately printed, 1910), pp. 890, 894–95.

11 Knight, *Knight's American Mechanical Dictionary*, 1:695.

12 Charles R. Beard, "Lancaster Snuff and Tobacco Boxes," *Apollo* 17 (1933): 261–64, discusses this type of box as being peculiar to the Lancashire area of England.

13 Rees, *Cyclopaedia*, 40:s.v. "William III."

14 The number of portraits of William III still in existence is in excess of two hundred. Among them, a possible source for the image on this box is the painting completed by Gerard Terborch in 1672, when William was experiencing a peak of popularity, having successfully prevented Louis XIV's armies from overrunning Holland.

15 As quoted in Jerome E. Brooks, *Tobacco: Its History Illustrated by the Books, Manuscripts, and Engravings in the Library of George Arents, Jr.*, 5 vols. (New York: Rosenback Co., 1943), 2:226.

16 *The Works of the Author of Whipping Tom . . .* (London: S. Briscoe, 1723) as quoted in Brooks, *Tobacco*, 3:139.

17 The Beekhuysen box is illustrated in Norman S. Rice, *Albany Silver* (Albany, N.Y.: Albany Institute of History and Art, 1964), p. 59. Fueter advertised in the *New-York Gazette, and Weekly Mercury*, July 31, 1769. The vignette on the lid depicts two fishermen casting nets, while that on the back shows two housewrights at work. Both are flanked by short texts in Dutch that probably offer moral or comical insight into the scenes.

18 I am indebted to Daniëlle Kisluk-Grosheide for the translations. A similar box made by the Amsterdam silversmith Jacobus de Konig in 1764 was offered in New York at Sotheby's sale 5311 (April 20, 1985), lot 32.

19 As quoted in Rees, *Cyclopaedia*, 15:s.v. "fishery."

20 As quoted in Rees, *Cyclopaedia*, 15:s.v. "fishery."

21 I thank Daniëlle Kisluk-Grosheide for kindly providing me with the translation.

22 *The Child's Bible* (Philadelphia: Henry F. Anners, 1834), pp. 11–16.

23 Jgs. 13:20.

24 I am grateful to Daniëlle Kisluk-Grosheide for the translation. *The Works of the Author of Whipping Tom . . .* (London: S. Briscoe, 1723), as quoted in Jerome E. Brooks, *Tobacco: Its History Illustrated by the Books, Manuscripts, and Engravings in the Library of George Arents, Jr.*, 5 vols. (New York: Rosenback Co., 1943), 3:139. This box is the subject of a research paper by Catherine Anne Jacobs, object folder 61.895, Registration Office, Winterthur; see also Daniëlle Kisluk-Grosheide, "Dutch Tobacco Boxes in the Metropolitan Museum of Art: A Catalogue," *Metropolitan Museum Journal* 23(1988): 204–5.

25 As quoted in Rees, *Cyclopaedia*, 16:s.v. "Frederick III." On the extensive production of brass tobacco boxes in Iserlohn, see Dossmann, *Iserlohner Tabakdosen Erzählen*; Könenkamp, *Iserlohner Tabakdosen.*

26 On Dutch and German brass tobacco boxes by Geise and other identified makers, see Katherine Morrison McClinton, "Brass Tobacco Boxes," *Antiques* 50, no. 3 (September 1946): 176–77. I am most grateful to Daniëlle Kisluk-Grosheide for providing me with Dutch translations. Borysthenes is the ancient name for the present-day Dnieper River, which extends from the region around Moscow south to the Black Sea. The inscription is meant to impress the reader with the extent of Frederick the Great's influence. I am grateful to Gerald E. Culley for helping me to interpret this phrase.

27 The other Winterthur box is acc. no. 67.906. On Morel, see Leonard Forrer, *Biographical Dictionary of Medallists*, 8 vols. (London: Spink and Son, 1909), 4:146.

28 The image almost certainly derives from one of the many plaster, terra-cotta, or bronze busts made of the subject in Paris by Jean-Antoine Houdon. The details of Houdon's working relationship with Washington are detailed in Charles Henry Hart and Edward Biddle, *Memoirs of the Life and Works of Jean-Antoine Houdon* (Philadelphia, 1911), pp. 182–225.

29 *Encyclopaedia; or, A Dictionary of Arts, Sciences, and Miscellaneous Literature*, 21 vols. (Philadelphia: Thomas Dobson, 1798), 6:667.

30 Ephriam Chambers, *Cyclopaedia; or, An Universal Dictionary of Arts and Sciences* (London, 1738), 2:s.v. "toilet."

31 As quoted in Rees, *Cyclopaedia*, 34: s.v. "soap."

32 As quoted in Diderot, *Encyclopédie*, 1:1207.

33 As quoted in William Dunlap, *A History of the Rise and Progress of the Arts of Design in the United States*, 3 vols. (1834; reprint, Boston: C. E. Goodspeed, 1918), 1:371.

34 Fiske Kimball, "Joseph Wright and His Portraits of Washington," *Antiques* 15, no. 5 (May 1929): 382. An example of the Wedgwood medallion is pictured in Fiske Kimball, "Joseph Wright and His Portraits of Washington," *Antiques* 17, no. 1 (January 1930): 38. The quote on the maker appeared in *Aris's Birmingham Gazette*, December 13, 1784.

35 Trade catalogue TS573 B61F* no. 2 TC, Downs collection, Winterthur Library. The notation accompanies pl. 3.

36 Stacy B. C. Wood, Jr., Stephen E. Kramer III, and John J. Snyder, Jr., *Clockmakers of Lancaster County and Their Clocks, 1750–1850* (New York: Van Nostrand Reinhold Company, 1977), p. 2.

37 Wood, Kramer, and Snyder, *Clockmakers of Lancaster County*, p. 2

38 Trade catalogue 7392 s19 vol. 3, Peabody Essex Institute, Salem, Mass. On the partnership, see Stevie Young, "Broadhead, Gurney, Sporle and Company," *Bulletin of the Pewter Collectors Club of America* 8, no. 3 (March 1981): 93–95.

39 The use for such a box is conjectural. It may have contained watch parts or clock lubricants.

40 H. M. Brackenridge, *History of the Late War* (Baltimore: Cushing and Jewett, 1817), p. vii.

41 On Perry, see *The Naval Temple* (Boston: Barber Badger, 1816), p. 159. On Decatur, see Brackenridge, *History of the Late War*, pp. 67, 68, 69.

42 As quoted in Brackenridge, *History of the Late War*, p. 48. Thomas Fletcher to Charles Fletcher, August 31, 1815, box 1, Thomas Fletcher Papers, Athenaeum of Philadelphia.

43 Forrest R. Holdcamper, *List of American-Flag Merchant Vessels That Received Certificates of Enrollment or Registry at the Port of New York, 1789–1867* (Washington, D.C.: National Archives, 1968), p. 61.

44 On Kelsey, see Janice P. Cunningham and Elizabeth A. Warner, *Portrait of a River Town* (Middletown, Conn.: Greater Middletown Preservation Trust, 1984), p. 56. Facts about Kelsey's career were gleaned from "Inscriptions from Monuments in the Greenwood Cemetery, Town of Haddam Conn." (Middlesex County Historical Society, Middletown, Conn., typescript).

45 A related example in silver is pictured in Martha Gandy Fales, *Early American Silver* (New York: Funk and Wagnalls, 1970), p. 178. It was made by the Charleston, S.C., silversmith Louis Boudo in 1825. Another in japanned sheet iron, acc. no. 59.2062, is in the Winterthur collection. It was owned by John Harbeson Barnes, a shipbroker in Philadelphia during the 1820s.

46 As quoted in Adrian Oswald, "English Clay Tobacco Pipes," *Archaeological News Letter* 3, no. 10 (April 1951): 153.

47 Joseph Fume, *A Paper: Of Tobacco* (London: Chapman and Hall, 1939), p. 51.

48 The engraved Waldo advertisement is owned by the American Antiquarian Society, Worcester, Mass. Jackson advertised in the *Boston Gazette*, September 27, 1736.

49 Both inventories are noted in Cummings, *Rural Household Inventories*, pp. 191, 254.

50 On his graduation, see the *New-England Historical and Genealogical Register* (Boston: Samuel G. Drake, 1847–), 10:153. Clifford K. Shipton, *Biographical Sketches of Those Who Attended Harvard College*, 17 vols.

(1933; reprint, Boston: Massachusetts Historical Society, 1972), 6:476.

51 James Edward Greenleaf, *Genealogy of the Greenleaf Family* (Boston: Printed by Frank Wood, 1896), p. 83.

52 J. Bennett Nolan, *Benjamin Franklin in Scotland and Ireland* (Philadelphia: University of Pennsylvania Press, 1938), p. 15.

53 As quoted in Charles Coleman Sellers, *Patience Wright: American Artist and Spy in George III's London* (Middletown, Conn.: Wesleyan University Press, 1976), p. 50.

54 Leonard Forrer, *Biographical Dictionary of Medallists* (1904; reprint, London: A. H. Baldwin and Sons, 1980). The Gosset wax profile, owned by the Victoria and Albert Museum, is illustrated in Charles Coleman Sellers, *Benjamin Franklin in Portraiture* (New Haven: Yale University Press, 1962), pl. 9. For references to Wedgwood and Tassie's work, see Sellers, *Benjamin Franklin*, p. 374. See also cabinet knobs and cloak pins in entry 316.

55 Edgar Stanton Maclay, *A History of the United States Navy from 1775 to 1898*, 2 vols. (New York: D. Appleton and Company, 1898), 1:418–21.

56 *The Weekly Register* (Baltimore) 5, no. 21 (January 1814): 355.

57 Georgia S. Chamberlain, "Moritz Fürst, Die-Sinker and Artist," *The Numismatist* 67, no. 6 (June 1954): 591. Georgia S. Chamberlain, "Medals Made in America by Moritz Fürst," *The Numismatist* 67, no. 9 (September 1954): 937–43. Winterthur owns the single example in gold, acc. no. 64.145, that commemorates Lt. Stephen Cassin's victory on Lake Champlain on September 11, 1814. These commemorative medals in copper are available today at the Philadelphia Mint. While those being sold at present appear identical to this example, they are not. The dies used to stamp this medal would have had a relatively short life span, perhaps 20 years. When they begin to chip and crack, evidence of which is visible on both sides of this medal, new dies are cut. The obverse of the illustrated medal has a Latin inscription that translates as "James Lawrence. It is sweet and proper to die for one's country." The inscrip-

tion on the reverse translates as "Clemency is greater than victory" and "Engagement between the *Hornet* of the American navy and the *Peacock* of the British navy, the 24th of February 1813." I am grateful to Gerald Culley for his assistance with the translations.

58 Theresa A. Singleton, "The Slave Tag: An Artifact of Urban Slavery," *South Carolina Antiquities* 16, nos. 1, 2 (1984): 42.

59 Singleton, "Slave Tag," pp. 45, 46, 47.

60 On the specifics of a badge, see Singleton, "Slave Tag," p. 50. Archibald Miller, ed., *Digest of Ordinances of the City of Charleston from 1783–1818, Extracts of Legislation Which Relate to the City of Charleston* (Charleston, S.C., 1818), p. 182. This information was kindly supplied to me by Theresa Singleton.

61 Singleton, "Slave Tag," p. 55. In addition, there are two badges known that were intended for free blacks. This small number represents immense attrition, since one extant badge issued in 1821 bears the number 5,081.

62 Henry Wansey, *Excursion to the United States of North America* (Salisbury, Eng.: J. Easton, 1798), pp. 121, 123.

63 Peale's advertisement appeared in *Paxton's Philadelphia Annual Advertiser*, supp. to John Adems Paxton, *The Philadelphia Directory and Register for 1818* (Philadelphia: E. and R. Parker, 1818); *Paxton's Philadelphia Annual Advertiser*, supp. to *The Philadelphia Directory and Register for 1819* (Philadelphia: John Adems Paxton, 1819).

64 The medal presented to Moore is owned by the United States Mint in Philadelphia. Winterthur owns a silver example, acc. no. 57.92.1, which appears never to have been engraved with the name of its recipient.

65 Catherine Thomas Masetti, "The Copper Admissions Token for the Philadelphia Museum," object folder 66.78, Registration Office, Winterthur. Two of the paper tickets are illustrated in Charles Coleman Sellers, *Mr. Peale's Museum* (New York: W. W. Norton, 1980), p. 218.

66 On the union's mission and organization, see *Transactions of the American Art-Union for the Year 1848* (New York:

George F. Nesbitt, 1849), p. 19. *Transactions of the American Art-Union for the Year 1849* (New York: George F. Nesbitt, 1850), p. 13.

67 The first medal is discussed in *Transactions of the American Art-Union for the Year 1847* (New York: George F. Nesbitt, 1848), pp. 17–18. On the second medal, see *Transactions . . . for the Year 1848*, p. 44.

68 Maybelle Mann, *The American Art-Union* (Otisville, N.Y.: Privately printed, 1977), p. 26.

69 Rees, *Cyclopaedia*, 15:s.v. "flint."

70 Rees, *Cyclopaedia*, 15:s.v. "flint."

71 *Sketchley's and Adam's Tradesman's True Guide; or, An Universal Directory for Birmingham, Wolverhampton, Walsall, Dudley, and the Villages in the Neighborhood of Birmingham* (Birmingham, Eng.: J. Sketchley, 1770).

72 As quoted in Rees, *Cyclopaedia*, 5:s.v. "bleeding."

73 Rees, *Cyclopaedia*, 5:s.v. "bleeding."

74 The Greenleaf advertisement appeared in the *Pennsylvania Gazette* (Philadelphia), January 21, 1752. The Vogler fleam is owned by Old Salem, Winston-Salem, N.C. The Derr fleam is pictured in Lester Breininger, Jr., "The Works of Peter Derr," *Spinning Wheel* (July–August 1972): 48. The Tiemann example is pictured in Kauffman, *American Copper and Brass*, p. 220.

75 As quoted in *The American Edition of the New Edinburgh Encyclopaedia*, 36 vols. (New York: Samuel Whiting, 1831), 17: pt. 2, s.v. "surgery."

76 Johnson, *Dictionary of the English Language*, 1:s.v. "barber," "barber chirurgeon."

77 François-Alexandre-Pierre Garsault, *Art du perruquier* (Paris, 1767), trans. J. Stevens Cox, *The Art of the Wigmaker* (London: Hairdressers' Registration Council, 1961), p. 5. Close examination of this basin's surface indicates it was originally tinned.

78 Holme, *Academy of Armory*, 1:438.

79 *New-York Gazette*, April 16, 1764.

80 English lobed salvers dating from the 1720s through the 1740s were also made in tin-glazed earthenware, mahogany, and brass. One American trefoil salver very similar to this standish is recorded. It was made by the Boston silversmith

Edward Winslow (1669–1753) and is currently owned by the Art Institute of Chicago.

81 John Wilton-Ely et al., *Apollo of the Arts: Lord Burlington and His Circle* (Nottingham, Eng.: Nottingham University Art Gallery, 1973), p. 73.

82 *Inigo Jones on Palladio*, 2 vols. (Newcastle upon Tyne, Eng.: Oriel Press, 1970), 2:40.

83 Diderot, *Encyclopédie*, 4:159.

84 Edward Cocker, *England's Pen-Man; or, Cocker's New Copy-Book* (London, 1703), as quoted in Joyce Irene Whalley, *Writing Implements and Accessories* (Newton Abbot, Eng.: David and Charles, 1975), p. 22.

85 An identical example that retains its candle screen was offered at a Sotheby's New York sale (June 24, 25, 1983), lot 391.

86 Holmes account book, 3561, Downs collection, Winterthur Library.

87 Broadside advertisement, 1742, pictured in John William Wallace, *An Old Philadelphian: Colonel William Bradford, the Patriot Printer of 1776* (Philadelphia: Sherman, 1884), p. 16.

88 William S. Walsh, *Handy-Book of Literary Curiosities* (Philadelphia: J. B. Lippincott Co., 1893), p. 301.

89 Trade catalogue TS573B61F* no. 2TC, Downs collection, Winterthur Library, pictures many of the various types of wax jacks available throughout the eighteenth and early nineteenth centuries.

90 Rees, *Cyclopaedia*, 33:s.v. "seal."

91 As quoted in William Murrell, *A History of American Graphic Humor*, 2 vols. (New York: Cooper Square Publ., 1967), 1:39, 42, 41, 43.

92 On the corporation, see Frederic J. Wood, *The Turnpikes of New England* (Boston: Marshall, Jones Co., 1919), p. 248. On turnpikes, see Roger N. Parks, *Roads and Travel in New England* (Sturbridge, Mass.: Old Sturbridge Village, 1967), p. 5. This information is cited by Gail E. Nessell, research paper, object folder 61.6, Registration Office, Winterthur.

93 Parks, *Roads and Travel*, p. 23.

94 Smithers advertised in the *Pennsylvania Chronicle*, April 25, 1768. The Gilman seal is pictured in Charles S. Parsons, *New Hampshire Silver* (Warner, N.H.: Steve Petrucelli, 1983), p. 21. Similar examples are pictured in Donna-Belle

Garvin and James L. Garvin, *On the Road North of Boston: New Hampshire Taverns and Turnpikes, 1700–1900* (Concord, N.H.: New Hampshire Historical Soc., 1988), pp. 52, 57, 61.

95 *Pennsylvania Chronicle*, April 25, 1768.

96 Knight, *Knight's American Mechanical Dictionary*, 3:2301–2. The difference between a stamp and a seal is not always as distinct as described. Some hybrid stamps are cut intaglio and create a three-dimensional image, such as those used for embossing.

97 I am grateful to Gerald E. Culley for providing me with the translation. As quoted in Rees, *Cyclopaedia*, 12:s.v. "dog."

98 Rees, *Cyclopaedia*, 27:s.v. "pastille."

99 Harold Newman, "The Scented Fragrance of the Perfume Burner," *Antique Dealer and Collector's Guide* (February 1969): 71–73. On Kyston's house, see L. A. Shuffrey, *The English Fireplace* (London: B. T. Batsford, 1912), pp. 152, 153.

100 On Barton, see David D. Field, *Centennial Address* (Middletown, Conn., 1853), p. 285.

101 On single-piece casting, see *History of Middlesex County, Connecticut* (New York: J. B. Beers, 1884), p. 200. This bell does appear to be seamless, in accordance with the technique ascribed to Barton. So, too, do 3 other bells in the Winterthur collection, all made in East Hampton by Hiram or Hubbard Barton, acc. no. 53.155.45; Philo S. Parsons, acc. no. 53.155.44; and Joseph N. Goff and Amiel Abell, acc. no. 53.155.43.

102 On the history of harness bells, see Brears, *Horse Brasses*, p. 102. The English founders are discussed in Brears, *Horse Brasses*, pp. 112–17.

103 The Waldo broadside advertisement is owned by the American Antiquarian Soc., Worcester, Mass.

104 On the Gott family, see *Vital Records of Wenham, Massachusetts, to the End of the Year 1849* (Salem, Mass.: Essex Institute, 1904), p. 41. On Wenham, see Charles F. W. Archer, "Wenham Town History," in *Standard History of Essex County, Massachusetts* (Boston: C. F. Jewett, 1878), pp. 416–18. A reeve is a minor appointed official who oversees some aspect of the activities on a unit of land, in this instance, the deer popula-

tion. On Gott's appointment as surveyor, see *Wenham Town Records, 1730–1775* (Wenham, Mass.: Wenham Historical Soc., 1940), pp. 110, 115, 150.

105 Henry B. Wheatly, ed., *The Diary of Samuel Pepys*, 8 vols. (London: George Bell and Sons, 1986), 1:27. Timmins, *Birmingham and the Midland Hardware District*, p. 214.

106 Broadside advertisement, 1748, American Antiquarian Society, Worcester, Mass.

107 *Pennsylvania Gazette* (Philadelphia), December 14, 1752.

108 *Sketchley's and Adam's Tradesmans True Guide* (Birmingham, Eng.: James Sketchley, 1770), p. 19.

109 Mention of the president's clothing was made in the *Gazette of the United States* (New York), May 2, 1789. On Rollinson, see William Dunlap, *A History of the Rise and Progress of the Arts of Design in the United States*, 2 vols. (New York: George P. Scott Co., 1834), 1:158.

110 The reference to veneration later appeared in the *New-York Evening Post*, February 23, 1832. *The Constitution and Laws of the Washington Association of Philadelphia* (Philadelphia, 1811). *A Summary Statement of the Origin, Progress, and Present State of the Washington Benevolent Society of Pennsylvania* (Philadelphia, 1816), p. 10.

111 *Constitution and By-Laws of the Light Artillery Corps of Washington Grays* (Philadelphia: R. D. DeSilver, 1838), art. 1. Writers have traditionally stated that these buttons were made for Washington's first and second inaugurations; see William L. Calver, "Washington Inaugural Buttons," *Bulletin* (New-York Historical Society) 9, no. 4 (January 1926): 124–26; J. Harold Cobb, *George Washington Inaugural Buttons and Medalets, 1789 and 1793* (Hamden, Conn.: Privately printed, 1963); Sally C. Luscomb, *The Collectors Encyclopedia of Buttons* (New York: Crown Publ., 1967), pp. 214–18; Elizabeth Hughes and Marion Lester, *The Big Book of Buttons* (Boyertown, Pa.: Boyertown Publishing Co., 1981), p. 671. No documentation to support this assertion has been offered, however.

112 Horace Greeley et al., *The Great Industries of the United States* (Hartford, Conn.: J. B. Burr and Hyde, 1872), p. 1048.

113 As quoted in Brecher, Lombarde, and Stackhouse, *Brass Valley*, p. 46.

114 The compositional material included in this entry is gleaned from 3 randomly selected buttons. Analyses of individual buttons can vary widely since some are gilded and others are silver plated.

115 R. K., *Observations on the Use of Spectacles* (London: Printed for P. Stevens, 1753), p. 5; see also Richard Corson, *Fashions in Eyeglasses* (Chester Springs, Pa.: DuFour Editions, 1967), pp. 17–21.

116 Rees, *Cyclopaedia*, 35:s.v. "spectacles."

117 *The Bazar Book of Decorum* (New York: Harper and Bros., 1870), pp. 120–21.

118 Rees, *Cyclopaedia*, 35:s.v. "spectacles." On the form of spectacles, see R. K., *Observations on the Use of Spectacles* (London: Printed for P. Stevens, 1753), p. 22.

119 As quoted in *Longworth's American Almanac, New-York Register, and City Directory* (New York: Thomas Longworth, 1832), adv. supp.

120 Johnson, *Dictionary of the English Language*, 2:s.v. "shoehorn."

121 Winterthur owns a third example in brass, acc. no. 59.2699.

122 As quoted in François-Alexandre-Pierre Garsault, "Art du perruquier," *Decription des Arts et Metiers Faite on approuve par MM de L'Academie Royale des Sciences* (Paris, 1767). Translated edition by J. Stevens Cox (London: Hairdressers' Registration Council, 1961), p. 12.

123 Diderot, *Encyclopédie*, 4:743.

124 Diderot, *Encyclopédie*, 4:838. Combs of this type were also used as late as the nineteenth century for combing one's own hair. Comly Rich includes a comb very similar to this in his advertisement in the 1837 issue of Archibald McElroy's *Philadelphia Directory*.

125 Clifford K. Shipton, *Biographical Sketches of Those Who Attended Harvard College*, 17 vols. (Boston: Massachusetts Historical Society, 1972), 16:405.

126 A sword with similar pommel made by Targee for presentation to Alfred Davis is owned by the Metropolitan

Museum of Art and is pictured in Berry B. Tracey, *Nineteenth-Century America* (New York: Metropolitan Museum of Art, 1970), ent. 33.

127 George W. Sheldon, *The Story of the Volunteer Fire Department of the City of New York* (New York: Harper and Bros., 1882), p. 2.

128 On the duties of the fire warden, see M. J. McCosker, *The Historical Collection of Insurance Company of North America* (Philadelphia: Insurance Company of North America, 1967), pp. 91, 90.

129 Staff heads are pictured and described as "brass club-stick knobs" in brass-founder's trade catalogue TS 573 B61F* no. 2, Downs collection, Winterthur Library. One of these is included among the fire-fighting implements at the top of a notice of meeting of the Relief Fire Society in Boston on March 4, 1782. That notice was engraved by Paul Revere and is in the collection of the American Antiquarian Society, Worcester, Mass. It is pictured in Donald J. Cannon, ed., *Heritage of Flames* (New York: Doubleday, 1977), p. 197.

130 William C. Hunneman account book, Boston National Historical Park, Charlestown Navy Yard, Boston.

131 *Constitution and By-laws of the Good Will Fire Engine Company, Philadelphia, Pennsylvania* (Philadelphia: Printed for the company, 1839), preamble; Jack Robrecht to Donald L. Fennimore, January 19, 1985. On the name change and history of the company, see Robrecht to Fennimore.

132 *Constitution and By-laws of the Good Will Fire Engine Company*, pp. 7, 8, 11.

133 Birmingham city directory, 1816, Birmingham City Library.

134 Ledger account, April 1789, sale to Eliphalet Chapin, as recorded in Hoopes, *Shop Records of Daniel Burnap*, p. 79. The Thompson daybook is owned by the manuscript department, New York Public Library.

135 Bailey advertised in *Rivington's New-York Gazetteer*, July 29, 1772. The Hutt advertisement is in *Rivington's New-York Gazetteer*, February 17, 1774.

136 Charles J. Hoadly, ed., *The Public Records of the Colony of Connecticut*, 15 vols. (Hartford, Conn.: Care, Lockwood, and Brainard Co., 1881), 12:181. I am indebted to Susan Burrows Swan, who told me of this and the Philadelphia quote. The Philadelphia law appeared in the *Pennsylvania Gazette* (Philadelphia), May 1, 1811.

137 A similarly engraved brass collar is pictured in *Four Centuries of Dog Collars at Leeds Castle* (London: Philip Wilson Publishers, 1979), fig. 33; see also Charles R. Beard, "A Collection of Dog Collars," *Connoisseur* (March 1940): 102-6; Charles R. Beard, "Dog Collars," *Connoisseur* (July 1933): 29-34.

138 John Doggett, Jr., *The New-York City and Co-Partnership Directory for 1843–1844* (New York: By the author, 1844), p. 87. On the nature of his business, see Charles M. Wetzel, *American Fishing Books* (Newark, Del.: Privately printed, 1950), p. 84.

139 James A. Henshall, *Book of the Black Bass* (Cincinnati: Robert Clark, 1881), pl. 1.

140 Thaddeus Norris, *The American Angler's Book* (Philadelphia: E. H. Butler, 1864), p. 27.

141 This reel is the subject of a research paper by Gabrielle M. Lanier, object folder 60.246, Registration Office, Winterthur. John Doggett, Jr., *Doggett's New-York City Directory for 1846 and 1847* (New York: By the author, 1848), adv. supp.

142 As quoted in Charles Eliot Goodspeed, *Angling in America* (Boston: Houghton, Mifflin Co., 1939), p. 159.

143 The term *sad* here means solid, dense, or compact. On Goelet, see *New-York Mercury*, March 7, 1768. Smith advertised in the *Pennsylvania Gazette* (Philadelphia), June 27, 1754. A description of the iron appears in Webster, *Encyclopaedia of Domestic Economy*, p. 1061. A. H. Glissman, *The Evolution of the Sad-Iron* (Carlsbad, Calif.: Privately printed, 1970) illustrates numerous examples and discusses the various ways of using flatirons prior to the advent of electricity.

144 A typically plain example can be seen in use in the English painter Henry Robert Morland's study *A Laundry-Maid Ironing Shirt Sleeves*, painted about 1760 and illustrated in the Victoria and Albert Museum's exhibition catalogue *Rococo Art and Design in Hogarth's England* (1984), p. 233. A brass tea caddy and warming pan with a similar design are pictured in Turner, *Introduction to Brass*, cover, p. 30. Alexis Loir, *Diverse Pannaux d'Ornements et Rinceaux de Feuillages* (Paris: P. Mariette, n.d.).

145 Alexis Loir, *Desseins de Brasiers dont les Ornements peuvent servir aux Cuvettes, Tables, et autres Ouvrages d'Orfevrerie* (Paris: P. Mariette, 1700).

146 Catherine E. Beecher, *The New House-keeper's Manual* (New York: J. B. Ford, 1873), p. 539. Leslie, *House Book*, p. 12.

147 On William Barton, see David D. Field, *Centennial Address* (Middletown, Conn.: William B. Casey, 1853), p. 285. On the sons, see *History of Middlesex County, Connecticut* (New York: J. B. Beers, 1884), p. 200; Ronald V. Jackson and Gary R. Teeples, eds., *Connecticut 1830 Census Index* (1830; reprint, Bountiful, Utah: Accelerated Indexing Systems, 1977), p. 9. Ronald V. Jackson and Gary R. Teeples, eds., *Connecticut 1840 Census Index* (1840; reprint, Bountiful, Utah: Accelerated Indexing Systems, 1978), p. 10. It should be noted that only heads of households are included in this census. It might be, therefore, that Hubbard was a boarder in his younger brother's house at the time the 1830 census was taken.

148 *History of Middlesex County, Connecticut*, p. 200.

149 Florence B. Jack, *The Art of Laundry Work* (Edinburgh, Scot.: T. C. and E. C. Jack, 1898), p. 25.

150 Edward Deming Andrews, *The People Called Shakers* (New York: Oxford University Press, 1953), p. 136.

151 Leslie, *House Book*, p. 30.

152 As quoted in Leslie, *House Book*, p. 30.

153 An English trade catalogue, TJ1200 B61B TC, p. 79, Downs collection, Winterthur Library, pictures an example. A German example can be seen in the exhibition catalogue "*Mein Feld Ist Die Welt" Musterbücher Und Kataloge, 1784–1914* (Dortmund, Ger.: Westfälisches Wirtschaftarchiv, 1984), p. 305.

154 Rees, *Cyclopaedia*, 34:s.v. "shot."

155 Rees, *Cyclopaedia*, 5:s.v. "bullet." These molds, their use, and the alternate technique of making shot by dropping into water, are illustrated and discussed in Diderot, *Encyclopédie*, 4:453, 784-85.

156 Another closely related example by the same maker is pictured and discussed in Dean F. Failey, *Long Island Is My Nation* (Setauket, N.Y.: Society for the Preservation of Long Island Antiquities, 1976), p. 200, fig. 229.

157 Rees, *Cyclopaedia*, 17:s.v. "gunpowder."

158 Rees, *Cyclopaedia*, 14:s.v. "eprouvette."

159 Simon Edgell's shop inventory is transcribed in Laughlin, *Pewter in America*, 2:155. On Byles, see Laughlin, *Pewter in America*, 2:156-58. Boardman's and other Connecticut pewterers' production figures are found in John Carl Thomas, *Connecticut Pewter and Pewterers* (Hartford, Conn.: Connecticut Historical Society, 1976), pp. 35-39.

160 On Smith, see *Pennsylvania Gazette* (Philadelphia), December 14, 1752; on Gregory, see *Pennsylvania Gazette*, May 3, 1753.

161 Winterthur also owns a pewter table-spoon, acc. no. 65.1695, with "P. DERR 1820" cast on the back of the handle.

DETAIL, CLOCK BALL, 1750–90

ENTRY 293

HARDWARE

Architectural and furniture hardware, in that order, make up this section. Within each group, objects in which function predominates are cited first, followed by those that are largely ornamental. As will be seen, however, the line between the two is often indistinct. The architectural hardware represented includes both interior and exterior features. Furniture hardware covers a wide range from unobtrusive elements such as hinges and castors to highly or even exclusively decorative items such as chair ornaments and clock balls. Represented in the first group are cloak pins, curtain pins, jamb hooks, bell-pull ornaments, door porters, rim locks, door latches, door knockers and nameplates, and rainspouts. The second includes castors, hinges, cabinet handles and knobs, lifting handles, keyhole escutcheons, chair nails, knife-box and trunk hardware, finials, chair ornaments, cabinet mounts, and ornamental borders.

CLOAK PIN

261

ENGLAND, PROBABLY
BIRMINGHAM, 1761–1820
BRASS (COPPER 70.37, ZINC 26.21,
LEAD 2.38), IRON

H. 5 5/8" (6.6 CM), W. 2 3/8"
(6.0 CM), L. 3 3/4" (9.5 CM)

58.2406

GEORGE III ASCENDED THE THRONE of Great Britain on October 26, 1760. His coronation took place on September 22, 1761. The English engraver and medalist John Kirk (1724-70) created silver medals, depicting the king in profile, to commemorate both events. The image on the coronation medal almost certainly served as the model for the portrait on the cast cloak pin illustrated here.[1]

Kirk was not the only artisan to make profiles of George III. Isaac Gosset, in 1776, and William Hackwood, in 1789, created examples in jasperware for Josiah Wedgwood. Kirk's work was, however, the earliest and relates more closely to this cloak pin than any other.

A printed image of this pin appears in a Birmingham brass-manufacturer's trade catalogue that has the inscription "Samuel Curwen his book" penned inside the front cover.[2] Curwen, a lifelong Salem, Massachusetts, resident during the eighteenth century, was a hardware merchant by profession and accumulated a number of trade catalogues from which he ordered goods.

Architectural hardware picturing the reigning monarch would have been a fashionable fixture in American households until the Declaration of Independence was written, which cited "the history of the present King of Great Britain [as] a history of repeated injuries and usurpations." With the reading of those words publicly in New York on July 9, 1776, the gilt lead equestrian statue of the king erected there six years earlier was torn down and dismembered. At that time any demand for a cloak pin that pictured George III would have evaporated in America, although such an item would have continued to sell in England. Nonetheless, the catalogue in which the pin was illustrated had continued usefulness for the less-politically charged objects pictured in it.

CLOAK PIN
262

ENGLAND, PROBABLY
BIRMINGHAM, 1768–97
BRASS (COPPER 70.73, ZINC 25.30,
LEAD 2.98, IRON 0.57), IRON

H. 2 1/2" (6.3 CM), W. 2 1/8"
(5.4 CM), D. 3" (7.6 CM)
69.3604

THE IMAGE OF JOHN WILKES (1727–97) on this cast cloak pin is probably copied from an English engraving done in 1768 as part of a tract commemorating his fight for freedom of the press. Wilkes was lionized by the general populace in England because he championed enfranchisement and individual liberty. During the Revolution he was equally outspoken in favor of the colonial cause, making him much admired in America, as evidenced by publication of his statement that "the two important Questions of Public Liberty, respecting General Warrants and the seizure of Papers, may perhaps place me among those who have deserved well of mankind."[3]

The cloak pin shown here is illustrated in a late eighteenth-century Birmingham, England, brass-goods trade catalogue that was owned by the Salem, Massachusetts, hardware merchant Samuel Curwen (b. 1715).[4] Curwen probably acquired the catalogue and others when he traveled in England between 1775 and 1783 making contacts with manufacturers whose goods he could profitably import and sell in Salem. During his trips, Curwen wrote regularly to correspondants in America, observing that his efforts were not always successful. Manufacturers, fearing that he might be a competitor's agent sent to steal trade secrets, would refuse him admittance to their factories.[5]

In spite of his difficulties, Curwen, like numerous other ambitious hardware merchants, managed to arrange business with English manufacturers, through which large quantities of stylish and useful brass goods were made available in America.

CLOAK PINS
263

THOMAS HANDS AND WILLIAM JENKINS
BIRMINGHAM, ENGLAND, 1791–1805
BRASS (COPPER 80.31,
ZINC 19.31), IRON

L. 3 1/4" (8.3 CM),
DIAM. 2 1/16" (5.2 CM)
58.130.1, .2

THOMAS HANDS AND WILLIAM JENKINS were partners as "man-ufacturers of commode handles, cloak pins, picture frames, looking glasses, &c" for about a decade and produced a substan-tial amount of identifiable stamped brassfoundry.[6] Although marked furniture and architectural brass hardware is uncommon, most extant signed examples bear the initials of these two men.

Like many Birmingham brass workers in the late eighteenth and early nineteenth centuries, Hands's and Jenkins's use of weight-driven stamping machines enabled them to produce hard-ware more quickly and cheaply than with the older method of casting. One such "stamp in good repair whose hammer is near

210 pound weight and is released at any height with pleasure from 3 inches to near 7 foot, so that almost anything is [stamped] with ease" was offered at auction in Birmingham on July 22, 1765. The ad further states that "two boys may do the operation it being made in so complete a manner." Using such stamps, Hands and Jenkins made a large variety of cabinet handles, finials, box lids, ornaments, and other accessories, which could be used inter-changeably as cloak or surplice pins, jamb hooks, looking-glass supports, and curtain knobs for the American market.[7]

CLOAK PINS

264

NATHANIEL MARCHANT (1739–1816)
AND LEWIS PINGO (1743–1833)
BIRMINGHAM, ENGLAND, 1805–9
BRASS (COPPER 31.93, ZINC 15.70,
IRON 0.79, LEAD 0.34,
GOLD 0.34,NICKEL 0.13), IRON

L. 2 3/4" (7 CM),
DIAM. 2 1/8" (5.4 CM)
62.94.1, .2

THOMAS JEFFERSON was elected third president of the United States in 1801 and was subsequently reelected to a second term. In 1804 Charles-Balthazar-Julien Fevret de Saint-Mémin executed Jefferson's portrait in profile using a physiognotrace. At the same time, he engraved a small circular copper plate depicting a reduced version of the sitter.[8] The engravings struck from it were widely sold and circulated.

That smaller image probably served as the inspiration for the design of the pair of cloak pins shown here. Their small size, circular shape, and low profile all relate in appearance to coins and medals. The creation of the latter two was the principal work of artisans at the Royal Mint in London, among whom were Nathaniel Marchant—one of the principal engravers until 1811–

and Lewis Pingo—chief engraver until his retirement in 1815.[9] Marchant and Pingo collaborated in creating British coins and presentation medals. They did the same with the design for these cloak pins, Marchant probably creating the design and Pingo engraving it.

The dies thus created were then probably sent to Matthew Boulton's Soho manufactory in Birmingham, which he advertised as being not only a silversmithing firm but also a "button company, mint for government coin [and manufactory] of medals." The small circular images were incorporated into cloak pins, mirror knobs, chimney hooks, curtain knobs, cabinet handles, and box lids.[10]

CURTAIN PINS

265

ENGLAND, PROBABLY
BIRMINGHAM, 1810–30
BRASS (COPPER 74.35, ZINC 24.54,
LEAD 0.75, TIN 0.15), IRON

H. 6" (15.2 CM), W. 5 1/2"
(14.0 CM), D. 6" (15.2 CM)

65.2127.1, .2

DESIGNS FOR SPREAD EAGLES that held draped fabric appeared in England as early as 1803, when Thomas Sheraton created a canopy bed with three eagles holding the swagged head piece.[11]

The lightweight, stamped sheet-metal eagles shown here, described as "stampt'd eagle curtain pins," appeared in an anonymous and undated Birmingham brass-manufacturer's trade catalogue at about the same time Sheraton was publishing his furniture patterns. They were offered in pairs for use on window jambs or "for cornices . . . with iron screw [or] with rings."[12]

Stamped brassfoundry was said to have been invented by "John Pickering of London, a jeweller, or gilt toy maker [who on] March 7th, 1769 patented a 'new method of performing that kind of work called chasing for . . . brass . . . ornaments for coaches,

chariots, cabinet brass work and domestic furniture.'" The process used a two-part steel die. The face of one half had a design cut into it cameo-fashion. The other, being cut intaglio, fit precisely into its mate. The first half was placed so as to slide vertically on two upright rods. The second was on a horizontal bed under it. When a thin sheet of brass was laid on the latter, the movable half would be dropped, stamping an ornament. As a result "the work is executed in a much more expeditious manner, and far superior in beauty and elegance to anything of the kind (not being actual chasing) ever yet performed by any other method."[13]

CURTAIN ORNAMENTS
266

ENGLAND, PROBABLY
BIRMINGHAM, 1825–50
BRASS (COPPER 83.33,
ZINC 15.30, LEAD 1.14,
IRON 0.13), IRON

H. 10" (25.4 CM),
DIAM. 5 1/2" (14.0 CM)
62.188.1, .2 GIFT OF MRS.
REGINALD P. ROSE

RUDOLPH ACKERMANN established himself as an arbiter of fashion and taste in London when, in 1809, he began publishing his periodical *The Repository of Arts, Literature, Commerce, Manufactures, Fashions, and Politics*. In the May 1, 1819, issue he illustrated a set of curtains for a dining room window. The curtains hung from a horizontal rod that "may be of mat gold or covered with black velvet; in the center and ends of which are pineapples, with their natural leafing." These pineapple ornaments and a great variety of other designs were incorporated into stylish curtain pelmets during the early nineteenth century to provide "varied, easy, and elegant . . . forms . . . arranged for effect and harmony."[14]

Decorative flourishes of this type were also designed for placement on beds, the "cornices [of which] may be either mahogany carved, carved and gilt, or painted and japanned. The ornaments over the cornices may be in the same manner; carved and gilt, or japanned [and] will produce the most lively effect." An impressive example of this detailing is depicted in a design for a grand "English State Bed" in Thomas Sheraton's *Appendix to the Cabinet-Maker and Upholsterer's Drawing Book*, showing compositions of carved and gilt "spreading oak leaves and roses" at each corner of the tester.[15]

Although such ornamental amenities were desirable, the high cost of carving and gilding placed them beyond the reach of many. Less expensive substitutes were available in brass, as exemplified by the subject of this entry. These lightweight cornice ends or bed ornaments were offered through trade catalogues issued by brass manufacturers in Birmingham as seen in the illustration here. Each unit consists of twenty-one separate die-stamped, cast, and die-rolled parts, all held together with an internal iron rod threaded at each end. They were made in a considerable variety of designs and cost a reasonable 9s. to 20s. per pair.[16]

JAMB HOOKS

267

PROBABLY ENGLAND, POSSIBLY
AMERICA, 1750–80
BRASS (COPPER 75.12, ZINC 20.15,
LEAD 3.35, TIN 0.93, IRON 0.38), IRON

H. 4 1/4" (10.8 CM), D. 2 3/4"
(7.0 CM), W. 2 1/4" (5.7 CM)
58.2332.1, .2

JAMB HOOKS HUNG beside the fireplace and supported a shovel, tongs, poker, and hearth brush. Those illustrated here are made almost entirely of wrought iron, but as with many contemporary andirons, their ornamental uprights are brass. The brass parts were cast in halves vertically, brazed together, and then fitted over and peened to an iron rod in the same manner that contemporary andirons were constructed. The design of the uprights, a faceted cube under a flame, was often used on andirons and handles of fire tools.[17]

These items were largely the work of men who described themselves as fire-iron makers, an area of specialty within the founding business that dealt with shovels, tongs, pokers, and andirons. All of England's major industrial centers employed such men, who enjoyed continuing demand for their work both locally and overseas. Americans bought

a great deal of English hearth equipment through hardware merchants such as Garrit Abeel and John Byvanck. At their store near Coenties market in New York City, they "imported in the Jamima . . . from London and the Prince George . . . from Bristol . . . neat brass and iron head shovels & tongs [and] chimney hooks."[18]

A widespread and efficient network of hardware merchants enabled Americans living outside East Coast port cities to buy English hardware locally. John and Joseph Shotwell of Rahway, New Jersey, about twenty-five miles by water and unpaved roads from New York City, serve to illustrate. On November 25, 1773, they informed potential customers that they had just imported "brass and iron chimney hooks . . . in the latest vessels from London, Bristol, Liverpool and Hull."[19]

JAMB HOOK

268

SAMUEL DREW
BOSTON, MASSACHUSETTS, 1800–1810
BRASS (COPPER 84.53, ZINC 6.69,
LEAD 4.72, TIN 3.03, ANTIMONY 0.64,
IRON 0.51, SILVER 0.10)

H. 4 5/8" (11.7 CM), W. 2 3/4"
(7.0 CM), D. 3 3/4" (9.5 CM)
95.49 FUNDS FOR PURCHASE
THE GIFT OF MR. AND MRS.
SEYMOUR SCHWARTZ

"HOOKS FOR HOLDING up the shovel and tongs, a hearth brush and bellows and brass knobs to hang them on, should be furnished to every fireplace." Brass was acceptable, but "steel is more genteel, and more easily kept in order."[20] In spite of that author's preference, brass was the predominant metal for chimney hooks like the illustrated example.

Trade catalogues issued by Birmingham brass founders for circulation among factors and hardware merchants in England, Europe, and America during the late eighteenth and nineteenth centuries include numerous examples that are usually described as "chimney bows" and "chimney hooks." Others, like this example, which allow the curved arm to be lifted and removed from the plate, are called "take off chimney hooks."[21]

William Hardenbrook, a New York brass worker, stated in the May 26, 1798, issue of the *Weekly Museum* that he would undertake "casting agreeable to any pattern." His work probably included jamb hooks. David

Phillips was another founder who worked in New York from 1802 until his death in 1818. The inventory of his estate, executed on August 19 by fellow brass founder Richard Whittingham, lists over two hundred "tong pins" and "tong coves," now outmoded terms for the illustrated hook.[22]

While no jamb hooks are presently attributed to William Hardenbrook or David Phillips, the illustrated example, cast in red brass and with a removable bow, almost certainly originated in the shop of the Boston brass founder Samuel Drew. He is recorded in Boston city directories as plying his trade at various addresses between 1800 and 1810, after which he is no longer listed.

BELL-PULL ORNAMENT

269

ENGLAND, PROBABLY
BIRMINGHAM, 1810–40
BRASS (COPPER 76.90,
ZINC 22.31, LEAD 0.60)

H. 5" (12.7 CM), W. 4 1/8"
(10.5 CM), D. 1 1/8" (2.8 CM)
59.555

PULLS OF THE TYPE shown here were installed in most well-to-do English and American houses during the late eighteenth and nineteenth centuries. They were located in the parlor, dining room, library, bedrooms, and other living areas and were attached with iron wires that passed inside walls to a row of bells in a central service area, usually the kitchen or pantry. Each pull or crank had its own bell, and with it a householder could summon a servant.

It was believed by those who could afford servants and the means to call them that "no room should be without a bell; as there is no part of the house in which a bell may not be useful, particularly in case of accidents, or of persons being taken suddenly ill in the night. . . . Much trouble may be spared to the domestics by establishing different modes of ringing the bell, so as to apprize them of what is wanted before they come up stairs. For instance, let it be understood that if a servant is to come for the purpose of receiving a message or an order, the bell is to be pulled once: and if fuel is wanted, let it be pulled twice: if lights, three times; if water, four times. In some families the manner of ringing the bell is so regulated, as to denote not the thing, but the servant that is wanted; as one ring for the waiting-man; two for the boy; three for the chamber maid, &c."[23]

The brass ornament illustrated here and its mate at the other end of the pull are of thinly stamped metal, while the ring at the bottom appears to be of seamed tube. Ornaments for pulls, cranks, and bells are depicted in considerable numbers in most nineteenth-century English brass-manufacturer's trade catalogues.[24]

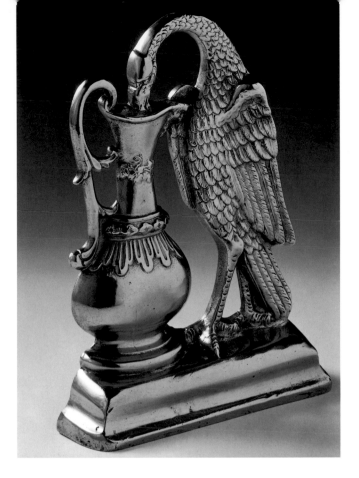

DOOR PORTER
270

PROBABLY ENGLAND, 1820–60
BRASS (COPPER 72.69,
ZINC 25.64,
TIN 0.92, LEAD 0.64), LEAD

H. 10 5/8" (27.0 CM), W. 7 7/8"
(20.0 CM), D. 1 7/8" (4.8 CM)
58.2828

AESOP IS BELIEVED to have been born about 620 B.C. in Greece, where he lived until murdered by a mob in Delphi about 560 B.C. He is said to have been physically deformed and born into poverty, living most of his life as a slave. These conditions should have relegated him to an unremarkable life, soon forgotten after his death. Even so, he made a lasting place for himself in history through his many entertaining fables in which he used animals to illustrate both human foibles and virtues.

One story features a fox and a stork. The fox invited the stork to dinner and, at the latter's expense, served "soup in a wide shallow dish [which he] could lap up with a great deal of ease; but the Stork who could just dip in the point of his bill" went hungry. The stork returned the compliment a few days later and served "some minced meat in a glass jar, the neck of which was so deep, and so narrow, that, the Stork with his long bill" ate his fill, but the fox could only look on in frustrated hunger.[25] The moral offered was to do unto others as you would have them do unto you.

Aesop had a strong appeal in England during the eighteenth and nineteenth centuries, evidenced by the fact that more than forty editions of his *Fables* were published there between 1704 and 1860. The stories were widely circulated and most were accompanied by engravings. One volume printed for the bookseller John Stockdale in 1793 included an engraving by Philip Audinet (1766–1837) of the stork and fox fable that relates to the design of this cast and partially lead-filled door porter, which was used to hold a door open.[26]

RIM LOCK
271

CLEMENT HARDWICK AND
THOMAS NEWMAN
WOLVERHAMPTON, ENGLAND, 1770–1817
BRASS (COPPER 70.10, ZINC 28.14,
LEAD 1.46), IRON

L. 7 1/8" (18.1 CM), H. 3 3/4"
(9.5 CM), D. 7/8" (2.2 CM)
82.207
GIFT OF MR. AND MRS.
ROBERT T. TRUMP

AS LATE AS 1860 it was observed that "the lock manufactory of [England] is confined almost exclusively to Wolverhampton and the neighboring village of Willenhall."[27] Clement Hardwick was one of numerous men working in the locksmithing trade in Wolverhampton, most of whom identified themselves as specialists, such as box- and trunk-lock maker, cabinet-lock maker, splinter-padlock maker, iron rim-lock maker, brass and iron mortise-lock maker, plate stock-lock maker, warded inside-lock maker, and brass desk-lock maker.

Hardwick was a "brass rimlock maker" as early as 1770, and he was still active in 1817.[28] The brass rim lock shown here typifies what he offered his customers. Its works are well finished, carefully fitted, completely of iron, and use a warded keyhole to throw a rectangular bolt. A now-missing knob with square shank retracted the spring-operated latch, and a small secondary bolt is operated manually with a tab that slides along the bottom edge of the case.

The "Lock-Smith [makes] The Keys, Wards, Springs, and Plates . . . himself; and employs the Founder to cast his cases, if in Brass."[29] This lock illustrates that relationship; the case bears the cast initials of the man Hardwick employed to make it. Although not positively identifiable, he might have been Thomas Newman, a contemporary of Hardwick's in the neighboring village of Willenhall.

While Hardwick, Newman, and their contemporaries sold much of their work throughout England, they sought an overseas market as well, of which America was an important part. This is well documented in American newspapers, many of which carried hardware advertisements for merchants, such as Daniel Robertson, who noted in the *Pennsylvania Gazette* that he had "just imported from London . . . cased brass locks."[30]

RIM LOCK AND KEEPER

272

JAMES CARPENTER (1775–1844)
AND JOHN YOUNG
WILLENHALL, ENGLAND, 1830–44
BRASS (COPPER 66.02,
ZINC 31.02, LEAD 2.69), IRON

L. 8 3/4" (22.2 CM), H. 5"
(12.7 CM), D. 5 3/4" (14.6 CM)
82.208
GIFT OF MR. AND MRS.
ROBERT T. TRUMP

WILLENHALL WAS a "town in the Borough of Wolverhampton. The manufacture of the place consists principally of locks and padlocks of every description from the smallest kind to those more ponderous and massive for gates and prisons. The chief branches are brass and other padlocks, South American rim, mortice, cabinet, Dutch, portfolio, trunk, dead, iron gate, and carpet bag locks . . . for home and foreign trade. These are exported in large quantities."[31]

Although James Carpenter first entered business as a manufacturer of curry combs, by the early nineteenth century he had branched into locksmithing. After about two decades manufacturing various types of locks, curry combs, elastic horse scrapers, and singeing lamps, he and

his partner John Young requested and received a patent for "improvements in the construction of locks, by combining in the same lock a sliding bolt and a lever spring bolt" that work independent of each other.[32]

This improvement was well received and incorporated into the work of numerous Birmingham, England, area manufacturers during the mid to late nineteenth century. As many as thirty different varieties, each bearing a different manufacturer's name, have been recorded.[33]

When Carpenter died in 1844, the firm was taken over by his son-in-law James Tildesley, who continued to operate it under the name Carpenter and Tildesley.

RIM LOCK AND KEEPER
273

WILLIAM PYE
NEW YORK CITY, 1810–40
BRASS (COPPER 74.98,
ZINC 22.11, LEAD 0.67, TIN 0.21,
ANTIMONY 0.13), IRON

L. 8 3/4" (22.2 CM), H. 4"
(10.2 CM), D. 6 3/4" (17.2 CM)
86.111

A LOCK IS "A WELL-KNOWN instrument for securing doors and preventing them from being opened, except by means of the key adapted to it."[34] Because of the security they offered, locks were in constant demand and were routinely fitted to interior and exterior doors of public and private buildings.

William Pye was one of many men who supplied that trade. He first listed himself in the New York City directories in 1810. During his thirty-year career he described himself variously as a hardware merchant, bellhanger, and locksmith. George, John, Thomas, William M., and Simeon Pye also engaged in the locksmithing trade in New York at the same time, but none for as long as William. His first shop was located at 415 Pearl Street, where he remained until 1819, when he relocated to 6 Chamber Street. By 1825 he was working at 12 Chamber Street but for only one year. In 1826 he was at 16 Augustus Street, again for one

year. He listed himself at 101 Canal Street in 1827 and remained there until 1833. In 1834 he had moved to 6 Wooster Street. At that time he attempted two partnerships, one with a Mr. Gledney and a second with Thomas Whaley at another address, 46–48 Mott Street. By 1838 both partnerships had been dissolved, and Pye was working at 107 Walker. In 1840 he moved to 162 Centre Street, after which he no longer appears in the city directories.

The rim lock shown here has a substantially cast brass case that houses iron and brass works. It is related to its English counterpart but does differ in two significant features. The case has two half-rounded, pierced countersunk tabs at the handle end to attach it to a door. English locks do not. Secondly, the bolt and keeper are brass, unlike English examples, which are iron.

DOOR LATCH
274

JOHN T. BURROWS
PHILADELPHIA, PENNSYLVANIA, 1831–49
BRASS (COPPER 81.83, ZINC 8.70,
TIN 5.30, LEAD 3.30,
IRON 0.20, SILVER 0.15), IRON

L. 6 1/2" (16.5 CM),
H. 3 1/2" (8.9 CM),
D. 2" (5.1 CM)
61.425

THE LOCK IS "A WELL KNOWN instrument for fastening doors . . . generally opened with a key. [It] is reconed the master piece in smithery; a great deal of art and delicacy being required in contriving and varying the wards, springs, bolts, &c. and adjusting them to the places where they are to be used. . . . Those placed on outer doors are called stock locks; those on chamber doors, spring locks."[35]

The door latch illustrated here was made for an interior door by John T. Burrows, who identified himself as a bell-hanger and locksmith in Philadelphia for eighteen years. He was one of twenty-nine men who listed themselves as pur-

suing these two professions concurrently in that city during the second quarter of the nineteenth century.[36]

This latch was nailed to the inside of a chamber door, allowing it to be opened from the inside by simply lifting the knob affixed to the latch bar. It was opened from the outside with a removable knob (now missing) that was rotated, causing the cam to lift the latch bar.[37] With the removal of the knob, which slid over a cylindrical shaft, the latch became a simple but effective lock, since the bolt could not then be lifted from the outside.

DOOR KNOCKER
275

ENGLAND, PROBABLY LONDON,
1740–75
BRASS (COPPER 76.24, ZINC 20.39,
LEAD 2.16, TIN 0.90), IRON

H. 12 1/4" (31.1 CM), W. 5 1/2"
(14.0 CM),
D. 8 1/4" (21.0 CM)
65.1500

DURING THE 1750S numerous designers including George Bickham, Matthew Darly, Thomas Johnson, and Francis Vivares created and published in London a flurry of design books in the rococo taste. While their titles varied, all delineated a multitude of asymmetric compositions made up of leafy scrolls, shells, falling water, and other stylized naturalistic motifs. These designs were intended "for ye use of Artificers in General," which included brass founders.[38]

Matthias Lock (ca. 1710–65) was among the most creative and prolific of these men. His designs, both abstract and for furniture, appear in many published works dating from the third quarter of the eighteenth century. During the 1750s a collection of his designs was published in London by Robert Sayer under the title *A New Drawing Book of Ornaments, Shields, Compartments, Marks, &c.* Many of the illustrations depict cartouches, a pervasive motif used extensively on architecture and the decorative arts. As such, it is perhaps the single design element that best epitomizes the essence of rococo taste. The cartouche that Lock drew for plate 6 of the Sayer book is very similar to the substantially cast plate of this door knocker.

DOOR KNOCKER
276

PROBABLY ENGLAND, POSSIBLY
AMERICA, 1770–1810
BRASS (COPPER 69.19, ZINC 26.23,
LEAD 4.14, IRON 0.33), IRON

H. 9 3/4" (24.8 CM), W. 3 3/8"
(8.6 CM), D. 7" (17.8 CM)
69.3602

ON AUGUST 24, 1772, Mary Eddy informed readers of the *Pennsylvania Packet* that she had "removed her ironmongery store [to] the west side of Second Street between Market and Chestnut Streets [in Philadelphia, where she sold] brass knockers for street doors." Those knockers might have been made locally by men like "Phillip Syng, Brass founder, from Philadelphia [who] makes (or repairs) all sorts of Brass-work, such as . . . knockers for doors," but they could just as readily have been a mass-produced import from England.[39]

Door knockers are often depicted in Birmingham trade catalogues. Most are practically identical to the one illustrated here, apparently the most popular model of all those offered. They were made in virtually every general brass foundry in Birmingham throughout the second half of the eighteenth century to the middle of the nineteenth century.

Described simply as "Brass Knockers," they were offered in at least eleven different sizes ranging from 4 1/2 to 10 inches in length.[40]

It must have been this type of knocker that was the subject of a notice in the *Pennsylvania Journal* on February 20, 1765, that "last week some villans broke and carried off, from the houses of [Philadelphia], between 20 + 30 brass knockers." They may have been wrenched from their doors for mischief or possibly to turn in as scrap for cash. Apparently in response to that violation, the Philadelphia brass founder Daniel King announced that he made "new constructed Brass Knockers for Front Doors . . . not the sort which have an iron staple over them," which were theft proof.[41]

DOOR KNOCKER
277

ENGLAND, PROBABLY
BIRMINGHAM, 1800–1825
BRASS (COPPER 71.18,
ZINC 27.08, LEAD 1.28,
TIN 0.12), IRON

H. 4 15/16" (15.1 CM), W. 4 5/8"
(11.8 CM), D. 3 1/4" (8.3 CM)
65.1492

THIS KNOCKER, probably meant for a front door, although possibly for a chamber door, is pictured in a Birmingham brass-founder's trade catalogue owned by the Victoria and Albert Museum. A related example that uses a fist to suspend the knocker is pictured and described as a Wellington knocker in another anonymous Birmingham brass-manufacturer's trade catalogue at Winterthur.[42]

Throughout the eighteenth century, brass or iron knockers were the only type of fixture on front doors. During the first decade of the nineteenth century, they began to be supplanted by the front door bell, but "on account of the ineffiency of the door-bell . . . it was difficult to obtain admittance [to some] houses."

A bell could not be heard from all areas of the house. In spite of this drawback, "brass knockers [were] considered old fashioned [by the 1840s], but they have at least the advantage of being easily sounded and never getting out of order."[43]

In addition to a brass knocker, the properly fitted nineteenth-century front door had "a slit for the reception of newspapers, letters, &c. . . . Over it should be placed a movable brass or silver-plated cover [and] a name-plate. . . . The want of [the last of these] frequently causes much inconvenience to strangers, particularly in a row of houses that are all alike, and in streets whose similarity is so great as in Philadelphia."[44]

DOOR KNOCKER
AND NAMEPLATE

278

ENGLAND OR PHILADELPHIA, 1830–70
BRASS (COPPER 77.78,
ZINC 18.83, LEAD 2.07,
TIN 0.58, IRON 0.17), IRON

KNOCKER: H. 9" (22.9 CM), W. 4 7/8"
(12.4 CM), D. 3 3/8" (8.6 CM);
NAMEPLATE: H. 3 1/4" (8.3 CM), L. 8"
(20.3 CM), D. 3 1/4" (8.3 CM)
82.248.1, .2
GIFT OF MR. AND MRS. ROBERT T. TRUMP

PHILADELPHIA CITY DIRECTORIES list numerous residents who might have owned this entrance door knocker and nameplate. Jacob, Jonathan, several Johns, and James Lukens are all potential candidates for original ownership during the mid nineteenth century.

Architectural hardware like this was among the extensive production of most English brass founders, as recorded in numerous trade catalogues that picture such items in a wide variety of styles and sizes. Through those catalogues, American hardware merchants such as Isaac B. Baxter at 224 South Second Street in Philadelphia ordered and imported "all kinds of building materials and cabinet mountings, such as Knob-locks, Latches, Hinges, Screws, Brass Knobs, Bed Caps, Brass

Nails, &c &c."[45] Although not specifically mentioned, knockers and nameplates were without doubt among his and his competitors' offerings.

While these merchants did not personalize door hardware for a purchaser, they would, if requested, offer names of craftsmen who could provide that service. Such work was the province of specialists such as "John Hutt, from London, engraver in general and copper plate printer [who] engraves all sorts of arms, crests, seals & cyphers [and] door plates."[46]

DOOR KNOCKER
279

INCREASE WILSON (D. 1861)
NEW LONDON,
CONNECTICUT, 1831–55
BRASS, IRON

H. 8 1/2" (21.6 CM), W. 4 3/8"
(11.1 CM), D. 4" (10.1 CM)
89.19

GEORGE RICHARDSON observed in his *Iconologia; or, A Collection of Emblematical Figures* that "when it is required to paint a fabulous divinity, it is necessary to have recourse to mythology, to select the proper attributes . . . . The attributes are distinctions, invented to render every figure the more easily known." Among the more popular and readily recognized of the ancient dieties was Bacchus, the son of Jupiter and Semele. "As Bacchus was the god of vintage, of wine and of drinkers, he is generally represented crowned with vine and ivy leaves," and his followers are usually depicted as young priestesses called Bacchantes.[47]

The image of Bacchus or his Bacchantes was extensively employed as ornament during the early nineteenth century, commonly as iron and brass door knockers, of which a number are depicted in English metalworker's trade catalogues. Through catalogues these knockers, and all other hardware included therein, were marketed widely. Their influence is readily apparent in the subject of this entry, which was made in New London, Connecticut. The knocker was cast–probably using an imported English example as the pattern for the mold–in the brass manufactory of Increase Wilson.[48]

While it is visually identical to its English counterpart, the knocker does differ in construction. Wilson applied for and was granted a United States patent on March 11, 1831, for its mode of construction. The specifications outline his improvement. "The usual mode, heretofore, of manufacturing cast iron door knockers, with brass plates, has been to fasten on the brass plates after the knockers are cast, by means of solder, screws, or rivets. My improvement consists in casting the knockers directly on the brass plates; which may be done by first casting the inside of the brass plates with tin, lead or other metals which fuse at a lower temperature than brass. The brass plates are then secured in their proper place in the moulds, and the iron poured in, (as is usual in casting iron) which will readily unite to the brass plates, and secure them on more firmly, and better than is done in the usual way with rivets, &c."[49]

Most knockers of this type, whether made in England or documented to Wilson's foundry, are of cast iron with a brass plate, which is readily understood because of relative cost. Examples made entirely of brass cost upwards of seven times their counterparts in iron.[50]

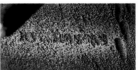

DOOR NAMEPLATE
280

UNITED STATES,
POSSIBLY PHILADELPHIA,
PENNSYLVANIA, 1840–50
BRASS (COPPER 73.53,
ZINC 22.77, LEAD 2.58, TIN 0.65)

L. 6 3/4" (17.2 CM), H. 3"
(7.6 CM), D. 1 1/4" (3.2 CM)
82.247
GIFT OF MR. AND MRS.
ROBERT T. TRUMP

CASPER BOCKIUS WAS A CABINETMAKER; Christopher Bockius was a saddler; and Charles Bockius was a fancy-leather manufacturer. All worked in Philadelphia during the mid nineteenth century. Any one of them might have had this cast brass, silvered nameplate on the entry door to his house. "Door & number plates, brass and silver door plates of every description from 2 to $40 elegantly engraved" were made in all major American cities at that time by men like S. J. Creswell, brass and iron founder, at 221 Arch Street in Philadelphia.[51] Such items were also imported from England and available through hardware merchants such as Harbeson and N. W. Hickman, located at 12 North Third Street in Philadelphia.

The nameplate shown here has what appears to be the surname Hickman cast into the reverse. It is not likely that the Hickmans, hardware merchants, made this plate. They probably commissioned it as part of a bulk order from a jobbing smith such as Creswell, who made "brass castings, plain and ornamental, for Gas fitters, Lamp Makers, Sword Mounters, &c.; best quality Composition for Locksmiths [and] Iron Castings for Machinists."[52] During the nineteenth century, retailers like the Hickmans often had their names, rather than those of the wholesaling manufacturers, placed on the objects they sold.

RAINSPOUT
281

UNITED STATES, PROBABLY
PHILADELPHIA,
PENNSYLVANIA, 1792
COPPER

H. 9' 6 1/2" (291.0 CM),
W. 13 1/2" (34.3 CM), D. 8" (20.3 CM)
59.1834

"THE DRAINS OF A BUILDING demand great attention from the architect who plans them in the first instance, and they also require to be kept in the most perfect order, to ensure the safety of the building, and the comfort, and even health of the inhabitants."[53] Their essential purpose was to catch and direct rainwater away from building walls and foundations.

The cheapest and most readily obtainable spouts were made of wooden boards, but metal hardware was more substantial and longer lasting. Lead and tinned sheet iron were the most common of these, but cast iron and copper were also used. Depending on the amount of rainfall and size of the roof, the Birmingham coppersmith Charles Wyatt offered rainwater pipes of tinned copper or leaded iron from 2 1/2 inches to 4 inches in diameter and gutters from 6 to 12 inches in girth for local use or export.[54]

American metalworkers also offered this type of hardware. The Alexandria, Virginia, coppersmiths George M'Munn and Isaac Sittler stated in the *Columbian Mirror and Alexandria Gazette* that "they have just received . . . from Liverpool an excellent assortment of copper in sheets . . . suitable for spouts and gutters which will come cheaper than lead."[55]

At about the same time the coppersmith and tin-plate worker William P. Atlee advertised in the *Lancaster Journal* that he was familiar with the methods of making and putting up "house pipes as practiced in Baltimore and Philadelphia." One of the Philadelphia craftsmen whom Atlee may have had in mind was Henry Harbenger, Jr., who advertised that he was located at "No. 406, Market Street, near the Centre Square [and had] constantly on hand, wholesale and retail . . . all kinds of house work in general, such as Copper and Tin Spouts, and Spout Heads."[56]

A.

B.

CASTORS
282 a,b

A. ENGLAND, 1720–80
BRASS (COPPER 69.78, ZINC 21.39,
IRON 5.25, LEAD 3.41), IRON, LEATHER
H. 1 1/8" (2.8 CM), DIAM. 1 3/8" (3.4 CM)
86.97.1
GIFT OF STANLEY BLOCK

B. ENGLAND, 1750–1810
BRASS (COPPER 73.96, ZINC 16.95,
LEAD 7.30, IRON 1.48, TIN 0.17,
SILVER 0.10), IRON
H. 1 1/8" (2.9 CM), DIAM. 1 3/8" (3.5 CM)
57.633

IN 1627 MATHURIN JOUSSE published a design of an armchair on small offset wheels that he described as a new "invention of a chair in which one can advance, back up and turn in all directions, with a simple and single movement." While primitive castors are stated to have been used on furniture in Europe as early as 1520, Jousse's design appears to be among the earliest representations detailing their purpose.[57]

Few illustrations document the use of castors on seventeenth- and eighteenth-century furniture, but evidence clearly proves their presence. R. Campbell noted in the *London Tradesmen*, published in 1747, that "the Upholder . . . employs the smith for castors, hinges, and locks to his beds, tables, cabinets &c," implying such amenities were commonplace. Campbell's assertion is amply illustrated in Thomas Chippendale's accounts to his patrons that specify castors on beds,

chairs, sofas, tables, and a "very large mahogany counter with folding doors & shelves."[58]

A number of his entries specifically describe castors. On May 5, 1759, Chippendale sold William Dumfries a "large mahogany . . . bedstead . . . with . . . strong triple wheel castors."[59] Castors of this type were preferred on heavy furniture like beds, since their two supplementary wheels not only eased rotational movement but very effectively prevented the shank that held the offset horn in place from bending.

On June 13, 1766, Chippendale submitted a bill to Sir Rowland Winn for repairing and cleaning furniture and replacing "a leather wheeled castor." Laminated leather wheels were apparently used for only a few decades during the mid eighteenth century, presumably because brass wheels eventually proved to be easier and cheaper to make and withstood moisture and heavy wear much better.[60]

A.

B.

CASTORS
283 a,b

A. ENGLAND, 1750–1810
BRASS (COPPER 71.63, ZINC 21.70, LEAD 4.41,
IRON 1.45, TIN 0.64, SILVER 0.10), IRON
H. 1 3/4" (2.9 CM), DIAM. 1 3/8" (3.5 CM)
69.3601

B. ENGLAND, PROBABLY BIRMINGHAM, 1810–25
BRASS (COPPER 75.88, ZINC 20.75,
LEAD 2.15, TIN 0.30, NICKEL 0.30), IRON
L. 3 7/8" (9.8 CM), W. 1 7/8"
(4.8 CM), H. 4" (10.1 CM)
51.145

CASTORS GREATLY FACILITATED the moving of furniture but often lost their ability to adjust to the direction of movement fairly quickly. This problem arose because the spindle bent under the weight of the object, preventing the fork or horn holding the wheel from rotating. Many men devoted their attention to alleviating that difficulty. Perhaps the most successful solution was written about in 1803 by Thomas Sheraton, who noted that "there is a caster lately introduced, which [has] the wheel . . . nearly perpendicular to the socket, and is supported by a small roller, which runs round with it."[61]

James Harcourt, a brass founder in Birmingham, is one of those who attempted to capitalize on the idea. He applied for and obtained a patent on June 21, 1820, entitled "an improvement in castors applicable to tables and other articles." In describing his innovation, Harcourt specified that it "consists in the adoption of antifriction rollers which

are intended to take off the friction when the castors turn horizontally." He went on to say that "the same contrivance is applicable to the various kinds of castor with either round or square sockets, or to any other description of castor for claw or paw furniture."[62]

The two castors pictured here each use a single small wheel, built into the crotch of the horn, that rotates against the flat underside of the plate or foliate *sabot*. The wheel not only eases rotation but also provides supplemental support to prevent the spindle arm from bending. Competitors saw the advantage of this improvement and incorporated it into their work by buying the rights to the patent. Castors made under such a provision were sometimes marked "PATENT" and were noted in brass-founders' trade catalogues as being "upon the patent principal."[63]

A.

B.

CUP CASTORS
284 a,b

A. ENGLAND, 1770–1810
BRASS (COPPER 74.07, ZINC 22.00,
LEAD 3.58), IRON, LEATHER
H. 2" (5.1 CM), W. 1 1/2"
(3.8 CM), D. 1" (2.5 CM)
86.99 GIFT OF STANLEY BLOCK

B. ENGLAND, PROBABLY BIRMINGHAM, 1812–50
BRASS (COPPER 70.43, ZINC 28.78,
LEAD 0.57), IRON, PORCELAIN
H. 2 5/8" (6.7 CM), W. 2 1/8" (5.3 CM),
DIAM. 1 1/2" (3.8 CM)
86.98 GIFT OF STANLEY BLOCK

DURING THE EIGHTEENTH and nineteenth centuries, furniture castors were normally made of brass. The metal was sturdy and decorative, and its price was also relatively modest, with weight of metal used being the principal cost factor. Nonetheless, other materials were used, normally with a view to making more affordable castors. Iron was the main alternative, but it was not nearly as decorative as an elaborate cast-brass lion paw or even a plain cup coated with tinted lacquer.

John Loach, a brass founder in Birmingham during the early nineteenth century, attempted an innovative marriage of iron and brass to make less expensive but equally decorative furniture castors. On May 8, 1812, he was granted a patent for his improvement. In justifying and describing his innovation, he noted that he makes "the heaviest parts of the castors . . . (which have heretofore been made all of brass) . . . of cast or wrought iron, and afterwards case or cover them with . . . rolled

or sheet copper or brass." He went on: "The way in which I cover them is this: I raise or form the metal coverings by means of a stamp press or any similar method in die moulds. . . . I then solder the part together that is to go round the outside of the iron socket, and by fixing it in a chuck in a lathe turn over the edge at the top of the socket; I then take a piece of metal . . . of a proper size, and fix it to the outside of the bottom of the iron socket, by turning the bottom edge of the metal covering over upon it, so as to cover and conceal the iron."[64]

The round socket castor illustrated here conforms precisely to Loach's process and, in theory, represents a cost saving. In practice, however, his castors seem not to have supplanted those of solid cast brass, such as the leather-wheeled example shown here with the square socket, which is made of seven layers of leather held in place on the axle by a thin conforming brass cap on each side.

CUP CASTOR
285

ENGLAND, PROBABLY
BIRMINGHAM, 1820–30
BRASS (COPPER 73.85, ZINC 24.00,
LEAD 1.44, NICKEL 0.26), IRON

H. 3 3/8" (8.6 CM), W. 2 1/2"
(6.3 CM), DIAM. 1 1/2" (30.8 CM)

57.753.1

THROUGHOUT THE EIGHTEENTH century in both England and America, wheels were attached to the legs of furniture with some degree of frequency. The inventory of John Penn, Jr., of Philadelphia, taken in 1788, records "1 writing table standing on brass castors [and] 1 field bedstead on castors." These small offset wheels were "usually applied and used on the feet or supports or the lower parts of massive articles of domestic furniture, or any other articles of domestic furniture, or any other articles which require to be moved with safety from place to place on a floor or hard surface."[65]

Castors became increasingly popular in the first decades of the nineteenth century, possibly testifying to more routine movement of furniture within households. In recounting the history of brass manufactur-ing in Birmingham in 1866, William C. Aitken observed that "the making of castors for furniture purposes absorbs a considerable amount of labor in the cabinet brass foundry trade; formerly these were of a more obtrusive character than they are now. In the old days of pillar and claw tables and curved out sofa legs, castors were prominent objects and decorations of the piece of furniture." The castor shown here is of the elaborate type to which he was referring. It is similar to the "Stamp't Round Socket Castors with Improved Horns and Steel Collars" sold in sets of four and illus-trated in a Birmingham trade catalogue that is water-marked with the date 1824.[66]

Numerous American hardwaremen imported English castors, which were enumerated in advertise-ments like that of Benjamin Davis of Philadelphia in the *Pennsylvania Packet*. On May 4, 1772, he offered "brass castors . . . just imported." Although not nor-mally marked, at least one importer is known to have placed his name on these wares. Two plain, cup castors on a small three-drawer table in the Museum of the City of New York bear the impressed name "A. THORP."[67] Andrew Thorp was a New York City hardware mer-chant active between 1822 and 1866.

The castor illustrated here undoubtedly passed through the inventory of a Philadelphia or Baltimore hardware importer. It was purchased by a Baltimore furnituremaker, who used it and seven others on the legs of a pair of painted window seats.[68]

CASTOR
286

JOHN LOACH AND CHARLES CLARKE
BRASS (COPPER 73.42,
ZINC 21.56, LEAD 2.15,
IRON 1.33, TIN 1.13), IRON

H. 2 1/4" (5.7 CM),
W. 1 3/4" (4.5 CM),
DIAM. 1 5/16" (3.3 CM)
69.3714

IN HIS *American Mechanical Dictionary*, Edward H. Knight defined a castor as "a small wheel attached to the leg of a table, chair or other piece of furniture, in order to facilitate its being moved without lifting."[69] As suggested in Knight's comment, the size of a piece of furniture was not a factor in the use of castors. Both large, heavy objects like beds and small, easily moved objects like side chairs frequently stood on castors. Although a helpful aid, little attention was paid to castors by householders, which resulted in their quickly becoming damaged or distorted.

Although a small and relatively inexpensive amenity, castors were in such demand that many inventors felt considerable profit was to be made designing and patenting improved models.

The Englishman John Walker successfully devised an improved design for which he received a British patent in 1827. The specifications state that in his "improved castor for funiture the point of the main pin of the castor bears upon a steel cup, fitted into the bottom of the socket, and which said steel cup, as well as the point of the pin, being both formed of hardened steel, it makes them more durable. I likewise fit a loose cylindrical collar upon the upper part of the pin of the castor, which turns upon the pin as a centre in the manner of a horizontal friction roller, and against which said collar a circle, or a portion of a circle, formed upon and above the horns which carry the roller of the castor, presses or acts so as to keep the bearing of the pin of the castor in the socket perpendicular, or nearly so, the circle or

portion of a circle having a lateral pressure upon the collar, and thus permitting the roller and horns to turn in the proper direction with facility."[70] That specification describes the castor illustrated here exactly.

Walker's countryman John Loach also had ideas for which he sought patent protection. Between 1812 and 1847 he was granted six patents for hardware. Two of those dealt with furniture castors, but neither relates to the salient features of this castor. It is probable, therefore, that Loach and his partner Charles Clarke, who worked together on Little Charles Street in Birmingham from 1827 to about 1860, purchased the rights to make and market this patented castor directly from the inventor or through a patent agent.

CUP CASTOR

287

JOHN AND CHARLES COPE AND
ABRAHAM COLLINSON
BIRMINGHAM, ENGLAND, 1841–62
BRASS (COPPER 65.52, ZINC 23.15,
LEAD 1.03), IRON

H. 3 1/8" (7.9 CM), W. 2 3/4"
(7.0 CM), DIAM. 1 5/8" (4.1 CM)
ONE OF FOUR
86.96.1
GIFT OF STANLEY BLOCK

IN 1827 JOHN WALKER, esquire, was granted British patent number 5562 in recognition of his improved furniture castor that included "a loose cylindrical collar . . . upon the upper part of the pin . . . which turns in the manner of a horizontal roller . . . to keep the bearing of the pin . . . perpendicular."[71] The purpose of this collar was to ease the lateral rotation of the horns that held the wheel. The inventor stipulated that it should be made of hardened steel to last longer.

Walker was apparently not a brass founder at the time he received his patent, as judged by the term *Esquire* following his name on the record, and, like "Mr. Pinchbeck of Charing Cross, London [who] obtained his Majesty's Royal Letters Patent . . . transferred the whole power of making his castors to others upon payment of a licensing fee." As seen by the stamped inscription on the cup of the castor shown here, one of Walker's licensees was the Birmingham firm of John

and Charles Cope and Abraham Collinson. The former, brothers born in 1783 and 1784 respectively, listed themselves as brass founders in Birmingham as early as 1816. They subsequently entered into numerous short-lived partnerships, finally forming an alliance with Abraham Collinson about 1841, as "military and cabinet brass founders."[72] This arrangement apparently suited them, for they remained together for more than a decade, during which time their firm made this substantial cup castor in accordance with the provisions of Walker's patent. Although the iron collar has rusted, the brass parts have remained relatively bright under their lacquered finish, which imitates gilding.

CASTOR
288

ATTRIBUTED TO LEROY S. WHITE
CHICOPEE, MASSACHUSETTS, 1854–70
BRASS (COPPER 65.30, ZINC 31.80,
LEAD 2.30, TIN 0.30), IRON

L. 2 1/16" (5.2 CM), W. 1 1/2"
(3.8 CM), D. 1" (2.5 CM)
73.308
GIFT OF HARRY D. BERRY, JR.

CASTORS SEEM TO HAVE BEEN invented at a very early date and are routinely depicted in illustrations of sofas as early as 1794. When Thomas Sheraton published his *Cabinet Dictionary* in 1803, their use had become so widespread that he devoted several detailed paragraphs to them, noting that "of this useful article in brass work, there are a great variety [including] plate casters . . . square and round socket casters, claw casters [and] two and three wheel plate . . . casters."[73]

Regardless of their configuration, all were designed to ease the movement of furniture. This they did well, but not without drawbacks. Furniture supported permanently on wheels moved not only when needed but at other times as well. As a result, numerous individuals in England and the United States attempted to perfect and patent an improved castor that would overcome the problem.

Among the 133 patents issued for castors by the United States Patent Office between 1850 and 1873 were two to LeRoy S. White of Chicopee, Massachusetts. On January 31, 1854, he was granted a patent for "New and Improved Method of Attaching and Detaching Shanks of Furniture Casters to and from their sockets."[74]

This improvement entailed fitting a spring inside the socket that encircles the shank of the castor and holds it in place. When the object it supports is to remain stationary, the castor is simply removed by pulling it out of its socket. Shortly thereafter, White sought another improvement, which was granted on August 6, 1854. In it he fitted the "holding spring . . . in the exterior of the [shank] instead of . . . the interior of the socket [making it] cheaper and more convenient" than his earlier version.[75]

CASTOR
289

JOHN TOLER, SONS AND COMPANY
NEWARK, NEW JERSEY, 1848–1905
BRASS (COPPER 67.77, ZINC 28.63,
LEAD 2.25, TIN 0.77, IRON 0.43), IRON

H. 2 3/8" (6.0 CM), W. 2 1/8"
(5.4 CM), DIAM. 1 3/8" (3.5 CM)
69.4056

IN 1878 JOSEPH ATKINSON recorded in the *History of Newark, New Jersey* that "from the smallest beginnings fifty years ago, there have grown up in Newark nearly a score of hardware and tool factories. . . . In the manufacture of edge tools such as carpenters use, the house of William Johnson is one of the very oldest in the country. It was founded by the present proprietors father in 1834. M. B. Provost, in the same line, was established about the same time. M. Price started in 1846, and Henry Sauerbier in 1848. Several years before this, John Toler began the manufacture of castors."[76]

Toler's business seems to have prospered, for within twenty years he had brought his sons Francis and Charles as well as Joseph III into partnership, and his firm was given a good rating, capitalized at

$100,000, by Dun, Barlow, and Company.[77] The company was out of business, however, by 1905, possibly in part because its area of specialty was so narrow.

A trade catalogue issued by the firm in 1883 indicates its stock was extensive and suggests that the business enjoyed a market that was national in scope.[78] The catalogue describes and pictures a broad range of castors for varied uses. Included are plate castors, round and square shallow-socket castors, round and square deep-socket castors, bed castors, bracket bed castors, and patent lounge castors. In addition, the firm offered what were called english style, french style, common philadelphia french, and patent-improved philadelphia french castors. The last two seem to have derived the designation philadel-

phia from the presence of a beaded decorative collar above the wheel.

All castors, regardless of type, were offered with iron or brass cups, plates, and horns. They could also be ordered in combination, such as an iron plate fitted to a brass horn. Additionally, they could be fitted according to the purchaser's preference with brass, porcelain, rubber, enameled, or lignum vitae wheels. All were available in graduated sizes. The castor illustrated here, pictured on page 10 in the 1883 catalogue, is described as a round deep-socket castor. It was made in seven variations of materials in eight sizes, from a 7/8-inch to a 2-inch cup. This 1-inch example, with brass socket, horn, and wheel, was priced at $.75.

BUTT HINGE

290

ENGLAND, PROBABLY
BIRMINGHAM, 1795–1810
BRASS (COPPER 71.88, ZINC 22.61,
LEAD 4.74, IRON 0.56, SILVER 0.12)

L. 2 7/8" (7.3 CM), W. 1 1/2"
(3.8 CM), D. 1/4" (0.6 CM)
ONE OF THREE
57.945

OF ALL THE OBJECTS made by the general brass founder, hinges were among the most widely used. Illustrative of this is an early nineteenth-century brass-founder's trade catalogue owned by Winterthur that contains a total of 211 engraved pictorial pages. Thirty depict hinges, of which there are twenty-five different types. Itemized are butt, rising butt, worm rising butt, narrow butt, strong butt (with thick plates), loose butt (one plate removable from the pintle), clock case, tumbler, round-top tumbler, rule joint, H, coach, desk, portable desk, stop (plates open only to 90 degrees), center (for swinging doors), square head, square top, double joint, french, spring, pew, milk pail, supper tray, and sandwich tray. In addition, the catalogue includes iron hinges and iron hinges "covered with brass." Each hinge illustrated is assigned its own number, which was often cast into the object and used for correct identification when ordering.[79]

The aforementioned catalogue pictures a total of 202 brass hinges, with no two the same. The smallest is 1/2-inch long with two holes in each plate; the largest is 6 inches, with five countersunk holes in each plate. Most are butt hinges, like the example shown here, which is one of three original to, and holding the top in place on, a Philadelphia-made display table.[80] The hinges allow the mirror-lined lid to be opened to a vertical position, exposing an elaborate compartmentalized interior. Normally, a stop hinge would be used to hold a lid like this open, but the innovative maker of this table chose to use these standard cast and lacquered butts in such a way that the lid itself becomes the stop against the back of the case.

STOP HINGES
291

PAUL MOORE
BIRMINGHAM, ENGLAND, 1843–50
BRASS (COPPER 69.92, ZINC 28.00,
LEAD 1.17, IRON 0.75)

H. 1" (2.5 CM), W. 11/16"
(1.7 CM), D. 1/8" (0.3 CM)
69.3759.1, .2

THOMAS SHERATON stated in the *Cabinet Dictionary* that the "hinge [is] a most useful article in cabinet-making, of which there are a great variety."[81] The most universal type was the butt hinge, which had widespread application on cabinet and bookcase doors, trunk and box lids, drop-leaf tables, and fall-front desks. In the eighteenth century and before, the two halves of brass cabinet hinges were cast individually, then shaped, finished, and fitted together. In the nineteenth century, changes in their fabrication were developed to speed production. The plates began to be cut from rolled sheet metal instead of being cast, and knuckles were shaped by machine instead of by hand.

A specialized variant of the butt hinge called "stop-but hinges, are so named because the door or top of any piece of work only turns a little more than perpen-dicular to the edge or surface on which they are set–if they are pressed further the hinge will break." Precisely when the idea of a stop hinge was conceived has not been established, but they are pictured in numbers of nineteenth-century Birmingham brass-manufactur-ers' trade catalogues. A. W. Gillet offered fifteen gradu-ated sizes of "Brass hinges with Stop Joints" priced from 2 to 14*s*. per dozen in his pattern book, which is date watermarked to 1829. Although no comparable pattern book is currently recorded for his competitor Paul Moore, the pair of stop hinges shown here, made from rolled sheet brass, attest to his making them as well. In fact, he may have specialized in such items, as suggested in the *Directory of Birmingham* for 1846, which lists "Paul Moore and Co. [as] metal rollers, wire drawers, manufacturers of brass stop butts and brass hinges, stair rods, solder, gilding, dipping and German silver wires and all kinds of tubing."[82]

The hinges illustrated here have the unusual feature of being stamped with the maker's name, "September 27, 1843," and "REGISTERED." This marking was allowed under the provision of the British Patent Office's Design Copyright Act of 1839. That act was amended with the "Designs Act [of] 1843 [that] offered protection to useful, as distinct from ornamental manufactured articles, and gave them 3 years protection."[83] In this instance Moore used that act to protect the design of his stop mechanism, which consists of interlocking offsets on two adjoining knuckles.

HINGE
292

ATTRIBUTED TO DANIEL BURNAP
(1759–1838)
EAST WINDSOR, CONNECTICUT, 1786–1805
BRASS (COPPER 76.87, ZINC 17.59,
LEAD 4.66, IRON 0.41, TIN 0.23,
SILVER 0.14, ANTIMONY 0.10)

H. 1 1/4" (3.2 CM), W. 2 1/8"
(5.4 CM), D. 1/4" (0.6 CM)
ONE OF A PAIR
64.585

CABINET HARDWARE was among the most important staples of the English brass worker. "Locks of all sorts, Hinges of various kinds . . . chases and handles for Cabinet-Work" were in constant and widespread demand. The products found an active market not only in England but also in America, as evidenced by the Boston hardware merchants Joseph and Daniel Waldo, who in 1748 "just imported from London [to be] sold by Wholesale and Retail at the cheapest Rates . . . hinges [and] all sorts of brass furniture for desks, book cases, &c." Similarly, in 1773 John and Joseph Shotwell of Rahway, New Jersey, offered "brass H hinges [and] clock case ditto [which they] just imported . . . in the last vessels from London, Bristol, Liverpool and Hull."[84]

American metalworkers also competetively sought to supply the need for cabinet hardware. Although Daniel Burnap thought of himself as a "clock and watch maker," his ability with brass allowed him to make other things as well. Among the extensive collection of his manuscripts, tools, and shop equipment now owned by the Connecticut Historical Society are thirteen wood patterns for clock parts and forty-five wood patterns for hardware. Four of the latter were used to make hinges, and one is identical to the subject of this entry.[85]

In addition to supplying his own needs for hinges, Burnap also sold them to others. Eliphalet Chapin, an East Windsor cabinetmaker, is recorded several times in Burnap's ledger as buying "pr of card table hinges," which were almost certainly cast in the clockmaker's shop.[86]

A.

CLOCK BALLS

293 a-c

A. ENGLAND, 1750–80
BRASS (COPPER 70.23, ZINC 22.83,
LEAD 6.23, IRON 0.55), IRON
H. 6 1/8" (1.5 CM),
DIAM. 2 1/8" (5.4 CM)
69.3603

B. PROBABLY ENGLAND, 1750–90
BRASS (COPPER 74.41, ZINC 21.09,
LEAD 2.59, IRON 0.81, TIN 0.77,
ANTIMONY 0.13)
H. 6 3/8" (16.2 CM),
DIAM. 2 3/8" (6.1 CM)
ONE OF A PAIR
65.1487.2

C. ENGLAND OR AMERICA, 1740–80
BRASS (COPPER 73.49, ZINC 23.79,
LEAD 1.85, TIN 0.50, IRON 0.23)
H. 6 1/4" (15.9 CM),
DIAM. 2 3/8" (6.1 CM)
65.1489

THOMAS SHERATON defined the vase, alternately called an urn, as "of roundish form with a large swell in the middle. A term used for ancient vessels . . . in architecture, the appelation vase is also given to those ornaments placed on cornices, pedestals &c. representing vessels of the ancients."[87]

Furniture that overtly manifested architectural principles in its design—such as tall-case clocks—needed freestanding ornamental elements on the cornices in order to be seen as complete. Consequently, eighteenth-century English and American tall clocks were routinely fitted with finials. Many were made of turned wood, which was sometimes carved and gilded, but brass was also used extensively.

The finials illustrated here, called *clock balls* in mid eighteenth- to early nineteenth-century Birmingham brass-founders' trade catalogues,

represent the types most often used.[88] Although similar in purpose and appearance, all three differ significantly in construction and, as such, demonstrate alternate solutions to the fabrication of this form. The example shown here with a stylized spiral flame was cast hollow in halves vertically along the entire length, and the two parts were brazed together. That with a belted sphere was cast hollow in halves horizontally; the two parts, the spire, and the base section are all held together with an internal iron rod that is threaded at both ends. The third example has the ball cast hollow in halves vertically. The two halves were brazed together, the spire was threaded, and the base was brazed in place. All three were originally coated with tinted lacquer to simulate gilding and prevent tarnishing. Only the example with the belted sphere retains any lacquer.

B.

C.

CLOCK BALL

294

BIRMINGHAM, ENGLAND, 1810–30
BRASS (COPPER 73.81, ZINC 18.79,
LEAD 4.16, IRON 0.68, SILVER 0.31,
TIN 0.26), IRON

H. 5 7/8" (15.0 CM),
DIAM. 2 3/16" (5.6 CM)
ONE OF A PAIR
57.921

THIS CLOCK BALL and its mate, although basically the same as their eighteenth-century counterparts, differ in a number of significant ways. Among the most obvious is the presence of graduated discs incorporated into the design of the cast spire, which is circular in section. Earlier examples had spires that were square in section with only a single small diameter fillet near the top. A second difference is visible in the ball. The entire surface has been ornamented. Earlier examples were plain, with an occasional encircling fillet at the outermost diameter.

The Greek key decoration around the center of the ball is die rolled while the tapering panels of reeding above and below it are die stamped. Whereas the spheres of eighteenth-century clock balls were cast in halves, these are made of thinly rolled sheet

metal that was die stamped to shape, thus effecting a significant reduction in weight with consequent savings in cost.

Such die-stamped clock balls were offered both with and without the Greek key border, which is easily removed when the ball is disassembled. They were sold in sets and were available in at least four different sizes. They had matching "Capitals & bases & Quarter Collumns." The capitals and bases were fitted onto the upper and lower ends of the small columns flanking the face of a clock, while the "Quarter Collumns" served in the same capacity on the quarter columns to either side of the door in the waist of a clock case.[89]

A.

FINIAL, CLOAK PINS,
CABINET KNOBS
295 a-c

A. BIRMINGHAM, ENGLAND,
1790–1810
BRASS (COPPER 77.75,
ZINC 21.41, LEAD 0.47), IRON
DIAM. 1 9/16" (4.0 CM), H. 6" (15.2 CM)
ONE OF THREE
57.521

B. BIRMINGHAM, ENGLAND,
1790–1810
BRASS (COPPER 76.66, ZINC 20.56,
LEAD 2.52), SHEET IRON
DIAM. 1 9/16"
(4.0 CM), L. 2 7/8" (7.3 CM)
64.2082.1, .2

C. BIRMINGHAM, ENGLAND,
1790–1810
BRASS (COPPER 76.29,
ZINC 23.08, IRON 0.14)
DIAM. 1 9/16" (4.0 CM),
L. 2 1/2" (6.3 CM)
TWO OF SIX
57.521

PLATE THIRTY-FIVE in a Birmingham brass-manufacturer's trade catalogue owned by the Victoria and Albert Museum pictures numerous circular drawer pulls with a threaded central post and stamped ornament. They are accompanied by the notation that "these knobs may be had of any cloak pin patt[er]n same sizes if so desired."[90]

The incorporation of an ornamental motif–such as the portrait of Washington shown here–into a variety of forms was easily accomplished through the use of downfall presses. These gravity-operated, die-stamping machines were capable of making dozens of identical images in a short period of time. Such mass production encouraged the proliferation of household objects.

A close examination of the numerous illustrations in brass-stampers' catalogues reveals that, even though not specifically stated, the same stamping was used when possible to make a large variety of objects. A circular stamping such as the one illustrated could, for instance, appear on drawer pulls, knobs to hold a looking glass in place on a dressing bureau, bed bolt covers, handles on architectural door locks, latches on cupboard doors, lids for boxes, and even finials for furniture.[91]

B.

C.

CHAIR ORNAMENT
296

BIRMINGHAM, ENGLAND, 1800–1820
BRASS (COPPER 75.04,
ZINC 20.54,
LEAD 3.99, SILVER 0.21, IRON 0.17)

L. 6 3/8" (16.2 CM),
H. 2" (5.1 CM),
D. 5/8" (1.6 CM)
56.580

THE ORNAMENT ILLUSTRATED HERE, on a painted arm chair, and a similar but smaller example on the crest rail of a matching side chair in the Winterthur collection are both depicted on the pages of a Birmingham trade catalogue owned by the Victoria and Albert Museum.[92] The two chairs are part of a large suite of seating furniture made in New York between 1810 and 1815, other parts of which are owned by the Brooklyn Museum and the Metropolitan Museum of Art. All are fitted with ornamental brass mounts.

These mounts are cast and, as noted by the caption accompanying the illustration in the catalogue, have "spikes to drive" them into the furniture. The spikes, square in section and tapered, are cast integrally with the mounts, unlike their Continental counterparts, which are fitted with separate steel spikes that thread into the backs.

Although advertised as chair ornaments, enterprising cabinetmakers used these mounts on other furniture as well. The catlogue's English-language captions imply an English-speaking market, and undoubtedly most of the objects depicted were used on Anglo-American furniture. These ornaments were occasionally circulated more widely, however, as evidenced by a Chinese painting of European factories in Canton. The painting, from about 1810, retains its original frame, also Chinese, which is fitted with identical mounts.[93]

CABINET MOUNT

297

PARIS, FRANCE, CA. 1814
BRASS (COPPER 72.00, ZINC 14.85,
IRON 1.40, TIN 1.29, LEAD 0.50, GOLD 0.40
ON REVERSE, 17.65 ON OBVERSE,
NICKEL 0.30, SILVER 0.10), STEEL

H. 1 7/8" (4.8 CM), W. 6 1/4"
(15.9 CM), D. 7/8" (0.9 CM)
62.237
GIFT OF MR. AND MRS.
DAVID STOCKWELL

THOMAS STANFORD, a publisher of New York City directories, listed Joseph Brauwers, cabinetmaker, at 163 William Street in 1814. A competing directory did likewise for a Joseph Brauwer at the same address. Although Brauwers is not mentioned in subsequent directories, a John Brower, bandboxmaker, is present in 1816 and again in 1817 but with no profession given. Both times the address remained 163 William Street. These entries probably all refer to the same man and provide a narrow date context for two card tables bearing the label illustrated here.[94] The tables have brass capitals and bases fitted over supporting columns as well as decorative mounts applied to the facade. The largest, a cast ornament in the form of a pair of peacocks flanking a basket of flowers, is attached to the skirt of the table with small chisel-pointed steel nails that are threaded into the back.

Brass ornaments composed of mirror-image animals, humans, or mythological creatures flanking a central motif were favored for use on early nineteenth-century French furniture. While imported brass mounts were also placed on American furniture, their design was rarely so symmetrical. The peacock is an unusual motif infrequently incorporated into furniture design prior to the late nineteenth century, since the lore associating peacocks with ill luck discouraged widespread popularity.[95]

While a considerable amount of stylish American furniture dating from the early nineteenth century was fitted with imported brass hardware, the sources and individuals involved in its supply are rarely so well documented as this instance. Instead of using his trade label to itemize the furniture forms he was capable of making—as was routine practice—Brauwers chose to note on his label that he could supply "the richest ornaments just imported from France."

COLUMN CAPITALS, BASES, AND BORDERS
298

ENGLAND, PROBABLY BIRMINGHAM, 1816–33
BRASS
CAPITAL: H. 2 3/8" (6.0 CM),
DIAM. 3 3/4" (9.5 CM);
BASE: H. 1 1/4" (3.2 CM), DIAM. 4" (10.2 CM);

STAR: H. 3/8" (1.0 CM);
GUILLOCHE: H. 5/8" (1.5 CM);
STRINGING: H. 1/16" (0.2 CM)
EACH ONE OF A PAIR
74.2

DURING THE EARLY nineteenth century, brass was used extensively for ornament by American cabinetmakers in East Coast cities having close trade connections with European metalworking centers. Among the most dramatic examples are the "richest [allegorical and mythological] Ornaments, just imported from France" that were nailed to furniture by Charles-Honoré Lannuier, who worked in New York; by Antoine-Gabriel Quervelle of Philadelphia; by Thomas Emmons and George Archibald of Boston, and others.[96]

A superlative mount depicting Eos, the Greek goddess of dawn, being drawn in her chariot across a cloud-filled sky, is centered on the skirt of the pier table shown here labeled by the New York cabinetmaker Michael Allison (1773–1855). Although the mount dominates the table's repertoire of ornament, there is a considerable amount of addi-tional brass used in the design: capitals and bases for the two columns at the front corners and two pierced and four solid borders that are inlaid entirely across the facade. All of these were readily available through trade catalogues from brass manufacturers in Birmingham, England. The cast capitals and bases for the columns were to be had in sets of two each, with or without square tops (without on this table), ranging from 1 1/2 inches to 3 inches in diameter, in 1/4-inch increments.[97]

The "ornamental strips of metal for letting into wood furniture, for decorative purposes . . . now known as 'buhl work' [was] produced by a process [known as] 'book piercing.'" The strips were sold in rolls and could be cut to length for placement on furniture such as that illustrated.[98]

CLOCKWISE STARTING IN UPPER LEFT

CABINET MOUNTS
299 a-e

A. MARKED "GA"
GERMANY, PROBABLY ISERLOHN, 1825–35
BRASS (COPPER 78.40, ZINC 17.02,
LEAD 2.24, TIN 1.85, GOLD 0.17,
ANTIMONY 0.12, SILVER 0.11), STEEL
H. 2 3/4" (7.0 CM), W. 2 3/8"
(6.0 CM), D. 1/2" (1.2 CM)
57.946.1

B. MARKED "GA"
GERMANY, PROBABLY ISERLOHN, 1825–35
BRASS (COPPER 75.49, ZINC 19.31,
TIN 3.67, LEAD 1.30), STEEL
H. 2 3/4" (7.0 CM), W. 2 3/8"
(6.0 CM), D. 1/2" (1.2 CM)
57.946.1

IN 1779 GEORGE RICHARDSON published *Iconology; or, A Collection of Emblematical Figures*, in which he personified "the Passions, Arts, Sciences, Dispositions of the Mind, Virtues, Vices &c . . . [to] not only amuse and instruct the mind, but inspire the Love of Virtue and the hatred of Vice."[99] The continents and the seasons are among the figures depicted.

Europe wears "a crown of gold . . . the horn of plenty allude[s] to the fertility of the soil [while] a horse . . . signifys the warlike disposition of the inhabitants," as does her mantle of armor. Asia has a "camel by her side. . . . The vase of incense, indicates the variety of odiferous spices produced in many of [its] provinces."[100]

Summer, "crowned with . . . ears of corn [is] holding a . . . sickle, . . . sheaves of corn allude to its being the principal fruit produced in this season." Autumn has "a garland of vines on her head; she holds a cornucupia of fruits in [one] hand and a bunch of grapes in the other . . . [which] signify the plenteous produce of this season, for the use of mortals." Spring, "the first and most agreeable season, is . . . crowned with myrtle [and] has various flowers in one hand."[101]

C. MARKED "GA"
GERMANY, PROBABLY ISERLOHN, 1825–35
BRASS (COPPER 73.88, ZINC 20.62,
TIN 2.43, GOLD 2.40, LEAD 0.55), STEEL
H. 2 1/2" (6.4 CM), W. 2 1/4"
(5.7 CM), D. 1/2" (1.2 CM)
57.946.2

D. MARKED "GA"
GERMANY, PROBABLY ISERLOHN, 1825–35
BRASS (COPPER 77.01, ZINC 18.63,
LEAD 2.38, TIN 1.61, SILVER 0.10), STEEL
H. 2 3/4" (7.0 CM), W 2 3/8"
(6.0 CM), D. 1/2" (1.2 CM)
57.946.2

E. MARKED "GA"
GERMANY, PROBABLY ISERLOHN, 1825–35
BRASS (COPPER 74.19, ZINC 17.79,
TIN 4.12, GOLD 3.10,
LEAD 0.48, SILVER 0.10), STEEL
H. 2 5/8" (6.7 CM), W. 2 1/4"
(5.7 CM), D. 1/2" (1.2 CM)
57.946.2

Although Richardson's stated intent was to inspire and instruct, the personifications could also be adapted for other use, as with designs for furniture ornament. Indeed, the text quoted above accurately describes the salient features of the mounts under discussion. Brass figural mounts depicting mythological, allegorical, or contemporary figures were imported into the United States from a number of metalworking centers in England, France, and Germany and were offered as optional ornament on furniture made in the larger East Coast cabinetmaking centers during the early nineteenth century.

The five cast vignettes shown here are selected from six affixed to a pair of New York stands that date stylistically between 1820 and 1835. The mounts are probably German and appear in an anonymous brass-trade catalogue believed to have originated in Iserlohn, an ancient metalworking town near the confluence of the Ruhr and Lenne rivers in the northeast corner of that country. All bear the initials of their founder, presently anonymous, cast into the backs.[102]

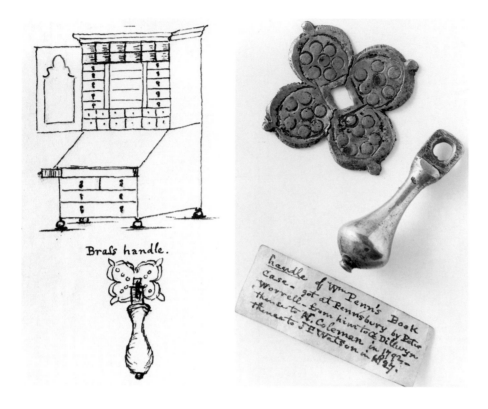

CABINET HANDLE
300

ENGLAND, PROBABLY LONDON OR
BRISTOL, 1680–1700
BRASS (COPPER 75.48, ZINC 20.00,
LEAD 2.67, IRON 0.72, TIN 0.34,
ANTIMONY 0.10, GOLD 0.10)

DROP: L. 1 3/4" (4.5 CM);
PLATE: W. 1 3/4" (4.5 CM)
58.102.20

JOHN FANNING WATSON (1779-1860) is best remembered as one of America's first antiquarians. In his *Annals of Philadelphia*, first published in 1830, he recorded that "William Penn and his family lived [at Pennsbury] . . . in the years 1700 and 1701. . . . His furniture was long preserved there, and finally got sold and spread in Bucks County. His clock and his writing desk and secretary I have seen."[103]

Watson examined and recorded Penn's desk before 1829 in the shop of "Nath[anie]l Coleman, a silversmith in Burlington [New Jersey, where it was] used as a shop-closet . . . in very old & unsightly condition." At that time, he apparently persuaded Coleman to give him one of the drawer handles–the one pictured here. Not wanting its significance to be lost, Watson executed a

detailed drawing of it and noted its genealogy from Penn through Peter Worrell, George Dillwyn, and Nathaniel Coleman to himself.[104]

The handle shown here is typical of English drawer hardware dating from the late seventeenth century, having a fully rounded cast pendant held to the drawer front with a cotter pin, which passes through a cast plate having a chased surface. In this instance, the handle was surely affixed to the drawer in England. English-made examples were also available for placement on American case furniture, as evidenced by the "112 drops" and "53 scutcheons" itemized in 1708 in the inventory of the Philadelphia cabinet-maker Charles Plumley.[105]

A.

CABINET HANDLES, ESCUTCHEON
301 a-c

A. MARKED "ET"
ENGLAND, PROBABLY LONDON, 1700–1740
BRASS (COPPER 74.87, ZINC 21.62,
LEAD 2.34, TIN 0.30, IRON 0.30, NICKEL 0.20)
H. 2" (5.1 CM), W. 2 1/2"
(6.3 CM), D. 1 3/4" (4.4 CM)
69.3605

THE FOUNDER'S "business is to cast all works that are made of brass. . . . There are various sorts of founders . . . who all work after the same manner and upon the same principles; but apply themselves to particular branches, for no other reason, but that they are not furnished with moulds for other articles."[106]

This tendency to specialize is not normally apparent in the advertisements of English and American brass founders. Most tried to give the impression that they could supply a variety of objects, such as the Boston founder William Coffin, who "makes and sells . . . knockers for doors . . . brass dogs of all sorts, candlesticks, shovels and tongs, small bells and all sorts of founders ware."[107]

Some founders did present themselves as specialists, however. *The Universal Director*, published in London in 1763, listed eleven brass

founders working in the city. Nine referred to themselves as general brass founders, but the remaining two, Butts and Company and John Jenkin, were specifically listed as "cabinet founders," implying that they specialized in making handles, escutcheons, hinges, and other furniture hardware.[108]

Edward Tiper may have been such a specialist and may have made the illustrated handles and escutcheon. Although practically nothing is known about him, he was granted freedom to pursue the brass foundry business in London on February 7, 1686. He is the only brass founder currently recorded working in London during the late seventeenth and eighteenth centuries with the initials "ET."[109]

B.

C.

B. MARKED "ET"
ENGLAND, PROBABLY LONDON, 1720–1740
BRASS (COPPER 74.88, ZINC 20.62,
LEAD 2.98, TIN 0.58,
IRON 0.27, ANTIMONY 0.16)
H. 1 7/8" (4.7 CM), W. 3 1/2" (8.9 CM),
D. 1 3/4" (4.4 CM)
52.146

C. MARKED "ET"
ENGLAND, PROBABLY LONDON, 1700–1740
BRASS (COPPER 71.89, ZINC 23.65,
LEAD 2.43, IRON 0.97, TIN 0.61)
H. 2 3/8" (6.0 CM), W. 3" (7.6 CM),
D. 1/16" (0.1 CM)
69.3607

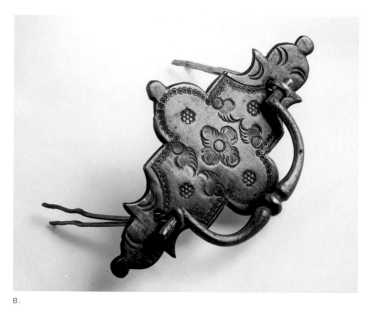

B.

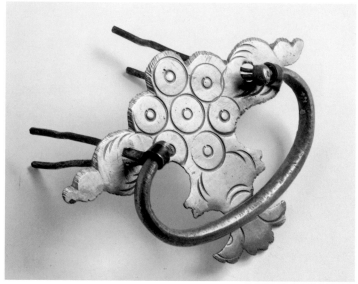

A.

CABINET HANDLES
302 a-d

A. MARKED "IG"
ENGLAND, PROBABLY LONDON, 1730–50
BRASS (COPPER 78.10, ZINC 16.87,
LEAD 2.89, IRON 0.80,
TIN 0.65, NICKEL 0.10), IRON
L. 2 3/4" (7.0 CM), H. 1 7/8"
(4.8 CM), D. 1 5/8" (4.1 CM)
69.3606

B. MARKED "IG"
ENGLAND, PROBABLY LONDON, 1730–50
BRASS (COPPER 74.77, ZINC 20.45,
LEAD 2.57, TIN 0.80, IRON 0.65,
NICKEL 0.22, ANTIMONY 0.20)
L. 3 3/4" (9.5 CM), H. 2 1/8"
(5.4 CM), D. 1 3/4" (4.4 CM)
69.3609

THE FOUR CABINET HANDLES illustrated here, each in a different pattern, were cast in the same shop and suggest the variety that a founder needed to offer to remain competitive. This diversity is even more apparent on the pages of English brass-founders' trade catalogues, which frequently depict dozens of patterns of cabinet handles, each available in different sizes.[110]

Cabinet handles and escutcheons were produced in great quantities throughout the eighteenth and nineteenth centuries. Many are unmarked by their manufacturers, but plates are encountered with pattern numbers cast into the backs. These numbers were always appended to a corresponding image in the manufacturer's pattern book and provided easy identification for ordering by a customer or hardware merchant.

On occasion, cabinet brass founders cast their initials into the reverse of the drawer-pull plates they made as evidenced by the four shown here, which were marked in accordance with an ordinance of the Worshipful Company of Founders in London that stipulated that every person working in copper and brass register his mark at Founder's Hall and place it on all his wares.[111] The guild apparently had difficulty enforcing that rule, however, resulting in few marked examples.

The rolls listing those brass founders freed in London between 1682 and 1750 mention seventeen men with the initials "IG." One was almost certainly responsible for these handles, which were probably all made at about the same time, presumably by one of those founders who began working in London after about 1730: Job Grimshaw, James Goring, John Giles, James Grape, and James Gamble.[112]

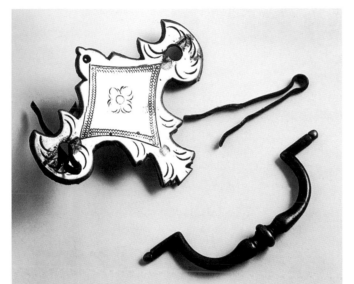

C.

D.

C. MARKED "IG"
ENGLAND, PROBABLY LONDON, 1730–50
BRASS (COPPER 70.51, ZINC 22.88,
LEAD 3.43, TIN 1.70, IRON 0.58,
ANTIMONY 0.25)
L. 3 1/8" (7.9 CM), H. 2 3/8" (6.0 CM),
D. 1 3/4" (4.4 CM)
69.3608

D. MARKED "IG"
ENGLAND, PROBABLY LONDON, 1730–50
BRASS (COPPER 73.64, ZINC 22.31,
LEAD 2.62, IRON 0.56, TIN 0.47)
L. 4 5/8" (11.7 CM), H. 3 1/8" (7.9 CM),
D. 2 7/8" (7.3 CM)
ONE OF EIGHT AND SIX ESCUTCHEONS
60.1134

CABINET HANDLE
303

MARKED "IP"
ENGLAND, PROBABLY LONDON, 1735–45
BRASS (COPPER 73.85, ZINC 19.60,
LEAD 2.53, TIN 1.51, IRON 0.61,
ANTIMONY 0.20, SILVER 0.19)

H. 1 7/8" (4.7 CM), L. 4"
(10.1 CM), D. 1 1/2" (3.8 CM)
ONE OF SIXTEEN AND
FIVE ESCUTCHEONS
57.1084

THE JAPANNED HIGH CHEST on which this handle was originally placed was made in the Boston cabinetmaking shop of John Pimm for Joshua Loring in the early 1740s.[113] Upon leaving Boston at the outbreak of the Revolution, Loring gave the chest to his wife's brother, the Reverend Phillip Curtis, from whom it passed through five generations before being bought by Henry Francis du Pont.

In 1892 a family member recorded that "the carving on the [chest's] two center drawers is considered very fine, as is also the color of the gold on the decoration and the old brass of the handles."[114] Each of those handles consists of a cast plate and bail held to the drawer front with two cotter pins. The abstract foliate and geometric decoration on the plates was executed by hand with chasing tools. The matching escutcheons are held in place with brass pins.

Pimm most likely bought this hardware from one of the specializing merchants in Boston, such as Mary Jackson and her son William, who in 1757 advertised that they had just "imported from London and Bristol . . . desk and bookcase furniture, viz. handles and scutcheons of various sorts . . . locks . . . desk buttons [and] brass pins."[115]

At least one of these handles has the maker's initials, which appear to be "I.P.," cast into the back of the plate. While the maker may have worked in Bristol or Birmingham, he was more likely located in London. The rolls of the Worshipful Company of Founders in London contain the names of several men with those initials. The most likely candidate is John Pulley, who was apprenticed to William Gardner, "citizen and founder of London," in 1724. After serving a seven-year apprenticeship, he was freed on August 2, 1731.[116] Pulley may have made these brasses in London for export to the American colonies.

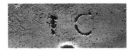

KEYHOLE ESCUTCHEON
3 0 4

MARKED "IC"
ENGLAND, PROBABLY LONDON, 1725–40
BRASS (COPPER 72.15, ZINC 19.66,
LEAD 6.24, TIN 1.03,
IRON 0.40, ANTIMONY 0.33, SILVER 0.12)

L. 2 3/16" (5.6 CM), H. 1 5/8"
(4.1 CM), D. 3/32" (0.2 CM)
ONE OF THREE
54.522

THIS KEYHOLE ESCUTCHEON, its mates, and fourteen cabinet handles appear to be original to the drawer fronts of their Massachusetts-made high chest. They are typical of the "book case escutcheons, brass desk handles, escutcheons to do [and] brass escutcheon pins [that] John and Joseph Shotwell . . . have imported . . . in the last vessels from London, Bristol, Liverpool and Hull . . . and have for sale at their store in Rahway, New Jersey."[117]

While typical in appearance, this escutcheon is somewhat unusual in that it bears the initials of its founder, "IC," cast into the reverse. The identity of that man is unknown, but he is probably among the sixteen with those initials recorded on the rolls of the Worshipful Company of Founders in London who attained freedom to practice their craft between August 4, 1718, and August 7, 1749.[118]

CABINET HANDLE

305

MARKED "IM"
ENGLAND, PROBABLY LONDON,
1720–40
BRASS (COPPER 70.58, ZINC 22.73,
LEAD 5.37, TIN 0.68, IRON 0.46)

L. 3" (7.6 CM), H. 1 3/8"
(3.5 CM), D. 1 1/2" (3.8 CM)
ONE OF A PAIR
69.3581

THE MAN WHO MADE THIS cabinet handle and its mate cast his initials into the back of the plates in compliance with the Worshipful Company of Founders dictum that he record his mark with the company and use it on every object he made. Although he cannot be positively identified, he was probably one of the ten men with the initials "IM" to whom the company granted freedom to practice the craft between 1713 and 1749.[119]

The maker may have offered his work for sale directly to customers but probably worked with a middleman. That middleman was "the Brazier, or Ironmonger [who] never makes nor is supposed to be capable of making all the different Articles in his Shop. . . . He employs the several Classes of Workmen who apply themselves to the particular Articles he wants . . . what part of them is cast is executed by the Founder." In London during the mid eighteenth century, "the Braziers and Ironmongers Shops are generally united, and in them you find [a great variety of wares including] chases and handles for Cabinet-Work . . . and all Sorts of Brass . . . Work that are useful for Furniture, or any Part of Furniture."[120] By entering a mercantile arrangement such as this, the ambitious founder could effectively enlarge the number of outlets for his wares at minimal cost.

A.

B.

CABINET HANDLES
306 a,b

A. ENGLAND, PROBABLY
BIRMINGHAM, 1750–80
BRASS (COPPER 75.11,
ZINC 20.71, LEAD 2.22, IRON 1.24)
L. 3 1/2" (8.9 CM), H. 2 7/8"
(7.3 CM), D. 1 1/4" (3.2 CM)
69.3610

B. ENGLAND, PROBABLY
BIRMINGHAM, 1750–80
BRASS (COPPER 76.00, ZINC 19.13,
LEAD 3.23, IRON 0.90, GOLD 0.14, TIN 0.12)
L. 3 5/8" (9.2 CM), H. 2 15/16"
(7.5 CM), D. 1 3/8" (3.5 CM)
69.3611

ALTHOUGH OFTEN FAINT and illegible, one-, two-, three-, and some-times four- digit numbers were often cast into the back of cabinet-handle plates made in Birmingham after the mid eighteenth century, and possibly before. These numbers also accompanied illustrations of the cabinet handles in pattern books, some of which contained as many as several hundred different images.[121] Although all different, the vari-ations in these cabinet handles were often slight. To help avoid ambi-guity or misunderstanding when ordering from the catalogues, the num-bers in question served as a common language for buyer, middleman or factor, and manufacturer.

Their utility is well illustrated in a letter written by Paul Revere on January 19, 1784, to his factor, Frederick Geyer, in England. Revere stated that he had recently received "a book with drawings which is a very good direction for one to write by. I should be very glad if you would send me eight pair of plated branches, four of No. 103 and four of No. 178, as marked in said book. If they have drawings different from the book I received [I] should be glad [if] they would send me one more book."[122]

If a pattern offered by a manufacturer proved popular, competi-tors would adapt it to their inventory. Although cabinet-handle designs seem not to have been patented, imitations were normally altered slightly. This is true with the plate illustrated here. Number 125 is vir-tually identical to number 287, except for reduced dimensions.[123]

CABINET HANDLE
307

JOHN GOLD
BIRMINGHAM, ENGLAND, 1760–70
BRASS (COPPER 77.98,
ZINC 17.56, LEAD 3.20,
TIN 0.70, IRON 0.16)

H. 2 7/8" (7.3 CM), L. 3 3/4"
(9.5 CM), D. 1 3/8" (3.5 CM)
ONE OF TWENTY
67.1445

IN COMPILING THE Birmingham directory for 1767, James Sketchley described the city's brass founders as "ingenious artists [who] make an infinite variety of articles as sconces, cabinet handles, escutcheons, hinges, cloak pins, &c &c, and this is the only place for merchants and others, to be provided."[124] John Gold at Colmore Row was among the men listed under this heading.

While Gold surely produced all the objects enumerated by Sketchley and probably more, his currently documented output consists of the handle illustrated here and another on a Charlestown, Massachusetts, high chest at Winterthur; two other identically pierced examples; and one with an unpierced plate.[125] While only two handles on Winterthur's high chest bear Gold's name, the other eighteen are identical in every detail, and all appear to be original to their respective drawers. The unmarked examples can therefore be assumed to have originated in Gold's shop.

Not all cabinet handles of this pattern can be assigned to Gold, however. The design was apparently popular and is depicted in numerous trade catalogues. Many brass workers took a promising or popular design from another and sold it as their own. Consequently, the eighteenth-century Salem hardware merchant Samuel Curwen found that there was jealousy and suspicion of strangers in all the manufacturing towns of England, making it difficult to gain admittance to manufacturers' workshops.[126]

CABINET HANDLE
308

ENGLAND, PROBABLY LONDON OR
BIRMINGHAM, 1750–80
BRASS (COPPER 73.00, ZINC 24.00,
LEAD 2.13, IRON 0.76)

L. 4 3/8" (11.1 CM), H. 3"
(7.6 CM), D. 1 5/8" (4.1 CM)
ONE OF EIGHT
56.23

ON NOVEMBER 11, 1771, the Philadelphia hardware merchant William Barrel advertised that he just "imported in the very last ships from London and [had for sale] on the most reasonable terms . . . at his store in Second Street between Walnut and Chestnut Streets . . . varnish'd chest handles."[127]

The handle shown here, lacquered to look as if it were gilded, was probably represented among those offered by Barrel and his counterparts in New York, Boston, and Charleston. Such handles and their matching keyhole escutcheons are among the most elaborate found on American case furniture, with their surfaces completely sculpted with Chinese and, somewhat less blatantly, rococo motifs. They were apparently quite popular, as judged by the frequency with which closely related variants of the pattern appear in early pattern books.[128]

Although the men who designed and made these cabinet handles remain anonymous, they clearly derived their inspiration from the work of the English engraver, satirist, and wallpaper manufacturer Matthew Darly, who published *A New Book of Chinese, Gothic, and Modern Chairs . . .* in 1751. It was Darly's second effort, however, *A New Book of Chinese Designs Calculated to Improve the Present Taste*, that codified the popular English interpretation of this style. The title and the note that it was available from "Print and Booksellers in Town & Country" clearly imply its intended instructive use for artisans and designers in all media.[129]

The symmetrical design of the handle illustrated here, with a central pagoda flanked by foliate elements and with fretwork below, was a favored design formula of Darly's and captures the essence of "the boundless panegyricks . . . lavished upon the Chinese . . . arts" during the mid eighteenth century.[130]

LIFTING HANDLE
309

ATTRIBUTED TO
JOHN CLARKE AND SON
BIRMINGHAM, ENGLAND, 1785–1809
BRASS (COPPER 65.10,
ZINC 33.37, LEAD 1.21), IRON

L. 6" (15.2 CM), H. 2 7/8"
(7.3 CM), D. 7/8" (2.2 CM)
69.3613

LIFTING HANDLES WERE PLACED on the sides of case furniture–principally chests-on-chests, high chests, and desks-and-bookcases, but also occasionally on chests of drawers–to facilitate moving them. When these handles were fitted with an ornamental back plate, they were termed *plate-lifting handles*. If the handle portion had shoulders where it entered the sockets, as is the case with the example illustrated here, it was called a *stop-lifting handle*. The purpose of the shoulder was to stop the handle in a horizontal position so persons using it would not pinch their fingers when lifting the furniture.[131]

This handle, which retains a portion of the original lacquer finish, has the maker's initials "JC&S" cast into the back of the plate. John Clarke first listed himself as a brass founder in Birmingham at 28 Halloway Head in 1770. Sometime between 1785 and 1791 he was joined by his son, and the two continued to be listed together as such until the 1809 directory, when their entry became "JS&AG Clarke, brass founders, Moor Street." Also cast into the reverse of the plate is the number 1497, which identifies this size and pattern handle.

CABINET-HANDLE PLATE
310

JOHN STOW (1727–54)
PHILADELPHIA, PENNSYLVANIA, 1747–54
BRASS (COPPER 80.22, ZINC 15.50,
LEAD 2.18, IRON 1.00, TIN 0.60)

H. 2 1/2" (6.3 CM),
W. 4 1/16" (10.3 CM),
D. 3/32" (0.2 CM)
85.53

IN OCTOBER 1751 the Pennsylvania State Assembly directed its trustees Isaac Norris, Thomas Leech, and Edward Warner "to order a bell from England" to hang in the State House, then being built. The trustees requested that the bell "be cast by the best workmen, and examined carefully before it is shipped." Even so, it cracked with the first stroke of the clapper. The committee "concluded to send [the bell] back by Captn Budden but he could not take it on board upon which two ingenious Work-Men undertook to cast it here."[132] Those men were John Pass and John Stow. The bell they cast still hangs in Philadelphia and is known as the Liberty Bell.

Stow, born in Philadelphia in 1727, advertised as early as 1749 "that he makes and sells all manner of brass work [at his shop] in Third Street a little above Market Street, Phildelphia." It was not until 1752, however, when he "removed from Third Street to the sign of the Three Bells in Second Street" that he enumerated a fuller range of his

products. Among his extensive listing he included "brass fire dogs, shovel & tongs, candlesticks, gun furniture, best brass shoe buckles and sleeve buttons . . . spoon moulds of all fashions, bell metal skillets and kettles of all sizes . . . house spring bells . . . dog collars, brass heads for iron dogs [and] joiner's furniture of several sorts."[133]

The last of these included cabinet handles of the type illustrated here. The substantial plate has Stow's name deeply cast into the back, which relates to the contemporary English founder's practice of casting initials or pattern numbers into the reverse of cabinet-handle plates. This plate is virtually identical to examples depicted in English trade catalogues and was almost certainly cast using an imported English cabinet handle as its pattern. It and the few other examples that bear Stow's name probably represent the bulk of his work that has survived, since his short career ended at the age of twenty-seven in March 1754.[134]

CABINET HANDLE

311

PROBABLY BIRMINGHAM,
ENGLAND, 1780–1810
BRASS (COPPER 75.13,
ZINC 22.76, IRON 1.60, NICKEL 0.18)

H. 2 1/4" (5.7 CM), L. 3 1/4"
(8.2 CM), D. 1 1/2" (3.8 CM)
ONE OF EIGHT
57.844

THE PUBLISHER OF THE 1779 Birmingham city directory felt compelled to editorialize in a section entitled "Coffin and Ornamental Furniture" that "the manufacture of these articles, till very lately, was confined principally to the metropolis. London, it must be confessed has within its walls, artists of unrivalled excellence. . . . Their introduction into this town (but a very few years ago) has been attended with singular advantage. The old process [casting] is utterly laid aside, and a more easy cheap and expeditious one is substituted. Artists of inventive minds and unwearied application, have called in the aid of dyes, presses and stamps" to fabricate a great variety of useful and ornamental brass work.[135]

The oval handle shown here typifies the type of cabinet hardware made by dozens of artisans working in Birmingham during the late eighteenth and early nineteenth centuries who made cabinet handles and

plates by the hundreds of thousands with gravity-operated downfall presses. The threaded posts used to hold the plate and handle to the drawer continued, however, to be cast in sand molds.[136]

The allegorical scene stamped into this plate, although marketable anywhere in the Western hemisphere, was probably intended to appeal specifically to American sensibilities. The recumbent female figure ultimately derives from the Greek universal mother, or mother earth, Cybele. When accompanied by cornucopia and sailing vessels, she was often used by Americans to symbolize prosperity through trade, agriculture, and enterprise.[137]

CABINET HANDLE

312

ATTRIBUTED TO THOMAS HANDS
AND WILLIAM JENKINS
BIRMINGHAM, ENGLAND, 1791–1805
BRASS (COPPER 76.77, ZINC 20.55,
LEAD 1.49, IRON 0.40, NICKEL 0.10)

L. 4 1/8" (10.5 CM),
H. 2 3/8" (6.1 CM),
D. 1 1/2" (3.8 CM)
ONE OF EIGHT
57.564

SOMETIME BETWEEN 1791 AND 1797, Thomas Hands, a die sinker and engraver, and William Jenkins, brass founder, joined partnership as "manufacturers of commode handles, cloak pins, picture frames, looking glasses, &c." By 1805 they were no longer recorded together in the city directories although each continued to be active individually in brass working. They are not the only Birmingham brass workers with those initials who worked together during the late eighteenth and early nineteenth centuries but were most likely the makers of numerous stamped cabinet handles with bails marked "H.J."[138]

Even though these men were together a maximum of fourteen years, the frequency with which their mark is encountered testifies to the speed with which downfall presses could replicate objects.

Hands's and Jenkins's mark is typically located on the reverse of semi-circular bails that are affixed by threaded posts to oval plates in a great variety of stamped patterns. Included in the patterns are Roman temples, dolphins, paterae, and even a variant of the great seal of the United States. The sources of inspiration for these motifs are readily apparent but not so with the genre scene stamped into this plate. It is tempting, however, to speculate on the influence that the sign hanging outside Mary Lloyd's Hen and Chickens Inn in New Street, Birmingham, had on the makers of these cabinet handles.[139]

CABINET HANDLE
313

ATTRIBUTED TO THOMAS HANDS
AND WILLIAM JENKINS
BIRMINGHAM, ENGLAND, 1791–1805
BRASS (COPPER 77.77, ZINC 20.82,
LEAD 1.17, NICKEL 0.25)

L. 3 1/8" (7.9 CM), H. 2 3/8"
(6.1 CM), D. 1 1/4" (3.2 CM)
ONE OF A PAIR
59.8

WHEN THE AMERICAN entrepreneur Thomas Fletcher visited England in 1815, he toured the manufactory of James Vickers and Company in Sheffield. There he noted that their "lower room or cellar contains about 20 stamps, or downfall sliding weights and a vast quantity of steel dies used for striking up parts of articles of various kinds."[140] He just as easily might have been describing the manufactory of Thomas Hands and William Jenkins, who worked together from about 1791 to about 1805 in Birmingham, where this cabinet handle was made. Fletcher went on to say that the process of stamping metalwares appeared "extremely simple and easily obtained by those who have been in the habit of making [objects by hand, but that] the principal obstacles to such an establish-

ment in [America] are first the great capital required—secondly the high price of labor."[141]

The basis of these observations in part supported an active transatlantic trade in cabinet hardware, as represented by this handle. It and its mate are original to an enclosed pier table made by Mark Pitman, who worked in Salem, Massachusetts, from about 1799 to his death in 1829. Pitman would have bought the handles from a hardware dealer in Salem or Boston such as Richard Bolton and John Grew, who in 1795 had "imported . . . an assortment of cabinet brass foundry goods, viz.–desk & drawer handles, hinges, pendant & screw rings . . . lifting handles [and] common and three wheel casters."[142]

CABINET HANDLE

314

ATTRIBUTED TO WILLIAM JENKINS
BIRMINGHAM, ENGLAND, 1805–20
BRASS (COPPER 78.45, ZINC 20.74,
LEAD 0.41, NICKEL 0.13)

L. 3 7/8" (9.8 CM), H. 2 1/4"
(5.7 CM), D. 1 3/8" (3.5 CM)
69.3612

WILLIAM JENKINS FIRST APPEARS in the Birmingham city directories in 1797 as partner to Thomas Hands. By 1801 the two listed themselves as manufacturers of stamped brass foundry. The 1803 directory lists Jenkins still in partnership with Hands at Loveday Street but also on his own as a button caster in Livery Street. By 1805 both men are listed separately. Jenkins continued to be entered independently until 1823, when his son joined him. Together they advertised themselves as "manufacturers of brass toddy and maslin kettles, battery pans, candlesticks, house bells, brass, copper and dipping wire, brass, copper and tinn'd tubing, sheet, rolled and ingot brass, dipping, gilding and rolled metals, cabinet brass foundry, &c."[143]

The handle shown here is typical of the type Jenkins made, most of which do not bear his initials. Although he made a general line of brass work, he seems to have specialized in cabinet hardware, handles being the only brass work bearing his mark. His interest in cabinet hardware is underscored in English patent records that document his being granted patent number 3450 for "manufacturing flat backed handles and rings, used with or affixed to cabinet and other furniture and things" on May 21, 1811; patent number 3483 for "manufacturing drawer and other knobs, used with or affixed to cabinet and other furniture and things" on September 9, 1811; and patent number 3698 for "making socket casters, used with or affixed to cabinet and other furniture and things" on May 22, 1813.[144]

CABINET HANDLE

315

ENGLAND, PROBABLY
BIRMINGHAM, 1790–95
BRASS (COPPER 80.19,
ZINC 18.77, LEAD 0.50)

DIAM. 2 5/8" (6.7 CM),
D. 1" (2.5 CM)
ONE OF EIGHT
57.520

THIS CABINET HANDLE and its mates were fitted to a Massachu-setts-made chest of drawers before the drawers were lined with pages of the Boston newspaper *Columbian Centinel* that date from July 18 through September 18, 1795. The front pages are filled with shipping notices, advertisements of imported British goods, and engravings of ships for sale. Some of the ships depicted are three-masted, square-rigged vessels like that stamped into the plates of these cabinet handles.

Ships of this type were built in England, but "the business of ship-building is one of the most considerable which Boston or the other seaport towns in New England carry on. . . . Merchants . . . have them constructed . . . and . . . send them out upon a trading voy-age to Spain, Portugal or the Mediterranean; where having dis-posed of their cargo . . . sell the vessel herself to advantage. They

receive the value of the vessel . . . and . . . the cargo . . . in bills of exchange upon London."[145]

The ship design that is stamped into this cabinet handle, which is depicted in pattern books, is a simplified and idealized interpre-tation of those vessels plying the Atlantic. The handle was designed and made in Birmingham to appeal to Americans involved in that trade, such as Asa Hunting, the probable maker of the chest of draw-ers to which this handle is attached.[146]

While circular cabinet handles are less frequently encountered than oval ones on American furniture dating from the early fed-eral era, "pendant and screw rings" for drawers were offered by the Boston hardware dealers Richard Bolton and John Grew for cus-tomers such as Hunting.[147]

CABINET KNOBS,
CLOAK PINS

316

BIRMINGHAM, ENGLAND, 1766–1810
BRASS (COPPER 71.00,
ZINC 28.40, IRON 0.14)
L. 2 5/8" (6.6 CM), DIAM. 1 9/16"
(3.9 CM)
68.630.1, .2 (LEFT)

BIRMINGHAM, ENGLAND, 1766–1810
BRASS (COPPER 69.90,
ZINC 29.80), IRON
L. 3" (7.6 CM), DIAM. 1 9/16"
(3.9 CM)
68.599.1, .2

"STAMPED BRASS FOUNDRY . . . is the invention of John Pickering of London, a jeweller or gilt toy maker, who, on March 7, 1769, patented a new method of performing that kind of work called chasing for gold, silver, brass, tin and other metals, but more especially to be used in the production of coffin furniture: also ornaments for coaches, chariots, cabinet brass work and domestic furniture."[148]

The development of brass stamping, actually an outgrowth of die stamping, which had been used for making medals and coins since before the time of Christ, allowed fabrication of thin repoussé ornaments to be "executed in a much more expeditious manner, and far superior in beauty and elegance to anything of the kind (not being actual chasing) ever yet performed by any other method."

The images on the cabinet handles and cloak pins shown here were stamped with the die used for the plaque in entry 221, depicting "one of the three most delineated characters in history." Although the die cutter did not sign this work, there were a number of men in London and Birmingham involved in cutting dies for medals and coins to whom it might be assigned. Nathaniel Marchant and Lewis Pingo, both of whom worked at the Royal Mint in London, and Peter Wyon, who worked at the Soho Mint in Birmingham, made many such medals and coins, but they also created and signed steel dies used to strike up household artifacts of this type.[149]

COMMODE KNOBS
317

PROBABLY BIRMINGHAM,
ENGLAND, POSSIBLY
UNITED STATES, 1805–30
SILVERED COPPER, BRASS

L. 2 1/4" (5.7 CM),
DIAM. 1 13/16" (4.6 CM)
TWO OF EIGHT
57.567

DURING THE EIGHTEENTH and early nineteenth centuries, metal cabinet handles were usually designed to fit as flush as possible against the fronts of drawers and doors of case furniture. They normally employed a simple type of pivot or hinge mechanism and were readily accessible when needed but otherwise were not in the way.

During the first few decades of the nineteenth century, however, a vogue arose for fixed ornamental knobs that extended–sometimes as much as three inches–beyond the front of a drawer or door. These commode or drawer knobs were made in a great variety of patterns; some were quite elaborate with deeply stamped floral patterns, and others incorporated stylized borders like the Greek key or simple moldings. They were usually described in trade catalogues as being "all brass."[150]

A typical example has a die-stamped front with crimped edge around a die-stamped back, a cast and threaded post, and a wide die-stamped circular collar. The knobs illustrated here are constructed in such a manner but are unusual in that they are of silvered copper instead of brass.[151]

Brass examples, either oval with bails or the circular post type, were used in considerable numbers on early nineteenth-century American furniture, but their counterparts in silvered copper seem never to have achieved a significant measure of popularity. They are occasionally pictured in trade catalogues issued in Sheffield, England, and at least one American is connected with their production. The Philadelphia silverplater George Armitage advertised "silver plated knobs for cabinet ware of the newest fashion and warranted superior to any imported, manufactured and sold on the lowest terms" in the January 3, 1809, issue of the *Aurora General Advertiser*.[152]

CHAIR NAILS
318

ENGLAND, 1770–90
BRASS (COPPER 77.24, ZINC 15.92,
LEAD 5.73, TIN 0.55, IRON 0.43,
SILVER 0.12)

L. 1/2" (1.2 CM), DIAM. 7/16"
(1.1 CM)
59.123

CATALOGUES PUBLISHED by Birmingham brass manufacturers during the late eighteenth and early nineteenth centuries picture a large variety of furniture hardware, including small, cast, hemispherical-headed nails. They were variously called trunk nails, chair nails, and coach nails but were most often described as "coffin nails." They were made in a range of sizes–with heads from 3/8 to 1 inch in diameter–of lacquered brass or prince's metal and were priced from 2s. to 10s. per thousand. Most were made by specialists such as John Collins, "brass chair nail and curtain ring manufacturer," on New Town Row in Birmingham.[153]

Such nails were used by chairmakers to hold fabric on chair frames in an ornamental fashion. On January 20, 1769, Thomas Chippendale charged the Earl of Shelbourne for "14 Mahogany Chairs with Antique backs & term feet very richly carved with

hollow seats stuffed and covered with Red Morocco leather & double Brass naild."[154]

Birmingham-made chair nails were also available in America. The Philadelphia hardware firm of James and Drinker offered them as "garnishing nails." Their counterparts, "Bolton and Grew, platers and brass founders [in Boston informed] their friends and the Public, that they have lately received from their manufactory a fresh assortment of plated and Brass Foundry Articles consisting of commode handles . . . brass hinges, trunk and chair nails and cabinet brass trimmings."[155] Those chair nails were similar to the ones pictured here, which, with 1,090 others, "double nailed," hold original black Morocco leather on a set of four hollow-seat side chairs made in Massachusetts between 1770 and 1790. The nail heads retain their tinted lacquer in imitation of gilding.

ORNAMENTAL BORDERS
319

ENGLAND, PROBABLY
BIRMINGHAM, 1785–93
BRASS (COPPER 73.16, ZINC 26.29,
LEAD 0.70)

W. 3/8" (0.5 CM),
D. 1/8" (0.3 CM)
67.151.1–.6

DURING THE EIGHTEENTH CENTURY, decorative brass nails were widely used to hold upholstery on seating furniture, as illustrated by the "mahogany chair stuff'd and cover'd with Spanish leather & brass nail'd" billed by Thomas Chippendale to the Earl of Shelbourne on December 10, 1770.[156] The nails were hemispherical headed, varying in diameter from about 1/4 to 3/4 of an inch. Each was cast individually with a square, tapered, pointed shank centered on the hollow side. They were enumerated in brass-founders' pattern books and usually sold at the relatively modest price of several shillings per thousand, calculated on weight.

Although nails were inexpensive, it was time-consuming to drive each one individually into the frames of a set of chairs or a sofa. A less expensive and quicker alternative did become available in the 1760s with the advent of downfall stamping presses, in which a narrow strip of thinly rolled sheet brass was stamped in a steel die to look like a row of nail heads. These strips, containing considerably less metal than a comparable row of individually cast nails, could be cut to proper length and quickly tacked to a chair or sofa frame. As such, they created the same effect at a greatly reduced cost.

Such borders were offered in brass-workers' catalogues in conjunction with more elaborate gadrooned, guilloche, acanthus leaf, shell, and fluted examples. They were described as "stamp'd metal Edgings of a fine burnish'd Gold Colour for Commodes &c."[157]

The strips illustrated here ornament what appears to be original black oil cloth upholstery on a set of six side chairs documented in a bill as being purchased on December 10, 1793, by Mrs. Selah (?) Dickerson of Berlin, Connecticut, from the Hartford cabinet- and chairmakers Samuel Kneeland and Lemuel Adams.[158]

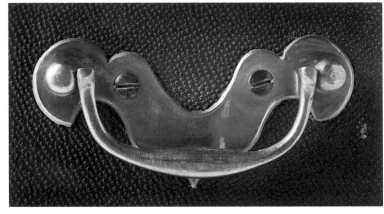

KNIFE-BOX HARDWARE
320

MARKED "TT"
ENGLAND OR UNITED STATES, 1780–1800
BRASS (COPPER 78.93, ZINC 15.25, LEAD 3.98,
IRON 0.92, TIN 0.71, ANTIMONY 0.13,
SILVER 0.11), WOOD, FABRIC, SHAGREEN

H. 13 3/4" (34.9 CM), W. 8 1/2"
(21.6 CM), D. 8 1/2" (21.6 CM)
65.1824

IN 1701 RANDLE HOLME drew and described a "case of knives" in his *Academy of Armory*. He depicted the case as a lidless inverted cone on a circular base and stated that it was the symbol of the edgetool-maker's profession. Containers for sets of table knives, forks, and spoons developed from that prototype and became part of the well-appointed English and American dining room. By the mid eighteenth century, the design had evolved to a modified rectangular box with hinged lid, similar to the example shown here. George Hepplewhite offered three designs for this variety in *The Cabinet-Maker and Upholsterer's Guide*, observing that they were to be "placed at each end on the sideboards, or on a pedestal [and that] the universal utility of this piece of furniture renders a particular description not necessary."[159]

Knife cases were always fitted with locks, testifying to the value of the contents, which in this instance consisted of twelve silver tablespoons, a condiment or marrow scoop, twelve forks, and twelve knives, each meant to stand upright in individual compartments. Knife-box hardware was made of silver, silver gilt, fused plate, or brass, the last of which could be lacquered, silvered, or simply polished bright. The case discussed here is fitted with four feet, three bails, two hinges, and a lock with hinged clasp, all of cast brass and most having the initials of their founder, "TT," cast into the backs.

Hinges, cabinet handles (like that on the lid), lifting handles (like those on the sides), and "Polished Brass Plate Trunk Locks with iron keys & inside work" were commonplace illustrations in brass-manufacturers' catalogues and were a staple in the trade between England and America. Although no American brass workers are presently recorded

as stating that they made knife-case hardware, the late eighteenth- and early nineteenth-century New York City brass founder, coppersmith, and ironmonger John Bailey pictured a knife case among other brass artifacts on his billhead, implying pictorially that he was capable of doing so. His competitor "Thomas Thomas, Tinman, Coppersmith and Brass Founder [at] No 206 Queen-street opposite Burling Ship [noted that he] has entered very extensively into the manufacturing part of the above Branches of Business, superior to any imported and equally as cheap. He has on hand a very large and extensive assortment of all kinds of Tin, Copper, Brass, and Pewterware."[160] The hardware on this knife box may have been among that assortment.

TRUNK HARDWARE
321

BIRMINGHAM, ENGLAND, 1811–50
BRASS (HANDLE: COPPER 77.60, ZINC
21.86, LEAD 0.24;
ESCUTCHEON: COPPER 76.86, ZINC 18.93,
LEAD 3.10, TIN 0.40, IRON 0.40)

BOX: H. 5 1/4" (13.3 CM),
W. 11 7/8" (30.2 CM),
D. 6 3/4" (17.2 CM)
64.2168

"THE MANUFACTURE OF TRUNKS . . . consists chiefly in lining the inside of a box with paper . . . and covering the outside with a skin, or leather, which is fastened to the wood . . . with brass nails, by way of ornament. . . . In the United States, this branch of business is very commonly united with that of the saddler and harness-maker."[161]

Trunk, chair, coach, or coffin nails, a staple of the Birmingham brass trade, were made in many sizes with either low or "high top" heads and priced from 2s. to 10s. per thousand. Although they were among the stock of general brass founders, there were a few men who specialized in them, such as John Collins of Birmingham, "brass chair nail and curtain ring manufacturer."[162]

The cast, square-shank brass nails, grouped with locks, hinges, keyhole escutcheons, and drawer handles as cabinet trimmings, were imported in quantity by hardware merchants such as the Boston firm of Richard Bolton and John Grew, who, on June 11, 1796, advertised that "they have lately received . . . a fresh assortment of . . . commode handles . . . brass hinges, trunk and chair nails."[163]

Commode handles are routinely attached to the lids of small trunks to facilitate opening. The handle shown here, while typical in form and ornament, is of special interest because the bail is stamped with "PATENT" on the underside. On July 15, 1811, the Birmingham brass founder William Jenkins was issued British patent number 3450 for "an improved method of manufacturing flat-backed handles and rings of different shapes and forms used with or affixed to cabinet and other furniture and things." This patent recognized Jenkins's improved method of making handles so that "a great part of . . . labor . . . [was] prevented [and a considerable amount of] metal . . . saved."[164]

Although the inscription on the escutcheon of this box holds promise of easy identification, the naval record of J. M. Allen has not yet been determined. He may have been James M. Allen, a one-time auctioneer and commission merchant in Boston and related to Benjamin L. Allen, partner in the firm of Allen and Beal, which sold "dress and fancy boxes and cabinet trimmings" along with furniture and other household goods.[165]

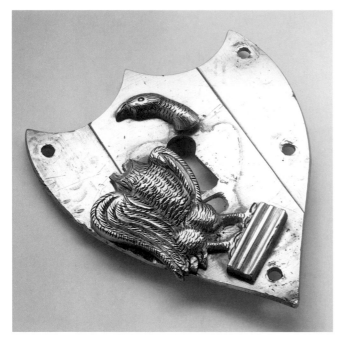

KEYHOLE ESCUTCHEON

322

UNITED STATES, 1800–1850
BRASS (COPPER 72.89,
ZINC 24.94, LEAD 1.24,
TIN 0.69, IRON 0.14)

H. 3 5/8" (9.2 CM), W. 3 1/16"
(7.8 CM), D. 3/8" (0.5 CM)
65.2222

MORTICE LOCKS ON BUILDINGS and furniture required the addition of a metal escutcheon to protect the wood around the keyhole from being damaged and disfigured from the constant insertion of the key. Leather-bound trunks also required such protection. Brass escutcheons were the norm, although other metals including silver, silver plate, and iron were also used. While they varied greatly from simple to elaborate, small to large, and unobtrusive to stylish, most were pierced with an unobstructed key-shape hole.

The example illustrated here is somewhat more complex in that it not only protects the wood or leather around the keyhole but also provides an added measure of security. The maker realized that "the security of locks . . . and their comparative excellence, are determinable by the number, variety and disposition of the wards, or other impediments inserted in the passage by which the lever, or key is conveyed to the bolt."[166] Accordingly, he designed this trunk escutcheon with a cast bird to hide the keyhole. It is of two parts, both spring loaded and attached to the cast plate with small bolts. The parts interlock at the neck in such a way that the head must be raised for the body to rotate to the left, exposing the hole for insertion of the key. The brass springs affixed to each part provide enough resistance to their movement so that the idly curious or even mildly larcenous might be dissuaded from attempting further entry.

This type of ornamental cover has a long history of use in European locks. One of the most widely published is of brass and was made by the Birmingham locksmith John Wilkes about 1685.[167]

1 Alternately called a surplice pin, mirror knob, or curtain pin, cloak pins were used for hanging coats in a hallway, supporting a looking glass, or tying back curtains on a window or bed.

2 Catalogue 739.4B82, Peabody Essex Institute, Salem, Mass.

3 As quoted in the *New-York Journal, or General Advertiser*, May 19, 1768. A second newspaper article testifying to American sympathies with Wilkes appeared in the March 19, 1798, issue of the *Boston Gazette*. It quoted and editorialized the inscription on his tombstone in London "Here lies John Wilkes, a friend to liberty!!"

4 Catalogue 739.4B82, Peabody Essex Institute, Salem, Mass., as cited in Robert W. Symonds, "An Eighteenth-Century English Brassfounder's Catalogue," *Antiques* 19, no. 2 (February 1931): 102–5.

5 Specifics of Curwen's difficulties are outlined in George Atkinson Ward, *The Journal and Letters of Samuel Curwen, an American in England, from 1775 to 1783* (Boston: Little, Brown, 1864), p. 149.

6 Birmingham city directory, 1801, Birmingham City Library.

7 The advertisement appears in *Aris's Birmingham Gazette*, July 22, 1765. The ornament on the face of these cloak pins varies significantly from the great seal of the United States in that the eagle faces the talon that clutches arrows, signifying a warlike attitude, rather than facing the talon clutching an olive branch, signifying peace. Winterthur owns four other cloak pins identical to these: acc. nos. 65.2232.1, .2, 61.642.2, and 64.94.2, all marked by Hands and Jenkins.

8 Alfred L. Bush, *The Life Portraits of Thomas Jefferson* (Charlottesville, Va.: Thomas Jefferson Memorial Foundation, 1902), p. 66, illustrates the full-size portrait; Fillmore Norfleet, *Saint-Mémin in Virginia: Portraits and Biographies* (Richmond, Va.: Dietz Press, 1942), p. 111, illustrates the reduced profile.

9 Laurence Brown, *A Catalogue of British Historical Medals, 1760–1906* (London: B.A. Seaby, 1980), p. 153; Lewis Forrer, *Biographical Dictionary of Medallists*, 8 vols. (London: Spink and Son, 1909), 3:560.

10 As advertised in *Holden's Triennial Directory for 1809, 1810, 1811* (London: Printed by John Davenport, 1811), p. 23. The stamping used as cabinet handles is illustrated in James F. Jensen, "Eighteenth- and Early Nineteenth-Century American Furniture at the Honolulu Academy of Arts," *Antiques* 113, no. 5 (May 1978): 1093, 1096; Wallace Nutting, *Furniture Treasury*, 3 vols. (Framingham, Mass.: Old America Co., 1928), 2:3619.

11 The design, dated November 9, 1803, appeared in Thomas Sheraton, *The Cabinet-Maker, Upholsterer and General Artist's Encyclopedia* (London, 1807).

12 Original trade catalogue, M61e, Victoria and Albert Museum, London; xerox, TS573 B61e* TC, Downs collection, Winterthur Library.

13 As quoted in Aitken, *Early History of Brass*, p. 68.

14 As quoted in Rudolph Ackermann, *The Repository of Arts, Literature, Commerce, Manufacture, Fashion, and Politics* 7, no. 41 (May 1, 1819): 310; 9, no. 50 (February 1, 1820): 113.

15 As quoted in George Hepplewhite, *The Cabinet-Maker and Upholsterer's Guide* (London: I. and J. Taylor, 1794), p. 18. Thomas Sheraton, *Appendix to the Cabinet-Maker and Upholsterer's Drawing Book* (London: Printed by T. Bensley, 1802), p. 31, pl. 19.

16 For cornice-end designs, see A. W. Gillet trade catalogue, Birmingham, ca. 1829, pls. 172–74, TS575 G47* TC; for bed ornament designs, see Birmingham trade catalogue, 1822, TS573 B61F* no. 2 TC, Downs collection, Winterthur Library. A similar pair is illustrated in Charles L. Venable, *American Furniture in the Bybee Collection* (Austin: University of Texas Press, 1989), pp. 136, 137.

17 A pair of andirons, acc. no. 59.2872.1, .2, and a shovel and tongs, acc. no.

59.2875.1, .2, in the Winterthur collection illustrate this uniformity of materials, style, and construction.

18 *New-York Journal, or General Advertiser*, October 6, 1768.

19 *Rivington's New-York Gazetteer*, November 25, 1773.

20 Beecher, *Treatise on Domestic Economy*, p. 280.

21 Trade catalogue TS573 M58d* TC, Downs collection, Winterthur Library.

22 David Phillips estate inventory, 54.67.171, Downs collection, Winterthur Library.

23 Leslie, *House Book*, p. 332.

24 A Birmingham brass-manufacturer's trade catalogue, ca. 1822, TS573 B61f* no. 2 TC, Downs collection, Winterthur Library, pictures 47 bell pulls of this type on pls. 132 through 137, in conjunction with more than 100 other bell-pull parts.

25 *The Fables, of Aesop*, 2 vols. (London: Printed for John Stockdale, 1793), 2:145–46.

26 Door porters, called door stops today, continued to be made in England until well into the twentieth century. For an 11-inch-high version called "The Pelican" see Pearson-Page Company trade catalogue, Birmingham, 1925, sec. 33, p. 4, item 1621, TS573 P36*, Downs collection, Winterthur Library.

27 Robert Hunt, ed., *Ure's Dictionary of Arts, Manufacturers, and Mines*, 3 vols. (London: Longman, Green, Longman, and Roberts, 1860), 2:730.

28 *Sketchley's and Adam's Tradesman's True Guide* (Birmingham, 1770), p. 82. A rim lock was applied to the face of a door; a mortice lock was set into a door. *Holden's Biennial Directory, Class Third* (London: Thomas Underhill, 1816–17), p. 241.

29 Campbell, *London Tradesmen*, p. 166.

30 *Pennsylvania Gazette* (Philadelphia), April 30, 1752.

31 As quoted in *Slater's Classified Directory* (Manchester, Eng.: Isaac Slater, 1850).

32 Specification of Letters Patent, no. 5880, January 18, 1830, British Patent Office, London.

33 Robert T. Trump, "The Carpenter-type Lock," *Antiques* 66, no. 6 (December 1954): 482.

34 Rees, *Cyclopaedia*, 22:s.v. "lock."

35 As quoted in Alexander Jamieson, *A Dictionary of Mechanical Science, Arts, Manufactures and Miscellaneous Knowledge*, 2 vols. (London: Printed for Henry Fisher, Son, 1829), 2:587.

36 Maurice Bywater, *Bywater's Philadelphia Business Directory and City Guide* (Philadelphia: By the author, 1850), p. 102.

37 A right-hand chamber latch made by Burrows is pictured in Herbert Schiffer, *Early Pennsylvania Hardware* (Whitford, Pa.: Whitford Press, 1966), p. 24. The subject of this entry is a left-hand example.

38 George Bickham, *A New Book of Ornaments* (London, 1752), title page.

39 Syng advertised in the *Maryland Gazette*, March 15, 1759.

40 All of these are depicted on pls. 118–24 and 209 in a Birmingham brass-founder's catalogue, TS573 B61c* TC, Downs collection, Winterthur Library.

41 The King advertisement appeared in the *Pennsylvania Chronicle*, April 20, 1767.

42 Catalogue M60d, pl. 172, Victoria and Albert Museum, London. The Winterthur catalogue is TS573 M58d* TC, Downs collection, Winterthur Library.

43 As quoted in Leslie, *House Book*, p. 333.

44 Leslie, *House Book*, p. 332.

45 *Desilver's Philadelphia Directory* (Philadelphia: Robert Desilver, 1831), adv. supp.

46 *Rivington's New-York Gazetteer*, February 17, 1772.

47 George Richardson, *Iconologia; or, A Collection of Emblematical Figures*, 2 vols. (London: Printed by C. Scott, 1779), 1:iii. *Heathen Mythology, Illustrated* (London: Willoughby, 1844), p. 64.

48 See Birmingham trade catalogue, TS573 B61c* TC, Downs collection, Winterthur Library, which depicts the Bacchus drawing.

49 *Journal of the Franklin Institute of the State of Pennsylvania; Devoted to the*

Mechanic Arts, Manufactures, General Science, and the Recording of American and Other Patented Inventions, n.s., 8 (1831): 13.

50 The analyzed areas of this knocker contained copper, zinc, tin, nickel, silver, iron, and high concentrations of cadmium. The object was probably cadmium plated and possibly nickel plated in the twentieth century.

51 As noted in the *New-York Daily Advertiser*, March 21, 1820.

52 Archibald McElroy, *McElroy's Philadelphia Directory for 1845* (Philadelphia: Edward C. and John Biddle, 1845), adv. supp., p. 3.

53 Webster, *Encyclopaedia of Domestic Economy*, p. 54.

54 Broadside advertisement, ca. 1800, Birmingham, Eng., 3-VIBD, New York Public Library.

55 *Columbian Mirror and Alexandria Gazette*, May 5, 1797.

56 *Lancaster Journal* (Pennsylvania), June 24, 1795. *Paxton's Philadelphia Annual Advertiser*, supp. to John Adems Paxton, *Philadelphia Directory and Register for 1818* (Philadelphia: E. and R. Parker, 1818).

57 As quoted in Simon Jervis, *Printed Furniture Designs before 1650* (London: Furniture History Society, 1974), pp. 43, 313. On castors, see Ralph Edwards, *The Dictionary of English Furniture*, 3 vols. (1927; rev. ed., London: Barra Books, 1983), 1:220.

58 Campbell, *London Tradesmen*, p. 176. Christopher Gilbert, *The Life and Work of Thomas Chippendale* (New York: Macmillan Co., 1978), p. 192.

59 Gilbert, *Life and Work of Thomas Chippendale*, p. 137.

60 As quoted in Gilbert, *Life and Work of Thomas Chippendale*, p. 184. The brass-wheeled castor in this entry appears to be original to a four-legged lectern, which is believed to be American made. It is illustrated in Montgomery, *American Furniture*, pp. 394–95. The other castor wheel is made of three layers of leather flanked on each side by a thin brass plate.

61 Sheraton, *Cabinet Dictionary*, 1:139.

62 On the Harcourt patent, see Specification of Letters Patent, no. 4481, June 21, 1820, British Patent Office, London.

63 See trade catalogue TS573 M58i*, Downs collection, Winterthur Library. The leaf-decorated castor, which was originally finished with tinted lacquer–giving it a gilded appearance–is one of four on a Baltimore painted window seat that is illustrated in Montgomery, *American Furniture*, pp. 313–15.

64 Specification of Letters Patent, no. 3548, May 8, 1812, British Patent Office, London.

65 "Inventory of the Household Effects of John Penn, Jr., 1788," *Pennsylvania Magazine of History and Biography* 15, no. 3 (1891): 374. As quoted in patent for John Lebrecht Steinhauser, Specification of Letters Patent, no. 4008, April 13, 1816, British Patent Office, London.

66 Aitken, *Early History of Brass*, p. 54. The trade catalogue is discussed in Nicholas Goodison, "The Victoria and Albert Museum's Collection of Metal-Work Pattern Books," *Furniture History* 11 (1975): 20, 30, pl. 58.

67 "Collectors Notes," *Antiques* 111, no. 4 (April 1977): 698.

68 The subject of this entry and its mates are original to their two window benches, which were made in Baltimore. These window seats are illustrated in Montgomery, *American Furniture*, pp. 314–15.

69 Knight, *Knight's American Mechanical Dictionary*, 1:498.

70 Specification of Letters Patent, no. 5562, November 17, 1827, British Patent Office, London.

71 Specification of Letters Patent, no. 5562, November 17, 1827, British Patent Office, London.

72 On Pinchbeck's invention and transferral of manufacturing rights, see *Aris's Birmingham Gazette*, November 28, 1768. On the brothers, see *Holden's Biennial Directory* (London, 1810–17), p. 94. On the partnership with Collinson, see *Pigot and Co.'s Royal National and Commercial Directory* (London: J. Pigot, 1841), p. 24.

73 George Hepplewhite, *The Cabinet-Maker and Upholsterer's Guide* (London: I. and J. Taylor, 1794), pls. 21, 23. Sheraton, *Cabinet Dictionary*, 1:138–39.

74 Specification of Letters Patent, no. 10,488, January 31, 1854, United States Patent Office, Alexandria, Va.

75 Specification of Letters Patent, no. 11,506, August 6, 1854, United States Patent Office, Alexandria, Va.

76 Joseph Atkinson, *The History of Newark, New Jersey* (Newark: William B. Guild, 1878), pp. 227–28.

77 *The Merchantile Agency Reference Book* (New York: Dun, Barlow, 1876).

78 Trade catalogue TS405 T64 TC, Downs collection, Winterthur Library.

79 Trade catalogue TS573 B61c* TC, Downs collection, Winterthur Library.

80 That table is pictured and discussed in Montgomery, *American Furniture*, pp. 366–67.

81 Sheraton, *Cabinet Dictionary*, 2:251–52.

82 Stop hinges are cited in Sheraton, *Cabinet Dictionary*, 1:112. The Gillet volume is pattern book TS573 G47* TC, Downs collection, Winterthur Library. *Directory of Birmingham* (Birmingham, Eng.: Wrightson and Webb, 1846), p. 71.

83 "Designs and Trade Marks: Registers and Representations," October, 1977, p. 2, Public Record Office, London.

84 On cabinet hardware, see Campbell, *London Tradesmen*, p. 177. On the Waldos, see broadside advertisement owned by the American Antiquarian Society, Worcester, Mass. The Shotwells advertised in *Rivington's New-York Gazetteer*, November 25, 1773.

85 As advertised on Daniel Burnap trade card, featured on the cover of Hoopes, *Shop Records of Daniel Burnap*. The copper plate Burnap made to print his trade card is owned by the Wadsworth Atheneum. On the Burnap patterns, see Hoopes, *Shop Records of Daniel Burnap*, pp. 162, 165. These hinges hold the waist door in place on a tall clock, the works of which are signed by Daniel Burnap. The clock is pictured and discussed in Downs, *American Furniture*, p. 209.

86 Hoopes, *Shop Records of Daniel Burnap*, p. 79.

87 Sheraton, *Cabinet Dictionary*, 2:328, 330.

88 See catalogues TS573 M58cf TC, TS573 B61F* no. 2 TC, and TS573 B61e* TC, Downs collection, Winterthur Library.

89 Three sizes of die-stamped clock balls are pictured in trade catalogue TS573 B61F* no. 4 TC, published in Birmingham, Eng., ca. 1813, Downs collection, Winterthur Library. See trade catalogue TS573 B61F* no. 2 TC, pl. 27, Downs collection. The capitals and bases were offered in 5 sizes and the quarter columns in 3. These clock balls are on, but not original to, a New York wardrobe attributed to the cabinetmaker Michael Allison. It is pictured and discussed in Montgomery, *American Furniture*, pp. 440, 441, 443.

90 Illustrated in catalogue M65j, Victoria and Albert Museum, London.

91 The finials and cabinet knobs shown are on, and may be original to, a Massachusetts-made secretary-bookcase that is pictured and discussed in Montgomery, *American Furniture*, pp. 233, 234.

92 The Winterthur chair is acc. no. 57.581. The trade catalogue, M61e, ca. 1810, bears the ink inscription "Bock fct Birmm." It is listed in Nicholas Goodison, "The Victoria and Albert Museum's Collection of Metal-Work Pattern Books," in *Furniture History*, 30 vols. (London: Furniture History Society, 1975), 11:17. Plate 47 in the same publication pictures the matching mount on Winterthur's side chair. Winterthur also owns a copy of the catalogue, TS573 B61F* no. 4 TC, Downs collection, Winterthur Library.

93 Winterthur owns a New York–made high-post bed, acc. no. 55.789, with numerous brass mounts, several of which are identical to those used on these chairs. The armchair on which this mount is placed is pictured and discussed in Montgomery, *American Furniture*, p. 456. The Chinese painting,

acc. no. 65.1601, is in the Winterthur collection.

94 The directories are the *Citizens Directory and Strangers Guide* (New York: Printed by George Long for Thomas N. Stanford, 1814), p. 108; and *Longworth's American Almanac, New-York Register, and City Directory* (New York: David Longworth, 1814), p. 35. One table was published by Benjamin Ginsburg, "Bronze Mounts and a New Label," *Antiques* 83, no. 4 (April 1963): 459; the Winterthur table, acc. no. 62.237, is pictured in Montgomery, *American Furniture*, pp. 339–40.

95 Geoffrey Warren, "Revered and Feared: The Peacock in Art," *Antique Dealer and Collector's Guide* 26, no. 12 (July 1975): 82–86. Peacocks are occasionally depicted in early designs, as on pl. 36 of *Various Birds and Beasts Drawn from the Life by Frances Barlow* (London: Robert Sayer, ca. 1760).

96 The quote appears on a label affixed to a card table at Winterthur, acc. no. 62.237, by the New York cabinetmaker Joseph Brauwers, ca. 1814.

97 Trade catalogue M61j, Victoria and Albert Museum, London, and trade catalogue NK7899 Y34* TC, Downs collection, Winterthur Library. The placement of the brass on the table prevents its analysis.

98 As quoted in Aitken, *Early History of Brass*, p. 84. A book-pierced border of this type is pictured in trade catalogue M60d, Victoria and Albert Museum, London.

99 George Richardson, *Iconology; or, A Collection of Emblematical Figures* (London: Printed by G. Scott, 1779), preface, p. ii.

100 Richardson, *Iconology*, pp. 31–32.

101 Richardson, *Iconology*, pp. 10, 11, 9. Corn, in this instance, is used generically to mean a seed of one of the cereals.

102 The brass-trade catalogue is owned by the Missouri Historical Society and was acquired as part of the archives of the Mesker Brothers Iron Company in St. Louis; microfilm copy, Downs collection, Winterthur Library. Such figures were also made in France and England,

but current evidence supports a Germanic origin for the illustrated examples. The mottling is not equal to French work, while the threaded steel spikes were not used in English mounts. The German exhibition catalogue "*Mein Feld Ist Die Welt,*" *Musterbucherbücher und Kataloge 1784–1914* (Dortmund, Ger.: Westfalisches Wirtschaftsarchiv, 1984) documents America as a market for German work of this type.

103 John Fanning Watson, *Annals of Philadelphia, and Pennsylvania* (Philadelphia: J. M. Stoddart, 1877), 2:101.

104 As quoted in Frank Sommer, "John F. Watson: First Historian of American Decorative Arts," *Antiques* 83, no. 3 (March 1963): 303. The drawing is preserved in the manuscript notes for the *Annals of Philadelphia* at the Historical Society of Pennsylvania, as cited in Sommer, "John F. Watson," p. 301.

105 William Macpherson Hornor, Jr., *Blue Book, Philadelphia Furniture* (Philadelphia, 1935), p. 9.

106 Campbell, *London Tradesmen*, pp. 178–79.

107 *Boston News-Letter*, February 17, 1737.

108 *The Universal Director* (London, 1763), p. 37, Guildhall Library, London.

109 Tiper is mentioned in "An Alphabet of the Commissions and Freedoms of the Worshipful Company of Founders, London," L37, MS 6337, Guildhall Museum, London.

110 Catalogue TS573 M58g* TC, Downs collection, Winterthur Library.

111 Parsloe, *Wardens' Accounts*, p. xxx.

112 "An Alphabet of the Commissions and Freedoms of the Worshipful Company of Founders, London," L37, MS 6337 and 6338, Guildhall Museum, London, list John Goode, freed February 4, 1683; John Godfrey, freed October 5, 1686; John Greenly, freed October 26, 1686; John Garish, freed August 24, 1687; John Goudet, freed April 29, 1690; John Gowne, freed September 19, 1691; John Grime, freed May 8, 1704; John Gibbs, freed May 3, 1707; John Giles, freed September 24, 1716; Job Gadbury, freed August 5, 1727; Jackson Grove, freed

February 5, 1727; Job Grimshaw, freed September 27, 1736; James Goring, freed May 6, 1745; John Giles, freed July 29, 1746; James Grape, freed February 5, 1749; and James Gamble, freed May 7, 1750. It is remotely possible these handles and escutcheons were made in Birmingham by John Gold. Two cabinet handles marked "I • GOLD," original to a high chest signed by the Charlestown, Mass., cabinetmaker Benjamin Frothingham, acc. no. 67.1445, are in the Winterthur collection (entry 307). The cabinet handle, acc. no. 60.1134, is original to a Massachusetts-made desk-and-bookcase pictured and discussed in Downs, *American Furniture*, ent. 226.

113 Esther Stevens Brazer, "A Pedigreed Lacquered Highboy," *Antiques* 15, no. 5 (May 1929): 398–401. The high chest is also pictured in Downs, *American Furniture*, ent. 188.

114 Charles Weston to Ann Matilda Williams, object folder 57.1084, Registration office, Winterthur.

115 *Boston Gazette*, October 3, 1757.

116 *The Apprentices of Great Britain, 1710–1762* (London, 1921–28), 24:4762, as extracted from the Inland Revenue Books, Public Record Office, London, for the Society of Genealogists. On Pulley, see "An Alphabet of the Commissions and Freedoms of the Worshipful Company of Founders, London," L37, MS 6337, Guildhall Museum, London.

117 The high chest is pictured and discussed in Downs, *American Furniture*, ent. 190. The Shotwell advertisement appears in *Rivington's New-York Gazetteer*, November 25, 1773.

118 "An Alphabet of the Commissions and Freedoms of the Worshipful Company of Founders, London," L37, MS 6337 and 6338, Guildhall Museum, London, list John Cudmore, John Clayton, John Cooke, Joseph Cannon, John Carter, Joseph Cable, John Child, John Chapol, John Cuttridge, John Cole, John Combors, John Cawdell, John Chapman, John Chipman, John Crener, and another John Cole.

119 "An Alphabet of the Commissions and Freedoms of the Worshipful Company of Founders, London," L37, MS 6337, and 6338, Guildhall Museum, London, list Joseph Matthews, John Martin, John Marshall, John Marsh, Joseph Miles, Isaac Moad, John May, John Minott, John Meason, and Jacob Moad.

120 Campbell, *London Tradesmen*, pp. 177–78.

121 Birmingham trade catalogue TS573 M58g* TC, ca. 1770, Downs collection, Winterthur Library, serves to illustrate, with 243 depictions of cabinet handles, no two the same.

122 Roll 14, vol. 53, letterbook, 1783–1800, Revere Papers, Massachusetts Historical Society, Boston.

123 For pl. 125, see trade catalogue NK7899 B6lc*, 1789; for pl. 287, see trade catalogue NK7899 H26, 1787, Winterthur Library.

124 *Sketchley's Birmingham, Wolverhampton, and Walsall Directory* (Birmingham, Eng.: James Sketchley, 1767), p. 8.

125 Those not owned by Winterthur are recorded in DAPC. Winterthur's high chest was made by Benjamin Frothingham and is illustrated in Richard H. Randall, Jr., "Benjamin Frothingham," in Walter Muir Whitehill, Johnathan L. Fairbanks, and Brock W. Jobe, eds., *Boston Furniture of the Eighteenth Century* (Boston: Colonial Society of Massachusetts, 1974), p. 224. A two-arm, brass wall sconce is recorded that bears the stamped surname "GOLD." It may be the work of the same man. It is illustrated and discussed in Sotheby's sale catalogue 6716 (May 24–26, 1995), lot 659.

126 Winterthur owns 9 English trade catalogues that picture this pattern. Although all illustrations relate closely to one another, minute differences in size and detailing indicate that each is the product of an individual manufacturer. George Atkinson Ward, *The Journal and Letters of Samuel Curwen, an American in England, from 1775 to 1783* (Boston: Little, Brown, 1864), p. 149.

127 *Pennsylvania Packet, and Daily Advertiser* (Philadelphia), November 11, 1771.

128 See pattern books NK7899 B61, pl. 90, fig. 608; TS573 M58g*, pl. 55, fig. 1149, Downs collection, Winterthur Library.

129 George Edwards and Matthew Darly, *A New Book of Chinese Designs Calculated to Improve the Present Taste. . .* (London, 1754), title page.

130 William Chambers, *Designs of Chinese Buildings, Furniture, Dresses, Machines, and Utensils* (1762; reprint, New York: Benjamin Blom, 1968), p. 1.

131 Trade catalogue M60d, figs. 8, 5, Victoria and Albert Museum, London, depicts a plate-lifting handle and stop-lifting handle.

132 Harold Donaldson Eberlein and Cortlandt Van Dyke Hubbard, *Diary of Independence Hall* (Philadelphia: J. B. Lippincott Co., 1948), p. 41. On the request, see Harold V. B. Vorhis and Ronald E. Heaton, *Loud and Clear* (Norristown, Pa.: R. E. Heaton, 1970), p. 7. The committee is quoted in Isaac Norris letterbook, 1719–56, pp. 32–33, Historical Society of Pennsylvania, Philadelphia.

133 The advertisements appear in the *Pennsylvania Gazette* (Philadelphia), August 3, 1749; *Pennsylvania Gazette*, March 16, 1752. In addition to brass, Stow also worked in other metals as evidenced by the 100 lead fire marks he supplied in 1752 for the Philadelphia Contributorship, an insurance company, recorded in M. J. McKosker, *The Historical Collection of Insurance Company of North America* (Philadelphia: Insurance Company of North America, 1967), p. 60.

134 Three trade catalogues that depict variants of this handle are TS573 M58h*, TS573 M58e*, and NK7899 B61fa*, Downs collection, Winterthur Library. The last of these pictures 5 examples that vary only in minor details. Winterthur also owns a Philadelphia-made dressing table, acc. no. 53.68, that has cabinet handles almost identical to the example made by Stow. They appear to be original and are probably English imports. J. C. Stow, *Stow Family*

(Baltimore: Privately printed, 1931–32), p. 3. This handle was originally on a Philadelphia high chest in Sotheby's sale 3720 (February 1, 1975), lot 1010.

135 Birmingham city directory, 1779, pp. xxvi, xxvii, Birmingham City Library.

136 A bail with the same mark is illustrated on pl. 52 of Birmingham trade catalogue M61e, ca. 1810, Victoria and Albert Museum, London. It is accompanied with the note "Specimen of the under-side of the Handles which are all Stamp'd." Winterthur also owns a copy of the catalogue, TS573 B61F* no. 4 TC, Downs collection, Winterthur Library.

137 Richard Payne Knight, *The Symbolical Language of Ancient Art and Mythology* (New York: J. W. Boulton, 1892), p. 145. On the American symbolism, see E. McClung Fleming, "From Indian Princess to Greek Goddess: The American Image, 1783–1815," in Milo M. Naeve, ed., *Winterthur Portfolio 3* (Winterthur, Del.: Henry Francis du Pont Winterthur Museum, 1967), p. 50. This handle and its mates are on a Salem, Mass., secretary-bookcase pictured in Montgomery, *American Furniture*, pp. 222–23.

138 Birmingham city directory, 1801, Birmingham City Library. In addition to this and other bails and a pair of stamped brass cloak pins, acc. no. 58.130.1, .2, Winterthur owns a Massachusetts-made dressing table, acc. no. 57.569, with original stamped brass knobs, the backplates of which are marked "H.J." Other partnerships were those of Hanson and Jefferies, stampers, and Horton and Jarvis, who made patterns for sand flasks. As yet unexplained is the existence of a few bails with initials that appear to be "H.J.ʳ."

139 While bails bearing the initials "H.J." are more frequently encountered than other marked examples, it must be noted that unmarked cabinet handles outnumber them. The hen and chicken motif appears on oval cabinet handles in Birmingham brass catalogue TS573 B61F* no. 4 TC, Downs collection, Winterthur Library. The handles are on a Portsmouth, N.H., chest of drawers

pictured in Montgomery, *American Furniture*, p. 183.

140 Thomas Fletcher (Sheffield) to Baldwin Gardiner (Philadelphia), box 7, Fletcher Papers, Athenaeum of Philadelphia.

141 Fletcher to Gardiner, Fletcher Papers.

142 On Pitman, see Montgomery, *American Furniture*, p. 372. Bolton and Grew advertised in the *Independent Chronicle. And the Universal Advertiser* (Boston), November 5, 1795.

143 Although the Jenkins and Hands partnership most likely began in 1791, they were not listed in the city directories until 1797; no city directories were published from 1792 to 1796. *The Directory of Birmingham* (Birmingham, Eng.: Wrightson and Webb, 1833), p. 47. Maslin kettles are used primarily in boiling fruit for preserves.

144 Jenkins's mark is rarely encountered, yet he was in business for a long period of time and capable of producing both variety and quantity, as judged by his advertisements. Bennet Woodcraft, comp., *Alphabetical Index of Patentees of Inventions* (London: British Patent Office, 1854), p. 303.

145 Edmund Burke, *Account of the European Settlements in America* (London: Printed for J. Dodsley, 1757), 2:175–76.

146 This cabinet handle is pictured in trade catalogue M61i, fig. 4040, pl. 3, Victoria and Albert Musuem, London. Hunting, a Roxbury, Mass., cabinetmaker, penned his name in ink on the front pages of the newspapers he used to line the drawers of the chest, which is illustrated in Montgomery, *American Furniture*, pp. 182–83.

147 *Independent Chronicle. And the Universal Advertiser* (Boston), November 5, 1795.

148 Aitken, *Early History of Brass*, p. 68.

149 On the advantages of stamped brass foundry, see Specification of Letters Patent, no. 920, March 7, 1769, British Patent Office, London. On the depiction of Franklin, see Russell Walton Thorpe, "Benjamin Franklin, LL.D., F.R.SS.," *The Antiquarian* 8, no. 1 (February 1927): 39. According to the author, Franklin shares this honor with George Washington and Napoleon Bonaparte. In 1906 the

Grolier Club in New York City published a *Catalogue of an Exhibition Commemorating the Two Hundreth Anniversary of the Birth of Benjamin Franklin*, which listed 443 depictions of the man, with no. 439 being a "Brass mirror Knob. Bust, profile to left. Patience Wright type. Circular. Ben Franklin, LL.D." Fairly accurate reproductions of this pattern are illustrated in Israel Sack, *Antique Reproductions: Cabinet Hardware and Period Fittings* (Boston, ca. 1927), p. 22. A copy, FS405 512TG, is in the Downs collection, Winterthur Library.

150 One trade catalogue in the Downs collection, Winterthur Library, NK7899 Y34* TC, ca. 1821, Yates and Hamper, Birmingham, Eng., pp. 34–39, pictures 77 patterns of commode knobs that are described as being all brass.

151 These knobs are on the drawers of a dressing bureau labeled by the Boston cabinetmaker Levi Ruggles, which is pictured in Montgomery, *American Furniture*, p. 187.

152 A few plated commode handles are pictured on pl. 69 of a trade catalogue published in Sheffield, Eng., ca. 1800, NK7250 M58d F TC, Downs collection, Winterthur Library. A pair of Philadelphia commodes with plated handles, perhaps by Armitage, are pictured in Donald L. Fennimore and Robert T. Trump, "Joseph B. Barry, Philadelphia Cabinetmaker," *Antiques* 135, no. 5 (May 1989): 1217.

153 On coffin nails, see trade catalogue M62b, pl. 202, Victoria and Albert Museum, London. Collins is listed in the Birmingham city directory, 1823, Birmingham City Library.

154 As transcribed in Christopher Gilbert, *The Life and Work of Thomas Chippendale* (London: Cassell, 1978), p. 255.

155 James and Drinker advertised in the *Pennsylvania Gazette* (Philadelphia), October 1, 1761. Bolton and Grew advertised in the *Columbian Centinel* (Boston), June 11, 1796.

156 Christopher Gilbert, *The Life and Work of Thomas Chippendale* (London: Cassell, 1978), p. 256.

157 Catalgoue TS573 M58h*TC, pl. 9,
Downs collection, Winterthur Library.

158 A copy of this bill is in object folder
67.151.1–.6, Registration office,
Winterthur. The upholstery and iron
gimp tacks appear to be undisturbed.
Modern machine-made brass upholstery
nails hold these strips to the chair
frames, however, indicating they may
have been reattached.

159 Holme, *Academy of Armory*, 2:3.
George Hepplewhite, *The Cabinet-
Maker and Upholsterer's Guide*
(London: I. and J. Taylor, 1794), p. 8.

160 Trade catalogue NK7899 B61c* TC,
ca. 1789, Downs collection, Winterthur
Library. An example of the Bailey bill-
head is in the Downs collection, 65x668.
As advertised in the *Independent
Journal* (New York), May 26, 1787.
Thomas Thomas was listed in the
New York City directories from 1786
to 1793 although he may have been in
the city earlier.

161 Edward Hazen, *The Panorama of the
Professions* (Philadelphia: Uriah Hunt,
1837), p. 74.

162 The term *high top* and these prices are
on pl. 202 of the 1822 watermarked
Birmingham trade catalogue M62b,
Victoria and Albert Museum, London.
Collins is listed in the 1823 Birmingham
city directory, Birmingham City Library.

163 *Columbian Centinel* (Boston),
June 11, 1796.

164 The "Patent" handle is pictured on pl.
62 of the British trade catalogue TS573
B61e* TC, Downs collection,
Winterthur Library. Specification of
Letters Patent, no. 3450, July 15, 1811,
British Patent Office, London.

165 The only Allen in naval records at the
National Archives is a John M., midshipman, from February 1, 1823, to
February 13, 1824. These records do
not include enlisted men. On Benjamin
Allen, see George Adams, *The Boston
City Directory* (Boston: James French
and Charles Stimson, 1848), adv.
supp., p. 18.

166 Joseph Bramah, *A Dissertation on the
Construction of Locks* (London: Printed
for the author, ca. 1800), p. 8.

167 The lock is pictured in Gentle and Feild,
English Domestic Brass, p. 192.

GLOSSARY

ALCHEMY
archaic term for brass

ANNULAR LAMP
oil-burning lamp that uses an argand burner centered within a horizontal, cylindrical, tubular oil font

ARABESQUE
type of surface decoration consisting of flowing lines of branches, leaves, and scrollwork fancifully intertwined

ARGAND LAMP
oil lamp with a vertical cylindrical wick fed by air on both the inside and outside

BAIL
curved, hinged handle, as on a kettle, pail, or drawer plate

BALDACCHINO
structure in the form of a canopy above an altar

BATH METAL
brass alloy of about 80 percent copper and 20 percent zinc esteemed for its golden color and often used for making buttons

BELL METAL
alternate name for bronze

BILLET BAR
horizontal part of an andiron; supports burning logs

BOBECHE
shallow-dished element on a candlestick shaft, usually at the top, that catches molten wax or tallow

BOSS
projecting circular or oval ornament normally used to hide a structural element

BRANCH
archaic term for a wall sconce or chandelier

BRAZE
to solder, using a copper-zinc alloy

BURNISH
to polish a surface by rubbing with a smooth, hard tool

CHASING
decoration or ornamental features on a metal object, made with a hammer and small punches

CHASE
hollow groove of a hinge into which a pintle (pivot pin) fits

COLZEA OIL
lighting oil made from the seed of a species of the rape plant

CORBEL
projection from a wall to support a weight

COUNTERFLUTES
shallow, vertical grooves whose lower ends are filled with reeds–slender, convex rods

CIPHER
initials placed on an object for ornament and identification

DAPC
Decorative Arts Photographic Collection; a section of the Winterthur Library

DEER REEF
person appointed to protect and control the deer population in a given area

DOWNS COLLECTION
Joseph Downs Collection of Manuscripts and Printed Ephemera; a section of the Winterthur Library

DO
ditto

DOUTER
implement used to extinguish a candle

DOVETAIL
overlapping brazed joint whose segments appear triangular

DRAGON'S BLOOD
bright red gum or resin exuded from the fruits of certain plants

DRAWPLATE
iron plate with tapered holes of various sizes and shapes through which wire is drawn for sizing and shaping

DUTCH GOLD
malleable brass alloy used in very thin sheets as an inexpensive substitute for gold leaf

DYE (DIE)
engraved stamp, typically of iron or steel, used to impress a design into a piece of metal

ECHINUS
egg-and-dart molding

EPERGNE
ornament for the center of the dining table used to hold fruits, flowers, and sweets

ESCUTCHEON
metal plate fitted around a keyhole on a piece of furniture or door to protect the wood from becoming scratched by a key

FACTOR
purchasing agent

FENDER FOOTMAN
shelf hung from a fireplace fender or coal grate

FILLET
narrow molding serving as ornament

FLASH
extraneous irregularly shaped extensions on an object, caused by leakage of molten metal into the joints of the mold in which the object was cast

FLAMBEAU
ornamental candlestick

FORC'D MEAT
meat from animals that have been force-fed

FRENCH PLATE
brass or copper coated with a thin silver foil, which is applied using heat and a burnisher

FUSED PLATE
copper coated with silver; made by placing a thin sheet of silver on one or opposite sides of a thick copper ingot and heating to cause fusion; the fused ingot is then flattened into a broad sheet with a rolling mill; often called Sheffield plate

GADROON
border of tapered, curved, convex or alternating convex and concave lobes

GERMAN SILVER
copper-zinc-nickel alloy admired for its white color and so called because it was first commercially prepared in the Western hemisphere in Germany; also called paktong

GIRANDOLE
wall-hung lighting fixture; also a prism-hung candlestick or candelabrum

HANDIRONS
archaic misspelling for andirons

HEAD
ornamental terminal at the top of an andiron

INDIA METAL
copper-zinc-nickel alloy admired for its white color and so called because it was imported into the West from India; also called paktong

IRONMONGER
merchant in ironware and the other base metals

JAMB HOOK
horizontally scrolled metal hook fitted to the wall beside a fireplace; holds fire tools

KNOP
rounded knob on a shaft

LATTEN (LATTIN)
archaic term for brass

LUSTRE
lighting device made entirely or largely of faceted glass elements that refract and magnify light

MANHEIM GOLD
malleable brass alloy used in very thin sheets as an inexpensive substitute for gold leaf

NOZZLE (NOSSIL, NOSSEL)
socket on a candlestick used to hold the lower end of the candle

OCCUMY
archaic misspelling of alchemy; a synonym for brass

ORREL COAL
coal mined from the region around Orel in central Russia

OXALIC ACID
poisonous and sour acid from the wood of the sorrel plant

PAKTONG
copper-zinc-nickel alloy admired for its white color; the name derives from the Chinese term *p'ai tung*, meaning white brass

PASTILLE
aromatic paste that produces a pleasing scent when burned

PATERA
stylized circular, oval, or rectangular ornament in the form of a flower

PEEN
to create a rivet head, by hammering, for holding parts of a metal object together

PETCOCK
relief valve used to draw liquid from a container

PHYSIC
synonym for medicine

PINCHBECK
alloy of about 85 percent copper and 15 percent zinc popular for making watchcases and jewelry in imitation of gold; named for its inventor, Christopher Pinchbeck

PORTOR (PORTER)
bar whose end is used in forging or hammering an object

POSNET (SKILLET)
three-legged lidless cooking vessel with handle; used over an open fire

PRINCE'S METAL (PRINCE RUPERT'S METAL)
brass alloy containing about 75 percent copper and 25 percent zinc popularly used for buttons; named for its inventor, Prince Rupert of Germany (1619-82), cousin of Charles II

RAPE OIL
lighting oil made from the seed of the rape plant

RED BRASS
brass of a strong red color derived from its high copper content, usually in excess of 95 percent

REPOUSSÉ
type of hammered and chased decoration with the ornamental features raised above the surface of the object

SEALER
official who determines the accuracy of weights and measures used for commercial purposes

SIMILOR
brass of a reddish yellow color derived from a high copper content, usually about 90 percent

SINUMBRA LAMP
oil lamp with an argand burner centered in a horizontal, cylindrical oil font, elliptic in cross section to minimize its shadow; derived from the Latin *sine umbra*, meaning without shadow

SOLAR LAMP
oil lamp with an argand burner centered within a globular font; designed with the flame close to the illuminant so that it can burn concrete fuels like lard

SPELTER
brass alloy with a high zinc content used to braze copper and brass joints

SPRUE
cylindrical stump on a cast object; formed from the remains of the contents in the channel through which molten metal flowed in the fabrication process; when of a thin rectangular shape it is called a bladed sprue or gate

SWAGE
block over which a piece of metal is hammered or stamped to shape

TOMBAC
brass alloy of about 80 percent copper, 17 percent zinc, and 3 percent tin used to make buttons, sword hilts, and other personal objects

TRAGACANTH
gum obtained from various species of Asiatic plants and used in medicine and the industrial arts

TRIPOLI
silicious stone used in polishing metal

TUTENAG
copper-zinc-nickel alloy esteemed for its white color; synonym for paktong, zinc, and lapis calamanaris

WHORTLE (WORTLE)
drawplate or implement used in the drawing of wire

WHITING
chalk in a powdered state, used for polishing

WORM
spiral tube used with a still to make liquor; also a cylindrical gear with spiral teeth used to regulate power in a machine

BIBLIOGRAPHY

BOOKS

Agricola, Georgius. *De Re Metallica*. Basil, Switz., 1550. Reprint. New York: Dover Publications, 1950.

Aitchison, Leslie. *A History of Metals*. New York: Interscience Publishers, 1960.

Aitken, William Costen. *The Early History of Brass and the Brass Manufacturers of Birmingham*. Birmingham, Eng.: Martin Billing, Son, 1866.

Allen, George Cyril. *The Industrial Development of Birmingham and the Black Country*. London: Allen and Unwin, 1929.

Ash, John. *The New and Complete Dictionary of the English Language*. 2 vols. London, 1775.

Bailey, N. *An Universal Etymological English Dictionary*. London: Printed for J. and A. Duncan, J. and M. Robertson, and J. and W. Shaw, 1794.

Barton, Denys B. *A History of Copper Mining in Cornwall and Devon*. Truro, Eng.: D. Bradford Barton, 1961.

Baumann, Carl-Friedrich, et al. *"Mein Feld Ist Die Welt": Musterbücher Und Kataloge, 1784–1914*. Dortmund, Ger.: Stiftung Westfäliches Wirtschaftsarchiv, 1984.

Beecher, Catherine. *A Treatise on Domestic Economy*. New York: Harper and Brothers, 1849.

Beeton, Isabella. *The Book of Household Management*. London: S. O. Beeton, 1861. Rev. ed. London: Ward, Lock, 1880.

Biringuccio, Vannoccio. *De La Pirotechnia*. Siena, It., 1540. Reprint. New York: Basic Books, 1942.

Bishop, J. Leander. *A History of American Manufactures from 1608–1866*. 3 vols. Philadelphia: Edward Young, 1866.

Bonnin, Alfred. *Tutenag and Paktong*. Oxford, Eng.: Oxford University Press, 1924.

Book of the Household. 2 vols. London: London Printing and Publishing Co., ca. 1870.

Bradbury, Frederick. *A History of Old Sheffield Plate*. London: Macmillan, 1912.

Brand, William F. *The Life of William Rollinson Wittingham*. New York: E. and J. B. Young, 1886.

Brass Candlesticks. Birmingham, Eng., ca. 1780. Reprint. Wiltshire, Eng.: Privately printed, 1973.

The Brass Founder's, Brazier's, and Coppersmith's Manual. London, 1829.

Brears, Peter. *Horse Brasses*. London: Country Life Books, 1981.

Brecher, Jeremy, Jerry Lombardi, and Jan Stackhouse, comps. and eds. *Brass Valley: The Story of Working People's Lives and Struggles in an American Industrial Region*. Philadelphia: Temple University Press, 1982.

A Brief Essay on the Copper and Brass Manufacturers of England. London, 1712.

Brongers, Georg Alfred. *Van gouwenaar tot bruyere pijp*. Groningen, Hol.: Neimeyer Nederlands Tabacologisch Museum, 1978.

Brown, William Norman. *The Principles and Practice of Dipping, Burnishing, Lacquering, and Bronzing Brass Ware*. London: Scott, Greenwood, and Son, 1912.

Bucki, Cecelia. *Metal, Minds, and Machines*. Waterbury, Conn.: Mattatuck Historical Society, 1980.

Burgess, F. W. *Chats on Old Copper and Brass*. New York: A. A. Wyn, 1955.

Burks, Jean M. *Birmingham Brass Candlesticks*. Charlotteville: University Press of Virginia, 1986.

Campbell, R. *The London Tradesmen*. London: T. Gardner, 1747. Reprint. London: David and Charles, 1969.

Caspall, John. *Making Fire and Light in the Home pre 1820*. Woodbridge, Eng.: Antique Collectors' Club, 1987.

Chippendale, Thomas. *The Gentleman and Cabinet-Maker's Director*. London, 1762. Reprint. New York: Dover Publications, 1966.

Clark, Victor S. *History of Manufacturers in the United States*. New York: Peter Smith, 1949.

Cobb, J. Harold. *George Washington Inaugural Buttons and Medalets, 1789 and 1793*. Hamden, Conn.: Privately printed, 1963.

Cocks, Edward John. *A History of the Zinc Smelting Industry in Britain*. London: Harrap, 1968.

Cottingham, Lewis N. *The Smith and Founders Director*. London: Printed by C. Hullmandel, 1823-24.

Crom, Theodore R., ed. *An Eighteenth-Century Brass Hardware Catalogue*. Hawthorne, Fla.: Privately printed, 1994.

_____. *Trade Catalogues*. Melrose, Fla.: Privately printed, 1989.

Cummings, Abbott Lowell, ed. *Rural Household Inventories: Establishing the Names, Uses, and Furnishings of Rooms in the Colonial New England Home, 1675–1775*. Boston: Society for the Preservation of New England Antiquities, 1964.

Davis, John D. *English Silver at Williamsburg*. Williamsburg, Va.: Colonial Williamsburg Foundation, 1976.

Day, Joan. *Bristol Brass: A History of the Industry*. London: David and Charles, 1973.

Delieb, Eric. *The Great Silver Manufactory*. London: Studio Vista, 1971.

Dennis, Faith. *Three Centuries of French Domestic Silver*. 2 vols. New York: Metropolitan Museum of Art, 1960.

Diderot, Denis. *Encyclopédie, ou Dictionnaire raisonné des sciences, des arts, et des métiers*. 28 vols. Paris: Briasson, 1751-76. Reprint. New York: Readex Microprint Corp., 1969.

Donald, Maxwell Bruce. *Elizabethan Copper: The History of the Company of Mines Royal, 1568 to 1605*. London: Pergamion Press, 1955.

_____. *Elizabethan Monoplies: The History of the Company of Mineral and Battery Works from 1565 to 1604*. Edinburgh, Scot.: Oliver and Boyd, 1961.

Doorman, Gerard. *Patents for Inventions in the Netherlands during the Sixteenth, Seventeenth, and Eighteenth Centuries*. The Hague: N. Nijhoff, 1942.

Dossmann, Ernst. *Iserlohner Tabakdosen erzählen*. Iserlohn, Ger.: Verlag Hans-Herbert Mönnig, 1981.

Downs, Joseph. *American Furniture: Queen Anne and Chippendale Periods, 1725–1788*. New York: Macmillan Co., 1952.

Edwards, Frederick, Jr. *Our Domestic Fire-Places*. London: Longmans, Green, 1870.

Erixon, Sigurd. *Gammal mässing*. Vasteras, Swe.: ICA-Förlaget, 1964.

Erixon, Sigurd, and Sven Ljung. *Skultuna bruks historia II: 1. 1607–1860*. Stockholm, 1957.

Feild, Rachael. *Irons in the Fire*. Ramsbury, Eng.: Crowood Press, 1984.

Fremont, M. Ch. *Evolution de la Fonderie de Cuivre d'après les documents du temps*. Paris: Typographie Philippe Renouard, 1903.

Fuller, John. *Art of Coppersmithing*. New York: David Williams, 1894.

Galon,_____. *L'art de convertir le cuivre rouge ou cuivre de rosette, en laiton ou cuivre jaune, au moyen de la pierre calaminaire; de la fondre en tables; de la battre sous le martinet; et de la tirer à la filière*. Paris, 1764.

Gentle, Rupert. *G. Dallas Coons Candlestick Collection*. Richmond: Valentine Museum, 1975.

Gentle, Rupert, and Rachael Feild. *Domestic Metalwork, 1640–1840*. Rev. and enl. ed. Woodbridge, Eng.: Antique Collectors' Club, 1994.

_____. *English Domestic Brass, 1680–1810*. New York: E. P. Dutton, 1975.

Gilbert, Christopher, and Anthony Wells-Cole. *The Fashionable Fire Place, 1660–1840*. Leeds, Eng.: Leeds City Art Galleries, 1985.

Goodison, Nicholas. *Ormolu: The Work of Matthew Boulton*. London: Phaidon Press, 1974.

Goodwin-Smith, R. *English Domestic Metalwork*. Leigh-on-Sea, Eng.: F. Lewis, 1937.

Grant-Francis, Col. George. *The Smelting of Copper in the Swansea District of South Wales from the Time of Elizabeth to the Present Day*. Swansea, Eng., 1867. 2d ed. London: Henry Sotheran, 1881.

Grove, John R. *Antique Brass Candlesticks*. Queen Anne, Md.: Privately printed, 1967.

Guttridge, G.H., ed. *The American Correspondence of a Bristol Merchant, 1766–1776: Letters of Richard Champion*. University of California Publications in History, vol. 22, no. 1. Berkeley, Calif., 1934.

Haedeke, Hanns-Ulrich. *Metalwork*. London: Weidenfeld and Nicolson, 1970.

Hamilton, Henry. *The English Brass and Copper Industries to 1800*. London: Frank Cass and Company, 1967.

Hazen, Edward. *The Panorama of the Professions*. Philadelphia: Uriah Hunt, 1837.

Hazlitt, W. Carew. *The Livery Companies of the City of London*. London: Swan Sonnenschein, 1892.

Heyl, Allen V., and Nancy G. Pearre. *Copper, Zinc, Iron, Lead, Cobalt, and Barite Deposits in the Piedmont Upland of Maryland*. Baltimore: Maryland Board of Natural Resources, 1965.

Hibbert, William Nembhard, comp. *History of the Worshipful Company of Founders of the City of London*. London: Unwin Brothers, 1925.

Hileg, Edgar Nathaniel. *Brass Saga*. London: Denn, 1957.

Hiorns, Arthur H. *Metal-Colouring and Bronzing*. London: Macmillan, 1892.

A History of Useful Arts and Manufactures. Dublin, Ire.: W. Folds, 1832.

Hogarth, William. *The Analysis of Beauty*. 1753. Reprint. Oxford, Eng.: Clarendon Press, 1955.

Holland, John. *A Treatise on the Progressive Improvement and Present State of Manufactures in Metal*. London: Longman, Rees, Orme, Brown, and Green, and John Taylor, 1831.

Holme, Randle. *The Academy of Armory*. 2 vols. 1688. Reprint. London: Printed for the Roxburghe Club, 1905.

Holmquist, Kersti. *Nineteenth-Century Brass*. Stockholm: Nordic Museum, 1967.

Holroyd, John Baker. *Observations on the Commerce of the American States with Europe and the West Indies*. Philadelphia: Robert Bell, 1783.

Homer, Ronald F. *Five Centuries of Base Metal Spoons*. London: By the author, 1975.

Hoopes, Penrose R. *Shop Records of Daniel Burnap Clockmaker*. Hartford: Connecticut Historical Society, 1958.

Hopkins, Eric. *Birmingham: The First Manufacturing Town in the World, 1760–1840*. London: Weidenfeld and Nicolson, 1989.

Hornsby, Peter. *Collecting Antique Copper and Brass*. Ashbourne, Eng.: Moorland Publishing Company, 1989.

_____. *Pewter, Copper, and Brass*. London: Hamlyn, 1981.

Hume, Ivor Noël. *James Geddy and Sons: Colonial Craftsmen*. Williamsburg, Va.: Colonial Williamsburg Foundation, 1980.

Hutton, William. *An History of Birmingham to the End of the Year 1780*. Birmingham, Eng., 1781.

Jarmuth, Kurt. *Lichter Leuchten im Abendland*. Braunschweig, Ger.: Klinkhardt and Biermann, 1967.

John, William David, and Katherine Coombes. *Paktong: The Non-Tarnishable Chinese "Silver" Alloy Used for Adam Firegrates and Early Georgian Candlesticks*. Newport, Eng.: Ceramic Book Company, 1970.

Johnson, Samuel. *A Dictionary of the English Language*. 6th ed. 2 vols. London, 1785.

Kauffman, Henry J. *American Copper and Brass*. Camden, N. J.: Thomas Nelson, 1968.

_____. *Early American Copper, Tin, and Brass*. New York: McBride Company, 1950.

Kauffman, Henry J., and Quentin H. Bowers. *Early American Andirons and Other Fireplace Accessories*. Nashville: Thomas Nelson, 1974.

Knight, Edward H. *Knight's American Mechanical Dictionary*. 3 vols. Boston: Houghton, Osgood, 1880.

Könenkamp, Wolf-Dieter. *Iserlohner Tabakdosen*. Munster, Ger.: Westfälisches Musemsamt, 1982.

Kuile, Onno ter. *Koper en Brons*. Amsterdam: Rijksmuseum, 1986.

Lardner, Dionysius, comp. *The Cabinet Cyclopaedia*. 3 vols. London: Longman, Rees, Orme, Brown, Green, and Longman, and John Taylor, 1834.

Larkin, James. *The Practical Brass and Iron Founder's Guide*. Philadelphia: A. Hart, 1853. Reprint. Philadelphia: Henry Carey Baird, 1883.

Lathrop, William G. *The Brass Industry in Connecticut*. Sheldon, Conn.: By the author, 1909.

_____. *The Brass Industry in the United States*. Mount Carmel, Conn.: By the author, 1926.

_____. *The Development of the Brass Industry in Connecticut*. New Haven: Yale University Press, 1936.

Laughlin, Ledlie Irwin. *Pewter in America: Its Makers and Their Marks*. Vols. 1, 2. Boston: Houghton Mifflin Co., 1940. Vol 3. Barre, Mass.: Barre Publishers, 1971.

Lee, Jean Gordon. *Philadelphians and the China Trade, 1784–1844*. Philadelphia: Philadelphia Museum of Art, 1984.

Leslie, Miss Eliza. *The House Book; or, A Manual of Domestic Economy*. Philadelphia: Carey and Hart, 1841.

Libert, Lutz. *Von Tabak, Dosen und Pfeifen*. Leipzig, Ger.: Edition Leipzig, 1984.

Lindsay, J. Seymour. *Iron and Brass Implements of the English and American Home*. Boston: Medici Society, 1927.

Lockner, Hermann P. *Die Merkzeichen der Nürnberger Rotschmiede*. Munich: Deutscher Kunstverlag, 1981.

_____. *Messing 15–17 Jahrhundert*. Munich: Klinkhardt and Biermann, 1982.

Marcossen, Isaac. *Copper Heritage: The Story of Revere Copper and Brass Incorporated*. New York: Dodd Mead, 1955.

Martin, Thomas. *The Circle of Mechanical Arts*. London: Printed for Richard Rees by Gale, Curtis, and Fenner, and Sherwood, Neeley, and Jones, 1813.

Michaelis, Ronald F. *Old Domestic Base-Metal Candlesticks from the Thirteenth to the Nineteenth Century*. Woodbridge, Eng.: Antique Collectors' Club, 1978.

Minchinton, W. E., ed. *The Trade of Bristol in the Eighteenth Century*. Bristol, Eng.: Printed for the Bristol Record Society, 1957.

Montgomery, Charles F. *American Furniture: The Federal Period, 1788–1825*. New York: Viking Press, 1966.

Moore, N. Hudson. *Old Pewter, Brass, Copper, and Sheffield Plate*. Garden City, N.Y.: Garden City Publishing Company, 1933.

Moxon, Joseph. *Mechanick Excercises*. London: Printed for Daniel Midwinter and Thomas Leigh, 1703.

Mulholland, James A. *A History of Metals in Colonial America*. University, Ala.: University of Alabama Press, 1981.

Nilsson, Nils. *Ljussaxen*. Sweden, 1983.

Oresko, Robert, ed. *The Works in Architecture of Robert and James Adam*. 2 vols. 1778. Reprint. London: St. Martin Press, 1975.

Ottomeyer, Hans, and Peter Pröschel. *Vergoldete Bronzen*. Munich: Klinkhardt and Biermann, 1986.

Overman, Frederick. *The Moulder's and Founder's Pocket Guide*. Philadelphia: Moss and Brother, 1854.

Parsloe, Guy, ed. *Wardens' Accounts of the Worshipful Company of Founders of the City of London, 1497–1681*. London: Athlone Press, 1964.

Pascoe, W. H. *The History of the Cornish Copper Company*. Redruth, Eng.: Dyllanson, Truran, Cornish Publications, 1982.

Pazaurek, Gustav E. *Möbelbeschaläge aus Bronze und Messing*. Stuttgart: Julius Hoffman, 1923.

Perry, Evan. *Collecting Antique Metalware*. Garden City, N.Y.: Doubleday, 1974.

Perry, John T. *Dinanderie*. London: G. Allen and Sons, 1910.

Phelps, Noah A. *A History of the Copper Mines and Newgate Prison at Granby, Conn.* Hartford, Conn.: Case, Tiffany, and Burnham, 1845.

Price, F. G. Hilton. *Old Base Metal Spoons*. London: B. T. Batsford, 1908.

Purves, Alexander. *The Brass-Moulder Illustrated*. London: E. and F. W. Spon, 1915.

Raistrick, Arthur. *The Hatchett Diary*. Truro, Eng.: D. Bradford Barton, 1967.

Raymond, Robert. *Out of the Fiery Furnace: The Impact of Metals on the History of Mankind*. University Park: Pennsylvania State University Press, 1986.

Rees, Abraham. *The Cyclopaedia; or, Universal Dictionary of Arts, Sciences, and Literature*. 47 vols. Philadelphia: Samuel F. Bradford, 1810-24.

Rickard, T. A. *A History of American Mining*. New York: McGraw Hill, 1932.

Roberts, Robert. *The House Servant's Directory*. 1827. Reprint. Waltham, Mass.: Gore Place Society, 1977.

Rosenström, Per Henrik. *Gammal Koppar*. Vasteras, Swe.: ICA-Förlaget, 1965.

Rowlands, M. B. *Masters and Men in the West Midlands Metalware Trades before the Industrial Revolution*. Manchester, Eng.: Manchester University Press, 1975.

Russell, Loris S. *A Heritage of Light: Lamps and Lighting in Early Canadian Homes*. Toronto: University of Toronto Press, 1968.

Scarborough, Quincy. *Carolina Metalworkers*. Fayetteville, N.C.: By the author, 1995.

Schiffer, Peter, Nancy Schiffer, and Herbert Schiffer. *The Brass Book: American, English, and European; Fifteenth Century through 1850*. Exton, Pa.: Schiffer Publishing Limited, 1978.

Schivelbusch, Wolfgang. *Disenchanted Night: The Industrialization of Light in the Nineteenth Century*. Translated by Angela Davies. Berkeley: University of California Press, 1988.

Schumpeter, Elizabeth Boody. *English Overseas Trade Statistics, 1697–1808*. Oxford, Eng.: Clarendon Press, 1960.

Seven Centuries of Brass Making. Bridgeport, Conn.: Bridgeport Brass Company, 1920.

Sheraton, Thomas. *The Cabinet Dictionary*. 2 vols. London: Printed by W. Smith, 1803. Reprint. New York: Praeger Publishers, 1970.

Shuffrey, L. A. *The English Fireplace*. London: B. T. Batsford, 1912.

Shuster, Elwood Delos. *Historical Notes of the Iron and Zinc Mining Industry in Sussex County, New Jersey*. Franklin, N.J.: Privately printed, 1927.

Silliman, Benjamin, Jr., and J. D. Whitney. *Report of the Examination of the Bristol Copper Mine, in Bristol, Conn.* New Haven, Conn.: Ezekiel Hayes, 1855.

Simpson, Marc. *All that Glisters: Brass in Early America*. New Haven: Yale University Press, 1979.

Smith, E. *The Compleat Housewife; or, Accomplish'd Gentlewoman's Companion*. London: Printed for J. and J. Pemberton, 1737.

Smith, William Hawkes. *Birmingham and Its Vicinity as a Manufacturing and Commercial District*. London, 1836.

Stengel, Walter. *Die Merkzeichen der Nürnberger Rothschmiede*. Nuremberg: Germanischen Nationalmuseum, 1918.

Stickney, Edward G. *Revere Bells*. Bedford, Mass.: Privately printed, 1956.

Timmins, Samuel, ed. *Birmingham and the Midland Hardware District*. London: Robert Hardwicke, 1862.

_____. *The Resources, Products, and Industrial History of Birmingham and the Midland Hardware District*. London: Robert Hardwicke, 1866.

Tufts, Edward R. *Hundreds of Hunnemans*. New York: Carlton Press, 1978.

Turner, Eric. *An Introduction to Brass*. Owings Mills, Md.: Stemmer House, 1982.

The Uses of Nickel in the Brass Foundry. New York: International Nickel Company, 1926.

Van Canneyt, Ignace, and Angelo Verschaeve. *Vlaams Koper en Brons*. Bruges: Vitgoveri, Marc Van de Wiele, ca. 1960.

Veitch, Henry Newton. *Sheffield Plate*. London: George Bell and Sons, 1908.

Verlet, Pierre. *Les Bronzes Dorés Français du dix-huitième siècle*. Paris: Grand Manuels Picard, 1987.

Verster, A. J. G. *Brons in den tijd*. Amsterdam: J. H. de Bussy, 1956.

Webster, Thomas. *An Encyclopaedia of Domestic Economy*. New York: Harper and Brothers, 1845.

Whisker, James B. *Pennsylvania Workers in Brass, Copper, and Tin, 1681–1900*. Lewiston, N.Y.: Edward Mellen Press, 1993.

White, Philip L., ed. *The Beekman Merchantile Papers, 1740–1799*. 3 vols. New York: New-York Historical Society, 1956.

Whitman, Maxwell. *Copper for America*. New Brunswick, N.J.: Rutgers University Press, 1971.

Williams, William Meade, comp. *Annals of the Worshipful Company of Founders of the City of London*. London: Privately printed, 1867.

Wills, Geoffrey. *The Book of Copper and Brass*. London: Country Life Books, 1968.

_____. *Collecting Copper and Brass*. London: ARCO Publications, 1962.

Wiswe, Mechthild. *Hausrat aus Kupfer und Messing*. Munich: Keyser, 1979.

_____. *Hausrat aus Messing und Kupfer aus dem Braunschweigischen Landesmuseum*. Braunschweig, Ger.: Braunschweigischen Landesmusuem. 1980.

Woodhouse, James. *Woodhouse's Reply to Seybert's [Adam] Strictures on His Essay Concerning the Perkiomen Zinc Mine*. Philadelphia: Privately printed, 1808.

The Works of Alexander Hamilton. 3 vols. New York: Williams and Whiting, 1810.

Young, W. A. *Old English Pattern Books of the Metal Trades*. London: Victoria and Albert Museum, 1913.

ARTICLES

Abbott, Collamer M. "Early Copper Smelting in Vermont." *Vermont History* 53, no. 1 (January 1965): 223-42.

_____. "Isaac Tyson, Jr., Pioneer Mining Engineer and Metallurgist." *Maryland Historical Magazine* 60 (1965): 15-25.

Ackerman, Paul. "William Homes Webb, 1773-1868: Brassfounder-Warren, Maine." *Maine Antique Digest* 11, no. 4 (April 1983): 1c, 4c.

Barron, Edward Jackson. "Notes on the History of the Armourers' and Braziers' Company." In *Transactions of the London and Middlesex Archaeological Society*, n.s., 2. London, 1913.

Beard, Charles R. "English Warming-Pans of the Seventeenth Century." *Connoisseur* 91, no. 377 (January 1933): 4-9.

Bonnin, Alfred. "Paktong." Connoisseur 76, no. 301 (October 1926): 98-100.

Bowen, Richard L., Jr. "Job Danforth, Jr., Providence Brass Founder and Pewterer." *Pewter Collectors Club of America Bulletin*, nos. 92–93 (March–September 1986): 77–87.

———. "William Billings: Providence Pewterer and Brass Founder." *Pewter Collectors Club of America Bulletin*, nos. 90–91 (March–September 1985): 16–44.

Caine, Joseph. "Statistics of the Tin Mines in Cornwall and the Consumpton of Tin in Great Britain." In *Cornish Mining*, edited by Roger Burt, pp. 83–93. London: David and Charles, 1969.

Calver, William L. "Washington Inaugural Buttons." *New-York Historical Society Quarterly Bulletin* 9, no. 4 (January 1926): 124–26.

Cooper, Thomas, comp. *The Emporium of Arts and Sciences* (Philadelphia), n.s., 3, no.1 (June 1814); no. 2 (August 1814); no. 3 (October 1814).

Dodd, George. "A Day at a Copper and Lead Factory." In *Days at the Factories*. London: Charles Knight, 1843.

Dow, George F. "The Topsfield Copper Mines." In *Proceedings of the Massachusetts Historical Society*, vol. 65. Boston, 1940.

Fales, Dean A., Jr. "Notes on Early American Brass and Copper." *Antiques* 74, no. 6 (December 1958): 534–38.

Fiske, W. Sanders. "Tobacco Pipe Cases." *Connoisseur* 73, no. 289 (December 1925): 218, 221–26, 229–31.

Folk, Homer F. "Making Brass Kettles in Connecticut's Naugatuck River Valley." *Antiques* 125, no. 4 (April 1984): 896–99.

Ford, Worthington Chauncey, ed. "Commerce of Rhode Island, 1726–1800." In *Collections of the Massachusetts Historical Society*, 7th ser., vols. 9, 10. Boston, 1914–15.

Goodison, Nicholas. "The Victoria and Albert Museum's Collection of Metal-Work Pattern Books." *Furniture History* 9 (1975): 1–30.

Goodwin-Smith, R. "The Development of Old Brass Handles." *Antiques* 28, no. 5 (November 1935): 196–98.

Houston, R. J. "The Gap Copper Mines." *Lancaster County Historical Society Bulletin* (1896–97): 283–98.

Hughes, G. Bernard. "Old English Candle Snuffers." *Antiques* 50, no. 5 (November 1946): 316–18.

Hulbert, E. M. "Copper Mining in Connecticut." *Connecticut Quarterly* 3 (January–December 1987): 23–32.

Hummel, Charles F. "Samuel Rowland Fisher's Catalogue of English Hardware." In *Winterthur Portfolio One*, edited by Milo M. Naeve, pp. 188–97. Winterthur, Del.: Henry Francis du Pont Winterthur Museum, 1964.

Kauffman, Henry J. "Coppersmithing in Pennsylvania." *Pennsylvania German Folklore Society* 11 (1948): 83–153.

———. "The Pennsylvania Copper Tea Kettle." *Lancaster County Historical Society Journal* 89, no. 1 (1985): 2–7.

Kernodle, George H., and Thomas M. Pitkin. "The Whittinghams: Brass Founders of New York." *Antiques* 71, no. 4 (April 1957): 350–53.

Kisluk-Grosheide, Daniëlle O. "Dutch Tobacco Boxes in the Metropolitan Museum of Art: A Catalogue." *Metropolitan Museum Journal* 23 (1988): 201–31.

Leman, John. "The Statistics of the Copper Mines of Cornwall." In *Cornish Mining*, edited by Roger Burt, pp. 49–82. London: David and Charles, 1969.

Lloyd, Ferguson. "Furniture Escutcheons in England and America." *Antiquarian* 17, no. 5 (November 1931): 34–35.

Martineau, Harriette. "Tubal-Caine." *Household Words* (London) 5, no. 112 (May 5, 1852): 192–97.

McClinton, Katharine Morrison. "Brass Tobacco Boxes." *Antiques* 50, no. 3 (September 1946): 176–77.

Michie, Thomas S., and Christopher P. Monkhouse. "Pattern Books in the Redwood Library and Athenaeum, Newport, Rhode Island." *Antiques* 137, no. 1 (January 1990): 286–99.

Minchinton, Walter E., ed. "The Virginia Letters of Isaac Hobhouse, Merchant of Bristol." *Virginia Magazine of History and Biography* 66, no. 3 (July 1958): 278–301.

Moreno, Edgard. "Patriotism and Profit." In *Paul Revere-Artisan, Businessman, and Patriot: The Man behind the Myth*. Boston: Paul Revere Memorial Association, 1988.

Olive, Gabriel. "Brass Fittings, A Newly Discovered Catalogue." *Antique Dealer and Collectors Guide* (April 1977): 88–91.

Oman, Charles. "English Brass Chandeliers." *Archaeological Journal* 93 (1936): 263–83.

———. "English Brass Chandeliers in American Churches." *Antiques* 90, no. 2 (August 1966): 110–13.

Peal, Christopher A. "English Knopped Latten Spoons: Part I." *Connoisseur* 173, no. 698 (April 1970): 254–57.

———. "English Knopped Latten Spoons: Part II." *Connoisseur* 174, no. 701 (July 1970): 196–200.

Pearre, Nancy C. "Mining for Copper and Related Minerals in Maryland." *Maryland Historical Magazine* 59 (1964). 15–33.

Raymond, Percy E. "Latten Spoons of the Pilgrims." *Antiques* 61, no. 3 (March 1952): 242–44.

Riley, A. Beresford. "Old Flemish and Dutch Brass." *Connoisseur* 8, no. 29 (April 1904): 207–12.

Robinson, Eric. "Boulton and Fothergill, 1762–1782, and the Birmingham Export of Hardware." *Historical Journal* (Birmingham, Eng.) 7, no. 1 (1963): 60–79.

———. "Eighteenth-Century Commerce and Fashion: Matthew Boulton's Marketing Techniques." *Economic History Review*, 2d ser., 16, no. 1 (August 1963): 39–60.

Robinson, Ralph J. "Maryland's 200-Year-Old Copper Industry." *Baltimore* (July 1939): 23–30.

Sherlock, Robert. "Chandeliers and Posterity." In *The Connoisseur Year Book 1960*, edited by L. G. G. Ramsey, pp. 24–31. London, 1960.

———. "Chandeliers, Fine and Handsome." In *The Connoisseur Year Book 1961*, edited by L. G. G. Ramsey, pp. 44–51. London, 1961.

———. "Chandeliers and the Scrap-Yard." In *The Connoisseur Year Book 1959*, edited by L. G. G. Ramsey, pp. 91–98. London, 1959.

———. "Churches and Candlelight." In *The Connoisseur Year Book 1958*, edited by L. G. G. Ramsey, pp. 44–51. London, 1958.

———. "In Search of Chandeliers." In *The Connoisseur Year Book 1962*, edited by L. G. G. Ramsey, pp. 74–81. London, 1962.

Singleton, Theresa A. "The Slave Tag: An Artifact of Urban Slavery." *South Carolina Antiquities* 16, nos. 1, 2 (1984): 41–65.

Symonds, R. W. "An Eighteenth-Century English Brassfounder's Catalogue." *Antiques* 19, no. 2 (February 1931): 102–5.

———. "The English Export Trade in Furniture to Colonial America, Part II. *Antiques* 28, no. 4 (October 1935): 156–59.

Verlet, Pierre. "A Note on the 'Poinçon' of the Crowned 'C.'" *Apollo* 26, no. 151 (July 1937): 22–23.

White, D. P. "The Birmingham Button Industry." *Post-Medieval Archaelogy* 2 (1977): 67–79.

Woodhouse, Samuel W., Jr. "English Hardware for American Cabinetmakers." *Antiques* 20, no. 5 (November 1931): 287–89.

UNPUBLISHED

"The Art and History of Founding Brass, Copper, and Bronze." Ca. 1878. MS 6355. Guildhall Museum, London.

Bacot, Henry Parrott, Jr. "Brass Founders in New York City." Master's thesis, Cooperstown Graduate Programs, 1972.

Ehninger, Jillian. "With the Richest Ornaments, Just Imported from France: Ornamental Hardware on Boston, New York, and Philadelphia Furniture, 1800–1840." Master's thesis, Winterthur Program in Early American Culture, 1993.

Ernay, Renee L. "The Revere Furnace, 1787–1800." Master's thesis, Winterthur Program in Early American Culture, 1989.

Mitchell, James R. "Marked American Andirons Made before 1840." Master's thesis, Winterthur Program in Early American Culture, 1965.

Sipe, Brian M. "Coppersmithing in Nineteenth-Century Phildelphia: The Bentley Shop." Master's thesis, Winterthur Program in Early American Culture, 1987.

INDEX